MW00368608

# How America Fought Its Wars

# How America Fought Its Wars

## Military Strategy from the American Revolution to the Civil War

*Victor Brooks*
*and*
*Robert Hohwald*

COMBINED PUBLISHING
*Pennsylvania*

## PUBLISHER'S NOTE

The headquarters of Combined Publishing are located midway between Valley Forge and the Germantown battlefield, on the outskirts of Philadelphia. From its beginnings, our company has been steeped in the oldest traditions of American history and publishing. Our historic surroundings help maintain our focus on history and our books strive to uphold the standards of style, quality and durability first established by the earliest bookmakers of Germantown and Philadelphia so many years ago. Our famous monk-and-console logo reflects our commitment to the modern and yet historic enterprise of publishing.

We call ourselves Combined Publishing because we have always felt that our goals could only be achieved through a "combined" effort by authors, publishers and readers. We have always tried to maintain maximum communication between these three key players in the reading experience.

We are always interested in hearing from prospective authors about new books in our field. We also like to hear from our readers and invite you to contact us at our offices in Pennsylvania with any questions, comments or suggestions, or if you have difficulty finding our books at a local bookseller.

For information, address:
Combined Publishing
P.O. Box 307
Conshohocken, PA 19428
E-mail: combined@dca.net
Web: www.dca.net/combinedbooks
Orders: 1-800-418-6065

Copyright 1999 by Victor Brooks and Robert Hohwald
All rights reserved. No part of this publication may be reproduced, stored in a retrieval system or transmitted in any form or by any means, electrical, mechanical or otherwise without first seeking the written permission of the publisher.

*Library of Congress Cataloging-in-Publication Data available.*

ISBN 1-58097-002-8

Printed in the United States of America.

# Contents

# MAPS

# Introduction

$O$n the chilly, early spring afternoon of April 9$^{th}$, 1765, King George III requested that George Grenville become the prime minister of the British government. This humorless brother-in-law of the famous William Pitt was appointed with the specific mandate to devise a plan to generate revenue from His Majesty's American colonies that seemed either unwilling or unable to defend themselves against French or Indian aggression. Grenville agreed with his king that the Americans might be industrious farmers, but these "country people" seemed incapable of ever becoming effective soldiers comparable to the redcoats recruited form the British Isles. The result of this set of beliefs was the passage of a Stamp Act designed to raise money to support several regiments of British regulars in garrisons throughout the colonies. Grenville and the king were certain that any colonial opposition to this modest tax would be disorganized and brief and His Majesty's regulars could be expected to maintain order in the colonies for decades to come.

Exactly one hundred years to the day after a British king set in motion a chain of events that would ultimately cost the crown its most valuable colonies, an American general wearing a mud splattered uniform met with his gray coated counterpart to accept the surrender of the Army of Northern Virginia. Ulysses Simpson Grant commanded an army that was over ten times the size of the British army of a century earlier and had just defeated a Confederacy that had fielded an army just as brave, resourceful and tenacious as its Union opponents. Now the northern and southern descendants of the men who had opposed Grenville's Stamp tax and defeated the British army sent to force the rebel colonists into submission were once again united in a single republic. As the guns around Appomattox, Virginia were silenced, Robert E. Lee spoke to his defeated army and, as tears came to his eyes, told his men to "be as good citizens as you have been good soldiers," a charge that set in motion a reconciliation between the two sections of the American republic. The America that King George and Lord Grenville had considered incapable of defending itself a century earlier was now poised to become the greatest and most prosperous nation in history.

The purpose of this book is to present a narrative and an analysis of this vital century of the American experience, particularly in the field of the young nation's military endeavors. Much of the impetus for this project began during the childhood of the authors in the 1950's and early 1960's when the adventures and exploits of fathers and uncles in World War II combined with ready access to their helmets, knapsacks, ammunition pouches and even insignia of rank produced imaginary campaigns against Axis aggressors. These activities led in turn to exposure to letters and diaries from earlier ancestors who had served in earlier wars. These first person accounts included the observations of a British surgeon during the War of 1812, a Pennsylvanian who defended Cemetery Ridge against the Confederates at Gettysburg and a young volunteer in the war against Spain who was killed at San Juan Hill and left behind a widowed teenager who would eventually become one author's grandmother.

These exploits seemed far more vivid and real than the dull descriptions of these wars presented in school textbooks and encouraged both authors to investigate these campaigns and battles from a wide variety of sources and accounts. This volume is a tangible result of that early curiosity and we the authors hope to share that sense of excitement with the readers of this book. We hope to provide a unique combination of battle narratives, campaign analysis and speculative discussion concerning possible alternatives to the events that actually occurred. In order to accomplish these goals, we have veered somewhat from more traditional military history texts. First, we have made no attempt to cover every aspect of every battle in the four wars chronicled in this book. A work of this scope does not allow coverage of the exploits of every unit in each phase of every engagement. Instead, while most reasonably well known battles in each war are included, we have concentrated on discussing in greater detail engagements that seemed to have the most impact on the outcome of the war. Second, we have attempted to stake out a position regarding the descriptions of each battle that constitutes a middle ground between a highly technical discussion intended for military professionals and the dramatic license that might be found in a popular historical novel. On the one hand, we have not overly concerned ourselves with the muzzle velocities of British six pounders or the proper construction of a Civil War breastwork. However, we have taken every precaution to ensure that designation of units, strength of armies and casualty totals are as accurate as possible and that generals who are mentioned were actually on the field where we placed them. Third, while we made extensive use of the memoirs of significant leaders in each war, we also actively sought out battle accounts by less exalted participants wherever possible. The accounts of newly recruited enlisted men, women who lived in a town on the edge of a battle and similar participants provide a sort of "from the ground up" perspective that generals' narratives sometimes entirely omit.

Two other aspects of this book that were decided upon early in the writing process are also worthy of explanation in an introduction. First, we devoted enormous discussion time and late night phone conversations to the alternate scenarios presented in this work. Each possible alternative outcome was approached relatively conservatively; we made no attempt to consider how George Washington would have employed ground to ground missiles in his attack on the Hessians in Trenton or how J.E.B. Stuart would have deployed tanks in his raids on the Army of the Potomac! However, we felt that it *was* legitimate to speculate on the impact of Federal or Confederate use of repeating rifles at First Manassas or Shiloh or the impact of colonial acceptance of the quite real, and quite generous British peace offer in the wake of Burgoyne's surrender at Saratoga, as these were quite tangible options that were available but not utilized. We also developed the same relatively conservative approach to our grading of Revolutionary War and Civil War generals. In our rating process, we attempted to assign a grade on the overall impact of each particular general on the eventual defeat or victory of his side in the war. Individual personalities were only included to the extent that they affected specific military outcomes. Therefore, for example, we feel that Albert Sidney Johnston, whom we rated near the bottom of Confederate generals, was as courageous, chivalrous and intelligent as Robert E. Lee but his military activities significantly weakened the Confederacy that he served. On the other hand, General John Pope's personality traits that produced his bluster, egotism and unchivalrous attitude toward Southern civilians had a major impact on his rating since it is obvious that these characteristics spurred Robert E. Lee to particularly energetic activities designed specifically to "suppress" an opponent whom the Virginian considered operating outside the boundaries of acceptable behavior for 19th century warfare. Lee's attitude toward Pope seems far different than his relationship with George McClellan, who, although a military antagonist, exhibited a chivalrous attitude toward non-combatants, prisoners and wounded opponents with which the Virginian could readily identify.

Finally, the extensive investigation of documents that this project entailed prompted the authors to detect several common factors in the American pursuit of warfare. First, we detected an ongoing strain of pragmatism and shunning of pomp and show that was often missing in European conflicts. It is almost impossible to imagine Ulysses Grant marching around a Union campsite bedecked with row upon row of gaudy medals and carrying a jeweled sword. Similarly, it is difficult to picture Robert E. Lee flanked by bodyguards as he moved among his men or posting deep rows of armed sentries to keep soldiers at a distance from his tent. Even the somewhat more aristocratic George Washington exhibited far more genuine concern for his men than most European generals and he willingly shared many, if not all, of the privations of his men.

A second common thread in this chronicle is the generally quite noticeable humanity of American soldiers who proved to be daunting opponents in battles but preserved an element of chivalry not always evident in other societies. Research for this book revealed numerous uplifting accounts of extensive medical treatment of British and Hessian prisoners who had been told by their officers that Americans scalped captives; Confederate and Union officers calling cease fires to enable enemy wounded to be evacuated from spreading fires or rising waters; and generals who were in a position to impose much more humiliating terms of surrender than they did with an eye toward possible reconciliation when the fighting was over.

Last, but certainly not least, the authors discovered an ongoing commonality of the concept of the citizen soldier, the civilian who volunteers to fight for his country as long as there is danger but counts the days until he can return to his "real' life. These were men who did not fight for booty or pleasure but for an idea, a situation far different from many European armies and wars, and this tradition extended from the lowliest private to the highest general. In this respect the authors believe one of the defining moments in American history occurred far from a field of battle when George Washington, at the height of his power and prestige, returned his commission to the Congress that appointed him and hurried back to Mount Vernon to celebrate Christmas. This simple yet profound act, which seems impossible for Alexander the Great, Julius Caesar or Napoleon is, we believe, a microcosm of the American military experience and a reason why it is unique in the annals of war.

A project of this scope would not have been possible without many kinds of support. Particular acknowledgment should be given to Dr. Henry Nichols, chairman of the Department of Education and Human Services, Rev. Kail Ellis, O.S.A., Dean of the College of Liberal Arts and Sciences and Dr. John Johannes, Vice President of Academic Affairs at Villanova University for their support of research underloads to support the research for this book. Dot Romano of the Department of Education and Human Services merits special praise for not only typing but also deciphering this manuscript. Dr. Keith Hoskin of Manchester University provided valuable insights into British perspectives of the Revolution and Civil War in numerous discussion. A number of friends and family members provided vital moral support through the various drafts of this book. Marianne and Nicholas Dallas, Laurie, David and Daniel Hohwald and Lynn, Donna, Craig, Matthew, Gregory and Stephen Brooks have all contributed a special part of themselves to this exciting project.

# CHAPTER 1

# The Shot Heard 'Round the World

## *The Battles of Lexington and Concord*

General Thomas Gage was convinced that April of 1775 would mark a major turning point in the fortunes of his family. For centuries the Gages had chosen the losing side in a succession of British power struggles as they supported King John against his barons, Charles I against his Parliament and James II against his daughter. Now, as commander of His Majesty's forces in America, General Gage would have the opportunity to direct elite British regiments in a punitive expedition against those deluded provincials who questioned imperial authority.

The crisis of 1775 seemed to be the most current installment in an almost traditional every-three-decade rebellion against the central government in London. Previous challenges including the 1685 uprising by the Duke of Monmouth against his uncle James II, the 1715 Scottish uprising against George I and the 1745 attempt by Bonnie Prince Charlie to unseat George II had been crushed by disciplined redcoats and had made national heroes of their generals. Now Massachusetts was becoming the most likely setting for a new rebellion and Thomas Gage had the good fortune to command the probable victors in the dispute.

Several miles from General Gage's Boston headquarters, Captain John Parker was thinking more about his family's long term survival than about his reputation. Parker knew that he was dying of consumption and in fact had less than six months to live. Yet Parker's experience in the siege of Louisburg and the conquest of Quebec was an invaluable asset to his fellow militiamen as they awaited the arrival of a large British expeditionary force on Lexington village green.

The transition from civil disobedience to open warfare which began on April 19, 1775 might have occurred in several previous confrontations between redcoats and provincials. During the summer of 1774 Gage had begun to plan a series of missions against the arsenals and powderhouses of New England in order to make it impossible for the people of the region to make a stand against him. Expeditions against the Provincial Powderhouse in Sommerville in September 1774 and the Salem munitions stockpile in February 1775 had barely avoided pitched battles as redcoats and rebels leveled muskets at one another but backed off at the last moment. Now Gage had just received direct orders from Lord Dartmouth, Secretary of State for the Colonies, to implement an armed suppression of colonial defiance to the Constitution of the Empire. The opening campaign in a war which would ultimately cost Britain much of its American empire was ordered by a government that viewed Gage's repeated requests for huge reinforcements as absurd and hysterical. At a time when only 12,000 regulars were stationed in all of Britain, Gage asked for 20,000 reinforcements and large drafts of hard currency. Lord Dartmouth responded to these requests with 700 Royal Marines, 3 regiments of infantry, several companies of light dragoons and orders to raise any additional forces from "friends of Government" throughout New England before launching an offensive against "proceedings that amount to actual revolt." Dartmouth emphasized that "the King's dignity and the honor and safety of the Empire require, that in such a situation, force should be repelled with force."

Gage's response to ministerial directives was to assemble a force of 21 light and grenadier companies, about 900 men, to march out into the Massachusetts countryside, arrest Samuel Adams and John Hancock in Lexington, and then proceed to Concord to destroy the ammunition dump, cannon and food supplies that scouts and spies had located in the village. This force consisted of picked men, who were all considered to be elite shock troops, as the grenadiers were specialists in assaults against fortified positions while the light infantry was used for rapid maneuver and speed of attack. The key to British success would be that the expedition would move at night, capture the rebel leaders in their beds and destroy the Concord munitions before the provincials could organize any effective resistance.

The British attack plan could have easily produced a sharp setback to rebel mobilization plans and could have provided proof of the superiority of regulars against amateur militia. However, three successive failures dramatically reduced the prospects for success. First, the selection of flank companies instead of entire regiments for the expedition reduced the cohesiveness of the British units which operated most effectively on a regimental structure. British officers were assigned to command men who were largely strangers, most officers and sergeants had no idea of their mission and what was expected of them and the order of march for the units was not fully clarified. Second, the Royal Navy did not provide enough boats for the troops to get from Boston to the mainland in one crossing, so that the entire force was not assembled on the Cambridge landing zone until 2 A.M.—four hours later than planned. Third, while Gage's security plans provided for cavalry patrols on the roads approaching Lexington and Concord, there was no real ability to prevent rebel messengers from leaving Boston for the mainland so that well before the British were fully organized for a march, Paul Revere and William Dawes were alerting the countryside that the regulars were approaching.

The initial British strike force was commanded by Lt. Colonel Francis Smith, who was considered by many of his subordinates to be fat, slow, stupid and self indulgent. However, General Gage valued his prudence and caution for a delicate mission through a countryside technically at peace. The troops under Smith's command were excellent soldiers, but they were soaked to the skin because of their landing in deep marshes, were overburdened with far too much equipment for a rapid march, and were forced to march in the dark over unfamiliar roads. As they marched over the country roads the British soldiers heard increasing numbers of alarm bells and other warning signals and they realized that the surprise of a night raid had already been lost.

Colonel Smith now ordered Major John Pitcairn of the Royal Marines to take six companies of light infantry and seize the Concord bridges until the rest of the force arrived. Pitcairn's force would first have to march through Lexington and the 240 Redcoats arrived near the village just as dawn was breaking over the Massachusetts farmland, while in the distance they began to hear a military drum beating a call to arms.

The British advance was opposed by Captain Parker's Lexington militia company, which mustered between 75 and 80 men for the confrontation on the village green. This unit was not actually an official force of "minutemen," as Lexington town officials had rejected provincial suggestions to divide community militia forces into second line alarm companies, first line conventional companies and elite rapid deployment men designated as minutemen. Most of the men who faced Britain's regulars had little ability to form up in a proper military formation but they were experienced in the use of firearms and were reassured by the presence of their relations and neighbors in line with them.

The dramatic confrontation which led to the "shot heard around the world" has been the subject of substantial argument for over two centuries. On the one hand, the Lexington militia were awed by the potential power of the forming lines of redcoats and Captain Parker ordered his men to let the British pass by without molesting them. However as British officers began to demand that the provincials throw down their weapons and leave, Parker issued his famous orders "The first man who offers to run shall be shot down. Stand your ground! Don't fire unless fired upon! But if they want to have a war let it begin here!"

Despite Parker's challenge, many of the Lexington men decided to return to their homes, although refusing to drop their weapons. As one militiaman told his captain "there are so few of us it is folly to stand here." Parker finally relented and ordered the militia to disperse. At this point, as the cheering regulars moved to close on the dispersing provincials, both sides heard the sharp report of a gun. While nearly everyone, British and American, agreed that the first shot did not come from the ranks of Captain Parker's militia or from the rank and file of the British infantry, a bloody confrontation had now begun.

While the Lexington men were convinced that the first shot was fired by the pistol of one of a group of mounted British officers and some swore that the shot came from Major Pitcairn himself, there are two other possibilities that seem more likely. One possibility is that several of the Lexington militia had still not left the comfort of Buckman's tavern on the village green and that one of these men decided to shoot a redcoat from the safety of a tavern window. Firearms and alcohol were certainly an explosive mixture which could provide a ready incentive for an unauthorized shot. The other possibility is that one of the worn or defective muskets on either side simply misfired and created an accidental discharge. The unreliability of 18th century firearms was legendary and this would hardly have been an unusual occurrence.

Whatever the cause of the famous shot, the result was a one-sided "battle" that did little for the reputation for bravery of the British regular. The front ranks of the light infantry companies began a volley fire against the dispersing provincials, killing eight men within a few seconds. Nine more men were wounded in the first volleys while a few Lexington men managed to fire back and slightly wounded one regular. A moment later Colonel Smith arrived on the scene and witnessed his soldiers running wildly out of control as they bayoneted wounded rebels and forced their way into buildings with little restraint from the officers. Smith ordered a drummer to sound assembly, and the redcoats reluctantly formed up in front of their furious commander. As the regulars formed up behind Smith and disappeared into the west, the people of Lexington identified their dead and wounded neighbors and Captain Parker's company prepared to shadow the redcoats and give battle again on more favorable terms.

The British assault force now proceeded to Concord to locate and destroy the rebel munitions depot in the village. While Hancock and Adams had escaped, American muskets and cannon would be much more difficult to move away. Smith's men secured the two main bridges into the town and began their search while officers sat on lawn chairs and bought breakfast from local inhabitants. While some of the regulars chopped down and burned the town's Liberty Pole, other companies located and destroyed three cannons, a few gun carriages and several barrels of flour. This minor destruction appeared far more serious to the hundreds of militia gathering in the hills around the village and within a short time entire companies of provincials were moving toward the Concord bridges.

As three advance companies of regulars under Captain Laurie began tearing up the planking of North Bridge in order to secure a British withdrawal, over 400 Concord militia under Major John Buttrick closed in on the span. A scene initially similar to Lexington Green quickly followed. British regulars opened fire without orders from their officers and six Americans went down, two with fatal wounds. However, this time the rebels were not in the process of dispersing, and Buttrick's men quickly dropped four officers and a dozen privates in their first salvo. To the amazement of the Americans, the redcoats suddenly turned and ran for their lives. A picked force of British infantry was now running from the despised provincial militia that was expected to run from them if they merely fixed their bayonets for a charge. As British Ensign Jeremy Lester admitted, "the weight of their fire was such that one was obliged to give way and then run with the greatest precipitancy."

The British withdrawal from Concord bridge to Lexington village has created an intertwined set of myths and realities that has been difficult to separate for two centuries. On the one hand, the patriotic tapestry of stoic redcoats being mowed down as they marched by the highly mobile "embattled farmers" does have a strong element of truth. The regulars were mauled as company after company of provincial militia selected fences, trees or barns and picked off substantial numbers of redcoats. The casualty toll among British officers was particularly heavy as within an hour the light infantry company of the 5th Regiment of Foot was down to one officer and a few moments later the 4th Regiment had suffered the same level of casualties. Every bend of the road from Concord to Lexington was a potential ambush, and by the time Smith's men were nearing Lexington, their casualty rate was threatening the whole command with disintegration. Both Smith and Pitcairn had been wounded, most of the other officers were down, and the expedition was nearly out of ammunition. However, a total American victory which might have eliminated 25% of the available British army in one afternoon was prevented by two major factors.

First, despite the mobility and superior use of cover of the militia, most "minutemen" were using weapons that were no more accurate than their British adversaries. Over four thousand provincials seem to have been involved in at least some part of the American attack on the British withdrawal between Concord and Charlestown and most of these men probably were able to fire from a number of ambush sites. Yet slightly less than 250 British soldiers were hit in this massive display of firepower. While the conditions of this battle would have been ideal for the employment of the much feared American long rifles, in reality, few Massachusetts militiamen were armed with this weapon. The natural ability of these militiamen to use mobility and cover combined with a longer range weapon might have been devastating to the British on this already disastrous march.

Second, as Smith's column staggered toward the dubious safety of Lexington village, their deliverance from the worst of the American assault had already been assured. General Gage had begun to worry about the Concord expedition even before it left Boston and, despite a number of bureaucratic errors, by 7 A.M. on April 19th a brigade of reinforcements was ready to march. Gage had provided Lord Hugh Percy with 1200 reinforcements including three infantry regiments, a battalion of Royal Marines and two six-pounder cannon. This substantial column had arrived on Lexington Green shortly before Smith's column began to emerge from the Concord road, and Percy formed his force into a large square that provided cover for the exhausted Concord expedition. Using his two cannon to keep the rebels at a distance, Percy reorganized the two detachments and prepared to fight his way back to Charlestown.

Percy's tactics were far removed from the stereotyped overburdened redcoats marching stoically in perfect order as militia swarmed around them. He formed his main force into three columns with strong advance parties and a powerful rear guard while the rest of the regiments formed a sort of mobile British square. Five companies of the 4th King's Own Regiment were ordered to take the high ground south of the road while a strong force of the 47th Regiment held the north side of the pike. The 23rd Royal Welsh Fusiliers composed the rear guard while the Marines were used as a mobile reserve to reinforce any side of the formation that might be threatened. Percy could now shift his reserves from one side to another more quickly than the Americans could move around the outside of the formation. He also slowed down the pace of the march to rest his men and allow the flank forces to clear houses, barns and tree groves close to the highway.

While Percy's tactics probably saved the British force from far higher casualties, the actions of his regiments produced enormous psychological consequences on both sides of the Atlantic. The regulars now smashed into any house or barn that was even suspected of harboring rebel marksmen and both armed and unarmed provincials were bayoneted or shot. Other redcoats engaged in frenzied plundering as the entire populace of villages was terrorized and at least some captured militia were executed on the spot. Lt. Mackenzie of the 23rd Foot noted that "many houses were plundered by the soldiers, notwithstanding the efforts of officers to prevent it. I have no doubt this influenced the rebels and many of them followed us further than they would otherwise have done." Lt. Col. James Abercrombie wrote "I cannot commend the behaviour of our soldiers on the retreat. They began to plunder and paid no obedience to their officers."

As the British column entered Charlestown and rested under the guns of the British fleet, it had left behind the beginning of the ruin of Britain's American empire. While Lord Percy had saved the regulars from virtual annihilation, the Americans had gained two substantial victories on the same day. First, in a military sense, the Americans had clearly won the engagement between the two forces. The British loss of 73 killed and 174 wounded was a significant proportion of an army of only slightly more than 4000 men available to hold all of Massachusetts and was considerably higher than the 49 killed and 41 wounded lost by the provincial militia. A significant number of colonists had witnessed elite regiments of the world's greatest military power bordering on outright panic, ignoring officers' commands and barely avoiding annihilation.

On a second level of confrontation, the provincials secured an even more important victory. The fast schooner *Quero* carried the American version of the battle to London two weeks before Gage's official account reached Parliament. The news of Lexington and Concord caused a sensation in London. Not only was the British government caught by surprise, unable to confirm or deny the rebel accounts, the provincial documents included a deposition from a mortally wounded British officer who generally supported the American version of events and praised the humanity of his captors. The Americans embellished actual British atrocities with graphic descriptions of peaceful citizens being plundered, raped and murdered in their homes by murderous ministerial soldiers. A supporter of Lord North complained that "the Bostonians are now the favourites of all the people of good hearts and weak heads in the kingdom—their saint-like account of the skirmish at Concord has been read with avidity and believed." Even Lord George Germain, no friend of the colonists, wrote that "the news from Americans occasioned a great stir among us yesterday—the Bostonians are in the right to make the King's troops the aggressors and claim a victory."

While British officials tried their best to compete in the contest for public opinion, the rebel cause was clearly the victor in the propaganda war. The war of depositions, newspapers, broadsides and sermons was a devastating victory for the provincials. Not only were Americans stimulated to armed resistance by the confrontation, a substantial portion of British society was repulsed at the actions of their regular army. Members of Parliament, city officials and even military and naval officers castigated the government, supported the American arguments and even refused to some against their fellow subjects in this "unnatural war." Thus a relatively small skirmish along rustic village roads had changed a provincial protest movement into a full fledged conflict over the future of the British Empire.

# CHAPTER 2

# The Response to Military Confrontation

## British and American Strategies and Resources in 1775

$S$oon after the arrival of the official reports of the armed confrontations in Lexington and Concord, the *London Morning Chronicle* declared that "the sword alone can decide the dispute, we must prevent the ruin of the British empire." Captain John Bowater, stationed with Gage's forces in Boston, wrote to Lord Denleigh in London concerning the role of colonials in a future British empire. "I every day curse Columbus and all the discoveries of this diabolical country—the natives are such a levelling, underbred, artful race of people that we can not associate with them. Throughout America they are a sad set of Presbyterian rascals, their words come up so slow that I frequently long to shove a soup ladle down their throats. I think nothing but a total extirpation of the inhabitants of this country will ever make it a desirable object of any Prince or State." The realization in Whitehall and Westminster that colonial demonstrations and protests had now transformed into open armed hostilities initiated a major policy debate on how to force the submission of the rebels within a single military campaign. American insurgency between the Stamp Act crisis of 1764 and the Spring of 1775 had called for the use of troops in a form of police action designed to overawe disaffected subjects with the military might of the British empire. This strategy was based on the belief that most of the trouble was the fault of a few recalcitrant individuals who unfortunately seemed to command a measure of sympathy in some parts of Massachusetts. Now the ministry officials were beginning to realize that the rebels had control over fairly well organized military units and that George III's insistence on the subordination and submission of the Colonials toward the mother country would have to be enforced through some level of armed conflict.

The evolving decision to employ a major military expedition to secure peace in the American colonies produced mixed reactions among British civil and military officials. On the one hand, officers such as Lt. William Fielding emphasized military enthusiasm for opening conventional warfare against the rebels. "I hope the rebels will get heartily thrashed, I would be content to lose a leg and an arm to see them totally defeated and their whole country laid to waste." On the other hand, the mother country was hardly geared up for a massive conflict. One minister noted that "there are no more troops in the country than are absolutely needed for securing the peace and collecting the revenue." According to Adjutant General Edward Harvey, dependence on the limited number of available troops to crush the rebels would produce a disaster as "America is an ugly job, a damned affair indeed!"

Thus during the second half of 1775 and the early months of 1776, First Minister Lord North, Secretary of State for the Colonies Lord Germain and His Majesty George III began to evaluate the challenges and opportunities associated with using massive conventional force to bring the deluded rebels to some form of submission to King and Constitution. The first step in this process was to mobilize all available military units in the empire and to locate new sources of manpower as quickly as possible. The entire British military establishment in 1775 included 49,000 soldiers based on a force of 39,000 infantry, 7000 cavalry and 3000 artillerymen. The army was scattered around the globe with 16,000 men in England and Scotland, 12,000 in Ireland, 9,000 in overseas garrisons from Gibraltar to India and 8,000 in North America and the West Indies with small additional units on detached duty or invalids. This force was divided into 72 infantry regiments averaging 477 men in ten companies and 25 cavalry regiments averaging 231 men in 6 troops. Enlisted men included substantial numbers of convicted felons, petty criminals, unemployed laborers on public relief and a sprinkling of more successful men who were attracted to the army by impressive uniforms and a desire for adventure or glory. The government now proposed to reinforce the army through shorter terms of enlistment, more generous enlistment bounties, lower standards of physical fitness, exemptions from all parish service for veterans and almost any other expedient that a relatively open society could employ.

The individuals leading these enlisted men had seldom received any formal military training but were members of the upper class or comfortable gentry who had purchased commissions in regiments for substantial monetary investments. For instance, a lieutenant colonel in the Foot Guards went for over $500,000 in modern currency and even a captaincy in an average regiment cost about $160,000. Thus many talented but relatively less wealthy middle-aged lieutenants served under the young sons of rich and noble families, who in turn held seats in Parliament which furthered their military advancement.

The expanded recruitment of British subjects for duty against the rebels was expected to be supplemented by hiring mercenaries from other European princes. While Catherine the Great contemptuously refused George III's request for Russian regiments, family ties to German rulers produced a stream of regiments from Hesse-Cassel, Hesse-Hanau and Brunswick. Over 30,000 men were soon rented from these sources and the unwilling mercenaries were soon on their way to an alien and seemingly hostile land.

The third anticipated source of reinforcements for the British war effort was presumed to be already on hand in the American provinces. Between 20% and 25% of the colonial population actively supported the Crown in its confrontation with Congress and this group included many of the most distinguished names in America. Loyalist recruits were expected to be found in all classes of society. Many provincials echoed the sentiments of Walter Dulany, a Loyalist officer from Maryland. "My duty as a subject, the happiness which America enjoyed under the British government and the miseries to which she would be reduced by independence were the motives which induced me to join the army, nor are there any dangers or difficulties that I would not cheerfully undergo to effect a happy restoration." Innkeepers, farmers, mariners, tradesmen, laborers, merchants and professional men were recruited to enlist in loyalist units. Over 40 regiments ranging from the Royal Greens and the Royal Highland Emigrants to the Roman Catholic Volunteers and the Black Pioneers eventually rallied to the royal standard. Under ideal circumstances, this force would provide a significant addition to British military power in America.

The basic plan developed by the British ministry for reducing the rebels to submission during 1776 revolved around a building of military strength to 96,000 men including 33,000 men to secure Britain and Ireland from potential French intervention, 8,000 men to prevent Spanish mischief in Minorca or Gibraltar, and 55,000 men designated for service in America including 14,000 for General Guy Carleton in Canada and 41,000 for General William Howe in the rebel colonies.

Carleton's army of 6,000 Germans and 8,000 British regulars would eliminate rebel units threatening Montreal and Quebec and then move south from Lake Champlain to the Hudson River, splitting New England from the southern provinces. Meanwhile, Howe's 2,000 loyalists, 13,000 Hessians and 26,000 regulars would land at Staten Island, capture New York City and compel the rebels to fight an open battle in which the colonial army would be annihilated.

The ultimate success of this expedition was expected to come from the sheer overwhelming psychological impact of the rebels being forced to contend with a far larger army than they could possibly imagine. North and Germain were not interested in a half-hearted show of strength but oversaw the building of the largest overseas military expedition up to that point in British history. This was a logistics enterprise comparable to the Normandy invasion of 1944 in its relative scope and intensity and was expected to crush the rebellion in a single campaign season. The British government believed that the far from united colonies simply could not repel this level of military force and thus would relatively quickly seek some form of political accommodation. After the rebel armies had been smashed in one or two major battles, the British government would offer relatively generous peace terms including free pardons to most colonists, some vague promises of redress of American grievances and hints of some level of representation in Parliament in return for unqualified acceptance of the sovereignty of King and Ministry. While the British leaders never seem to have contemplated the massive retaliation of executions and property destruction imposed on the defeated Scottish rebels after Culloden in 1746, they were also unlikely to allow the colonists to maintain enough autonomy to present a serious threat to imperial rule in the foreseeable future.

The formulators of British strategy in the opening stage of the Revolution realized that they possessed a number of inherent advantages in their efforts to suppress the rebellious provinces. The Mother Country had a well developed economy, a large population, the world's most formidable navy and an army that was confident and used to winning battles and wars. The colonists' record in the French and Indian War seemed to indicate that few Americans had a real talent for military exploits and provincial militia would probably disintegrate in the face of determined assaults by regulars. Britain simply had more money, more industry and more organization than anything the colonists could produce. Yet even fairly optimistic officials such as Lord George Germain acknowledged the difficulties facing the prepared expeditionary force.

The first challenge facing a British intervention would be the fact that England's three to one population advantage over the colonists would be partially negated by the 3,000 miles separating the provinces from the mother land. Most British uniforms, weapons, bullets and rations would have to be transported across the stormy Atlantic at enormous cost in time and money. Every replacement for a wounded or dead soldier in Carleton or Howe's armies would have to endure a two to four month voyage while vulnerable to attacks by American privateers or warships.

A second factor limiting British power was the simple fact that the king and ministry had authorized the use of force to retain a particularly valuable segment of the empire. The American provinces would be of little value to the mother country if the British army turned them into corpse strewn, burned out deserts. The government was sending an army to restore a perceived legitimate government and thus mass executions, substantial plundering and mistreatment of civilians would destroy any possibility of a profitable reconciliation. A significant number of British leaders were convinced that the mass of the American population was loyal to the King and merely needed proper encouragement to throw off the yoke of a tyrannical Congress. Even George III warned that notes of triumph after victories would not be proper since such success would be "against subjects, not a foreign foe." While the awesome military power of Britain might be

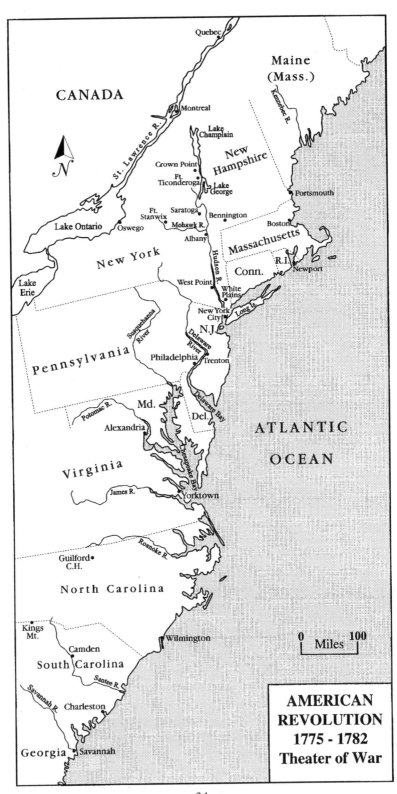

AMERICAN
REVOLUTION
1775 - 1782
Theater of War

24

displayed and even unleashed to some extent, the crushing force of total warfare would have to be held in check for the indefinite future.

The final complicating factor facing British strategic planners was the nature of the American population compared to other subjects within the empire. The British army of 1775 was used to putting down domestic insurrections and had on a number of occasions crushed rebellions in England and Ireland in which under-armed and untrained peasants had been annihilated by regiments of regulars. However, the uprising of Scottish highlanders in 1745-46 had shown that a small number of poorly armed rebels who possessed at least some organization and tactical skill could embarrass the British military establishment. Now the British army was about to face a rebel population that was far more heavily armed than most Europeans, was used to utilizing weapons for survival in a hostile environment and had developed at least some level of military organization. These provincials, "numerous and armed" could prove a formidable adversary to a British army that became too overconfident of easy victory.

While ministerial and crown officials debated a variety of strategies to suppress the rebellious provinces, leaders from the thirteen colonies were meeting in Philadelphia to organize plans to expel Gage's army from American soil and repel any further British attempt to impose a military solution on the dispute between King and Congress. During June of 1775 the Continental Congress approved two major actions that would profoundly affect the expanding military hostilities between Britain and America. On June 14 the Congress approved a petition by the Massachusetts Provincial Congress to adopt the militia regiments surrounding Boston as an American Continental Army. The provincial representatives supplemented this approval with an authorization to raise 10 companies of riflemen from Pennsylvania, Maryland and Virginia and send these units as a national reinforcement to the mostly New England troops confronting General Gage.

The day after it voted to adopt the New England army, Congress chose George Washington to be Commander in Chief of the newly designated Continental forces. New England leaders such as John Adams had promoted Washington's appointment as a means of attracting southern support for the military confrontation with England while the Virginian's impressive appearance and notable contribution to the Congressional military committees inspired the confidence of his fellow members.

A significant portion of the members of the Continental Congress were determined to develop some form of formal military organization to oppose His Majesty's armies, yet these men had also inherited from their English and Colonial ancestors a strong aversion to a standing army and a professional officer class. Regular armies brought corruption, brutality and violence to an otherwise peaceful society and constantly threatened the liberties of the citizens. On the other hand, a British army was occupying a major American city and it was quite likely that the Ministry would send additional units to suppress the colonial population. Thus some form of military strategy, even including a distasteful organization of regular forces, was necessary to preserve property and freedom.

The initial military strategy developed by the American political leaders was based on two significant, and potentially devastating, miscalculations. First, most influential colonists were convinced that the British government had neither the will nor the resources to launch a truly massive expeditionary force against the rebel provinces. England's need to defend other Colonial possessions, fear of French or Spanish military intervention, threats of rebellions in Ireland or Scotland combined with the relatively anti-military tradition of much of British society would probably limit a trans-Atlantic expedition to about 20,000 men, including the garrison already stationed in Boston. Amateur strategists in America began devising manpower formulas that determined a two to one colonial manpower advantage as a virtual guarantee for military success for the rebels. Thus a proposed American army of 55,000 men would provide Washington with a 25,000 man main army, 20,000 soldiers to be sent to secure Lake Champlain and threaten Canada, and a 10,000 man "flying camp"which would provide emergency reserves or conduct operations in the South. While this plan assumed that the Americans would enter battle with an almost 3 to 1 advantage over the regulars, unfortunately, most of the necessary regiments remained as paper forces. When General Howe began threatening New York in the summer of 1776 the ratio was closer to 55,000 to 20,000 in favor of the British.

A second major misconception in American strategy was based on the assumption that relatively untrained colonial volunteers would be more than a match for brutalized, unthinking, ministerial regulars simply because they were more virtuous. Newly commissioned General Charles Lee told the colonists what they wanted to hear when he emphasized the innate superiority of zealous citizen soldiers against the European regulars flogged into a "Prussian discipline" like dogs. Lee felt that Americans would restore to the world the ancient virtues of Roman citizen soldiers and through their military victory redeem a world corrupted by greedy officials kept in power by their dehumanized mercenaries.

These assumptions of American moral superiority and a less than absolute British commitment to military victory almost destroyed the Revolution when Washington's army was nearly annihilated in the New York campaign. However, beyond the limitations of too few soldiers and too little training, the American rebels also faced additional handicaps in a military confrontation with the mother country.

For example, since America was primarily an agrarian society, most colonists worked on farms that needed constant attention and could only spare adult males for short periods of military service. Any sort of standing army of professionals would have to be recruited from fringe areas of the American population which would set finite limits on the size of a regular army. The very prosperity of colonial society made long term military service even less attractive to Americans than their English counterparts as the boredom, danger and physical discomfort of army life was a stunning contrast to the relative affluence and comfort of many colonial lifestyles.

A second significant handicap challenging American strategies was that colonial society was simply not very well developed to support a military conflict even on a limited 18th century level. Americans made few cannon or muskets, did not have a transportation system that could provide dependable food and clothing supplies to a modest sized army, and didn't have enough raw materials to assure an adequate supply of gunpowder. The colonies didn't possess a professional governmental ministry or an experienced cadre of military officers that could deal with the minute details of maintaining an army in the field and then using that army to overwhelm the enemy. The colonists were challenging a mother country that possessed highly confident regiments of regulars who were used to winning military campaigns and a Royal Navy that was the most potent maritime force on the planet.

While these strategic handicaps presented a daunting challenge to the emerging Revolutionaries, a number of important advantages to the rebel cause were discerned over time. A particular asset to the provincial forces was the vast size and peculiar geography of the American continent. While the Royal Navy could land British regiments at virtually any point on the seacoast and support the army with formidable naval gunfire, the navy could not penetrate very far into the interior of the colonies. Whenever the army attempted to move too far inland, supply lines would be more difficult to maintain and the wooded country would be far from suitable for maximum effectiveness of conventional regiments. While the rebels wouldn't usually be able to offer the British equal battle in open field engagements, the regulars couldn't usually penetrate into the countryside to destroy vital rebel bases and magazines.

Another quickly recognizable rebel advantage was the realization that the three to one population advantage enjoyed by the mother country would be at least partially nullified by the 3,000 miles separating London from the scene of the conflict. The colonists needed to maintain a regular army to represent continuity, stability and the dignity of the Revolutionary cause and to provide a permanent nucleus around which militia and irregulars could rally. However, this regular nucleus could often be expanded substantially in an emergency by calling in local levies of militia and short term volunteers. General Burgoyne at Saratoga and General Cornwallis at Guilford Court House found themselves facing far larger armies than they expected as new companies and regiments of rebels simply kept pouring into the American lines. This access to rapid reinforcement also lessened the potentially disastrous repercussions of several American defeats. For example, the large garrisons surrendered at Fort Washington and Charleston included many soldiers who held short term enlistments and would have to be replaced soon even if they had not been captured. On the other hand, the large British armies at Saratoga and Yorktown were primarily irreplaceable regulars who were then totally removed from the chessboard of the war.

A third gradually realized American advantage was based on the reality that colonial population centers were so relatively unimportant to the rural society that British capture of some or all of the rebel cities would be far less decisive than in a conventional European conflict. While the Americans almost lost an army trying to hold New York and did lose an army in an ill-advised attempt to defend Charleston, the European precedent of declaring the war over when enough cities had been captured by the opposing army simply didn't seem to occur to the Americans. When General William Howe informed his ecstatic monarch that the war had been won because the British had captured Philadelphia, George III could not understand that the only real accomplishment of a year long campaign was that the rebel army had been pushed back about 20 miles and would merely regroup for the next round of the contest.

While some of the challenges, handicaps and opportunities facing the British Ministry and the American Congress were quickly appreciated, other key factors were not originally foreseen and emerged only as the war developed and expanded. As strategy discussions filled candle-lit meeting rooms on both sides of the Atlantic, a group of Yankee militia leaders were about to provoke the first major battle of the infant Revolution.

CHAPTER 3

# The Bunker Hill Dilemma

## *The Emergence of William Howe*

$T$ he ministerial response to the crisis caused by the armed insurrection around Lexington and Concord was an immediate dispatch of reinforcements to the British garrison at Boston. This force was spearheaded by the HMS *Cerebrus* which carried three generals who would play significant roles in the upcoming conflict. The arrival of Henry Clinton, John Burgoyne and William Howe represented a vote of no confidence in the ability of General Thomas Gage to deal with the expanding confrontation and served as a demonstration of British determination to crush the rebellion. Lord North insisted that "I don't know what the Americans will think of them, but I know that they make me tremble!"

Each of these major generals possessed a level of confidence and self assurance nurtured by a lifetime of association with the ruling class of Britain, yet each man also voiced some aversion to an assignment to make war on fellow British subjects. General Henry Clinton, the youngest of this group at 45, was the grandson of the sixth Earl of Lincoln, a cousin of the second Duke of Newcastle and the son of the former governor of New York. Clinton had grown up in New York City, attended school on Long Island and joined a New York militia regiment. After returning to England, Clinton purchased a commission in the Coldstream Guards and was soon promoted to the post of aide-de-camp to Sir John Ligonier, the 77 year old commander-in-chief of the British army. Ligonier and Clinton represented opposite ends of the spectrum of tolerated behavior for a British officer. Ligonier had flaunted his relationship with a 13-year-old mistress and now kept a country residence that included four mistresses with a combined age of less than 60. While Sir John expected junior officers to join him in his country frolics, Clinton was somehow able to condemn his commander's antics while still maintaining his position. The young aide subsequently became a loyal and devoted husband when he married the daughter of a minor nobleman, but by 1775 he was a grieving widower with four young children and a somewhat reluctantly accepted assignment to go back to American to crush the rebel colonists.

The second notable passenger on the *Cerebrus* was General John Burgoyne, the fifty-two-year-old probable illegitimate son of Lord Bingley who had been the Chancellor of the Exchequer, one of the most powerful men in the realm. Burgoyne's active and colorful career as an officer in the Horse Guards was soon undone by a tumultuous relationship with Lady Charlotte Stanley, the attractive and popular daughter of the Earl of Stanley, one of the wealthiest men in England. After Burgoyne was virtually thrown out of the Earl's house when he was attempting to court Lady Charlotte, the couple eloped in the middle of the night and escaped to France to avoid the wrathful father-in-law and the bridegroom's numerous gambling creditors. An eventual reconciliation of Burgoyne and Derby produced a colonelcy in an elite regiment, a seat in Parliament and an open door to every important manor in the kingdom. By 1775 Burgoyne was a distinguished cavalry officer, a rising amateur playwright and a famous man about town who somehow seemed to be able to balance a genuine deep affection for his ailing wife with a constant string of affairs around the capital city. Burgoyne had also developed a close relationship with George III, who indulgently ignored Burgoyne's high profile support of the rights of the colonists.

The senior general in this new triumvirate was Hon. William Howe, the 45 year old younger son of the second Viscount Howe who had served as a senior officer under Wolfe at the storming of Quebec and had in turn married the probable illegitimate daughter of King George I. Thus William Howe enjoyed an easy access to the reigning monarch despite his staunch anti-government and pro-colonist speeches as a Member of Parliament for Nottingham. Howe's pro-American sympathies were probably made even more emotional when the General Court of Massachusetts voted £250 to erect a statue in London of William's older brother George who had been killed at Ticonderoga in 1758. When Howe agreed to accept the King's assignment as a general in an expeditionary army sent to suppress the rebellion in America, he consistently stressed his probable employment as a peacemaker authorized to mediate the dispute between the Americans and the British Ministry and King.

These newly assigned generals were thus not obscure officers ordered to command troops in an obscure war, but were members of the most elite element of British society. Each man was competent, well known and comfortable in the exertion of authority. However, it also seems that each of these men would have much preferred a role in a traditional 18th century conflict against a real enemy such as France or Spain to a complex and rather vague assignment to suppress fellow subjects who claimed rights as Englishmen that these generals acknowledged to be legitimate. This was a twilight war for men dreaming of the glory gained in leading ornately uniformed men against opposing forces of ornately uniformed men on a sunny, open battlefield in Europe.

A more specific examination of the personality and military potential of the emerging leader of this triumvirate, William Howe, reveals a commander who would come tantalizing close to defeating the rebellion before it was much more than a year old. In fact, Howe's talents, limitations and opportunities bear a striking resemblance to an equally controversial Union commander three generations later—George Brinton McClellan. Howe and McClellan were each placed in command of the most formidable military force available to their nations and became extremely popular among the men who served in those armies. Each man came from a comfortable and highly influential family and was permitted a level of criticism of the nation's leader which few other military commanders could hope to enjoy. Howe's amphibious expedition against the colonial capital of Philadelphia entailed weeks of delay comparable to McClellan's glacial pace in the move up the Peninsula toward Richmond. Howe trapped a demoralized rebel army against the banks of the East River and then delayed a final assault while Washington extricated his army from inevitable destruction. McClellan pinned a fragmented and vastly outnumbered rebel army against the banks of the Potomac and squandered a chance at gaining a smashing victory when he allowed poorly coordinated and badly delayed assaults to be parried by the more aggressive Robert E. Lee. Thus Howe, like McClellan, offers the model of the military commander who *did* win substantial successes in some instances and *should* have won the war against a numerically inferior and poorly supplied opponent.

The emergence of William Howe, and the controversy that surrounded him, began as Thomas Gage and his three new major generals surveyed possible opportunities to end the embarrassing encirclement of His Majesty's forces in Boston. Howe and his fellow passengers on the *Cerebrus* realized that General Gage's long term role in the upcoming conflict was sure to be a limited one. Lord Chatham had already described Gage in a Parliamentary speech as "an impotent general with a dishonored army trusting solely to the pickaxe and the spade for security against the just indignation of an injured and insulted people." Now the newly arrived generals were prodding Gage to use his newly reinforced army of 5700 men to secure three key points of high ground surrounding Boston. The British seizure of Dorchester Heights, Breed's Hill and Bunker Hill could provide a springboard to a more general assault on the rebel defenses with a particular focus on the capture of American headquarters at Cambridge.

Unfortunately for the British high command, the intelligence system operated by the Massachusetts Committee of Safety had provided the rebels with details of the projected offensive and the provincial leaders were prompt to react. General Artemus Ward, the commander of provincial forces, ordered Colonel William Prescott to take three regiments of infantry and a small detachment of artillery and fortify Bunker Hill under cover of darkness. Prescott marched his men onto the Charlestown Peninsula after dark on the evening of June 16, 1775, but when he surveyed the terrain across the neck, he became convinced that Breed's Hill was the proper location for a fort. While artillery employed on Bunker Hill would have trouble reaching British positions in Boston, Breed's Hill commanded the northern section of Charlestown and could prove a real threat to enemy fortifications.

Prescott's regiments climbed up to a meadow on top of Breed's Hill and plodded through uncut grass that was almost to their waists. Colonel Richard Gridley, the engineer officer assigned to the detachment, inspected the ground by starlight and staked out a planned redoubt 136 feet to a side with a southern wall pointed toward Boston and an eastern side facing the sea. As Prescott urged his men to muffle the sound of their shovels, the Massachusetts soldiers worked in shifts to complete a formidable fortification before the sun rose. At dawn on June 17th the officers of the watch on the British warships in Boston harbor stared in amazement at a menacing new fort that seemed to be emplacing guns aimed directly at the fleet.

While HMS *Lively* opened fire with all available cannon, General Henry Clinton rushed into Gage's headquarters to report the rebel threat. Soon a room full of British and Loyalist officers was discussing the most effective response to the amazing American accomplishment. Clinton argued that the rebels had provided the British army with a golden opportunity, as their new position was probably virtually undefended in the rear so that the colonies had put themselves in a bag and "all we have to do is squeeze it." Clinton proposed that a British landing force of 500 men would use the guns of the fleet for cover and seize the narrow neck that separated Charlestown from the mainland. This would cut off either retreat or reinforcement for the Americans and the defenders of Breed's Hill would either surrender or starve. If the rebels attempted to break out of the trap or if the rest of the army at Cambridge tried to reinforce them, the guns of the fleet would annihilate the whole force. While Loyalist Colonel Timothy Ruggles supported Clinton's plan because it avoided the prospect of heavy casualties that would be incurred in a frontal assault, Gage and Howe insisted that Clinton had never led an amphibious attack and hadn't considered the dangers of this type of operation. Gage emphasized that this plan could easily place a British army between two rebel forces, especially if the Americans were hiding large numbers of men on the far side of Bunker Hill. Howe insisted that British ships moving up the Mystic River to support an amphibious landing would be sailing in water that might be too shallow for safety and that troops might land in a stretch of mud flats and flounder ashore with wet powder and useless muskets. Gage and Howe also agreed that from a political point of view, the Americans should be met on a battlefield of their own choosing—the reputation of the regular troops had been tarnished at Concord and could only be restored by thrashing the rebels on an open battlefield.

The council of war's less than enthusiastic response to Clinton's plan provided an opportunity for William Howe to propose an alternate strategy. Howe suggested a British landing on the beach below the American fortifications where the guns of the fleet could smash any rebel sortie from the redoubt while the provincial troops on the far side of the neck would be too far away to intervene. A flying column of light infantry would rush up to the Mystic River beach, knife across the American line of retreat and open fire on the redoubt from the rear. Once the rebels were engaged from the rear, the armed transport *Symmetry* would move close in and provide artillery support as the battalion companies rushed the fort just as the colonists were ducking for cover from the bombardment. The result would be a rout of the rebel defenders which could then be utilized as a spring-board for pushing inland to Cambridge with the subsequent capture of American headquarters and perhaps much of the colonial army. The success of Howe's plan would depend on the speed of the light infantry in getting behind the rebels, the capability of naval and army artillery to silence American batteries and the probability that the colonists' fort couldn't possibly be finished within one night. As Howe insisted, "never in my experience have I heard or seen even regular troops capable of building a complete redoubt in a single night's work."

While Howe and his fellow British generals tended to underestimate the fighting capabilities of their colonial opponents, they were also serving in an army in which it was considered an essential characteristic of talented leadership to hold casualties to a minimum because of the difficulty in securing replacements among an unenthusiastic British populace. Although a frontal assault was an acceptable tactic in a battle, it was seldom carelessly or casually executed and was almost always attempted within a broader context of flanking movements, diversionary tactics and artillery support in order to expose the assaulting column to as little enemy fire as possible. Unfortunately for the British regiments designated to launch the assault on Breed's Hill, the auxiliary factors so crucial to a successful attack were beginning to unravel in the hot June sun.

As General Howe supervised the embarkation of 2300 British regulars assigned to make the crossing from Boston to Charlestown, the rebel defensive positions were being strengthened considerably. Prescott's position on Breed's Hill provided him with a vast panoramic scene from the Charles River to the Mystic River and from the Charlestown streets to the opposite shore in Boston. While Prescott considered the redoubt as the centerpiece of the American defense position, he ordered Captain Thomas Knowlton to take a company of Connecticut reinforcements and two artillery pieces to fortify a gap between Breed's Hill and the Mystic River, while other companies were detailed to build a breastwork intended to provide fire support for the fort. As Knowlton's men began to reinforce stone and wooden fences and stuff loose straw between the rails to give the appearance of a solid wall, Colonel John Stark arrived on the scene with his New Hampshire reinforcements. Stark ordered some of his men to reinforce the fence line while the remaining troops were ordered to descend to the narrow beach eight feet below. The New Hampshire colonel was convinced that the British would launch a bayonet charge at any Americans defending the beach and this attack would slash the colonists to pieces if they had to pause to reload their muskets. Stark ordered his men to build a waist high breastwork with rocks and stones hauled down from the adjoining fields and then marked out stakes 50 yards from the new wall. He then set up his men in three firing lines so that there would be no respite from the volleys when the British attacked.

The American defense force now numbered about 1400 men, with about 150 troops in the redoubt, 300 colonists defending the adjacent breastwork, 150 snipers placed in houses throughout the deserted town of Charlestown and the remainder positioned along rail fences, stone walls and on the beach. While Prescott was in tactical command of the position, two senior officers were on the scene in more complicated capacities. Dr. Joseph Warren of Boston had recently been commissioned a general in the Massachusetts forces and was now walking among the defenders while refusing to supersede Prescott. General Israel Putnam of Connecticut was directing the first trickle of reinforcements toward the line of rail fences near the Mystic.

Prescott's panoramic view of his defenses was soon transformed by the sight of 28 landing barges moving across the water from Boston to Morton's Point on the peninsula. Two rows of 14 boats each carried hundreds of soldiers with bayonets glistening in the sun and red coats providing a colorful contrast with the blue water. The 2300 soldiers of the first landing party landed on the beaches to the music of fifes and drums while General Howe disembarked and began to study the American defenses. While the general appeared supremely confident to his staff and subordinates, he was already shaken by the fact that Admiral Samuel Graves, commander of the British fleet in Boston, refused to allow his ships to enter the Mystic River to provide fire support. A few minutes later Howe was informed that his batteries of supporting artillery had been issued with the wrong sized cannonballs in Boston and any artillery support would have to be postponed.

The lack of naval and ground artillery support was a major blow to Howe's planned assault, but the British general quickly formulated a revised scheme of attack. While Lt. Colonel Robert Pigot marched part of the army through Charlestown and pinned down the redoubt's defenders, Howe would lead the grenadier and battalion companies against the rail fences as the light infantry came up behind the American lines by way of the beach.

As the 11 light infantry companies moved along the Mystic River beach in groups of four men across, Colonel Stark took position behind his three lines of defenders. His men could hear the rattling of drums around the bend but they didn't see the redcoats until they were almost even with the firing stakes. The American commander yelled that "not a man is to fire until the first regular crosses the stake" and the colonial marksmen prepared to aim at their enemies' waistcoats.

The lead company of the British assault force, from the Welsh Fusiliers, leveled their bayonets as they prepared to charge the rebel breastwork. At that moment Stark's men opened fire and killed or wounded most of the attacking company. The light infantry from the King's Own Regiment then stepped over the bodies of their comrades and broke into a run. A second rebel volley decimated this company before they could get near the Americans. Finally, the men from the 10th Regiment of Foot managed to scramble over an alarming number of writhing redcoats and launch a third attempt to capture the beach. The Americans' third volley exploded in their midst and eliminated this company as an effective unit. Now Stark's men began to fire in relays and the front ranks of the regulars simply melted away. Within minutes 96 British soldiers were dead, dozens more wounded, and the survivors were dragging their comrades out of range of the deadly American fire.

While the light infantry companies were marching along the narrow beachfront, the grenadier and battalion companies were sweating up Breed's Hill encumbered with 60 pound packs and dazed by the effect of the hot sun on their woolen uniforms. Howe's men finally got within firing range and fired a volley at the defenders behind the rail fences. Most of the bullets merely whistled over the Americans' heads as the grenadiers were forced to start knocking down rows of fences in order to move in for closer shots. As the redcoats struggled through the broken fences, a yellow sheet of flame erupted from the rebel defenses and huge gaps began to appear in the British lines. The battalion companies' officers now began leading their men up to support the grenadiers but the officers started dropping in alarming numbers. Within a few minutes every officer on Howe's personal staff was dead or wounded and the blood spattered general ordered his men to drop back from the fences.

The confusion and alarm spreading among the troops on the British right wing was matched by equal distress on the left side of the assault force. Colonel Pigot's units moving through the deserted streets of Charlestown were met by ferocious sniper fire from upper story windows throughout the town. As Pigot's casualties mounted rapidly, an urgent message for naval support was finally acknowledged and British warships began firing red-hot shot and carcass balls filled with pitch into Charlestown. Soon the town was a blazing mass of buildings as choking rebel snipers began to fall back to Breed's Hill. By 3:30 P.M. the British regiments had stumbled through the smoking outskirts of the town and were ready to attack the American redoubt. The redcoat assault on the American fort followed the same dismal pattern as the move against the enemy beach and fence defenses. The British fire was invariably too high to hit most of the rebels yet when the regulars tried to move in for closer shots, they were slaughtered by American volleys. Almost every officer who attempted to rally his men for a fresh attack was killed or wounded within seconds. Soon Pigot's shattered units were pulled back to regroup for a new attack.

Contrary to American textbook narratives, General Howe did not simply order a second mindless charge up the hill with the hope that the rebels couldn't kill all of his men before they reached the top. Howe realized that the beach assault had failed so he redeployed his remaining light infantry companies for a more mobile assault on the rail fences while fresh Marine reinforcements were sent to Pigot to support a new attack from that direction. The Marines and light infantry were Howe's most mobile forces and their speed might allow them to flank the Americans before the rebel marksmen could do much damage. This second assault force was able to move rapidly toward the colonists' positions, but the Americans responded by developing a constant rotation of rows of marksmen which produced an almost continuous volley that smashed the advancing redcoats. Light infantry and Marine companies were quickly reduced to 8 or 9 men with most of the officers now out of action.

By four o'clock in the afternoon of June 17th, it appeared that the American rebels had smashed a major element of the British army at almost no loss to the defenders. A British retreat after two assaults would have produced shockwaves that would have rolled to the very heart of the British Ministry. A modest number of fresh reinforcements and more ammunition would probably have made the American position invulnerable to further assaults. However, during the late afternoon of this critical day in the American Revolution the tide of battle started to move very much in the British favor.

On the American side of the battlefield, the defenders were stunned by the enormous casualties they had inflicted on the redcoats. However, they were also hungry, thirsty and nearly out of ammunition. Most of the gathering reinforcements that could be seen on Bunker Hill simply came no closer and an increasing trickle of front line defenders made their way to Charlestown neck with the expectation that it was someone else's turn to risk his life against the regulars. Israel Putnam had stormed back from the front lines to Bunker Hill to try to organize a reinforcement for the defenders. While Putnam was able to convince two companies of men to march to the redoubt, most of the Americans simply milled around the far side of the hill waiting for something to happen.

The prospects for William Howe during the late afternoon were becoming noticeably brighter. The British landing force had been reinforced by the fresh 63rd Regiment and two additional companies of Royal Marines. The British artillery batteries had finally received the right size ammunition and the Royal Navy was now ready to be in a position to provide fire support without any danger to the fleet. Howe now addressed his soldiers and ordered them to remove all packs and other equipment other than a musket and bayonet. The men were permitted to shed their bulky red coats and were told that one final charge would win unending glory for their regiments. The general now felt confident that every piece of the plan was coming together to produce a quick victory. The new plan was to launch a mere token gesture toward the rail fences while most of the now unencumbered troops would assault the redoubt from both flanks and front. Naval and Royal Artillery cannon would keep the rebels pinned down while the regulars went over the fort's walls and trapped the remaining defenders.

The final assault on Breed's Hill produced some hint of what the British army could accomplish if every element of a battle plan fell into place. While the defenders behind the rail fences were pinned down by a British skirmish line, the main assault force moved in to surround the redoubt. When the regulars got to within 20 yards of the fort, Prescott's men fired one last massive volley and almost stopped the British advance. However, most of the provincials had used their last bullets and now British artillery grape-shot started to explode among the defenders at a moment of peak vulnerability.

British soldiers now started to drop down from the redoubt walls to try to bayonet defenders who had only rifle butts and fists. One of the last Americans who still had ammunition, Peter Salem, a black soldier from Prescott's command, shot Major Pitcairn, the Marine commander, as he was directing the British assault from the top of the wall. Colonel Prescott backed out of the rear entrance of the redoubt as he parried the bayonet thrusts of several redcoats with his sword. Joseph Warren formed a rear guard which held back the British long enough for most of the provincials to escape, and then died with his last few men under a wall of enemy bayonets. Finally, as the American survivors sprinted from the reverse slope of Breed's Hill to the relative safety of Bunker Hill, the redcoats closed ranks and fired a series of volleys at their retreating adversaries. Only a brilliant fighting withdrawal by Stark's New Hampshiremen prevented a British assault on the disorganized Americans staggering toward Charlestown neck and safety. Even General Burgoyne commended Stark's actions insisting that "Stark's retreat was no flight, it was even covered with bravery and military skill." As Stark's men withdrew across Charlestown neck, the regulars moved up to the crest of Bunker Hill waiting orders to move on to Cambridge. When Howe surveyed his exhausted regiments and saw the huge number of dead and wounded soldiers covering the fields and meadows around Breed's Hill, plans for carrying the attack toward Cambridge were postponed indefinitely.

Within hours after darkness descended on the burned out buildings and smashed breastworks of Charlestown peninsula, the leaders of both the British and colonial forces were faced with the dilemma of deciding who indeed had won the first major battle of the Revolutionary War. While Howe and his British regulars held the actual battlefield, almost one half of the assault force was dead or wounded. The 2500 British troops engaged in the battle had lost 1054 men with the 226 dead including a large proportion of officers. The 1400 colonial defenders who actually saw action on June 17th had suffered almost no casualties during the first two British attacks and had ended the day with 140 killed and 310 wounded or captured.

Howe's claim of a decisive victory over the rebels was not even acknowledged enthusiastically at British headquarters in Boston. Henry Clinton dispatched a series of letters to friends in Parliament emphasizing the bungling activities of Gage and Howe. Clinton informed his cousin the Duke of Newcastle that the British enlisted men had shown a high degree of courage, but little else had gone well. "The men lacked a high order of discipline and displayed wild behaviour when advancing under fire. During the battle all was confusion, anarchy and wretchedness." Thomas Gage dispatched an official account to Lord Barrington in London and admitted, "you will receive an account of some success against the rebels, but attended with a long list of killed and wounded on our side; so many of the latter that the hospital has hardly hands sufficient to take care of them. These people show a spirit and conduct against us they never showed against the French, and everybody has judged of them from their former appearance and behavior when they joined with the King's Forces in the last war; which led many into great mistakes."

The dilemma of attempting to evaluate victory or defeat on June 17th was equally challenging to American leaders and participants. William Prescott was so convinced that the British army had been decimated in the day's assaults that soon after the last Americans had withdrawn from Charlestown peninsula, the Massachusetts colonel was attempting to gather reinforcements and more ammunition for an immediate counterattack. Artemus Ward, who seemed more interested in simply holding Cambridge, overruled his subordinate and began planning new defensive positions. Prescott and Colonel John Stark were convinced that the huge British casualty rate had provided the Americans with an enormous propaganda victory at the minimal cost of a redoubt and a few breastworks. Future Continental general Nathanael Greene exemplified this attitude by declaring, "I wish we could sell them another hill at the same price."

On the other hand, the battle of "Bunker Hill" was not a day of uninterrupted glory for the patriot cause. The British army had dislodged the rebels from what was then considered a vital position and the redcoats had threatened to continue to roll up American defenses back to Cambridge. Israel Putnam's attempts to encourage large numbers of Americans milling on Bunker Hill to join the defenders of Breed's Hill had largely been a failure. Artemus Ward had vacillated all day between sending reinforcements or evacuating the defenders of the peninsula. Thus the commendable steadfastness of the New England militia in the face of determined attacks by trained regulars was somewhat counterbalanced by a huge void in the American command structure. Fortunately for the patriot cause, a new general was now on his way from Philadelphia to Cambridge. William Howe's emergence as commander of His Majesty's forces in America would soon be challenged by the talents of a newly appointed Virginia planter.

# CHAPTER 4

# Boston Redeemed and New York Damned

## *The Emergence of George Washington*

$T$ he day before Colonel Prescott's men began their fortification of Charlestown peninsula, the Continental Congress chose a new commander-in-chief for the provincial forces besieging Boston. While the president of Congress, John Hancock, hoped and expected to be offered the command of an almost exclusively New England army, fellow Massachusetts delegate John Adams was equally determined to procure the position for a southern planter. Adams was convinced that the appointment of George Washington of Mount Vernon was the only logical choice for an army that had any pretensions of Continental scope. Thus despite Hancock's resentment "about Adams' back room negotiations," George Washington, Esquire, was appointed "General and Commander in Chief of all the forces raised and to be raised in defence of liberty."

The nomination of a Virginian to the supreme command of the newly established Continental Army provided a happy convergence of interests for key northern and southern members of the Continental Congress. On the one hand, a number of New England delegates believed that there was no better means of obtaining vital southern financial and military support for the rebellion in Massachusetts than by choosing a supreme commander from outside of the northern colonies. Even northern delegates noted George Washington's impressive appearance and his excellent record in the military committees of Congress. Compared to men with more or less equal military experience, no single individual gave evidence of the same well rounded personality, steadfast character and political sagacity.

While northerners viewed Washington's appointment as a device to secure more broad based support for the challenge to British rule, men from the middle and southern colonies viewed the Virginia planter as a barrier to

New England hegemony. Many influential patriots from New York to Georgia were uneasy about the prospect of the New England army defeating and expelling the British and then imposing their own peculiar laws and lifestyles on the rest of the colonists. The appointment of Washington would serve as a deterrent against the possibility of substituting King Stork for King Log.

George Washington's reaction to his appointment to commander-in-chief reflected the Virginian's complex personality. He had been the only member of Congress to wear a military uniform to each session, and he had let it be known that he would accept the supreme command if it were offered. However, his response to his fellow delegates was filled with trepidation. "I feel great distress at the position. I do not feel myself equal to the command I am honored with." The sobering reality of independent command encouraged him to challenge Patrick Henry to discover a more unrewarding appointment than general of a newly formed army. "From the day I enter upon the command of the American armies, I date my fall and the ruin of my reputation." While Washington expressed mixed feelings about both his own aptitude for the position and the long term impact of the appointment on his reputation, an objective examination of the choices available to the colonial leaders at that moment in time reveals the simple reality that Washington was the most prominent military figure from one of the most prominent colonies in the new alliance. No other competitor for the position possessed the right combination of attitudes, experiences and personality that George Washington offered to an infant nation. He had developed the vital combination of life experiences, ambition for command and sense of American identity that would eventually make him the personification of the whole Revolutionary cause.

Virtually every stage of Washington's first 43 years of life had provided experiences that would be invaluable to commanding troops during the long and draining conflict that was just emerging. He had explored and surveyed wilderness territories when sheer survival depended on adaptability, flexibility and courage. His quick response to the bloody ambush of General Edward Braddock's army near Fort Duquesne during the French and Indian War had saved most of the British troops from virtually certain annihilation. He had supervised slaves, artisans, tutors and overseers on his extensive plantation lands and had become comfortable in managing large numbers of people. He had mastered the critical art of engaging less prominent freeholders to view him as one of their kind while electing him to a seat in the House of Burgesses.

On a second level, Washington's dealings with the regular military establishment provided substantial motivation for wanting to convince his Revolutionary War opponents that they had made a major mistake in treating his talents so lightly in his earlier service on their behalf. Washington spent much of his military experience in the French and Indian War as a colonel of Virginia militia who was frequently enraged when British lieutenants, captains and majors ignored or ridiculed his authority because he wore the blue uniform of a provincial officer rather than the red coat of a regular. His initial response to these insults was to use every tactic that he could imagine to secure a commission in a regular regiment. These requests for admission to the close-knit circle of professional officers were continually rejected and Washington left military service feeling very much an outsider. Now with the British Empire in a virtual state of civil war, he had been appointed to command an army that would challenge the most powerful regiments in the world. A triumph over those professionals would provide Washington with the ultimate opportunity to cause the British high command to regret their cavalier attitude toward a talented but unrecognized provincial.

Finally, Washington's experiences as a colonial planter had exposed him to the petty discrimination suffered by British subjects who lived on the wrong side of the Atlantic. He paid annoying import duties on products that could be made more cheaply in America; he was constantly overcharged by London merchants who sent over goods of poor quality; he noted the condescending attitude of British tailors and craftsmen as they supplied orders from an obviously unsophisticated provincial. By 1775 Washington had developed an increasingly clear conviction that Americans were different from and better than their counterparts in England.

While Washington had never before commanded a particularly large body of men in combat he brought to his appointment a tenacity of character and abilities as a leader that were crucial to any long term prospect of military success. His determination and steadfastness of purpose rooted in an unshakable conviction of the righteousness of the American cause, a scrupulous sense of honor and duty and a dignity that inspired the respect and confidence of those around him more than compensated for the tactical errors caused by a lack of command experience. In fact, his consciousness of his own defects and his willingness to profit by any military experience allowed him to learn the essentials of strategy, tactics and military organization that far surpassed his initial capabilities against the British regulars.

Soon after he arrived in the American camp outside Boston on July 2nd, 1775, George Washington realized the appalling difficulties facing the commander of an embryo army. While the soldiers were generally well fed and relatively healthy, there were few other positive developments that were apparent. Discipline in the army was lax and officers and men were almost indistinguishable; drunkenness and malingering were common; ammunition was so scarce that most men had only three rounds apiece. The camps were filthy and poorly guarded as sentries frequently walked away from their posts before they were relieved. Perhaps the greatest challenge facing the new general was the fact that most of the regiments had only enlisted until the end of the year and thus much of the army might be on their way home just as the British finally decided to risk another assault on the rebel defenses.

The new American commander was soon sending a steady stream of letters to relatives and friends bemoaning the problems of organizing a rabble in arms into a army capable of meeting the British regulars on an open battlefield. "Could I have foreseen what I have experienced and am likely to experience, no consideration on earth would have induced me to accept the command. In short, they are no means such troops as you are led to believe of them from the accounts which are published. I daresay the men would fight very well if properly officered although they are an exceedingly dirty and nasty people." While Washington was less than enthusiastic about the personal characteristics of New England soldiers, he was still convinced that they could be formed into a decent fighting force under certain conditions. He agreed with Colonel Prescott that the battle of Bunker Hill might have been won if the forward troops had been more fully and aggressively supported by officers and units which shrank from the conflict. Now the worst disciplined units could be disbanded and new regiments organized with better officer material. As the Reverend William Emerson noted, "the strictest government is taking place and great distinction is being made between officers and soldiers. Everyone is made to know his place and keep it."

While Washington organized new companies and regiments on the fields around Cambridge, the British army in Boston was facing its own set of problems as the first frosts descended upon Massachusetts. William Howe had replaced Thomas Gage as the commander of British forces but the change in command did little to improve the soldiers' morale. The regulars were hungry, cold and bored. Robberies, housebreakings and rapes were followed by the inevitable round of floggings and hangings. British officers amused themselves with amateur theatricals and a generous supply of spirits while their general became fast friends with Mrs. Betsy Loring, the attractive wife of a minor Loyalist official. Howe had been given permission by the British government to evacuate Boston if he deemed it a military necessity, but the new commander was toying with a number of possible plans to destroy the rebel besiegers.

The American commander-in-chief was also considering a number of potential offensive strategies to drive the British from Boston. Washington requested 3000 reinforcements from the middle and southern colonies. These new forces included a number of companies armed with the vaunted Pennsylvania long rifles. While these weapons were very slow to load and couldn't carry a bayonet, they had a fantastic range that could pick off British pickets, scouts and officers which added a major psychological feeling of encirclement for the regulars in Boston.

While the riflemen kept the British behind their breastworks, Washington approved Colonel Henry Knox's plan to travel to Fort Ticonderoga and bring back every usable cannon from that captured fort's arsenal. Knox spent six weeks dragging heavy artillery pieces through snow, mud, swamps and streams and finally arrived back at Cambridge with 59 invaluable cannons including siege howitzers, mortars and other guns that could devastate British defensive emplacements. Now Washington was ready to attempt his first major confrontation with the British army. On the night of March 2nd, 1776 an advance force of 800 American soldiers swarmed over the unoccupied Dorchester Heights and took up defensive positions. A short time later, 1200 men under General John Thomas moved up the hills with 300 carts filled with fascines, barrels, rocks and pressed hay. While Knox's newly acquired artillery began a diversionary bombardment of Boston, the rebels dug a number of forts to protect them from British grapeshot and musket fire. At 3 A.M. fresh working parties relieved the first shift of troops and erected additional fortifications at a feverish pace. A hazy mist shielded the Americans from British lookouts until slightly past dawn when astonished English officers confirmed the presence of a series of fortifications that dwarfed the earlier operation on Breed's Hill. One British officer insisted that it would take 20,000 men to build such formidable fortifications, while another redcoat described the feat as "an exploit equal to the genie in Aladdin's lamp."

General Howe immediately began planning an extremely risky frontal assault designed to push the rebels out of Dorchester. Hundreds of stoic regulars numbly waited for the orders to embark from city wharves on their way to a bloody replay of Bunker Hill. Howe was actually risking a major catastrophe, as Washington had already formulated a contingency plan to launch a 4000 man amphibious attack on the weakly held Boston defenses while the main British army was slogging up the Dorchester hills. The resulting battle may well have pinned most of the British army between two larger rebel forces and resulted in the annihilation or capture of Howe's entire army. This sort of overwhelming disaster might have brought the King's friends in Parliament to the brink of major concessions to the colonies well before independence became the only feasible alternative policy for the rebels.

Just as the British assault force was embarking from the Boston docks, a torrential rainstorm pounded the region and canceled both the British attack and the American counterstroke. The provincials now had ample time to perfect their emplacements and by the morning of March 6th, American mortars were dropping shells on the British defenses. When Howe concluded that Boston wasn't worth a major battle, scores of transports began evacuating the British regiments, hundreds of terrified Loyalists and as much equipment as could be loaded. On March 17th in "an astonishing silence" the first American troops cautiously entered the streets of Boston just as the British fleet disappeared beyond the horizon. Washington's army had captured huge stores of military supplies, 250 cannon and crucial quantities of powder and flints. They had also redeemed the spiritual capital of colonial resistance to ministerial tyranny.

The evacuation of the British army from Boston marked the end of the first of two distinctive stages of the American War of Independence. As

British historian Jeremy Black has correctly observed, the American campaign to expel British military power from the united colonies actually produced two separate struggles for independence. The first struggle ended less than a year after the opening shots at Lexington when the withdrawal of Howe's army temporarily left the 13 colonies totally free of British military occupation. The rebel leaders now possessed the enormous psychological advantage of gaining physical control of the entire American land mass from New Hampshire to Georgia, while Crown officials and sympathizers had been stripped of any military support to back their demands for inhabitants' demonstrations of loyalty to the government of Britain. A substantial expeditionary force of the world's most powerful empire had been forced to evacuate a major city and European powers such as France were already beginning to realize that permanent estrangement of Britain and her colonies was a real possibility.

Washington's first campaign had ended in a breathtaking success. Now the American general and most of his fellow patriot leaders realized that the British king and ministry would most likely expend enormous reserves of manpower and money to retake their most valuable overseas possession. It was readily apparent that a larger, better equipped British expeditionary force would soon be crossing the Atlantic to suppress the rebellion in one massive campaign. Now the second, and far more complex segment of the American Revolution was about to begin.

The British ministers and military leaders who designed the strategy for operations in America during 1776 had already received a sobering analysis of their task from newly returned General Thomas Gage. The former British commander insisted that the government leaders must realize that "the Americans are now spirited up by a rage and enthusiasm as great as people were ever possessed of, and you must proceed in earnest or give the business up. A small body acting on the spot will not avail. You must have large armies making diversions on different sides to divide their force. A large army must at length be employed to reduce these people, including the hiring of foreign troops. I fear it must come to that or else avoid a land war and make use only of your fleet." The basic plan devised by the British officials in Westminster and Whitehall was to utilize a large force of British regulars and German mercenaries to strike the rebellion from two directions. General Guy Carleton would lead an army from Canada to capture Lake Champlain and then move down the Hudson River to threaten the rebels from north of New York City. Meanwhile, an army of almost 35,000 men under General William Howe would land on Staten Island and threaten Manhattan while hopefully engaging the main colonial army in the process.

When General Washington moved 10,000 Continentals and militiamen from Boston to New York during May of 1776, his first instinct was to bypass Manhattan and plan a campaign using the Hudson Highlands as a base of operations. A number of his subordinates urged Washington to remain in Manhattan only long enough to burn New York City and thus deny its port facilities to the British. However, Congress viewed the city as an important psychological symbol of American resistance and a fairly rapid reinforcement of an additional 9000 men persuaded Washington to try to defend the community.

Washington's main objective in his strategy for holding New York seems to have been based on a hope to entice Howe into a replay of Bunker Hill by holding key pieces of high ground around the city. This plan might have had some merit if General Howe had obliged with another frontal assault against American entrenchments, but that general had sworn off this tactic after the Massachusetts campaign. Now the British commander could use his brother Admiral Richard Howe's huge naval flotilla to land at any point of his choosing around New York while the rebels couldn't possibly defend every threatened position. The enormous advantage of total control of the sea was merely enhanced by the almost 2 to 1 military superiority held by the British army, and the possibility of victory was even further augmented by the fact that much of the American army consisted of raw recruits who had never fired a shot in anger.

Any objective analysis of the strengths and weaknesses of the British and American forces in the summer of 1776 shows that there were far more reasons for Washington to abandon New York rather than risk an almost irreplaceable patriot army to defend the city. A town filled with Tory sympathizers, difficult to defend and open to British naval power was hardly the ideal location for a climactic battle. Any moderately effective defence of threatened landing beaches would have required an army of 60,000 men while Washington had less than a third of that number. The American commander now compounded the risk of annihilation by dividing his army into two contingents with one each on Manhattan Island and Long Island.

Washington seemed fascinated by the possibility of luring the British into a frontal assault on Brooklyn Heights near the tip of Long Island, so he ordered an extensive series of forts and breastworks built along the Brooklyn line. Unfortunately for the Americans, the defence of Long Island was entrusted to a revolving door list of rebel generals. Nathanael Greene was Washington's first choice for the key responsibility but the Rhode Islander came down with malaria and had to be replaced by the far less talented John Sullivan. After carefully reviewing Sullivan's many drawbacks, Washington suddenly added General Israel Putnam to the command mix although Sullivan was kept in command of the main wing of the defending army.

Putnam knew exactly nothing about the topography of Long Island, and his subsequent troop dispositions were terrible. He placed 4000 men in the Brooklyn Heights fortification where the soldiers would be in a good spot to repel a British frontal assault but couldn't support any other provincial units. A 1700 man force under General William Alexander, a claimant to the title of Lord Stirling, was utilized as the right wing of an outer defence perimeter placed along a ridge of hills about two miles from the Brooklyn fortification. Three thousand men under General Sullivan were dispatched to form a center for the outer defenses while a single Pennsylvania rifle regiment was designated as the left flank well out of supporting range of Sullivan's men. After placing his forces in poorly chosen positions, Putnam compounded the error by assuming that Sullivan had placed adequate defence forces on each of the roads leading up to the American positions so he didn't bother to check the approaches himself.

Putnam and Sullivan had now set up a series of defensive dispositions that were so weak that William Howe couldn't have asked for a better target if he had designed the American emplacements himself. On August 26th, 1776 Howe landed 22,000 men at Gravesend at the tip of Long Island and set in motion a huge flanking operation which if it had been fully implemented would have ended the war within 24 hours. At eight o'clock that night the British advance forces began to move into their assigned positions. A 5000 man force under General James Grant was positioned to occupy Stirling's wing while an additional 5000 British and Hessian regulars gained the attention of Sullivan's regiments. Meanwhile a column of 10,000 redcoats was marching toward Jamaica Pass in an attempt to get behind the American defenders. By 2 A.M. the British advance force had moved up to Jamaica Pass and expected a fairly formidable American defence. However, Sullivan had allocated only five men to hold the position and these rebels were quickly swept up by an amazed force of mounted British and Tory scouts. The main attack force now marched along Jamaica Road just out of earshot of Colonel Samuel Miles' regiment guarding the American left flank. Soon they were in position to strike the rebel outer defenses from behind.

The outcome of the battle of Long Island was largely decided before the first shot was fired. Over 20,000 British troops had virtually encircled fewer than 5000 colonial soldiers. Now a rapid succession of British maneuvers began to take shape. First, several British warships occupied the American artillery on Brooklyn Heights with a dawn bombardment of the rebel positions. Then the Hessian regiments positioned in front of Sullivan's men enticed the Americans to advance a short distance against them after hearing the signal that the British main force had flanked the colonials. Suddenly green coated jaegers and blue coated grenadiers sprinted towards the provincials with a massive volley of rifles and muskets. Just as Sullivan's men were engaging the Germans, they heard the cheers of Scottish regiments that were brandishing bayonets and claymores and attacking from the rear. The Americans were sandwiched between two enemy forces, and the Flatbush Road, the main retreat route to Brooklyn Heights was cut off. Within moments the center of the American army was disintegrating. Hessians were spitting terrified rebels to trees with bayonets and striking down whole groups of men attempting to surrender as they reacted to British claims that Americans didn't take prisoners and mutilated wounded enemies. While the main escape route had been cut, numbers of colonials fled across the fields and entered the Brooklyn defenses causing panic among the mostly untrained militia garrisoning the fortifications.

The American right wing was more heavily outnumbered but the larger numbers of Continental regiments were able to make a much more ferocious stand. General Grant refused to even launch a serious demonstration against the rebels until his 5000 man contingent was reinforced by 2000 Marines and naval frigates had raked the Americans artillery emplacements. The 1700 men from the crack Delaware and Maryland regiments formed a V formation on the high ground while they exchanged volleys with 7000 enemy soldiers. Finally Lord Cornwallis was able to maneuver 4000 redcoats behind the American defenders and soon the dwindling American force was being hammered from front, flank and rear. Stirling ordered most of his surviving men to head for the swamps and marshes around nearby Gowanus Creek, the only escape route not cut by the enemy. While a significant number of Colonials were able to make their escape, dozens of men drowned as they struggled through the morass.

Stirling's last act of defiance was to draw his sword and rally the 250 Marylanders under Mordecai Gist. This small force launched a frontal assault against 11,000 stunned redcoats and an ever smaller number of Americans regrouped for four more attempts to break through the British lines. As most of the Americans were killed or wounded, Gist was able to break through with a mere eight survivors while Stirling and a few other walking wounded held back the enemy. George Washington had recently arrived close enough to watch the final spectacle of American bravery and exclaimed "good God! What brave fellows this day I must lose!"

The entire outer defence of the American position on Long Island had now collapsed with over 600 rebels killed or wounded and over 800 men captured with a total British loss of about 300 killed and wounded. While Howe's assault on Breed's Hill had cost the British army about 45% of its attacking force, the percentage of casualties on this August day was less than 4% of the men engaged. Now terrified remnants of Sullivan's division were racing through the American defenses while their commander was being captured by a company of Hessians. While Washington rode up and down the American lines brandishing two pistols and threatening to shoot the first man who fled, Israel Putnam cried out his now familiar caution to withhold fire until the men could see whites of the British eyes. Just as historians have speculated for years about Union and Confederate chances for victory during the never launched Federal assault on Lee after Pickett's Charge, the non-event of a British assault on Brooklyn Heights on August 27th, 1776 provides fascinating alternative scenarios.

While the American position looked like a formidable obstacle from a distance, one more push by Howe's already victorious regulars might have virtually ended the Revolution. The American troops were inexperienced, disorganized, terrified of British and Hessian bayonet attacks and hemmed in by the guns of the Royal Navy. Washington's main garrison was outnumbered almost five to one by an enemy that was now almost certain it was invincible. However, Howe simply ignored the pleas of subordinate officers and directed his men to make preparations for a siege of Brooklyn. By the morning of August 28th, the first muddy hills thrown up by British digging were within 600 yards of the American defenses.

Washington's response to the establishment of a British siege of Brooklyn was one of his critical decisions of the war. Rather than accepting a European style siege based on sending out sorties and hoping to delay the British approaches, the American commander simply refused to follow accepted military conventions and instead ordered a highly risky evacuation of his army. On the night of August 28th, Colonel John Glover's Marblehead regiment of Massachusetts mariners began to evacuate the American army from Long Island to Manhattan. While successive lines of colonial defenders gradually leapfrogged back to the Brooklyn ferry terminal, a steady stream of barges and small boats pulled the embarking troops across the East River. A providential early morning fog provided vital extra hours to pull out the rear guard units and the first British advance scouts didn't arrive at the shoreline until the last Americans were embarking.

Washington had saved his army to fight another day but momentum was clearly on the British side. As Washington noted to a member of Congress, "the militia are dismayed, intractable and impatient to return home. Great numbers have gone off, in some instances by whole regiments—with the deepest concern I am obliged to confess my want of confidence with the generality of the troops." The illness or capture of several general officers encouraged Washington to reorganize his army into three divisions. Israel Putnam's division was assigned to defend New York City, William Heath's division was charged with securing the Kingsbridge link with the mainland and Joseph Spencer's contingent was deployed to contest a British landing between the city and the northern tip of the island.

The activities of these division commanders didn't seem to inspire Washington to much confidence in his ability to hold Manhattan for an extended period. He notified Congress that "we should on all occasions avoid a general action and never be drawn into a necessity to put anything to risk. That the enemy means to winter in New York there can be no doubt; that they can drive us out is equally clear; nothing seems to remain but to determine the time of their taking possession."

Howe may have planned to spend the winter in Gotham, but his leisurely schedule after the American evacuation of Long Island frustrated any British officer who possessed a sense of urgency about the war. A disgruntled British naval captain complained that "for many succeeding days did our brave veterans, consisting of 22,000 men, stand on the banks of the East River, like Moses at Mount Pisgah, looking at their promised land, a little more than half a mile distant." The commander of the British army had been receiving steady reports of huge desertions in the American army and when one piece of intelligence revealed that 6000 of the 8000 members of the

Connecticut militia had simply vanished, Howe's delaying tactics seemed to be working.

On September 15th, 1776 William Howe concluded that the American positions on Manhattan had been sufficiently weakened by desertion to attempt the next British assault. A fleet of British frigates provided covering fire as General Clinton landed at Kip's Bay with a battalion of light infantry, a battalion of grenadiers, three battalions of Hessian jaegers and a brigade of British Guards. Howe chose the landing spot because he was convinced that the rebel defenders had no artillery emplaced and the Americans would be forced to fight on an open plain with little available cover. The American area commander, General Spencer, was proving his high level of incompetence by failing to develop any real plan of beach defence while he sat waiting for a more convenient British landing at Turtle Bay.

A dawn cannonade by 86 guns on British ships signaled the landing of 4000 British and Hessian soldiers on Manhattan Island. Within minutes the 900 American front line defenders had lost 60 killed and 60 captured while the rest of the force conducted a panicked retreat. As the redcoats began to consolidate their beachhead, Washington arrived on the scene to direct the deployment of nine regiments of New York and Connecticut recruits. While their general galloped around the field giving orders for the men to defend a series of fences and cornfields, the American army simply disintegrated. At one point 2500 patriots were routed by a charge of 70 British light infantry who were soon following a trail of hats, packs, canteens and muskets. Washington exploded with rage as he lashed out at his sprinting men and he managed to land blows on a wide spectrum of troops ranging from terrified privates to a particularly speedy brigadier general. Redcoat infantry now began to close in on the almost dazed general and at one point he seemed to be considering a one-man attack on the British regulars. Finally, a nearby aide grabbed the reins of Washington's horse and pulled his commander to safety just as British muskets exploded around him.

This crucial moment in a disastrous battle might have come close to ending the Revolution. An entire American division had crumbled within minutes at a loss of over 400 men while only 12 redcoats were injured in the attack. The 5000 colonial troops defending New York City were now almost cut off from their only escape point as British soldiers swarmed across the width of Manhattan. The most important figure in the American cause seemed to prefer a glorious death to command of a disorganized rabble As the many New York Loyalists anticipated the raising of the Union Jack in their city, the stunning American success in Boston seemed to have become ancient history. It was now quite apparent that one more major British victory could consign the Declaration of Independence to the obscurity of a defeated cause.

# CHAPTER 5

# Rekindling the Flame of Liberty

## *Harlem Heights to Princeton*

*T*he American struggle for independence from England suffered a number of significant crises that in each case saw the patriot cause lurch dangerously close to submission to royal authority. The disintegration of the American outer defenses at Long Island, the surrender of the large Continental garrison at Charleston, and the barely avoided loss of West Point due to Benedict Arnold's treason are examples of particularly bleak periods in the revolutionary conflict. However, if one searches for a specific day in which the prospects for final victory seemed most bleak, September 15, 1776 could easily serve as a candidate for the darkest day of the war. By the late afternoon of that date, it seemed that the British conviction that an amateur rabble could never stand against a professional army had been proved convincingly and few men on either side could have predicted that the last flickering flames of rebellion would be soaring anew less than sixteen weeks later.

At dinner time on September 15th General William Howe was directing a huge, confident army in what appeared to be the final major action of the American Revolution. The American defenders at Kip's Bay had been routed after inflicting only a dozen casualties on the British landing force, the commander of the American army had narrowly avoided death in battle and almost half of the American army was virtually trapped in New York City. The American soldiers had panicked so quickly in their defence of the beaches that a dazed George Washington had momentarily lost his desire to live to fight another day. As General Nathanael Greene insisted, "General Washington was so vexed at the infamous conduct of his troops that he sought death rather than life." When the psychologically devastated American commander returned to his headquarters on Harlem Heights he was informed that the British beachhead was expanding so quickly that Israel Putnam's division was almost sure to be trapped and captured.

However, soon after nightfall the whole attitude of Washington and his army began to undergo a dramatic transformation. Small units of Putnam's division began to straggle into the American camp and as the night continued almost all of the "lost" American regiments reported for duty. In an incredible stroke of luck for the rebels, Howe had halted the expansion of the British lines just short of covering the entire width of Manhattan Island. While Howe and his subordinates enjoyed their food and ale, Putnam's soldiers had slipped through a narrow strip of fields next to the Hudson River, carefully avoided British roadblocks and patrols, and filed back toward the main American positions. They had left behind huge supplies of food and ammunition and had abandoned over half of the entire artillery strength of the Continental forces, but by the morning of September 16, 1776 several thousand soldiers were members of Washington's army and not future residents of the British prison hulks in the adjoining rivers.

A newly invigorated commanding general now ordered a force of 120 elite rangers under Col. Thomas Knowlton to investigate British troop dispositions in the Harlem Heights area with a promise of rapid reinforcement if Knowlton ran into trouble. Soon after the American rangers moved into the woods and hollows separating the contending armies, they were attacked by over 400 British light infantry who were on a similar probing mission for General Howe. Within a few minutes the outnumbered Americans were retreating to the taunting bugle calls of the British scouts who were using the signal given during a fox hunt when the fox has skulked into his hole. This supreme insult to a disintegrating American army transformed the patriot commander into an enraged combatant determined to extract vengeance for such a humiliation.

Washington quickly dispatched three rifle companies to support Knowlton's rangers and when the American marksmen began picking off the advancing British officers, the light infantry panicked and began to withdraw. The wavering redcoats were soon stiffened by the arrival of the famed Black Watch regiment of Scotsmen who arrived on the scene with bagpipes playing and claymore swords glistening in the late summer sun. The American rangers and riflemen pitched into the overconfident Scots and in a brawl of rifle butts against bayonets and swords, Knowlton went down with a fatal wound. Just as the American defenders were collapsing, a sweating and panting force of 800 rebel reinforcements slammed into the redcoats who were soon fighting for their lives. Only the arrival of a large force of Hessian grenadiers saved the British from annihilation.

The heavily reinforced King's troops now began a gradual withdrawal toward their main lines but suddenly two Maryland regiments managed to get around the enemy flank and the British lines began to crumble. Now whooping and cheering rebels were chasing the British and Germans through a series of fields and orchards and the regulars were bordering on panic. The last minute intervention of two elite British infantry battalions and two grapeshot firing artillery pieces was able to slow down the American charge until the redcoats and their allies could retreat to the cover of the guns of the fleet.

The vigorous American attack at Harlem Heights provided an enormous lift for the whole rebel army. Slightly more than 2000 rebels had virtually routed almost 5000 British and Hessians during a battle in which 130 Americans and 170 redcoats were killed or wounded. Howe was forced to admit that the battle was "an unfortunate business" which caused "a good deal of concern." For the first time in the New York campaign, the American rebels had bested a British force. Now an even more cautious British commander spent almost a month fortifying the newly captured American port while Washington's army was able to refit and reorganize.

While the engagement on Harlem Heights raised American morale and showed that the provincial soldiers could stand up to British regulars, that day's action provided one of the rare bright spots in the New York campaign. Quite simply, Washington's strategy, tactics and troop deployments during the summer and autumn of 1776 were far short of brilliant. The American commander utilized a four week hiatus to pull his army back to White Plains, where he directed the construction of a series of fortifications and virtually dared Howe to attack him there. Most of the American positions had been well chosen but near perfect emplacements weren't good enough when confronting a more numerous and more experienced enemy. Washington' engineers had for some reason failed to fortify an elevation called Chatterton's Hill which, in enemy hands, could dominate the whole American right flank. When Washington finally realized the importance of the hill, the British were already assaulting the American lines. A militia regiment rushed up the hill to delay the redcoats but ran right back down when a few British shells landed nearby. Before a force of regulars could be dispatched to the critical point, Howe's men had stormed up the other side and were beginning to blast the exposed American lines. The British were now in position to roll up the entire American army regiment by regiment. However, Howe decided that it was time for a siege and the rest of the British army simply stood in place as Washington's army slipped away.

The British commander had squandered another opportunity to crush the American rebels but Washington's next move soon provided Howe with another chance for victory. The Virginian's strategy after White Plains seems particularly confused as he divided his outnumbered army without any real expectation of a major gain to compensate him for the risk. Washington left 8000 men under the command of General Charles Lee to hold a base near West Chester. This contingent didn't seem to particularly threaten any British force and was ultimately knocked out of the war for the next several months. The rest of the army, about 3000 men, was dispatched to New Jersey to supplement the American garrisons at Fort Washington and Fort Lee on opposite sides of the Hudson River. The attempt to utilize these forts to harass the British during November, 1776 would mark one of the lowest points of Washington's military career.

Washington's first instinct when he surveyed the defensive capabilities of Fort Washington was to abandon the fortification and combine the 2000 man garrison with his own force to deter a British invasion of New Jersey. However, a trio of subordinate generals, Nathanael Greene, Israel Putnam and Hugh Mercer, convinced their chief that the fort was impervious to British assault. Unfortunately, the American generals were more than a little over optimistic, as the structure was a gigantic military millstone. The fort possessed no well and water had to be hauled up from the Hudson. There were no bombproof trenches, no fuel supplies and almost no sanitation. The British navy was virtually untouched as English ships could easily sail out of range of the fort's artillery. Despite all of these drawbacks, a dithering commanding general not only failed to evacuate the position, he actually permitted another several hundred soldiers to be deployed in the potential trap.

Even William Howe could not resist this opportunity for an easy victory, and on the morning of November 16th he dispatched an army of 8000 men to storm the fortress. As British naval and land artillery started to bombard the fort, Washington and several of his lieutenants were rowed across from New Jersey to evaluate the situation. The outer American defenses were now crumbling under a Hessian assault and Colonel Robert Magaw, the garrison commander, urged Washington and the other generals to leave. One by one the outer trenches were overrun by British and German assault parties and soon the entire 3000 man American defence force was crossing into the small main bastion. At this point General Knyphausen, the commander of the assault force, demanded Magaw's surrender under threat of executing the garrison if the fort was taken by storm. The panicky and disorganized Americans now threw down their weapons and over 2900 rebels became prisoners of war.

The American attempt to prevent the British capture of New York had virtually decimated the entire Continental army. Washington's erratic strategy decisions and the generally poor performance of most American combat units had provided William Howe with a truly spectacular victory. The British expeditionary force of 32,000 men had lost only 200 killed and 1000 wounded in the series of battles from Long Island to Fort Washington. In New York City the Union Jack was flying over every public building and an enthusiastic British officer remarked that "the inhabitants carried the King's officers on their shoulders; they have felt so much of real tyranny since the New England rebels came among them that they are at a loss even to enjoy their release."

George Washington's retreating American army was a shadow of its pre-Long Island strength. The rebels had lost 500 men killed, almost 2000 wounded and over 4000 men captured in the past three months. Not only had one third of the American army been lost on the battlefield, whole companies and regiments of provincial militia were deserting every day. At this point the virtually disintegrating Continental Army bears a striking resemblance to John Bell Hood's Army of Tennessee as it retreated from Tennessee after being decimated in the battles of Franklin and Nashville. Both Washington's and Hood's armies were literally disintegrating as they retreated through a barren December landscape. However, while the Army of Tennessee was effectively finished as a fighting force by December, 1864, the equally ragged winter soldiers of 1776 were still capable of inflicting unpleasant surprises on their British pursuers.

The rebel army that marched through the Watchung Mountains during the endless rainy days of December 1776 was now reduced to about 3000 men. When this straggling handful of men reached the Delaware River at Trenton, Washington ordered the destruction or removal of all available boats to delay a British advance into Pennsylvania. The American commander gradually realized the error of giving command of most of his army to Charles Lee as the English veteran simply ignored Washington's messages to rush his men to Pennsylvania. Luckily for the American cause at the very moment when Lee was most likely to emerge as the new commander of the Continental army, his eccentric lifestyle would rob him of the opportunity.

Charles Lee has consistently been vilified by admirers of George Washington as an incompetent semi-traitor who performed no positive service for the American cause. This evaluation is probably overly harsh as Lee did prove to be a genuine asset in the critical first stage of the war. The former British officer combined energy, experience and enthusiasm for American liberty to benefit the rebel cause. He was instrumental in strengthening the American emplacements around Boston, had a major role in defeating a British attempt to capture Charleston and was an effective spokesman for the value of mobile militiamen against trained regulars. Unfortunately, Charles Lee was also one of the most eccentric personalities during a century that seemed to revel in strange behavior. Lee was filthy, obnoxious, sarcastic, obscene and incredibly ugly. The possibility of a triumphant Charles Lee's image on the American dollar bill would probably terrify most citizens of the United States. However, Lee's biggest drawback was that by the late fall of 1776 he was convinced he was a far better general than Washington and seemed perfectly willing to allow the Mount Vernon planter to lose an army to prove his point.

Lee moved his large detachment of the American army at a glacial place during the early weeks of December, 1776. Apparently he was beginning to formulate a plan to gain command of the Continental Army as he stopped at Mrs. White's tavern in Basking Ridge, New Jersey on the night of December 12th. Although he spent the night almost five miles from the protection of his army, Lee had no inkling that he was soon to be a guest of His Majesty's army. A British cavalry patrol that included the soon to be notorious Lt. Banastre Tarleton intercepted an American dispatch rider who after being threatened with decapitation, obligingly revealed Lee's less than secure lodgings. On the snowy morning of December 13th, two dozen British light dragoons crept up on the tavern, routed Lee's bodyguard and captured the American general in a bathrobe and slippers. While Lee would finally be exchanged 18 months later, his major role in the American Revolution was now virtually over.

George Washington had two reasons to be thankful to the British cavalry for their dawn raid on Basking Ridge. First, the American commander was now freed from the intrigues of his major competitor for supreme command. Second, Washington was able to utilize part of Lee's command to initiate one of the most brilliant counter strokes of the War of Independence. Washington could now consider a more aggressive behavior because his British nemesis had essentially decided that the 1776 campaign season was officially over. William Howe had intercepted a number of Washington's dispatches to Congress warning the legislature that most of the army was due to be discharged on New Year's Day. Howe apparently decided that good food, warm quarters and the amiable companionship of Mrs. Betsey Loring in New York were far more congenial than chasing after a soon to disintegrate rebel army through snow covered fields and frigid rivers. Thus Howe deployed some of his regiments in a series of strong points from Burlington to Trenton and ordered the main part of his army into winter quarters in New York.

When George Washington realized that Howe had decided to end active campaigning for the year, the aggressive American commander immediately began to explore opportunities for a counteroffensive. He explained to a friend that "I am wearied to death with the retrograde motions of things" and determined to use his army in battle before much of it simply melted away with the new year. Washington was able to combine regiments from Lee's division, a reinforcement of Pennsylvania militia and the remnants of his own force to collect almost 6000 men for an attack on the British outposts in New Jersey.

The operational plan which emerged would be initiated with a surprise attack on the Hessian brigade defending Trenton with possible follow-up assaults on the British garrisons at Princeton and Brunswick. The attack on Trenton was designed to begin on Christmas night after the German garrison had been isolated from other enemy outposts. During the week before Christmas, American advance parties had gradually severed the links between Trenton and other garrisons by ambushing enemy cavalry patrols, capturing dispatch riders and attacking Hessian pickets. This harassment became so effective that Colonel Johann Rall, the brigade commander at Trenton, was finally forced to use an escort of 100 infantry and an artillery detachment just to protect a letter to the British commander in Princeton. Rall's subordinates were convinced of an impending American attack, but the colonel ignored their warnings and boasted that one good bayonet charge would send the American rabble fleeing in panic.

Washington's planned assault was based on three columns crossing the

Delaware River and launching coordinated attacks from three directions. A force of 900 infantry and two artillery companies under General John Cadwalader would mount a diversionary attack against the British garrison at Bordentown to block any reinforcements from that direction. General James Ewing would take 700 Pennsylvania and New Jersey militia across at Trenton ferry, seize the bridge over the Assunpink Creek at the south end of town and seal off any possible enemy escape. The main assault force of 2400 men would cross at McKonkey's Ferry, nine miles north of Trenton, split into two columns under General Sullivan and General Greene and launch a pre-dawn attack.

At 2 o'clock on the clear, cold afternoon of December 25th, 1776, Washington's main force began to form up for the river crossing. By mid-afternoon each brigade had moved to its embarkation point as Colonel Glover and his Marblehead men readied a fleet of large Durham boats for the crossing. As the first companies began to embark, a light snow began to fall and within an hour a major snowstorm had developed. The most difficult part of the loading operation was the backbreaking process of loading 18 heavy artillery pieces on the boats. Washington and Henry Knox, the Continental artillery commander, had agreed that the inclusion of a large artillery contingent was vital to the success of the plan. Continental artillerymen had a high morale as members of the most prestigious arm of the American army and they knew that their ability to plug the vents and muzzles of their pieces in wet or snowy weather provided a much more reliable weapon than the failure prone muskets.

The crossing of the ice-clogged Delaware River proved to be the first major hurdle for the shivering rebels. Contrary to the popular illustrations of the crossing, George Washington did not strike a dramatic pose in the front of the boat. The American commander and his men were firmly planted in their seats as they huddled against a stinging combination of snow and sleet while the boats banged up against drifting ice. The appalling weather conditions delayed the landing in New Jersey until 3 A.M. on December 26th and Washington now realized that a pre-dawn attack was out of the question.

George Washington would have been depressed by more than the late arrival of his men if he had known that both General Cadwallader and General Ewing had taken a long look at the raging snowstorm and decided to call off their missions. Now the one remaining landing force enjoyed a much smaller numerical advantage than originally envisioned and a key escape route had been left open to the enemy. The 2400 assault troops now divided into two columns with Sullivan's division assigned to attack the town from below while Greene's contingent would come in from above. Luckily for Washington, the disrupted marching schedule and lack of reinforcements were counterbalanced by Colonel Rall's blunders. Rall had permitted his three regiments to enjoy a huge Christmas celebration that included generous supplies of seasonal spirits. Not only was most of the garrison sleeping off a major hangover, their commander had spent the night playing cards and guzzling punch and was barely functioning the next morning.

The American assault on Trenton began just after 7:30 A.M. when an advance force of 60 American infantry dispersed the few Hessians placed on guard duty. Lt. Jacob Piel heard the initial shots and woke Colonel Rall who stumbled into the street and tried to organize a German attack. Rall ordered his own blue-coated regiment to advance up King Street, the Lossberg regiment to move up Queen Street and the Knyphausen regiment to form a reserve. Just as the Hessians were forming into their ranks, a six gun battery commanded by Captain Alexander Hamilton began blasting the bewildered enemy. When the Lossbergs started dragging up their own cannons to reply to the American fire, a company led by Captain William Washington and Lieutenant James Monroe charged the Hessian gunners and captured the pieces although both American officers were wounded. The confusion in the German ranks allowed the Americans to occupy an increasing number of houses and outbuildings and American marksmen were picking off enemy soldiers by the dozen. A few minutes later the Hessian commander went down with a mortal wound and the first sign of panic swept through the German regiments.

While these two regiments were being decimated by American cannons and rifle fire, the Knyphausen regiment fixed bayonets and prepared to rush to their comrades' aid. At that moment Col. John Stark's New Hampshire regiment charged from behind and soon caught the Germans in a crossfire. Elements of all three Hessian regiments were now rushing through the streets trying to locate a way out of the trap. Since Ewing's detachment had never arrived, the Assunpink Bridge remained temporarily open and several hundred Hessians and a few British light dragoons were able to run to safety. The battle of Trenton was now less than 90 minutes old and most Hessian resistance had ended.

The failure to cover a critical escape route had allowed Rall's brigade to escape total annihilation, but Washington's army had still inflicted a devastating defeat on His Majesty's cause. The Hessian garrison had lost 25 killed, 90 wounded and 920 captured with a loss of 3 regimental colors and several pieces of artillery. The American attackers had lost a minuscule four men wounded including future president James Monroe. Washington's surprise attack had pumped new life into a dying American cause and had disproved Howe's claim that the war was virtually over. However, while many other generals would have been satisfied with this major accomplishment, Washington was determined to continue the American offensive. Washington ordered his army back to the Pennsylvania camps after the capture of Trenton and immediately began activities designed to hold his army together after the end of the year. The general called upon Robert Morris of Philadelphia to provide 50,000 paper dollars and $150 in hard currency to offer bounties to extend the enlistments of the departing New England regiments. He praised the assembled men by admitting that "you have done all I asked you to do and more than could be reasonably expected" and then promised every soldier a $10 bonus in return for an extra six weeks of duty. This bounty was a generous offer of almost two months pay and was enough to convince about half of the men to remain until February.

Now Washington crossed back into New Jersey with about 1400 regulars and 3000 Pennsylvania and New Jersey militia and deployed his army along Assunpink Creek. While the Americans were reinforced by a few additional companies of militia, they were no match for a rapidly advancing British division of 8000 men under Lord Cornwallis. Washington had placed his army in a potential trap as the Americans had the Delaware River at their back and Cornwallis was pushing his troops far more rapidly than the ever cautious Howe. The American general was able to avert disaster by ordering two critical operations. First, Washington rushed a crack brigade of riflemen and rangers to delay Cornwallis' planned assault. When the initial brigade commander, Frenchman Mathias de Fermoy staggered back to Trenton in a drunken stupor, one of the regimental leaders, Colonel Edward Hand, was quickly assigned to replace him. Hand's skilled riflemen were able to pick off large numbers of the British advance force and Cornwallis was forced to re-deploy on every creek and stream from Princeton to Trenton. When the Americans retreated into Trenton they quickly began sniping from every window and fence, compelling the redcoats to conduct a house to house fight. Cornwallis finally broke free of the village streets but it was almost dark and he was faced with the choice of a night assault on Washington's lines or a postponement until the morning. The British were already battered by American riflemen and exhausted from the constant deployments so the British commander easily convinced himself that he would "bag the old fox" in the morning.

Washington's response to this British threat was typical of his ability to innovate and extemporize in a crisis. The general ordered 400 of his men to build bonfires and make as much noise as possible with picks and shovels to convince Cornwallis that he intended to defend his positions after daybreak. Meanwhile the bulk of the army was marching quietly to the Quaker Bridge several miles beyond the left flank of the British army. Soon over 4000 American soldiers were accompanying muffled wagons and artillery caissons in a night march to attack the British rear guard at Princeton while the enemy army in Trenton prepared to attack phantom defenders.

At dawn on January 3rd, 1777, Washington called a halt to the march on the outskirts of Princeton and prepared to assault the three British regiments reported to be holding the town. General Mercer was ordered to tear down the bridge at Stony Brook to delay Cornwallis if he returned north; General Sullivan's column was ordered to enter Princeton from the east and surprise the British garrison from the rear while Nathanael Greene's column would launch a simultaneous frontal assault.

Washington's plan was well conceived and the Americans would have the same advantages of superior numbers and surprise that had produced the victory at Trenton. Unfortunately, most of the British garrison was no longer in the village but was marching on a collision course with the American columns. The British commander at Princeton, Colonel Francis Mawhood, had apparently decided during the night that Lord Cornwallis might need additional troops for his attack on Assunpink Creek and thus the British colonel hurried south with two of his regiments and 30 light dragoons to provide support. Mawhood was stunned to see part of Mercer's advance unit marching toward him in the frigid early morning and he ordered his men to seize the nearest high ground which dominated the road. The Americans spotted the same hill and cut across the frozen fields to grab the position. The rebels won the race but the British had three times as many men and were equipped with artillery. The arrival of men from Colonel John Haslet's Delaware rifle regiment and an artillery battery under Captain Daniel Neill evened the odds somewhat, but the British infantry launched a bayonet charge against an American force that had less than 20 men with bayonets. The redcoat assault killed Mercer and Haslet and routed the survivors. Soon the panicked Americans were running across the fields towards Quaker Road and only the arrival of Captain Joseph Moulders' cannons turned back the triumphant English attackers.

The American line near Quaker Road was now starting to crumble and Mawhood's regulars were forming for another bayonet assault to carry the day. At this critical moment George Washington arrived with reinforcements and began to organize an American counter thrust. Elite units such as Hitchcock's brigade of Continentals and Hand's Pennsylvania riflemen were now interspersed with the reorganizing militia units. As American rifle companies worked their way around the British flank and started to pick off officers and sergeants, Washington formed an extended assault line and marched his men to within 30 yards of the redcoats. At this point the American frontal volleys combined with effective rifle fire on the flank began to annihilate the British defenders. The redcoat line wavered and then disintegrated as an exuberant Washington, yelling "its a fine fox chase boys," charged after an enemy force that was running for their lives.

While two British regiments were collapsing on Quaker Road, the remaining force of redcoats was deploying along a stream called Frog Hollow. Messengers straggled in reporting the disaster to Mawhood's command and the men from the 40th Regiment were soon retreating from Sullivan's attacking division. When a running battle erupted through the streets of the town, some of the redcoats broke off the engagement and fled toward Brunswick. However, most of the regiment barricaded itself in Nassau Hall, the main building of the College of New Jersey, and the largest structure in America in 1777. The redcoats knocked the glass out of the windows and prepared to pick off the first wave of attackers. However, Alexander Hamilton and Joseph Moulder wheeled up their artillery pieces and soon cannon balls were flying through the building. The first ball tore through the prayer hall and beheaded a portrait of King George II, which was a less than positive omen for the British defenders. Finally, Captain James Moore, a New Jersey militia officer whose Princeton house had been looted by the British, led an infantry assault on the wavering garrison. A few minutes later the 194 surviving redcoats had surrendered and the Americans had gained their second stunning victory in little more than a week.

The American commander was now faced with one of the more challenging dilemmas of his military career. The huge British supply depot at Brunswick contained mountains of equipment, thousands of muskets and an extremely tempting war chest of £70,000 in hard currency. Washington admitted that "with six or seven hundred fresh troops upon a forced march would have destroyed all their stores and magazines, taken their military chest and put an end to the war." Unfortunately, there were no fresh troops available as the American soldiers began slipping into barns and silos and disappearing into the woods to seek warmth, food and sleep. The third and final throw of the dice during the New Jersey campaign was never attempted.

Notwithstanding the failure to bag the Brunswick cornucopia, the American victory at Princeton was only a little less spectacular than the earlier battle of Trenton. The British 4th Brigade had been virtually eliminated as an effective force with a loss of 60 killed, 150 wounded and 244 captured, against an American casualty total of 30 killed and 75 wounded. Within less than two weeks, an apparently disintegrating rebel army had eliminated six enemy regiments, inflicted over 2000 casualties at a loss of only slightly more than 100 men, and had recovered 75% of New Jersey for the patriot cause. Frederick the Great of Prussia analyzed the campaign in glowing terms. "The achievements of Washington and his little band of compatriots between the 25th of December and the 4th of January were the most brilliant of any recorded in the history of military achievements."

William Howe could still field an army of over 30,000 men and American militia units continued to return home in alarming numbers, but the American victories in New Jersey infused new life into the patriot cause and provided George Washington with his first substantial triumphs after a string of near disasters. All in all, Trenton and Princeton proved that the results of the New York campaign had not been so disastrous as it first appeared. The British did hold New York and some of the surrounding country, but only there and at Newport, Rhode Island, did they have footholds at the end of 1776. The Americans could well afford to trade a little space for a great deal of time.

CHAPTER 6

# Alternative Strategies and Outcomes

## *Rebels and Redcoats 1775-1776*

$T$he first two years of the American Revolution are viewed in retrospect as a more critical period in the formation of political policy rather than an era of decisive military engagements. While this initial period of the patriot struggle produced the dramatic events surrounding the debate and ratification of the Declaration of Independence, there was no climactic battle of the scope of Saratoga or Yorktown which determined the eventual outcome of the war. However, although neither the American rebels nor the British ministerial army was able to terminate the conflict in their favor between the spring of 1775 and the spring of 1777, each army did have several opportunities to inflict such a decisive defeat on the enemy that the war indeed might have ended in its first stage with either de facto American independence or British suppression of the rebellion as the two widely divergent outcomes.

The first major opportunity for the American patriots to gain most of their desired concessions from King and Parliament occurred during the 11 month struggle for control of Boston and its outlying regions. American military resistance during the Massachusetts campaign caught the British military establishment at its weakest point in the conflict. The Royal Navy's battle strength was enormously weakened by the poor physical condition of many of its ships, the transport ships needed to ferry a large expeditionary force to America were not yet available and large numbers of infantry regiments were at their low peacetime establishments. The main projection of British force in the colonies centered around the 5700 man garrison at Boston which was virtually besieged by a much larger, if far less professional, colonial army. The American rebels not only enjoyed a large numerical advantage, the colonies were also swept by the rage militaire which for the only time during the war suspended the natural aversion of the provincials to military organization and military discipline. A decisive American victory over the one available British army would send shock-waves through Westminster and Whitehall and create a clear opportunity for a negotiated peace largely on American terms.

The first opportunity to turn a military embarrassment into a full scale disaster occurred during the Battle of Bunker Hill. The American defense of Breed's Hill on the afternoon of June 17, 1775 had scored a major psychological triumph, as William Howe's assault force lost over 40% of its strength while failing to push the British offensive beyond Charlestown peninsula. However, more effective overall command decisions by General Artemus Ward, more successful encouragement of disorganized reserve companies by General Israel Putnam and the timely arrival of supplies and ammunition on the front line defenses might have resulted in the near annihilation of half of the British army in America.

William Howe's strategy for capturing Breed's Hill had largely failed after two redcoat assaults had been devastated by American marksmen. The success of the third and final assault was not due to any brilliant maneuvers on the part of the British leadership but was based on the simple fact that the rebel soldiers had no more ammunition. A third assault launched against a reinforced and resupplied American line would most likely have been repulsed with enormous casualties with a disorganized and decimated British army then ripe for a provincial counterattack that might have largely eliminated Howe's whole assault force. The capture of a senior British general and most of his army would have been a devastating blow to opponents of compromise in the British cabinet and Parliament and would have left the remainder of His Majesty's forces in America at enormous risk. A Boston garrison of barely over 3000 men that had just witnessed the defeat of half of its army would have been opposed by almost 18,000 triumphant rebels soon to be commanded by an aggressive George Washington.

A second opportunity for a decisive patriot victory emerged during the first week of March, 1776. When Washington ordered the construction of extensive artillery emplacements on Dorchester Heights, William Howe immediately drafted a plan for a British assault on the rebel fortifications. The scheme focused on a British night assault utilizing most of the army while a smaller contingent held the city of Boston. Howe didn't realize that Washington had planned for just such a contingency and was ready to launch a 4000 man assault force against the Boston defenses while the British were climbing toward the Dorchester emplacements. This scenario would have created a real possibility for British disaster as Washington's defensive emplacements were far stronger than the Breed's Hill fortifications, while a successful American landing in Boston would have trapped the British army between two superior rebel armies.

The decisive defeat of the British army in Boston would have forced a massive crisis on the crown and ministry in London. The King might have used the virtual annihilation of a British army as an emotional spur to British patriotism. He could have hoped for a groundswell of popular enthusiasm to avenge this stain on British honor through a massive retaliation against the American rebels. On the other hand, it is somewhat more probable that moderates in the cabinet, supported by pro-American Whigs and wealthy merchants concerned with loss of their colonial markets, would have devised a comprehensive peace offer acceptable to the majority of patriot leaders. An offer of conciliation that included removal of all Parliamentary taxes, formal recognition of the Continental Congress and Continental Army and some offer of compensation for destruction of property during the war would have redressed most colonial grievances, while British expectation of some pro forma provincial expression of loyalty to King George would have guaranteed an American presence in a trans-Atlantic commonwealth. A serious offer of conciliation presented to the American colonists before the late spring of 1776 would have essentially fulfilled most of the initial war aims of the rebel cause. Thus it is ironic that a major British defeat in Massachusetts might have prompted the very concessions that would have maintained American political ties to Britain for the foreseeable future.

While the possibility for an early peace settlement favorable to colonial expectations was most apparent during the Massachusetts campaign, the prospect for a termination of the conflict on terms more agreeable to ministerial hard liners was a strong likelihood during the ensuing struggle for New York and New Jersey. A more energetic British response to glaring American strategic and tactical errors during the 1776 campaign would probably have resulted in a virtual collapse of the rebel military effort. The preponderance of British ships, guns and men combined with the disadvantages suffered by a largely untrained American army and inexperienced rebel commander should have produced ample opportunities to restore royal authority to the rebellious colonies.

The arrival of General William Howe and Admiral Richard Howe at Staten Island during the summer of 1776 symbolized British determination to suppress the rebellion during one campaign season. General Howe commanded an army that could use British naval supremacy to land troops at any location of his choosing and then outnumber the colonial defenders by a 2 to 1 margin. His force was supplemented by Loyalist regiments who were familiar with local topography, roads and landmarks and could easily infiltrate rebel units. Howe commanded an army that was composed of far more diverse units than the stereotypical robot-like infantry that was incapable of any flexible movement. Military units included contingents of German jaegers, English light infantry, Scottish highlanders and Tory rangers that could move as quickly as most rebel formations. Howe's primary target was a city that was very difficult to defend and contained a large Loyalist population that would welcome the British regulars as liberators from Congressional tyranny.

This long list of British assets contrasts sharply with the state of American affairs in 1776. Washington was an inexperienced general consulting subordinate officers who were largely incompetent or unsure of themselves at this stage of the war. The American Continental units were outnumbered almost 6 to 1 by British regulars so that the possibility of colonial success often depended upon untrained militia who could desert the regular army at the first crisis in a battle. The Congressional insistence on defending Manhattan Island had forced Washington to attempt to hold a position that was simply untenable without adequate naval support.

This enormous disparity in British and American capabilities clearly provided William Howe with the means to destroy the poorly deployed rebel army in one campaign and thus allow the British government to impose a reconciliation with the colonies very much on terms acceptable to King and Parliament. The British commander had at least three opportunities to effectively end the war in 1776 and thus become a pivotal figure in the annals of British military history.

The first clear-cut opportunity for British annihilation of the rebel cause appeared during Howe's brilliant flank attack on the American forces at Long Island. The British attack plan had worked splendidly as the outer perimeter of the provincial army simply disintegrated and several of the most valuable Continental regiments were eliminated from the conflict. The remainder of the American army had retreated behind a system of defenses on Brooklyn Heights that was little more than a hollow shell. Washington had allowed almost 10,000 colonials to be trapped in a position with no effective escape route and one spirited British bayonet charge would have utterly destroyed the cohesion of the rebel forces. However, rather than annihilating the American army on that sultry August afternoon, Howe called back his victorious army to prepare for classic siege operations against the patriot defenses. This command decision is simply incomprehensible. The British army had suffered only minor casualties during the battle while several of the most experienced American units had been utterly destroyed. Unlike the redcoats who faced a near victorious and highly confident rebel army on Breed's Hill which had twice devastated the attacking regulars, the British army on August 27, 1776 faced a demoralized and panicky enemy with a potential assault force almost ten times the size of the contingent deployed at Charlestown. The battle that should have ended the American Revolution was transformed by Howe's caution into a mildly satisfying demonstration of British superiority on an open field of battle.

Most less fortunate military commanders would never have been granted a second chance to secure total victory at virtually no loss to their own forces. However, William Howe clearly demonstrated his exceptional good luck when barely three weeks later the American army again presented itself for quick elimination. The British landing at Kip's Bay seemed to confirm the conviction among British leaders that the American rebels could never defeat a regular army in an open field engagement. Only a dozen British soldiers were injured in an assault that killed or captured hundreds of rebels and almost resulted in the death of George Washington. Much of the remainder of the American army had been poorly deployed around New York City and an energetic expansion of the British beachhead across Manhattan Island would have cut off their final escape route. However, Howe halted the British advance with plenty of daylight remaining and allowed the American garrison to escape to Harlem Heights.

The American retreat across New Jersey after the disastrous capitulation of Fort Washington provided William Howe with a final opportunity to terminate the war during the first full campaign season. Washington's army was disintegrating during the early winter of 1776 and even the commanding general was beginning to admit in private that the end was near. Yet Howe's failure to seize the initiative allowed the rebels one last opportunity to save the dying revolution.

The first setback to British intentions occurred when Howe allowed his German mercenaries to practice the kind of warfare that visited havoc on the civilian population. Just as large numbers of New Jersey residents were flocking back to the royal standard with guarantees of amnesty and protection, the Hessian units began a systematic campaign of plunder and looting that devastated Loyalist and rebel households alike. Since the mercenaries didn't seem to know or care whether they were pillaging friends or enemies of the king, a growing number of Jerseyites realized that royal protection offered few benefits and many risks. Soon large numbers of fence sitters were enrolling in rebel militia units to supplement a Continental Army desperately short of manpower.

The second weakness in Howe's strategy for New Jersey was the inability of the British commander to pursue Washington beyond the Delaware River. While Washington was able to collect most of the boats around Trenton before he evacuated to Pennsylvania, this move was a very temporary expedient. Howe's army possessed a large number of barges in New York City that could have been transported to the shores of the Delaware. There were also plenty of carpenters and artificers who could construct additional craft on site. The British army had both the naval capability and the manpower to chase Washington back to Philadelphia and capture the colonial capital by Christmas. The loss of Philadelphia at this point would have been a much larger psychological blow to the patriots since there would be no offsetting victory in another theatre as there was when the British were capturing the city just as they were about to lose an entire army at Saratoga.

Howe's ultimate choice of strategies was the worst of both worlds as he neither pushed his army into Pennsylvania nor completely withdrew to New York. The policy of placing small garrisons around the frontiers of New Jersey was a dramatic invitation to a gambler such as Washington who would turn Howe's error into a dazzling psychological victory for the patriot cause.

Thus by the first week of 1777 the War of Independence had entered a phase in which the possibility of a relatively early and easy victory for either of the contending forces was now greatly diminished. The patriot "rage militaire" of 1775 which might have encouraged a chastened British government to seriously consider a generous peace settlement with its disaffected colonists had not survived the first year of the war and now American hope for eventual victory rested on an unstable mix of small numbers of long term professionals, larger numbers of unpredictable amateurs and the ultimate aid of foreign powers. On the other hand, the British expeditionary force that landed in New York in 1776 had been provided with the manpower, weapons, money and naval support that should have beaten an over-matched enemy lead by an inexperienced general. The peculiar set of circumstances that would provide Britain with every reasonable opportunity to win the war in an single campaign would never quite be repeated during the remaining five years of war.

# CHAPTER 7

# The War for the North Country

## The Genesis and Climax of the Saratoga Campaign

William Howe's offensive against New York and New Jersey during 1776 was expected to play the dominant role in forcing the rebellious colonists to submit to imperial rule. However, this campaign had been designed in Whitehall as part of a two pronged advance that would not only secure New York City as a major base, but also effectively split the New England provinces from the rest of the rebel alliance. The British attempt to coordinate parallel campaigns against the American rebels would not only demonstrate the ineptitude of the ministry in exercising control over imperial military resources, but would ultimately result in the loss of an entire field army in one of the most decisive turning points of the entire revolution.

The sequence of events that entered a climax with the surrender of 7000 British and German soldiers at Saratoga, New York had its genesis in an aborted American offensive initiated almost two years earlier. During the autumn of 1775 George Washington and a number of congressional leaders developed an increasing interest in the potential political and military benefits of adding the province of Canada to the thirteen colonies already in conflict with the British ministry. Eventually two American expeditionary forces were raised and equipped to invade Canada from different directions. While a New York based column under General Richard Montgomery marched from Fort Ticonderoga up Lake Champlain and on to the St. Lawrence River, a contingent of New England volunteers under Colonel Benedict Arnold followed the far more treacherous route up the Kennebec River toward the Chaudiere Valley near Quebec. The Americans were convinced that the Canadian governor, Sir Guy Carleton, could not effectively cover two invasion routes with less than 1000 available regulars and that many of the French inhabitants would rally to the rebel cause when given the opportunity.

Richard Montgomery's brigade was able to subdue the British garrison at St. John's on November 3rd, 1775 and ten days later the Americans had possession of Montreal. However, Arnold's column was struggling through one of the most difficult marches in military history. The planned 20-day expedition soon stretched to 45 days as incessant rains washed out primitive paths and food supplies ran so low that the men were forced to eat their candles and moccasins. Large numbers of volunteers turned back, scores died of exposure and only slightly more than half of the original 1100 man force arrived on the Plains of Abraham outside the walls of Quebec. Meanwhile, Montgomery's brigade was being decimated by disease and the need to garrison captured posts, so that the former British officer was able to bring only 300 men to reinforce Arnold's exhausted New Englanders. The Americans were soon conducting a "siege" of Quebec while they were actually outnumbered by the British defenders who had been receiving a steady stream of reinforcements. The two American commanders decided to launch a desperate New Years Eve assault during a raging blizzard. While some rebel soldiers were able to penetrate the town's defenses, Montgomery was killed, Arnold was badly wounded and newly emerging hero Daniel Morgan was forced to surrender much of the assault force.

While Benedict Arnold was attempting to direct American operations from a hospital bed, General Carleton was organizing his substantial relief force that had embarked from England. His Majesty's forces in Canada soon numbered over 10,000 men including regular German and British regiments, Canadian woodsmen and Indian auxiliaries. During the spring and early summer of 1776 this force not only pushed the last American units from Canadian soil but continued down Lake Champlain with the objective of capturing Fort Ticonderoga and Albany. Carlton had assembled an impressive freshwater fleet of 24 gunboats, 2 schooners and an 18 gun flagship which threatened to sweep rebel defenders from the 135 mile length of the lake.

The American soldiers who formed the Northern Army of the newly proclaimed United States were just as poorly equipped, poorly deployed and outnumbered as their counterparts in Washington's army around Manhattan. There were only about 3500 men available for duty between Albany and Canada and their effectiveness was further diminished by a Congressional feud which alternately placed Horatio Gates and Philip Schuyler in command of the theatre. The only senior officer in upper New York who was convinced that the British invasion could be frustrated was the energetic but perplexing Benedict Arnold. Arnold was given command of an unfinished rebel shipyard at Skenesborough, New York and ordered to cobble together some sort of naval unit that might at least delay Carlton's invasion. The former New Haven pharmacist wheedled supplies, bullied subordinates and eventually constructed a motley fleet of gondolas and row galleys that at least produced an American naval presence on Lake Champlain.

Arnold knew that his jury-rigged fleet could never challenge the British squadron in an open battle, so he chose to base his ships in a small defendable bay at Valcour Island where the American vessels might escape detection. On the morning of October 17, 1776 the British fleet passed Valcour on its way to Ticonderoga and after the ships had passed, Arnold ordered an American attack on the enemy rear. The under-gunned rebel ships were able to damage a few British opponents but enemy gunfire soon smashed all but five of the American vessels to pieces. During the night Arnold was able to maneuver his surviving ships through the British pickets and begin a headlong retreat to the south. Unfortunately, the British ships were fast enough to compensate for the patriot head start and by the next day the powerful flagship *Inflexible* began obliterating the surviving vessels. Arnold beached the remaining ships and ordered his largely army based crews to rendezvous at Fort Ticonderoga. Carleton ordered a cautious land and maritime pursuit and was soon within three miles of the outer defenses of the American bastion.

The subsequent actions of the British commander seem incredible for a victorious commander who had decisively defeated a crumbling and outnumbered enemy force. Carleton called off a planned assault on Ticonderoga with the excuse that it was too late in the season to march to Albany and holding the American fort for the winter wasn't worth the effort. He informed Lord George Germain that "the season is so far advanced that I cannot yet portend to Your Lordship whether anything further can be done this year." Carleton's attitude seemed a perfect match to the hesitation surrounding William Howe's activities further south. Arnold's defeat, with the loss of his entire fleet, had produced a British withdrawal that would delay any effective attempt to capture Albany for almost a full year and produce the same unsatisfying results that the main British army had accomplished in the vital campaign of 1776.

Sir Guy Carleton had not only fumbled an opportunity to split the rebellious colonies in two, he had also given Lord Germain the perfect opportunity to diminish the Canadian governor's future role in British military operations. The Secretary of State for the colonies had never forgiven Carleton's role in a court martial which had ended Germain's military career and almost resulted in his execution after the battle of Minden in 1759. The hiatus in British campaigning during the winter of 1776-77 provided General John Burgoyne with an opportunity to return to London and provide Germain and George III with a self serving proposal to end the rebellion through a massive expedition initiated on Canadian soil. Burgoyne's "Thoughts for Conducting the War from the Side of Canada" detailed a three pronged offensive in which one British column of 2000 men would drive east through the Mohawk Valley while a picked force of 14,000 men descended from Canada and moved down the Hudson toward Albany to link up with a third army commanded by Howe that would move upriver from its New York City base. George III agreed with Burgoyne's premise that if Washington tried to stop Howe he would be an easy target for the combined British armies, while if he didn't move, New England could be invaded and knocked out of the war. After receiving a gala send-off and the King's personal good wishes, John Burgoyne embarked for his role in reuniting the colonies to England.

Burgoyne arrived in Quebec on May 6, 1777 confident of success but already short of men. While the king had provided tokens of his personal affection, he had also insisted that an 8000 man contingent of regulars was wasteful to the treasury and promptly sliced a thousand men from the total. When Burgoyne arrived in Canada he expected Carleton to fill out the expedition with an additional 6000 men equally divided among Loyalist volunteers, Indian auxiliaries and Canadian woodsmen. Unfortunately, the great expedition had stimulated little energy for recruiting on Carlton's part and a startled Burgoyne counted only 150 Canadians, 100 Tory rangers and 400 Indians to supplement his regulars. Thus the actual strength of the great invasion column was barely over half of its intended level, a shortcoming that would haunt the British commander in future weeks.

On June 16, 1777 the British expedition moved out in sparkling , clear Canadian summer weather with delightful breezes, moving the dozens of flapping regimental flags and banners. The 3700 British regulars represented seven elite regiments while the 3000 Germans were organized into five regimental units. A force of over 500 artillerymen shepherded over 130 cannons while Indian allies moved along water routes accompanied by over 200 Batteaux. One enthusiastic British officer described the panorama before him, "the army was in the best condition that could be expected or wished, the troops in the brightest spirits, admirable, disciplined and remarkably healthy."

Burgoyne's first major objective on American soil was the bastion at Fort Ticonderoga now commanded by General Arthur St. Clair and garrisoned by a mixed body of 2500 Continentals and militia. Most of St. Clair's men had no bayonets, food supplies were low and there were too few men to fully man the defensive perimeter. While the fort was generally well situated, a nearby height, Sugar Loaf Hill, rose 800 feet on the west side of the defenses and dominated both Ticonderoga and all the adjacent out-works. The artist John Trumbull, who was inspecting the fort in his capacity as Gates' adjutant general, quickly spotted this vulnerability and urged St. Clair to fortify the heights. However, the post's incompetent engineer, Jeduthan Baldwin, convinced his commander that the British could never drag cannons up so steep a mountain. On July 2, 1777 an advance party of British engineers scouted the Ticonderoga defenses and convinced Bur-goyne that Sugar Loaf Hill could be occupied if blocks and tackles were employed to lift the artillery into position. The backbreaking process took almost three days to complete but by the morning of July 5th British batteries were looming down on the American fortress. St. Clair finally realized that his emplacements were now useless and ordered an evacuation to the west shore of Lake George. The first major barrier to British control of the Hudson had now disappeared.

While the bulk of the Ticonderoga garrison marched south in relatively good order, Colonel Seth Warner was ordered to remain near Hubbardton, Vermont with a rear guard to delay British pursuit. At dawn on July 7th Warner's largely sleeping force of 600 men was startled into action by a British assault force under General Simon Fraser. The rebels were able to hold the 750 attackers at bay for most of the morning, but the subsequent arrival of a strong reinforcement of German jaegers flanked the American defenses and threatened to annihilate the whole rear guard. Although Warner's force inflicted over 200 casualties, he left behind over half of his men as casualties or prisoners and abandoned 12 artillery pieces. During the next several days, the main contingent of the American army retreated from Skenesborough to Fort Edward as St. Clair desperately attempted to reorganize an increasingly dispirited column of rebels. Burgoyne now had the option of moving his army a short distance back up to Fort Ticonderoga and then reembarking by water down Lake George. This move would have put the British army on the upper reaches of the Hudson River with no major American units between his expedition and Albany. However, in one of the most heatedly debated decisions of the American Revolution, Burgoyne rejected even a minor retrograde movement as disastrous to morale and insisted on pushing forward on a land route through the difficult terrain of the northern New York wilderness. The current American theatre commander, Philip Schuyler, immediately dispatched hundreds of American axmen and pioneers to contest every foot of the British march. While the rebels felled trees, flooded roads and destroyed bridges, Burgoyne's column crawled toward Fort Edward at the rate of just over a mile a day. By the end of July the British army had marched only 23 miles closer to Albany and the first sign of serious American resistance was about to appear in the crucial upper reaches of the Mohawk Valley.

The first significant obstruction to the British master plan for 1777 occurred at the gateway to the Mohawk River on the site of modern Rome, New York. Colonel Barry St. Leger's 2000 man wing of the British expeditionary force had landed at Oswego on Lake Ontario and quickly moved toward the American stronghold of Fort Stanwix. The mixed force of British regulars, Hessian jaegers, Tory Royal Greens and Indian warriors expected to confront an American garrison of no more than 60 men. When St. Leger's force arrived in front of the patriot defenses they were startled to be confronted by several regiments of Continentals fully manning the walls. The energetic and resourceful American commander, Colonel Peter Gansevoort, had a garrison of only 750 men, but his men were committed to a last ditch defense of their post rather than risking a surrender to an enemy that included almost a thousand Indians who might easily massacre their prisoners. Gansevoort's determination to maintain his position was heightened by the arrival of messengers sent by General Nicholas Herkimer who reported that an additional force of 800 Tryon County militia was hurrying up the Mohawk Valley to support the defenders.

At nightfall of August 5th, 1777 four regiments of American militia had arrived near present-day Utica, New York and expected to complete the final 14 miles of their march to Stanwix the next day. Gansevoort informed Herkimer's scouts that he would fire three cannon sometime the next day to signal the start of a sortie designed to distract St. Leger while the Tryon men approached the fort. The next morning Herkimer was content to proceed at a cautious pace while he waited for the sortie, but his regimental commanders and other subordinate officers wanted to move much faster. Stung by charges of cowardice and inaction among his men, Herkimer reluctantly ordered a more rapid advance through the woods between the Sauquoit and Oriskany Creeks.

St. Leger's Indian scouts reported the poor security around the American column and the British commander was convinced that he could ambush the approaching rebels with little threat to his own men. A relatively small force of 100 Tory rangers and 400 braves under Sir John Johnson were deployed on the approach route near a deep ravine in Oriskany Creek. As the August sun pushed the temperature into the mid 90's, the less than security conscious Americans entered a 700 foot ravine which was over 50 feet deep with plenty of dense undergrowth. Suddenly Colonel Ebenezer Cox's lead regiment was almost annihilated by volley after volley fired by the unseen green coated Tories. The flank and rear of the American column was smashed by rapidly moving Indians who continually fired and moved to a new place of concealment. Herkimer fell from his horse with an ultimately mortal leg wound and the panicked militia were about to disintegrate as a fighting force.

The battle of Oriskany might have produced the most complete annihilation of an American army during the Revolution but a number of factors intervened to spare at least part of Herkimer's army. First, the enemy trap had been sprung before the rear American regiment had entered the ravine. As scores of terrified militia ran from the closing ambush, large numbers of Indians broke from their cover and chased the fleeing Tryon County men. Soon two miles of fields and woods were littered with the bodies of tomahawked and scalped patriots. However, this carnage provided a respite for the men trapped in the ravine and the dying Herkimer was able to organize the survivors into two-man teams that enabled one man to fire while the other reloaded, thus keeping the Indian knives and tomahawks somewhat at bay.

The rebel militia was able to organize a final defensive line to counter an impending assault by an enemy, now reinforced by additional Tory companies. However, in the midst of the climax to the battle an enormous summer thunderstorm pelted the region and temporarily slowed the vicious combat.

As the warriors and Loyalists began to reorganize for a renewed assault against the few remaining battle-worthy rebels, Indian messengers arrived from Stanwix with the startling news that their camps were being plundered. A 200 man sortie under Lt. Colonel Marinus Willet had slipped out of the fort, dispersed a company of British pickets and plunged into the Indian encampment. Willet's force carted off 21 wagon loads of vital weapons, ammunition, blankets and cooking utensils and began to destroy anything that couldn't be removed. The Indians assaulting Herkimer's column soon abandoned the field to attempt to salvage their vital equipment and the relatively small contingent of Tories was forced to withdraw to Stanwix. Although Herkimer's army held the battlefield, the American loss in killed and wounded was one of the highest of the war. Only 150 Americans remained capable of marching to Stanwix and the four regiments had lost as many as 400 dead while inflicting only a third as many casualties on their assailants. However, Fort Stanwix was still a fully operational bastion and St. Leger's Indian auxiliaries were strongly considering the advantages of leaving His Majesty's regulars to fight the war on their own. The final blow to the St. Leger offensive occurred several days after Oriskany when Benedict Arnold began a drive up the Mohawk Valley with a crack force of almost a thousand New York and Massachusetts Continentals. The Indian warriors received exaggerated reports of American reinforcements and abandoned their role in the siege with a final flourish of looting the British camp. St. Leger's outnumbered regulars were now in a headlong retreat to Oneida Lake and the Mohawk Valley prong of the great offensive was effectively eliminated from the campaign.

The American defense of Fort Stanwix had substantially negated the role of one major wing of Burgoyne's expedition, but the commanding general was confident that his main body would suffer no such embarrassment. However, Burgoyne's enormous supply train and unwieldy artillery units would need vast numbers of additional horses in order to make any progress in the increasingly inhospitable wilderness. General Friedrich von Riedesel, commander of the German brigade, eventually convinced Burgoyne to organize a large scale raid employing his mercenaries to sweep the Vermont countryside for cattle and horses. Lieutenant Colonel Friedrich Baum was assigned a mixed force of 800 men to undertake a "stealthy" foraging expedition to the east of the Hudson. The 300 Tory rangers and Indian scouts might have been appropriate to the spirit of the mission, but the employment of a large unit of dismounted Brunswick dragoons marching with 12 pound jackboots and tripping over huge broadswords seems more than a little ludicrous for a mobile striking force. On an even more incredible note, a German band accompanied the raiding party with all of its instruments, presumably to scare away the militia at the Germans' approach. Baum's scouts informed him that the town of Bennington was well stocked with horses and cattle and was defended by only 300 newly recruited militia. Unfortunately, these scouts reported back to their commander before they spotted the arrival of a far more formidable American force of 1500 New Hampshire volunteers under the command of Colonel John Stark. An additional brigade of Vermonters under Seth Warner was also on its way to Bennington to provide the Americans with added support. The German raiders arrived in the outskirts of Bennington on the rainy morning of August 15th and Baum quickly realized that he was facing an impressive enemy formation. He ordered his men to construct breastworks on a nearby ridge and dispatched a message to Burgoyne to send up reinforcements.

At noon on August 16th, 1777 the battle of Bennington opened with an American assault on Baum's hastily constructed breastworks. Stark's relatively inexperienced men were able to carry out an amazingly well coordinated series of attacks against the enemy flanks while American riflemen initiated panic among the Germans by picking off most of their officers. The turning point in the battle probably occurred when Loyalist Major Philip Skene, commanding a key section of the British defenses, noticed a party of men wearing the Tory insignia of white paper in their hats and welcomed them as reinforcements. The "Loyalist" unit quickly proved to be one of Stark's units and smashed through the enemy defenses before they could be fired upon. Now the Loyalist and Indian units melted into the woods leaving Baum to hold the emplacements with the remaining Germans. Stark rallied his men for a final assault with the cry, "there my boys are your enemies, we'll beat them before night or Molly Stark will be a widow." Mrs. Stark's marital status remained unchanged as the American volunteers pushed through the collapsing enemy line, killed the German commander and began looting the campsite and chasing after fleeing survivors.

The battle of Bennington seemed to end as a great American victory, but just as the New Hampshire volunteers scattered over the adjoining fields, a German relief column under Lt. Colonel Heinrich Breymann arrived at the battle scene and tore into the disorganized rebels with a furious bayonet charge. The 700 disciplined regulars were on the verge of scoring a stunning counterstroke when Seth Warner's first contingent of Vermont troops sprinted onto the field. While Warner's hard fighting volunteers parried German bayonet attacks with rifle butts and tomahawks, Stark reorganized his New Hampshire brigade and started a flanking movement against Breymann. The German colonel was able to rally a rear guard that held open an escape route for part of his column and about 2/3 of the relief force was able to escape the fate of Baum's men.

The battle of Bennington had crushed Burgoyne's hopes for a rapid British advance to Albany. At a cost of only 30 killed and 60 wounded Americans, Stark's army had inflicted almost a thousand casualties on Burgoyne's expedition. When these losses were added to the dispersal or retreat of the nearly 2000 men in St. Leger's army , the total force available for the capture of Albany had been cut by almost 30% in the single month of August. Just as the British invaders were losing irreplaceable men around

Stanwix and Bennington, the American defenders were gaining strength due to a senseless murder near Burgoyne's own headquarters.

Miss Jane McCrae was the daughter of a patriot farmer who fell in love with her neighbor, Daniel Jones, a member of a Tory family. When Jones became an officer in Burgoyne's army, McRae journeyed to Fort Edward to be near her fiancé. During Jane's visit at the home of a female cousin of British General Simon Fraser, a party of Indian auxiliaries entered the isolated house and carried off the two women. Fraser's cousin, a Mrs. McNeil, was led to Fort Edward while a second party of Indians took charge of Miss McCrae. Apparently these braves began to argue about the share of the reward each warrior would receive for bringing in their captive to the British camp and they settled the dispute by killing the young woman and then wandered into camp trailing her scalp of blond hair. The livid British generals Burgoyne and Fraser planned to hang the culprits but their subordinates convinced them that any punishment would result in the desertion of most of their fellow braves. The outcome of this incident enraged frontier settlers who were now convinced that Burgoyne planned to unleash an Indian massacre of provincials, and thus flocked to recruiting depots to protect their homes and families.

While the murder of Jane McRae stimulated a wave of recruiting successes in New York settlements, the appointment of a new commander of the Northern theatre encouraged a steady stream of reinforcements from east of the Hudson. On August 19, 1777 Horatio Gates replaced Philip Schuyler in the latest installment of a power struggle between New Yorkers and New England men in Congress. Schuyler had begun to organize a formidable American army at Stillwater, New York but the evacuation of Fort Ticonderoga had encouraged his New England opponents in the legislature to insist on a change of command. Schuyler's role in the defense of Fort Stanwix, the dispatch of pioneers to disrupt Burgoyne's advance and his organizational skill in raising New York militia regiments were ultimately vital to the eventual American victory at Saratoga. However, the appointment of Gates, who probably shared Schuyler's solid, but not outstanding, abilities offered the prospect of large scale reinforcements from New England to tip the manpower balance against the British invaders.

The American army that Gates inherited at Stillwater was beginning to develop into a formidable fighting force. The 7000 men available by August 19th already outnumbered Burgoyne's remaining troops and new arrivals were augmenting their strength every day. George Washington dispatched an invaluable reinforcement to the northern army by sending 550 Virginia riflemen under Daniel Morgan and several companies of elite light infantry under Major Henry Dearborn. While reinforcements streamed into the American camp, embittered Schuyler loyalist Benedict Arnold surveyed possible alternative defensive sites with engineering officer Tadeusz Kosciuszko. They convinced Gates to move his army to Bemis Heights which was three miles north of the Hudson's confluence with the Mohawk. This position provided thick hilly forests that would prevent the British from getting around the American left flank while the right wing could be protected by the Hudson River.

The Bemis Heights position featured a plateau with steep bluffs rising almost 300 feet above the Hudson and dominating the narrow defile of the river on its way to Albany. Gates' engineers designed a series of trenches and breastworks along a three sided open square with a formidable artillery redoubt in support of each position. The only possible vulnerability of the defensive network was on its western approaches where a higher plateau could threaten the emplacements if the British could flank the Americans and then scale the highest ridge.

Gates' and Arnold's concurrence on the best location for the northern army was the last major area of agreement between these two headstrong and touchy individuals. Arnold apparently viewed Bemis Heights as nothing more than a secure base from which to launch an attack on the advancing British army. The Connecticut general was convinced that the British advantage in siege practices and heavy artillery would encourage Burgoyne to move up his big guns and demolish the static American positions if given an opportunity to do so. On the other hand Gates was convinced that the British had to attack quickly in order to reach Albany before the onset of freezing weather. Unless Burgoyne could smash through the American lines and gather fresh supplies, the British would be forced to retreat back to Canada and postpone their invasion for another year.

Each of these convictions had a solid basis in fact. On the one hand, Gates was perfectly correct in assuming that Burgoyne's timetable for capturing Albany was so badly delayed that he simply couldn't afford the luxury of a leisurely 18th century siege against an enemy that already outnumbered his own army. However, Arnold was also quite correct in insisting that the strength of the American army that was developing during the late summer of 1777 might not be duplicated during a subsequent British invasion attempt in 1778 or in 1779. The combination of New York militia, New England volunteers, elite units from Washington's army and other contingents of the northern force presented a unique opportunity to an aggressive general. While the controversy between Arnold and Gates simply created more ill will between the two generals, John Burgoyne forced the issue with the first assault on the American defenses.

On the morning of September 19th, 1777, the American position at Bemis Heights was held by slightly more than 10,000 men divided into three general contingents. Brigadier Generals Glover and Patterson deployed their brigades to cover the river approaches to the camp, a center wing under Brigadier General Ebenezer Learned held the most open stretch of ground and General Benedict Arnold supervised a left wing which was charged with preventing the British from seizing the adjoining hills. Burgoyne's attack plan was based on a compromise between a reconnaissance in force and an all out assault which ultimately would involve two thirds of his army. A center assault force of about 2000 men was ordered to march on the ground between the hills and the Hudson and feel out the American defenses. This force would be operating in thick woods which precluded European style maneuvers and effectively canceled out the British advantage in artillery. A flank force consisting of 10 companies of light infantry, 10 companies of grenadiers, a team of Brunswick riflemen and British sharpshooters and a contingent of fast moving Indians and Tories was expected to work its way around the American left and try to capture any defensible high point. A third wing under the command of General von Riedesel would utilize 3 regiments of Brunswick regulars, 6 British light infantry companies and 8 cannons to cover the river road in case of an American counterattack, while searching for a weak point in the enemy defenses near the Hudson.

The morning of September 19th dawned chill and foggy making it difficult for Burgoyne and his staff to get a clear look at the Yankee position. By 11 o'clock the sun had burned off the mists and the British units began moving toward their initial assigned objectives. The advance companies of the British assault force emerged into a field called Freeman's Meadow and promptly fell out to prepare a leisurely lunch. While the British pickets lounged nonchalantly an elite American strike force of Morgan's riflemen and Dearborn's light infantry shattered the early afternoon silence, as they shot dozens of redcoats and chased the startled British soldiers through a series of fields and orchards. Suddenly the Americans emerged into a clearing where they faced a far larger British brigade which promptly scattered the attackers. Burgoyne now sensed that he could trap Morgan's invaluable rifle corps if he deployed enough men quickly and soon almost 3000 British and German troops were fixing bayonets and waiting for orders to advance on the rebels.

The American riflemen were outnumbered and carried no bayonets to parry an enemy assault but their incredibly accurate marksmanship kept dropping so many British officers that the British attack was delayed. Soon Benedict Arnold dispatched seven regiments of Continentals to support Morgan and the arrival of the fresh American units threatened the hot and exhausted redcoats with disaster. While Gates dithered between committing his reserves and containing the engagement, General von Riedesel risked the loss of the British supply trains along the River by moving his forces inland to help Burgoyne. Riedesel climbed a hill with 500 infantry and two cannons and descended into the supposedly impassable Mill Creek ravine below. The advancing regulars had smashed into one of the few weak spots in the American line and they were gradually able to push the rebels back toward the edge of the battlefield and round up small numbers of wounded Yankee prisoners.

The battle of Freeman's Farm had ended with an American withdrawal from the field, but Burgoyne's claim of victory was clearly exaggerated. The British advance had not located a significant weak point in the American defenses and Burgoyne lost another 160 killed and 450 wounded from an already outnumbered army. The patriot army had lost only 63 killed and 240 wounded and the British commander admitted "no fruits, honours excepted, were attained by the preceding victory, the enemy working with redoubled ardour to strengthen their left, their right was unattackable already." A British subordinate echoed his commander's growing concern for the army, "the courage and obstinacy with which the Americans fought were the astonishment of everyone and we now became fully convinced that they are not that contemptible enemy we had hitherto imagined them, incapable of standing a regular engagement and that they would only fight from strong and powerful works."

Horatio Gates' hesitation in committing more than a fraction of his available forces had permitted Burgoyne to escape virtual annihilation during the first battle of Saratoga. However, Burgoyne's caution during the next several days would more than outweigh the impact of the American general's dithering. The former cavalry officer was always attracted to sweeping attacks and his first instinct after Freeman's Farm was to renew the assault on the American defenses. The preparations for another attack were interrupted by messengers arriving from New York City with the news that British soldiers were moving up the Hudson. General Henry Clinton informed Burgoyne that the long awaited operation against the American defenses in the highlands of the Hudson had finally begun as 3000 redcoats were now preparing to storm Fort Clinton and Fort Montgomery. Burgoyne was convinced that this new threat to the American rear would compel Gates to strip the Bemis Heights defenses in order to rush troops to meet the oncoming Clinton. A reasonable amount of patience might result in a British assault against undermanned American emplacements and produce a glorious triumph with very little risk. The British army settled in to construct almost three miles of fortifications while waiting for scouts to confirm that Gates was dispatching much of his army south.

Burgoyne's assumption that Gates would weaken the entrenched army to cover his rear proved to be one of the most serious miscalculations of the entire war. The American commander not only maintained the forces already in position but also integrated a steady stream of reinforcements that were checking into the American camp virtually every day. The 10,000 rebel soldiers available at the battle of Freeman's Farm had increased to almost 12,000 men two weeks later and would ultimately reach 20,000 by the end of the campaign. A British council of war on the evening of October 4th produced a heated debate among the officers concerning the dwindling options facing His Majesty's northern army. American patrols had now become so bold that they circled the right wing of the British and even carried off some English soldiers digging potatoes five hundred yards behind headquarters. Desertions increased, and the Americans sent agents into camp to lure the British from their hard service with promises of lenient treatment. As foraging parties were ambushed by rebel patrols, the daily food ration was cut by a third. To keep the men's spirits up Burgoyne announced that "there is reason to be assured that other powerful armies are actually in cooperation with these troops" and distributed twelve barrels of precious rum to the regiments.

The rum provided a temporary lift for the sagging spirit of the British army but the relief force further down the Hudson was still too far away to provide tangible aid. Thus at the October 4th conference a group of officers led by General von Riedesel and Fraser suggested a British withdrawal. Burgoyne cringed at the idea of retreat and apparently viewed another winter in Canada as worse than surrender. He still believed that his 5000 remaining regulars could defeat any number of amateur soldiers and he was able to convince his subordinates to support another assault on the American defenses. The attack would feature a three pronged attack on the high ground near the American left flank with the expectation that a successful assault would allow British artillerymen to blast the rebels from the newly captured heights.

At ten o'clock on the morning of October 7, 1777, the final British offensive of the Saratoga campaign lurched into motion. The advance units of British regulars marched a mile toward the American defenses, entered a field of tall cornstalks and immediately halted. The infantry regiments lounged in the grass, waited for the expected artillery support to arrive and exchanged comments about the leisurely lifestyles of cannoneers. Suddenly the far end of the field exploded in a wall of flame from Morgan's riflemen. While the British soldiers tried to evade the spattering bullets, Enoch Poor's brigade of Continentals charged through the grass and delivered a series of short range volleys which shattered the startled redcoats.

The major units of Burgoyne's assault force now extended themselves in a line that stretched for over a thousand yards. On the right under General Fraser and Lord Balcarres were the British light infantry companies, the 24th Regiment of Foot and two 6 pounders. The center position was held by General von Riedesel with detachments of regular German infantry, Colonel Breymann's grenadier contingent, two British 12 pounders and two German 6 pounders. The left flank was held by Major John Acland's grenadier battalion, two British 6 pounders and two howitzers. This combined force had a strength of just over 1700 men while another detachment of about 200 Indians and Tories had been sent ahead to circle the enemy rear and create a diversion.

While Poor's Continentals were chasing the British advance units back to their main lines, Gates sat dining on his lunch and trying to develop the most effective response to a British move that might be either a reconnaissance in force or a full scale assault. The arrival of fresh militia units during the past three days had now swelled his army to over 17,000 men, including almost 7000 Continentals. Arnold argued for a major counterattack which could provide an opportunity to get behind Burgoyne and split his army in two. Gates preferred to wait for Burgoyne to advance. "If undisciplined militia were repulsed in the open field, and the enemy pressed them in their retreat, it would be difficult to form them again, even behind their own breastworks; for if they were under a panic, they would keep on retreating, even after they had passed their own lines." Arnold was finally able to secure Gates' permission for a limited counterattack, provided it did not commit the mass of militia reserves. Arnold insisted "pray, let me go; I will be careful and if our advance does not need support I will promise not to commit you." When Arnold seemed to give the impression that he was intent on far more than a limited attack, the two generals entered into another of their frequent shouting matches and Arnold was virtually relieved of his command. The Connecticut general rode off toward the sound of the approaching battle while Gates sent aides to force his recall.

By 3 o'clock in the afternoon, a fairly static firefight had developed between Poor's and Learned's Continental brigades and the main British assault force. Finally Poor decided to break the stalemate by advancing to a hill facing Acland's grenadiers and organizing his men for an all-out charge. While Acland's jittery men rained grapeshot on the Continentals, the New Hampshire patriots "charged madly and blindly in the face of a furious fire." Acland was shot through both legs and the British were driven back in disarray. The collapse of the British grenadiers had now uncovered the center positions held by the Germans, and at this point Benedict Arnold arrived to lead a charge of Learned's brigade against this exposed front. When the American attack threatened to obliterate the German defenses, Lord Balcarres' men were ordered to swing over to hold the collapsing center. As the redcoat light infantry rushed to relieve their German allies, they were caught in a deadly crossfire by Morgan's riflemen and Dearborn's infantry.

The last effective British unit that could slow the onrushing Americans was the 24th Foot which was now under the direct command of Simon Fraser. While Fraser galloped about in an attempt to rally the men for one last charge, Morgan ordered his riflemen to bring down the British general. Three shots rang out, and as the charismatic Scotsman slumped to the ground, Burgoyne ordered a withdrawal of the entire assault force. Colonel Breymann now slipped into a frenzy of orders as he tried to organize a rear guard action with his grenadiers, but after slashing several of his panicky men with his sword, he was shot down by his own soldiers. Arnold now galloped into the main British defenses and went down with a leg wound as his ecstatic men overran the retreating redcoats. The way to the British rear was now open, but Arnold was out of action and Gates was still determined to withhold his militia from an open field engagement. Burgoyne was allowed to stagger back toward a new defense position while the exuberant rebels tallied their accomplishments.

The action of October 7th which became known as the battle of Bemis Heights had cost Gates' army a loss of 50 killed and 150 wounded. The slightly less than 2000 British and German soldiers who had been involved in the assault had lost 176 men killed while 250 more were wounded and 200 others taken prisoner. The British position on the Hudson was now near a state of collapse. Burgoyne continued to hope that Clinton's slow advance up the Hudson would rescue his beleaguered army, but even though the southern force was believed to be within 50 miles of Albany, the addition of 2000 additional redcoats would do little to counterbalance Gates' continuing reinforcements. Burgoyne now had fewer than 5000 effectives to defend a position encircled by 20,000 rebels. Apparently the emergence of a four to one deficit in manpower provided Burgoyne with a legitimate excuse to propose an honorable capitulation and when Gates softened his original terms to label the action a "convention" instead of a surrender, the British general accepted the offer. At ten o'clock on the morning of October 17, 1777 the defeated British army marched in strict formation from their trenches with redcoat musicians pounding on dozens of drums. As the victorious Americans lined the road to observe their passing, a German officer admitted his admiration for his antagonists. "There was not a man among them who showed the slightest signs of mockery, malicious delight, hate or other insult." The American musicians struck up a rendition of Yankee Doodle, which was still considered a British tune. John Burgoyne presented his sword to Horatio Gates, who immediately returned the weapon but accepted the surrender of 5895 men, 7 generals and dozens of field guns. A tenacious American struggle against a far more seasoned army had resulted in the elimination of the second largest British army in North America for the lost of fewer than 600 patriots killed and wounded.

The American victory at Saratoga not only eliminated an important part of the British army and delivered into the hands of the Americans large quantities of miliary stores, it also removed the danger of a British advance that might have split the American states in two. Most important of all, it convinced the French court that the time had come to enter the war on the side of the Americans. A civil war within the British Empire would soon become a conflict with global implications.

# CHAPTER 8

# The Philadelphia Campaign

## The Final Confrontation between Howe and Washington

$S$ir William Howe spent a comfortable winter in newly captured New York City following the campaign of 1776. While he enjoyed the congenial company of the numerous Loyalist prominent families and continued his affair with Mrs. Betsey Loring, the wife of his newly appointed commissary of prisoners, Howe began to explore a possible operational plan for the next campaign. On April 2nd, 1777, the British general wrote to Lord George Germain with a proposal to capture Philadelphia using the main part of his army while leaving a small force behind to hold New York. This plan suggested the advantage of a seaborne assault on the rebel capital which would eliminate the need to maintain a 100 mile long supply line from New York through New Jersey if an overland campaign was attempted. A waterborne expedition would make maximum use of Britain's enormous naval superiority but would also place the main British army in North America out of supporting range of Burgoyne's proposed expeditionary force from Canada. Since Howe was convinced that the Canadian operation was Burgoyne's "private show," which was drawing troops, supplies and attention from his own more important campaign, the prospect of operating out of supporting range of a competing general was hardly an undesirable situation for the British commander.

The British army in the early spring of 1777 was a military force that was still far superior to its rebel adversary in numbers and training. Despite the setbacks at Trenton and Princeton the previous winter, Howe's regiments comprised a magnificently equipped, supremely confident corps that could concentrate 20,000 men for a battle with the Americans while still maintaining large garrisons around New York City. However, prospects for ultimate victory were diminished by the development of a command structure that was becoming hopelessly divided between London and New York. While Howe was utilizing his position as commander-in-chief in America to set up one set of goals and objectives for the upcoming campaign, Lord Germain and the king were developing their own strategy for the capture of Albany with little regard for Howe's plans, intentions or capabilities. As letters and replies crossed each other in the Atlantic Ocean during the critical planning stages of the upcoming campaign season, the vital coordination between the two principal British armies in North America had virtually disappeared.

While British ministers and generals debated their possible strategies for ending the rebellion in 1777, George Washington's army prepared for the upcoming campaign in its fortifications behind the Watchung Mountains of New Jersey. Washington's selection of Morristown as a winter camp was a brilliant move since the formidable location discouraged the far larger British army from launching a serious attack. The arrival of spring weather brought a much needed influx of recruits for the Continental army. The earlier Congressional authorization for an army of 88 regiments containing 76,000 men had become a fireside joke in the American camps, but the arrival of a few thousand volunteers and a shipment of uniforms, gunpowder and muskets from France eventually provided Washington with a minimally acceptable army of 10,000 men. The American commander horded his strength during the spring as Howe attempted a series of maneuvers designed to lure Washington out of his defenses for a stand-up battle that the British were sure to win. When the rebels refused to take the bait, Howe returned to Staten Island and waited for his final contingent of reinforcements before initiating his great seaborne expedition.

General Henry Clinton arrived back from London in June of 1777 with an additional 2500 men designated for the Philadelphia expedition. Clinton was appointed garrison commander at New York with vague instructions to support Burgoyne's advance if practicable. Howe completed preparations for loading most of his army on his brother's massive transport fleet, and on July 23, 267 vessels set sail with 13,000 regulars on board. When the British fleet disappeared into the mists of the Atlantic, George Washington was gravely concerned about Howe's intentions. He wrote a friend that "the amazing advantage the enemy derive from their ships and their command of the water keeps us in a state of constant perplexity and the most anxious conjecture." Washington realized that his adversary could use his naval superiority to launch an attack on the rebels from almost any point on the coast. At first the American general was convinced that the fleet was headed north to the Hudson and thence to Albany to link up with Burgoyne and sever the colonies north from south. Then his informers in New York reported that Howe was carrying supplies for a month which could indicate an attack on the Virginia coast or a move against Charleston. The possibility of a British offensive too distant for the intervention of Washington's army encouraged the general to seriously consider ignoring Howe's intentions and marching the Continental forces into New York to trap Burgoyne.

On July 25th, Washington's scouts reported sighting 70 British ships off Egg Harbor near present-day Atlantic City, New Jersey. This location seemed to indicate an approach to Cape May 35 miles further south, which provided access to Delaware Bay and ultimately the Delaware River. Washington could scarcely believe that Howe was sailing away from Burgoyne with no attempt to support the northern army, so he still suspected that the British would double back to New York at the last minute. He informed Horatio Gates that "Howe's abandonment of Burgoyne is so unaccountable a matter that until I am fully assured it is so, I cannot help casting my eyes continually behind me!" Washington began a cautious move toward Trenton where he could be in a position to move toward either Pennsylvania or New York depending on the next sighting of the British fleet.

A pilot at Lewes, Delaware provided Washington with even more contradictory information over the next several days. A message dispatched on July 31st informed the general that the British fleet had arrived at the mouth of Delaware Bay and seemed ready to move toward Philadelphia. However, two days later the same pilot reported that the fleet had disappeared to the east. Howe had forsaken the most obvious approach to the capital and could be headed anywhere; perhaps this whole drama was merely a ruse to draw Washington away from New York and the Hudson Highlands. The somewhat befuddled American army spent much of the month of August marching back and forth along the Delaware River shoreline as contradictory reports streamed into Washington's headquarters. After three weeks of marching and countermarching, Washington lost patience with this waiting game and issued preliminary orders for a march to New York. However, just as his advance units were starting north, the American commander received startling news that British ships had been spotted at the entrance to Chesapeake Bay. The march to the Hudson was immediately canceled, and the Continental Army marched south to defend the national capital.

The morning of August 24th, 1777 dawned clear and hot as the Grand Continental Army of the United States formed ranks about a mile outside the city of Philadelphia. Washington had ordered his men to wash their clothes and directed each soldier to wear a green sprig in his hat as an emblem of hope. The collection of American regiments marched down Front Street to Chestnut Street and then passed a reviewing stand on the way to the Common. The 11,000 men in Washington's army took two hours to complete the march while John Adams noted that "the army looked extremely well armed, pretty well clothed and tolerably disciplined but much remains to be done." The Massachusetts congressman suggested that his nation's warriors were not yet a professionally trained army as "our soldiers have not yet quite the air of soldiers. They don't step exactly in time. They don't hold up their heads quite erect. They don't all wear their hats in the same way."

The morning after the grand review of the American army, the first

AMERICAN
REVOLUTION
Brandywine Campaign
August - September
1777

Pennsylvania

Whitemarsh

Valley
Forge

Germantown

Schuylkill River

Philadelphia

Brandywine
Creek

Battle of
Brandywine

Kennett
Square

Chadd's Ford

Chester

Howe

Washington

Wilmington

DELAWARE RIVER

Maryland

Newark

New Jersey

Head of the Elk
(Elkton)

Cooch's
Bridge

Delaware

N

0    5    10

Miles

landing party of British soldiers disembarked near Elkton, Maryland. The anticipated 10-day voyage had been transformed into a 32-day endurance contest in which thousands of His Majesty's best troops had been subjected to the hell holes of British transports. Howe had originally intended to off-load his troops when he arrived at Delaware Bay, but had changed his mind at the last minute. The British commander suddenly envisioned massive rebel river defenses obliterating his support ships, when in reality the Americans had only four small vessels and a few light guns to contest a British advance. The Chesapeake seemed to offer the advantage of surprise since it seemed that no general in his right mind would go so far out of his way to attack Philadelphia.

The exhausted, enervated redcoats landed on an "exceedingly hot" Monday morning and the freedom from confinement on ships made the soldiers "riotous as satyrs" despite the hangings and floggings meted out to seven of the men to discourage plundering. Howe's maritime strategy had certainly surprised the Americans but it had resulted in the loss of most of his vital horses during the voyage, had erased any possibility of supporting Burgoyne's army and had placed the British expeditionary force exactly 10 miles further from the center of Philadelphia than when the campaign had begun. Now the exhaustion of his men and a series of torrential late summer thunderstorms delayed the British advance for another two weeks and provided George Washington with ample time to prepare a response to the invasion. The 11,000 available Americans were soon deployed in a series of emplacements that stretched for several miles along the Brandywine Creek in southern Pennsylvania.

Washington's decision to confront the British advance using the Brandywine as a natural barrier to an enemy attack has encouraged an ongoing debate among historians and military analysts. On the one hand, the Creek was 50 to 150 yards wide and deep enough to discourage an enemy assault anywhere but at a series of fords that provided access to the American position. Washington could concentrate his forces at those points and possibly inflict heavy casualties on a British frontal attack. However, Washington committed a series of tactical errors which invited disaster if Howe used any imagination in planning his offensive. First, Washington had finally built up his cavalry arm to a strength of four first class regiments. Yet rather than assigning them to the scouting and screening duties that were expected of mounted soldiers, he held his horsemen close to headquarters where they provided virtually no early warning of British intentions. Second, the American commander seemed to easily dismiss the fact that Howe had conducted the New York campaign with a series of brilliant surprise flanking attacks that demonstrated the minimal likelihood of a replay of the frontal attack on Breed's Hill. Washington was waiting in vain for Howe to oblige him with another Bunker Hill when the British general had far more sophisticated plans. Washington's army was not badly outnumbered but it was deployed poorly if Howe attempted an imaginative attack.

The American defensive deployment centered on Chadd's Ford where Washington placed his center divisions under the command of Nathanael Greene. The left flank was defended by General Armstrong's Pennsylvania militia who had fortified Pyle's Ford, while divisions led by generals Sullivan, Stirling and Stephens formed a right flank in positions from Painter's Ford to Brinton's Ford. A light infantry corps under Brigadier General William Maxwell was deployed on the far side of the Brandywine to provide early warning of a British approach, while smaller forces were employed in the defense of a series of fords to the north of the main American position. Unfortunately, the American defenses extended only six miles upstream, while Howe had selected a crossing site a mile above the end of the patriot line.

William Howe was convinced that his opponent would deploy most of his army to challenge a direct frontal assault, so the British commander developed an ingenious plan to attract Washington's attention while he executed a daring flanking attack. While Earl Charles Cornwallis marched north along the Brandywine with 8200 men and crossed the creek at Jeffries Ford, General Knyphausen would make a demonstration attack on the American position at Chadd's Ford which would occupy Washington until the British army was in his rear and had cut off the main escape route to Philadelphia. Cornwallis marched out of Kennett Square, Pennsylvania at 4 A.M. on September 11, 1777 with a column that was accompanied by Howe and included the 3rd and 4th infantry brigades, 2 battalions of grenadiers, 3 squadrons of light dragoons, a detachment of Hessian jaegers and a contingent of pioneers to clear away any road obstructions. At about the same time, General Knyphausen left camp with 6800 men to deploy directly across the creek from the American center.

Cornwallis' men marched north through open countryside covered with a dense ground fog that screened his movement from the limited number of American patrols. The column finally arrived at Jeffries Ford which was about a mile north of the nearest American position. Washington had ended his line at Buffington's Ford because local informants had assured him that there were no good crossings for several miles beyond that point. The locals were right to the extent that Jeffries Ford was a difficult crossing point with water up to a man's waist and was served by roads that were difficult to reach. However, Loyalist inhabitants of the area had informed Howe that the creek was fordable and a Tory named Curtis Lewis led Cornwallis' men directly to the ford which was totally unguarded by the patriots.

While Cornwallis' men were resting and drying themselves and advance patrols were sent ahead to locate the American defenses, George Washington prepared his main wing to fend off a developing frontal assault. Knyphausen's 6800 men included the 1st and 2nd brigades of foot, the Hessian brigade, the Queen's Rangers, a detachment of elite riflemen, a contingent of light dragoons, and a powerful supporting force of artillery. This assault force first encountered Maxwell's light infantry deployed on the west side of the creek and a massive artillery bombardment followed up by a spirited bayonet charge drove the Americans back to the main provincial defenses. At 10 A.M. this British contingent opened fire on the Americans across the creek while they waited for confirmation that Cornwallis was in the enemy's rear. While the two armies blasted at each other across the water, Washington began receiving conflicting reports of British units threatening his flank. When a local farmer named Thomas Cheyney rode into headquarters at about 2 P.M. with word that he had barely escaped from a British cavalry patrol on the east side of the creek Washington was faced with the dilemma of whether the story was genuine or Cheyney was a Loyalist spy.

Washington was finally convinced that Cheyney's story was genuine when American scouts began reporting large numbers of redcoats marching south from the near bank of the Brandywine. The American general delegated the defense of Chadd's Ford to Wayne's division, designated Greene's division as a reserve to be employed in an emergency and ordered the three right flank divisions to hurry to Birmingham Court House and entrench before the British arrived. The divisions commanded by Stirling and Stephen arrived near Birmingham in time to occupy a ridge known as Plowed Hill, but Sullivan's division became lost on the way when their commander rode ahead to direct the location of artillery emplacements. The two American divisions formed a strong line flanked on each side by dense wooded areas. When Howe arrived with his redcoats he admitted, "the damn rebels form well." However, when Sullivan's men finally arrived, they began to displace men from the other division and the American line started to degenerate into confusion. The British column had just occupied the next ridge called Osborne's Hill and Howe chose this moment of partial chaos among the patriots to launch his first attack. Howe's first contingent of Guards, grenadiers and light infantry advanced in ominous silence as they marched down the slope of Osborne's Hill, across a stretch of flat ground and up the side of Plowed Hill.

This scene represents a classic portrait of stoic redcoats marching in tightly organized lines against the sustained volleys of entrenched American defenders. However, Howe's bold flanking maneuver guaranteed the regulars a huge numerical advantage over a confused detachment of Americans attempting to form a defense in the face of British bayonets. The Americans had fewer than 3000 men available to resist over 8000 redcoats, and while their initial volleys dropped dozens of advancing British soldiers, the weight of numbers quickly took effect. A contingent of three Maryland regiments holding the American right flank was overwhelmed by hundreds of British bayonets and a reinforcing brigade rushed in by General Prudhomme de Borre was caught in a crossfire by British Guards and Hessian Grenadiers. General de Borre signaled an American retreat on that end of the line and became one of the first rebels to run—an action that ended his military career three days later. General Sullivan desperately attempted to cobble together a new flank but "no sooner did I form one party than that which I had before formed would run off." Hazen's regiment of Canadian volunteers became the only unit to maintain its cohesion when their commander simply pulled his men away from the growing stampede and reformed them on the American center.

Stirling's division had been able to pin down the units advancing on the American center but Cornwallis simply ordered more and more regiments to launch attacks on the remnants of the enemy line. The relatively few men under Stirling and Hazen held off the main force of Cornwallis' corps for almost an hour in some of the heaviest fighting of the war. As these units pulled back under the threat of thousands of British bayonets, a brigade of Virginians under General Woodford formed a temporary position which allowed the retreating rebels to pass through their ranks as they held open a line of retreat.

Once Washington realized that his army had been flanked, he responded decisively to the crisis. Anthony Wayne was ordered to hold Knyphausen at bay while Greene's division was rushed 4 miles in 45 minutes to support the collapsing American right wing. Washington accompanied Greene's fast marching brigades and when he arrived at the village of Dilworth he came in contact with Sullivan's men retreating from Plowed Hill. Washington and Greene agreed that the battle was as good as lost, and the only hope was to save the army from annihilation. Greene ordered the 1000 men in Weedon's and Muhlenberg's brigade to form a new defensive position which would delay the 8000 redcoats until Sullivan's men could move up the road toward Philadelphia. Some of Weedon's men were able to conceal themselves in a nearby woods and when Cornwallis' column advanced to launch a bayonet attack, the hidden patriots blasted the forward units. For over half an hour the heavily outnumbered rebels stopped the British advance while hundreds of their comrades scrambled to safety. By the time the redcoats were able to bring up artillery support and break through the American defenses, the majority of Washington's right wing had escaped up the Chester Pike.

The final push by Cornwallis' contingent was accompanied by a less than enthusiastic cross creek assault by Knyphausen's detachment. When the German general finally heard Cornwallis' guns at about 4:30 P.M., he let loose with his own artillery barrage which screened an attack across the Brandywine. Anthony Wayne's division was heavily outnumbered and the American commander reverted to a fighting withdrawal using every stone fence and local building as a strong point to delay the British advance. Wayne's tactics had almost succeeded in stopping Knyphausen's offensive when a contingent of Cornwallis' infantry came blundering through the woods after they had become lost in their pursuit of Sullivan's men. Wayne was able to extricate most of his regulars from the British encirclement but the supporting force of Pennsylvania militia was trapped and forced to fight its way out with heavy casualties.

Nightfall found most of the American army streaming east on Chester Pike. A night march for a defeated army fearing close pursuit created a certain level of chaos but at no point did the retreat become a rout. The Americans withdrew about 12 miles to Chester Creek where newly commissioned General Lafayette organized a straggler control point and halted the army's retreat. The American army had been hurt but hardly annihilated with a loss of 200 killed, 750 wounded and 400 captured, compared to 570 total British casualties including 90 killed. The British advance had not been halted, but the panic and evaporation of American defenses that had plagued the Americans during the New York campaign was far less evident in the fields of southern Pennsylvania.

Howe had planned and fought a masterful battle. He boldly divided his command in the face of an enemy almost his equal in size and successfully conducted a lengthy flank march and attack. He handled his troops superbly and the outcome of the battle was never in serious doubt once the crossing had been accomplished. The only real criticism should go to Knyphausen who failed to sustain his initial holding attack long enough to tie down Washington's troops all day, and then launched an unenthusiastic final attack that allowed most of the American defenders to escape in the darkness. Washington, on the other hand, fought a fairly poor battle. His decision to fortify a line along the Brandywine was not necessarily a bad one but his failure to reconnoiter the creek properly, his unwillingness to fully employ his cavalry and his insistence on the likelihood of a British frontal attack were major shortcomings that might have cost him an even more severe defeat. Washington spent too much of the day worrying about Knyphausen and by the time he decided to confront Cornwallis he was doing little more than averting the total annihilation of the army.

Howe's rough handling of the American army did not end with the battle of Brandywine. When Washington marched most of his army toward the Schuylkill River, he deployed Anthony Wayne's division to guard his flank at Paoli Tavern. During the early morning hours of September 21st, a British force of 5000 men under General Charles Grey began a silent approach toward the 1500 Americans camped at Paoli. Grey ordered his men to remove the flints from their muskets in order to prevent accidental discharges that would alert the sleeping rebels. The British assault force had somehow obtained Wayne's password for the night so that the redcoats were able to silence the American pickets after they gave the correct countersign. The Yankee soldiers were silhouetted against their campfires and became easy targets for lunging British bayonets. Captain John Andre noted that "the British troops rushed along the line putting to the bayonet all they came up with, and overtaking the main herd of fugitives, stabbed great numbers and pressed on their rear till it was thought prudent to order them to desist."

The scene that night was a grisly one punctuated by screams and the clashing of swords and bayonets more than musket and rifle shots. A British soldier observed "the Americans running about barefoot and half-clothed in the light of the fire. They showed us where to chase them while they could not see us. I stuck them myself like so many pigs, one after another, until the blood ran out of the touch hole of my musket." Wayne was able to organize a rear guard that fired several volleys while the rest of the force escaped the British encirclement. However, American casualties in the so called "Paoli Massacre" were relatively heavy with a loss of 53 killed, 100 wounded and 71 captured compared to a trifling enemy loss of seven men wounded. While the surprise bayonet attack produced a particularly grisly encounter between the two forces, Grey was not the brutal killer depicted in later American accounts, as he left most of the wounded prisoners in houses along the road and then reported their location to Washington in order to send medical assistance.

Howe followed up his success at Paoli with a rapid advance to Valley Forge which confused Washington, who was uncertain whether the British army was headed toward Philadelphia or was positioning itself to threaten his supply base at Reading. The American commander was now forced to choose between protecting the American capital and covering his main supply depot since he didn't have the mobility or numbers to screen both targets. While Washington and his generals debated the merits of the two possible courses of action, Howe recrossed the Schuylkill and occupied a position on Stony Creek at Norristown which placed the British army squarely between the Americans and Philadelphia. There was nothing that the Continental Army could do to save the capital from enemy occupation as the American force was too exhausted and too outnumbered to intercept the redcoat advance. Washington's only option was to protect his supply base and find a secure camp from which to monitor enemy movements, await reinforcements and wait for an opportunity to catch Howe at a vulnerable moment.

At this point, Howe was totally in control of the campaign and he knew it. He rested his men all day on September 24th and on the 25th marched his men the 11 miles from Norristown to Germantown which was about 6 miles north of the center of Philadelphia. The morning of September 26th, 1777 dawned bright and cool following a heavy rainstorm the previous night. At 8:30 A.M. Howe ordered Charles Cornwallis to take the British and Hessian Grenadiers, two squadrons of light dragoons and some light artillery units and enter the rebel capital. Most of Philadelphia's most ardent patriots had evacuated the city while Congress had relocated to York and the Liberty Bell was moved to Allentown. Cornwallis marched into the city and was greeted "by the acclamations of some thousands of the inhabitants mostly women and children." A number of the town's most prominent Tories came forward to embrace Cornwallis who took formal possession of the city at 10 A.M. A loyalist merchant named Samuel Shoemaker was appointed mayor while former conservative member of the Continental Congress Joseph Galloway was named police commissioner. While General Burgoyne's army was preparing a last desperate attempt to break through the American encirclement at Saratoga, William Howe savored the accomplishment of his capture of the enemy capital with minimal loss to His Majesty's forces. According to the traditions and expectations of 18th century European warfare the capture of an enemy capital usually signified the end of a war and the beginning of a complicated series of negotiations to produce a treaty, which saved the honor of the defeated nation but gave the victors most of what they wanted. Unfortunately for William Howe the triumph of capturing Philadelphia was shortly to be negated by the British surrender at Saratoga while George Washington was determined to make the British occupation of the American capital a short and unpleasant experience.

George Washington was embarrassed by the successive disasters of Brandywine, Paoli and the enemy capture of Philadelphia, but a number of developments quickly restored his determination to change the course of the war. First, Washington realized that the loss of the capital of a decentralized American confederation was far less vital than the surrender of London or Paris to a European enemy. The Americans still held their main supply depot at Reading and the daily arrival of reinforcements from Pennsylvania and New Jersey militia units would soon push his effective strength back over 10,000 men. His growing army was further heartened by news of Burgoyne's failure to break through the American lines at Freeman's Farm, which merited a 13 gun salute and a generous ration of rum for the entire corps. When Washington learned that Howe had sent 3000 men to the New Jersey side of the Delaware River while keeping Cornwallis' division stationed in Philadelphia, he began to develop a plan to launch a surprise attack on the British encampment at Germantown. While the American commander was optimistic that he could repeat his triumph at Trenton on an even larger scale, he didn't seem to fully appreciate the fact that two of the three columns in that operation had never arrived on the battlefield, while this attack would be even more complex and daring.

Washington's basic plan for the attack on Germantown envisioned a four pronged American advance along four widely separated approach routes. Nathanael Greene would march 6000 men down Limekiln Pike and strike the right flank of the British defenses while a parallel column of 2000 Maryland and New Jersey militia under General Smallwood would advance through Jenkintown and distract the British units deployed on the extreme right of their line. Washington would accompany a force of 3000 men including divisions commanded by Wayne, Sullivan and Stirling on a march straight down Germantown Pike to attack the center of the British line at Market House in Germantown, while being supported by several Pennsylvania militia regiments under General Armstrong who would distract the British left near the Schuylkill River.

At 6 P.M. on the evening of October 2nd, the four columns of the American assault force marched out of their encampment on Methacton Hill in Montgomery County and began a 20 mile march toward Germantown. The best prospect for an American victory would be if the army achieved complete surprise and all four columns struck Howe's defenses in a coordinated attack. However, any serious delay to the attacking columns would simply allow the British commander to shift his troops from one threatened position to another and destroy the attacking columns piecemeal. Howe had been informed by spies that Washington was planning some sort of offensive operation but the British general underestimated the scope of the enemy plan. The British defensive works were quite formidable, with a left flank protected by the Wissahickon Creek's steep banks, a center position manned by three brigades of infantry supported by a large artillery contingent, and a right flank protected by strong emplacements and defended by such elite units as the Queen's Rangers and the British Guards. Howe had also deployed a strong outer picket line about two miles north of his main position and this force located at Mount Airy was designed to serve as an early warning to any American approach.

Washington's column approached Mount Airy from Bethlehem Pike at dawn on the morning of October 3rd but the dense ground fog that covered the region prevented the American commander from securing any information about the three other detachments. The patriot commander decided to assume that the other columns had arrived at their starting points and ordered Captain Allen McLane to use his dismounted light dragoons to attack the British pickets. The redcoats were driven back in a panicky retreat through two miles of fog shrouded fields with the Americans in close pursuit until they smashed into the outer works of the main British position. Wayne's division now pitched into a confused unit of British light infantry that had no idea of the size of the American assault force as the rebels drifted in and out of the white mist. The lead elements of the British army gradually gave way and retreated back to Market Square just as their commanding general arrived on the scene.

Howe quickly chided his elite troops for retreating from shadows as he exclaimed "for shame, light infantry, I never saw you retreat before; Form! Form! It is only a scouting party." The British commander learned that his men were facing more than American scouts when an American artillery battery was deployed and started dropping grapeshot around a large tree where Howe and his staff were standing.

The initial American attack was making good progress as British troops had difficulty locating targets in the fog and entire redcoat regiments were becoming cut off from their main body. However, the American offensive began to lose momentum when Colonel Thomas Musgrave's 40th regiment of British infantry found itself isolated from the rest of its brigade. Musgrave could hear the rebel attackers closing in through the fog and he quickly decided to defend the most formidable looking building that he could identify. Six companies consisting of about 120 men followed their colonel through the entrance to Benjamin Chew's imposing mansion called Cliveden. Musgrave ordered his redcoats to close the window shutters and barricade the doors on the first floor while he deployed sharpshooters at the windows of the second and third floors. The British troops had moved so quickly that they had escaped the notice of the advancing Americans and Musgrave could have remained unnoticed in his formidable fortress. However, the British colonel boldly chose to reveal his position when he directed his sharpshooters to open fire on the rear of Washington's column as it marched down the road nearby.

The discovery of Musgrave's presence presented a major dilemma for Washington and his subordinates. While a number of officers urged their commander to ignore the small British force and concentrate on moving toward the main enemy line, Henry Knox insisted that all of his military textbooks cautioned against leaving an armed fort in an army's rear. While Cliveden was hardly a medieval castle garrisoned by an army of threatening knights, Washington agreed with Knox's reasoning and detached Maxwell's light infantry from the American advance toward Market Square and ordered him to capture Cliveden. When adjutant Lieutenant William Smith was killed while attempting to persuade Musgrave's men to surrender, the Americans responded with a massive artillery barrage in preparation for the infantry assault.

The "siege" of the Chew House proved to be a disaster for the nearly victorious American offensive. Knox's artillery accomplished little more than knocking a few tiles from Cliveden's roof while the main structure remained intact. Maxwell's infantry assault was annihilated by British sharpshooters who killed 56 Americans and wounded dozens of others before the attack was suspended. Attempts to burn the house with a wagon load of flaming hay and pitching lighted kindling through the windows resulted in the death of Major John White and the wounding of Colonel John Laurens with no real damage to the British refuge.

This preoccupation with eliminating a mere 120 redcoats who provided a small hindrance to the rebel advance effectively impeded the momentum of the entire offensive. However, Wayne's division was exerting so much pressure on the British position at Market Square that Howe was thinking seriously of abandoning the field and retreating back to Philadelphia. Unfortunately for the Americans, at this critical moment Stephens' division from Greene's wayward column drifted onto the battlefield pursuing retreating redcoats through the fog. General Stephens was leading his division while in a drunken stupor and he gave orders to fire volleys into the fog with little concern for the potential targets. Stephens' men fired a number of volleys at soldiers who turned out to be the rear echelon of Wayne's advancing corps. These troops promptly countered with their own volleys against the "enemy" soldiers who had apparently gotten into their rear. Howe and his subordinates glimpsed part of this devastating shootout between the American divisions and the British general promptly called for a British counterattack supported by reinforcements dispatched by Cornwallis in Philadelphia.

The British attack swept out of the fog and caught several American regiments as they had just expended the last of their ammunition. The divisions under Washington's direct command began a gradual withdrawal back up Germantown Pike until they reached Chestnut Hill about four miles north of Germantown. Several regiments from Greene's column had advanced much further than the rest of the army and were actually in the process of ransacking British campsites when the British counterattack swept over them. The most forward American unit, the 9th Virginia regiment, was engaged in plundering the huts of the British light infantry when it was surrounded by several enemy regiments whose volleys killed dozens of Americans and forced the surrender of the entire unit. Greene now realized that Washington's column had already retreated along with most of the militia on his flank so he was hard pressed to extricate his remaining regiments before the British trapped the entire division.

The American attack had failed to annihilate Howe's forces at Germantown but when Washington's soldiers were forced to withdraw there was no semblance of panic or rout. Pamphleteer Thomas Paine was serving as a volunteer aide to General Greene and his description of the fall back captured the new spirit of the army. "The retreat was extraordinary. Nobody hurried themselves. Everyone marched at his own pace. The enemy kept a civil distance behind, sending every now and then a shot after us, and receiving the same from us." Anthony Wayne's rearguard division formed a solid firing rank at Whitemarsh Church about seven miles north of the battlefield and opened a lively musket and artillery volley at the British advance regiments who decided that this was a good place to halt the pursuit.

Washington's exhausted but still belligerent troops continued past their previous campsite at Methacton Hill and established a new encampment six miles away at Paulings Mills on the Perkiomen Creek. The Americans had marched over 40 miles and fought a fierce five-hour battle in the space of little more than 24 hours and yet were eager to fight again as soon as possible. Most of the army became convinced that a few unlucky breaks such as the inability to capture Cliveden, Stephens' on-field drunkenness and the accidental firing on friendly troops had prevented a possibly decisive victory over the redcoat forces. Washington admitted that "upon the whole, it may be said that the day was unfortunate rather than injurious. The enemy are nothing better by the events and our troops are not the least dispirited by it, having gained what all young troops gain by being in such actions." The bold attempt to surprise Howe had resulted in a loss of 152 Americans killed, 521 wounded and 400 men captured while the British losses totaled 70 killed and 465 wounded or captured. The coincidental patriot victory at Saratoga and near defeat of Howe at Germantown produced an awesome challenge to a British ministry that now began to suspect that the internal imperial struggle for control of the American colonies would soon be transformed into a much more risky international conflict. Howe's last major confrontation with George Washington had enabled the British to hold the American capital at least on a temporary basis, but the commanding general's successor would be obliged to face a far more confident and experienced adversary in the next campaign.

# CHAPTER 9

# Climax in the North

## *Valley Forge to Monmouth*

$T$he surprise attack on the British camp at Germantown initiated a series of maneuvers between Washington and Howe that eventually produced the American withdrawal to the hallowed fields of Valley Forge. When General Howe decided to pull his exposed regiments from Market Square to the more defendable environs of Philadelphia, Washington established a campsite at Whitemarsh about 13 miles from British headquarters. During most of the autumn of 1777, the main American army was largely undisturbed by English sorties as His Majesty's forces were occupied in the dangerous and tedious business of opening up the Delaware River to British shipping. A series of combined army and navy assaults on the rebel bastions of Fort Mercer and Fort Mifflin resulted in the loss of the 64 gun-ship *Augusta*, a tally of 500 men killed and wounded, and a diversion of much of the British army before both forts were eventually evacuated by the badly outnumbered defenders.

The establishment of a secure supply line from the Atlantic Ocean to the rebel capital city enabled the British commander to turn his attention to Washington's defenses during the last weeks of the 1777 campaign. Howe and his staff officers utilized the home of Quaker housewife Lydia Darragh to discuss a complex plan to surprise the American army in a pre-dawn attack planned for December 5th. However, Mrs. Darragh was hardly a disinterested bystander, as once she overheard the British conversation she quickly determined to transmit the vital information to an American army that included her son. Mrs. Darragh wrote down a detailed summary of the British operational plan and then boldly requested a pass from her cousin, Captain Barrington of Howe's staff, to procure some flour from the mill at Frankford, north of the city. Carrying an empty flour sack to reinforce her ruse, Mrs. Darragh trudged five miles through the snow to Frankford and then quickly headed east toward the outer perimeter of the American lines.

She contacted the commander of her son's regiment, Colonel Thomas Craig, and handed him a notebook containing a description of the British plan to surprise the rebels by sending 10,000 men and 13 artillery pieces on an all night march which would strike the American defenses just before dawn.

The arrival of this vital information at Washington's headquarters convinced the American general that his suspicions of some form of British offensive were accurate, and every regiment was placed on high alert. During the pre-dawn darkness of the frigid morning of December 5th, 1777, Lord Charles Cornwallis led a confident advance force of redcoats over snow covered roads on their way to reverse the American winter assault on Trenton just under two years earlier. The British regulars were able to snap up an exposed picket force of Pennsylvania militia and were pressing on to the main defenses, when a series of volleys erupted from Daniel Morgan's recently arrived rifle corps. As the English infantrymen attacked the fully alerted provincial soldiers, General Howe climbed to the bell tower of a nearby church and sourly noted that the Americans had prepared a formidable series of strong points. For the next two days the British regiments launched a series of flanking assaults on the American positions at Militia Hill, Fort Hill and Camp Hill but each move was checked by a well placed force of rebel riflemen or light infantry. On the afternoon of December 8th Howe reluctantly conceded that his winter offensive had failed and pulled back to Philadelphia, after losing 350 men while inflicting few casualties on the rebels. While Lydia Darragh was suspected of treason, almost arrested by Captain John Andre and expelled from her Quaker congregation, her bold adventure had been substantially responsible for deflecting William Howe's last serious attempt to defeat George Washington in a major battle.

The Whitemarsh action had provided a major lift to American morale, but Washington had no intention of using this position as his winter headquarters. The American defenses were believed to be uncomfortably close to Howe's much larger army and the general and his staff began to explore alternative options. A council of senior generals considered two possible sites for a winter encampment—a withdrawal to a base of operations near the main supply depot at Reading which was about 60 miles from central Philadelphia, or a march to Valley Creek which was only about a third as far from the British defenses. The majority of American generals strongly supported the Reading option as it guaranteed the availability of ample supplies and provided the prospect of housing at least part of the army in comfortable dwellings in the region. However, Anthony Wayne insisted that a base over 60 miles from Philadelphia would confirm Howe's assumption that he had routed the rebel army while an encampment at Valley Forge would provide a visible symbol of continued American resistance. Washington utilized Wayne's argument to support his own conviction that a soft billet at Reading would dull the hard won fighting edge of his army while a certain degree of hardship and adversity would encourage the offensive spirit that had already begun to be apparent at Germantown. The American commander's decision to opt for Valley Forge may have been one of his most colossal blunders of the war, as the experiences of the next few months would result in the death of more American soldiers than all of the battles that Washington directed over seven years of war.

Valley Forge offered a reasonably good defensive position relatively close to occupied Philadelphia, but in every other respect, selection of this site was a disaster. The camp had no readily available water supply except for the laborious process of dragging buckets by hand from Valley Creek. The region provided little available forage for horses so that at one point Henry Knox insisted that any serious British assault would cost the patriots their entire artillery corps as the horses were too weak to move the cannons. Baron de Kalb was so unimpressed with Washington's choice of a camp that he noted "it must have been selected at the insistence of a speculator or on the advice of a traitor or by a council of ignoramuses." The relative fertility of the region was negated by a road network that was totally inadequate to handle large numbers of wagons, while snow covered roads and flooded rivers halted transport of provisions from Reading for days at a time. Private wagon drivers charged exorbitant rates to deliver supplies to the American encampment and often simply dumped their cargoes just part way to their destination. The farmers and merchants of the area preferred to sell their goods to Howe's forces for hard currency rather than accept almost worthless Continental Scrip, yet Washington was reluctant to use his authority to simply commandeer supplies since he was convinced that such actions would turn the citizenry against the patriot cause.

The combination of erratic food supplies, absence of warm clothing and the onset of a moderately cold and snowy winter produced an escalating sick list that threatened to exterminate Washington's army. A surgeon attached to the patriot forces lamented "poor food, hard lodging, cold weather, fatigue, nasty clothes, nasty cooking, vomit half the time, smoked out of my senses—why are we sent here to starve and freeze? Why sweet felicities have I left at home—here all is confusion, smoke, cold, hunger and filth." By Christmas of 1777 Washington admitted that there was absolutely no meat available in the entire camp, with only 25 barrels of flour still on hand. There were periods of three or four days at a time when no rations were issued to the famished soldiers, while even in "good" weeks the men subsisted on a diet of "firecake" which was merely flour and water heated on a fireplace. When General von Steuben arrived in camp he noted that "the men are literally naked... the officers who had coats had them of every color and make. I saw officers at a grand parade in a sort of dressing gown made of old blankets or woolen bed covers."

This atrocious supply system made even the ramshackle Confederate commissary during the Civil War seem efficient in comparison, as the failure to provide rations and warm clothing left the men extremely vulnerable to disease. Colds turned into pneumonia, unsanitary conditions in the huts led to dysentery, typhus and typhoid fever. Smallpox spread despite crude attempts at inoculation. Hospital rooms designed for 6 men were soon crammed with 20 or 30 soldiers, many of whom died within a few days of beginning their medical "treatment." One contingent of 40 hospitalized Virginians was reduced to only 3 survivors within a week of hospitalization. Cemetery carts rattled through the camp as men of the graves detail picked up the bodies of soldiers who had starved or frozen to death during the night. Most of these men were totally naked as their surviving comrades removed every article of clothing from the corpses. The lack of pay for months on end merely enhanced the feeling of disgust among entire companies and regiments and the desertion rate was soon at epidemic proportions. Thus the result of Washington's misguided attempt to harden his men through deprivation was the threatened annihilation of the Continental Army as an effective military force.

The death rate among American regiments during the Valley Forge winter was a staggering 25% with over 3000 men buried in the camp between December and March. Considering the fact that the largest patriot fatality list at any single battle was the 300 lost at Long Island, the death toll at Valley Forge was overwhelming for the relatively small American force. The high desertion rate and the large number of men on sick call reduced the number of available soldiers to less than 5000 men during several periods of the winter of 1777-78. Washington had unknowingly placed his men in a charnel house that almost ended their military capability. Any British general with even a modicum of initiative and energy could have used a system of spies and informers to verify Washington's plight and marched his far larger, better fed, better equipped army toward a final confrontation with the emaciated skeletons defending American liberty. Fortunately for the cause of American independence, Howe was content to spend the winter attending amateur theatricals produced by his officers and enjoying the pleasures of his relationship with Betsey Loring. The Continental Army was almost at the point of collapse but Howe was not the sort of general who could deliver the final, fatal blow to the American cause.

During the late winter and early spring of 1778 a number of events began to restore the cohesion of Washington's army and provide the survivors of the brutal winter encampment with new hope for fighting the British on more equal terms. First, the American commander finally realized the fact that malnutrition was destroying his regiments and allowed commissary and quartermaster detachments to forage the Pennsylvania and New Jersey countryside to commandeer food and other supplies. Nathanael Greene accepted a temporary appointment as quartermaster general of the army and employed an energetic and ruthless contingent under Anthony Wayne to sweep through farms and towns in order to secure adequate supplies for the troops. American morale was further augmented when Washington was able to secure enough money from Congress to pay the men their back wages and supplement this action with a newly approved one month bonus for the men who had survived the winter encampment.

The military disposition of Washington's army was enhanced with the arrival of Frederick von Steuben as the new Continental drillmaster. This middle aged veteran of Frederick the Great's Prussian army was typical of many foreign volunteers, as he grossly exaggerated the rank and importance of his European service. While von Steuben had only been a company commander in the German army, he did possess excellent leadership qualities which he displayed on the frozen fields around Valley Creek. The new drill supervisor initiated a rigid training schedule which utilized model companies trained under his personal control to promote a higher degree of discipline and precision in an increasing number of American regiments. Steuben's combination of knowledge and showmanship won over the initially skeptical patriot soldiers and soon men were competing for praise from the rather eccentric German.

Steuben's plan to instill some level of European-style discipline and tactical precision in the highly individualistic American units was actually a calculated risk enthusiastically supported by Washington. A more traditionally configured army would become less unpredictable in a crisis, better able to form and hold formations and more adept at maneuvering under fire and marching quickly on open roads. A disciplined army could be extracted more readily from a possible trap and could more rapidly develop a critical counterattack. However, these tactics would sacrifice much of the inherent Yankee individualism that so often frustrated the strategies of the less flexible and less innovative British armies. The rebel ability to use cover and concealment, maximize the impact of excellent marksmanship and move rapidly through fields and forests often provided an effective counterweight to superior British numbers, equipment and naval power. The approach of spring would soon provide Washington and Steuben with the opportunity to determine whether the survivors of Valley Forge could use their new expertise to challenge the British professionals.

While William Howe clearly had no initial intention of abandoning his hard won prize of Philadelphia after going to the trouble of repulsing Washington at Germantown and clearing the Delaware River of American defenses, the British commander's plans and preferences soon dropped to secondary status when the policy makers in Whitehall began to review their options for the 1778 campaign. Howe suspected that he had not received proper support from his government and proper commendation from the King after his dramatic capture of the rebel capital. He felt that George III and Lord Germain favored Burgoyne's plans and operations while the subsequent debacle at Saratoga had merely negated the benefits of Howe's victorious campaign against Washington. Now all Howe had to show for his brilliant battles was a half empty conquered city that would be extremely difficult to hold with the expected arrival of a French army and fleet. The British commander in America decided that this would be an ideal time to return to London and reclaim his seat in Parliament before his splendid triumph melted away with French intervention.

Howe submitted his resignation to Lord Germain and was given a spectacular going away party in Philadelphia which included a mock medieval tournament and banquet designed by Captain John Andre. Even at the climax of this extravagant "Mischianza," an American raiding party proved that Washington was far from defeated, as the rebels penetrated redcoat positions and set fire to a number of British held structures. The new British commander, Sir Henry Clinton, would soon face a confident and invigorated adversary.

The American alliance with France which was formalized during the winter of 1778 forced a major revision of British strategy. Instead of trying to suppress the rebellion by defeating rebel armies and occupying their major cities, the British government was forced to consider the necessity of defending the entire empire against possible attack from one or more powerful European enemies. Since large numbers of reinforcements were not readily available in a society that did not employ conscription, the defense of Canada, Florida and the West Indies would have to come primarily from forces already transported to North America. Thus Henry Clinton was ordered by the British government to evacuate Philadelphia as soon as possible, while dispatching almost one third of his army to positions in the West Indies. Clinton realized that his army would have little initial opportunity for military success and was quite prepared to resign and follow Howe back to London. However, a royal appointment to membership in Lord Carlisle's newly designated peace commission, together with hints of royal generosity at the conclusion of any sort of face saving peace settlement, prompted Clinton to maintain his command and initiate a plan to evacuate the army back to New York. While the British government had ordered the new commander to transport his army by a sea route, Clinton decided that he would use his available shipping to evacuate over 3000 panic stricken Loyalists while the main part of the army marched overland through New Jersey.

While the British army prepared to evacuate the American capital, Washington called a council of war, inviting 16 of his generals to suggest the most appropriate response to the enemy withdrawal. The Virginia general assumed that he could oppose Clinton's 14,000 regulars with a mixed force of 11,000 Continentals and militia. Possible options included an immediate attack on the British rear as the enemy left Philadelphia, a peaceful occupation of the capital with major campaigning delayed until the arrival of French reinforcements, or a move toward New Jersey with the intention of getting in front of the slow moving enemy army and provoking a climactic confrontation with Clinton. Most of the assembled generals expressed their desire to wait until their new French allies showed up, but a few more bellicose subordinates such as Wayne and Lafayette felt that the newly hardened rebel army could defeat the retreating British on their own, and perhaps end the war before the alliance provided the French government with excuses to demand American concessions. Washington finally agreed to a compromise plan which would allow the American forces to shadow Clinton's march and turn an anticipated rear guard confrontation into a major battle if circumstances seemed to favor an American victory.

Clinton's long columns of scarlet coated regulars snaked through the Jersey countryside as the men cursed an early summer heat wave that pushed temperatures into the mid-90's. The disgruntled redcoats marched with the nearly 500 slow moving wagons driven by sweating, cursing teamsters who urged their horses on to New York. The new British commander was less than enthusiastic concerning the prospect of a running battle with the rebels as his men trudged toward the Atlantic, so he deployed half of his army as a rear guard to discourage an American assault. A series of relatively short marches moved the army from Philadelphia to Haddonfield to Monmouth Court House, as patriot scouts and cavalry patrols dispatched their intelligence back to Washington's more rapidly moving army.

As the British army moved toward Monmouth Court House, Washington called another council of war to formalize American attack plans. General Charles Lee, the American second in command who had recently been exchanged, presented an emotional argument for a push to the Hudson Valley with only a token move against Clinton's force. Lafayette insisted that "it would be disgraceful and humiliating to allow the enemy to cross the Jerseys in tranquility" and offered to lead an attack on the British rear guard. Greene and Wayne supported their French colleague in a suggestion that a strong detachment should be sent to intercept Clinton, with a major reinforcement held on standby status if favorable circumstances developed. Washington finally agreed to give Lafayette command of a detachment of 5000 men including Morgan's rifle corps, Maxwell's veteran infantry brigade, Wayne's division and selected units of New Jersey militia to exert pressure on the retreating British column. While Lee opposed the American plan, he insisted that he would be disgraced if such a large force was deployed under the command of a general junior to himself in rank and experience. Washington relented to the extent that while he maintained Lafayette in field command, he designated the British veteran as overall detachment commander. This awkward organizational structure was an invitation to disaster if Clinton decided to seriously challenge the patriot advance.

The British general knew that Washington's army was marching to contest his passage to New York but Clinton seemed to exhibit mixed feelings concerning the desirability of accepting the rebel challenge. The British army was formed in battle formation to meet an expected American assault on Monmouth on June 27th, but when the patriot army didn't arrive, Clinton ordered a continuation of the British withdrawal. The next morning, Lee's detachment was on the road by 4 A.M. and was marching from Englishtown to Monmouth to intercept the rear units of the British column. The American regiments moved at a leisurely pace as the torrid heat pushed the temperature to 90 degrees by 10 A.M. with an expectation of 100 degrees by afternoon. The advance patriot units arrived in Monmouth Court House at just before noon—in time to see the final few redcoats disappear down the road.

Charles Lee occupied the village while most of his men were rested and fed. However, a mobile unit led by Anthony Wayne pressed ever closer to a British rear guard of 600 redcoats. While Wayne was closing in on this relatively small enemy unit, Henry Clinton was finalizing his plans for the day. The British commander had determined to embark his men on ships docked at relatively nearby Sandy Hook rather than marching all the way to New York. On the other hand, he dispatched Charles Cornwallis with an additional 1500 men to discourage a close American pursuit. Thus while Wayne's men converged on the enemy rear guard, both Lee and Cornwallis were deploying reinforcements destined to expand a skirmish into a full fledged battle. An initial British cavalry attack on the lead patriot units was repulsed by controlled volleys that dropped dozens of enemy horsemen. Wayne and Lafayette tried to convince Lee that this initial victory should be expanded into an all out assault on a temporarily outnumbered British column. However, Lee resisted any offensive moves as he insisted "you do not know British soldiers. We cannot stand against them. We shall certainly be driven back at first. We must be cautious." Since Lee had neither a plan of attack nor a real grasp of the situation, the larger American units were milling around in confusion as Cornwallis initiated a British flanking assault against the poorly deployed rebel line.

George Washington's first news from the scene of the battle seemed to indicate a triumphant American advance against an outnumbered adversary. However, when the patriot general arrived at the site of the confrontation, he was shocked to see large numbers of Americans, retreating from the advancing redcoats. Washington quickly dispatched his aides to bring forward the rest of the army while the general himself roared his displeasure with Lee's tactics. The legendary temper was soon boiling over as he insisted that Lee should not have requested command of the advance force unless he really meant to fight a significant battle. A lively string of obscenities may or may not have peppered Washington's encounter with his subordinate, but the general did calm down sufficiently to ask Lee to take charge of the forward defenses while the rest of the army moved into place.

By 3 o'clock on the afternoon of June 28th, the battle situation was becoming critical for the patriot army. Lee's detachment was fragmented and disorganized and Clinton began to realize that a substantial reinforcement for Cornwallis might smash the rebel defenses. A succession of fresh British regiments threatened to roll over the outnumbered Americans until Lee ordered a general retreat back to a new position at Tennant Church. As Lee's disorganized and weary men pulled back, Washington was forming a formidable defense line on high ground behind a causeway crossing a swampy area called the West Morass. This new position was defended by

Greene's division holding the right flank, Stirling's division on the left with Washington retaining personal command of the center brigades. Lafayette was given command of a second line which was largely out of sight of the British units while Wayne's regiments held an advance position behind an outer series of hedges and fences in front of the main army.

The heavily reinforced British assault force now advanced toward positions that were assumed to be defended by Lee's exhausted and disorganized regiments. The redcoats expected a rapid American retreat until they came within musket range of Stirling's division. Large formations of the Black Watch and elite light infantry companies simply evaporated in a hail of American bullets. Dozens of other redcoats dropped of heat exhaustion or heat stroke in the 100 degree temperatures. Clinton now shifted a number of regiments to an assault on the positions held by Greene's men. Lord Cornwallis personally led a number of elite units in a futile attack that was disrupted by a number of well placed rebel artillery batteries. Now the action shifted to the center of the line where Wayne's men used their excellent cover to pour volleys into a perfectly formed contingent of advancing British soldiers. Lt. Col. Henry Monckton organized a succession of redcoat assaults on Wayne's well protected patriots and died along with many of his subordinate officers in a futile attempt to break through the American hedges. Clinton now brought in units from other parts of the battlefield to overwhelm the stubborn Continentals, but Wayne pulled his units back to the main defenses under cover of massive American artillery fire.

The redcoat tide had now crested and Washington began to suspect that an American counterattack might unhinge the whole British army. An initial assault launched by three Pennsylvania regiments routed a weary force of British grenadiers and only Clinton's ability to rush reinforcements to the crumbling unit prevented a disastrous patriot breakthrough. Washington now initiated a huge artillery duel between the two armies as he used his cannon fire to cover the formation of a large scale assault force. However, scores of American soldiers were now dropping from heat exhaustion and the American commander reluctantly ordered his men to sleep on their arms and initiate a new attack at dawn on June 29th. Clinton had no desire to continue an engagement that might annihilate his poorly positioned army and he ordered a withdrawal toward Sandy Hook during the night. The British not only abandoned the field to the Americans, but they also left behind 250 dead redcoats and 400 men too badly injured to be moved. Another 600 Hessian and British soldiers deserted during the retreat while dozens of others were captured by American patrols. Washington's army had held the field at the end of the battle but each side claimed some level of success at the confrontation around Monmouth Court House. The Americans had not captured the British wagon train and the major part of Clinton's force was able to retire to the New York defenses. However, the British general had lost almost one fifth of an irreplaceable army while his adversary could easily replace his battle losses. The Continental soldiers had reasserted an aggressiveness that had begun to emerge in the earlier engagements around Philadelphia while Clinton began to realize that an all out confrontation with Washington's army was probably too risky for his very finite expeditionary force. However, while Washington considered new options for his increasingly formidable army, the war in the North virtually came to a halt. The northern states would continue to be the site of Indian uprisings, British amphibious attacks and small scale skirmishes but the major focus of the war was about to shift southward.

The ambitious British campaign plan of 1777 which envisioned a capture of the rebel capital and control of the vital Hudson Valley had produced few tangible benefits to the English war effort. During the 12 months following the onset of Burgoyne and Howe's offensives, the British ministry had been stunned by the loss of one army and the decimation of a second contingent; the evacuation of a newly conquered enemy capital; and the formalization of a Franco-American alliance which threatened the very existence of Britain's 18th century empire. The slender hope for some acceptable outcome to this crisis now rested on a plan to recover the southern colonies and negotiate some form of face-saving accommodation with the rebel government. The war in the north had produced few permanent British gains and had encouraged the emergence of George Washington as a truly formidable adversary. The American commander had learned the craft of military leadership while directing an army that was consistently outnumbered, outgunned and often outmaneuvered. The patriot leader had fought the military forces of the world's most powerful empire to a standstill and instilled a dramatically lowered expectation for victory among the ministers and officials in Whitehall and Westminster.

CHAPTER 10

# Alternative Strategies and Outcomes

## *British and American 1777-1778*

$T$he most likely opportunity for a decisive British military triumph in the American Revolution occurred between the summer and late autumn of 1776. During this period George Washington was not yet very confident of his abilities, the Continental army was plagued with incompetent division and brigade commanders, and American soldiers were terrified of meeting British bayonet attacks on open battlefields. The newly issued Declaration of Independence was only "permanent" as long as there was a patriot army to enforce the language of the document. Thus a British victory which resulted in the capture or disbanding of the bulk of the American army combined with a generous peace settlement that addressed most of the colonists' long standing grievances, would have quite likely relegated the Revolution to the status of an unpleasant but brief anomaly in the long term relationship between American provinces and English motherland.

The ministerial expectation that a single, overwhelming utilization of British military force would end the rebellion in one campaign season was condemned to disappointment when William Howe allowed his American adversary to escape outright annihilation on at least four separate occasions during the New York and New Jersey campaigns. The flickering rebellion was given a respite which Washington and the Congressional leaders utilized to regroup and redeploy their resources to meet the expected renewal of the British offensive in 1777. While British victory had been at least temporarily thwarted, the King's forces still maintained the ability to successfully terminate the war during the next campaign. The United Kingdom still fielded a powerful army that outnumbered and outgunned the relatively small corps of American professionals who were always uncertain about the level of militia support that would be available in the next critical battle. A British government that was willing to take a few more risks and ensure an adequate level of communication between ministerial offices and field armies could still win the war despite the embarrassing setbacks at Trenton and Princeton.

The basic British plan to terminate the war during 1777 was, on the whole, a fairly intelligent document. Burgoyne's proposal to capture Albany and split the colonies in two would have been a devastating blow to the rebel war effort, while Howe's scheme to force Washington to fight in the open by threatening the American capital would be a brilliant stratagem if it was accomplished quickly enough to permit the redcoats to march north and support the expedition from Canada later in the summer. The campaign plan for 1777 had a better than average opportunity to provide a military victory for the British government if Howe, the ministry and Burgoyne each played their expected role in expediting the planned offensives. Unfortunately for the imperial officials, each link in this crucial chain of command failed at a critical moment.

The major defect in Howe's operation was the British general's incredible decision to move his army by sea all the way down to the Chesapeake to attack an enemy capital that could be much more easily approached from a number of other routes. This strategy effectively removed any opportunity to cooperate with Burgoyne without providing any substantial advantage in the expected confrontation with Washington's forces. Howe also overestimated the size of the force that he would need to deal with the Continental army defending Pennsylvania. A relatively risk-free detachment of three or four thousand men from the Philadelphia expedition to Clinton's command in New York would have provided enough manpower to defeat Washington at Brandywine, while allowing his second in command to dispatch nearly seven thousand men up the Hudson to disrupt the American lines around Saratoga. A force of this magnitude would have forced Horatio Gates into the unenviable position of confronting equally large enemy armies to his front and rear and might have at least allowed Burgoyne to withdraw to the north without surrendering his army.

While Howe's actions were less than praiseworthy, the British crown and ministry frustrated at least some key elements of Burgoyne's invasion from Canada. King George III eliminated a number of key units from Burgoyne's command, when the expenditure of modest funds to raise and train new regiments in Britain would have released vital experienced units for service in the Hudson River expedition. The official willingness to spare no expense in crushing the rebellion during the preparation for the 1776 campaign seems to have given way to traditional British parsimony in this subsequent campaign. The reluctance to provide a full compliment of regulars embarking from England was exacerbated by the failure of the key support force under Barry St. Leger to adequately assist Burgoyne's expedition. St. Leger's deployment of 2000 regulars, Loyalists and Indians in the Mohawk Valley might have delayed the mobilization of the New York militia units reinforcing Gates' army. However, the British colonel allowed himself to be checked by an outnumbered but much more determined Colonel Gansevoort at Fort Stanwix and then effectively pushed out of direct involvement in the Burgoyne campaign by Benedict Arnold's small contingent of Continentals.

Howe's capture of the American capital could not counteract the impact of British disaster at Saratoga in the ministerial offices around London and Paris. However, a subsequent annihilation or capture of a substantial segment of Washington's army might have provided encouragement in Whitehall and second thoughts about an American alliance in Versailles. The British commander displayed uncharacteristic energy when he initiated an early winter surprise attack against the American camp at Whitemarsh and might have produced an important victory if he had simply repeated this strategy a few weeks later against the Valley Forge fortifications. Howe received a steady stream of reports from spies, Loyalists and deserters describing the gradual disintegration of the American forces around Valley Creek. He might have utilized this information to prepare a massive assault on Washington's defenses during the darkest days of the Valley Forge encampment. Contrary to the mythology surrounding that dreadful American experience, while food and clothing were in short supply, the winter of 1777-1778 in southeastern Pennsylvania was slightly above normal in temperature and slightly below normal in snowfall. Thus a British winter march from Philadelphia to Valley Forge would have been undertaken in relatively dry weather with temperatures in the high 30's or low 40's, hardly the conditions facing Napoleon's army in the retreat from Moscow. A well planned and well coordinated British assault with 13,000 or 14,000 available soldiers might have inflicted a staggering blow on the patriot cause. Washington's army seldom had more than four or five thousand effectives available due to lack of food and winter clothing and the American cavalry and artillery units were practically immobilized by poorly fed horses. Rather than emerging as a symbol of heroic endurance against terrible conditions, Valley Forge might have been the site of a significant blow to American hopes for independence. Fortunately for the patriot cause, Howe chose to utilize his extensive information resources to convince him that the rebel army was so close to disintegrating of its own accord that British inaction during winter would result in a bloodless victory by spring.

Burgoyne's surrender at Saratoga combined with the survival of Washington's army during the crisis at Valley Forge probably ended the last realistic opportunity for a clear cut British military resolution of the American rebellion. However, the overwhelming disaster of Yorktown was still several years in the future and an intelligent political and diplomatic response to the crisis caused by the defeat at Saratoga could have yet produced an accommodation with the rebel provinces that would satisfy both ministry and general public. The continuum between total military suppression of the American rebels and abject capitulation to patriot demands contained a number of less extreme outcomes that might have satisfied the adversaries in both London and Philadelphia.

The initial stunning announcement of the loss of almost 8000 British regulars in a forest along the Hudson River swept through a startled population in the autumn of 1777. Major General Frederick von Lossberg, one of the commanders of the German expeditionary force in America, summarized the military dilemma facing his British allies. "We are far from an anticipated peace because the bitterness of the rebels is too widespread, and in regions where we are the masters, the rebellious spirit is still in them. The land is too large and there are too many people. The more land we win, the weaker our army gets in the field. It would be best to come to an agreement with them." Lord Chatham (William Pitt) summarized the critical state of military affairs for his colleagues in the House of Lords. "No man thinks more highly than I of the virtue and valor of British troops. I know they can achieve anything except impossibilities and the conquest of America is an impossibility! You cannot conquer America. We know that in three campaigns we have done nothing and suffered much. You may swell every expense and every effort still more extravagantly; accumulate every assistance you can buy; traffic and barter with every pitiful prince that sells his subjects—you are forever vain and impotent—doubly so from this mercenary aid in which you rely; for it leads to an incurable resentment in the minds of our enemies. If I were an American as I am an Englishman, while a foreign troop was landed in my country I would never lay down my arms!"

Charles Fox subsequently appeared before the House of Commons with a bill to declare that all those who supported the war were as criminally responsible as the ministers and demanded that the orders which had been given to Burgoyne should be laid before the House. While this motion was rather narrowly defeated, the opposition members of Parliament were able to demand a debate on the state of the nation which was scheduled for February 2nd, 1778. On that raw, frigid afternoon large crowds began to gather outside of Parliament clamoring for admittance to what promised to be one of the most exciting and entertaining debates in years. A select group of wives, mistresses and well connected friends of MP's stampeded into the galleries to watch a three hour performance by Fox. The famous orator began slowly and then warmed up during the evening. "I would wish gentlemen to forget their animosities and consider themselves neither friends nor enemies to America but regard with a calm and dispassionate mind its part as a very considerable part of the British Empire." Fox insisted that a British concession of independence to the colonies would not necessarily harm the nation's economic interests as "an independent America could be a powerful friend. To continue to seek blood in America would endanger the hope of that friendship. Now that France is about to enter the war, no more regiments should be allowed to leave England to serve in America."

Lord North and his benefactor, George III, had arrived at a crisis moment in the war with the American provinces. While Fox's motions to end the war in the colonies were temporarily tabled, even a Tory leader admitted "we are in a damned bad way." On the one hand, North insisted that all rational Europeans should support England's attempt to put down insurrection or "one day all of Europe will find itself ruled by Americans imbued with democratic fanaticism." However, Benjamin Franklin held a more realistic view of European feelings concerning Britain. "Every nation in Europe wishes to see England humbled, having all in their time been offended by her insolence." As dispatches crossed the English Channel with news of increasing belligerence toward Britain on the part of a number of nations, North began to petition his monarch to resign from a seemingly impossible job. George III was horrified at the prospect of an imminent Pitt ministry and briefly considered abdication as he insisted "if the nation will not stand by me, they shall have another King." The monarch was finally persuaded otherwise to the extent that he was able to secure an extension of the North regime by offering the prime minister almost a million dollars to pay off outstanding debts while locating another million dollars in the secret service fund to create a string of sinecures for the minister and his relatives.

While the friends of the King provided enough votes in Parliament to allow the government to continue military operations in America after Burgoyne's surrender, the ministers now began to consider a number of scenarios that could minimize further damage to an increasingly fragile empire. The candle-lit drawing rooms from Kensington to Green Park were the backdrops to animated discussions concerning the future direction of British operations against the seceded provinces. The first strategy which emerged from ministerial conversations included a tacit admission that the British army could not eliminate Washington's forces from the military chessboard. A number of British officials suggested that it was time to abandon the interior of America and use the remaining regiments to hold possible naval strongholds. This tactic included a blockade of all American shipping combined with intensive raiding along the coastline of the rebel provinces, while naval commanders would be given full power to negotiate peace terms when the disaffected colonists finally came to their senses and accepted a compromise settlement. The implementation of a naval blockade presented a number of challenges to British policy makers. The government would have to decide which American ports should be held and which ones should be abandoned; what kinds of ships would be most effective in blockading and raiding duties; and the extent of military commitment needed to secure the necessary bases. General Jeffrey Amherst, who had emerged as the king's chief military advisor and de facto commander of the British army, insisted that even the defense of a limited number of ports would require 33,000 regulars with an additional 12,000 men needed if Philadelphia was retained. Since Halifax was too remote to service the expected blockade squadrons, New York would have to receive upgraded dockyard facilities while Norfolk was proposed as a worthwhile southern naval base.

Ministerial proponents of the maritime strategy to end the rebellion insisted that their scheme would reduce the risk of losing another entire British army while effectively employing the might of the Royal Navy in a war of commercial and maritime attrition that would hopefully induce the financially strangled American provinces to accept a negotiated settlement short of total independence. However, in its original format, this plan contained a number of deficiencies. The maritime proposal assumed that the Americans would weary of the struggle first when it was quite possible that war weariness would affect British politicians and merchants well before their American counterparts were ready to capitulate. Any attempt to produce an effective blockade of the American coastline would require far more than the 90 ships now serving in the western Atlantic which would in turn possibly strip the maritime defenses of the motherland against a possible Franco-Spanish invasion. Finally, a policy of holding British troops in a limited number of enclaves might tempt the always aggressive Washington to launch American offensives against the still loyal British territories of Canada and Florida.

The obvious potential drawbacks of the initial maritime proposal encouraged Lord North to seek the tacit approval of the king for a more comprehensive strategy that included direct negotiations with the rebel Congress. North was convinced that Britain was not equal to a war against the combined forces of France, Spain and America as "Great Britain will undo herself while she thinks of punishing France." George III agreed that removal of an aggressive menace from the rebels was worth pursuing as "it is so desirable to end the war with America to be enabled with redoubled ardour to avenge the faithless and insolent conduct of France." The three year conflict with the rebel colonies had now produced a fascinating turnabout in the priorities of key British leaders as the initial determination to suppress the rebellion at all hazards had now given way to a more traditional British desire to punish France for interfering with the internal affairs of the empire even if it required virtual abandonment of the American war to accomplish this end. This enormously important change of attitude is often underestimated in American chronicles of the Revolution and yet it led to a pivotal decision in the British government that might well have ended the war five full years before the ratification of the Treaty of Paris in 1783.

During the late winter of 1778 King George authorized Lord North to appoint a peace commission that would offer the Continental Congress terms so generous that the Americans would hopefully jump at the opportunity to enjoy all the advantages of being British subjects without any of the burdens. The list of proposed concessions to the American provincials was comprehensive and impressive. The peace commission would be authorized to propose a renunciation of parliamentary supremacy and their right to tax for revenue purposes; the acknowledgment of Congress as a legal body representing the will of the American people; the renunciation of any standing British army in the provinces in time of peace without the consent of the colonial legislature; an acknowledgment of the legitimacy of the Continental Army with permanent commissions offered to Continental officers; reservation of all government offices in America for American citizens; and finally, acceptance of American demands for representation in Parliament on a proportional basis of overall imperial population. The financial difficulties plaguing both American citizens and the Congress would be ameliorated by an offer to exchange Continental dollars for British currency while the debts of the colonies and national government would be paid by Parliament.

While this list of concessions was generous and focused directly on the issues that had caused the estrangement between Britain and America in the first place, the king and Lord North expected some concessions from the Americans in exchange for these conciliatory gestures. American participation in a newly restructured empire would be based on a willingness to accept Parliamentary authority to regulate trade and tax non-British imports to the colonies in order to maintain a protected market for British manufacturers; officers in the Continental army would agree to accept the King's commission; the Americans would agree to forego the development of a separate naval force; American debts to British merchants would be honored; and Loyalists would be restored to their estates and properties. The peace proposal authorized by Lord North and the King was a serious attempt to encourage a new direction for British military objectives at this time of crisis for the empire, and this package represented what should have been an ideal point of departure for a negotiated settlement approved by the American Congress. Unfortunately, two significant factors intervened to disrupt the peace process and ensure the continuation of a war that was rapidly exhausting the resources of both British and American adversaries.

The first flaw in the British plan to produce a negotiated settlement to the war appeared in the very process of selecting the members of the proposed commission. The Earl of Carlisle, who was apparently famous for being one of the best dressed men in England, was chosen to head this vital mission. The Earl was a heavy gambler with huge debts and apparently looked upon his appointment as an opportunity to recoup his fortune in America. The second member of the group was Commodore George Johnstone, an ill tempered former governor of West Florida who had already fought one duel with Lord George Germain and was hardly likely to exhibit the tact so necessary to producing a sense of trust among the American congressional leaders. The final appointment went to William Eden, who was apparently included because he happened to be a school classmate to Carlisle and was a close friend to the Earl. North's inability to appoint truly talented diplomats to this crucial commission which might hold the future of the British Empire in its collective hands appears to be one of his most dismal failures of the war. This less than August body simply could not impress the far more talented members of the Congress with the seriousness of the

British desire for peace and thus the Americans tended to dismiss the Conciliatory Act as a ministerial plot to encourage the rebels to disband their army and then attempt to reconquer a defenseless nation.

The other major defect in North's strategy revolved around the instructions given to the Carlisle Commission before they sailed from Britain. Contrary to the popular depiction of George III as an obstinate monarch who vowed never to concede the loss of his American colonies, the King had secretly authorized North to concede independence to the rebels if they refused to accept the initial offer of de facto dominion status. The King had largely accepted General Amherst's conclusion that "the object of the war now being changed and the contest in America being a secondary consideration, our principal object must be distressing France." King George reluctantly concurred in this opinion and admitted that "should a war with France be our fate, the only means of making it successful would be withdrawing the greatest part of troops from America and employing them against the French and Spanish settlements. But if we are to be carrying on a land war against the rebels and against these two powers, it must be feeble in all points and consequently unsuccessful." The increasing likelihood of war with the Bourbon states prompted the king to authorize a highly classified final proposal to the colonists which would agree to American independence in return for a guarantee of British sovereignty in Canada and Florida and some form of protection and amnesty for Loyalist subjects. According to most available accounts of the brief negotiations between the Carlisle Commission and Congress this ultimate concession was never even hinted at during the talks and the British diplomats seem to have taken the initial American rejection of their first proposal as a final response. The commissioners simply headed back to England without presenting any further suggestions for a settlement. A more talented and sophisticated body of negotiators might have at least hinted that further concessions were possible and kept the peace process alive until the last best offers were divulged.

While the British advantage in manpower and financial support forced the Americans to primarily react to their adversaries' military and diplomatic initiatives during much of this period, it is apparent that the patriots had at least one opportunity to possibly win the war before the struggle shifted to the southern states. The American victory at Saratoga was so decisive that it forced the British government to seriously consider abandoning the colonies in the wake of Burgoyne's surrender. However, the opportunity to confront the crown and ministry with an even more devastating crisis just missed emerging during Washington's surprise attack on Germantown. The American assault was initially so successful that William Howe was just about to order a full scale retreat when the key American attack units began to shoot each other in the fog. A British abandonment of their Germantown defenses could have easily resulted in the loss of two or three thousand British soldiers, with the probable result being Howe's evacuation of Philadelphia shortly thereafter. It is not difficult to imagine the crisis atmosphere that would have swept through Parliament during an almost simultaneous announcement of defeat at Saratoga and Germantown with a subsequent evacuation of the just captured rebel capital. This succession of disasters would have nullified the immense ministerial effort to suppress the rebellion during 1777 and would have seriously jeopardized the future of the North government. This chain of events might have forced the British ministry to dispatch a more talented, high profile peace commission to America with the last ditch concession of independence placed on the negotiating table at a much earlier point.

While the American victory at Saratoga encouraged a decisive uplift of hopes for eventual independence due to the onset of French intervention, an additional patriot victory at Germantown might have obviated the need for Bourbon assistance. For the small price of a more formalized policy of leniency toward the Loyalists and a mutually advantageous commercial agreement, the American revolutionaries might well have secured their independence five years before the actual termination of the war. Unfortunately, the combination of a missed military opportunity in the fog at Germantown and a botched diplomatic opportunity in the wake of the Carlisle envoy ensured that the War of Independence would evolve into an even more bitter and bloody struggle as the contest shifted to the southern colonies.

CHAPTER 11

# Southern Stars Fall from the American Constellation

### *The British Offensive from Savannah to Camden*

*T*he surrender of General Burgoyne at Saratoga and the ensuing alliance between France and the rebel colonies convinced the British ministry in London that a total military triumph over the Americans was becoming a more remote possibility. However, a number of civil and military leaders became increasingly intrigued with the prospect of redeploying the British army in an attempt to recover one or more of the southern provinces to royal authority. A southern strategy offered a number of potential benefits for the increasingly hard pressed British military machine. First, a progressive series of offensives designed to reconquer Georgia, the Carolinas and Virginia might encourage the Continental Congress to accept a compromise peace settlement that exchanged some minimal acknowledgment of contin- ued royal authority for British evacuation of the southern states. On the other hand, if the Congressional leaders insisted on total independence, the crown could maintain control over a substantial portion of North America.

The decision to shift the focus of the war from the northern to the southern provinces was based on fairly sound reasoning. Georgia, the initial British objective, was the least enthusiastic member of the American confed- eration and had provided few recruits for the Continental Army while raising large numbers of Tory regiments. It is quite possible that any full scale referendum on the issue of independence from Great Britain would have revealed a majority of Georgians more committed to the maintenance of political ties to the British Empire.

Rebel plans for the defense of the lower south were complicated by the existence of a very scattered population, while British encouragement of Indian raids and potential slave uprisings tended to siphon off a large portion of the patriot population for local defense. The leaders of the British government were fascinated with the prospect of having the British army treated like liberators while King George was convinced that a southern offensive would prove his assertion that most Americans, given a free choice, would support a continued allegiance to the Crown.

The government eventually agreed upon a strategy in which British regulars would gradually reconquer the disputed regions in the southern provinces and then recruit loyalist defense forces that would assume control of each community and permit the redcoats to move on to the next logical objective. As successive counties were pacified, they would be restored to full civil government which would provide an expanding base of loyal territory behind the advancing screen of British military power. Once the southern colonies had been restored to a normal relationship with the imperial government, the available British regulars could either be used for a new offensive against French possessions in the West Indies or for a possible northward thrust against the main Continental Army under Washington.

The British southern strategy was essentially a sound plan, but it suffered from a shortage of manpower that was not evident when the royal government attempted to reconquer the northern provinces in 1776. At the time of the Declaration of Independence, the entire effective strength of the British army was just under 96,000 men, with over 54,000 men assigned to William Howe and Guy Carleton to crush the rebellion in an overwhelming pincers movement. However, as the British government prepared to initiate its southern offensive at the end of 1778, the total strength of the army had risen to 180,000 men with 78,000 regulars stationed in either North America or the Caribbean. Yet at no point between the attack on Savannah and the siege of Yorktown did any British army employed in the southern colonies exceed 14,000 men and most of the key battles were fought with a total combined strength of Tories and regulars of between 1000 and 4000 effectives. While the British ministry clearly benefitted from the inability of the patriots to raise or maintain very large forces in the south up to the confrontation at Yorktown, the future of imperial rule in North America was placed in the hands of an incredibly small number of redcoats and Tories.

The opening engagement in the British southern offensive occurred five months after the battle of Monmouth Courthouse, when Sir Henry Clinton dispatched Lt. Colonel Archibald Campbell with 3500 men to capture the important port city of Savannah. This Georgia city would provide a gateway to the southern colonies while serving as a link with British naval squadrons in the West Indies. Although the Continental Congress realized that Savannah would become a likely British target, the American government had done next to nothing to defend the town. A tiny force of 1000 untrained Georgia and South Carolina militia commanded by General Robert Howe had been deployed east of the city with its right flank resting on a swamp and the left flank next to a series of rice paddies. While one of Campbell's assault columns feinted a move through the rice fields, a cooperative slave led the main force through the swamp, which allowed the redcoats to emerge on the patriot rear. The two British columns launched a combined attack that simply obliterated the American defenders as over 500 rebels were killed, wounded or captured at a loss of 3 killed and 10 wounded for the redcoats. Campbell's army promptly marched into Savannah and raised the Union Jack over the first major southern prize.

The British army spent most of the next nine months pacifying Georgia and southern South Carolina with regular garrisons deployed throughout the region. As the ministerial forces expanded their hold on the provinces, French and American commanders in the northern states grew increasingly alarmed. Count Jean Baptiste d'Estaing, commander of French naval forces in America, insisted, "the American cause is now in great peril and all hopes are based on very early arrival to aid the cause." George Washington wanted to use French assistance to attack Clinton in New York City, but the French admiral was far more interested in an allied assault on Savannah. On the 16th of September, 1779, 3500 French soldiers joined General Benjamin Lincoln's army of 800 Continentals and 850 militia to prepare for an attack on General Augustine Prevost's 1500-man garrison holding Savannah. Admiral d'Estaing had provided an impressive naval squadron of 20 frigates and 25 ships of the line and also offered to provide 1000 additional marines to assure the success of the allied campaign.

The British garrison at Savannah was now facing an army almost four times as large as their own numbers, supported by an impressive array of naval firepower. However, Prevost was an able and energetic officer who had no intention of simply handing this prize to the rebel army. Prevost sent messengers to other British units garrisoning much of South Carolina and Georgia and ordered them to march immediately to reinforce Savannah. Within a few days Colonel John Maitland slipped through the allied lines with 900 invaluable regulars, which boosted the British garrison to 2400 men. Army engineer James Moncrief was directed to supervise the construction of a powerful defense network which included formidable breastworks, 13 redoubts and a number of artillery emplacements mounting over 100 cannons.

While the British engineers were constructing their works, French and American soldiers were hauling over 50 heavy guns from d'Estaing's fleet and by the morning of September 23rd, the heavy artillery, siege mortars and supporting naval broadsides were pounding the British fortifications. The allied barrage was effectively shattering the Savannah defenses and, given time, Prevost might have been forced to surrender the city. Unfortunately, d'Estaing began receiving exaggerated intelligence reports concerning a huge British relief squadron that was heading for Savannah to break the siege and a panicking French admiral now decided to risk a frontal assault before the enemy fleet arrived.

At 4 A.M. on the morning of October 9th, 1779, a picked detachment of

French infantry began a pre-dawn assault on the British redoubt at Spring Hill. The allied attack plan was based on an initial assault by French volunteers who would chop through the British abatis and then wait for 1100 support troops to follow in a double quick rush. A second column of French soldiers would try to penetrate to the Savannah River and then turn Prevost's right flank, while American troops would attack the British left flank and hopefully siphon redcoats from the formidable center defenses.

The complex allied attack plan devolved into a disorganized disaster as each element of the offensive disintegrated in the face of stiff British resistance. A steady stream of American deserters had provided Prevost with essential information concerning virtually every aspect of the intended assault, and the British commander deployed his troops to smash each successive threat. An elite unit of Tory sharpshooters supported by rows of cannon loaded with grapeshot lined the parapets of the Spring Hill redoubt. The French advance force was shattered by volleys of rifle fire from the Loyalist sharpshooters while the support units couldn't advance through the hail of grapeshot that was tearing them to pieces. As the allied attackers began stacking up in the hail of bullets and shells, d'Estaing went down with several bullet wounds while Casimir Pulaski, the American cavalry commander, received a mortal wound when a hail of grapeshot hit him in the stomach and groin. Prevost held back most of his best bayonet men until the American militia forces became disorganized during their attack on the British flank, and then let loose wave after wave of redcoats who killed or captured much of the patriot corps.

Within an hour, the allied assault had degenerated into chaos as Prevost's cheering, exuberant redcoats bayoneted or shot the few enemy soldiers who attempted to penetrate into the city. The painfully wounded French admiral was carried off a battlefield that contained almost a thousand allied casualties including almost 300 French or American killed. The British garrison had lost only 40 killed and 63 wounded and the redcoats eagerly awaited another assault. Admiral d'Estaing had no intention of obliging Prevost and he quickly pulled his men and guns from the trenches and loaded them back aboard the French fleet. Benjamin Lincoln was in an increasingly desperate position. He was now besieging an enemy force that outnumbered his own army while dispatches from the north informed him that British reinforcements from New York City were headed towards South Carolina. The American general called off the siege and marched his shattered army back to its base in Charleston. This retreat would soon turn the tables between besiegers and the besieged.

Henry Clinton's plan for the upcoming campaign during 1780 was based on utilizing the newly restored province of Georgia as a base for an operation against Charleston and a subsequent march through North Carolina and Virginia. Clinton was convinced that Sir Peter Parker had failed in his earlier attempt to capture the South Carolina port because he had landed his troops too far away from the key bastion of Fort Moultrie, had challenged a heavily defended fort with an unsupported naval squadron, and had underestimated the will of the American defenders to fight for the city. The British commander was determined to avoid those blunders and add the capture of Charleston to the growing list of successes in the southern provinces.

On December 26, 1779 General Clinton finished his lavish celebration of the Christmas holiday, turned command of the New York garrison over to General Knyphausen and set sail for South Carolina with 90 British transports carrying 13 regiments of regulars, supported by large detachments of artillery, cavalry and Loyalist auxiliaries. Five ships of the line and 9 frigates convoyed Clinton's 8500 men on their southbound voyage, which included the usual number of storms, becalmings and ships being blown off course. The British expeditionary force landed near Charleston on February 11, 1780 and began to link up with elements of the garrisons already holding much of the south.

The American defense of Charleston bears a striking resemblance to the patriot experiences around New York City during the 1776 campaign. The rebel commander, Benjamin Lincoln, could deploy only 800 regular soldiers who were supported by 2800 poorly trained short term militia. Lincoln was under enormous political pressure to hold a poorly defended city against an overwhelming number of better trained and better equipped professionals. Clinton had pulled together an expeditionary force that numbered 14,000 men and provided the British commander with something on the order of a 20 to 1 advantage in regular soldiers for the upcoming campaign. The forts defending Charleston harbor had been allowed to fall into disrepair while a land defense was supported by few natural barriers. Lincoln used his more rational periods to propose a total evacuation of the city, but the South Carolina legislature and Governor John Rutledge consistently overruled his suggestion.

While George Washington debated whether a slow moving land reinforcement column could reach Lincoln before the city fell, Henry Clinton pushed his forces ever closer to the outer defenses of Charleston. The redcoat army seized the Stono River ferry, occupied Johns Island and erected artillery batteries on the west bank of the Ashley River. Clinton's relatively leisurely pace allowed Washington to dispatch 1500 North Carolina and Virginia regulars to assist the garrison, but Clinton countered this move by summoning an additional seaborne detachment of 3500 men from New York City. By the beginning of April Lincoln had completed his defensive preparations by deploying seven small frigates for harbor defense, mounting 250 cannons in 13 forts and redoubts and recruiting additional militia to raise his entire force to 5000 men. However, the American commander had largely ignored the need to maintain an open line of communications with the north while placing his weakest units in the most advanced and vulnerable positions. When Clinton finally got down to business, the whole succession of American defenses began to crumble like a house of cards.

The first British objective was to close off Charleston harbor to prevent French naval support from arriving at a critical moment. On the morning of April 8, 1780 Charlestonians rose early to find a good observation spot on the Battery or on nearby rooftops to watch the expected duel between the American harbor forts and the Royal Navy. The almost festive atmosphere bore an eerie resemblance to an April morning 85 years later when the first Palmetto State artillery shells burst over Fort Sumter. The 1780 incarnation of the battle of Charleston harbor was a much shorter contest as Admiral Arbuthnot's ships pounded the American fortifications to rubble while the main batteries at Fort Moultrie scored only one hit on the attacking fleet. By early afternoon the British navy had sealed off the city by sea and Charleston harbor was useless to the patriot cause.

The naval victory in Charleston harbor prompted Clinton to summon his adversaries to surrender the city to "prevent the useless effusion of blood," while Lincoln politely declined to accept the initial British offer. A more energetic and imaginative American general would have taken one good look at the sea of British masts in Charleston harbor and evacuated his army through the still open northbound road network. However, Charleston's civic leaders insisted that they would open fire on any Continental soldiers attempting to evacuate the city and Lincoln meekly stayed put.

The British sappers and engineers completed the first approach parallel three days after the naval engagement and soon 24 pounders and heavy mortars began to shell the city. While the Royal Engineers constructed a second parallel, Clinton directed his artillery batteries to fire the same pitch-filled carcass balls that had obliterated much of Charlestown, Massachusetts during the battle of Bunker Hill. Large numbers of Charleston stores and homes began to blaze as the rain of flaming shells increased in intensity each day. While British artillery pounded the city, mounted forces commanded by Colonel Banastre Tarleton and Major Patrick Ferguson began to cut off the vital escape routes north of the city. In one particularly grim encounter, a force of Tory riflemen and saber wielding cavalry attacked a key American defense position and killed or wounded over 150 patriots within 15 minutes while losing only 3 men slightly wounded. Lincoln's last line of communication was severed and the British trap was ready to be sprung.

The completion of the British investment of Charleston in early May left Lincoln with only two remaining alternatives: reopen the roads to the north or surrender the city. The American general ordered a massive artillery barrage to cover a sortie by 200 picked light infantry to attempt to spike the enemy siege guns and open an evacuation route for the army. However, an assault force of 200 men attacking 14,000 besiegers was little short of ridiculous, and the patriot force was soon back in its own emplacements after accomplishing little more than the temporary elimination of two or three British guns. Lincoln now opened serious negotiations with General Clinton, but Sir Henry bluntly refused to consider the capitulation of the city in return for the free evacuation of the American army. Finally, the British commander conceded the immediate parole of all patriot militia units and on May 12, 1780 the Continental Army marched out of Charleston with its colors cased and piled thousands of muskets beside the Citadel. The siege operations had cost Clinton's army only 76 men killed and 138 wounded, and had resulted in the largest disaster to American arms in the entire War of Independence. Benjamin Lincoln surrendered 5500 men, 391 cannons, 6000 muskets and 7 frigates while losing 89 Continentals killed and 138 wounded, although the total loss among the militia was less than a dozen.

The American general's conduct of the siege of Charleston was one of the most inept episodes in the nation's military history. Lincoln organized only one small scale attack on the British lines during the entire siege and then failed to support the assault force. He insisted on attacking the enemy siege parallels with howitzers that sailed their shots harmlessly over the British lines when his substantial number of available mortars might have done real damage to the redcoat emplacements. He deferred to city and state officials when he should have been listening to the advice of his talented subordinates, who were urging him to evacuate the invaluable Continentals. Washington's sensible policy of avoiding battles with a superior British force when a convenient line of retreat was not available was simply ignored by his southern theatre commander. Now most of the effective American military power south of the Potomac was residing in British prison camps and the next few months would mark the nadir of the patriot cause.

While Lincoln's surrender of the Continental garrison allowed the redcoats to occupy a vital port, one last humiliating defeat awaited the Americans at the close of the Charleston campaign. Washington had belatedly dispatched a column of 400 Virginia regulars under Colonel Abraham Buford to reinforce the Charleston garrison. Buford's small army had just crossed into South Carolina when a messenger informed him of the disastrous surrender and he immediately ordered a countermarch to the north. The Virginia infantry were marching through the Waxhaws district near the Carolinas border when they were overtaken by about 300 mounted Tory light dragoons commanded by Banastre Tarleton. Buford halted his men in a field next to the road he was following, and gave orders to open fire on the horsemen when they had closed to within ten paces. Allowing a mounted opponent to get that close to infantry armed with single shot muskets was an invitation to disaster, as Tarleton's men charged right through the American line and began slashing the Virginians with their sabers while the patriots tried to reload their unwieldy weapons. Within less than 10 minutes the Continentals had been defeated and when the patriots began to raise their arms in surrender the Tory rangers simply kept hacking their enemies to pieces as Tarleton sat and watched. The American force was annihilated with over 100 men killed, most after they had surrendered, 200 badly wounded, and the rest of the force marched off into captivity. One of the youngest prisoners was 13-year-old Andrew Jackson, who was severely slashed on the arm and face by a British officer when he refused to clean his boots while claiming to be a legitimate prisoner of war. While Jackson's mother was ultimately able to secure his release because of his youth, Jackson swore a revenge that would be fulfilled on the ramparts of New Orleans 35 years later.

The surrender of Charleston stunned George Washington and the Continental Congress into taking immediate steps to prevent the collapse of the entire southern theatre. However, while Washington wanted to name Nathanael Greene as the new commander of a reorganized southern army, Congress overruled his suggestion and appointed Horatio Gates, who was living in semi-retirement on his Virginia plantation. Gates was delighted with news of his important assignment but his neighbor and friend Charles Lee warned him that the command would offer little chance for glory, as "your Northern laurels may turn to Southern willows." Apparently Gates ignored this warning until he arrived at the ramshackle American headquarters in Rugeley's Mills, North Carolina. Horatio Gates had assumed command of the northern theatre in the summer of 1777 with an established army of 7000 men and new detachments of Continentals and militia joining him almost daily. The Southern department that he inherited three years later provided only 900 underfed, under-equipped, unpaid Continentals who were surrounded by hostile Tories. Gates later admitted that "I command an army without strength, a military chest without money, a department apparently defunct in public spirit and a climate that increases despondency instead of animating the soldiers' arm." The new commander was a competent administrator who knew how to handle prickly militia units and he was eventually able to induce about 3000 Virginians and North Carolinians to join the army although this was still a far cry from the 20,000 men that he had deployed at the end of the Saratoga campaign.

Gates was intelligent enough to realize that he had to start rolling back the tide of British expansion and he chose the large British supply depot at Camden, South Carolina as his first objective. The enemy base was commanded by a garrison of 700 men under Lord Francis Rawdon and the post seemed vulnerable to an attack by several thousand patriots. Gates' talented and competent subordinates, including Baron de Kalb, William Smallwood and Otho Williams, urged him to march through the Catawba and Wateree valleys in order to stay close to a source of supplies while keeping between the British army and the main American magazine at Charlotte. However, a group of South Carolina partisans including Thomas Pickney and Francis Marion insisted that the most logical move would be a shorter march straight through the Carolina Sandhills to Camden. While the route offered a higher probability of arriving at the enemy base before British reinforcements could be dispatched, the march would be conducted through sparsely settled, Tory dominated territory that offered little opportunity to gather supplies.

Gates elected to follow the advice of the partisan rangers and his 4000 men embarked on a nightmarish expedition which featured a diet of green corn, green apples and gourmet concoctions of candle wax and hair powder. While dozens of Americans fell out along the march route with predictable bouts of gastric distress, the Tory families along the roads quickly dispatched messengers to warn the British command that Gates was heading for Camden. Lord Rawdon strengthened his fortifications, emplaced his available artillery and waited for reinforcements to even the odds in the expected battle.

Lord Charles Cornwallis had assumed direct command of the southern theatre after Henry Clinton took much of his expeditionary force back to New York City following the surrender of Charleston. Cornwallis' life had been shattered by the recent death of his wife and he welcomed the responsibility of a new theatre command to dull the pain of his bereavement. The new British commander was competent, energetic and determined to eventually replace Clinton as commander in chief in America. Cornwallis rapidly organized a relief force for a march to Camden and his column was able to arrive at the threatened post slightly ahead of the patriot army.

The British general surveyed the available defenses and decided to order a night march in order to intercept Gates before he could actually attack the city. A column of 817 regulars, 844 Tory volunteers and 382 Loyalist militia marched through the moonlit pine forests as the advance cavalry units rode out to locate the patriot army. At 2 A.M. on the already hot and steamy morning of August 15th, 1780 a force of green-jacketed Tory light dragoons collided with a scouting party of patriot cavalry. Gates' army was straggling behind the advance screen for a distance of several miles as hundreds of rebels were afflicted with extreme stomach distress. Their commanding general had provided a pre-battle dinner of the usual green corn and apples supplemented by a special dessert of molasses and half cooked cornmeal which "seemed to purge as well as if we had taken a jalep." At least 25% of Gates' effective strength had been rendered useless by an affliction that had nothing to do with British bullets or bayonets.

As the sun rose over the sandy pinelands about five miles from Camden, about 3000 reasonably functioning patriots gathered to do battle with Cornwallis. Gates had no real knowledge of British plans or intentions and commanded an army that was top heavy with militia as only 800 regulars were available for duty. While the enemy force consisted of only 2200 men, Cornwallis had deployed a well trained, veteran army and Gates' subordinates advised a retreat to a more defendable battlefield. Gates had been convinced that he was going to confront an army of only 700 men and the shock of his new intelligence seems to have drained the American commander of his earlier enthusiasm and energy. When the American militia commanders insisted that their men would abandon the army during a retreat, Gates reluctantly ordered deployment for battle about 500 yards from the rapidly organizing British lines.

The coming engagement between Cornwallis and Gates represented a microcosm of the problems plaguing a largely amateur rebel army in their confrontation with the most powerful military force in the western world. The American militia units had been issued with bayonets only the day before, and the only practice with these weapons focused on using the instruments to spit food on campfires. Gates fortified a strong right flank when he deployed his Maryland and Delaware Continentals in that direction, but his center and left were held entirely by untrained militia, while his cavalry was posted too far back to provide support in case of a British breakthrough.

Cornwallis deployed his slightly outnumbered army in a far more effective pattern which stiffened each militia unit with a supporting unit of regular infantry or cavalry. The initial attack would be undertaken by 1200 redcoat regulars backed up by the Volunteers of Ireland and the Royal North Carolina regiment. A strong reserve force consisting of a regiment of Highlanders, Tarleton's light dragoons and a battery of light artillery could be rushed to the front if the first assault wave pierced the American lines. Cornwallis was convinced that he commanded a much better trained army and could afford to risk an assault on the American defenses. His initial reasoning was quickly validated.

The battle of Camden opened with an artillery exchange between the two relatively small artillery corps of the opposing armies. When Otho Williams noticed that the British regulars were beginning to form up for an assault, the American colonel urged Gates to order several Virginia regiments to attack the enemy before they were fully organized. The American militiamen were less than enthusiastic about the idea of a frontal assault on the impressive line of redcoats and only a few dozen reluctant Virginians straggled forward. Suddenly, the high pitched cheers of the Welsh Fusiliers warned the patriots that they were too late to attack and a devastating redcoat volley shattered the few advancing Americans. When the British regulars moved toward the rebel lines, the American militia fired a few harmless shots and promptly disappeared into the inviting swampland adjoining the battlefield. Once the left flank simply evaporated, the panic stricken North Carolinians holding the center position realized they were about to be flanked and the men from the Old North State joined their compatriots in heading for the swamp. Only a trail of discarded muskets, knapsacks and canteens indicating that there ever had been an American left flank or center.

Thirty minutes after the opening shot of the battle Cornwallis had dispersed most of the American army and had isolated the Continentals from any cavalry support. The American regulars, under the overall command of Baron de Kalb, and led by Colonels Otho Williams and Mordecai Gist formed a tight defensive line while they waited for the inevitable British bayonet charge. When the Continentals noticed the collapse of the entire militia contingent, they realized that their only possible support would come from Smallwood's reserve force of Maryland regulars. Williams raced to the rear of the battlefield to spur Smallwood's men forward but the Maryland colonel had mysteriously disappeared from his unit. Williams quickly assumed command and tried to organize a rapid march to the front lines, until a large force of enemy regulars cut off the advance with a ferocious bayonet charge.

Lord Cornwallis had now isolated the two remaining American detachments and was determined to successfully eliminate the pair of Continental units. Williams formed the reserve brigade into a tightly compacted square which was able to beat off several British attacks, but had no hope of breaking through hundreds of redcoats to relieve de Kalb's command. De Kalb and Gist tried to organize a last ditch defense but when they opened ranks to welcome the arrival of a force of North Carolina militia, the "friendly" soldiers revealed themselves as Tories and smashed the Continentals with several well aimed volleys. De Kalb organized an energetic American bayonet counterattack which finally succeeded in pushing a hole in the Tory lines. However, at this critical moment, Cornwallis released his reserve regiment of Highlanders who struck the Continentals with Claymore swords, bayonets and muskets. De Kalb was shot or stabbed at least 11 times and only avoided immediate death when Cornwallis personally intervened to save him for a more lingering death.

The final stand of the Continentals against almost 2000 near victorious British attackers was very reminiscent of the last act of the drama at Long Island four years earlier. The Americans fought bravely but were heavily outnumbered and gradually succumbed to sheer weight of numbers. While the subordinate Continental officers were being killed or wounded, the American commander was already far from the battlefield. When the American center and flank collapsed, Gates mounted his horse and rode toward North Carolina. The commanding general was able to cover the 65 miles to Charlotte in only one day and arrived in Hillsboro, 180 miles further away, 3 days later.

Horatio Gates had been appointed by Congress to recapture Charleston and turn the tide against Britain in the southern theatre. Instead of re-entering the Palmetto State in triumph, the American general had managed to lose the only remaining American army in the South in less than one hour. The almost irreplaceable Maryland and Delaware brigades had been virtually annihilated, most of the militia units had permanently deserted the rebel cause and thousands of neutral citizens were seriously considering accommodating the return of royal authority. Gates' offensive against Camden had resulted in a staggering casualty list of 650 Continentals killed or wounded, 100 militia battlefield casualties, 300 men taken prisoner and 1000 rebels missing in action or deserted. Cornwallis had virtually eliminated an American army of over 3000 men at the small cost of 70 killed and 250 wounded. Two days after the battle, Tarleton's Tory light dragoons had surprised Thomas Sumter's 500 man detachment while the rebels were sleeping and swimming near Fishing Creek. Tarleton's green coated horsemen charged out of the woods and killed or captured 90% of the patriot army at a cost of only 16 men lost. Sumter escaped only because he had been knocked unconscious by a Tory saber and was overlooked in the confusion. The final act in the Camden tragedy emerged a few days after Fishing Creek, when a large column of new patriot recruits marched south to reinforce Gates and received word of the American defeat and the general's subsequent flight. The entire detachment conducted an immediate poll, and voted unanimously to desert the patriot cause and offer their services to the British army.

The initial phase of the British attempt to reconquer the southern provinces must be evaluated as an almost flawless campaign. The succession of victories from Savannah to Camden had inflicted over 9000 casualties on the patriot forces at a cost of only 200 killed and 500 wounded for His Majesty's forces. Georgia and South Carolina were reduced to almost total accommodation with the imperial government, while North Carolina and even Virginia seemed in imminent danger of conquest. Large numbers of neutral and pro-Congress citizens had signed requests for royal amnesty. In January of 1779 Colonel Archibald Campbell had informed Lord Germain of his hope of soon reporting the first British military victory in the summer campaign. The ambitious colonel exclaimed, "I need not inform your Lordship how much I prize the hope of being the first British officer to rend a stripe and a star from the flag of Congress." By the autumn of 1780 two of the original stars had fallen from the American constellation and several more seemed to be in imminent danger of joining them. Only the determination of a frontier colonel, a former British army wagon driver and a New England Quaker would ultimately stand in the way of the dissection of large segments of the increasingly fragile American Confederation.

# CHAPTER 12

# The Year of Patriot Crisis and Triumph

*King's Mountain to Yorktown*

*O*n a crisp October morning in 1780 Sir Henry Clinton sat at the desk in his New York City headquarters and penned an enthusiastic summary of the southern campaign to Lord North. He chronicled the capture of Savannah and Charleston, the rout of American armies at Waxhaws, Camden and Fishing Creek and the defection of numerous rebels to the King's cause insisting "there are few men in South Carolina who are not either our prisoners or in arms with us." Several hundred miles to the south, Lord Charles Cornwallis was planning a new offensive which was expected to consolidate recent British gains in Georgia and South Carolina and encourage new victories in North Carolina which would gather even more Loyalist support. Once the Old North State was secured for the crown, Cornwallis envisioned a march into Virginia to link up with British naval forces and threaten Washington's army from the southern flank.

Cornwallis' strategic plan had considerable merit and could have severely threatened the patriot cause if all elements had fallen into place, but it was based on the erroneous assumption that British conduct in the newly conquered territories would ultimately convince a majority of residents to side with the King. Cornwallis, Clinton, Lord North and Lord Germain all essentially agreed that a policy of conciliation and amnesty would encourage far more Loyalist sentiments among undecided southerners than a policy of terror and reprisal. These men believed that any American who wasn't actively engaged to fighting the King's troops should be considered a potential ally while any sort of massive retribution would simply push the local residents into the rebel camp. On the other hand, a number of prominent British officials totally opposed a policy of coaxing Americans back into loyalty through generosity on the part of the royal government. Thomas Hutchinson, exiled former governor of Massachusetts, William Tryon, former governor of North Carolina and New York, and Admiral George Rodney, commander of British naval forces in the West Indies, attempted to convince the King and his advisors that anyone who wasn't clearly committed to a Loyalist stand should be considered an enemy of the crown and dealt with accordingly. These men were allied with subordinate officers in the British army such as Banastre Tarleton and Patrick Ferguson who were convinced that a policy of terror, reprisals and general harshness towards unrepentant rebels was the only way to convince the Americans that it was in their best interests to support the Crown in the virtual civil war that had erupted in the southern provinces.

Although Cornwallis was far too humane to condone extensive violence against the residents of the South, he seemed powerless to rein in the combination of subordinate officers and Tory leaders who found retribution against rebels or even suspected patriots as a far more congenial pursuit than did their general. Large numbers of Loyalists who had been driven from their homes, humiliated by the tarring-and-featherings inflicted by their rebel neighbors and jailed or exiled for their staunch royal sympathies simply could not accept a policy of mild reconciliation. Thanks to the recent successes of the British army these men were now back in power and they were determined to seek revenge on their former tormentors. The result was a series of shootouts, lynchings, bushwhackings and midnight house burnings that would have done credit to the legends of Dodge City and Tombstone a century later. Loyalist leaders such as "Bloody Bill" Cunningham and patriot rangers such as "Swamp Fox" Marion engaged in a bloody war within a war that had few rules and plenty of opportunities for atrocities. Cunningham terrorized South Carolina with a succession of violent acts including bayoneting surrendered prisoners, hanging civilians who furnished rebels with supplies and burning the homes of anyone remotely in sympathy with the patriot cause.

The Loyalist reprisals were able to crush rebel outbreaks as long as major British forces were within supporting distance, but the long term effect on Cornwallis' strategy was far more negative. Cornwallis' regulars would pacify a particular region, begin to restore civil government, enlist new Loyalist regiments and then move on to the next targeted area. As the zones of pacification were extended, it became easier for rebel partisans to get behind the British army and disrupt Tory government with the aid of locals who were now suffering at the hands of the Loyalists. Once the redcoats were out of supporting range, relatively small Tory military units could be ambushed and destroyed and the citizens they had mistreated could be recruited for a regenerated patriot militia. Thus an entire pacified region might crumble back into rebellion as Cornwallis' army moved to reconquer more distant regions in North Carolina or Virginia.

The one area in the reconquered provinces that resisted rebel counterattacks was the region of South Carolina commanded by Major Patrick Ferguson. Ferguson was a truly fascinating British officer who had developed a fully functioning breech loading rifle that was almost a century ahead of its time, proved chivalrous to defeated adversaries and developed a genuine rapport with frontier settlers who were willing to acknowledge royal supremacy. This Scottish officer was so charismatic that he was able to recruit seven full regiments of Tory volunteers who were organized into a formidable army of 4000 men to maintain ministerial authority in western South Carolina.

Ferguson was so successful in South Carolina that Cornwallis assigned the major to move into North Carolina and sweep the area between Charlotte and the western frontier in order to crush rebel bands and recruit additional Loyalist units. For some unknown reason, Ferguson chose to leave three-fourths of his corps in South Carolina to continue their training while advancing north with 1100 picked men. While the major marched north, he dispatched a captured American militiamen over the Blue Ridge mountains to warn the "over the mountain" men to either submit to royal authority or face a campaign of house burnings and executions.

Colonel Isaac Shelly had been elected colonel of the militia units in the East Tennessee area and he had received numerous reports of the plundering and killings that had accompanied the Tory expeditions. Shelly became convinced that the most effective deterrent to Loyalist raids would be a preemptive attack on Ferguson's army before the enemy could cross the mountains and destroy their farms. The East Tennessee frontiersmen were self-reliant individuals who were deadly shots with their Pennsylvania long rifles and could hit enemy targets at over 300 yards. On the morning of September 26th, 1780, over 1000 grim faced patriot settlers gathered at Sycamore Shoals, Tennessee and prepared to march east to attack Ferguson. Shelly and three other leading citizens were elected colonels of the four regiments that were organized and the buckskin clad men mounted their horses and rode towards North Carolina.

When Patrick Ferguson realized that a substantial patriot army was moving towards him, he sent messengers to Charlotte to alert Cornwallis and request the dispatch of substantial reinforcements, as he warned his general that "the backwater men have crossed the mountains so you know what you have to depend upon." As the frontier army crossed into North Carolina they were joined by a reinforcement of 400 militia under Colonel Charles McDowell, and the combined force duly elected Colonel William Campbell as the general of their army. Campbell was convinced that Ferguson would rush back to Charlotte to join forces with Cornwallis unless the Tories could be cut off by a highly mobile force. He selected 700 men who had the fastest horses and moved to intercept Ferguson. Campbell's arrival at a settlement called Hannah's Compass produced another reinforcement of 400 men and the startling news that the enemy was in the process of fortifying nearby King's Mountain.

Ferguson felt that King's Mountain was a formidable defensive position that could be held relatively easily while he waited for Cornwallis to provide additional units. However, the Tory commander didn't know that his superior was extremely ill and incapable of issuing the necessary orders to reinforce the threatened Loyalists. The Tory position was slightly more than a mile below the North Carolina border on the crest of a 600 yard long ridge which was 60-120 yards wide with virtually no trees on top but very heavily wooded approaches and lower slopes. Ferguson sent out foraging parties to gather supplies while he deployed 800 militia and 100 King's American Rangers and Queen's Rangers along the crest. The Loyalists had been equipped with bayonets and trained to fight as British regulars in close ordered ranks. However, since this training only emphasized the ability to move forward or rearward on command, this defensive position was a terrible location for a European style battle. Ferguson had not bothered to erect breastworks or abatis as he expected massed volleys and bayonet charges to carry the day and insisted that "I defy God Almighty and all the rebels out of hell to overcome me."

The Scottish major mounted a white horse, slid a hunting shirt over his uniform and grasped a silver whistle which would give the battle signals for his men. Ferguson's adversaries had ridden all night in a driving rainstorm and the next morning, as they approached King's Mountain, the patriot horsemen intercepted a Tory messenger who informed his captors that his commanding officer would be wearing a hunting shirt, riding a white horse and carrying his sword in his left hand. By noon on October 7th Campbell's columns had arrived within a mile of the Loyalist camp without being detected and the regimental colonels gathered to plan the upcoming attack. While Ferguson had deployed his loyalists to counter a fairly conventional frontal assault, the rebels had no intention of obliging him with inviting targets. Campbell approved a plan in which the Americans would divide into four groups and encircle the mountain, after which a war whoop would signal an Indian style duck and cover advance.

The frontiersmen raced uphill as the wet leaves provided excellent soundproofing against lax Tory sentries. Suddenly, the buckskin clad attackers swarmed over the Loyalist pickets with the only distinction in dress being the contrast in paper insignia on patriot hats while the Loyalists displayed pine twigs in their headgear. As the frontiersmen closed in on the crest of the hill, Ferguson deployed his men in a three sided square and ordered a series of volleys that hit plenty of trees and boulders but had little impact on the mobile attackers. Campbell roared, "here they are boys shoot like hell and fight like devils." and the rebels used excellent cover and their deadly rifles to pick off large numbers of Tories within a few minutes. The Loyalist commander was shocked by the large gaps forming in his ranks, and he quickly countered with an order to fix bayonets and charge downhill in a tactic reminiscent of Joshua Chamberlain's later exploit at Little Round Top. However, unlike the Confederates of a later generation, these rebels were prepared for Ferguson's gambit and possessed more accurate, although slower loading weapons than their opponents. Large numbers of Tories were killed or wounded when they ran down the slope as the patriots used the excellent cover to decimate the Loyalists. Ferguson's men gradually pulled back to the open crest and fired a succession of volleys which sailed over the heads of their antagonists while Campbell's men dropped ever larger numbers of their exposed opponents. As one patriot participant noted, "the hill was more assailable by the rifle than defended by the bayonet."

Ferguson ordered at least five increasingly desperate downhill bayonet attacks but each one gradually receded, with fewer Loyalists able to reform at the top. As the Tory commander tried to rally his men on the crest, all four detachments of patriots made a final rush and Ferguson went down with at least seven bullet wounds and died within minutes. Groups of Tories now tried to throw down their weapons, but their attempts to surrender were often ignored the enraged rebels screamed, "Tarleton's Quarter" and "Remember Buford" and shot down dozens of potential captives. Finally, Campbell started knocking down patriot rifles as he screamed "for God's sake, quit. It is murder to shoot them anymore." While several more prisoners were later executed, the worst of the carnage on King's Mountain had ended.

The entire battle between American Tories and patriots had lasted less than an hour but in that sixty minutes the entire strategy for British reconquest of the South was doomed. Ferguson's entire command was annihilated as the Loyalists suffered 157 dead, 167 mortally wounded and 698 prisoners, compared to a much smaller rebel loss of 28 killed and 62 wounded. Just as the surprising American victory at Trenton had rekindled the dying embers of the Revolution in the northern states, the spectacular defeat of Ferguson convinced large numbers of southerners that British rule in their province was far from permanent and it would be far more practical to accommodate to the authority of Congress.

The American victory at King's Mountain provides an excellent example of the advantageous combination of innovative commanders, flexible tactics and superior firepower being utilized to annihilate an opponent that seemed better trained and more experienced in traditional battle tactics. The sixty minute engagement was clearly the beginning of the end of the British hopes to absorb the southern provinces back into the empire and would encourage a series of events that eventually led to the debacle at Yorktown. Sir Henry Clinton wrote a realistic appraisal of the action when he insisted that "this battle had so encouraged the spirit of rebellion—the first link in a chain of evils that followed each other in regular succession until they at last ended in the total loss of America."

While Campbell's army was riding towards King's Mountain, the Continental Congress debated a strategy to force the British evacuation of the southern states. On October 5th, 1780, Congress passed a resolution to replace Horatio Gates with a general of Washington's own choosing. The American commander selected his original choice for the position, Nathanael Greene of Rhode Island. Greene arrived in Hillsboro to inspect 949 disgruntled, hungry, unpaid Continentals who formed virtually the entire strength of the Grand Continental Army of the South. The new southern department commander realized that this army would not seriously threaten Cornwallis unless it could be reinforced, retrained and refitted. Greene took a daring gamble and divided his small army into two wings and sent the separate detachments in separate directions in order to increase the odds of locating provisions. The new commander was convinced that this risky move would allow the Americans to hang onto Cornwallis flanks while they harassed British scouting parties and threatened the enemy line of communication. Greene would base one wing of the army at a camp in Cheraw Hill while Daniel Morgan would be assigned to march the other wing westward.

Greene's division of his small army was a calculated risk that offered reasonable prospects of deflecting any move that Cornwallis might initiate. If the British general struck Greene's detachment at Cheraw, Morgan's column could attack Augusta or Ninety-Six and threaten the British rear; if the redcoats marched against Morgan, Greene could threaten Charleston and the coastal supply line of the British army; if Cornwallis moved to reoccupy Charlotte, Morgan and Greene could each strike from a different flank; if the British remained in South Carolina, Greene could rest and reinforce his army and confront the enemy under more advantageous conditions the next spring.

Greene marched to Cheraw Hill with 650 Continentals and 450 newly arrived Maryland and Virginia militia while Morgan was assigned to command 320 Continentals, 200 Virginia militia and 80 light dragoons. Greene's subordinate was ordered to march to the west side of the Catawba River and set up a base which would serve as a rallying point for additional western volunteers while the detachment "annoyed the enemy in that quarter, collecting provisions and aiding the main army if it was attacked." Greene's strategy began to pay dividends on December 27, 1780 when a contingent of Morgan's light dragoons and mounted militia commanded by Colonel William Washington surprised an advance party of Tory raiders at a crossroads town called Hammond's Store and virtually annihilated the entire force of 250 men with almost no American casualties.

Cornwallis was stunned and furious when he was informed of the debacle to his advance corps and the British general began to suspect that Greene commanded a much larger force than his scouts had reported. Cornwallis decided to counter Greene's ploy with his own gamble which resulted in a division of the British army into three separate wings, each ordered to launch an attack against the enemy camps. A mobile column under Lord Rawdon would hold back Greene's wing if he ventured too far from Cheraw Hill, while a mixed force led by Tarleton would strike at

Morgan's camp with the main army under Cornwallis moving up to deal with Morgan and Greene in succession. The timely arrival of 2500 reinforcements from New York City provided Cornwallis with a substantial numerical advantage over either wing of the American army and the British general was convinced that he could destroy the last major organized resistance to British rule in the South.

The critical southern campaign of 1781 opened on January 6th when Banastre Tarleton moved north with 300 light dragoons, 250 light infantry, 200 Highlanders, a battery of 3 pounders and several regiments of Loyalist volunteers. The short, stocky redheaded Tarleton cut an imposing figure with his horsehair crested helmet and green cavalry coat, but he was seen as little more than a cold handed butcher among patriot residents of the south. After a number of incredibly easy one-sided victories, the glamorous commander of Tarleton's legion was becoming somewhat overconfident of his abilities and probably viewed Morgan's militia-dominated army as just one more inviting target for his ruthless and well trained regiments.

Daniel Morgan would soon emerge as a formidable opponent to Tarleton and his rapacious legionaries. Morgan had served in the French and Indian War as a wagon driver for the British army but his hair-trigger temper had almost resulted in his death. A disagreement with a British officer resulted in an altercation where the redcoat was struck and Morgan was sentenced to 500 lashes which was a virtually death sentence for many victims. The former wagon driver survived to become a prosperous Virginia planter and by the beginning of the revolution commanded an elite company of riflemen which was eventually expanded into a corps and played a vital role in the defeat of Burgoyne at Saratoga. By the autumn of 1780 Morgan was a newly commissioned general who now faced one of the most ruthless and talented officers in the British army.

On January 13th, 1781 Nathanael Greene warned Daniel Morgan that "Tarleton is on his way to pay you a visit. I doubt not but he will have a decent reception and a proper dismissal." Morgan quickly acted on Greene's intelligence and began a general withdrawal that would continue until he could locate a potential battlefield that offered an advantage to his militia-dominated army. By 6 A.M. on January 16th the British army had moved to within six miles of Morgan's detachment and Tarleton was convinced that he could smash the Americans as they attempted to cross the major barrier to a successful retreat—the Broad River. The American brigadier was tempted to attempt to outrun Tarleton's Legion but he suspected that his men would either be attacked at mid-crossing or desert soon after they reached the far side of the river, so he accepted a monumental risk and chose to turn and meet the oncoming redcoats.

Morgan deployed his small army of 1000 men with an eye toward the probability that Tarleton would attempt some form of massive cavalry attack in order to panic the American militia and then cut them to pieces. The Virginian found a three tiered defense position designed to hide his cavalry units while allowing mutually supporting lines for the infantry. The first line of defense would be a picked force of 150 riflemen who would stay under cover until the enemy moved to within 50 yards and then pop up from cover and fire two volleys before they fell back. A second line formed around Andrew Pickens' 300 militia would be placed 150 yards behind the riflemen. These inexperienced volunteers would be asked to get off two volleys at 50 paces and then withdraw to reform at the rear as an emergency reserve. The main battle line would be placed a further 150 yards back just below the crest of a ridge of sandy hills where cattle wandered in open fields called the Cowpens. The Maryland and Delaware Continentals would anchor the line at the center as they protected the main road back to the river, Tate's Virginia militia would hold the right flank, while Triplett's regiment of Virginians supported by a company of Georgians would defend the left side of the main line, with the entire formation under the command of Colonel John Howard. Morgan's ace in the hole was a force of 125 light dragoons and mounted militia under Colonel William Washington who were concealed from British observation on the far side of the hills and were ordered to stay hidden until the critical moment of the battle. The American commander insisted, "the whole idea is to lead Benny (Tarleton) into a trap so we can beat his cavalry and infantry as they come up those slopes. When they've been cut down to size by our fire, we'll attack them."

During the frigid night of January 16-17, Morgan went from campfire to campfire to tell every soldier his personal part in the battle and emphasize that the men who fought in the upcoming engagement would be long remembered by their countrymen. In a scene reminiscent of King Henry V on the eve of the St. Crispin's Day battle with the French at Agincourt, the Virginia planter exhorted his men to play their glorious role in what might become an equally improbable victory against a superior foe. "Two fires and you are free! And then when you return to your homes, how the old folks will bless you and the girls kiss you for your gallant conduct."

Banastre Tarleton arrived at the Cowpens shortly before daybreak on January 17th and was surprised to see the rebels drawn up for battle rather than running for the Brood River. He deployed a cavalry unit in the front to make an initial mounted assault while his British regulars, Loyalist regiment and artillery units were formed into a solid attack line. The varied units presented a colorful yet terrifying sight to the waiting patriots as one observer noted "a brilliant army of scarlet, green, blue and white with glittering rows of bayonets and drums rolling with regimental colors rippling in the wind" was marching inexorably toward their target.

The first engagement of the day occurred when a company of British cavalry lined up and charged the barely noticeable American marksmen. A patriot volley quickly dropped one third of the mounted attackers and Tarleton signaled his main assault force to support the mounted unit. The British line of almost 1000 bayonet-wielding men had closed the range on the American riflemen when an alarming number of officers began to fall from the ranks. Morgan had ordered his sharpshooters to aim for enemy leaders and their deadly fire initially disrupted Tarleton's attack plan. While the surviving officers were attempting to reform their units, the American riflemen pulled back toward the ridge and opened a field of fire for Pickens' militia. At this point Morgan's gamble began to pay off. He had purposely selected a battle site that had no swamps or woods nearby so that the raw militia units would have no inviting refuge if they panicked at the sight of British bayonets. Pickens' men knew their exact assignment and carefully squeezed off two fairly accurate volleys and then filed off behind the riflemen. The American militia tore gaping holes in Tarleton's assault line and then promptly marched off the field before the redcoats could retaliate. Tarleton's only compensation for the loss of dozens of men and 40% of his front rank officers was that he became convinced that the Americans were retreating in panic and that one more push to the crest of the ridge would produce a rout that would match the triumph at Camden.

At 7:15 A.M., twenty minutes after the opening shot of the battle, Tarleton issued orders for a massed bayonet attack on the final American position on the crest of the ridge. Howard's Continentals knelt along the ridge and blasted the oncoming rows of red and green coated attackers. However, while the Americans were kept occupied by the assault, Tarleton sent his elite reserve unit of Scottish Highlanders around the British left flank in order to hit the rebels from the side. The exuberant Scotsmen charged up the side of the hill, slashed through the covering screen of militia with their claymores and bayonets and threatened to roll up the exposed Continental flank. This was the crisis moment of the battle and Tarleton, despite incurring heavy casualties, was sure that he was about to smash Morgan's army to pieces. However, a succession of rapidly occurring events turned the expected British triumph into one of the most one sided American victories of the war.

John Howard saw that the Highlanders were threatening the Continental position and he immediately ordered his men to retreat and form into a new firing line. Just as Major McArthur's Scots became disorganized as they chased the "defeated" patriots, Howard's men halted their withdrawal, faced about and fired a point blank volley that decimated the 71st Highland regiment, and many of the survivors were cut down during a subsequent American bayonet charge. As the Maryland and Delaware Continentals pushed the enemy back down the ridge, Colonel Washington rode up to Howard and Morgan as they were discussing their next option. The American cavalry commander insisted "they're coming on more like a mob. Give them one more fire and then I'll charge them." Morgan immediately agreed to the plan and ordered Howard's men to charge down the hill at the disorganized Highlanders while the American cavalry emerged from behind the ridge and smashed the enemy flanks.

Within a few minutes, Tarleton's most elite unit had been virtually annihilated while his main attack force was still trying to regain its cohesion after losing so many key officers. When the redcoats and Tories saw that the Scots had been defeated, they began their own retrograde movement just as the reorganized men of the militia and the rifle companies re-entered the battle and blasted the British flanks. A substantial force of patriot cavalry cut off the main line of retreat back to the British camp and soon the panicked and demoralized English and Loyalists began surrendering in droves as they were now hemmed in by Continentals, riflemen, militia and light dragoons.

Banastre Tarleton was a bold officer, but he apparently had no intention of surrendering to what he considered a rabble in arms. The British colonel raced from the battlefield with a company of escorts and was soon engaged in a running battle with Washington and his hard charging American horsemen. A dramatic duel worthy of most film epics ensued as the opposing commanders slashed at each other with their sabers. Just as Tarleton was on the verge of being cut off by Washington and several Americans, he pulled out his pistols and shot the patriot commander's horse while riding through the closing ring of steel. Banastre Tarleton would live to fight another day, but his rapacious army of redcoats, Tories and Scotsmen had been eliminated from the chessboard of the American Revolution.

Daniel Morgan's relatively small force of Continentals and militia had inflicted a devastating defeat on the British southern army. In just about one hour Lord Cornwallis had lost the entire left flank of his advancing force and the earlier victory at King's Mountain had been provided with a worthy sequel to bolster the American hope of ultimate victory. Morgan had directed an enormously impressive battle in which he had lost only 12 killed and 60 wounded and had deployed his army in perfect relation to its makeup and resources. Tarleton's overconfidence had enabled the Americans to annihilate his army as the British casualty list came to 100 men killed, 229 wounded and 829 captured.

Charles Cornwallis spent the morning of January 17th camped about 25 miles from the battlefield waiting for Tarleton's signal to move in and destroy Morgan's surviving units as they retreat north. When the British commander was informed of the disaster at Cowpens, he was torn between a desire to immediately march on Greene's relatively small detachment or pull back south to deflect a possible American attack on the major supply depot at Ninety-Six. Cornwallis finally decided to gamble that he could smash Greene before his own bases were endangered. He ordered the destruction of all heavy equipment in the British camp, burned most of the wagons, all of the tents and any food the men could not carry and ordered a forced march northward through the snow and rain of a particularly harsh Carolina winter.

When Nathanael Greene received almost simultaneous reports of Morgan's victory and Cornwallis' response, he personally rode over 125 miles to confer with his chief subordinate while he barely avoided capture by Tory light dragoons during the journey. Greene urged Morgan to link up with the main army and then begin a staged withdrawal towards Virginia while enticing Cornwallis further and further away from his base. The next few weeks produced an exciting drama as Greene virtually dared Cornwallis to catch him as the patriot army stayed just ahead of their British pursuers while avoiding a decisive battle. The American army crossed the Catawba, the Yodkin, the Deept and the Dan Rivers while Cornwallis' cold and hungry redcoats would frequently catch glimpses of the rebel rear guard leaving a town just as their own advance force entered the settlement.

Greene abruptly halted his retrograde movement when he crossed the Dan River and established a formidable camp in southern Virginia while deploying his cavalry units to harass the British flanks and discourage recruitment of Tories. The most impressive dividend from the strategy occurred on February 25th when Colonel Lighthorse Harry Lee spotted a large force of mounted Loyalists riding to join the main British army. Lee rode forward with a party of dragoons who wore the same green coats as Tarleton's Legion and the Tory leader, Colonel John Pyle, mistakenly believed that he had encountered an escort dispatched to guide him to Cornwallis' camp. While Pyle dutifully lined his men up to be inspected by the "Tory" cavalry commander, Lee's men quietly got behind their adversaries and suddenly pulled out their sabers and pistols. Within five minutes the startled Loyalists had lost 100 dead, 302 wounded and dozens captured with no loss to Lee's cavalry. News of this daring maneuver virtually dried up the flow of Loyalist recruits for Cornwallis' increasingly disgruntled army, and the British commander was forced to admit, "I am amongst timid friends and adjoining to inveterate rebels."

Greene utilized his secure base in Virginia to resupply his army and process new units of militia and Continentals. General von Steuben sent 400 picked men from his Virginia regulars, 1700 new Virginia volunteers streamed into camp, and almost 1100 additional North Carolinians joined the rebel cause. By the end of February, Greene commanded a fairly impressive army of 4400 men, although only slightly more than 10% of these volunteers could be categorized as fully trained regulars. Cornwallis had dispersed scouting parties and garrisons throughout North Carolina so that his main army was reduced to less than 2000 men, although virtually all of them were first line troops. When Greene and Morgan discussed the possibility of confronting the redcoats with a largely untrained army, Morgan insisted, "when the volunteers fight, you beat Cornwallis, if not he will beat you."

Morgan advised Greene to select a battle site that would force Cornwallis to attack him and then deploy his army in a formation similar to the one that proved so successful at Cowpens. Greene selected Guilford Court House, North Carolina as the most advantageous location for a major confrontation and promptly deployed his army in three successive defense lines. However, while Greene was perfectly willing to try to duplicate Morgan's success against Tarleton, the region around Guilford was quite different from the Cowpens area. A dense forest dominated the whole area so that control of each firing line would be more difficult and the possibility of mutual fire support was greatly diminished. The first line of defense was composed of the North Carolina militia who were considered the weakest element of Greene's army. These men were deployed behind a rail fence next to a wooded area that contained a concealed force of American cavalry under Colonel William Washington and Lighthorse Harry Lee. The second line was 300 yards further back and defended by the somewhat better trained Virginia militia supported by a rifle corps which was under orders to pick off either advancing redcoats or retreating militia who were inciting a panic. Almost six hundred yards behind this second line was a curving line of Continentals commanded by Isaac Huger and centered on the hill that contained the local court house.

The morning of March 15, 1781 dawned bright and cold with freezing temperatures and some snow covering the ground. Cornwallis' advanced scouts had reported that Greene had recrossed the Dan River back into North Carolina and seemed determined to force an engagement on the British army. The British general was delighted that the Americans seemed eager to expose themselves to a bayonet assault by his 1900 hardened regulars, and he ordered an approach to Guilford with a massive employment of drums, fifes and bagpipes in order to overawe the many American novice warriors. Greene and Morgan went among the patriot defenders and assured them that they held strong positions and outnumbered their adversaries; if all went well, they should repeat the Cowpens triumph.

Cornwallis' redcoat regiments spent most of the morning assembling their attack formations and then promptly halted to enjoy their noon meals. Finally at about 1:30 P.M. the crimson line began to march toward the North Carolinians who were leveling their muskets on the long rail fence. As the redcoats closed to within fifty yards, the Old North State militia blasted two volleys that cracked through the frigid air and large gaps began to appear in the scarlet ranks. The patriots fled toward the woods a few steps ahead of the enraged regulars who largely ignored an assault against the second line to chase their tormentors into the snow covered forest. However, when the British soldiers charged through the woods to skewer their adversaries, the mounted squadrons under Washington and Lee came galloping out of their concealed position and opened fire with pistols and carbines which created chaos in the redcoat ranks. Only the long conditioned discipline of the regulars combined with the herculean efforts of their officers enabled Cornwallis' men to reorganize on the open plain and continue their advance on the American defensive lines.

The British assault line gradually regained its momentum and closed in on the Virginia militia who fired their prescribed two volleys and then retreated behind the court house hill. Now Isaac Huger gave the order for his Continentals to take aim on the oncoming redcoats and the crest of the hill exploded with the massed volleys of the Delaware and Maryland regiments. The disciplined Continental volleys tore through the redcoat lines and the Americans followed their fire with a spirited bayonet charge which sent the shaken redcoats fleeing for their own start line.

Nathanael Greene now faced the most difficult decision of his military career. The entire main assault force of the British army was in disarray after being decimated by three successive lines of American defenders, and a patriot counterattack could possibly smash Cornwallis' army and capture the commanding general. However, while the British commander had engaged every unit in his command, Greene was convinced that Cornwallis was concealing a large body of reserves that would fall on the charging Americans and smash their flanks. The Rhode Island Quaker was aware that his small army was the last organized patriot force south of the Chesapeake and the loss of this force would insure British sovereignty in most of the region. Thus Greene reluctantly recalled his charging regulars and Cornwallis was given the opportunity to reform his depleted units for one last assault.

Cornwallis was determined to sweep the rebels from a field now littered with redcoat casualties and the British general was not squeamish about incurring even more losses among his stoic regulars. The scarlet line advanced back across the blood-drenched field toward the only remaining American position, the crest of Court House Hill. When the redcoats and Continentals were engaged in a wild melee with bayonets, rifle butts and even fists, Cornwallis ordered his remaining guns to fire grapeshot into the swirling mass of combatants. The general's subordinates begged him to reconsider such deliberate killing of his own men but Cornwallis ignored their pleas and deadly missiles tore through rebels and redcoats like. As volley after volley of deadly iron balls ripped through the contending armies, the less experienced Americans virtually acknowledged the desperation of the British and pulled back to a final fall back position, abandoning the field to their adversaries.

The two British wing commanders, Generals Webster and O'Hara, now led their badly battered units in a desperate assault on the last ditch American strong point, but the blue coated patriots smashed the faltering attackers and even chased them back toward Cornwallis and his orderlies. Greene carefully studied the reforming redcoat lines and was again convinced that his opponent was laying a clever trap for any further American assault. The majority of militiamen had either left the field or were too disorganized to launch a counterattack, while the remaining Continentals were still outnumbered by Cornwallis' redcoats. The American general decided that he had accomplished his purpose of damaging the enemy army and delaying an invasion of Virginia, so the patriot units were ordered to abandon the field and march north toward the Dan.

The British army now held the Guilford Court House battlefield and Lord Cornwallis wrote exuberant messages of triumph to his superiors in New York and London. However, a more dispassionate observer would have been dubious of the claim of British victory. The British loss of 143 killed, 389 wounded and over 100 missing represented almost one third of Cornwallis' army and crippled his ability to continue a northward offensive. The American army loss of 78 killed and 183 wounded constituted about one twentieth of the effective strength of Greene's army and left a potent force to reconquer the Deep South. Elite British units such as the Guards and the Welsh Fusiliers had been virtually eliminated as effective units and would be of little use in subsequent operations. Cornwallis was soon forced to evacuate his "victorious" battlefield and retreat 200 miles to the British enclave at Wilmington.

The series of battles and skirmishes between Campbell's assault on King's Mountain and Cornwallis' retreat to Wilmington totally reversed the tide of British success that had peaked at Camden. From November 1780 to March 1781, the British army had lost over 3300 irreplaceable men while inflicting only 260 casualties on the rebel armies. This was an attrition rate that simply could not be maintained for any extended period of time, as it was becoming increasingly obvious that ministerial support for the war was rapidly weakening. The only advantage that Cornwallis had realized from this unfortunate turn of events was that Greene's aggressive maneuvers to recover the south had left the back door to Virginia open and the British theatre commander was determined to use this opening to eventually link up with General Philips on the Chesapeake and threaten the main rebel army under Washington from its southern flank.

While the American victories at King's Mountain and Cowpens reversed the tide of British successes in the South, influential members of the allied French government were increasingly certain that it was time to negotiate a peace with Great Britain that ceded less than total independence to the rebel provinces. The Comte de Vergennes, the French foreign minister, planned to approach neutral nations such as Austria and Russia to mediate a peace settlement based on the status quo in North America as it existed in January, 1781. Since the British still held most of Georgia, the Carolinas, New York City, Long Island, Maine and the Great Lakes region, Vergennes' plan would result in the recognition of a United States that was limited to 9 or 10 states and hemmed in on every side by British territory. When George III's ministers were informed of the French peace overtures, they welcomed the proposals as a realistic basis for a peace treaty.

Rumors of the Anglo-French communications reached Washington's headquarters outside of New York City in the spring of 1781, and the American commander realized that the best he could hope for from his French allies was assistance in planning one final campaign before a probable general truce froze the contending armies in their positions. Washington admitted that most Americans were sick of the interminable war as "instead of having the prospect of a glorious offensive campaign before us, we have a bewildered and gloomy defensive one, unless we receive a powerful aid of ships, land troops and money from our generous ally." On May 22, 1781 Washington held a conference with the Comte de

Rochambeau in Wethersfield, Connecticut and the French commander strongly hinted that this would be the last campaign in which the Americans could expect help from Paris. However the Gallic general also casually mentioned that a large French fleet under Admiral de Grasse would be available for cooperation with the allied land forces for a brief time during September and early October before it was recalled to more important duties in the Caribbean. Washington immediately proposed a joint assault on British held New York City but the French general was convinced that Henry Clinton had made that target virtually invulnerable, and he suggested consideration of an alternative campaign that would be less risky and more rewarding.

The alternative objective began to emerge during the late summer when General Lafayette, commanding a small army screening Cornwallis' movements in Virginia, reported that the British general appeared to be building a naval installation at Yorktown. Cornwallis had combined a number of British detachments with a reinforcement from Clinton to form an army of over 7000 men and Washington realized that any significant defeat of this army could produce political shock waves in Britain even more dramatic than those after Saratoga.

Washington provided Clinton with a number of clues that he was planning a joint attack on New York City and then promptly disappeared on a 450 mile march toward Virginia before the British commander realized he had been duped. At about the same time, Sir Samuel Graves arrived off the Virginia capes with orders to resupply Cornwallis' army and destroy a small French squadron thought to be operating in the area. Graves was startled by the appearance of a massive French fleet that included 27 ships of the line to his own 22. During the ensuing "Battle of the Capes," de Grasse's superior fleet sank only one British ship, but it suffered no losses and effectively blocked Graves from reinforcing or resupplying the Yorktown garrison when the frustrated British admiral called a halt to the battle and sailed back to New York to make repairs.

Sir Henry Clinton finally realized that the enemy army was no longer facing his garrison and he immediately began to assemble a 7000 man relief force while he waited for Graves' fleet to arrive and refit. Meanwhile Cornwallis deployed his own 7000 men in a six mile line of breastworks extending from Wormley Creek to the York River. Cornwallis was supported by two large 44 gun frigates, three armed transports and about 1000 armed sailors and Marines, but he faced an allied army that had now been reinforced by de Grasse to a total of 11,000 Americans and 8800 Frenchmen with additional forces on their way.

On the morning of September 17th, 1781, Washington and Rochambeau were rowed out to de Grasse's flagship, the *Ville de Paris* which at 110 guns was the largest warship in the world. During the cordial meeting, de Grasse agreed to extend his stay for a reasonable period to aid in performing siege operations and consented to land additional marines and siege artillery to further tip the balance against to British defenders. When the now increasingly confident allies began to deploy their advance units around Yorktown, Cornwallis stunned Washington by abandoning his extremely formidable outer works in order to shorten his lines while he waited for reinforcements from New York. This startling move eliminated the need for almost two weeks of preliminary digging of siege lines for the allies and Rochambeau assured his American counterpart that the defeat of Cornwallis was now reducible to the calculations surrounding each successive line of parallels and the proper utilization of the appropriate types of siege artillery.

The first allied siege works were begun on October 6th and within three days the engineers had pushed to within 600 yards of the lower end of Yorktown. Heavy siege guns were dragged into position and Washington ceremoniously fired the first round in the formal siege. Within a few hours 52 heavy siege guns were battering British emplacements and damaging the naval support vessels. Cornwallis informed Clinton that reinforcements were desperately needed as "we have lost about seventy of our men and many of our works are considerably damaged; with such works on disadvantageous ground, against so powerful an attack one cannot hope to make a very long resistance. We continue to lose men very fast." Clinton was increasingly aware of the peril of the Yorktown garrison but a need for repairs to British transport ships and the general laxity of dock workers in New York harbor delayed the sailing date for the relief force by almost two critical weeks.

While Clinton paced in his New York headquarters reading the increasingly alarming dispatches from his southern theatre commander, the allied army had completed the second siege line only 300 yards from the British works. The only impediments to an even closer investment of the town were two British redoubts that could sweep a third siege parallel with deadly artillery fire. Washington ordered separate French and American detachments to capture redoubts number 9 and 10 in a daring night assault. A brief but bloody attack cost 10 American and 50 French lives but both strong points were seized and the British defense was at a critical point. On October 14th, Cornwallis ordered a desperate counterattack using 350 picked light infantry who captured parts of the new siege line, spiked a few guns and promptly fell back when the expected support units failed to arrive. The British commander was left with only one more card to play and on the next evening he prepared to ferry his men across to the Gloucester side of the river and strike an alleged weak spot in the siege lines manned only by American militia. Cornwallis hoped to smash through the allied cordon and then rapidly march toward New York by abandoning all excess baggage. Unfortunately for the British cause, the night of the planned assault a violent storm flooded the area and damaged much of the available transport equipment, effectively stranding most of the garrison on the wrong side of the river. Cornwallis was now reduced to an effective force of less than 6000 men with the probability that the final allied siege line would smash his army before Clinton could arrive with reinforcements. When his last substantial artillery units were destroyed in the latest allied barrage, the British commander realized that it was time to negotiate.

On October 18th, 1781, a British drummer boy climbed on a damaged parapet and began to beat the signal for a parley. A blindfolded officer was led to Washington's headquarters with a request for a twenty-four hour truce to conduct negotiations for surrender. The American commander allowed a two hour respite and offered his British counterpart reasonably generous terms which Cornwallis promptly accepted. The next morning, while Cornwallis displayed incredible bad form by pleading illness and staying in his headquarters, General Charles O'Hara rode out at the head of the British army to surrender to the allied army. O'Hara promptly rode toward General Rochambeau, hoping to capitulate to a fellow professional European officer, but the Frenchman politely directed his adversary to Washington as the commander of allied forces. Washington, ever on the lookout for slights from British officers, then directed the British subordinate to his own second in command, Benjamin Lincoln, who accepted O'Hara's sword and then quickly returned it. While the British bands played a variety of tunes which may or may not have included "The World Turned Upside Down," 8061 soldiers and sailors, 244 pieces of artillery, 24 regimental standards and seven generals were stricken from the rolls of His Majesty's military command. The disgusted redcoats smashed in drums, stomped on their cartridge boxes, broke their muskets on the ground and tried to avoid the gaze of their American captors, turning instead to face the more acceptable view of French professionals. While Englishmen from commanding generals to the lowliest privates could try to gain solace from the myth that they had only been beaten by a superior force of equally well disciplined Frenchmen, the harsh reality was that at a cost of 23 killed and 65 wounded, George Washington had eliminated one of the two major British armies in North America from the war and had presented His Majesty's loyal opposition in London with the ammunition needed to finally convince George III and his ministers that even if the world had not entirely turned upside down, the future of the British empire would be determined in places other than the 13 rebellious colonies.

# CHAPTER 13

# Why Did the World Turn Upside Down?

## The Strategy and Tactics of American Victory and British Defeat

While the defeat at Yorktown did not immediately force the British government to recognize the independence of their colonies, Cornwallis' surrender set in motion a chain of events that eventually produced a Treaty of Paris which proved enormously advantageous to the new American republic. Almost as soon as this treaty formalized the new place for the United States in the world community, citizens of the nation sat in taverns, parlors and drawing rooms and debated how the rebel provinces had been able to secure their freedom from the most powerful empire in their contemporary world. This discussion has continued for over two centuries and has revolved around both the actual military engagements that ultimately resulted in patriot success and the abilities and weaknesses of the leaders who directed the opposing armies during the contest.

The actual American military success during the War of Independence presents a complex and multi-dimensional series of issues. Historians and military analysts have credited the patriot victory variously to innovative American battle tactics, incompetent British leaders, the alliance with France and numerous other factors. For example John Ferling's excellent collection of essays in *The World Turned Upside Down* includes contributions on the role of logistics, the impact of politics, the influence of the frontier and the consequences of naval warfare on the outcome of the war. Although there is probably no single cause for American victory or British defeat, an intensive review and analysis of all of the major campaigns and battles of the conflict reveals that the patriots developed just enough advantages over their adversaries to produce a paper thin margin of victory which could have swung in the opposite direction even in the last stages of the war.

The most popular and enduring myth of the War of Independence has been the assumption that innovative and highly mobile patriot forces were able to devastate a much more conventional and static professional army of redcoats. Much of this myth is indeed based on reality. The Americans frequently did use thin skirmish lines, highly mobile forces, night marches, winter campaigns and hit and run tactics to engage in fighting methods alien to the conventional practice of 18th century European armies. The patriot ability to rapidly erect fortifications on Breed's Hill and Dorchester Heights was critical to the eventual British evacuation of Boston; Washington's willingness to gamble on an enormously risky night crossing of an ice clogged Delaware River was vital to the triumph at Trenton; and the mobile operations of Daniel Morgan's riflemen opposing the British advance at Saratoga were crucial in forcing Burgoyne's surrender. However, the British forces were never completely tied to European tactics and redcoat generals employed rifle companies, mounted rangers, night attacks with bayonets and winter raids at various points during the war. However, the more innovative British tactics never seemed to produce quite so decisive results as the more publicized rebel actions. General "No Flints" Grey's midnight attack on Anthony Wayne's sleeping troops at Paoli Tavern was a brilliant stroke that just missed annihilating an American corps, William Howe's daring winter march from Philadelphia to Whitemarsh over snow covered roads almost caught Washington's army by surprise and Charles Cornwallis' gamble of destroying all of his baggage in order to trap Nathanael Greene's army fell just short of its planned objective. Unfortunately for the British cause, none of these innovative British actions produced the sort of victory that would crush the rebel cause while American deceptions, night attacks and perilous river crossings often seemed to produce major psychological rewards for the patriots.

While the authors agree that these innovative tactics and actions were vital to the ultimate American victory, much of the success of these operations revolves around the complex yet effective makeup of the patriot armies who fought the war. George Washington's voluminous correspondence during the war reveals his virtual obsession with developing and commanding an army of long term professionals who would differ from their British adversaries in little but the color of their uniforms. The American commander always seemed to hope that he could match the enemy redcoats with equally disciplined bluecoats of his own and ultimately defeat the British army in a titanic battle of musket volleys fought out on an open plain. However, for better or worse there simply never were nearly enough Continentals to match the available number of redcoat regiments and thus produce a "conventional" victory before the massive French intervention which produced the triumph at Yorktown. The reality of American operations during the War of Independence is that the patriot forces when at optimum strength for battle actually constituted a three tiered organization that could not fully function with one element absent.

Just as American defense policy in the nuclear age called for a triad of land based missiles, manned bombers and missile equipped nuclear submarines, the patriot forces during the Revolution were dependent on a triad of Continental regulars, short term militia regiments and specialized units of riflemen and rangers and related auxiliaries. The effective employment of this diversified military force seems to constitute a potential key to the American ability to defeat the much more professional British army.

The clear cut organization of choice in Washington's estimation was the small nucleus of Continental regiments who somehow survived eight years of privation and official indifference to constitute an amazingly resilient organization that even evoked the reluctant admiration of their British adversaries. While the American regulars were generally able to escape the draconian punishments and the sense of being treated little better than dogs that redcoats were forced to endure, the Continental line was subjected to a regimen of privation, starvation and nakedness that was shocking even by British standards. The combination of no pay, no food and no equipment guaranteed that the Congressional authorization to raise a regular army of 74,000 men enrolled in 88 regiments would become a grim running joke around American military campfires. Europeans had emigrated to the New World to escape the regimentation and discipline of the Old World and were seldom likely to readily surrender their personal freedom for an indefinite term of military service in an army that exemplified the word deprivation.

A Continental establishment was certainly necessary to prove to both the British adversary and potential European allies that the Revolution was something far more serious than a short term peasant revolt; to demonstrate the professional nature of the American miliary; and to provide potentially decisive volley fire at certain crisis moments on a battlefield. However, there would never be enough Continentals to match the redcoats on a typical battlefield and thus American hopes for victory usually relied on the contributions of the two less professional elements of the triad. A detailed analysis of the numbers of soldiers engaged in the opposing armies during Revolutionary War battles reveals the simple fact that on most occasions when there were more patriots on the field than redcoats, the Americans generally won the battle. The British army usually beat the rebels when the Americans were unable to mobilize enough units at the right place at the right time and the outnumbered patriots retreated and/or panicked when they realized that there were simply too many redcoats marching against them. Thus, the deployment of as many militia units as possible tended to counteract the British numerical advantage and provide some possibility of expecting a patriot victory. Something over 200,000 Americans appear to have served at least a brief time in state militia units and even though many of them served for only 30 days or during one battle, they could still provide the margin of victory in a critical engagement.

The key to American victory in a battle was not so much whether militia were employed, for they were involved in virtually every battle, but whether they stayed on the field long enough to do some real damage to their British adversaries. For example, Horatio Gates was able to use massive lines of New England and New York militia to defeat Burgoyne at Saratoga. Gates' numerical advantage allowed him to cut off most possible British attack routes and then force the enemy to fight under unfavorable geographic conditions. The American ability to utilize mobilization of short term militia units could provide a manpower advantage in the crisis moment of a battle while the very fact that most of these men tended to return home shortly thereafter relieved the always critical supply situation for patriot commissary and quartermaster officers.

The final leg of the triad consisted of the relatively small but vitally important units designated as rifle or ranger corps. These unconventional forces provided a major psychological boost to the patriot cause. While most of these men carried weapons that could not be utilized with a bayonet, and could not be fired as rapidly as a musket, these technical drawbacks were more than compensated by their ability to provoke terror in the ranks of British officers and enlisted men. European battles featured a stand-up exchange of massed vollies which culminated in one of the contending armies launching a bayonet assault that often sent the opposing force scurrying off the field to regroup at some later time. The use of unconventional American soldiers who fired long range weapons from the cover of trees or fences and tended to hit a disproportionate number of officers disrupted the command and control structure of the British army and made the almost mathematical equations of victory or defeat in European warfare far less certain in the American wilderness.

## Grading the Generals

While the differences in types of soldiers utilized and tactics employed between the two adversaries played a major role in the American victory in the Revolution, the relative leadership abilities of the commanders of the opposing armies is at least equally important to the outcome of the struggle. An evaluation of military leaders is limited by the same factors which affect the value of ratings of quarterbacks, pitchers or point guards; namely, how crucial is this single individual to the outcome of a game (or battle) involving a larger number of participants? This analysis of military commanders will attempt to rate each general's overall impact on the ultimate outcome of the war based on factors such as ratio of victories to defeat, ratio of casualties inflicted to casualties suffered, psychological impact of the battle on the contending sides and ability to maximize the fighting abilities of men under command. While any number of criteria can be used in identifying "important" leaders during the Revolution, this analysis is based on an assumption that the individuals selected substantially influenced the outcome of at least one major battle of the war although a few of these men go far beyond those perimeters.

An evaluation of British military commanders would probably begin with the general responsible for the initiation of military operations at Lexington and Concord—General Thomas Gage. Gage appears to have been an intelligent, engaging officer who had some sympathy for the colonists and some perception of their long term military capabilities. However, his role in the crucial engagements at Lexington-Concord and Bunker Hill were little short of disastrous to the British cause. Gage's plan of operations against the rebels in the Massachusetts countryside was generally well developed but failed miserably in implementation. A series of missed orders, poor communications and questionable naval support was exacerbated by the selection of overweight, slow, self indulgent Colonel Francis Smith to lead the assault force. While Gage's timely dispatch of Lord Hugh Percy's relief column saved the expedition from possible annihilation, his succession of mistakes in execution provided the rebels with a crucial psychological victory. Gage's performance in the subsequent Charlestown peninsula expedition did little to restore the general's reputation. While Gage outranked the newly arrived triumvirate of Burgoyne, Clinton and Howe, he largely faded into the background as these three generals argued over the proper response to American fortification of Breed's Hill. Gage appears to have had some concerns regarding Howe's ultimate strategy, but the British commander merely stood aside to allow his subordinate to undertake his disastrous assault. While Gage's rating is somewhat improved by the fact that his Lexington expedition was not annihilated and Bunker Hill resulted in a technical, if costly, victory for the British, a grade above "D" would probably be too generous.

While Thomas Gage was facing the consequences of American mobilization around Boston, his counterpart in Canada, Sir Guy Carleton was attempting to parry a patriot determination to add a fourteenth colony to the new alliance. Carleton was extremely successful in utilizing his pathetically limited manpower to cobble together a mixture of regulars, retired veterans, provincial seamen and local militia in order to counter the threat of a two pronged American invasion of Canada. Carleton's defense of Quebec in the famous patriot New Year's Eve assault resulted in the loss of more than half of the attackers against only five British deaths.

Carleton followed this success with a spirited attack down Lake Champlain which destroyed Benedict Arnold's hastily mobilized fleet and placed the British army within striking distance of Albany. However, in a moment of inexplicable hesitation comparable to Joseph Hooker's change of heart just as he had flanked Lee's outnumbered army, Carleton canceled an assault on poorly defended Fort Ticonderoga and order his army to retreat back to Canada. While Carlton's role in the defense of Canada surely merits an "A," his failure to exploit a fantastic opportunity to split the colonies in two deserves an "F" which would produce a composite rating of "C."

The first general to confront George Washington was also one of the most controversial British military leaders of the 18th century. William Howe's face to face encounters with Washington resulted in a series of victories in which the British commander in chief in America inflicted over 7700 casualties on the patriot army while losing only 2100 of his own redcoats and Hessians. Howe was able to capture both New York and Philadelphia with minimal threat to his army while developing a series of flanking maneuvers that consistently foiled his adversaries' plans.

However, Howe's substantial tactical success over the rebels was substantially marred by two major failings. First, each time the British commander was on the verge of crushing the last remnants of the patriot army, Howe allowed a combination of indecision, caution and a desire for personal comfort to postpone the decisive victory. Second, his insistence that the roundabout expedition to capture Philadelphia was more important than his expected support of Burgoyne's northern army led to the most decisive British defeat before Yorktown and essentially traded occupation of a half empty capital for the loss of a 7000 man army and the addition of France to the list of Britain's opponents. Thus Howe's rating of "A" for overall tactical success must be combined with an "F" for his contribution to British strategic objectives to produce a "C" grade.

Howe's determination to push the needs of the northern army to the bottom of his priority list for the 1777 campaign produced a dramatic impact on the reputation of rival general John Burgoyne. This general's rating is slightly elevated by the failure of his chief to provide adequate support which was a key element in the planned Hudson Valley expedition. However, Burgoyne has little else to support his reputation. The amateur playwright and high stakes gambler led an army that was weighed down with impediments ranging from heavy artillery that was useless for a battle in a forest to silver tea services designed for the general's triumph in Albany.

Burgoyne's incredible pace of one mile a day allowed the patriots plenty of time to organize effective counter measures and obliged the British army to halt short of its final objective. During the battles of Freeman's Farm and Bemis Heights, Burgoyne seemed to launch a series of improvised engagements which were somewhere between reconnaissances in force and outright attacks and resulted in a marked disadvantage for the British troops who were as unsure of their objectives as their commanding general. There is also considerable evidence that Burgoyne rejected attempts to force a passage back to Canada because he preferred an upcoming winter in England as a paroled general of a surrendered army to another season in the north country as commander of a retreating army. Just as Howe allowed a desire for personal comfort to hinder offensive operations against Washington, Burgoyne was perfectly willing to allow 7000 soldiers to enter captivity in order to ensure a better venue for his own activities. Burgoyne's surrender at Saratoga was a disaster of the first magnitude and only Howe's major culpability in failing to provide support raises Burgoyne's grade to a barely passable" D-."

Sir Henry Clinton was confronted with the dubious distinction of being promoted to replace William Howe as commander in chief in North America at the same time that the British ministry had decided to de-emphasize the struggle against the rebellious provinces in favor of a war against the traditional French adversary. Clinton was almost immediately ordered to evacuate his army from Philadelphia to New York and his march across New Jersey produced a mixed outcome in which most of the force did arrive but only after the battle of Monmouth inflicted relatively high casualties on the expedition. The new commander followed this assignment with a subsequent move against the city of Charleston which resulted in the most substantial British victory of the war. However, at this moment of personal triumph, Clinton abandoned the southern theatre to Charles Cornwallis and spent most of the next two years vainly attempting to draw Washington into a battle of annihilation. When Cornwallis ultimately found himself besieged at Yorktown, Clinton made some effort to dispatch a substantial relief force but was frustrated by a combination of insufficient dockyard facilities and the need to repair damaged Royal Navy vessels. A more talented and aggressive general might have found a way to accelerate the repairs and move the reinforcements to Virginia in time to make a difference in the outcome of the siege.

An evaluation of Clinton's overall impact on the outcome of the War presents the contrasts so common to a number of British leaders. While the British captured Charleston by deploying almost seven times as many regulars as Lincoln's beleaguered army, the victory was nonetheless the most impressive triumph of the war for His Majesty's forces. Clinton did not direct a brilliant campaign, but he committed no serious blunders and prevented any large scale escape from the city. Sir Henry's collision with Washington's newly reorganized army at Monmouth Court House was much less successful than the Charleston campaign, but he was able to transport most of his army to New York while avoiding a truly massive disaster. The composite of commanding the British army during its most significant victory of the war, leading a somewhat successful evacuation of Philadelphia and being somewhat responsible for the failure to reinforce Cornwallis at Yorktown produces a relatively respectable "C+" for Henry Clinton.

The British leader most hated by the American rebels was also responsible for a succession of fairly impressive ministerial victories in the southern province. Banastre Tarleton was vain, arrogant, rapacious and brutal in his conduct of military operations, but he was also an energetic and innovative commander. Tarleton produced an impressive string of victories at Monck's Corner, Lenud's Ferry, Waxhaws and Fishing Creek which inflicted over 1000 American casualties at a loss of only 39 redcoat and Tory killed and wounded. Tarleton's aggressive actions in the battle of Camden smashed the American militia units and allowed the British regulars to virtually annihilate the Continental regiments on the scene.

However, Tarleton's spectacular run of success clearly produced an overconfidence that would critically affect the colonel's judgement in his confrontation with Daniel Morgan at Cowpens. Tarleton completely misunderstood his adversary's tactics and then turned and rode away from his army rather than attempting to save as many units as possible. While the defeat at Cowpens totally reversed the favorable ratio of casualties enjoyed by Tarleton before this battle, a composite record of several small to medium victories marred by one major defeat would most likely produce a "C" grade.

The British field commander most often associated with the loss of the American colonies is, of course, Charles Cornwallis. The famous depictions of the "World Turned Upside Down" at the surrender of Yorktown burned a lasting impression on American citizens of Lord Cornwallis as the man who "lost America." However, an accurate evaluation of Cornwallis' long term impact on the war must also include a complicated series of contributions including a brilliant battle as wing commander in the British victory at Brandywine, a decisive defeat of Horatio Gates' army at Camden and a technical victory, although at very heavy cost, at Guilford Court House.

Cornwallis entered the Virginia campaign of 1781 with a generally better than average reputation as a field commander but his dubious place in history would be assured by the Yorktown campaign, which resulted in the loss of almost 9000 British soldiers and seamen at little cost to the allied besiegers. Clinton's inability to provide a promised relief column somewhat mitigates Cornwallis' responsibility for the disaster but even his earlier success can only push Cornwallis' final evaluation to a barely passable "D."

A summary evaluation of the British commanders during the Revolution reveals a relatively composite of one "C+," three "C's," two "D's" and one "D-." No single leader was assigned a failing grade largely due to the mitigating circumstances of victories in other battles while in field command or lack of promised support from other generals during an unsuccessful campaign. However, no British general could be readily awarded a "good" or "excellent" evaluation in an ultimately totally disastrous attempt to reduce the American rebels to submission. There is simply no British equivalent of a Robert E. Lee who radiates genius even in the middle of a losing effort. Most of the British commanders during the War of Independence were competent and occasionally even innovative, but they were primarily a group of arrogant, self-satisfied, complacent aristocrats who exemplified the evils of a hierarchical British society that was just beginning to reform with the advent of the Industrial Revolution. However, unfortunately for the future of the first British Empire, the energetic, often brilliant self made men who were beginning to revolutionize the economy of England were not yet welcome in the inner circles of political and military decision making for the kingdom. On the other hand, this new type of English speaking citizen was already becoming influential in the legislatures and military camps of the American patriots.

The first American leader who commanded patriot troops in a direct battlefield encounter with the redcoats was John Stark of New Hampshire. While Artemus Ward held the title of overall commander of the rebel army besieging Boston and Israel Putnam was responsible for the American units deployed on Charlestown peninsula, neither man exercised the actual combat leadership that fell to Stark on that hot June afternoon. Stark's performance at the battle of Bunker Hill and during the engagement two years later at Bennington was little short of brilliant. At Bunker Hill Stark displayed a talent for improvisation in a crisis that characterized the most distinguished patriot leaders during the entire war. His use of successive lines of marksmen deployed behind natural and man made barricades virtually annihilated entire units of Howe's assault force and encouraged British commanders to avoid potentially decisive frontal assaults in future battles based on their nightmarish experiences on Breed's Hill.

During the Saratoga campaign Stark again utilized his army of volunteers to devastate a combined force of redcoats and Germans and deprive Burgoyne of a crucial source of supplies necessary to his move toward Albany. Stark's overall impact on the war is somewhat incomplete due to his reluctance to serve for long periods with the main patriot army, but a grade of "A-" seems to be a reasonable evaluation for this extremely valuable militia leader.

A second person who seems to be an excellent example of the value of a self taught amateur who provided invaluable service to the patriot cause is Henry Knox of Massachusetts. Knox had been a Boston book dealer before the war and had tapped into his large inventory of military volumes to become an authority on a number of aspects of strategy and tactics. When Washington was faced with the unpleasant prospect of attempting to maneuver Howe's army out of its Boston defenses, the rotund bookseller volunteered to lead an expedition to Fort Ticonderoga in upstate New York to transport the siege train that had been captured in that recently captured British stronghold. Knox overcame flooded rivers, blizzards and ice storms to drag over 50 pieces of siege artillery to Washington's headquarters at Cambridge. These howitzers and mortars, when used in conjunction with the patriot ability to rapidly construct impressive earthworks, provided a series of fortifications on Dorchester Heights which forced the British evacuation of Boston with virtually no loss to the rebel army.

Just under a year later, Knox was the driving force behind the transport of 18 vitally important pieces of artillery across the ice clogged Delaware River, which provided much of the margin of superiority over the Hessian defenders of Trenton and produced another almost bloodless triumph for the American army. The only time during the war in which Knox's self-taught knowledge of military history proved to be an impediment to the patriot cause was during the battle of Germantown, when the American artillery commander convinced Washington that the tiny British force occupying the Chew House constituted a "fortress" in the American rear and should be destroyed before the advance continued. Washington's ensuing pre-occupation with the neutralization of Cliveden reduced the momentum of the far more important assault on Howe's main defenses and probably prevented a major American victory. Beyond this one blot on the general's reputation, Henry Knox's enthusiasm, expertise and energy provided the patriot cause with an artillery army that was crucial to the rebel victory and should rate at least an "A-."

While Banastre Tarleton represents the British leader Americans most loved to hate, Benedict Arnold seems to fill that role among native born figures in the War of Independence. Arnold has been alternately depicted as both the most brilliant field commander for the patriots when he supported the rebel cause and the most heinous villain of the war when he chose to switch sides for the promise of a generous reward and a commission in the British army. However, the authors are convinced that while Arnold's treason should not be underestimated, his military contributions to the patriot cause before the West Point drama have been historically overrated.

Arnold was certainly energetic, bold and aggressive during his tenure as an American field commander, but a closer examination of the impact of his actions reveals a rather mixed picture. The former Connecticut pharmacist's role in the invasion of Quebec was certainly an active one, as he led a column of New England militia through the Maine wilderness to provide a "back door" threat to the British defense of Canada. However, almost half of the force either died or turned back, and Arnold's 600 survivors were hardly enough to turn the tide of the campaign even when added to Richard Montgomery's New York corps. The ensuing New Years Eve attack on Quebec City was daring and exciting but was a first rate military disaster which resulted in the loss of 500 of the 600 attackers against a minuscule British loss of 5 killed and 13 wounded. One of the ironies of the famous assault was that Richard Montgomery, who was killed in the first moments of the battle, emerged as a hero while Arnold, who was severely wounded, lived long enough to become regarded as an arch-villain. Montgomery, who seemed to possess genuine military talent, was actually an ardent opponent of American independence, insisting he fought only to protect the rights of the colonies as English subjects. It is quite possible that had Montgomery lived, he might have either retired from the army or possibly even have switched sides rather than serve in an army attempting to completely secede from the British empire, possibly rivaling Arnold for infamy in American opinion.

Arnold himself survived to take over command of the remnants of the American invasion force and eventually conduct a withdrawal to Lake Champlain in the face of a British counteroffensive in the spring and summer of 1776. Arnold's subsequent role in the battle of Valcour Island revealed his usual aggressiveness and energy, but when the smoke cleared, the acting "admiral" had lost all 15 of his ships against only 3 British vessels destroyed and only Carleton's incredible last minute panic attack prevented a major British threat to Albany.

Arnold's most vital contribution to American victory occurred when he served as a wing commander in the patriot army facing Burgoyne at Saratoga. The Connecticut general's actions at Freeman's Farm and Bemis Heights were crucial to the rebel victory and should have received much more prominence in Gates' post battle dispatch to Congress. However, Arnold's subsequent actions, though partially justified by the quite real unfairness of Congress in promptly promoting the brigadier to major general, are hardly filled with valor. It is quite apparent that Arnold was utilizing his position as military commander of Philadelphia to improve his own social and financial prospects and he was consistently bordering on outright illegal acts. His subsequent relationship and marriage to Loyalist sympathizer Peggy Shippen simply accelerated a slide toward outright treason which forever stained his earlier reputation in patriot circles. Arnold's actions in the battles around Saratoga were certainly critical to the American cause, but the Connecticut leader presents a more erratic picture in other engagements which, even when attempting to separate his contributions from his later treason would reduce his possibly outstanding rating to a somewhat less impressive "B-."

One of Arnold's principal rivals for the position of most flawed patriot leader is General Charles Lee. Lee, like Arnold, was a general who is so controversial that it is difficult to properly evaluate his actual impact on the American victory. The former British major's reputation has been colored by the fact that he was a repulsive, conceited, foul-mouthed eccentric who apparently actively conspired to replace Washington as commander of patriot armies. Lee essentially exercised field command during three significant occasions during the war, and none of these experiences were particularly beneficial to the patriot cause.

The summer of 1776 found Lee in command of the defenses around Charleston harbor as it was threatened by a British amphibious attack. While the former British officer was able to successfully organize the diverse militia units into a semblance of an army, only Colonel William Moultrie's absolute refusal to follow Lee's order to evacuate Sullivan's Island allowed the rebels to repulse the enemy assault. Later that year Lee was entrusted with the major wing of the American army when Washington divided his forces and attempted to counter the British threat to Fort Washington and Fort Lee. When the American commander began his retreat toward Pennsylvania, his orders for Lee to rejoin him were totally ignored. This disobedience provided Howe with a golden opportunity to successively destroy the two separate portions of the rebel army. Only Lee's incredibly foolhardy decision to spend the night far from his army, with his subsequent capture, released desperately needed reinforcements to Washington's disintegrating corps. Lee's exchange after 18 months of captivity provided the eccentric general with one last opportunity for command. Washington reluctantly appointed his second ranking general to command the large advance element of the army as it moved toward Clinton's retreating redcoats near

Monmouth Court House. Lee botched a major opportunity to annihilate the British rear guard and then was in turn nearly routed by the redcoat counterattack which was only stemmed by Washington's personal intervention. A general for which so much was expected at the beginning of the conflict fizzled into a barely possible passable rating before his ultimate court martial and retirement.

A more successful, but no less controversial, veteran of the British officer corps who chose to side with the rebel colonists was Horatio Gates. While Gates was a personally more attractive and congenial figure than Charles Lee, his involvement with military and Congressional opponents of Washington combined with his famous retreat from Camden battlefield permanently blemished his reputation in American military annals.

Gates seems to be a beneficiary of enormous good luck and a victim of substantial bad luck at different points of the war. When the Congressional leaders of New England were able to exert enough influence to replace the competent New Yorker Philip Schuyler with their own favorite in the position of commander of the Northern army, the former British officer benefited from his predecessors' energetic activities. Schuyler had already blunted Barry St. Leger's Mohawk Valley thrust, recruited and raised a large number of New York militia regiments and prepared a formidable set of defenses on the Hudson River. Gates fine-tuned Schuyler's valuable preparations and produced one of the two most decisive American victories of the war. While subordinates such as Daniel Morgan and Benedict Arnold played crucial roles in producing this epic triumph, Gates should be credited with the administrative skill and strategic vision which orchestrated the British defeat.

Gates' significant contribution to ultimate American victory was tarnished by a general bungling of the Camden expedition and his subsequent hurried retreat from the site of the battle when he left his subordinates behind to salvage something from the developing disaster. The virtual annihilation of Gates' army was a major defeat for the patriot cause, but the numbers involved in the opposing armies were much smaller than in most northern engagements and the importance of Saratoga outweighs this embarrassing episode in Gates' career and leaves him with a still respectable grade of "B-."

While Horatio Gates' southern misadventures were compensated for by a great northern victory, Benjamin Lincoln enjoyed no earlier laurels to offset the American disaster at Savannah and Charleston. When Lincoln was given command of the southern theatre in September of 1778 he was regarded as a general who exhibited integrity, temperance and diligence but was also overweight, slow and methodical. Lincoln seems to have developed a decent working relationship with his French counterpart, Admiral D'Estaing, but the American general and the French admiral orchestrated one of the most embarrassing engagements of the war when they attempted to assault the heavily outnumbered British defenders of Savannah. Neither

Lincoln nor D'Estaing enhanced their reputations with the botched attack which cost the allied armies almost ten times as many casualties as the enemy defenders and resulted in the French admiral's less than heroic departure with his entire fleet.

Lincoln's subsequent defense of Charleston produced one of the most feeble American responses to a British threat and resulted in the worst single patriot setback of the war when the Massachusetts general surrendered over 5000 men and 7 ships while inflicting only minimal casualties on Clinton's army. While Lincoln's string of southern disasters was at least minimally balanced by a reasonable level of success as a corps commander in the northern theatre, this general must share an unenviable category with Burgoyne and Cornwallis as a commander who managed to lose an entire major army during a siege operation. A rating of "D-" is the most generous grade that can be awarded to this unlucky general.

While command of southern armies badly tarnished the reputations of Gates and Lincoln, the conflict in the Carolinas and Georgia was far more congenial to the stature of former wagon driver Daniel Morgan. Morgan's role in the American victory in the War of Independence is one of the most vital of any patriot leader. His rifle corps played a critical role in the defeat of Burgoyne at Saratoga and deflected Howe's intended major assault on Washington's lines in the engagement at Whitemarsh. When the newly promoted brigadier general was assigned to an independent command in the aftermath of Nathanael Greene's bold division of his forces, he responded with one of the most impressive operations in American military history.

Morgan selected a battle site at the Cowpens which seemed to totally favor his antagonist Banastre Tarleton. However, the Virginian's deployment of a mix of militia units, riflemen and regulars was one of the most effective of the war and inflicted almost 15 British casualties for every American killed or wounded. Cowpens annihilated a British army and inflicted a psychological blow on the enemy from which the redcoats never totally recovered. Morgan must be rated as one of the authentic geniuses of the American Revolution with a grade of "A."

The other American general who utilized the complex southern war to dramatically enhance his reputation was Rhode Islander Nathanael Greene. The former manager of an anchor making firm had developed a somewhat mixed record as a corps commander under Washington. Greene was at least partially responsible for convincing Washington to commit reinforcements to Fort Washington and arrived almost an hour late for the battle of Germantown as his men became lost in the fog. On the other hand, Greene played a significant role in defeating the Hessians at Trenton and conducted a last ditch defense at Brandywine that saved the rest of the army.

Greene inherited a decimated, dispirited army from Horatio Gates and quickly turned the tide in the south with a series of daring maneuvers. The Rhode Islander's game of cat and mouse with Cornwallis' better trained army greatly diminished British striking power, while battles such as Guilford Court House and Eutaw Springs inflicted enormous casualty rates on the enemy even if the redcoats held the battlefields at the end of the day. While Greene produced few clear cut victories during his tenure, his orchestration of the southern campaign was incredibly successful and produced enormous strategic advantages for the patriot cause. Greene should share Morgan's equally well deserved "A" rating.

No analysis of Revolutionary War military commanders would be complete without an evaluation of the most dominant figure of the entire era—George Washington. One of the most persistent myths of the War of Independence is the impression that Washington was a general who lost most of his battles but emerged victorious when the British decided to quit the war after Yorktown. A more detailed examination of the Virginian's military activities during the course of the war reveals a quite different picture of a general who clearly merited his reputation as the "indispensable man" in the quest for American independence.

Washington's impact on the patriot victory should be viewed from a number of perspectives. The first salient point regarding Washington's military leadership is that his army emerged victorious in more engagements than it lost. An analysis of the major battles in which Washington held field command reveals five fairly definite British victories—Long Island, Kip's Bay, Fort Washington, Brandywine and Germantown; and five American triumphs—Harlem Heights, Trenton, Princeton, Monmouth and Yorktown. The eleventh major battle, White Plains, was essentially a draw as the British forced the Americans to retreat but lost twice as many men as their opponents and then withdrew from their newly captured position. Two other engagements, Dorchester Heights and Whitemarsh, should be listed as victories for Washington precisely because they did not involve a major battle with large numbers of casualties on both sides. At Dorchester, Washington was able to force Howe to evacuate Boston at virtually no loss to the American forces, while at Whitemarsh the British commander's attempt to force a decisive engagement was deflected by excellent intelligence and a well deployed Continental Army. Thus we see that of the 13 engagements that offered the possibility of a fairly substantial impact on the course of the Revolution, the British were able to actually defeat Washington on only five occasions.

An examination of the balance sheet of casualties inflicted versus casualties suffered under Washington's field command is an even more impressive indicator of the American commander's impact on the patriot victory. The thirteen major battles and engagements listed above resulted in the deaths of just over 1000 Americans and just under 1000 British and Hessians. Washington was hardly profligate with the lives of his men and three of the most decisive American victories resulted in minimal numbers of killed in action, including 30 dead at Princeton, 23 at Yorktown and no battle deaths at Trenton. A comparison of total killed, wounded and captured during the battles in which Washington commanded the Continental Army reveals a casualty list of just under 8300 Americans and French soldiers as opposed to 13,800 British and Hessian losses in the thirteen major confrontations. Thus Washington's army was able to inflict about 3 enemy casualties for every 2 it lost, which was an enormously favorable exchange in a conflict in which the British faced such enormous difficulties in recruiting and transporting reinforcements.

Beyond the favorable balance of casualties enjoyed under Washington's leadership, there is little doubt that the Virginian's charisma and personal magnetism almost single-handedly held together the patriot cause at the moments of crisis. There is little doubt that Washington tended towards favoritism concerning certain subordinates, viewed even minor criticism as a significant threat to his reputation, and underemphasized the value of militia in most battles. However, long after other generals and leaders had returned to the comfort of their homes, the commander in chief remained at the head of his army and shared in their danger. Washington may have generally had more comfortable quarters, better food and more amusing diversions than most of his soldiers, but by 18th century standards he shared far more hazards and endured far more discomfort than his aristocratic European counterparts. He was a master of the dramatic gesture, ranging from his personal chase of fleeing redcoats at Princeton to his donning of spectacles to convince the Newburgh officers corps to retract their demands on Congress. A general who refused pay for his services, showed deference to sometimes exasperating Congressional committee members and still managed to defeat the most powerful military machine of his time, could merit nothing less than a rating of "A."

While Washington was the indispensable man in the accomplishment of American victory, George III was the essential person to ensure British defeat. The traditional American depiction of the English king as a tyrannical, ruthless despot determined to enslave the Colonists is patently untrue. The grandson and great-grandson of corrupt, ill tempered monarchs, George III was a devoted husband and father who was generous and loyal to his friends and had developed a primitive notion that each of his subjects might actually be important in some vague and not yet fully determined fashion. However, while George III was not a classic tyrant, he was quite definitely the wrong leader to maintain the overseas colonies in the face of an armed insurrection. This King inhabited an uncomfortable middle ground between two types of British monarchs. A more warlike and daring leader such as Henry V would probably have sailed across the Atlantic at the head of a massive battle fleet and army and personally commanded his troops in the climactic battles against the rebels. A more diplomatic successor such as Queen Victoria would have directed her ministers to arrange a compromise settlement with the disaffected Americans in much the same style as the granting of dominion status and virtual independence to Canada with the Confederation Act of 1867.

Unfortunately for the British empire, George III was neither a Henry V nor a Victoria. He was the first British king in centuries to live through a reign without having once commanded his forces in battle as captain general of the armies. While his predecessors frequently mounted horses and fought their enemies on muddy or snowy battlefields, George III directed his armies from a desk and exercised command through a thick layer of ministers, bureaucrats and equally desk bound generals. Royal appointees such as Lord North, Lord Germain and William were probably competent enough to deal with poorly organized Irish rebels or poorly armed Highland Scots but were out of their depth directing a war against a determined, well armed, reasonably well organized American adversary. Their spoiled, stubborn monarch issued contradictory directives, vacillated between priorities against the French or the rebel colonists and appointed decidedly second rate diplomats to deal with the far more single-minded Congressional negotiators. While His Majesty blustered, threw tantrums and periodically threatened to abdicate his throne, George Washington and his patriot colleagues won a war of independence and virtually stole a generous peace from their former motherland.

# CHAPTER 14

# The Shore Dimly Seen

## *The American Invasion of Canada, 1812*

$T$he War of 1812 represents the paradox of a seemingly inevitable yet also highly avoidable second conflict between the United States and Great Britain. Each nation had far more to lose than gain in a war with the other major English speaking society. The United Kingdom was already fully absorbed in a life or death struggle with the forces of Napoleon and could ill afford to divert even minimal military and naval resources from the Continent to North America. On the other hand, the United States in 1812 was about as unprepared for a serious conflict as at any point in the history of the republic. The American navy could deploy fewer than a dozen warships, none larger than a frigate, to confront a Royal Navy that boasted over a thousand ships including 180 powerful ships of the line. The United States army could muster a force of only 5000 regulars scattered in posts and forts throughout the country. A substantial number of Americans vehemently opposed a war with Great Britain and a number of state governments would refuse to supply any financial or military support to the Federal government. Because of all of these limitations the young republic simply could not afford to engage in a lengthy contest with Great Britain; if England was able to defeat Napoleon and turn its vast military power on the United States before a peace settlement had been negotiated, the very existence of the federal union could be imperiled.

While the immediate causes of the second war between Britain and America were generally viewed as revolving around British impressment of American seaman and attempts to control the trade policies of the United States, combined with the desire of frontier region Americans to annex Canada to the federal republic, citizens from both nations had developed negative stereotypes about their trans-Atlantic counterparts long before the outbreak of actual hostilities. Americans generally viewed the residents of their former motherland as stuffy, hidebound, snobbish, dedicated to the acceptance of inconvenience and hopelessly impractical. Britons often viewed their former colonists as brash, boastful, crude, money-hungry upstarts who had the unfortunate good luck to strike it rich in an incredibly abundant continent.

British newspapers were particularly adamant with their censure of American lifestyles. The Edinburgh *Review* informed its readers that "America is less popular and less esteemed among us than the base and bigoted Portuguese or the ferocious and ignorant Russians." A British lord was quoted as particularly opposed to "that spirit of encroachment, that indiscriminate thirst for gain, that sordid jealousy" that marked residents of the United States. Even Augustus John Foster, the relatively well liked British ambassador to Washington emphasized the rivalry between the two competing societies. "They and we are now rivals in what has always given power whenever it has extended—commerce—but I trust that still for a long time we shall maintain the immense superiority that we do now. They are next to us in this race, but in nothing else are they near us. We drove them into being a nation when they were no more fit for it than the convicts of Botany Bay." Thomas Jefferson probably echoed the sentiments of a large number of Americans concerning their acceptance of the British opinion of the United States when he tersely noted, "the British government is the most corrupt and corrupting mass of rottenness which ever usurped the name of government."

Despite this relatively common exchange of pleasantries between the two nations, there was little overwhelming sentiment for open warfare beyond the relatively limited number of Congressional War Hawks in America and the most violent America haters in Britain. When Prime Minister Spencer Percival was assassinated by a disgruntled British merchant in May of 1812, Percival's successor, Robert Jenkinson, Earl of Liverpool, initiated a Parliamentary re-examination of the controversial Orders in Council which essentially barred the United States from trading with France and its allies. The debate exposed an incredible mismanagement of foreign policy on the part of the ministry when the House of Commons could not identify a single member of that body who would actually admit to ever supporting the orders and no one could even remember who had authorized the legislation in the first place. On June 23, 1812 Lord Liverpool signed a document repealing the Orders in Council and the British government trumpeted the importance of this action in preventing a war with the United States. Unfortunately, five days earlier, President James Madison had listed those same now-defunct Orders as the reason for his declaration of war against the United Kingdom.

While the British Parliament had been debating the shadowy birth and enforcement of an incredibly unpopular piece of legislation, the United States Congress had voted 19 to 13 in the Senate and 79 to 49 in the House to initiate a war with England. This was hardly a unanimous mandate for a conflict and the vote was dramatically closer than subsequent votes in 1917 and 1941 which plunged the nation into far larger wars. Generally the war was most popular in the South and the western and northern frontier regions, while most of the population of New England and the Middle Atlantic states either opposed the war or was lukewarm about the potential benefits of a confrontation with Britain. The arrival of the news of the repeal of the Orders in Council might have changed enough pre-war voters' minds to have avoided the conflict, but much of the War Hawk leadership was probably more interested in the annexation of Canada than whether or not American goods would have a more open foreign market. Since the impressment issue would not disappear until Napoleon was safely deposed and a large number of frontier representatives were enthralled with the idea of new territories opening up in an annexed Canada, it is still debatable whether or not Parliament's actions would have prevented a war.

The relatively reluctant president James Madison and the much more enthusiastic Republican legislators led by Henry Clay had generally agreed that the basic strategy in a war with Britain would be to launch an immediate invasion of Canada and then use part or all of the newly acquired province as a bargaining chip in negotiations with the British government to end impressment and repeal the Orders in Council. The one essential element that has never fully emerged from the available documents and correspondence from the era is whether the American government intended to keep all of Canada, keep part of Canada, or give back the whole territory to Britain in the wake of a peace settlement with His Majesty's government. Perhaps the general sentiment of the time was to first conquer the north land and then figure out what to do with it sometime later.

On the surface, the population disparity between 7 ½ million Americans and the mere 500,000 residents of Canada seemed to indicate that British North America wouldn't remain British for very long after a declaration of war. Thomas Jefferson assumed that Canada could be conquered almost as soon as an invasion army was mobilized since "the acquisition of Canada this year as far as the neighborhood of Quebec will be a mere matter of marching." Henry Clay told his Congressional colleagues that "the conquest of Canada is in your power. I trust I shall not be deemed presumptuous when I state I believe the militia of Kentucky are alone competent to place Montreal and Upper Canada at your feet."

Jefferson, Clay and their over optimistic associates simply ignored a long list of impediments to the easy conquest of Canada. First, while the United States enjoyed a 15 to 1 population advantage over its northern neighbor, the 6400 immediately available regulars were almost matched by the 5600 British regulars and trained Canadian militiamen that could be deployed by Governor General Prevost. The key stronghold of Quebec was defended by a formidable force of 2300 men and as long as that city was in British hands and the Royal Navy controlled the sea, the American invaders simply could not exploit their conquests south of this citadel. The minimal manpower advantage of a projected American invasion force was complicated by policy makers' ignorance of the probable impact of the interminable Canadian winter on proposed offensive operations. It would be virtually impossible for the Americans to capture both Quebec and Montreal in one campaign, so the army would have to spend at least one winter in the frigid north land and then possibly confront a British relief force that would be dispatched by His Majesty's government.

Another obstacle facing the Yankee invaders was the fact that British North America was filled with exiled Loyalists who wanted no part of being tied to the United States and would flock to join military units to resist an American invasion. There were settlers from the United States in many Upper Canadian communities, but they would most likely remain fairly neutral in any actual combat, while the families of the Tories were united in their determination to fend off republican rule. On the other hand, the American population residing near the Lake Champlain invasion route generally opposed the war and would probably provide minimal aid to the invasion force.

The final obstacle to a relatively easy American victory was the generally horrendous quality of the leaders of the military establishment. Secretary of War William Eustis was a former surgeon who was appointed mainly for his loyalty to Jeffersonian principles and his ability to pinch pennies in every area of the army budget. Eustis was a borderline incompetent who was hated by almost every other member of Madison's cabinet. The senior American general, Major General Henry Dearborn was a sixty-one year-old-relic of the War of Independence who had been enticed back to command the army from his post as collector of customs for the port of Boston. Nicknamed "Granny" by his troops, Dearborn was hardly the epitome of a young, enthusiastic republican general. Senior Brigadier General James Wilkinson was a 55-year-old master of self promotion who had already moved dangerously close to treasonable activities on a number of occasions and would have been court-martialed and cashiered by most other armies in the world. Most of the other significant generals were either alcoholic, senile or simply burned out and were simply incapable of directing an energetic enterprise such as the invasion of Canada. These American leaders would be confronting a British officer corps that was generally unspectacular but competent and possessed a field commander who totally overshadowed any of his American counterparts. Major General Isaac Brock was an energetic, intelligent, gifted officer who was convinced that his combination of regulars, embodied militia and Indian allies could deflect initial American assaults until substantial aid from Britain would permit him to begin a counter invasion of the enemy northern and western frontiers.

Madison, Eustis and Dearborn agreed on a plan for an invasion of Canada that would revolve around a series of well coordinated offensives directed toward Montreal, eastern Lake Ontario, the Niagara frontier and the western part of Upper Canada that would hopefully prevent the British from concentrating against any single American column. After all of these objectives had been captured, the armies would regroup for an advance down the St. Lawrence against Quebec. Each segment of the invasion plan contained a specific purpose. The thrust up along Lake Champlain would seize Montreal and block the St. Lawrence River from any British reinforcements while isolating the enemy western posts from their main supply route; an offensive from Sackett's Harbor across the eastern end of Lake Ontario combined with the assault on the Niagara frontier would pin down British forces in those areas so they could not be rushed to the relief of Montreal; a move from Fort Detroit toward the Thames valley would secure the loyalty of the American settlers in the border communities and overcome the western Indians. General Dearborn agreed to take command of the Army of the North and strike for Montreal while General Stephen Van Rensselaer would lead the Army of the Center across the Niagara River and Brigadier General William Hull would organize the expedition designed to capture Upper Canada.

The proposed use of a series of well coordinated offensives had a reasonable possibility of success if the timing of the American armies allowed them to confront each enemy force piecemeal. However, the planned concerted effort almost immediately deteriorated into a series of unsupported attacks that produced an embarrassing disaster for the American army in 1812. William Hull initiated the first stage of the invasion of Canada when he rode to Urbana, Ohio to assume command of an army of three regiments of Ohio militia, one regiment of Michigan volunteers, a regular army regiment and a small contingent of Ohio cavalry. Hull was actually still serving as governor of Michigan territory and he had been a reasonably competent administrator. However, the new brigadier general was in his sixties, in fairly poor health and confronting severe bouts of alcohol induced depression. He was realistic enough about his own limitations to oppose Eustis' proposed appointment of him as commander of a major American army but by the early summer of 1812 Hull was leading an army of 2000 men to Fort Detroit on the Canadian-American border.

When the American army arrived in Detroit on July 5th, 1812, the commanders of the Ohio militia regiments, Colonels Duncan Mc Arthur, Lewis Cass and James Findlay, urged Hull to immediately cross the Detroit River and capture the small British garrison at nearby Fort Molden. The American general delayed the crossing for a week while he ruminated about possible attack plans. When Hull finally ordered his men into Upper Canada, he ignored the expanding garrison at Fort Molden and contented himself with issuing bombastic proclamations to the local farmers and sending scouting parties up the Thames River. Isaac Brock arrived on the scene startled and overjoyed at Hull's lack of action and quickly proceeded to cobble together an army from several companies of the 41st Regiment of Foot, Canadian embodied militia, and Indian auxiliaries serving under the legendary Chief Tecumseh. While Brock scrounged up small numbers of reinforcements, British Captain Charles Roberts led a column of 200 Cana-

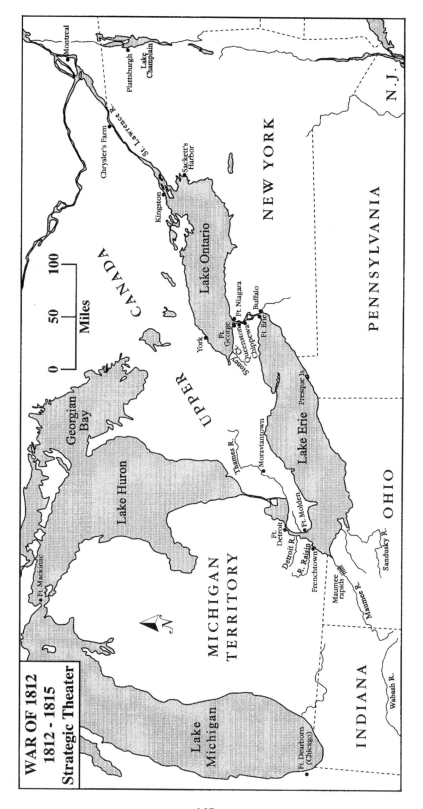

WAR OF 1812
1812 - 1815
Strategic Theater

Montreal

Plattsburgh

Lake
Champlain

N.J.

St. Lawrence R.

Chrysler's Farm

Sackett's
Harbor

Kingston

NEW YORK

Lake Ontario

100

Miles

50

CANADA

PENNSYLVANIA

0

York

Ft. Niagara

Buffalo

Ft.
George

Queenston
Chippewa

Stoney Cr.

Ft. Erie

UPPER

Presque Is.

Georgian
Bay

Thames R.

Moraviantown

Lake Erie

Ft. Mackinac

Lake Huron

Ft. Malden

OHIO

Ft.
Detroit

Detroit R.

Sandusky R.

R. Raisin

MICHIGAN
TERRITORY

Frenchtown

Maumee
rapids

Maumee R.

N

Lake
Michigan

INDIANA

Ft. Dearborn
(Chicago)

Wabash R.

dian woodsmen and 400 Indians toward the American stronghold of Fort Mackinac which commanded the entrance to Lake Michigan. Early on the morning of July 17th Roberts landed on Michilimachinac Island, deployed several cannons within firing range of the fort, and demanded the surrender of American Lieutenant Porter Hanks and his garrison of 61 men. Hanks called a council of his few officers who almost unanimously voted to capitulate before they were massacred by the large number of Indians outside the fort. Hanks hauled down the American flag and marched out of the fort, which provided the British forces with the first of a long series of victories in 1812.

The report of the American surrender at Fort Mackinac further weakened Hull's already shaky resolve as he was convinced that the fall of the northern stronghold would unleash thousands of hostile Indians and Canadian voyagers on his exposed rear. The general promptly called off a planned assault on Fort Molden and ordered his startled subordinates to pull their units back to the Detroit side of the river only 24 days after the "permanent" occupation of Upper Canada had begun. Once Hull pulled his cursing and humiliated soldiers back to Michigan, Isaac Brock sensed that he could accomplish much more than the mere defense of Fort Molden. Brock largely accepted Tecumseh's insistence that the American general was a fool and coward and they agreed to begin offensive operations against Detroit as soon as modest reinforcements could be deployed. When Hull ordered a force of 200 Ohio militiamen to march south to meet and escort a supply convoy coming up toward Frenchtown, Brock and Tecumseh set up an ambush that sent the panicked volunteers running back to Detroit and threatened to cut off the main American supply route. The American general compounded the confusion surrounding his army when he dispatched Colonel James Miller's 4th regular regiment to guard the still threatened supply train. Miller's column was ambushed by a combined force of British regulars and Indians about 14 miles from their destination, but this time the redcoats were facing well trained opponents and the Americans turned the tables and routed the ambushers. However, just as the regulars were ready to continue the pursuit, Hull sent an inexplicable order to call off the action and retreat back to Detroit.

At this point, even though the Americans outnumbered Brock's available forces by 2 to 1, Hull had totally lost command of the situation. While Miller and the Ohio colonels debated relieving their general and then backed down at the last minute, William Hull retired into his headquarters and apparently refused to come out for days at a time. The American army of over 2300 men was now operating without a leader, and Brock was energetically bringing up two small warships and several batteries of artillery to begin a siege of Detroit. Brock's force of 330 regulars, 370 militia and 300 Indians was less than half of the size of his opponent but Brock possessed a seemingly bottomless bag of tricks to considerably even the odds. First, he issued all of his militiamen the spare red coats owned by his regulars and then began to march this newly embellished force of 700 redcoat "regulars" in plain sight of the American defenders. Next he ordered a scout to allow himself to be captured while carrying a fake message that Tecumseh was expecting an additional 5000 Indians to join the "large force" that he already deployed around Fort Molden. Finally he sent couriers to Hull with dire predictions that unless Hull immediately surrendered Detroit, Brock wouldn't be responsible for the actions of the "thousands" of Indians who were already surrounding the American defenses.

General Isaac Brock opened fire on the American defenses on the morning of August 15th, 1812 and William Hull simply lost his ability to issue a military command. The American general didn't bother to deploy his considerable number of artillery pieces along the waterfront where they could challenge the British guns. While the British gunners actually hit relatively few defenders, the Yankee militia were gradually becoming pushed tightly into the narrow confines of the main fort while failing to take positions that could deter an enemy river crossing. When Brock began to cross the river with his British and Canadians, Hull became convinced that he was being attacked by over 10,000 enemy soldiers and he immediately sent out his most trusted aide, his son, to negotiate a capitulation. After a short conference, the Americans agreed to surrender terms and the Stars and Stripes were lowered from one of the key bastions of the American frontier.

A startled but ecstatic Isaac Brock accepted the surrender of 2300 men, 33 cannons and huge numbers of surplus muskets, balls and barrels of powder. He informed Governor General George Prevost "when I detail my good fortune, your excellency will be astonished." The opening American thrust into Canada had produced one of the most embarrassing defeats in the nation's military history at virtually no cost to the British defenders. One of Hull's few rational actions during the whole campaign was to request supporting offensives from the other two American columns, but when Dearborn and Van Rensselaer failed to budge, the American Army of the West was doomed to almost total annihilation, as Brock deftly shuttled his few invaluable regular units from less threatened fronts to the critical Detroit theatre. While the two opposing armies deployed about the same number of regulars, the American army enjoyed an enormous superiority in the size of its militia force. However, the American volunteers seemed to veer between confidence that they could conquer all of Canada without outside assistance and almost mindless panic at the thought of hordes of Indians massacring their entire army. Colonel Miller and the Ohio regimental commanders could probably have forced the inept Hull to resign if they had been more energetic, but they simply stood back and watched the entire campaign degenerate into something between comic opera and tragedy.

The next phase of the "concurrent" American invasion of Canada did not occur until October and proved no more successful than Hull's move across the Detroit River. General Stephen Van Rensselaer had assembled an impressive army of 6000 along the Niagara frontier including almost 1700 regulars under Brigadier General Alexander Smyth. Neither of these leaders of the Army of the Center were professional military men. Van Rensselaer was an ardent Federalist who opposed the war and held this important command merely because of his membership in one of the richest, most influential families in New York. Smyth was a successful Virginia attorney who had developed strong political connections with Jefferson and Madison and was rewarded for his loyalty with a general's commission. Smyth apparently despised Van Rensselaer and considered his regulars as almost a separate army that might or might not be included in a move into Canada.

Van Rensselaer had taken several months to fully deploy his forces, but by mid-October he was ready to launch a two-pronged assault into Canada. A large militia force supported by a small contingent of regulars would form up on the Niagara River directly across from the Queenston ferry terminal on the Canadian shore. The assault force would capture the ferry terminal, seize the high ground on the ridge above, and cut the main road between Lake Ontario and Lake Erie. Smyth's regulars would move out of Fort Niagara and utilize a water approach to come up at the rear of British held Fort George. The capture of this stronghold would eliminate the possible reinforcement of Queenston and allow the Americans to rapidly expand their beach-head along the whole Niagara frontier.

Isaac Brock had arrived in the Niagara theatre after his triumph at Detroit accompanied only by a few companies of British regulars. The British general had gradually assembled a defense force of 1600 British regulars and Canadian militia supplemented by 300 Indian auxiliaries. Brock was convinced that the most likely target of an American assault would be the bastion of Fort George, and he had concentrated over half of his relatively meager force in that fortification leaving the Queenston area only lightly defended. However, in at least one respect the talented British general could continue to rest easily, the great American invasion of the Niagara frontier would not in the least threaten Brock's fortress headquarters.

The initial American assault was scheduled to begin sometime in the pre-dawn hours of October 11, 1812, but this attack never began as the American officer responsible for distributing the oars for all of the American assault craft simply defected to the Canadian side, carrying all of the vital rowing equipment in his escape vessel. Van Rensselaer initiated an urgent search for new oars and the next evening the great attack actually got underway. The American general's cousin, Colonel Solomon Van Rensselaer, led an assault force of 300 regulars and 300 New York volunteers across the rain-swept Niagara River. Solomon Van Rensselaer was wounded almost as soon as he landed on the Canadian shore, but regular army captain John Wool was able to locate a sheep path, which he utilized to lead a small force up the nearby ridge and behind a key British artillery battery which was pounding the American attack force.

While the Americans were attempting their initial landings, Isaac Brock was awakened by the noise from Queenston as he slept in his Fort George headquarters. Brock was convinced that the American landing was merely a feint designed to draw British regulars from the real target. However, Alexander Smyth decided that conditions were not favorable for a crossing by his regulars, so the most powerful units in the American army sat idly in Fort Niagara while Brock started to organize the relief of Queenston. The British commander rushed toward the ferry terminal with a small advance party and arrived in the vicinity of the newly captured British artillery position just as the Americans were attempting to shift the guns to fire on the redcoats. Brock led a frenzied counterattack in which the Americans began to withdraw, but not until a rifleman had killed the redcoat commander. Brock's death was a profound loss to the British defenders, and the incident granted a breathing space to the badly disorganized American attackers. General Van Rensselaer used the lull in the fighting to come across the river on an inspection tour and quickly realized that substantial British reinforcements were on their way up from Fort George.

A small trickle of Americans were continuing to cross the icy river but only Lt. Colonel Winfield Scott's detachment of regular artillerymen seem to have arrived without serious loss. A major wave of 13 assault boats was dispatched from the New York shore and disaster struck quickly. Three boats spun out of control and landed on the Canadian shore into the very arms of British defenders who quickly captured the bewildered occupants. The remaining ten vessels were ripped by enemy fire and soon the ferry terminal was covered with American casualties. Stephen Van Rensselaer rushed back across the river to supervise the embarkation of the large militia units standing along the waterfront but as the volunteers uneasily watched the off loading of dozens of new casualties being ferried back from Canada, they suddenly remembered their constitutional right to refuse service outside of their state. General Van Rensselaer stormed up and down the American lines, but no one would budge. As the American militia debated their citizen rights, the British relief force under General Roger Shaeff was about to crush the now outnumbered invasion force.

Shaeff was far more cautious than his deceased commander, but the new British general gradually tightened a cordon around the American held ridge above the Queenston ferry terminal. The British were able to concentrate nearly 2000 men around less than half as many Yankees who were gradually drifting down to the terminal seeking boats to evacuate them back to New York. Finally, Winfield Scott formed a rear guard with his 140 remaining regulars and the one still-functioning cannon and tried to buy time for the escape of the rest of the assault force. However, virtually no evacuation vessels had been moved across to Niagara River, and the scene down at the ferry terminal degenerated into panic as hundreds of apprehensive militiamen waited in vain for their rescue. Scott's force was ultimately overrun when an overwhelming force of redcoats, militia and Indians flanked his last defense line and the American commander was almost tomahawked when he attempted to surrender his small contingent. Once the American regulars capitulated, the militia units quickly followed suit and General Shaeff found himself in charge of a large haul of prisoners and equipment.

The failed Niagara invasion rivaled Detroit for a one-sided British victory as Shaeff's men counted 958 enemy prisoners and 90 killed and 150 wounded among the American assault force compared to their own loss of only 14 killed and 77 wounded. Almost 5000 American soldiers had never gotten into action including Alexander Smyth's crack brigade of United States regulars. When Von Rensselaer resigned his command after the embarrassing disaster, Smyth replaced the failed Federalist Patroon and promptly evacuated Fort Niagara in the wake of two more aborted attempts to move an assault force into Canada. While the Army of the Center had not suffered quite the same fate as its western counterpart, Van Rensselaer and Smyth had failed to take advantage of a 3 to 1 superiority in manpower to establish a beachhead on the Canadian side of the river. The prospects for the American cause in western New York at the end of 1812 were just as grim as in Michigan territory.

A month after the failed American attack on Queenston, the third prong of the planned invasion of Canada ponderously jerked into action. General Dearborn had mobilized an impressive assault force of nearly 8000 men including 7 regiments of regulars, to move up Lake Champlain and strike across the border to Montreal. The American army confidently moved out from Plattsburgh, New York and soon arrived at the New York-Quebec border, where it collided with an enemy force of 1900 men composed primarily of Canadian militia. Dearborn's army crossed the La Colle River and promptly captured an enemy blockhouse while routing the advance force of defenders. However, the follow up attack soon degenerated into a mob scene as American units became lost in the fog and darkness and individual militia units began firing on other Americans. The disgusted militiamen suddenly decided that it was unconstitutional for them to serve in a foreign country and Dearborn was faced with the choice of continuing to march toward Montreal with his 2000 remaining regulars or heading back to Plattsburgh for the winter. The American general decided that the capture of Montreal wasn't all that important and ordered his men into winter quarters while hoping for better success in 1813.

The great American invasion of Canada had been an abysmal failure, with virtually no success to mitigate the unbroken string of disasters along the frontier. The only morale boosting news that American citizens received during the dismal summer and fall of 1812 came from distant locations in the middle of the Atlantic Ocean as the tiny American navy counteracted the land fiascos with a series of brilliant maritime victories. The nautical successes began in August when Captain Isaac Hull, General Hull's nephew, set sail in the USS *Constitution* and encountered HMS *Guerriere* about 700 miles east of Boston. Captain James Dacre's 49 gun frigate was considered one of the most impressive ships in the Royal Navy, and Dacre was confident that superior British discipline would more than compensate for the five extra guns mounted on his American opponent. However, the Constitution's superb gunners quickly blew apart the British vessel's masts, damaged her hull and killed or wounded most of her crew in less than a half hour. Two months later the USS United States, commanded by Captain Stephen Decatur, confronted the HMS Macedonian about 600 miles west of the Canary Islands. Decatur was able to outmaneuver Captain John Carden's ship and then use his 56 to 49 advantage in cannons to blow the British vessel apart with a series of well aimed long range broadsides that induced the enemy frigate to strike her colors and be sailed into Newport Harbor as a prize of war.

The amazing string of American naval victories continued only three days later when, on October 18, 1812, the sloop of war *Wasp* encountered the British sloop *Frolic* 500 miles off the Virginia coast. The Yankee gunners utilized their amazing gunnery to shoot down 80 per cent of the enemy crew and then add another British ship to the lengthening list of American triumphs. Several days after Christmas, the USS *Constitution* ended the year on a bright note when new captain John Bainbridge attacked the HMS *Java* off the coast of Brazil. *Java* was carrying an impressive list of supplies and passengers including the royal governor of India but the American frigate turned the British vessel into a smoldering wreck within 30 minutes, and His Majesty's governor and his fellow dignitaries were barely able to transfer to the *Constitution* before their vessel slipped under the waves.

The Anglo-American naval confrontations during the opening months of the war were almost as embarrassing to the British government as the land engagements were to Madison's supporters during 1812. The first seven months of the war produced the British capture of three American sloops at a cost of three frigates, two sloops, a brig, an armed transport and over 50 merchant ships lost to the small American navy. This one-sided balance sheet was simply intolerable to a British ministry and public that had grown up listening to stories of the invincibility of English nautical forces. Since the opening of the Napoleonic wars, the Royal Navy had lost only 5 out of 200 engagements with the French navy, which largely matched the British fleet in number of ships and total armament. Now the tiny American navy was accomplishing naval feats that the French squadrons had never been able to attain. As one cabinet minister admitted, "it is a cruel mortification to be beat by these second-hand Englishmen upon our own element." The *Times of London* gloomily reported that "the Americans must be possessed of some secret in the management of their guns, in the fabrication of their powder or in the size and constitution of their shot," and hinted that the Yankees were actually using some kind of secretly developed "super frigate" that was actually a ship of the line in disguise. The London *Chronicle* noted that "every individual in the country must feel humiliated at this succession of disasters which mock our boasted naval superiority." The British Admiralty did not treat the menace of the American navy lightly, as naval officials ordered the immediate construction of a dozen specially designed heavy frigates intended to challenge the Americans on a more even basis. The ministry also ordered British frigates not to cruise alone or to engage, single handed, the larger class of American ships "which though they may be called frigates, resemble line of battle ships." The government ordered all merchantmen sailing the Atlantic to cross in convoys and hoped that 1813 would redress this embarrassing threat to Britannia's mastery of the sea.

While the impressive American naval victories of the early stage of the world salvaged at least some pride in the nation's fighting ability, the unvarnished truth is that in most cases, the year 1812 represented one of the most disastrous periods in United States military history. The string of defeats on the Canadian frontier had dashed all hope for a quick and an easy victory and had exposed the nation to the inevitable wrath of the world's most formidable military power once the conflict with Napoleon had been resolved. A disgusted Ohio senator admitted that "our affairs are in a miserable way, defeated and disgraced, the revenue extravagantly expended, the war not managed at all."

The three pronged invasion of Canada had employed a fairly impressive American assault force of over 17,000 men in three armies with fairly substantial cavalry and artillery support. The United States forces had been opposed by a much smaller enemy army of about 4500 British and Canadian soldiers and 700 Indians. However, while the British army fully utilized almost every one of its limited number of available regulars, the Americans seldom employed their own best trained men to any real advantage. Although the Americans deployed over 4000 regulars in their three invasion columns, only the 300 men of the 5th U.S. Infantry at Detroit and 300 men under Winfield Scott at Queenston saw any actual combat, leaving almost 3500 trained regulars out of combat situations. While the American regulars did not fight because they were never committed to battle, an alarming number of militiamen saw no action because they refused to enter Canada. Only Hull's four Ohio and Michigan regiments seemed eager to engage the enemy on his own ground while over 10,000 volunteers on the Niagara and Lake Champlain fronts added nothing to the American military effort. The result was that the huge American numerical advantage which existed on paper was actually a virtual parity of forces during a battle situation.

The American superiority in manpower was also canceled out by a truly abominable lineup of Yankee generals and leaders. The incompetent secretary of war William Eustis issued orders to the equally ineffective theatre commanders Dearborn, Van Rensselaer and Hull, which virtually guaranteed battlefield disasters. While Captain Zachary Taylor's brilliant defense of Fort Harrison, Indiana and Lt. Colonel Winfield Scott's brave rear guard action on Queenston Heights provided glimpses of more talented and energetic officers on the horizon, the campaign of 1812 was led by antiquated, tired, unimaginative generals who couldn't even match the middle level of British commanders, let alone defeat someone as energetic and talented as Isaac Brock. The British defenders of Canada had inflicted an incredible 40 to 1 casualty ratio on the American invaders as only 20 British Canadians and Indians were killed and an additional 98 wounded in a series of engagements in which United States forces counted over 4000 killed, wounded and captured, with absolutely no territorial gains to show for their efforts. As each side prepared for the campaign of 1813, it was clear that His Majesty's forces held an enormous psychological advantage over their republican adversaries.

CHAPTER 15

# The Battles' Confusion

## Triumph and Frustration in the Campaign of 1813

James Madison and the Republican leaders of Congress were intelligent enough to realize that already diminished public support for war with Great Britain in early 1813 would be even further eroded unless the American armies were soon able to win some clear cut victories over the redcoats. A number of solid, though not spectacular, improvements in the organization of the republic's military forces enabled the United States to enter the second year of the war in a stronger position than the previous summer. Madison initiated a serious search for a replacement for Secretary of War William Eustis, who was increasingly denounced as a total incompetent. One Congressman insisted that "the president must be content with defeat and disgrace in all his efforts during the war if the Secretary remains long in office." The President sounded out Secretary of State James Monroe, Senator William Crawford and General Henry Dearborn about the post, but none of these men were willing to assume the title on a permanent basis. The chief executive finally settled on John Armstrong, a leading Republican politician from New York who was an abrasive, hot-tempered intriguer who was despised by every other member of the cabinet, but was at least a better administrator than his predecessor. Armstrong's appointment produced a modest improvement over Eustis' disastrous tenure but he was still not the ideal person to contend with the potential military might of the United Kingdom.

The changed leadership at the war office was accompanied by a series of bills designed to increase the size of the American army for the upcoming campaign. Recruitment had lagged far behind authorized strength levels during the first months of the campaign. Army pay was low, army life was hard and militia service was far less onerous for Americans who wished to become involved in military activities. A Federalist legislator noted that "money usually can command men, but it will take millions to make soldiers of the happy people of this country; nothing short of a little fortune will induce our farmers and their sons to enter a life which they cordially despise—that of a common soldier."

The Madison administration offered a number of proposals to improve the regular military establishment and most of these measures were enacted into law. One bill provided for raising an additional 22,000 regulars for one year to increase the total authorized strength of the army to 57,000. The legislation offered a bounty of $26 for recruits who would enlist for a 12-month tour of duty. Army pay was raised from $5 to $8 a month for privates which was still lower than the $10 a month expected by unskilled laborers. Long term enlistees would be offered a $16 induction bonus, three months' pay in advance and 160 acres of land after discharge with the option of signing up for three years or the duration of the war. Regulars who were willing to extend their enlistments were offered a bounty of $40 plus additional land bounties after the war. Congress also authorized more officers for each regiment so that a portion of the officer corps could always be involved in recruiting activities.

Congress also endorsed an unprecedented level of naval expansion after savoring the unexpected successes of the naval arm in 1812. An American army officer noted that "our brilliant naval victories have contributed to place that description of force in a proper point of view" and the result was an enthusiasm for naval operations that eventually included President Madison. A grand naval ball held on the USS *Constitution* and attended by the President and cabinet set the stage for a series of bills designed to permit the American Navy to challenge the Royal Navy in at least some limited circumstances. Congress authorized four ships of the line, six new heavy frigates and even began to investigate the feasibility of constructing steam propelled warships. Unfortunately, most of these ships would require extended construction periods and would have virtually no impact on the upcoming campaigns.

The final attempt to provide a more serious challenge to British military superiority focused on a modest restructuring of the officer corps for the next round of engagements. While the Army of the North and the Army of the Center continued to be plagued by incompetent generals in the 1813 campaigns, the energetic William Henry Harrison replaced William Hull in the Northwest and the controversial but effective Andrew Jackson assumed responsibility for most of the southern frontier. Also, talented young officers such as Zebulon Pike and Winfield Scott were given extensive responsibilities for the upcoming campaign and these men were able to partially offset the continued failures of their unsatisfactory superiors.

While this modest list of reforms had mitigated some of the worst problems of the previous year, the road to victory was still beset with far too many obstacles. The series of disasters on the Canadian frontier had finally convinced American leaders that Britain would not simply cave in to United

States demands. One Republican Congressman noted, "I have no belief in an honorable peace till we give them a drubbing on land." Speed was essential because the tide in Europe was now moving clearly in Britain's favor, and once England was freed from the commitments in Europe, substantial reinforcements could be rushed to North America. The American strategy for 1813 thus evolved into a scaled down and somewhat more realistic operational plan in which Quebec and Montreal were initially ignored in favor of an attack on Kingston, Britain's principal naval base on Lake Ontario, York, the provincial capital of Upper Canada and Fort George and Fort Erie which were the key strongholds on the Niagara frontier. Only if these objectives were safely occupied would Lower Canada become an American target. However, before any of these goals were realized, the first order of business was to recapture Detroit in order to eradicate the embarrassment of William Hull's disastrous surrender.

Hull's stunning capitulation had catapulted William Henry Harrison into prominence as the potential savior of the West. Harrison, who was already governor of Indiana, now assumed a position as major general of Kentucky militia and brigadier general of the regular army, in order to take charge of the new forces being mobilized to invade Michigan. Harrison organized an impressive army of 9000 men who were deployed in four separate columns: 2500 regulars and Kentucky militia under Brigadier General James Winchester would move north from a base camp at Fort Wayne; Brigadier General Edward Tupper would follow Hull's old route from Urbana with 1200 Ohio militia; Brigadier General James Leftwich would lead a column of 3500 Virginia and Pennsylvania volunteers down the Sandusky River; while Brigadier General Samuel Hopkins would lead 2000 mounted Kentuckians on a campaign to destroy Indian villages along the Wabash and Illinois rivers.

William Henry Harrison was a dynamic, energetic officer but his initial campaign plan began to disintegrate almost immediately. His four columns were hopelessly out of mutual support distance and could be subject to annihilation by any concentration of British and Indian forces. The constant rain and flooding during the fall and early winter of 1812 disrupted Harrison's supply lines to the extent that almost a third of his force went home because of inadequate food supplies. Nevertheless, Harrison was convinced that the onset of freezing weather would allow him to get closer to Detroit, and soon after the first substantial snowfall he ordered his left wing, Winchester's column, to move north toward the Maumee rapids. Winchester's sullen, almost mutinous troops marched through snow two feet deep, harnessing themselves to sledges to pull their meager supplies and equipment. Men floundered through drifts, skidded on icy spots and then slogged through slush or mud while living on half rations. When they reached their objective on January 10, 1813, Winchester was prepared to let his half starved men recuperate while waiting for Harrison's main force to arrive. However a few days after Winchester's arrival, two refugees from the village of Frenchtown, Michigan staggered into camp with startling news. These messengers informed the American general that British commander Henry Proctor had just ordered a small force of redcoats and Indians to strip Frenchtown of all of its supplies and livestock and these men begged the Americans to march to the town and expel the enemy before the British could act.

Winchester called a hurriedly convened council of war and his subordinate officers all agreed that a relief expedition would be a perfect activity for their bored, mutinous soldiers. Since the messengers had reported that Frenchtown contained over 3000 barrels of flour and ample livestock, a march to the village would also solve most of the American supply problems. The general quickly agreed to dispatch Colonel William Lewis with about 560 of his 1300 available men and at about 2 P.M. on January 18th Miller's men surprised about 250 Canadian militia and Indians and cleared the town after a bloody skirmish in which 67 Americans were killed or wounded and at least 12 Indians were scalped by the Kentucky militiamen.

Two days later Winchester arrived with the rest of his column and he promptly managed to practically invite Proctor to annihilate his command. The American general deployed his Kentuckians throughout the homes in the town so that it would be impossible to concentrate his men on short notice. Winchester then agreed to Lt. Colonel Samuel Wells' demand that the regulars be stationed on a totally undefendable field outside of town because that position was to the right of the militia and regulars always were expected to be to the right of volunteers. Finally, Winchester himself took one look at the unimpressive houses in the town and quickly decided that he would be more comfortable staying at a larger home on the other side of the river almost a mile from his command. The general then solidified his incompetence by failing to post pickets on most approaches to the town.

Henry Proctor was far from the most brilliant general in His Majesty's service, but he was intelligent enough to realize that the American defense of Frenchtown was a disaster waiting to happen. Proctor concentrated every redcoat and Canadian woodsman that he could find at Fort Molden and promptly marched out with 597 men supported by a sledge-drawn artillery battery and about 500 Indians. While the British-led force groped its way toward Frenchtown in a major snowstorm, Winchester's men ate hearty meals, sampled the local whiskey and then promptly fell into a deep sleep. When Proctor's men arrived on the outskirts of the town at 4 A.M. on January 21st, they had come upon an enemy garrison that was possibly even more unprepared for an attack than the Hessians at Trenton. However, Proctor was determined to conduct the assault by the book and he lined his men up in perfect rows and then held off the signal to advance until he had brought up his artillery from the rear of the column. The whole time-consuming ritual was noisy enough that one of the few fully awake defenders saw the redcoats forming in the snow and quickly gave the alarm. This timely warning allowed the Americans to organize a few small groups of riflemen, and a small number of redcoats and Canadians fell before a few well aimed volleys. However, Proctor's Indians were able to slip around both flanks of the incredibly exposed American regular regiment and the bluecoats were soon dropping by the dozen as they were butchered before they could form a defense. Once the right flank crumbled, the Kentuckians in the town were surrounded and outnumbered and the crude rail fences available for cover didn't prevent them from being overwhelmed rather quickly, while Winchester was captured after he crossed the river to rally his men.

Within about 30 minutes, the only serious opposition to Proctor's assault was a concentration of about 400 men under Major George Madison. These men used a large barn and a number of nearby outbuildings to organize a serious threat to the attackers, although the Kentuckians had lost all contact with the rest of the army. After an intensive firefight, Madison was convinced that he had the British on the run when a redcoat officer marched forward with a white flag. The American major assumed that the British were going to surrender and was startled to learn that Winchester had ordered the capitulation of the whole column and the Kentuckians must throw down their arms. Madison was convinced that the Indians meant to slaughter the prisoners and he quickly became engaged in a shouting match with Proctor, claiming that his men would rather die fighting than be butchered after they surrendered. An equally adamant Proctor screamed obscenities at the American major but finally assured him that their lives would be spared. While Madison's men were marched safely off the field, the battle of Frenchtown was about to become the massacre at River Raisin.

Madison's detachment and some other units of American prisoners were marched to Fort Molden under British protection. However, dozens of other American captives, marched off in small groups escorted by the Indians never came anywhere near a British prisoner of war camp. For no apparent reason, while some prisoners were relatively well treated by the warriors, others were simply butchered ten or twelve at a time by Indians searching for more scalps and trophies. The carnage reached a climax back in Frenchtown when 80 wounded Americans left behind because of their wounds were massacred by Indians who either tomahawked them or locked them in houses and then burned them inside. The grisly massacre of prisoners probably added another 200 dead Americans to the 200 men killed in the actual fighting. Another 900 men were marched off as prisoners while 33 men escaped to inform Harrison that his entire left wing had been annihilated. Proctor's casualty list was a relatively modest 24 dead and 161 wounded. The goal of liberating Detroit was as elusive as ever and "Remember the River Raisin" would become a grim battle cry in future American charges.

While Harrison attempted to consolidate the surviving columns of his decimated army, other American forces began to creak into action. Captain Isaac Chauncey, commander of naval forces on Lake Ontario, and General

Henry Dearborn, commander of the Army of the North, had been directed to cooperate in a combined expedition to capture Kingston and York and then support a planned general offensive on the Niagara frontier. When the American leaders received intelligence that the British garrison at Kingston was 6000 men, triple its actual strength, they decided that York presented a much more inviting target. On April 22, 1813 an American expeditionary force sailed from Sackett's Harbor, and five days later the force was ready to disembark four miles from the provincial capital. Since Dearborn was suffering from one of his seemingly endless bouts of illness, real or imagined, General Zebulon Pike was given command of the 1600 man landing force. Pike's column marched to within two miles of the town and then encountered an enemy fort that was defended by about 600 redcoats. The garrison was on the point of being overwhelmed when a powder magazine accidentally exploded, spreading a shower of deadly missiles that killed 40 defenders and 53 Americans including Pike. The attackers eventually captured about half of the garrison and then moved on to destroy two new British frigates that were docked nearby. However, when the Americans entered the town, the relatively inexperienced officers who were now in command lost control of their men, who were now convinced that the magazine explosion had been a deliberate atrocity and proceeded to plunder and loot the community. The Yankees carried off the royal standard of Parliament and then set fire to most of the government buildings while they looted a number of private dwellings. While the Americans had gained a relatively minor military victory, they had more importantly sowed the seeds for the retaliatory burning of their own capital sixteen months later.

Dearborn's expedition across Lake Ontario had gained minor military success but had stripped the vital base at Sackett's Harbor of most of its defenders. British Governor General Sir George Prevost and Admiral James Yeo realized that most of the American army was out on the lake and they organized a force of 800 regulars and several militia units to attack Sackett's Harbor in late May. Brigadier General Jacob Brown had been assigned the unenviable task of holding the American base with only 400 regulars and a scratch force of New York militia. However, while Brown's men were outnumbered, they had plenty of artillery and knew how to use it, and their commander had done an excellent job of deploying his limited forces. Brown set up a three tiered system of defenses highlighted by a front line of Albany Volunteers supported by the cannons and under orders to pick off as many redcoats as possible and then fall back. A second line of regulars and militia was deployed in two small forts that were loaded with heavy guns and protected by a line of felled trees. The final line of entrenchments featured a large ditch backed up by earthworks designed to repel any redcoats that broke through the defensive gauntlet.

Admiral Yeo sighted Sackett's Harbor in the early evening of May 26th and Prevost's men were immediately landed. However, the British naval commander had failed to maneuver his ships in close enough to shore to provide effective fire support to the landing force. The redcoats suffered heavy casualties in their assault on the Albany Volunteers who then retreated back to the second line of fortifications. The British regulars then encountered devastating artillery fire from the American forts but their disciplined advance finally drove the defenders back to the final line of entrenchments. Prevost launched two massive assaults on the American regulars but an even more concentrated employment of cannons smashed both attempts. Meanwhile, Brown had ordered his militia to slip around the enemy flanks and strike the British forces from the rear. This crossfire was simply too much to be long endured and the British general finally ordered his surviving men back to the assault boats with a loss of 48 killed and 211 wounded as opposed to half as many American casualties. Brown became the latest in a series of young American commanders who were gradually mitigating the disasters perpetrated by their incompetent senior generals.

On the same day that Prevost had set sail for his ill-fated attack on Sackett's Harbor, Dearborn's Army of the North had arrived at the western end of Lake Ontario to initiate operations against the British bastion at Fort George. While Dearborn remained in nominal command, he developed another medical indisposition and assigned operational responsibility to Colonel Winfield Scott. Scott, who had been a successful Virginia lawyer, had never received a formal military education although he had read Napoleon's works, and felt that he could rectify some of the mistakes that the Americans had been making in their encounters with the British army. Scott quickly developed an excellent working relationship with naval commander Oliver Hazard Perry and the two rising stars of the American cause developed an excellent assault plan designed to capture the enemy fortress at minimal loss.

Perry reconnoitered the enemy shoreline during the night before the planned attack in order to select the best landing spot and then planted buoys to mark the stations for the American warships during their supporting bombardment. British batteries were located and targeted and ships were designated to silence them before the landing began. Scott and Perry developed a three wave assault in which the first wave would include specially trained riflemen and one small cannon to gain a foothold on the beach, a second wave featuring large forces of light infantry and light artillery designed for mobility and speed, and a final wave of regular infantry and heavier guns that would take longer to disembark. Scott also deployed a force of several dragoon companies several miles above the fort in order to intercept the British garrison as it retreated.

Scott's 4000 man invasion force was opposed by a British garrison of 1200 regulars and 800 Canadian militia commanded by Brigadier General John Vincent. Vincent had received intelligence confirming the probability of an American attack but he had to spread out his defenders in order to contest the landing at a number of points. At 4 A.M. on May 27th, Perry's five warships began to bombard the fort while a number of smaller vessels towed the assault craft onto the beach. The American landing site was defended by 100 Glengarry fencibles who put up a spirited resistance but were overwhelmed by Scott and his first wave. Vincent rushed in a black pioneer company, five companies of the 8th Regiment of Foot and a small force of embodied militia, and this force was able to stall the American advance until they were in turn overwhelmed by the second wave of invaders. The British general now deployed his most elite unit, the 49th Regiment of Foot, and these superb regulars once again contested the enemy advance. However, a combination of effective American naval fire and the landing of the final assault column convinced Vincent that it was better to retreat and save his invaluable redcoats rather than try to hold a doomed fort. The fort's guns were spiked and the powder magazine was blown up just as Scott and his advance elements stormed into the bastion. Just as in the assault on York, the explosion downed the American commander although Scott escaped Zebulon Pike's mortal wound. Scott's incapacitation slowed the American advance so that Vincent was able to retreat toward Queenston. The American blocking force of dragoons was poorly deployed and the redcoats were able to brush past the Yankee horsemen and complete a successful withdrawal, although losing 52 killed, 44 wounded and 262 captured, compared to American losses of 39 dead and 111 wounded.

The American assault force had gained a fairly significant victory, but Scott's injury effectively ended any possibility of following up the initial success. Dearborn re-assumed operational command and promptly managed to turn a hard won victory into a near disaster. The American commander was convinced that Vincent's army was panic stricken and near collapse, so he sent half of his army under General William Winder to dispose of the remaining redcoats while he supervised the repair of the damaged British fort. Winder's pursuit force moved at a glacial pace, and Vincent became convinced that the Americans were ripe for a counterattack. On the night of June 5th, the British general put together a strike force of 700 of his best regulars and marched toward the American bivouac at Stoney Creek. Winder had provided almost no pickets or sentries and the redcoats stormed into the unsuspecting American camp with fixed bayonets. A wild nighttime battle ensued in which Winder blundered into a British unit and was captured, and his second in command suffered the same embarrassment a few minutes later. Vincent returned the courtesy by almost walking into an American unit but he turned away at the last minute, although cut off from the rest of his force. The British deputy commander, Colonel Harvey, seemed to be about the only senior officer on either side who could find the right army to lead and he wisely decided to call off the whole affair after losing 200 men to only 55 American casualties. However, soon after the redcoats retreated, the senior American officer decided that the British would be coming back with reinforcements and pulled the whole force back toward Fort George.

Vincent eventually found his own army and he was given another opportunity to discourage another American advance compliments of Mrs. Laura Secord. Mrs. Secord was married to a sergeant in the Lincolnshire militia which was serving under Vincent and she had remained at their home in Queenston when Dearborn's men had occupied the town. Laura overheard a group of American officers discuss a detailed plan to capture the nearby town of Beaver Dam and she bluffed her way through Yankee lines and ran to the British camp with her vital intelligence. This Canadian counterpart to Lydia Darragh had provided Vincent with a golden opportunity and he promptly set up an ambush for the less than security conscious American column. Lt. Colonel Charles Boerstler led his column of 600 regulars and militia toward Beaver Dam with virtually no advance scouts, flank guards or other warning measures. About a mile from the town the American force was ambushed by 50 redcoats and 500 Indians who quickly forced their opponents into an untenable open field. When the British lieutenant in command used a flag of truce to inform the American commander that "thousands" of Indians were ready to massacre their opponents unless there was an immediate surrender, Boerstler capitulated and added another embarrassing disaster to the annals of this war.

General Dearborn was now panic stricken after two successive British ambushes and he pulled his far larger army back almost to the gates of Fort George. When the American commander reported yet another indisposition to Madison, the President finally relieved him of his command and the Niagara front settled into a months long stalemate which largely nullified the initial triumph at the British fort.

The unsatisfying stalemate on the Niagara shifted American hopes for military success back to the western frontier under William Henry Harrison. Harrison realized that the recapture of Detroit would be useless without American control of Lake Erie, so he reorganized his army while waiting for the energetic Commodore Perry to provide the same excellent support as he had already demonstrated at Fort George. Perry's main base at Presque Isle quickly became a scene of almost manic activity as workers constructed four new vessels and converted five merchantmen to warships. The twenty-seven-year-old commodore was a dynamo who not only organized a furious shipbuilding program but also established fortifications and outposts and supplied them with local militia to frustrate British attempts to capture his shipyards. While Perry had produced nine ships, he was plagued with a shortage of crewmen. Commodore Chauncey had reluctantly sent about sixty men from the Ontario squadron but Perry noted that this contingent consisted of "a motley set of blacks, soldiers and boys," few of whom had maritime experience. Harrison took the commodore's requests for help more seriously and dispatched a hundred of his best sharpshooters and every seaman he could identify in his regiments.

Perry's fleet was tiny by salt water standards, but his nine ships were the key to the future of American ability to exercise some level of naval superiority on the critical Lake Erie front. The flagship *Lawrence* and the brig

*Niagara* each carried a moderately impressive 20 guns but no other American ship carried more than four cannons and three ships carried only one. The American commodore began a sweep of the lake and then proceeded to Put-in-Bay to replenish his food and water supplies. As dawn broke on September 10, 1813, American lookouts observed six British warships moving toward the Yankee fleet. British commander Robert Barclay was an energetic, capable officer who had served under Lord Nelson at Trafalgar and, like his admiral, had lost an arm in battle. Barclay had been harassed into action by British army officers who didn't appreciate that his fleet wasn't yet ready for offensive operations. Barclay had two impressive ships, the *Detroit* and the *Queen Charlotte* with 19 and 17 guns and two more mid-size vessels, the *Lady Prevost* and *Hunter,* deploying 13 and 10 guns, but he was short of ammunition, had very few Marine sharpshooters and was top heavy with long range guns.

As the two fleets closed for battle, Perry ordered his men to raise a large banner with the *Lawrence*'s namesake's famous last words "Don't Give Up The Ship." British naval bands played "Rule Britannia" as the American fleet maneuvered to gain the wind advantage. Perry was determined to use the favorable breeze to move in close and use his superiority in short range guns to blast the British vessels to pieces while American riflemen picked off the enemy crew members. However, while the *Lawrence* closed in toward the Royal Navy ships, Lieutenant Jesse Elliot, the captain of the *Niagara,* simply stood off and fired his limited number of long range guns. The *Detroit* and *Queen Charlotte* trapped the American flagship between their guns and simply smashed the *Lawrence* to pieces, killing or wounding 83 of the 103 crew members. Perry fired one last gun to convince the enemy that the ship wasn't ready to surrender and then scrambled over the side to a waiting longboat. The American commodore dodged musket shots and cannon as he was rowed out to the still undamaged *Niagara*. The flagship and three supporting schooners sailed back into the battle as Perry steered his major ship between *Lady Prevost* and *Chippewa* on one side and *Detroit* and *Charlotte* on the other, with his port guns blasting the first two enemies and his starboard cannons smashing the larger adversaries.

The British fleet was unprepared for this seemingly suicidal maneuver and within minutes the *Detroit* and *Charlotte* were steering so furiously that they ran afoul of one another and were dead in the water. Perry veered to starboard, passed along the other side of the two ships and raked them with additional broadsides. Barclay's only remaining arm was shattered and virtually every British officer on the ship was dead or wounded, and one by one the vessels began to strike their colors. The American commander's courage and coolness under fire combined with superior American short range gunnery and rifle marksmanship had gained a spectacular victory. An exuberant Perry grabbed an old envelope and scrawled an urgent message to Harrison that "we have met the enemy and they are ours, two ships, two brigs, one schooner and one sloop." While the capture of six relatively small ships didn't exactly decimate the Royal Navy, Perry's victory swept the lake of British naval power and produced a nationwide celebration of "every demonstration of joy and admiration that could be exhibited as far and as fast as the roar of cannon and the splendor of illumination could travel."

Perry's pithy message of victory convinced Harrison that the time had come to produce a land version of the victory of Lake Erie and the American general marched north with an army of 6000 men including 3000 regulars, 2000 Kentucky militia and a special corps of 1000 mounted riflemen. As the American column approached Detroit, Henry Proctor prepared to abandon both the Michigan town and Fort Molden; much to the undisguised disgust of Tecumseh, who now realized that his current British counterpart was no Isaac Brock. When the panic stricken British commander began to fall back up the Thames valley, the Indian leader reluctantly pulled his warriors back along with the redcoats. On September 26th, 1813, Harrison arrived at Detroit and raised the Stars and Stripes above the community for the first time in 14 months. While just under half of his force was deployed to garrison the town, the American general, accompanied by new hero Oliver Perry, advanced for a final confrontation with Proctor and Tecumseh.

On October 4th the redcoats and Indians had arrived in the village of Moraviantown, which was now jammed with the army's supply wagons and baggage; if Proctor didn't make a stand he would lose most of his equipment, and Tecumseh encouraged him to turn and fight the advancing Yankees. The position was actually a fairly strong one for the 2000 defenders as the probable battlefield was flanked by the banks of the Thames on one side and a large swamp on the other, forcing any attacker to charge in a fairly confined space. The British general placed his veteran 41st Regiment in a lightly wooded field adjoining the river, deployed Tecumseh's 1000 warriors near the swamp, and positioned his embodied militia and one artillery piece in the center backed up by a mounted force of 20 light dragoons.

General Harrison originally planned a fairly conventional infantry attack toward the center, but Colonel Richard Johnson, commander of the mounted riflemen, convinced him to concentrate a mounted assault on the two flanks where the enemy had no cavalry screen. Harrison readily agreed to this strategy and Johnson led one battalion of horsemen toward Tecumseh's position while the second battalion veered toward the redcoats. The British regulars were startled by the approach of a mounted force that could shoot accurately while in the saddle and the panicked redcoats were quickly scattered. When the Canadian militiamen joined their comrades in retreat, the Indian flank was now open to a mobile attack from both front and rear. Johnson's men, now screaming "Remember the River Raisin," galloped from two directions towards Tecumseh's waiting braves. The first Indian volley dropped perhaps two dozen of the mounted Kentuckians but the warriors' flank was now crumbling. While Proctor hurried from the battlefield in a carriage, Tecumseh directed a desperate last ditch action. Colonel Johnson went down with a bullet wound and his deputy, Colonel William

Whitley, was shot from his horse. According to a number of accounts, the wounded Whitley was confronted by Tecumseh himself and both men fired simultaneously, killing each other. The Indian chieftain's grief-stricken followers pulled their dead leader from the battlefield and retreated up the Thames valley while a group of Kentuckians mutilated the body of a dead warrior they mistakenly believed was the legendary chief.

The battle of the Thames produced a variety of military and political consequences. The British regulars were virtually annihilated with a total of almost 700 killed, wounded and captured, while the Indians lost a large number of warriors and their chief, compared to only 15 killed and 30 wounded on the American side. While Proctor's hasty retreat from his army resulted in a court martial, Johnson and Harrison became national heroes with subsequent political careers in which Johnson rose to the vice-presidency in 1836 while Harrison was elected president in 1840. Finally, the battle near Moraviantown threw the fledgling Indian confederation into disarray and allowed the Americans to establish a substantial beachhead on Canadian soil. Unfortunately for American hopes, this victory was the high point of 1813, with the remaining months bringing news of one disaster after another to the United States cause.

While the men serving under Harrison soon realized that their general was capable of directing a major victory, the soldiers on the Champlain front underwent the less congenial experience of having their incompetent commanding general replaced by two equally unsatisfactory generals. The newly retired Henry Dearborn was replaced by General James Wilkinson as theatre commander, while General Wade Hampton was assigned to direct the main field army based in Plattsburgh, New York. Wilkinson was basically a confidence man in uniform, who had no loyalty except to himself and was always walking a fine line between self-interest and treason. He had managed to bamboozle both John Adams and Thomas Jefferson into giving him major commands and was military commander of New Orleans when he received Secretary of War Armstrong's summons to "come quickly" to Washington. Wilkinson managed to take 83 days to arrive in the nation's capital and then began an equally leisurely pace to his new headquarters at Sackett's Harbor.

Armstrong assigned command of the main field army in the region to Wilkinson's bitter enemy, General Wade Hampton. Hampton was one of the wealthiest planters in America, a power in the Republican Party with a hair trigger temper, thin skinned sensibility and a rigid code of personal honor. The general was convinced that the new theater commander was a corrupt charlatan who was beneath the contempt of a real gentleman. The mutual loathing between the two leaders split the officer corps of the Army of the North into rival cliques, who seemed more interested in attacking one another than the British army. Armstrong had ordered Wilkinson to move up the St. Lawrence to threaten Montreal, while Hampton was expected to march north from Plattsburgh with 4000 men to combine with his rival's 7000 man column and then assault the enemy bastion.

Hampton's army was the first force to arrive at the Canadian border when his men crossed the Chateaugay River from Four Corners, New York. Sir George Prevost was determined to slow down the American advance while he concentrated his forces for the defense of Montreal and he dispatched a largely French-Canadian militia force of 800 men under Lt. Colonel Charles de Salaberry to harass Hampton's column. While the Americans were largely occupied with moving their artillery and supply wagons into Canada, the highly mobile inhabitants hit the Yankee advance units and sent them reeling back into New York in panic. Hampton had suffered only minor losses, but he was convinced that he was facing 8000 hardened regulars and pulled his entire army back toward Plattsburgh.

While Hampton's troops were marching back to their winter quarters, Wilkinson's men were moving in the opposite direction toward Montreal. Apparently, the commander of the Northern army had made many of his major military decisions under the influence of opium and this expedition was no exception. Willkinson kept ordering changes of direction and moves along the wrong roads while he battled with any subordinate who dared to question his judgement. Finally, on November 12th he sent General John Boyd's advance force of 2000 men into Canadian territory near a place called Chrysler's Farm. Boyd's men were slogging through knee deep fields of snow when they stumbled upon a smaller British force which had set up an impressive series of breastworks around the farm. A series of poorly coordinated American assaults cost Boyd over 400 men, compared to British losses of fewer than 170, and the column commander ordered his men back across the St. Lawrence. Wilkinson exploded into a rage in which he threatened to court-martial Boyd for not continuing his attack, then decided to arrest Hampton for not meeting his army, and finally condemned Armstrong for lack of additional support. The theatre commander then decided that he had enough scapegoats and promptly pulled his army back into winter quarters. The American soldiers began a winter encampment that featured inadequate quarters, bad food and poor uniforms, while Armstrong relieved both Wilkinson and Hampton of their commands and simply wrote off the whole northern theater as a hopeless disaster, unless and until the Secretary of War could maneuver himself into the actual field command of the army. Wilkinson and Hampton were certainly incompetent, but even a more talented general would have faced almost insurmountable challenges in any march on Montreal. Prevost had deployed a defense force that was huge by War of 1812 standards, with 6000 regulars, 12,000 militia, several Royal Marine rocket companies and a fleet of warships deployed around the city. An outnumbered, poorly supplied American army would have been easy prey for the redcoat defenders.

Wilkinson's botched northern campaign not only failed to capture Montreal, it also stripped the entire Niagara frontier of the regulars needed to hold the increasingly more energetic redcoats at bay. Brigadier General George McClure had been assigned the unenviable task of holding the American beachhead on Canadian soil with only tiny contingents of United States regulars. For example, while the British garrison of Fort George had included almost 2000 redcoats, McClure could spare only 60 bluecoats to hold the fortress. When McClure received intelligence that the enemy was ready to launch a counterattack on Fort George, the American general ordered his men to evacuate all of the Canadian communities in proximity to the fort. The American withdrawal produced some of the most senseless violence of the entire war as McClure's men burned the entire town of Newark while turning the inhabitants out into the snow on only two hours' notice and then proceeded to devastate the important community of Queenston in the same way. This savage brutality served no military purpose and merely enraged the Canadians enough to enlist in militia units in large numbers.

The British authorities were now determined to avenge the string of American plundering and arson incidents from York to Queenston, and their first objective was to expel the Yankees from their main position at Fort Niagara. On the frigid night of December 18th, Canadian sea fencibles ferried a 600 man assault force from Burlington Heights to the American shore and Colonel John Murray led his men to the outer defenses of the American fort. The British scouts had captured a dozing American picket and threatened to kill him unless he divulged the night's password. This vital information allowed the redcoats to gain entry into the works and they began to bayonet dozens of the sleeping garrison. Ten minutes of wild fighting resulted in 65 Americans killed, 14 wounded and 344 captured, compared to a minuscule British loss of 6 killed and 5 wounded. The crowning embarrassment to the American defenders was that the garrison commander, Captain Leonard, was found drunk and virtually unconscious in a house 2 miles from the fort.

The capture of Fort Niagara signaled the beginning of a series of violent punitive raids by redcoats, fencibles and Indians. Hours after the capitulation of the fort, a force of 50 redcoats and 500 Indians under General Riall crossed into New York and burned six towns to the ground. Five days after Christmas, Riall returned with 1500 men and burned Buffalo, after having routed 1200 American militia. By New Year's Eve, 1813, an area twelve miles wide and thirty-six miles long had been devastated, with over a dozen towns reduced to cinders smoking in the snow. The smoldering, burned out ruins along the Niagara frontier were hardly conducive to promoting American optimism concerning the upcoming campaign of 1814, and even some normally optimistic leaders were becoming convinced that the wrath of the British Empire would soon be truly fearsome.

The campaign of 1813 wasn't quite as disastrous to American arms as the previous year's engagements, but the United States had accomplished very little in the second year of the war. The young republic had recaptured

Detroit, neutralized the Indian menace on the Northwest frontier, gained a foothold in Upper Canada and secured control of Lake Erie. However, most of Canada was no closer to being American territory than 18 months earlier, the looting and burning of Canadian towns had left a virulent anti-American sentiment among many residents, and the United States was increasingly vulnerable to British attacks along the coast.

American senior generals had still exhibited very little skill in fighting battles or conducting campaigns, so that the relatively small number of victories was attributable to much younger officers such as Scott, Perry and Jacob Brown. The successful engagements at Fort George, Put-in-Bay, Moraviantown and Sackett's Harbor were more than outweighed by embarrassing defeats at Frenchtown, Stoney Creek, Beaver Dam, Chateaugay, Chrysler's Farm and Fort Niagara. A survey of the major battles of 1813 reveals a total American casualty list of about 3000 men compared to fewer than 1800 enemy soldiers lost. There were still far too many British ambushes and surprise attacks, too many drunk American leaders sitting in a stupor while their command was defeated and too many cases of militiamen disappearing at a moment of crisis. However, while the poor leadership qualities of American generals presented a major impediment to victory, two other factors provided even more reasons for concern in the upcoming year.

First, the American public in 1812 had been able to rationalize the embarrassing land defeats with a number of spectacular naval victories. However, once the British ministry and naval command began to take the American maritime threat seriously, the Royal Navy virtually swept the United States Navy from the ocean. Heavily reinforced British squadrons were able to defeat *Chesapeake*, blockade *Constitution* and *Congress* in Boston, pen *United States* and *Macedonian* in New London, bottle up *Adams* in Washington, and sink most of the smaller warships in a series of engagements. American naval power in the Atlantic was eventually reduced to *Enterprise*, *President* and *Essex* and while any one of these ships was probably superior to a single opponent, these vessels were now in danger of facing odds of 100 to 1 in overall naval strength. The American salt water navy had been virtually blockaded out of existence by the end of 1813 and whatever offensive capability remained was confined to the Great Lakes.

The advent of total British naval dominance in late 1813 was accentuated by a second looming crisis—the winding down of the interminable Continental war. Even a military genius of the caliber of Napoleon was unable to resurrect annihilated armies indefinitely and the French emperor was almost out of miracles by the winter of 1814. The British government now foresaw the very real probability that large numbers of army units and ships could soon be re-deployed to North America to unleash retribution against the impudent Yankees. The prospect for the upcoming year wasn't particularly bright for James Madison and his shrinking circle of enthusiasts, as the young republic prepared to meet a rapidly expanding British war machine.

CHAPTER 16

# The Perilous Fight

## *The Decisive Campaign of 1814*

*T*he final year of the War of 1812 opened in the shadow of monumental changes in the balance of power in Europe. The battle of Leipzig had forced Napoleon to retreat into France with the Allies in hot pursuit. At the same time, a British army under the Duke of Wellington had smashed the last French army in Spain and was marching toward Paris from the south. On March 31, 1814, the allies entered the City of Light and eleven days later Napoleon abdicated and began his exile to Elba. For the first time in more than a decade, Europe was at peace and the United States was now alone in the field against a militarily triumphant British empire. Even the most optimistic Republican supporters of war with Britain began to realize that this already unsatisfying conflict might soon turn into a disaster for the young republic.

The British government expected to deploy more than 40,000 regulars in North America by the end of 1814, and a substantial number of Britons were determined to utilize that force to punish the Yankees for their treacherous declaration of war in a moment of supreme crisis for the empire. Admiral Sir Alexander Cochrane articulated much of British public opinion when he insisted, "I have it much at heart to give America a complete drubbing before any peace is made." The *Times* of London declared that it was time for Britain to "chastise the savages, for such they are, in a much truer sense than the followers of Tecumseh or the Prophet."

However, while the United Kingdom held substantial advantages in the much greater experience of their regular army, total control of the seas and the psychological boost of recently defeating Napoleon, the United States was far from helpless. The Americans controlled Lake Erie, and its supply lines to the west were shorter and less exposed than the enemy. The battle of the Thames had destroyed Tecumseh's confederacy and greatly reduced the number of Indian auxiliaries willing to serve with the British army. The improvement of army pay and benefits was gradually increasing the size of the American regular forces which would reach over 45,000 by the end of the year. Thus the basic American strategy for the upcoming campaign was to retake Fort Mackinac, drive the British from the Niagara frontier, seize enemy strongholds on Lake Ontario, and then negotiate a favorable peace before the British could marshal their forces for a massive offensive against the United States.

The spring of 1814 was a period of reorganization and reinforcement for the two contending armies. The British ministry dispatched 14 of Wellington's regiments to North America and began making preparations for far more additional troops to be transported during the summer. The United States Congress increased the size of the authorized regular army to 55 regiments and expanded the number of generals to 8 major general positions and 16 brigadiers. As the incompetent leaders of earlier campaigns resigned or were dismissed, energetic, talented men such as Andrew Jackson, George Izard and Jacob Brown received a second star, while Alexander McComb, Winfield Scott and Edmund Gaines were among the new brigadiers.

The basic American operational plan for 1814 was to send Jacob Brown's reinforced army to capture Burlington Heights and York in concert with Commodore Isaac Chauncey's naval squadron. This expedition would in turn allow columns from Sackett's Harbor and Plattsburgh to invade Canada from additional points, thus spreading the British defenders into a dangerously thin line—Brown's assault force was assembled around two brigades of American regulars: 14000 men under Winfield Scott and 1000 soldiers led by General Eleazor Ripley, supplemented by additional units of Pennsylvania and New York militia under Colonel Peter Porter. The Niagara offensive was originally expected to commence in May, but Commodore Chauncey exasperated his army counterparts by constantly postponing the date at which his fleet could lend support. Scott utilized the delay to fine tune the regiments under his command into a superb fighting force. He emphasized good sanitation, tight discipline and good food as he brought his men to a peak of efficiency, with their only minor setback consisting of the gray uniforms they were forced to use when the expected consignment of new blue coats was diverted to Sackett's Harbor.

On July 3rd, 1814, the complicated American offensive was initiated. Several regiments of New York militia moved north from Buffalo and feigned an attack across the Niagara against Queenston, to draw off part of the Fort Erie garrison. The ruse worked perfectly and Brown used the diversion to push his main force against the British fort, which had been stripped of all but 137 of its defenders to meet the anticipated attack on Queenston. The heavily outnumbered garrison surrendered quickly and Brown pushed his force of about 3000 men toward the Chippewa River, as a first stop on the way to a link up with Chauncey's fleet and an assault on York, Ontario. Meanwhile, Brown's British counterpart, Lieutenant General Sir Gordon Drummond, was rapidly assembling detachments from all over

Ontario while he dispatched his deputy, Major General Phineas Riall, with just under 2000 regulars to confront the Americans on the Chippewa River.

Brown's scouts spotted the redcoat column deploying on the far side of the river, and the American soldiers spent Independence Day constructing a strong defensive position along a ditch which fronted the open plain that led to the Chippewa. When the enemy made no move to attack on July 4th, Brown started making plans for a further advance and Scott promised his brigade a dress parade before they started another march. While Scott was lining his men up for the grand review, Riall's redcoats slipped across the river and smashed into Porter's militia, which was the weak link of the American position. A spirited bayonet charge drove off the New Yorkers and Pennsylvanians, and Riall assumed he was confronting another militia unit when he encountered Scott's gray-coated men. Riall quickly found out otherwise when the American brigade advanced toward the redcoats, alternately stopping to fire and then moving forward to within sixty yards of the enemy force. The British commander exclaimed "those are regulars by God!" and hastily responded to the charging graycoats.

Winfield Scott's force was still somewhat outnumbered, but his well drilled men formed into a shallow U formation that caught the British troops in a devastating crossfire that shattered two enemy regiments within about five minutes. The surviving redcoats were able to reform and open a volley fire until Brown rushed in his second brigade, which hit the enemy flanks just as Scott ordered a bayonet charge on the British center. Riall was smart enough to sense a major calamity brewing and he quickly pulled his own well drilled troops back across the river before the American trap was fully sprung. Riall had saved most of his army, but left behind 148 killed, 221 wounded and 41 captured, compared to an American loss of only 44 killed and 224 wounded.

The first conventional slugging match between two relatively equal forces of regulars on an open field had produced a clear cut American victory. Brown now waited for a message from Commodore Chauncey that his squadron was in position to support an attack on Burlington Heights with a subsequent thrust at York. However, 19 days passed with no dispatches from Chauncey while scouts brought back alarming news of a massive buildup of British forces in the area. General Drummond received continuous updates on Brown's advance into Ontario from local citizens, and he began to devise a strategy that could annihilate the American army in one complex operation. The British commander dispatched one army across the Niagara River into New York to threaten Brown's supply depots, ordered a second column to cut off the American line of retreat at the Chippewa River, and marched a third army from Burlington Heights to either confront an enemy advance or strike him in the rear if he pulled back toward New York.

Jacob Brown began to receive intelligence of the British incursion into New York and he immediately dispatched Scott with part of the army to Queenston, in hope of drawing the redcoats back into Ontario and away from his precious magazines. Scott's column spent all day on July 25th marching back toward the Chippewa, but at 6 P.M. the startled Americans came face to face with a redcoat army that was heading for the vital crossroads of Lundy's Lane in order to cut off any enemy move toward New York. British and American units raced to occupy the ridges around the crossroads and the redcoats won the race, quickly placing almost 2000 men on a hill that would dominate the upcoming battle.

The energetic Scott dispatched messages to Brown reporting the emergence of this new threat and then ordered his outnumbered men to take the enemy hill before the redcoats could entrench their position. Major Thomas Jessup's 25th Regiment was able to march through a wooded area and hit a Canadian militia battalion on its flank, while the British regulars in the center were distracted by the main American assault. Jessup's men smashed through the fencibles and then confronted and captured General Riall, who was directing his regulars into position for a counterattack. However, Riall's deputy rushed in additional units and Jessup's flanking move was parried.

Scott continued to organize a succession of American assaults on the ridge but they were thrown back when newly arrived British artillery units cut down dozens of advancing bluecoats. At this point, just as darkness was setting in, Brown arrived with the rest of the American army, which was still being pursued by Drummond's more numerous main column. When the American rearguard deployed to meet Drummond's expected assault, the British general abandoned that plan and swung his men around the enemy flank so they could reinforce their comrades on the Lundy's Lane ridge, while assuming that additional units still marching from Burlington Heights could threaten Brown's rear the next morning.

The American position at nightfall on July 25th was increasingly perilous. A British force that outnumbered them 3 to 2 now held the key position on the battlefield, while another British column could threaten their rear when they arrived sometime the next morning. Brown would have to either smash through the British lines in order to march back toward the Niagara River, or pin down the redcoats long enough to allow the Americans to maneuver around the ridge and retreat before the enemy reinforcements arrived. This desperate situation produced a rare night battle, in which Scott's brigade was finally able to capture the vital ridge and then throw back a succession of British counterattacks by turning the captured enemy artillery on the redcoat attackers. However, during the night Scott went down with a severe wound and then Jacob Brown was hit by the staff of a misfired British rocket and had to be carried from the ridge. Soon after these events, Drummond was somewhat less severely wounded and his subordinate pulled the redcoats back from the ridge to regroup and reorganize.

The injured Drummond now began to plan an alternate strategy based on the expected arrival of his reinforcements, when an excited aide informed the startled general that the Americans had abandoned the hill. Apparently the American defenders had exhausted their ammunition and water and

Brown ordered them back to their supply wagons to resupply and rest. When the American commander realized that the decimated British were too exhausted to launch an early attack, he ordered his men to march to Fort Erie, allowing the surprised redcoats to re-occupy the ridge at daybreak.

The battle of Lundy's Lane produced both a confused engagement and a disputed outcome. Drummond had constructed an excellent trap with a numerically superior force holding the high ground against the Americans, while an advancing column threatened the enemy army from the rear. However, once Brown's forces were able to push the redcoats off the hill and inflict such heavy casualties that the American escape route could not be blocked, the Americans could rightly claim a tactical victory, as the British plan to annihilate them had failed. On the other hand, Drummond's energetic actions had blunted the American advance into Ontario and forced Brown to retreat to a small foothold around Fort Erie. The bloody engagement had resulted in a British casualty list of 81 killed, 562 wounded and 233 captured, while the Americans had suffered comparable losses of 171 killed, 573 wounded and 117 captured. While Brown hurriedly organized his survivors to challenge Drummond's obvious move toward Fort Erie, the focal point of the conflict shifted toward the American capital.

While most of the diversion of Wellington's regiments to North America was intended to deflect American threats toward Canada, the British government was also determined to carry the war to the enemy heartland to teach the Yankees a well deserved lesson and make them more amenable to accept a peace treaty largely on His Majesty's terms. President Madison and Secretary of War Armstrong were well aware of a British threat to the Mid-Atlantic region, but they were convinced that Philadelphia, New York or Baltimore were far more likely targets than the relatively small capital city. For example, Baltimore was a huge seaport, held a major naval base that was building the newly authorized capital ships and steam frigates, and would provide a huge cash ransom if it was spared from the torch. On the other hand, Washington city, which would ordinarily become the primary military target in a European war, was little more than a swampy hamlet that happened to contain a few government buildings.

General William Winder, who had recently been exchanged after capture, was appointed to command a newly authorized 10th military district which included Baltimore and Washington. Winder was a mediocre leader who had been appointed to this critical post mainly because he was a cousin to the governor of Maryland, who would furnish most of the men to defend the region. Armstrong was so convinced that Washington would never become a serious enemy objective that he had only stationed 380 of the army's 40,000 regulars in a position to protect the capital. Thus Winder was forced to rely on a motley collection of beached sailors, Marine gunners, volunteer cavalry and local militia units to defend the capital against Wellington's confident veterans. Vice Admiral Sir Alexander Cochrane, commander of British naval forces in North America, was determined to burn the American capital in

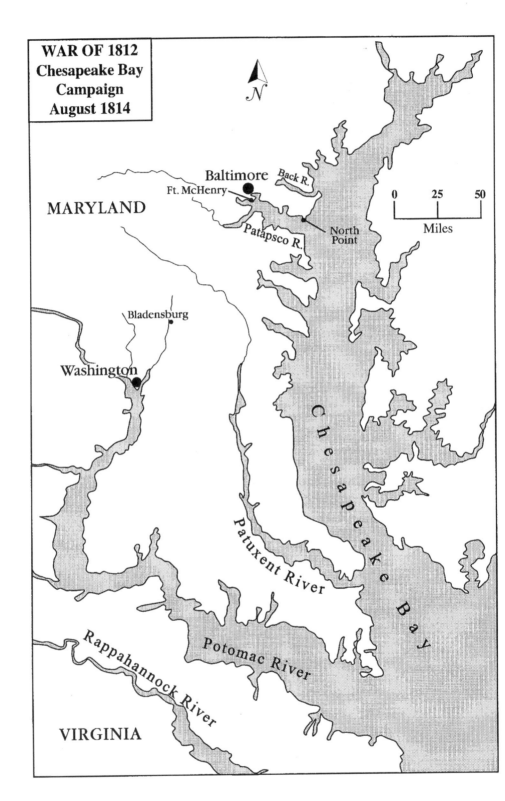

WAR OF 1812
Chesapeake Bay
Campaign
August 1814

Baltimore
Ft. McHenry
Back R.

MARYLAND

North
Point

Patapsco R.

0    25    50

Miles

Bladensburg

Washington

Chesapeake Bay

Patuxent River

Potomac River

Rappahannock River

VIRGINIA

retaliation for American outrages in Ontario, and this able, imaginative, bloodthirsty leader had been provided with an impressive array of land and naval forces.

Cochrane menaced the American coast with a fleet that was far larger than the combined strength of the United States Navy. His fleet of almost 100 warships included six ships of the line, twenty-one frigates and a large array of troop transports containing four veteran regiments commanded by Major General Robert Ross, one of Wellington's deputies during the Peninsular War. On the morning of August 15th, 1814, Cochrane dropped anchor near the head of Chesapeake Bay and waited for the arrival of Admiral Sir George Cockburn's fleet which would provide an additional 15 major warships and a brigade of Royal Marines. The next morning Sir George came aboard Cochrane's flagship *Tonnant* and the two admirals sat down to lunch with Ross and his deputies as they reviewed the objectives of the upcoming campaign. Cockburn agreed with his superior that Baltimore was the more important military target, but he had a personal score to settle in Washington, as it was the home of former Englishman Joseph Gale's notoriously anti-British *National Intelligencer,* which had taken particular delight in comparing Sir George to Attila or Genghis Khan. Cockburn was able to convince Cochrane and Ross that a raid on Washington would provide a huge psychological victory for the British army and navy, and he was even able to convince his superior that Sir George should accompany Ross on the expedition.

The British commanders agreed on a plan in which the fleet would enter the Patuxent River and land Ross' army at a location that would encourage the Americans to believe that the redcoats were headed for Baltimore. After the Yankees had deployed their forces toward that city, Ross would suddenly change direction, advance and capture the crossroads village of Bladensburg and then march on the American capital. As the late summer sun rose on August 14th, Ross led five infantry regiments, a Royal Marine brigade, and a Royal Artillery rocket regiment toward the outskirts of Bladensburg. The British force of 4400 men was marching toward an American army that contained 6000 men but which was in a state of tactical chaos. Winder had dispatched General Tobias Stansbury to Bladensburg with several regiments of Maryland militia. Stansbury led a force that had no combat experience and little military training, but the general had at least a rudimentary concept of deploying troops and placed his men in positions that might have given the enemy serious problems when they attempted to cross the Eastern Branch and advance toward Washington.

The first step leading to the infamous "Bladensburg Races" occurred when Secretary of State James Monroe arrived on the scene and promptly began to redeploy the startled Marylander's men. Monroe had just about finished placing every unit in a position where they had no concealment and no ability to support one another when Madison and Armstrong arrived, and the Secretary of War began to order the men into even worse positions while he unsuccessfully argued with the President over who should assume field command. Finally, Winder arrived and tinkered with the deployment by pulling the reserves so far back that they could never hope to support the front lines. The American defenders were now poorly deployed, had no idea what they were supposed to do when the British came, and were serving under a general who had no real reserves, no command post, and no rational plan of what to do when the British attacked.

At about one o'clock on the afternoon of August 24th the advance column of redcoats marched into the village of Bladensburg and observed their poorly concealed opponents across the stream. One officer noted "most of the American troops seemed like country people who would have been more appropriately employed in attending to their agricultural occupations than in standing with muskets in their hands." The men of Colonel Thornton's advance brigade began removing their knapsacks and prepared to open a battle that has become one of the most infamous, and somewhat misunderstood, chapters in American military history.

The veterans of Wellington's campaign began to advance across Bladensburg bridge when they were hit by Stansbury's artillery and riflemen. The combination of cannon balls and rifle shots staggered the redcoat line and might have even turned the tide of the battle if the American gunners hadn't forgotten to bring along the far more lethal canister shells that they had left behind in their supply wagons. Thornton's men were so bloodied from their first assault that they were pulling back across the bridge when a startled Ross arrived with the rest of the army. The British commander quickly ordered a heavily reinforced assault on the American left flank while the enemy artillerymen and sharpshooters were kept busy from the fire of the rocket launchers. The howling rocket attack from over 60 British launchers completely overshot the mark, but when they started landing in the American rear, entire militia regiments simply evaporated, although not a single man was hit by the noisy weapons.

While the main part of the army stampeded in panic, the British flank assault began edging around the American front line, which forced the artillerymen and riflemen to either withdraw or surrender. Madison now realized that the redcoats were preparing one of their terrifying bayonet assaults and the president and cabinet quickly began their own retreat, leaving fragments of the American army to delay the oncoming British advance. The small force of American regulars began an energetic delaying action as the last barrier to British capture of Washington was being strengthened. Commodore Joshua Barney of the United States Navy had arrived at the battle site with a battery of five large guns manned by Marines and supported by a force of naval "flotilla men." While most of the rest of the American army simply vanished, Barney placed his big guns astride the main road to Washington and deployed his 500 men to counter an overwhelming force of redcoats. Ross swept through the last line of American infantry and threw virtually his entire army at the front and flanks of the

Yankee battery. The Marine gunners and naval infantry dropped scores of redcoats and in turn were bayoneted at their guns with the fuses still lit. As the American line was being overwhelmed, Barney and a small rear guard held open an avenue of retreat until the commodore went down with several bullet and bayonet wounds. As Barney dropped to the ground still holding his sword, Cockburn, in a surprising act of chivalry, saved his fellow mariner from redcoat bayonets, paroled him on the spot, and ordered British sailors to carry him to the rear for medical treatment while congratulating him on his courage. As the rest of the American army vanished in the distance, Ross rested and reorganized his men and prepared for the march into Washington.

The battle of August 24th almost immediately acquired the less than heroic title of the "Bladensburg Races," but the British triumph was not nearly as one sided as it would initially seem. Ross lost about 500 men in the assault, including 18 of his most experienced officers. This loss effectively reduced his total strength by almost 15% while the American casualty list was a far smaller 26 killed and 51 wounded. Even a moderately large force of American regulars might have inflicted an embarrassing defeat on the advancing British column, which might have been forced to withdraw back to the supporting fleet. The highly publicized American advantage in total numbers is ludicrous when one considers that Ross deployed about 10 British regulars to every American bluecoat on the scene. The British commander had the advantage of commanding a far larger number of regulars against an opposing army that was woefully mishandled, poorly deployed and under the command of not one but a group of incompetent commanders. The military expertise of Madison, Monroe, Armstrong and Winder is almost laughable and would have been a farce if it wasn't for the number of American and British killed in the battle. Ross had gained his open road to Washington, but a battle in which the winning army lost seven men to every casualty in the losing force would hardly qualify as an epic triumph.

After a pause to allow the redcoats to rest, Ross and Cockburn mounted their horses and led two regiments of regulars into one of the most controversial episodes in the history of Anglo-American relations. The British column arrived in the partially abandoned American capital around dusk and while Ross searched for an official to negotiate a formal surrender of the city, Cockburn and a number of officers entered the President's mansion. The British raiders sat down to a meal that had been prepared for a scheduled cabinet meeting, helped themselves to a number of souvenirs, and called in demolition experts to burn the building. The admiral and his retinue then proceeded in turn to the Capitol building, the Treasury, the War and State Department offices and the Patent Office, destroying all but the latter when the British born superintendent of patents convinced Cockburn that the building contained large amounts of private property. This gleeful but relatively disciplined party also burned a private home that had sheltered snipers and was on its way to torch the Navy Yard when the

American commander of the facility burned the installation ahead of them. Cockburn then enjoyed his own personal revenge when he arrived at the *National Intelligencer* office and wrecked the printing presses and gutted the building while telling his men to make special note that all of the typeset with the letter "c" received special attention. Less than 48 hours later the 300 man occupation force marched back down the Bladensburg road and returned to the fleet, leaving behind a smoldering national capital.

The British destruction of public buildings in Washington became one of the most controversial elements of the entire war. While a number of Federalist papers blamed Madison for the disaster, most public opinion was focused on Armstrong, who had failed to provide adequate regular forces to defend the capital and thus saw his career effectively ended. A number of European papers condemned the burning of Washington and even the *London Statesman* noted that "the Cossacks spared Paris but we spared not the capital of America," although the Prince Regent ordered three successive days of artillery salutes to commemorate the "brilliant success." A review of the British action from the perspective of almost two centuries may offer a more complex judgement. On the one hand, the American plundering or destruction of Canadian towns such as Newark, Queenston and York was reprehensible and totally unjustified in a military sense. However, the looting and burning of public buildings in the provincial capital of Upper Canada was perpetrated under rather different circumstances than the sack of Washington. The commander of the American expeditionary force and scores of his men had just been killed in what the Americans (mistakenly) thought was a deliberate atrocity on the part of the defenders when the British powder magazine exploded. The surviving American officer in command had not yet consolidated his authority when an apparent minority of soldiers began plundering without orders. However, the burning of the White House, Capitol and other public buildings was an officially condoned operation encouraged by the British government when peace negotiations were already underway, and was under the personal supervision of a British admiral. The British had already retaliated for American plundering in Canada by burning over a dozen communities in New York, including Black Rock and Buffalo. A far more sensible approach would have been to gain the enormous psychological victory of capturing the enemy capital and then sparing the city as a sign of goodwill in ongoing negotiations. Instead, the British ministry used the burning of Washington as a terror weapon which merely backfired when large numbers of Americans became determined to avenge this insult and the American negotiating team dug in its heels and refused to be intimidated by the intended British display of awesome force. While the British government might have been justified in retaliating for the American destruction of the Royal Palace and Houses of Parliament, the burning of much of Washington was an enormous over-reaction to the admittedly needless plunder of a provincial capital. The destruction of the White House and Capitol would long delay the onset of more cordial relations between the two English speaking societies and only British willingness to spare most private dwellings prevented the rancor from this event lasting for generations.

Robert Ross did not have much time to savor his triumph as his naval counterparts began badgering him to duplicate his victory by capturing Baltimore. Admiral Cochrane was obsessed with the possibility of almost completely destroying the Maryland metropolis and he encouraged Ross and Cockburn to be far less humane in their treatment of what he considered a nest of pirates. The British naval commander offered the army commander a brigade of sailors to replace his casualties at Bladensburg and energetically prepared a detailed battle plan for the operation. The British raiders were opposed by General Samuel Smith of the Maryland militia, who essentially superseded Winder as commander of American defenses in the region. While Winder was lazy, slow and not particularly intelligent; Smith, a professional banker in civilian life, was the epitome of the best characteristics of a citizen-soldier. Smith utilized a combination of his military experience during the Revolutionary War and his vast business expertise to demand and receive proper Federal support for the defense of Baltimore.

Naval heroes Oliver Perry, David Porter and John Rogers were dispatched with naval infantry and Marines to add invaluable expertise in artillery emplacement and deployment of riflemen. Several hundred regulars were assigned to support Major George Armistead's garrison at Fort McHenry, and soon the fort was crammed with 1000 men and 57 guns to challenge a British naval assault. While Winder had radiated defeatism and confusion from the outset of his tenure; Smith was confident, well organized, and convinced that the British were overconfident and could be defeated. By Sunday, September 11, 1814, Smith had deployed 16,400 men in a series of defensive positions from North Point to Fort McHenry and he was determined to blot out the embarrassment of Bladensburg with a major American victory.

On Monday, September 12th the British fleet anchored off North Point at the tip of the peninsula between the Back River and Patapsco River, and Ross's columns of 3700 soldiers and 1000 mariners began to move inland. Samuel Smith had already anticipated the British move and he had dispatched Brigadier General John Stricker's column, reinforced by several rifle companies and a battery of 6 five pounders, which moved on to the Philadelphia road and then marched over to Long Log Lane, which led ultimately to North Point 14 miles from the city center. The peninsula was about a mile wide and was an ideal location for bloodying the enemy army before it reached the main American defense position.

Stricker deployed his brigade about half way between North Point and Hamstead Hill and sent out scouts to report on the location of the enemy. The American messengers reported back around 8 A.M. with the news that the British army was camping at Gorsuch's farm about three miles from Stricker's headquarters, but they were uncertain about Ross' next move. The American commander deployed his men between two small streams: Bear

Creek and Bread and Butter Creek, which offered cover from nearby woods and a long wooden fence near the main road. Stricker placed two regiments and his six guns in a front defense line, deployed two more regiments in support and held a fifth regiment in reserve. He wanted to avoid a repetition of the disintegration of the American line at Bladensburg, so he placed his men in mutually supporting positions while relying on numerous swamps and the two streams to discourage British flank attack.

The American column waited several hours for the British to march out from Gorsuch's farm and when a scout reported that the redcoats were busy preparing lunch, Stricker decided to provoke a fight rather than risk a possible British night assault. The brigadier selected Major Richard Heath to march toward the enemy position with 250 men including two companies of sharpshooters and one cannon, under orders to attack the redcoats and then draw them back to Sticker's main force. At about 1 P.M. this small task force hurried down the road until it smashed into British pickets near the farm where both sides exchanged volleys.

Ross and Cockburn had been enjoying a leisurely lunch when they heard the crackle of gunfire and when Mr. Gorsuch asked the general whether he would require dinner later in the day, Ross responded that "I'll eat in Baltimore tonight or in hell!" The two leaders then mounted horses and rode to the site of the skirmish while the redcoats tried to flush out the concealed American riflemen. Cockburn was becoming increasingly nervous about advancing further with no proper escort and Ross agreed to go back down the road and hurry on the main army. Ross was never able to reach his men as a volley of rifle fire suddenly exploded from the woods and the British general went down with a mortal wound in his chest. Ross ordered Colonel Arthur Brooke to assume command of the expedition, commended his wife to "my King and country" and died soon after. When word of their commander's death reached the newly arrived redcoats, an officer noted "a groan came from the column as the army had lost it mainspring."

The somewhat shaken Brooke was able to organize a continuation of the advance and by 3 P.M. his men were organized to assault Stricker's position. Brooke decided to use his three cannons and his rocket launchers to cover an attempt by the 4th Regiment to get around the American left flank while two more regiments and the naval brigade would assault the Yankee center. The Americans were fully prepared for the British frontal assault and they used their riflemen to drop scores of charging redcoats. Then the Yankee gunners loaded their cannons with pieces of broken locks, nails and horseshoes to spray a deadly wave of scrap metal among the already decimated attackers. While the British attackers took heavy casualties, their sacrifice was not in vain as the 4th Regiment was able to flank the American position and send most of the regiments fleeing to the rear in less than five minutes.

Stricker did a masterful job of evacuating successive American defensive positions as his units leapfrogged back to Hampstead Hill while pouring well aimed volleys at the advancing redcoats. Brooke advanced to within a mile of the main American position, but it was getting dark and he had lost 350 men compared to 160 Americans, and he decided to postpone his attack until the next day when Fort McHenry was expected to be neutralized. As Brooke and Cockburn settled down for the night, the British bombardment squadron began to converge for the attack on the American harbor fort. They had no trouble discerning their main target as Major Armistead had commissioned the construction of an enormous flag "so large that the British will have no difficulty in seeing it at a distance." Mrs. Mary Pickersgill, a widowed flag maker, had been paid $405.90 to supply a flag that had stars and stripes each 2 feet across. The flag was so large that the widow had to borrow the malt house of a local brewer to finish the project and the American defenders reveled in this highly visible act of defiance.

At 6:30 A.M. on the humid, cloudy morning of September 13, 1814, the British bombship *Volcano* opened fire on the American fort. Shortly after, the remaining 15 ships of the squadron were firing a wave of cannon balls, mortar bombs and rockets at their target, while Armistead and his frustrated gunners sat waiting for the British ships to move closer in order to return fire. A few American guns responded to the British attack, but by 10 A.M. Armistead called off his artillerymen because they were simply wasting ammunition. After five hours of unrelenting fire, Admiral Cochrane became impatient with the lack of apparent damage to the enemy fort and ordered his ships to close in for the kill. Almost immediately, the *Volcano* took five straight hits and soon other British vessels were pulling back with numerous hits in their sides and rigging.

When the dawn assault on Fort McHenry began, Colonel Brooke roused his sleeping army and prepared them for an attack on Hamstead Hill. Brooke and Cockburn climbed up the stairs of Judge Thomas Hill's house and surveyed the American position from a second floor bedroom. They noted a profusion of earthworks, ditches, palisades and fences defended by over 12,000 men and almost 70 cannons. While Cockburn kept badgering his army counterpart with the refrain that militia would break in any really serious bayonet attack, the British general knew he was outnumbered 3 to 1 and would only have adequate naval support if Fort McHenry was neutralized. Finally the British colonel agreed to order a 2 A.M. assault for the next morning under the assumption that the harbor fort would be neutralized by that time.

Brooke and his subordinates utilized most of the day to organize their assault units while they waited for news from Cochrane's flagship. Finally, the British admiral transmitted a vaguely worded message that Fort McHenry was not yet neutralized and to expect only minimal support from the navy in any full scale attack. This information was enough for Brooke and by 2 A.M. his regiments were not advancing toward the American lines but trudging back along the peninsula toward North Point and embarkation for their transports.

A careful analysis of the Chesapeake campaign reveals a level of British failure that has largely escaped full notice because of the dominant American concern with the burning of the White House. While the British government certainly encouraged Cochrane's force to terrorize the American coastal communities, the primary objective of the raids was to draw United States regulars away from the Canadian frontier. Since only 2000 regulars, about 5% of the American army, were utilized in the defense of Washington and Baltimore, the British strategy clearly failed. Madison and Armstrong diverted almost no regular units from the northern frontier to the Chesapeake during the summer of 1814, which doomed Washington to its fate but did very little to help Prevost or Dummond in their operations. Beyond this failure of strategy, the assaults on Washington and Baltimore cost Ross and Brooke almost 1000 casualties, which were about 25% of the regular army force available for the campaign and was far more damaging than the loss of 300 Americans, including only a few dozen regulars. Cochrane and Cockburn particularly seemed to enjoy themselves in this piece of 19th century buccaneering, but their tangible accomplishments were rather limited and they provided almost no diversion for operations in Canada.

The highest priority for His Majesty's government in the summer of 1814 was the utilization of the heavily reinforced armies in Canada to crush the American border defenses and hopefully, the establishment of a new boundary line far to the south in American territory. Sir George Drummond, commander of the Niagara theatre, had received substantial reinforcements from Britain during the summer, and he followed up the action at Lundy's Lane with a siege of the American garrison at Fort Erie. When Drummond advanced against the fort in early August, Jacob Brown rushed new regiments into the stronghold until the garrison was expanded to 2000 men under General Edmund Gaines. The British column numbered over 3000 regulars but they could deploy only half as many cannons as their adversaries, and after 10 days of ineffective bombardment, Lt. Colonel Weston Fischer was ordered to assault the works with 1300 redcoats. The assault was a total disaster as American artillery and riflemen inflicted over 900 British casualties in less than 30 minutes while losing only 84 of their own men. While Drummond maintained a tenuous siege line around the fort, General Brown dispatched a column under Peter Porter to cut a trail behind the enemy position and destroy or capture the British guns. At 3 P.M. on the rainy afternoon of September 17th, 1600 American soldiers came howling out of the woods and smashed two regiments of redcoats in the first ten minutes of the battle. However, while Porter's men were able to destroy almost every enemy cannon, the startled redcoats were able to consolidate their position after a loss of 600 men compared to just under 500 bluecoats. Drummond subsequently declared a victory but called off the siege and pulled back to Chippewa, while Brown was content to simply strengthen his lines around the last major American foothold on the Canadian side of the frontier.

Drummond's less than spectacular siege was one segment of a two pronged British thrust against American forces on the frontier of Canada. Sir George Prevost was in the process of launching a simultaneous drive against Plattsburgh with an impressive army of 12,000 men that far outnumbered the American garrison. General George Izard, the American commander in this region, had assembled 5000 regulars around Lake Champlain to contest the expected British advance, but even that modest force was dramatically reduced by the blunders of Secretary Armstrong. While the largely incompetent Secretary of War had stripped the national capital of regulars when he became convinced that Cochrane and Ross would ignore Washington, he concurrently ordered Izard to march almost his entire army to Sacketts' Harbor when he decided that Prevost would ignore Plattsburgh. A stunned Izard reluctantly obeyed Armstrong's incredible order and left behind Brigadier General Alexander Macomb with a skeleton force of invalids, new enlistees and men returning from leave.

Macomb had very few regulars available to confront the advancing British army, but he did possess three significant assets. First, Izard had left behind an impressive series of entrenchments supported by a substantial number of cannons, with enough provisions available to withstand a lengthy siege. Second, the energetic Macomb assembled several regiments of New York militia who would provide valuable reinforcements in a defensive capacity. Finally, the American land forces were supported by a small but excellent naval squadron under the command of the talented Commodore Thomas MacDonough. The Lake Champlain fleet included the flagship *Saratoga* with 26 guns, the brig *Eagle* mounting 20 pieces, the schooner *Ticonderoga* boasting 17 cannons and the sloop *Preble* armed with 7 guns. A small squadron of ten gunboats supplemented the firepower of the main fleet.

Prevost's column moved south from Chazy, Quebec on September 5th and by nightfall the British army was only eight miles from Plattsburgh. On the morning of September 6th Macomb retired to his Saranac River defenses and allowed the enemy to become temporary masters of a hamlet that boasted a church, a jail, an inn, a courthouse and about 150 residents. The British commander held a substantial numerical advantage over the few hundred convalescent regulars and 2000 more healthy militiamen that manned the American emplacements. However, Prevost was convinced that overwhelming the enemy land defenses would be a useless gesture unless the Royal Navy controlled Lake Champlain, and he ordered his army to dig in and await the arrival of Captain George Downie's naval flotilla.

Downie commanded a squadron that was led by the 37 gun frigate *Confiance* supported by the 16 gun brig *Linnet* and the twin 11 gun sloops *Cherub* and *Pinch*. A detachment of 12 gun-boats completed the British fleet. At 9 A.M. on Sunday, September 11th, as Stephen Smith prepared for the British landing at North Point, Downie's fleet sailed into action stations and waited for the enemy squadron to emerge from Plattsburgh Bay and engage the Royal Navy. MacDonough reasoned correctly that he would have to deploy his fleet in a formation that could counteract the firepower of the relatively much larger *Confiance*. Therefore, rather than emerging into the open water of Lake Champlain, he held his ships in a stationary line that would put them broadside to the approaching enemy. This meant that the British would be advancing against heavy fire from the start and that initially they would have a distinct disadvantage because they could return that fire only with a few of their forward guns and not with any broadsides.

The British fleet had moved to within 400 yards when MacDonough gave the order to commence firing and the *Confiance* bore the full broadside blast of the four American warships. Nevertheless, the British flagship used her superior firepower to pound the *Saratoga* from the forward guns then swerved just far enough to launch a fearsome broadside that killed or wounded 25% of the American crew. By 11 A.M. MacDonough's ship was badly battered and the commodore was down with wounds from flying splinters. However, the American squadron commander took an enormous gamble that turned the course of the battle. He ordered the stern anchor dropped and the cable to the bow anchor cut in such a way that the wind and current would swing the ship 180 degrees around. Now the guns on the other side of the vessel blasted into *Confiance* and Downie suffered a mortal wound. The now outgunned remaining British ships surrendered one after another and Lake Champlain was now dominated by the American fleet.

While *Saratoga* and *Confiance* were engaged in their slugging match, Prevost ordered his army to strike the American defenses in a two column assault. Prevost's chief deputy, General John Robinson, a feisty, opinionated protégé of Wellington, was ordered to ford the river west of the main American lines, outflank the New York militia and come driving down through the enemy artillery emplacements. The second column was given the task of a frontal assault against the American position which was expected to be supported by the guns of the victorious British fleet. Eager to be on his way, Robinson cursed Prevost for waiting for the ships to engage, and angrily drove his men forward. Unfortunately, the British scouts quickly became lost in the woods and the column wandered around the New York countryside looking for the elusive Americans.

Robinson's lost redcoats were still having better luck than the other assault column as the numerically superior British troops were attacking in vain against the well emplaced American artillery. Just as Robinson's detachment emerged from the woods to initiate their part of the assault, one of Prevost's aides galloped up and reported that the attack was canceled because of Downie's defeat. Prevost had lost 37 killed, 62 wounded and 300 captured, compared to American casualties of 35 killed and 47 wounded, but he still held an enormous numerical advantage over his adversaries. However, as long as the American fleet controlled Lake Champlain, the enemy could harass Prevost's supply lines and make Plattsburgh untenable as a British base.

The London *Times* called the British defeats around Lake Champlain "a lamentable event to the civilized world" and General Robinson, now back in Quebec with his troops, noted "I am sick at heart, everything I see or hear is discouraging, this is no field for a military man above the rank of colonel of riflemen .... nothing but a defensive war can or ought to be attempted here, and you will find that the expectations of His Majesty's ministers and the people of England will be utterly disappointed in this quarter." In just ten days the massive British offensive against the United States had collapsed as the summer of glorious prospects gave way to an autumn of harsh reality. The failed assaults against Baltimore, Fort Erie and Plattsburgh had resulted in over 2300 British casualties compared to about one third as many American losses. When this dreadful news reached London, the British government initially attempted to minimize its effect on determination to prosecute the war. However, when the Prime Minister attempted to persuade the Duke of Wellington to assume command in North America, the hero of the hour replied coldly, "you can get no terms from the American and your military operations .... do not entitle you to demand any," Lord Liverpool quietly instructed his negotiators at Ghent to make peace as quickly as possible, as "there is no disposition to exact any terms from the Americans inconsistent with their honor." The final barriers to the signatures on the "Peace of Christmas Eve" were now falling rapidly, but one more climactic battle would be fought over two weeks after the American and British envoys technically terminated the war.

The final, and perhaps most famous, campaign of the War of 1812 had its origins in the insistence of Lord Liverpool that the war must end on a note of British victory, and on the determination of Admiral Cochrane to conquer a prize as rich in opportunities for profit as the Baltimore capture that had been denied him. Thus Cochrane was able to convince the ministry to send him substantial reinforcements from Wellington's regiments, in order to attack the rich city of New Orleans with over 9000 men. Sir Edward Pakenham, the Iron Duke's brother-in-law, was assigned to this tempting expedition as the commander of the land forces. Pakenham and Cochrane were opposed by Major General Andrew Jackson, who had been assigned five regiments of regulars to deflect a British invasion of the Gulf Coast. However, Jackson was so convinced that the enemy would attempt the capture of Mobile before they attempted an assault on the Crescent City, that he rushed most of his regulars to Alabama while relying on his 2800 Tennessee volunteers to hold New Orleans in an emergency.

Early in the morning of December 23rd, 1814, a British advance force of 1600 men under Colonel William Thornton descended on the Villiere plantation only 8 miles from New Orleans, captured a few local militiamen, and seized the main house. The owner of the plantation, Major Gabriel Villiere, was enjoying a cigar on his veranda when the redcoats arrived, and he leaped through a window and made his way to Jackson's headquarters with his startling news. The American commander, as decisive and energetic as usual, declared "By the Eternal, they shall not sleep on our soil!" and immediately assembled a strong column for a counterattack. A detachment of Tennessee riflemen, a battalion of Creole militia, a battalion of free black volunteers and a group of Choctaw Indians marched through the swamps and struck Thornton at midnight. Brigadier General Coffee's Tennesseans, supported by fire from the American ship *Carolina*, smashed into the sleeping redcoats and forced the British to give up any idea of an immediate advance after losing 280 men compared to 210 Americans.

Pakenham waited for additional reinforcements and scheduled a grand assault for the morning of January 8th, 1815. Jackson utilized the hiatus to strengthen his main defense line along the Rodriguez Canal. The 3500 available defenders were kept busy emplacing cannons, stacking cotton bales and clearing a field of fire around the approaches. Pakenham called a conference of his commanders on the afternoon of January 7th and finalized the plan of assault. Contrary to popular American chronicles of the battle, the British general had no thought of a mindless, unsupported frontal assault in his plans, but had developed a fairly sophisticated operational scheme. Colonel Thornton was ordered to cross the river during the night and lead a force of 1400 men along the opposite shore where they would capture a number of American cannons and turn the guns on Jackson's flank. Major General John Keane would then advance with a column of elite soldiers who were ordered to capture a key redoubt that anchored the right end of the line. Keane's column was expected to hit the enemy from the side while the main assault force struck the American center under cover of a massive rocket barrage. The redcoat attackers would be carrying dozens of ladders designed to get the men over the barricades where they could bayonet the defenders, who were equipped with few bayonets of their own.

The foggy, frigid morning of January 8th, 1815 provided the backdrop to the last major battle between the two English speaking societies. Jackson knew that his men were heavily outnumbered, but the American barricades were defended by several batteries of artillery and hundreds of frontiersmen who had deadly long rifles that far outgunned the British muskets. When Pakenham gave the order to advance, the entire British assault operation began to disintegrate. First, Thornton's flank column had become lost on their way to the American positions and didn't begin to attack until the main assault was underway. Next, the American cannons fired a massive barrage against the British rocket launchers and smashed them to pieces before they could fully support the attack. Finally, Keane's column was advancing too slowly to distract the American defenders from Pakenham's main column. The result was one of the most one sided defeats in British military history.

The redcoats marched forward accompanied by the wail of Scottish bagpipes with some hope that the planned diversions would distract the American defenders. However, even the covering ground fog began to dissipate, and the redcoats were caught in the open as they endured the massive enemy barrage. Jackson's artillerymen switched their targets from the British rocket launchers to the advancing infantry and soon entire rows of redcoats were falling to the frozen ground. Then the Tennesseans shouldered their long rifles and picked off the advancing soldiers long before they could shoot back. Apparently a large number of the most celebrated riflemen were provided with newly loaded rifles as fast as they could shoot, and the effect was a devastating preview of the use of repeating rifles fifty years later. As American sharpshooters fired perhaps ten or twelve shots a minute, entire British regiments began to disintegrate. General Keane rode among the men of the 93rd Highland regiment and went down along with dozens of the Scots. Pakenham vainly attempted to reform one of his brigades and was mortally wounded within seconds of being sighted. As Jackson shouted "give it to them boys, let's finish this business today," the surviving redcoats began to either run or go down in a new hail of bullets. One of the most over-optimistic British officers must have been Captain Thomas Wilkinson who led a company of his men to the barricades and climbed over the cotton bales shouting "the day is ours!" Unfortunately, virtually the entire company following had been annihilated and the brave captain was killed on the ramparts. Wilkinson had been joined in death by so many of the senior British officers that there seemed to be no one alive to either order another suicidal advance or a mind numbing retreat. Finally, General Lambert, who commanded the still uncommitted reserve brigade, surveyed the bloody battlefield and ordered his entire army to withdraw to safety.

Within the space of about one hour in the cold Louisiana mist, Andrew Jackson and his diverse army of Indians, pirates, frontiersmen, African-Americans and Creoles had negated the bitter memories of Detroit, Queenston and Frenchtown. The American defenders had inflicted a defeat on the British that was as one-sided in casualties as Marathon or Agincourt. Pakenham's assault force had lost 291 killed, 1262 wounded and 484 captured against an incredibly small loss of 6 men wounded among the main American defense force. Candles gleamed from nearly every window along Pennsylvania Avenue in the evening of February 4th as Washingtonians learned of Jackson's triumph and these illuminations were quickly matched by citizens of Baltimore, Philadelphia and New York. Ten days later, Henry Carroll, an American official present at the peace negotiations, arrived in a coach that had been driven at top speed from New York. Carroll arrived in Washington at 4 P.M. and was taken to James Monroe's residence. A few moments later Carroll and Monroe were on their way to President Madison's temporary home at Octagon House, and shortly after 8 P.M. the President emerged to tell an excited throng of onlookers that the peace terms were acceptable and the war was about to end. Church bells rang, cannons boomed and dozens of skyrockets proclaimed the onset of peace. After almost three years of economic chaos, poor military leadership, weak direction in Washington and dangerous levels of dissension in many states, a nearly disastrous war had ended in the glow of emotional celebrations, courtesy of an energetic general in New Orleans and a resolute group of envoys in Ghent.

CHAPTER 17

# Alternative Strategies and Outcomes

## *British and Americans 1812-1815*

*T*he War of 1812 is often called America's "second war of independence" and many of the issues and the ideology of the conflict echoed those of the Revolution. An amateur army of Americans for a second time faced the might of the most powerful empire of its time, and many citizens of the republic were convinced that perfidious officials in Westminster and White-hall were determined to destroy the new nation. However, this alleged threat to the very existence of the United States was far more imagined than real, given the reality of power politics in the early 19th century. The British attitude toward the former colonies was arrogant and often exasperating, but His Majesty's government was almost totally pre-occupied with defeating Napoleon and viewed the conflict with America as a sideshow until the French emperor was defeated. Even some Americans began to realize that the citizens of the United States had inflated their importance in world affairs. Daniel Sheffey, a Virginia Federalist, warned his fellow members of Congress on the eve of the war that "we have considered ourselves of too much importance in the scale of nations. It has led us into great errors. Instead of yielding to circumstance, which human power cannot control, we have imagined that our destiny, and that of other nations, was in our hands, to be regulated as we thought proper."

The thirty-two-month conflict, that developed at least in part because of this inflated perspective of American influence and power, produced an awesome range of emotions for citizens as they reacted to ignominious defeats and thrilling victories. The War of 1812 was a classic example of a drawn conflict in which neither adversary was particularly happy about the final outcome, but both nations were forced to realize that they could easily have been subjected to far worse disasters. The *Morning Chronicle* of London condemned the Treaty of Ghent, declared that "the British government has humbled themselves in the dust and thereby brought discredit to the whole country." On the other hand, (American) envoy Henry Clay was convinced that the Americans had gotten the worst of the deal by signing "a damned bad treaty." However, Britons could point with pride to Brock's splendid victories at Detroit and Queenston while Americans tended to remember Perry's triumph on Lake Erie and Jackson's epic success at New Orleans. British officials were convinced that they had jettisoned an unnecessary war while maintaining the honor of the nation. Foreign Secretary Lord Castlereagh congratulated the Prime Minister on the peace treaty, calling the termination of the war "a most auspicious and reasonable event in which we have been released from the millstone of the American war." American leaders emphasized the moral victory inherent in fighting "Wellington's invincibles" to a draw in the campaign of 1814. Congressman Joseph Story insisted "never did a country occupy more lofty ground, we have stood the contest, single-handed, against the conqueror of Europe." Each nation could point with pride to certain heroic achievements accomplished by the soldiers and sailors of its armed forces, but realistic individuals in both countries were forced to admit that neither side won the war.

An appreciation of the fact that the War of 1812 was a military draw encourages the investigation of two fascinating questions. First why was neither nation able to win the war, and what were the factors that prevented either Britain or the United States from defeating the adversary? Second, which alternate scenarios might have emerged if either country had, in fact, been able to win the contest?

While the United Kingdom entered the War of 1812 as a reluctant participant, that nation did enjoy an immense military and naval superiority over its American antagonist. However, Britain failed to emerge victorious for a number of reasons. First, and possibly most important, the British government simply could never bring itself to treat the war in North America as anything more than a sideshow to the "real" war raging in Europe. Wellington's army always received priority for the best generals, the best equipment and the best men, and, at least until 1814, the North American theater received whatever remained in the military stockpile. Even Isaac Brock, the most talented British commander in North America, admitted that he hoped that his victories in that region would secure for him a coveted position in Wellington's camp. Most other British generals in North America tended to be mediocre because the empire simply couldn't spare their most talented men from the life and death struggle with the Napoleonic foe. British commanders on this side of the Atlantic tended to be cautious, unimaginative, older leaders who were only able to best their opponents when faced with the particularly incompetent American generals who staffed the army during the first half of the war. Prevost, Proctor, Pakenham and Drummond enjoyed very little success against rising American stars such as Winfield Scott, Alexander Macomb and Andrew Jackson.

This increasingly evident contrast between talented young American lead-ers and mediocre British commanders was very much paralleled on the diplomatic front. While the United States dispatched brilliant negotiators such as John Quincy Adams, Henry Clay and Albert Gallatin to Ghent, the British contingent consisted exclusively of second tier functionaries who were clearly outmatched by their American counterparts.

An obvious, but still important, possible cause for Britain's failure to win the war may be discerned in the attitude of the massive reinforcements that were sent to North America after the fall of Napoleon. The veterans of Wellington's campaigns were tough minded, experienced soldiers who were proud of their victory over the legendary French emperor. However, instead of being sent to England for a heroic welcome or at least posted to France as occupying conquerors, many regiments found themselves aboard over-crowded transports bound for a second rate war in a wilderness continent. While Wellington had allowed his men considerable freedom in choice of dress and personal action in return for obvious bravery on the battlefield, the mediocre British commanders in North America were virtual martinets who shocked the Peninsula veterans with their petty harassment and attention to minor uniform infractions. These redcoats saw themselves as forgotten soldiers forced to serve under incompetent commanders in the middle of nowhere, while their more fortunate comrades were enjoying victory parades in London or occupation duty in Paris. Thus it is ironic that at the point at which Britain was finally able to concentrate its largest, most experienced force in North America, the performance of its soldiers fell off relative to its American opponents.

A third, and largely inter-related, reason for Britain's failure to win the war was the inability of the United Kingdom to convincingly trounce the American forces during the crucial final six months of the war. While the British possessed a slight edge in the number of successful engagements in the war up to the spring of 1814, that advantage was clearly obliterated between July 1814 and January 1815. Between the battles of Chippewa and New Orleans, the only clear cut British victory occurred at Bladensburg, and even there the redcoats suffered much higher casualties than their American adversaries. Although a number of American chronicles of the last year of the war focus on the humiliation of the British capture and burning of Washington, the final campaign of the war brought a very creditable reputation to the United States forces. An analysis of comparative casualties suffered during the final six months of the war reveals the somewhat startling figure of over 6100 British soldiers lost, compared to only 1800 Americans killed, wounded and captured.

The British force that was initially expected to continue the war into 1815 was not overwhelmingly superior to its American opponents. The Royal Navy had successfully blockaded the coast of the United States, but an accelerated program of construction of steam frigates threatened to chal-lenge British naval supremacy. The British regular army in North America had been reinforced to 40,000 men but was facing an increasingly well led American regular army of 45,000 men supported by thousands of steadily improving militiamen. Thus the achievement of some clear cut level of military superiority over the American adversaries would probably have required an additional 30,000 to 40,000 veterans dispatched from Europe. This re-deployment of massive elements of the British army was technically feasible but politically almost impossible, given the political climate of Europe in 1815. A North American army of 70-80,000 men would have been larger than the British army commanded by Wellington at Waterloo and would have forced the British ministry to strip its European garrison just as Napoleon was re-emerging on the scene.

Given these realities of the Continental balance of power, it appears that the best opportunity for Britain to win a fairly substantial victory in North America would have occurred sometime during the year 1813. At this point the American army was still saddled with incompetent theatre commanders, the Royal Navy was driving the United States fleet from the ocean, Tecumseh and his Indian confederation was at its peak, and the Americans had relatively few ships available to contest British naval domination of the Great Lakes. Within this context it seems that the decisive period of that year centered around the battles of Lake Erie and the Thames, in which in the space of a few weeks, Oliver Hazard Perry smashed British naval dominance and William Henry Harrison not only recovered Detroit but occupied much of Upper Canada, and annihilated Tecumseh's significant alliance with His Majesty's forces. British victory in these two engagements might well have forced the United States to consider accepting peace on far less congenial terms than the following autumn.

His Majesty's government may not have been able to impose a conqueror's peace on the American republics but the United States clearly was unable to achieve military victory in the contest. Of the three most prominent American objectives during the war, the British had rescinded the Orders in Council before the war formally began, the impressment of American sailors was halted only because Napoleon had been defeated, and Canada was further away from annexation to the United States at the end of the war than it had been at the beginning. The American republic was successful in its conduct of the war only to the extent that it was able to prevent the more powerful United Kingdom from annexing large sections of the United States in the wake of expected British military victories. There are a number of possible reasons why the war ended no more triumphantly for the Americans than for their British opponents.

The primary reason for American lack of success in the War of 1812 was the limited government philosophy of the Jefferson-Madison Democratic-Republicans. The entire Republican theory of government revolved around the belief that significant federal expenditures were anathema to a truly republican form of government. One result of this policy was that the United States entered war with Britain with a ridiculously small military and naval establishment compared to its adversary. The United States entered a war with the United Kingdom with a much smaller disparity in population and wealth than is commonly assumed. Britain's population of 12 million was not overwhelmingly larger than the 7 ½ million residents of the United States. However, the United Kingdom, admittedly engaged in a titanic struggle with Napoleon, maintained a naval establishment that provided 50 times as many major fighting vessels as the American navy and deployed an army that could field 40 times as many infantry regiments as the United States. While Americans were justifiably proud of their small, highly efficient fleet, they could have been more proud of a large well organized navy; the 11 regular army regiments were well trained and energetic, but an additional 100 regiments would not have been unreasonable for a nation preparing to enter a war with the British empire.

The Madison administration presented the worst of both worlds to citizens concerned with the defense of the nation. The Republicans insisted on provoking a war with Britain without authorizing the forces necessary to engage in that conflict. Alexander Hamilton and his fellow Federalists held beliefs that were far less congenial to democratic principles than their opponents, but at least the first Secretary of the Treasury and his ideological heirs had a more coherent concept of national defense. The Federalists took the far more sensible view that the United States should either take all possible measures to avoid provoking a confrontation with Britain, or if a war did become inevitable, expand the army and navy to the point that the nation could have a reasonable expectation of victory.

The failure of the American government to authorize sufficient forces to fight the war in its early stages was compounded by the equally ruinous policy of staffing the most important military and naval leadership positions with an assortment of incredibly incompetent individuals. The nation entered the war with totally ineffective war and naval secretaries who were an embarrassment to the nation. The primary field commanders, including William Hull, Henry Dearborn, James Wilkinson, and Stephen Van Rensselaer, formed the most incompetent group of leaders in American military history. While most of the front line naval leaders were far more talented and energetic than their initial army counterparts, the naval high command continued to tolerate the failure of Commodore Isaac Chauncey, who was so ineffective in providing naval support to the crucial military campaigns around Lake Ontario that he permanently crippled the war effort on the Canadian frontier.

A third major contributing factor in the failure of the United States to win the war has received far less attention than it deserves. The United States mobilized an impressive military force during the course of the war which should have provided overwhelming numerical superiority in most engagements. A total of 57,000 regulars were enlisted between 1812 and 1814, while an incredible total of 458,000 Americans served at least some time in militia units in the various states. The total force of over half a million men represents an impressive total of over 50% of all males between the ages of 18 and 45 who resided in the nation at that time. This mobilization of military forces compares favorably with the far more high-profile deployment of men in the Civil War and World War II, especially when one considers the fact that almost half of the states opposed the war so vehemently that they refused to call out their militia. This manpower level should theoretically have provided impressive numbers of soldiers to challenge the British in every major battle of the war. Instead, the American army was never able to employ as many as 17,000 men in any single engagement and in most cases the United States forces entered battle with armies of only four or five thousand effectives. While much of the problem in concentrating militia forces may be traced to traditional problems of short enlistment periods, unwillingness to serve outside the state and a variety of transportation problems, the inability to concentrate any significant number of regulars is far more perplexing.

An example of this failure to concentrate available forces emerges in the ill fated defense of the nation's capital. The American army in August of 1814 could deploy over 40,000 regulars, yet only slightly more than 1% of these men were assigned to the protection of Washington. Admiral Cockburn and General Ross thus advanced on a national seat of power at a point in time when 99% of their opponent's army was unavailable for combat. During the same time period, Alexander Macomb was defending Plattsburgh with fewer than 1000 regulars and Samuel Smith was able to deploy only slightly more professionals around Baltimore. Thus something like 2500 regulars were engaged in the most crucial series of battles in the war, with over 37,000 other bluecoats employed in far less critical activities. This concentration presents a marked contrast with the situation in the Union Army in the vital campaign of exactly 50 years later. The National Army in May of 1864 deployed 513,000 men, with 130,000 advancing under Grant against Lee's army, 100,000 deployed with Sherman on the march toward Atlanta and an additional 90,000 committed to supporting advances under Benjamin Butler and Franz Sigel. Thus over 60% of the entire available strength of the Union army was directly involved in the two principal campaigns, compared to only 5% concentration at a similar period of crisis in 1814. The fact that so much of the American army was "missing" for much of the War of 1812 hardly contributed to a more victorious end to the conflict for the young republic.

The final outcome of the War of 1812 was only one of a number of possible scenarios that might have produced a quite different version of the chronicle of the American republic. One of the most intriguing alternatives to the war that was actually fought revolves around the ability of the Madison administration to have delayed the declaration of war against Britain for two or three years. The President and Congress might have decided to respond to British depredations with a more coolly thought-out military and naval buildup, rather than the obviously unfortunate insistence on entering a war without any serious attempt to expand the fighting capacity of the republic. A theoretical three year expansion program might have included a number of highly effective activities. One quite manageable improvement could have been the construction of perhaps 10 ships of the line and 20 heavy frigates between 1812 and 1815. This force would still have been considerably smaller than the Royal Navy, but would have provided some offensive capability for the American Navy, which could have used these vessels to disrupt British trade routes and perhaps even launch raids on the English coastline in order to force the enemy to re-deploy naval squadrons to protect the homeland. A second highly innovative tactic might have included the construction of a fleet of approximately 20 steam frigates as proposed by Robert Fulton. The launching of several squadrons of such technically advanced ships in 1814 or 1815 would have produced an extremely effective weapon against the imposition of a British blockade on the American coastline and, if actually used in combat against the Royal Navy, might have produced a technological breakthrough similar to the introduction of airplanes and tanks during the World War of a century later. It is not inconceivable that Britain's role as "mistress of the seas" might have been severely challenged by a fleet of war vessels capable of moving regardless of wind; certainly a duel between such novel vessels and the might of the British battle line would have produced a fascinating confrontation.

The American maritime expansion could have been complimented by an equally effective build up of land forces. Since the United States was able to raise 57,000 volunteer regulars during the course of the war, it would not be unreasonable to expect that the army could have undergone a staged expansion between 1812 and 1815 to deploy perhaps 50,000 regulars by the summer of 1815. A force of this size, if provided with proper training and equipment, would have provided an additional stimulation to a British government already confronting a powerful American navy to come to terms with its former colony. The authors believe that a rational, measured naval and military buildup between 1812 and 1815 would have produced a solution to the Anglo-American crisis with much more congenial results than emerged from the War of 1812. Either Britain would have been forced to fight an American adversary that deployed a powerful, well trained army, a substantial fleet of conventional war vessels and a powerful squadron of technologically superior steamships, or His Majesty's government would have bargained in good faith to settle disputes with the United States rather than impose an unpopular war on an increasingly contentious and war-weary, tax-paying citizenry. The most likely result would have been a grudging, but real, British concession of American rights on the high seas, and an equally grudging respect for the former colonials who were now obviously strong enough to back up their threats against British incursions.

While this initial scenario supposes the probability that a more powerful United States could have avoided war with the British antagonists, additional alternative consequences might include the possibility of outright

British or American victory in the war that was actually fought. Each alternative outcome might have dramatically changed the course of American history. The United Kingdom entered the War of 1812 with no desire to eradicate the American republic from the world map, but as the war progressed, the British government began considering the imposition of concessions on a defeated adversary that would have reduced drastically the size of the contemporary nation. British officials assumed that a clear cut military victory would produce a peace treaty in which most of the Midwest would either be annexed to Canada or turned into an Indian buffer state, most of Maine would be occupied in order to provide direct access between Quebec and Nova Scotia, and the Great Lakes would be acknowledged as British waterways.

A series of British victories during the crucial Chesapeake, Lake Champlain and Louisiana campaigns of 1814 might very well have allowed the United Kingdom to impose its terms on an American government that was almost bankrupt and faced with the possible secession of New England. Acceptance of British terms would have effectively eliminated almost one third of the territory of the United States, with the real possibility that future westward expansion might have been greatly reduced. One significant possible implication of this amputation of much of the republic might very well have been the increasing dominance of the slave states, as British occupation of the mid-west would have closed off the entry of additional free states, while southerners would have been free to expand their peculiar institution into more southerly areas. The loss of the Midwest would have significantly delayed the emergence of the Republican party and might instead have produced a secession movement in abolitionist New England as that region would have been shut out of its natural alliance with much of the upper Midwest. A threatened secession of the New England states might have forced the middle Atlantic states of New Jersey, New York and Pennsylvania into the same predicament experienced by Virginia, Tennessee and North Carolina after the cotton states quit the Union in 1861.

Another possible ironic outcome of a British victory in the War of 1812 revolves around the development of the Anglo-American alliance during the world wars of the 20th century. A continued British occupation of large portions of American territory most likely would have provoked a third war with the United States within another generation or two. However, even if war was somehow avoided, it would have been extremely difficult for an American president in 1917 or 1941 to have rallied the people of the United States into an alliance with a British empire that continued to occupy portions of the republic. Thus the relatively marginal gain of expanding Canadian frontiers in the 19th century might have come back to haunt England if that action had discouraged American military assistance in the crises of World War I and II.

While a British victory in the War of 1812 might have pushed both the United Kingdom and United States down very different paths during the next century and a half, a corresponding American triumph could have produced a whole different series of outcomes. One probable result of an American victory would have been the annexation of Canada into the Union. This would have created a new series of challenges, opportunities and problems for the already diverse inhabitants of British North America. The persons who would have most readily welcomed this change in sovereignty would have been the large number of recent emigrants from the United States who still maintained an emotional attachment to the Union and had moved north primarily to take advantage of cheap Canadian land. These residents would have welcomed a state of Ontario and some of them might have emerged as political leaders in the newly annexed territory.

The ecstatic welcome of those recently transplanted Americans would have been evenly matched by the feelings of grief displayed by earlier emigrants from the republic to the south. The Revolutionary era Tories who had fled to Canada to form the United Empire Loyalists had generally prospered in their new haven. Members of families who had contested the end of British dominion in America now constituted much of the ruling circle that governed Canadian society. While annexation into the United States was unlikely to bring any massive retribution from the American government for Loyalist activities in the earlier war, the Canadian Tories would have been faced with the challenge of dealing with hundreds and then thousands of land hungry Americans flowing across the former boundary line or initiating a long journey toward the ancestral motherland.

One of the most intriguing outcomes of a theoretical American annexa-tion of Canada revolves around the impact of such an event on the French speaking population of Quebec. While the Quebec Act of 1774 had guaran-teed religious freedom for the Catholic population of Canada, the French population paid a steep price for the maintenance of religious and cultural sovereignty. Until the middle of the twentieth century, the political power in the Canadian Confederation was based on an English speaking power base with most of the key governmental and industrial positions reserved for Anglophones. Therefore, an alternative scenario of annexation into the United States presents intriguing possibilities. On the one hand, the Franco-phone population of Quebec would have become an island of French speaking Americans in a huge English speaking sea of states. However, the American political system also offered the possibility that the French speaking residents of a state of Quebec would have exercised far more influence within their own state than they enjoyed as residents of a Canadian province until well into the present century.

A theoretical American annexation of Canada may have had as important an impact on the sectionalist crisis of the 19th century as the earlier mentioned British annexation of parts of the United States. The authors believe that the northward expansion of the free states of the Union may have provoked the slave owning states into secession earlier than the actual crisis of 1861. This confrontation might have resulted in a peaceful division of the Union as northern leaders in a period before the emergence of Abraham Lincoln might have been so pre-occupied with the development of the most recent of the new territories that the "erring" cotton states may have been allowed to depart unhindered. On the other hand, if an earlier emergence of the sectionalist crisis had resulted in armed conflict, the southern states would have gained the advantage of fighting a north that had not attained the superiority in technology, industry and population that it enjoyed in 1861-1865. Either a diplomatic or military resolution of the crisis that resulted in the successful creation of a Southern Confederacy would have produced an alternate North America in which a United States that extended from the Arctic Ocean to perhaps the Potomac River would be contiguous with a Southern Confederacy that in time might have faced the same challenge of economic and cultural dominance from its giant neighbor to the north as modern Canada has experienced with its colossal southern counterpart.

While these alternative outcomes provide intriguing possibilities for the emergence of a quite different United States of America, in real life, the Treaty of Ghent ended the war with far fewer permanent repercussions than might have occurred in a more clear cut victory by either nation. The American peace commissioners who walked through the cheery Christmas illuminations of Ghent to conclude the final negotiations with Great Britain on December 24th 1814, agreed enthusiastically with their British counterparts that they expected that this would be the last Anglo-American treaty of peace. Relations between the English speaking societies on the opposite sides of the Atlantic Ocean continued to be contentious and exasperating for some time to come, but Canada and the United States each gained an enhanced sense of identity from the often frustrating conflict.

The war ensured that Canada would never become part of the republic to the south, as an alternative, parallel form of emerging democracy grew out of the continued British presence. The failure of the American invasion of Canada encouraged an increasing awareness among Canadians that loyalty to the British way of life as opposed to American radical democracy and republicanism was preferable in their society. Concepts of peace, order and good government became viable alternatives to American life, liberty and happiness which seemed to many Canadians as both anarchistic and hedonistic. Organizations such as the Loyal and Patriotic Society of Upper Canada utilized heroes such as Isaac Brock to proclaim that British order was preferable to the American culture; that certain sensitive positions are better filled by appointment than by election; that order imposed from above has advantages over grass roots democracy. The result was a form of government based on state paternalism that created a alternative development from the more individualistic American way of life.

The United States may have failed to expand its sovereignty into British North America, but the War of 1812 did produce a number of tangible benefits. Despite the spotty military record displayed by the nation during the war, the conflict enhanced America's reputation in many of the capitals of Europe. English ambassador to Washington Augustus Foster admitted, "the Americans have had the satisfaction of proving their courage, they have brought us to speak of them with respect." Another British minister insisted that "the war has humbled the tone of our ministry and of the nation and made the United States much more respected in Europe."

The war may have been a tie in purely military terms, but the United States had the great good luck to win the final battle which was not less spectacular for being contested after the war was technically over. The battle of New Orleans not only pushed Andrew Jackson to the pinnacle of political power, it played an enormous role in forging the myth of American victory. French minister Louis Serurier noted, "the war with its spectacularly victorious ending, will have enormous consequences. Finally the war has given the Americans what they essentially lacked, a national character founded on a glory common to all." A new sense of national identity had emerged based on a war not seen as a futile and costly struggle in which the United States had barely escaped a serious defeat, but as a glorious triumph that ended with a victory of epic proportions against the conquerors of Napoleon. As one Congressman exclaimed, "the glorious adventures of the late war have sealed the destiny of this country, perhaps for centuries to come, and the Treaty of Ghent has secured our liberties, established our national independence and placed the nation on high and honorable ground." The War of 1812 may not have produced a genuine military victory, but the earlier defeats and humiliations were quickly forgotten in the euphoria of Ghent and New Orleans. *Niles' Register* probably captured the spirit of most Americans in the winter of 1815 when it rhapsodized on the twin messages of military victory in Louisiana and virtual diplomatic triumph in Belgium. "Who will not be an American? Long live the Republic! All hail! Last asylum of oppressed humanity!"

# CHAPTER 18

# Sam Houston's War

## *The Texas Campaign in the Mexican-American Conflict*

$T$he American war with Mexico has always occupied a controversial place in the historical consciousness of the United States. The conflict has been alternately condemned as a wicked war of aggression against a weaker neighbor and justified as an inevitable phase in the expansion of a freedom loving democracy. However, no matter which of these interpretations is closer to the reality of the event, the real confrontation between the two rival republics did not begin with the mutual declarations of war during the Spring of 1846, but more than 10 years earlier when the largely American settlers in Texas revolted against an increasingly aggressive government in Mexico City. Ironically, while most Americans of the 20th century have shown little interest in the formal war between the United States and Mexico, the struggle for Texan independence evokes a number of emotional images. The exploits of Jim Bowie, William Travis, Davy Crockett and Sam Houston have been chronicled in films, television programs and dramatic pageants, while the later activities of Zachary Taylor and Winfield Scott are largely ignored. Thus a comprehensive assessment of this conflict should probably focus on the war as a three phase confrontation which included the Texas revolution, the initial operations of the American army to secure the Texas border and gain a foothold in Northern Mexico, and finally, the expedition to capture the enemy capital and "conquer a peace."

The seeds of the Texas revolution and the subsequent American conflict with Mexico were sown during the 1820's when a newly independent Mexican republic decided to stimulate growth in its northern province of Texas by encouraging foreigners to settle in the region. The laws of 1824 and 1825 invited foreigners to establish themselves in the province by offering 4428 acres of land to each family for a minimal payment of $30. Soon "Texas fever" was sweeping the American states as land hungry citizens took advantage of this incredible offer and headed southward. By 1835 Texas had almost 30,000 people, of which over three quarters were Americans, but this steady stream of immigrants was becoming intolerable to the central government in Mexico City.

The succession of revolutions and coups which wracked Mexico City in the late 1820's and early 1830's had temporarily diverted attention from the Texas problem, but when newly installed president Antonio Lopez de Santa Anna consolidated his hold on the executive office, the American settlers were vulnerable to the wrath of this mercurial dictator. Santa Anna first jailed the most prominent Anglo leader in Texas, Stephen J. Austin, and then sent his brother-in-law, General Martin Perfecto de Cos with an army to confiscate colonists' weapons and arrest any prominent troublemakers. Lieutenant Jose Castenada was dispatched in late September, 1835 to the town of Gonzalez to retrieve a small cannon that had been provided to the settlement years earlier to discourage Indian raids. Castenada and his 100 man detachment were confronted by 18 armed Americans who had buried the cannon and then defied the Mexicans to "come and take it" if they dared. While the Mexican lieutenant and a group of colonists including local blacksmith Almaron Dickinson parlayed and dickered over ownership of the cannon, about 170 Texans from other settlements answered a call for help and formed themselves into a small army. During the early morning hours of October 2nd, the colonists dug up the now famous cannon, fired a few charges of nails and horse-shoes at the encamped Mexicans, and launched an assault that sent Castaneda's detachment rushing back to the main base at San Antonio.

The Texas revolution had now begun, and within ten days over 500 men led the recently released Stephen Austin were marching on Cos' headquarters. Cos had deployed most of his men in houses throughout the town, but had placed part of his 400 man army in the local mission which was popularly known as the Alamo. While the Texan rebels conducted a leisurely siege of the town, Austin went to the United States to drum up support for the new uprising. Pro-rebel rallies in Boston, Philadelphia, and New York raised large amounts of money for the cause, while the citizens of New Orleans raised two companies of volunteers called the "New Orleans Grays," who promptly left by steamboat for the scene of the contest.

General Edward Burleson, the newly appointed commander of the besieging army had little idea how to conduct military operations, and his men were becoming frustrated and bored. Finally, in early December, two American residents of San Antonio de Bexar, Sam Maverick and John Smith, escaped through the Mexican lines with detailed plans of the enemy defenses. While Burleson vacillated between immediate attack and continued siege, a colorful frontiersman by the name of Ben Milam gathered about half of the army and launched his own attack. The rebels were outnumbered and facing a heavily entrenched regular army, but Cos was a fairly incompetent commander, and the Texans were able to fight a vicious house to house

WAR WITH
MEXICO
1846 - 1847
Strategic Theater

TEXAS

Ft. Jessup

LOUISIANA

New Orleans

San Jacinto

San Antonio
de Bexar

Goliad

Neuces River

Rio Grande

Ft. Texas

Point Isabel

Camargo

Matamoros

Monterrey

Saltillo

Buena Vista

N

GULF
of
MEXICO

Tampico

MEXICO

0      100
Miles

Mexico City

Jalapa

Cerro Gordo

Vera Cruz

Puebla

battle that captured most of the town in a bloody four-day exchange which resulted in Milam's death. Early in the morning of December 9th, Cos called a halt to the action and agreed to surrender the town and mission in return for the safe conduct of his men back to the Rio Grande.

Eight hundred miles south of San Antonio, Santa Anna received word of his brother-in-law's embarrassing defeat and became determined to chastise the insolent Texans by sweeping northward with a large expeditionary force. The president arrived in the capital of Saltillo on January 7th, 1836 with over 4000 men drafted from every corner of the republic. The General-issimo was preparing to march the final 365 miles to Bexar when he was struck down with an intestinal disorder that delayed the advance for several weeks. This change of schedule would ironically prove fatal to the over 180 Texans who attempted to halt the Mexican drive to the Alamo.

General Sam Houston, commander in chief of Texan armies, was convinced that the only way to stop the huge Mexican army was to mobilize all available rebel units into one large mobile force capable of destroying the invaders' communications and supply lines. When Santa Anna's column linked up with additional detachments stationed closer to Texas, he would command nearly 6000 men, while the entire scattered rebel army could deploy less than one fourth of that number. Houston was determined to avoid a situation where small rebel contingents were destroyed piecemeal, and when the general received word that Colonel James Neill had fortified the mission at Bexar, he dispatched Colonel James Bowie and thirty men to blow up the fort and evacuate the mission's invaluable artillery. Houston emphasized to Governor Henry Smith "our forces must not be shut up in forts where they can neither be supplied with men nor provisions."

An immediate northward advance by Santa Anna during January of 1836 would have provided Neill and Bowie with few alternatives to the destruction of the mission, but when the expedition was delayed, Bowie allowed himself to be convinced by local volunteers that the Alamo could be defended. Bowie and the Bexar officers were probably overly impressed with the mission's huge arsenal of 25 cannons, including a massive 18 pounder. Unfortunately, the Texans seemed to gloss over a long list of negative factors that should have convinced them to evacuate long before the first Mexican lancers arrived within 10 miles of San Antonio. The Alamo was a mission designed to offer protection against hostile Indians but the walls were largely packed earth and the place included no firing steps, watch towers, bastions or redoubts to cover enemy approaches. On the other hand, the structure was so large and contained so many pieces of artillery that it would require at least a thousand soldiers to properly man the walls and an additional 200 or 300 men to service the cannons. Bowie and Neill were more than slightly short of that goal as they commanded just over 100 men or about one sixtieth the force that could concentrate against them.

On February 2nd, Texan scouts confirmed that Santa Anna had finally begun his march northward with San Antonio as the likely objective. Bowie wrote the Texas governor that "Colonel Neill and myself have come to the solemn resolution that we will rather die in these ditches than give it up to the enemy!" Apparently the Bexar commanders drastically underestimated the fighting potential of the Mexican invaders, and equally overestimated the number of rebel reinforcements that would arrive to aid them. Two columns of reinforcements did arrive before Santa Anna, but their numbers were incredibly thin compared to the size of the enemy. The day after Bowie's dramatic message, Colonel William Barret Travis arrived in Bexar with a company of 30 men who were designated "regular" soldiers even though they had no training and no uniforms. A week later an even smaller force arrived with an even more famous commander, the company of mounted Tennessee volunteers led by former Congressman and frontier hero David Crockett, and consisting of perhaps a dozen buckskin clad riflemen. Apparently Colonel Neill, intimidated by the luster of three such famous colonels, decided to let these luminaries worry about the mission and rode away on a vague extended leave of absence. While Crockett must have commanded one of the smallest contingents led by a colonel in American military history, the fort's co-commanders, Travis and Bowie, exercised leadership over a garrison that might easily have required the services of a captain. Despite the small size of the garrison and the poor construction of the mission, two members of the detachment, Green Jamieson and Almeron Dickinson, utilized their special talents to improve the crumbling structure. Jamieson erected a wooden stockade across a fifty yard gap between two of the Alamo walls, constructed a series of firing platforms on the walls and supervised the deployment of gun mounts for much of the artillery force. Dickinson deployed a number of batteries to cover each approach to the fort and positioned the formidable 18 pounder to command access to the town.

The rebel garrison celebrated the arrival of Crockett with a Washington's Birthday party in town that continued far into the night, but the festivities were interrupted when a scout entered Bexar with the startling news that the Mexican army was only a few miles away. The next morning, while the enemy cavalry began to deploy for a sweep into town, the Texan rebels grabbed extra rifles and as much powder as they could carry and headed for the mission. One of the most famous and controversial sieges in American history was about to begin.

The siege of the Alamo was relatively short by most historical standards; only 13 days elapsed between the arrival of the advance units of the Mexican army and the final assault on the mission. However, this confrontation more than made up in drama what it lacked in total number of days of crisis. First, few besieged garrisons in American history have faced the almost impossible odds that were stacked against them. Santa Anna was capable of concentrating a Mexican assault force that outnumbered the Texan defenders by over thirty to one, and yet this small group of rebels virtually unanimously elected to stay and fight to the end, even when some opportunity for escape still remained. Second, defenders such as Jim Bowie and Davy Crockett were colorful, well known personalities who died facing an enemy leader displaying particularly outrageous cruelty to his vanquished foes.

The chronicle of the siege of the Alamo presents a fascinating blend of myth and reality in which popular film and television images of the events surrounding those 13 days are alternately supported and disproved by the actual facts. The depiction of tightly drawn siege lines of Mexicans surrounding the besieged mission is somewhat exaggerated but not entirely inaccurate. Santa Anna had something over 5000 men available for his punitive operations, but his forces were so widely scattered and changing positions so frequently that it appears that only about half of this number was available for effective siege operations. Thus rebels were generally able to get in or out of the Alamo and even the relatively large force of 32 volunteers riding in from Gonzalez was able to slip through the Mexican lines with little serious trouble.

The image of wheel to wheel cannons blasting the besieged garrison is also a combination of fact and myth. On the one hand, Santa Anna brought only 12 cannons with his main force, while the Texans could theoretically deploy twice that number against the invaders. However, the defenders were consistently short of powder and cannon balls and had to minimize their fire until the final assault, while the relatively small number of Mexican guns were well supplied with ammunition and were able to open a number of breaches in the poorly constructed mission walls. Santa Anna could probably have waited until his larger 12 pounders arrived from the south and pounded the fort to pieces in a few days, but delay was simply not the dictator's style and he didn't seem to be overly concerned about wasting the lives of his men to gain his objectives.

The popular depiction of Davy Crockett and similar sharpshooters making life miserable for the besiegers with their shooting exploits is also based on strong elements of fact. It is apparent that a significant percentage of defenders was armed with some form of long range rifle which was greatly superior to the second hand Brown Bess muskets employed by the Mexicans. This enormous advantage of range would certainly have permitted men such as Crockett to pick off enemy gunners and cavalrymen from a distance and would have added greatly to the morale of the defenders. On the other hand, the massive sorties into the Mexican camp to destroy cannons, collect cattle and destroy enemy confidence which appear in virtually every film or program on the Alamo are clearly exaggerated. The few Texan sorties were generally fairly small scale actions designed to destroy nearby huts and shacks that could provide cover for Mexican troops and usually employed only a few men. Finally, the famous depictions of the feud between Travis and Bowie are based on some premise of fact but, again, greatly exaggerated. It is fairly evident from most accounts of the siege that Bowie was stricken with some vague fever or attack very early in the siege and Travis effectively commanded the garrison for most of the next two weeks. Bowie's major contribution to the defense of the Alamo, for better or worse, occurred mainly in the period before the siege was fully underway. On the other hand, it is probable that the famous knife fighter did provide moral support to the men during the last days and it is not at all unreasonable to assume that his final stand was every bit as dramatic as portrayed in films or television.

One of the most intriguing elements of the saga of the Alamo was the attempt, and subsequent failure, of Colonel James Fannin to relieve the garrison by marching a fairly large detachment from Goliad to Bexar. Fannin was one of the few West Point trained officers in the rebel army and he had developed the Goliad mission into a formidable bastion called Fort Defiance with a garrison of 420 men. When the detachment commander was informed of Santa Anna's arrival in Bexar, he almost immediately assembled a relief force of 320 men and four cannons and set out toward the Alamo 95 miles distant. A rapid march to San Antonio might have produced either an even worse massacre or the deliverance of the garrison but neither scenario ever developed, as the breakdown of Fannin's wagons quickly convinced the colonel to retreat back inside the walls of his bastion.

The failure of this relief expedition narrowed the options of the Alamo garrison to three bleak choices—surrender, escape or last ditch resistance. While the possibility of surrender may have been discussed among the Alamo's officers, the red flag of no quarter that Santa Anna had ordered flown from the tower of a Bexar church probably discouraged confidence in the Generalissimo's willingness to provide generous terms. The possibility of escape was probably available almost up to the final assault on the mission and apparently at least a handful of defenders slipped over the walls at one time or another during the siege. However, the vast majority of the rebels decided to defend the fort to the last extremity even though the dramatic gesture of Travis' line in the sand is not particularly well documented. While the authors agree with the conventional theory that the Texan defenders were determined to sell their lives as dearly as possible in a Mexican assault, we feel that it is reasonable to believe that the members of the garrison still maintained strong hopes that they could survive an enemy attack right up until the final moments of the battle. The Texans had survived a 13-day siege with no loss to their own force and relatively minimal damage to the Alamo. The defenders knew they had more and better artillery than the besiegers while their rifles had better range than their opponents' muskets. Virtually every member of the garrison was extremely familiar with the American victory at New Orleans, where the defenders' combination of superior artillery and rifles had devastated an army far better trained and more professional than Santa Anna's invaders. Thus it was quite possible that the Texans approached the end of the siege with some hope that the miracle of New Orleans could be re-enacted in San Antonio.

On the afternoon of March 5, 1836, Santa Anna decided to end the stalemate in Bexar by launching a massive assault on the Alamo scheduled for the pre-dawn hours of the next morning. The Mexican president planned to use an initial assault force of 1800 men deployed in four columns that would strike each of the mission walls. A screening force of cavalry would cut off any possible escape from the fort, while a reserve force of elite grenadiers remained in waiting to exploit the first Mexican success. Santa Anna expected the element of surprise to be decisive in the assault, but Travis and his men had expected an impending attack when the enemy batteries stopped firing on the evening of March 5th. The defenders deployed every possible gun that could be mounted and then stacked four or five rifles next to each firing position to provide maximum firepower during the attack.

Throughout the night, battalions of assault troops marched into position in the cold, wet grass outside the mission. The initial attack had been scheduled for 4 A.M. but the Mexican president ordered a last minute postponement for an hour to provide better light for the advance. This delay proved to be a crucial factor in the battle as the nervous attackers started yelling "Viva Santa Anna" as they waited for the order to advance, and the Texans were able to receive at least a brief warning of the impending threat. As the hundreds of assault troops jumped up and ran forward, Travis grabbed a sword and shotgun and yelled "Come on boys! The Mexicans are upon us and we'll give them Hell!"

The battle of the Alamo was essentially fought in three stages which lasted about as long as a play or film. The first stage of the engagement began as a major disaster for the attackers and threatened to provide the Texans with a huge psychological victory. The white coated Mexican infantry pushed toward the Alamo from all four sides, but the defenders met this first challenge with supreme success. A battery of 12 pounders began tearing through entire companies of attackers while the Texan sharpshooters calmly grabbed each successive loaded rifle and squeezed off another devastating round. However, just as the Texan fire reached a crescendo, William Barrett Travis was shot in the head as he directed the fire of an artillery battery.

Despite the loss of the fort's commanding officer, the defenders were slaughtering the Mexican troops so quickly that the whole army was on the point of disintegration. As the first streaks of gray sky brightened the early morning, the initial assault collapsed while one column commander, Colonel Duque, crumpled to the ground with several Texan bullet wounds and was trampled by his own men in the confusion. However, the surviving Mexican officers were able to regroup their companies and organize a second thrust at the Alamo walls that got off to a somewhat more promising start. It was now light enough for the attackers to spot the Texan sharpshooters and artillerymen and at least some of the defenders were now dropping from Mexican musket volleys. However, as the front line assault companies began to close on the mission walls, they were caught in a vicious crossfire of rebel guns and their own support troops who were now hitting more of their own men with their massed volleys than Texans. This second assault began to break apart in panic and confusion, and Santa Anna, who was sitting safely behind a redoubt, was faced with a situation similar to William Howe after the collapse of the second attack on Breed's Hill sixty-one years earlier. While Howe personally led his decimated redcoats against the rebel defenses, the self styled Napoleon of the West remained well protected but threw in every elite unit he could deploy for a gigantic concentrated push.

The final assault on the Alamo began with another volley of cannon and rifle fire smashing entire lines of Mexican troops as they groped toward the mission walls. However, the very intensity of the Texan fire prompted an unplanned maneuver that started to turn the tide of the battle. The columns under the command of General Cos, Colonel Romero, and the now deceased Colonel Duque all converged on one point of the Alamo wall as they almost blindly tried to escape the hailstorm of lead and broken horseshoes. Ironically, the nearly defeated Mexicans were concentrating on one of the weakest spots in the entire fortress. This part of the Alamo wall had received the heaviest damage from Mexican artillery, and there were a number of newly opened breaches that had only been partially repaired. Also, this part of the wall contained no firing steps so the rebel defenders were forced to either lie on top of the wall or dig holes in the parapet in order to get a clear field of fire.

When the three Mexican columns converged on this weak point, there were probably nearly 1000 assault troops engaging perhaps 20 or 30 Texans who were deployed in this particular spot. The defenders blasted volleys from the top of the walls and through their loopholes, and dozens of attackers went down within minutes. However the death of Travis left the fortress with no overall commander responsible for deploying the various defenders, and the garrison was so small that there was absolutely no reserve force to throw into a breach of the defenses. Thus while smaller groups of Mexicans were being shot and having their ladders pushed down on them by rebels in better defended locations, the largest single concentration of attackers was climbing over and through this vulnerable point. As wave after wave of Mexicans scrambled over the top of this wall, the available defenders went down in a wild melee of individual confrontations. At this point, the earlier disadvantage of the attackers' muskets quickly transformed into an enormous advantage. The Alamo defenders were generously armed with rifles that provided much greater accuracy than enemy muskets but were not equipped to carry a bayonet. As long as the fighting was occurring at a distance, the rifles were far superior, but now, as hundreds of attackers climbed over the walls, the deadly Mexican bayonets were more than a match for anything the Texans possessed for close-in fighting. Individual defenders pulled out single shot pistols, Bowie knives and even tomahawks, but these weapons, even combined with clubbed rifles, were no match for Mexican steel. A defender surrounded by five or ten assailants might kill one or two of his adversaries in a final burst of adrenalin, but invariably the outcome favored the Mexicans. While some of the white coated attackers engaged the rebels, others jumped to the ground and opened the main gate of the mission. Within minutes the whole defense of the north wall collapsed and hundreds of assault troops poured into the Alamo plaza.

While the defenders of the north wall attempted to hold back a rising tide of Mexican attackers, Davy Crockett and his Tennesseans were engaged in a desperate attempt to keep General Morales' column from over-running the southern perimeter of the fort. Crockett had agreed to command the defense of the most vulnerable point in the mission—the wooded palisade that had been built to cover the gaps in the mission walls. This wooden stockade looked particularly attractive to Morales' assault companies and the first ranks of attackers advanced toward this inviting target. Suddenly, volley after volley of rifle fire belched from the Tennesseans' guns and the Mexican attack disintegrated so quickly that Morales was about to signal a general retreat. A last desperate gamble allowed Morales to swing his survivors well clear of Crockett's palisade and toward a cluster of huts near the other end of the south wall. A picked force of elite infantry seized the huts, rushed across an open space between themselves and the Alamo's mighty 18 pounder, and then climbed into the rear of the barbette which protected the gun. The rebel artillerymen had no supporting riflemen near them, and the startled gunners were slashed to pieces by flashing bayonets with their invaluable gun now being swung around to blast the defenders.

Once the Mexican attackers had captured the main gate and gotten control of the Alamo's most powerful piece of artillery, the last hope for Texan victory virtually disappeared. However, a final, and in many cases most gruesome, act in the drama remained to be played out. The rebel defenders who were still manning the walls were now in an untenable position as they were being forced to engage hordes of attackers in hand to hand combat. Some of the Texans jumped over the sides of the walls that led to the surrounding fields and began to place as much distance between themselves and the fort as possible. General Sesma's cavalry screen had been waiting for this moment and the Mexican lancers skewered most of the retreating rebels. At least two defenders escaped immediate capture but were detected and executed later in the day, while it is somewhat possible that two other retreating Texans avoided the lancers and showed up in Nacogdoches later in that month with an emotional description of the final assault.

While some of the Texans took their chances with the enemy cavalry in the open, most of the surviving defenders retreated to a series of well prepared interior strong points. Many of the missions's rooms had been fitted with loopholes, earthen parapets and even shallow trenches to facilitate a last ditch stand. A number of fast moving defenders were able to retire into these strongholds and pour a devastating fire on the massed attackers who were filling the mission plaza. Dozens of well protected sharpshooters, supported by a few batteries of shrapnel firing cannons, started tearing huge holes in the Mexican formations as a gigantic crossfire began to develop. Once again the Mexican assault seemed on the verge of collapse, and once again, Santa Anna was too far from the action to produce a response. However, two of the senior Mexican leaders in the fort, generals Amador and Morales, turned the course of the battle. These men ordered massive assaults on most of the remaining rebel artillery batteries and then turned the captured guns on each of the Texan strong points. A grisly routine emerged in which Alamo guns would blast through rebel parapets, bayonet wielding infantry would storm an individual room and after a short, bloody engagement, wipe out the defenders. Room by room this procedure resulted in additional Mexican casualties but invariably captured the dwindling rebel strongholds.

The gradual elimination of Texan bastions soon reduced the number of rebel defenders to a hopelessly outnumbered handful concentrated in a few bypassed locations. One of these survivors was Jim Bowie who had been installed in a small room near the main gate with a brace of pistols and his famous knife. While some accounts of the siege suggest that the famous knife fighter was either unconscious or dead during the final assault, it seems more likely that the legendary final encounter really did take place in which the fort's co-commander died in a final struggle with a group of Mexican attackers who suffered at least some casualties in the process.

The last surviving defenders retreated to the heavily fortified Alamo church which featured the firepower of a battery of rebel 12 pounders. Almeron Dickinson's gunners opened salvos of nails and horseshoes at the massing Mexican infantry and a few remaining sharpshooters picked off attackers who tried to batter in the thick church doors. When dozens of Mexican attackers dropped to the ground dead or wounded, Morales ordered the 18 pounder swung into position and the huge balls started to batter the church. The double doors splintered and sagged as dozens of attackers streamed into the aisles and spread out through the smoke filled building. Not only were most of the remaining defenders stabbed or shot, at least three young boys were slaughtered by Mexican bayonets before officers could stop their men. After Dickinson and his remaining gunners went down in a final bayonet assault, the last effective defender, Major Robert Evans, sprinted toward the powder magazine with hopes of blowing up another mass of Mexican attackers. A volley of musket fire brought down the major before he could reach the powder kegs and a small group of non-combatants, including Mrs. Dickinson and her daughter and Colonel Travis' servant, were discovered in the rubble and escorted to the triumphant Santa Anna.

The legendary battle of the Alamo probably lasted just under two hours and ended before 7 A.M. on March 6th. The rising sun revealed about 180 defenders sprawled around the mission and the adjoining fields while the triumphant Generalissimo dismissed the engagement as a "small affair." While the Mexican president blithely informed his Congress that only 65 attackers had been lost in an assault that had killed 600 Texas rebels, his more sober minded subordinates were privately wondering how many more such victories it would take to eradicate their army. Santa Anna had indeed captured a rebel stronghold and massacred the garrison, but he had come very close to losing the battle and had suffered far more casualties than he was willing to acknowledge. American estimates of Mexican losses on that fateful March morning range between 600 and 1600 out of an assault force that has been calculated at something between 1800 and 5000 men. Mexican official reports for this period are appallingly exaggerated and incomplete and it seems that every Mexican general admitted to a different level of losses. The figure of 600 casualties has been based on the rather tenuous claims of a captured American physician who treated Santa Anna's wounded soldiers and a Mexican study of the siege released after the war with the United States. While this figure may be an approximation of the actual Mexican losses, the authors believe that it is quite possible that Santa Anna may have suffered considerably higher casualties. The rebel firepower, especially in the opening stage of the assault, must have been extremely formidable. Several batteries of shrapnel firing cannons supported by crack shot riflemen armed with several weapons each must have taken a fearsome toll of Mexican attackers who enjoyed virtually no cover or protection. The British losses of 45% of the assault forces at Bunker Hill and New Orleans may have been matched in the Mexican attempts to capture the Alamo walls. A Mexican loss of this percentage among the 1800 front line assault troops would calculate to about 800-850 casualties in the advance on the mission. Once the attackers had gained control of the walls, the casualty exchange would probably be much more even, but it is not unreasonable that each Texan defender would have killed or wounded at least one assailant before he died, thus adding another 150-180 Mexican casualties in the battle for the parapets and interior buildings. Thus is it certainly possible that a total loss of about 1000 soldiers verified Travis' prediction that "victory will cost the enemy so dear, that it will be worse for him than defeat."

The capture of a relatively small rebel fortress cost the Mexican dictator more than just the loss of a fairly high percentage of his invading army. American newspapers attempted to outdo one another in the invective against the Napoleon of the West and epithets such as "tyrant" and "butcher" were the mildest titles for the Generalissimo. Reports of Santa Anna's policy of no quarter filtered into the northern republic and they included hints of butchering of unarmed captives. Apparently at least six or seven defenders, possibly including Davy Crockett, were captured alive and presented to the commanding general by General Castrillon, who pleaded for their lives. Santa Anna let out a contemptuous sneer and turned his back as his staff officers and bodyguard fell upon the unlucky survivors with their swords and bayonets, almost killing Castrillon in the process. This complete contempt for the rules of war among civilized nations was shocking to a mid-19th century American public that had seen even the hated redcoats display at least some chivalrous conduct against captured

Americans. Thus the New York *Post* warned the Mexican dictator "he will shortly see that policy would have required that he govern himself by the rules of civilized warfare. Had he treated the vanquished with moderation and generosity, it would have been difficult if not impossible to awaken that general sympathy for the people of Texas which now impels so many adventurous and ardent spirits to throng to the aid of their brethren."

Santa Anna's reputation as a butcher in the American states was dramatically embellished by the subsequent events around Goliad. Colonel James Fannin, the timid commander of Fort Defiance, recovered enough of his nerve to attempt to leave the fortress to link up with Sam Houston's main Texan army. However, the column of over 500 men had marched only a short distance when wagons began to fall apart and the commander quickly ordered his men to camp in a virtually undefendable field even though a far more promising wooded region was only two miles away. The next morning, March 20th, when the Texans began to resume their advance toward nearby Coleto Creek and its inviting wooded position, General Jose Urrea's cavalry swooped down and attacked the rebels. The Texans were able to hold their own in a bloody all-day battle, but Urrea kept receiving additional units and by nightfall he had totally surrounded the rebels. The next morning, Fannin called a council of war among his officers to discuss the alternatives of breaking out of the trap or capitulation. Fannin's even more timid subordinates quickly suggested a surrender and the Texans gave up their arms based on Urrea's vague demand of "surrender at discretion."

The defeated Texans were marched back to Goliad where the uninjured rebels were imprisoned in a partially burned out church while about 100 wounded prisoners were accommodated in a makeshift hospital. The captured Americans were reasonably cheerful as they heard Mexican rumors that they would soon be repatriated to the United States as a goodwill gesture by Santa Anna. However, the Mexican president had far more malevolent plans for his prisoners. On March 26th, Santa Anna issued a directive to Urrea's temporary replacement in Goliad, Colonel Jose Portilla, to execute all of the rebel captives as soon as possible. The next morning, the uninjured prisoners were lined up and marched out of town toward a nearby forest. Suddenly a large detachment of Mexican cavalry surrounded the three columns of rebels while infantry units formed up behind the horsemen. A moment later volleys of musket fire began slaughtering the stunned Texans although about 20 men were able to escape in the initial confusion. Fannin and his second in command were accorded the "honor" of a separate execution although their bodies were burned with their men. A short time later the helpless wounded prisoners were either bayoneted in their beds or dragged outside and shot as the Generalissimo's vengeance against the rebel Texans reached its climax. An additional 400 rebels had been added to the tally at Bexar, and the Napoleon of the West was convinced that one more massacre would crush the Texas republic forever.

Since the only remaining rebel force in the field was Sam Houston's small army, this force became the next logical target for the Mexican invaders.

The massacres at Bexar and Goliad prompted thousands of Texas colonists to abandon their farms and homes and retreat eastward in a movement termed the Runaway Scrape. The tide of civilian evacuees roughly paralleled the withdrawal of Sam Houston's single remaining Texan army as it retreated in search of an opportunity to strike at Santa Anna without being annihilated. On March 17th Houston reached the Colorado River and took up a good defensive position in anticipation of a link up with Fannin's column, but when survivors of the Goliad massacre streamed into camp, the army began another withdrawal to the east. However, while the Mexican president was gobbling up vast expanses of rebel territory, his army was becoming divided into smaller detachments as additional troops were assigned to garrison the newly conquered areas. On April 14th Santa Anna's scouts reported that Texan president David Burnet and his entire cabinet were meeting at Harrisburg, only 30 miles from the Mexican advanced cavalry units. The Generalissimo quickly assembled a mobile force of 750 men and pushed toward his objective while additional elements were ordered to move forward as soon as they could be concentrated.

Burnet and his associates were able to abandon Harrisburg just before Mexican cavalry units swooped down to capture them, but Sam Houston now realized that his opponent's impetuous abandonment of most of his army was just the opportunity for which he had been waiting. Houston assembled his army of 800 volunteers and marched his men toward a position on the San Jacinto river that effectively cut off Santa Anna from his main army. On the afternoon of April 19th, he exhorted his men that "victory is certain, trust in God and fear not! Remember the Alamo!" An additional day of hard marching brought the Texans to Buffalo Bayou, which was directly astride the route that Santa Anna and his advance corps would have to follow to regain contact with the main body. The Texan army was deployed in a position that featured the 300 foot wide and 30 foot deep Bayou on the right, the San Jacinto River on the left and a marshy field in the front while a large forest of live oaks provided a valuable fall back position to the rear. The location of the bayou and river made a Mexican flanking attack almost impossible while the marshy fields would provide poor footing for a frontal assault.

The Texan army was barely able to set up its defenses when the first units of the Mexican army arrived on the scene. The afternoon of April 20th featured a number of cavalry skirmishes between Mexican lancers and mounted Texans while a mini-artillery duel raged between the rebel army's two 6 pounders and Santa Anna's single 9 pound gun. When the Mexican dictator's scouts reported the strength of the rebel position, Santa Anna decided to withdraw a short distance toward Peggy Lake and await the arrival of the only immediately available reinforcements, 400 men led by General Cos.

April 21st, 1836 dawned as a beautiful spring day and the Mexican army was observed throwing up a barricade of saddles, luggage and ration boxes while waiting for Cos' arrival. When the reinforcements arrived a combined force of just under 1200 Mexicans ate and rested while their general took a nap in preparation for his next move. Houston utilized his adversary's less than energetic response to the Texans' threat to accomplish two important tasks. First, the Texan general ordered a detachment to destroy nearby Vince's Bridge, which effectively cut off the only route of retreat for either army and guaranteed that a major confrontation would have to take place on this ground. Second, Houston called a council of war to solicit opinions whether the Texans should hold their ground or attack Santa Anna before he attacked them. When the discussion produced a tie vote, Houston broke the stalemate by jumping on his white horse, drawing his sword, and ordering his volunteers to advance in a ragged attack formation accompanied by their two artillery pieces.

The battle of San Jacinto began in the warmth of a late afternoon sun as the Napoleon of the West slept contentedly under a large oak tree. Virtually every man in the Texan army had a friend or relative killed at Bexar or Goliad and each volunteer knew he could expect the same treatment if Santa Anna emerged victorious on this April afternoon. At about 3:30 P.M. the line of rebels marched to within 200 yards of the Mexican camp and the two Texan cannons spewed salvos of horseshoe pieces and nails into the enemy fortifications. The flying missiles cut through the startled Mexicans and shredded their hastily constructed barricade. Then the Texans began shouting "Remember the Alamo!" and "Remember Goliad!" and they charged the enemy position before most of their adversaries could load their muskets. The result was an 18 minute melee in which the organization and leadership of the Mexican army simply evaporated and the Texans engaged in a bloody retribution for Santa Anna's barbarism.

The Mexican president awoke from his nap to discover rebel soldiers slaughtering his panic stricken men as most of his senior officers were either dead or retreating. Some of the terrified Mexican soldiers headed for the bayous and drowned in their attempt to escape while others were shot as they attempted to surrender to Texans who were determined to pay back the atrocities of March. While the painfully wounded Houston rode around attempting to stop the slaughter, many rebels simply ignored their general and killed anyone unlucky enough to be in a Mexican uniform. The impact of the Texan attack had been so surprising and so devastating that few Mexican soldiers ever fired back and only 9 of the attackers were lost in the frenzied battle while over 630 adversaries had been killed before some semblance of order was restored.

Houston's men continued to round up Mexican fugitives during the night and the next morning, and the most valuable capture occurred when a nondescript "private" in a faded coat and red carpet slippers was escorted to the hastily constructed prisoner compound. When large numbers of captured Mexicans began shouting "El Presidente" to this newly arrived captive, he was escorted to Houston and identified as Santa Anna. A Mexican bullet had inflicted a painful leg wound on the Texan commander and he was heavily sedated by large doses of opium. When the Napoleon of the West was brought to a tree under which Houston was sleeping, the former governor of Tennessee temporarily halted cries for Santa Anna's immediate execution and granted the Mexican general's request for some opium for his own use.

Houston may have been less than totally coherent when Santa Anna was brought before him, but he quickly regained enough awareness to conduct an enormously important negotiation with the Mexican president. The Generalissimo's earlier atrocities certainly made him a prime candidate for a particularly nasty execution envisioned by many of the Texan volunteers, but Houston was intelligent enough to realize that while he had annihilated one enemy army of 1200 men, there were still over 4000 more Mexicans to face his badly outnumbered army. In return for Santa Anna's safety and eventual return to Mexico, Houston extracted an agreement to withdraw all enemy forces from Texas and a promise of recognition of Texan independence. Houston probably suspected that Santa Anna would disavow his agreement as soon as he returned to Mexico City, but it would be difficult to assemble a new invasion force and any kind of truce would provide an opportunity for American aid to the new republic. Thus, given the cards that Houston had to play, he probably accomplished the best deal that the Texan colonists could get in the bloody Spring of 1836.

The Texan Revolution had been a glorious triumph of the relatively small number of rebels who had challenged the military might of the Mexican republic. However, the cost of victory had been incredibly high. Of the approximately 7000 adult males living in Texas at the beginning of 1836, more than 700 had been killed at Bexar and Goliad alone, while dozens of others had been lost in smaller skirmishes or executed when they were captured. The literal decimation of the Texan rebels had secured a new country, but equally important to the long term relations between Mexico and the United States, stimulated a sense of outrage among Americans that made a full scale war between the two North American republics increasingly likely within the next decade. The first phase of the conflict between Mexico and America may not have included a formal declaration of war, but it was a brutal, bloody opening stage of a confrontation that would deeply affect both nations for decades to come.

# CHAPTER 19

# Zachary Taylor's War

## The Northern Campaign in the Mexican-American Conflict

$T$he decade following the rebel victory of San Jacinto was a period of complex relationships between the republics of Texas, Mexico and the United States of America. While the Mexican government never launched a serious follow-up invasion of their breakaway province, a state of low intensity warfare simmered along the Texan-Mexican borderlands for years. The Lone Star Republic had been recognized by the United States and European powers such as Great Britain and France, but the majority of Texans leaned toward annexation to the American Union if the necessary legislation could be approved in Washington. The presidential election of 1844 presented clear cut alternatives to American voters, as Whig candidate Henry Clay generally opposed immediate annexation while Democrat James K. Polk supported a broad-based policy of expansionism that included statehood for the Lone Star territory.

At midmorning of March 4, 1845, newly elected President Polk stepped out from the lobby of the Coleman Hotel and, in a driving, cold rain, climbed into President John Tyler's open carriage for the traditional ride down Pennsylvania Avenue to the Capitol. The new president's inauguration address was triumphant yet moderate and conciliatory toward the Whig opposition. However, the new president clearly subscribed to the idea that the annexation of Texas would be merely a rectification of the mistake that had been committed in 1819 when the United States had ceded Texas to Spain in exchange for Florida. He insisted that "annexation is a matter between Texas and the United States alone," clearly warning Europe and Mexico to refrain from what was seen as an internal issue for the American republic. The Mexican government responded to Polk's speech with a terminating of diplomatic relations and a mobilization of forces to challenge American hegemony between the Knacks and Rio Grande rivers. The new president subsequently dispatched Brigadier General Zachary Taylor to Fort Jesup, Louisiana with over 2500 regulars to form an "army of Observation" pending Texan acceptance of the terms of annexation. When the Texas Republic approved union with the United States on July 4, 1845, Taylor's small army was ordered to advance to the Rio Grande and build appropriate fortifications to challenge Mexican advances into what was now claimed as American territory.

The Republic of Mexico insisted on two points concerning Texas that made war between the two North American republics increasingly likely by the spring of 1846. First, the Mexican government refused to concede the independence of its rebellious province and thus accused the American government of interfering with the internal affairs of its northern neighbor. Second, the Mexicans also claimed that the southern boundary of the province of Texas had been the Nueces River so that the stationing of American troops along the Rio Grande was a clear cut invasion of Mexican soil. Thus as Zachary Taylor completed a supply depot at Point Isabel on the Gulf of Mexico and a front line fortification at Fort Texas across the river from the city of Matamoros, a large Mexican army was being deployed on the opposite side of the Rio Grande. A series of incidents that began on April 9th, 1846 provoked an escalation of hostilities that produced open warfare between the two armies only three weeks later.

The first step toward all out combat occurred when Taylor's quartermaster, Colonel Truman Cross, failed to return from a horseback ride and an American search party was ambushed by Mexican cavalry with several casualties on each side. The subsequent discovery of Cross' mutilated body simply confirmed that the area north of the Rio Grande was rapidly developing into a war zone. On April 24th, newly arrived Mexican commander General Mariano Arista sent an imposing column of 1600 lancers under General Anastasio Torrejon on a sweep across the river above Fort Texas. The next day the Mexican horsemen collided with Captain Seth Thornton's patrol of 63 American dragoons and in a brief, one sided battle, 11 Americans were killed and Thornton and most of his men was captured. Taylor dispatched a message to Polk that "hostilities may now be considered as commenced" and requested immediate reinforcement from the governor of Texas. War between the two major republics of North America had finally become a reality, and each contending society began an official evaluation of its ability to emerge victorious in the upcoming conflict.

The United States entered hostilities with Mexico during a period of rapid population growth that had pushed the total population of the republic to just under 21 million people, which was about triple the size of the United States when it had challenged the British empire 34 years earlier. The United States of 1846 was a far larger, wealthier, and more technologically developed nation than the young republic of the early 19th century, but the country was still far less inclined toward military affairs than comparable European societies. The United States Army in 1846 was even smaller than the 1812 version with about 5300 troops available for deployment. The horrendous pay of $8 a month, the lack of prestige of a military career and the ready availability of easier, better paying jobs encouraged most native born citizens to view enlistment in the army as an extremely undesirable alternative to almost any other pursuit. About one adult male citizen in two thousand actually enlisted in the regular army, so maintaining even the extremely modest numbers that Congress authorized required recruiters to tap into the immigrant population to fill out the regiments. By the spring of 1846 as incredibly high 48% of the army was composed of foreign born recruits, almost half of whom had recently arrived from Ireland. Contemporary accounts concerning the morale of the American army on the eve of war are incredibly contradictory as observers noted the tight discipline and professionalism of the regulars but include comments that many of these men were less than enthusiastic about a career in soldiering. The fact that the Mexican War featured probably the highest desertion rate from the American army of any major conflict and that hundreds of these men actively joined the Mexican cause raises some interesting questions concerning the willingness of substantial numbers of soldiers to switch allegiances from one flag to another with few qualms about their actions.

The United States entered hostilities with Mexico armed with an array of weaponry that was relatively good but might have been much better. The army had recently adopted the Model 1841 percussion rifle which offered superior accuracy and the significant advantage of eliminating the use of the flint and its attendant problems in damp or stormy weather. However, due to budgetary constraints, only a few companies of regulars had been armed with this weapon, while most units fought the Mexicans using the last generation of flintlock muskets which were better than their adversaries' but far less reliable than the new percussion system. As Ulysses Grant noted, "at a distance of a few hundred yards a man might fire at you all day without you finding out."

While the American troops entered the war outnumbered by their opponents, suffering from relatively poor morale and armed with mediocre muskets, they did possess several substantial advantages that would emerge as the war progressed. First, the artillery arm of the American army had developed into one of the most effective units of any mid-19th century military force. Elements of the artillery forces had been organized into highly mobile "flying artillery" units which featured 6 pounder guns that could be rapidly transported from one point of the battlefield to another in a short time and then employed in either defensive or offensive modes, depending on the evolving nature of the engagement. At times it seems that this fast moving array of cannons could be used with the same shock effect in halting enemy attacks as the employment of tactical air support and armored units in 20th century battles. The excellent deployment of American guns turned more than one battle from a near defeat to a triumphant victory in a matter of minutes. A second weapon system that has been less amply documented in available literature but seems to have played a major role in several battles was the informal introduction of mass firepower to the battlefield with the introduction of the revolver. The recently developed invention of Samuel Colt, which allowed the owner of a six shooter to employ far more close-in firepower than the slow loading, unreliable flintlock pistols, was not generally recognized as an official weapon in most regular units. However, an increasing number of infantry officers, cavalrymen, artillerymen and, eventually, infantry enlisted men began to appreciate the enormous advantage of employing one or two revolvers in a close-in engagement. A relatively small number of dragoons armed with a pair of pistols apiece could devastate a much large unit of Mexican cavalry well before the enemy could employ their much more awkward lances and swords. In a similar vein, six shooters provided an ideal close-in weapon for American artillerymen who were attempting to parry the threat of enemy cavalry who were on the verge of overrunning Yankee guns.

Finally, in the numerous instances of street fighting that developed during the war, a rapid firing pistol was invaluable in house-to-house combat where a long barreled musket was difficult to handle. Thus the combination of mobile artillery to provide longer range firepower and revolvers to supply closer distance superiority proved an awesome addition to American fighting capabilities in 1846 and 1847, and permitted Zachary Taylor and Winfield Scott to counter much larger numbers of adversaries.

The Mexican army that was deployed to oppose the United States was, on paper, vastly superior to its northern adversaries. The government in Mexico City could field almost 32,000 regulars, which provided a 6 to 1 numerical superiority against the Americans. The Mexican army was battle tested from years of putting down revolts and being involved in a seemingly endless round of civil wars that plagued the republic. While these upheavals provided extensive combat experience for the soldiers, they also devastated the Mexican economy and ensured that the nation would enter the war with few modern warships, a tiny industrial base and little capacity to produce effective weapons systems. On the whole, Mexican tactics, weapons and equipment were simply not up to the demands of contesting a war with a increasingly technologically advanced mid-19th century economic power. Mexican soldiers went to war carrying left over Napoleonic era Brown Bess muskets that had been dumped by the British Army, and then charged those weapons with defective gunpowder that encouraged men to either fire from the hip or close their eyes during each less-than-effective volley. The Mexican cavalry included a number of effective horsemen but the men carried lances and sabers that were simply no match for opponents armed with revolvers, breach loading carbines and shotguns. The artillery arm was equally competent, but saddled with an awkward array of cannons that seemed too heavy to move easily on the battlefield and too light to do serious damage when finally deployed. During the Vera Cruz-Mexico City campaign the Mexican army relied increasingly heavily on the Irish deserters from the American army, who formed the famous San Patricio Battalion and played a key role in manning the available cannons.

The two contending nations also shared certain common points as they approached the outbreak of hostilities. The United States and Mexico each employed a large number of generals who consistently kept at least one eye focused on potential political advantage. Winfield Scott, commander of the American army in 1846, had already been considered for the Whig nomination for the presidency, while Zachary Taylor seemed to fight his battles with a view to their impact on a possible ticket to the White House. In turn, President Polk selected a number of significant field commanders simply because they were loyal Democrats and supported Senator Thomas Hart Benton's bid to become senior military commander in order to supersede the politically unreliable Scott and Taylor. The Mexican high command was, if possible, even more devious and politically motivated than their American counterparts. The appointment, dismissal and re-instatement of Mexican generals rivaled the later pattern of the Army of the Potomac and provided few really effective leaders. However, the political survival techniques of most American and Mexican generals paled in comparison to Antonio Lopez de Santa Anna, who rates a special niche in the pantheon of political generals. The Generalissimo's ability to appear to support two warring countries or factions simultaneously far outshone his rather dismal accomplishments on most battlefields. The Napoleon of the West could throw away an entire army in one idiotic gamble and then begin to recruit a new army without pausing for another breath.

The shared emphasis on political advancement displayed by the generals of both armies was matched by a common element of dissent on the war in each nation. American Whigs spent much of the war opposing Polk's conduct of the war and publicizing lack of administration support for the two premier generals. Future Civil War leaders such as Ulysses S. Grant and Abraham Lincoln consistently opposed the war along with much of the officer corps of the army. On the other hand, Mexican solidarity was threatened by secessionist impulses in northern provinces and potential coups in the capital. Finally, the citizens of both nations shared a misunderstanding of the hopes, capabilities and heritage of their neighboring republic. Americans viewed the Mexicans as lazy, idle, superstitious Catholics who seemed doomed to be subjected to a corrupt, unstable government. Mexicans often depicted Americans as greedy, shrewd, money hungry heretic Protestants who would not be satisfied until every acre of the New World was dominated by Washington. The myths and realities of both societies would soon be magnified in the arena of the approaching military conflict.

On April 22nd, 1846, tall redheaded General Mariano Arista arrived in Matamoros to take command of the Mexican army confronting Zachary Taylor on the Rio Grande. Arista had attended school in the United States, lived for a time in Cincinnati and felt that the understood the American temperament better than most Mexicans. The new commanding general knew that Taylor's most glaring weakness was that his major fortification, Fort Texas, was well garrisoned but didn't contain large reserves of food while his main supply base, Point Isabel, featured huge inventories of rations but was relatively weakly defended. Arista was convinced that he should push his army across the river and place it between Fort Texas and Point Isabel, in a position where Taylor would have to attack him at a disadvantage. Since the Mexican army was almost twice as large as its adversary, there was an excellent opportunity for a stunning victory to open the war.

While Arista's plan was well conceived, Zachary Taylor realized the danger of his situation just in time to march a large column back up to Point Isabel before the Mexicans could deploy against him. Taylor left Major Jacob Brown at Fort Texas with an infantry regiment, a battery of his heaviest guns and a number of smaller cannons, while the commanding general marched his main column of 3000 men toward the vital supply depot in the Gulf of Mexico. The Americans had just enough of a head start that Arista couldn't intercept the column, but the Mexican general ordered a bombardment of Fort Texas while most of his army deployed to catch Taylor on his way back to the Rio Grande.

The American march to Point Isabel began on the afternoon of May 1st, and by noon the next day Taylor's men had arrived at the Gulf port and began to load hundreds of wagons with supplies for the main base. The next morning, while the loading process was continuing, the troops in Point Isabel heard the sound of heavy artillery fire back at Fort Texas. Taylor had to decide whether to march his men south with half empty wagons, or trust that Brown's well armed garrison could hold the fort long enough to complete the re-supply activities. The American general dispatched Texas Ranger captain Samuel Walker to slip through Mexican lines to the besieged fort, and the intrepid fort was more than holding its own against the Mexican bombardment. Taylor took two more days to fully load his wagons while deploying Commodore David Conner's welcome gift of 500 Marines to garrison Point Isabel. On the morning of May 6th, Taylor dispatched 500 of his regulars to assist in the defense of his supply depot, and began a march to the Rio Grande with 2500 men and at least 300 wagons groaning with supplies and ammunition.

The small army marched across waist high grass in the shimmering Texas heat and by the next morning the advance units were rapidly closing on the Rio Grande. However, Arista had enjoyed almost a week to deploy his forces and he had positioned over 4000 men in a double line across the width of a plain called Palo Alto or Tall Timbers which straddled the main road back to the river and Fort Texas. Taylor's situation was particularly grim as he was outnumbered, cut off from his base and burdened with a huge, slow moving wagon train. Two of Taylor's young engineers reported back from a reconnaissance that Arista's flanks were anchored by a swamp on one side and a wooded knoll on the other, so that there was little recourse but an assault on the enemy center which probably contained Arista's strongest units. Taylor quickly responded to this threat by dispatching most of his dragoons to guard the vital wagon train, while ordering his infantry and supporting guns to attempt to break through the barricaded road.

The first of a series of lucky breaks for the Americans occurred almost immediately, when Arista's well concealed artillery batteries opened fire at the attackers from a range of over 700 yards, which reduced the impact of their guns so much that the approaching infantry simply sidestepped the balls as they bounced through the grass. The Mexican gunners had given away their positions and Taylor's "flying artillery" batteries quickly moved up and began dropping deadly salvos into the newly vulnerable enemy artillery positions. Major Samuel Ringgold ordered up additional support- ing guns and the massed artillery was soon cutting loose with devastating accuracy that began knocking out Mexican guns and then ripping through the massed ranks of infantry. Arista quickly countered this gambit with a massed cavalry charge, utilizing Colonel Torrejon's 1500 lancers to sweep past the American right flank and smash into the vulnerable enemy wagon park. However, the Mexican horsemen didn't sweep far enough and they were intercepted by the 5th United States Infantry regiment which hastily formed a square and began pouring accurate musket fire into the startled lancers. While their colonel attempted to find a weak point in this formation, Ringgold dashed up at the head of a battery of artillery and began pumping well placed salvos into the middle of the increasingly disorganized horse- men.

While Ringgold's artillery concentrated on the lancers threatening the right flank of the American line, Captain James Duncan deployed a battery of 6 pounders and a pair of heavy duty 18 pounders on the left side of Taylor's position. These American guns knocked out the enemy guns one by one and then began concentrating on the massed ranks of Mexican infantry. The U.S. artillery was soon dropping six to eight rounds a minute into the increasingly panicky enemy formation and when a flaming wad from one of Duncan's guns started a prairie fire, thick columns of black smoke began to engulf the choking musketeers. Arista wisely acknowledged that the Ameri- can gunners had nullified his defensive advantage and he began prepara- tions to withdraw to an alternative position. He had lost perhaps 10% of his army compared to an enemy loss of less than 50 men, but he could quickly summon additional troops from Matamoros while Taylor had little ability to secure reinforcements and his short list of 9 men killed in action included Samuel Ringgold, his brilliant artilleryman.

While Arista was withdrawing his men to a new position under cover of darkness, Taylor was holding a council of war to determine his next move. Most of his officers favored a very cautious advance toward Fort Texas while avoiding a confrontation with Arista if possible. However, a vocal minority led by artillery Captain James Duncan insisted that the Mexican army could be even more thoroughly trounced and they urged their general to initiate an immediate pursuit. Taylor needed little convincing and his small army moved rapidly across the grassland until they encountered the enemy deployed along an old dry river bed called the Resaca de la Palma. Arista had assumed that he had solved the problem of American artillery support by deploying his men along a 200 foot wide ditch that featured walls three or four feet deep and was protected on the flanks by dense formation of chaparral. The Mexican general deployed his infantry behind the ditch, positioned about a dozen cannons along the rim and then retired to his tent to work on the paperwork needed to complete his formation. Taylor carefully studied the formidable Mexican positions and selected 1700 men to launch an assault while the rest of his army was employed in defending the precious wagons.

Taylor assumed that his mobile artillery batteries could smash a hole in the enemy defenses which would allow the infantry to swarm through and split the Mexican line. However, Arista's men were so well entrenched that most of the cannonballs bounced harmlessly on the walls of the Resaca. The American general decided to break the deadlock by ordering Colonel Charles May's dragoons to overrun the Mexican batteries but the alert enemy gunners merely sprinted to safety when they saw the approaching horsemen and then turned their guns to shell the Americans' rear. While the dragoons attempted to extricate themselves from this developing trap, Colonel William Belknap was ordered to support the horsemen with a bayonet charge. Belknap's men were able to link up with the cavalry but the combined force was stalled by the Mexican gunners and riflemen. The whole American attack was on the point of disaster when a small force under Captain Philip Barbour located a well concealed footpath that led behind the Mexican lines and out onto the far side of the Resaca. Barbour's company positioned themselves in a well protected mass of chaparral on the far side of the Mexicans and then opened fire on the startled defenders. Belknap's men used this temporary diversion to launch a bayonet attack which threatened to pin a large number of defenders between two American forces. Suddenly, as the men from this threatened area began to panic and run down the ditch, the whole Mexican line began to unravel and entire units simply disintegrated as individual soldiers decided it was time to seek the safety of Matamoros. Arista's headquarters tent was captured just after he abandoned it, and the Mexican general watched helplessly as swarms of panic stricken soldiers swarmed onto overload ferries and rafts as they attempted to cross the Rio Grande. Dozens of soldiers drowned as they attempted to cross the muddy river and most of the survivors arrived in Matamoros without their weapons. Arista had lost almost 2000 men either killed in action, drowned, or wounded, and most of the survivors arrived on the other side too stunned to continue the battle. However, Taylor made no serious attempt to cross the river and annihilate the Mexican army, contenting himself with rounding up prisoners and tending to his 35 dead and 75 wounded. The final battle for Texas had ended with a devastating Mexican defeat and the scene of the rest of the war would now shift to Mexican soil.

The American public was electrified by the news of Palo Alto and Resaca de la Palma and Zachary Taylor was promoted to brevet major-general despite Polk's uneasiness with his general's rising political stature. Cities and towns across the nation passed resolutions nominating Taylor for president, and delirious Whigs saw a golden opportunity to regain the White House in 1848. However, the American general was facing a far more immediate challenge in his camp on the Rio Grande. Thousands of American volunteers were pouring into the encampment and most of them made it perfectly clear that they had not enlisted to perform fatigue duties or drill; they were simply to fight Mexicans as soon as possible. Politically ambitious regimental commanders were urging "Old Rough and Ready" to advance into northern Mexico as quickly as possible, while Taylor himself was appalled at the growing sick lists and death rates in his main camp at Camargo. Within a few weeks, 1500 men, about one eighth of the volunteers, had died from a variety of afflictions and one officer admitted, "the dead march is played so often on the Rio Grande that the very birds know it."

While Polk and Taylor shared few warm feelings for one another, both men had essentially agreed that the next logical campaign should revolve around a march into northern Mexico in order to secure the province of Nueva Leon and Couhuila while General John Wood's separate army would move into Chihuahua. Their assumption was that the occupation of northern Mexico, combined with American thrusts in California and the region around Sante Fe, would allow the United States to "conquer a peace" by inducing the Mexican government to accept a generous payment for cession of practically unpopulated regions while the northern states would be returned to Mexican sovereignty. However, Taylor's quartermaster officer calculated that an advance into Mexico would require over 2000 wagons and yet only 180 vehicles were available. The American commander spent much of the summer of 1846 searching for alternative campaign plans and by the end of August he was prepared for his next operation.

Zachary Taylor approved an expedition that would utilize most of his 3000 regulars and an approximately equal number of volunteers to march south and west toward the important provincial capital of Monterrey, and then use that city as a springboard for further operations. Taylor planned to use pack mules to supplement his limited number of wagons, but the majority of volunteers would be left behind in Camargo because of the shortage of transport. The American expeditionary force of just over 6000 men was divided into three divisions commanded by William Butler, a political ally of the president; David Twiggs, a big, heavy, intellectual lightweight who General Winfield Scott had claimed "is not qualified to command an army either in the presence or in the absence of an enemy;" and William Worth, a prickly, thin skinned officer who Ulysses S. Grant called "a nervous, impatient and restless man," who was personally brave but couldn't get along with most other officers. Thus, as Twiggs and Worth traded insults and Butler quietly tallied the political benefits of a successful campaign, the relatively small American expeditionary force lurched its way toward Monterrey.

Taylor's main adversary in Monterrey would be General Pedro de Ampudia, who had used his rival Mariano Arista's disasters at Palo Alto and Resaca to gain control of the northern army. Ampudia had garrisoned the capital of Nueva Leon with 7300 regulars and 3000 militia and had established a formidable string of strong points highlighted by the fortifications on Independence Hill and Federation Hill in the western approaches to the city, and the Tancria, El Diablo and Citadel strongholds guarding the northern and eastern roads.

Zachary Taylor arrived on the outskirts of Monterrey on September 20th, 1846 and promptly sent out parties of Texas Rangers and army engineers to study the city's defenses. He deployed his army in a local picnic grove that the Americans named Walnut Springs and began to assimilate the available intelligence. The American commander was convinced that Ampudia was committed to a static defense of the town, that would tend to tie down much of the garrison in fixed positions. Taylor's response to this scenario was to risk a highly controversial division of his outnumbered army into two completely separate wings, that would hit the Mexican defenders from both west and north.

On the afternoon of September 20th, General Worth moved out from Walnut Springs with a column of 2000 men that had been ordered to capture the western defenses of the city. Ampudia's scouts quickly informed their general that the American army had divided, but the Mexican commander ignored the opportunity to destroy his opponents in detail and ordered his men to hold their position and await the first enemy move. Worth's men had to march over extremely difficult terrain, and the American column wasn't ready for offensive operations until the morning of September 21st. Worth's first objective was to cut the Monterrey-Saltillo, road and he dispatched Colonel Hays' mounted Texas Rangers to occupy that route. Suddenly a party of over 1500 Mexican lancers commanded by Colonel Juan Najera wheeled into position to cut off the Texans from the rest of Worth's detachment. Hays' men quickly dismounted and deployed behind a series of fences and ditches while they pulled out a lethal assortment of double barreled shotguns, six shooters and Bowie knives and waited for the Mexican cavalry charge. Hays' fast firing weapons devastated the lancers before they could close in to skewer the Texans and while they were reforming for another attempt, Worth rushed in two artillery batteries to smash Najera's flanks. Najera went down in a torrent of grapeshot and his decimated horsemen broke toward the town. The opening engagement in the battle had lasted less than fifteen minutes and resulted in over 100 Mexican casualties, compared to the loss of one Texan killed and two wounded.

Worth had accomplished his first objective, cutting Monterrey off from its main supply route, but the next goal, the capture of the fortifications on Independence Hill and Federation Hill, was far more daunting. Worth and several of his engineers surveyed the imposing hills and the wing commander finally decided that the safest operation would be to cross the Santa Caterina river, assault Federation Hill, and then use artillery deployed on that newly captured elevation to support an attack on Independence Hill, which seemed to have more extensive fortifications. Captain C. J. Smith was ordered to lead three companies of regulars and six companies of Texas Rangers across the river to start climbing the steep incline of Federation Hill. The nine companies of Americans clawed and groped their way up the elevation while the Mexican defenders poured a largely ineffective sheet of musket and cannon fire down on the assault party. While Ampudia's men were increasingly focusing their attention on this detachment, Worth sent Colonel Persifor Smith's entire brigade up the other side of the mountain where they received little opposition. Apparently the Mexican defenders weren't alerted to this much more serious threat until the Americans were spilling over the crest of the ridge and shooting the garrison from behind. The defenders were now in danger of being trapped by two advancing enemy columns and they quickly fled toward Monterrey, leaving behind an intact 9 pounder cannon. The columns of Captain Smith and Colonel Smith met on the top of the ridge and immediately turned their invaluable captured gun on the main fortification on the hill, El Soldado. The single gun opened a breach in the Mexican redoubt and, as the Americans poured through the last stronghold on Federation Hill, the remaining defenders streamed down the slope toward the city. Worth's wing had ended a spectacular day in which they had cut the main enemy supply line and captured one of the two principal western fortifications at a cost of less than 20 casualties. Unfortunately, their counterparts approaching the northern defenses of Monterrey had a far more sobering and costly experience on that same September 21st.

Taylor had designated Worth's assault on the western approaches to Monterrey as the primary engagement of September 21st, but he had concocted a massive, complicated diversionary effort to prevent Ampudia from concentrating his garrison against Worth's operation. However, the American commander's plan for the rest of his army contained defects that were very similar to the weaknesses in General John Burgoyne's plans during the Saratoga campaign. Just as the British commander could never seem to make up his mind whether his operations against Horatio Gates were reconnaissances in force or full scale assaults, Taylor's plans were equally vague and overly complicated. The American general's main target on the northern front was a disused tannery, that had been converted into a massive fortification supported by additional redoubts. Apparently Taylor had sketchy information concerning the Mexican firepower available in two other strong points, the Citadel and El Diablo fort, and didn't appreciate the extensive nature of the enemy defense network. Thus when Colonel John Garland moved toward La Taneria with two regiments of regulars and a unit of Baltimore volunteers, his force was caught in a devastating crossfire from the tannery and the two supporting forts. Dozens of Americans fell writhing to the ground and every time the troops attempted to close in on the tannery walls, Mexican sharpshooters deployed on the roofs of neighboring houses begin picking off the advancing officers.

Taylor watched his diversionary attack crumbling before his eyes, and he quickly committed a force of Tennessee and Mississippi volunteers to support Garland. However, as the reinforcements moved through the Monterrey suburbs toward the tannery, most of Garland's force passed them as they retreated back toward Walnut Springs. One company of regulars, commanded by Captain Electus Backus, had managed to capture some of the outbuildings of the Taneria and this force either didn't hear or ignored Garland's order to withdraw. While Backus' men provided covering fire, the Tennessee volunteers rushed the tannery and lost over 100 men in less than five minutes. Just as the wavering Tennesseans were about to collapse, Colonel Jefferson Davis' red shirted Mississippi Rifles rushed in behind their decimated comrades and the two regiments made a bloody dash toward the tannery. Davis, who was Zachary Taylor's son-in-law, and his brigade commander, General John Quitman, initiated a series of rapid advances backed up by supporting volleys, and despite heavy casualties, the Americans were able to climb over the tannery walls and engage the defenders in a hand to hand melee. Most of the garrison retreated out of the rear entrance of La Taneria, but about 30 Mexicans were captured and Taylor now had a foothold in the northern defenses of the city.

The assault on La Taneria had indeed created a diversion for Worth's move on western Monterrey, but Taylor's casualties were appallingly high when compared to Palo Alto and Resaca. The northern wing of the American army had lost 394 killed and wounded and had gained only a very tenuous bridgehead for further operations. Taylor had underestimated Mexican fighting capabilities and had incurred casualties that couldn't easily be replaced. Although Ampudia had lost both Federation Hill and La Taneria, he knew that his adversary couldn't capture the city if it continued to lose men at this daily rate. If the first day of the battle of Monterrey was marked by a diversion that ended up a more hotly contested engagement than the expected main battle, the second day of the struggle was notable for a complete absence of support for Worth's wing. The communication between Taylor and Worth, who were hardly on friendly terms, was little short of non-existent once the junior general was given his orders to march westward. On September 22nd, as Worth was preparing to attack Independence Hill, Taylor's main wing of the army never left their camp at Walnut Springs.

Worth's men fell in at 3 A.M. and began an advance in the rain and wind while Taylor's detachment slept soundly in their encampment. A bolder and more observant commander of the Mexican forces might have realized that an unsupported detachment of 2000 Americans was launching an attack against a city that could deploy 10,000 defenders against the assault. However, Ampudia kept waiting for an attack that never came from Taylor, and the defenders of Independence Hill were left to their own devices. The Mexican position featured a series of breastworks along the crest of the hill supported by a main fortification, called the Bishop's Palace, which dominated the ridge that led down into the city. The American assault force gained an immediate advantage as the rain and gales discouraged the defenders from sending out scouts or pickets, and the attackers had climbed to the tops of the slopes before the Mexicans ever knew what hit them. The defenders rallied to hold the Americans at bay for a short time, but when it became obvious that Ampudia had no intention of sending reinforcements, the soldiers manning the outer works withdrew down the opposite slopes and left the Bishop's Palace surrounded and isolated. The palace was strong enough to withstand an unsupported infantry assault, but the American gunners had dragged a dismantled 12 pound cannon up the slopes and the single gun began to batter through the fortress walls. Colonel Francisco Berra, the fort's commander, could still have inflicted enormous casualties on the assault force if he had contested every square foot of the palace, but he was far too impatient to use this tactic and he foolishly led his entire 200 man garrison on a sortie right into lines of American riflemen. Most of Berra's force was either killed or captured, but about 50 Mexican soldiers were able to retreat back into the palace and hold the building for a few more hours. However, by 4 P.M. the American artillerymen had blasted a major breach in the palace walls and a final bayonet attack carried the fort. Ampudia quickly made a bad situation worse when he panicked at the sight of the American flag flying over the "impregnable" Bishop's Palace, and ordered all of the outer fortifications of the city abandoned.

By the morning of September 23rd the Mexican garrison had withdrawn to a defense perimeter in the residential section of the city, with the Citadel serving as the only remaining military fortification still held by Ampudia. Taylor was now ready to resume his advance into the northern and eastern section of Monterrey while Worth's men waited impatiently for orders to enter the city from the west. The American commander either didn't bother to inform Worth of his plans or his messengers were captured, but when the subordinate general heard the sound of gunfire coming from the other side of the town, he assumed he was expected to advance. Thus the final stage of the battle of Monterrey revolved around two totally independent wings of the American army advancing street by street with little idea what their counterparts were accomplishing.

Taylor's wing used the tannery as their staging area for a house to house operation that was implemented with the help of the Texas Rangers. The Texans had been engaged in street battles against Mexican forces of over a decade, and had reduced the operation to a precise science. The American attackers were advised to avoid using streets wherever possible and the advance usually proceeded through the interiors of rows of houses. The assault troops would break int into the first house in a row, shoot or disperse the Mexican defenders, and then use picks and crowbars to knock down the wall adjoining the next house. Once a hole had been created, the Americans would pitch a few lighted 6 pound shells into the neighboring home, jump through the opening and then rush up the steps to the roof to prevent any organized counterattack. The inexorable advance continued street by street as the Mexicans defenders withdrew to the central plaza of the city. The Texans attached to Worth's column were equally adept at street fighting tactics and by early afternoon the two wings of the army were only two blocks apart, with the Monterrey cathedral looming as the final objective. When Taylor ordered a supporting battery of artillery to begin lobbing shells at the city's dominant structure, Ampudia began to panic. The Mexican general had stored most of his reserve gunpowder in the cathedral and he knew that one lucky hit could send the entire center of the city up in one massive explosion.

Ampudia had been a less than spectacular field commander, but the general now emerged as a surprisingly good bargainer. He opened negotiations with Taylor and played his two remaining cards to the hilt. First, he emphasized to his American counterpart that the Mexican army still held the formidable Citadel, which the Americans had nicknamed the Black Fort. Taylor couldn't claim complete victory until he had captured this fortification and an assault on the work would significantly lengthen his already large casualty list. Second, Ampudia hinted that the Mexican government was ready to accept most of the American terms for peace and a generous treatment of the Monterrey garrison would solidify the opportunity for a settlement of the conflict. Taylor's small army had already lost 142 killed and 364 wounded and was still outnumbered by the Mexican defenders. Therefore he was clearly amenable to Ampudia's suggestions and he offered extremely generous terms for a Mexican evacuation. Ampudia was permitted to withdraw from the city with his army intact and was allowed to retain several batteries of cannons. The Mexican army would pull back toward Saltillo and a 60-day truce would be observed. Thus Zachary Taylor had won another important victory, captured a major Mexican city, and added another triumph to his political reputation even though the enemy army had largely escaped intact. While the capture of Monterrey brought another round of spectacular victory celebrations throughout the United States, Taylor's days as the senior field commander in Mexico were already numbered.

James Polk and his cabinet advisors received the news of Taylor's latest victory with mixed emotions. On the one hand, the capture of Monterrey affirmed that the administration's direction of the war was generally successful. However, this latest triumph clearly placed the politically minded Taylor one step closer to the White House in 1848. Also, it was becoming obvious to Polk and Secretary of War Marcy that the capture of

Mexico's northern province would not convince the enemy government to sue for peace. A march on Mexico City was looming as a more likely scenario and neither Democrat wanted Zachary Taylor to lead that advance. The president now authorized plans for a possible amphibious landing along the Gulf coast with a subsequent expedition inland toward the Mexican capital city. As this operation was being discussed, powerful Democratic Senator Thomas Hart Benton of Missouri offered Polk an intriguing possibility. Benton suggested that Congress should re-establish the position of Lieutenant General which had been dormant since the death of George Washington. The person who held the new commission would be senior to any of the largely Whig oriented general officers and would automatically assume command of field operations in Mexico. The impervious and self-confident Benton nominated himself for the post and secured Polk's tacit approval to implement his plan in Congress. However, Whig opponents of the war organized a massive resistance to the proposal and when a number of Benton's Democratic rivals balked at giving this level of power to their Missouri colleague, Polk was forced to turn to Winfield Scott as the lesser of two evils among his leading generals.

Although Scott shared Taylor's Whig political affiliation, the senior general in the American army didn't hesitate to push his subordinate into the background when it suited his purposes. The former Virginia lawyer secured the president's approval of an amphibious assault on the port of Vera Cruz and promptly ordered Taylor to dispatch 9000 men, including nearly all of his regulars, to Scott's command. Taylor was ordered to hold a defensive position around Monterrey with only 4700 men, of which Jefferson Davis' Mississippi Rifles was the only infantry unit that had ever seen combat. According to a plan agreed upon by Scott and Polk, the northern theater of operations was expected to become a sideshow in the war, but the two opposing generals: Zachary Taylor and Antonio Lopez de Santa Anna, were each determined for personal reasons to force one more titanic showdown in the Mexican republic's northern territory.

Taylor largely ignored Scott's "suggestion" that he confine his activities to defensive operations around Monterrey. Old Rough and Ready was still toying with his own march toward the enemy capital through the bleak country between Saltillo and San Luis Potosi, and he kept pushing his advance units further south while he moved his own headquarters well beyond the defenses of Monterrey. His almost totally inexperienced army was soon deployed in a precarious position that practically invited disaster if the Mexicans could concentrate any substantial forces. Meanwhile, Antonio Lopez de Santa Anna had returned from his exile in Cuba to assume effective command of the Mexican army and reclaim his title as president of the republic. The Generalissimo hurriedly assembled an impressive army of 20,000 men in Mexico City, and then marched north to San Luis Potosi in preparation for an audacious lunge at Taylor's outnumbered and overextended army.

Santa Anna was quite aware of the threat of an American amphibious landing, but he was convinced that the onset of yellow fever season in the coastal lowlands would effectively halt any impending American move inland, while the Mexican army could be employed in destroying Taylor's small army with a subsequent offer of a peace treaty much more favorable to Mexico. When a young American courier officer blundered into an ambush and the complete details of American troop strength and intentions was found on his corpse, the Mexican general was confident that Taylor's army was as good as eliminated. On January 28th, 1847, the huge Mexican army began a terrifying trek across almost 300 miles of desert and suffered alternating bouts with extreme heat and frigid ice storms. Hundreds died, thousands deserted, but by the third week in February about 16,000 haggard Mexican soldiers staggered into the town of Encarnacion more or less ready to crush the Gringos.

On February 20th a scouting party of American dragoons spotted a huge dust cloud that marked the advance elements of Santa Anna's army, and Zachary Taylor realized that the campaign for the north was not quite over. The American general was so confident of the superiority of his men that his initial inclination was to engage the enemy right in front of his forward base at Aqua Nueva, which offered no terrain advantages for the outnumbered defenders. However, newly arrived General John Wool, who Taylor admired deeply, convinced his superior to withdraw back to the Buena Vista ranch which was about 8 miles south of the city of Saltillo. Thus Taylor reluctantly approved a 10 mile retreat just as Santa Anna's cavalry closed in on the American advance base.

Wool had suggested the fall back to Buena Vista because he was convinced that the position maximized the capabilities of the outnumbered American forces. The only direct route from Aqua Nueva to the ranch went through a narrow defile that rivaled the famed Greek pass at Thermopylae for its ability to be held by a small number of defenders. This point in the road, called the Narrows, was bordered on one side by a high plateau and on the other by a maze of gullies fronting a mountain. While the only available road went through this narrow pass, the Mexican army could also approach Buena Vista by marching across the difficult terrain of a plateau that extended about a mile and a half from the Narrows and rose about 50 feet above the road, or could sweep about four miles further to the east and negotiate a series of steep ridges that ended almost directly in front of the ranch.

Taylor and Wool surveyed each of these approaches and began to deploy their limited number of defenders. The American commander was particularly concerned that Santa Anna would attempt to send his cavalry around Buena Vista and down behind Saltillo, so he hurried back to the capital of Coahuilla with Jefferson Davis' Mississippi Rifles and a contingent of dragoons to secure his flanks and rear. Wool took charge of the frontal approaches and placed a battery of guns outside the pass, while deploying two infantry regiments across the road and on the ridge facing the defile. Three infantry regiments and three batteries of guns were allocated to screen the plateau from a possible Mexican attack, while the more distant ridges were covered by riflemen posted on rooftops of the hacienda and its outbuildings.

Santa Anna had planned to launch an assault from all three approaches, but the initial engagement devolved into a sporadic series of skirmishes between the opposing cavalry forces. When the Mexican cavalry failed to appear on the outskirts of Saltillo, Taylor began a night time ride back to his front lines and sent word back to the town for the dragoons and Davis' regiment to move up to the ranch. The Mexican general initiated the main battle on the morning of February 23rd, when he moved four full divisions of infantry against a mere five American regiments. Blanco's division was charged with capturing the pass at the Narrows but a combination of devastating artillery fire from Washington's battery and the rifle volleys of Illinois infantry deployed on the heights above the defile stopped the Mexican advance in its tracks. However, two divisions of Santa Anna's infantry were able to pick their way across the rugged terrain of the nearby plateau and the full force of this column smashed against Colonel William Bowles' 2nd Indiana regiment, which virtually disintegrated when hit by a force about 20 times its size. The two other regiments that were deployed between the plateau and Buena Vista ranch were able to withdraw in reasonable order, but the entire left flank of the American line had simply vanished and thousands of enemy troops were smashing their way toward the critical hacienda.

At 9 A.M. on February 23rd, the American position around Buena Vista was in serious jeopardy, as survivors from the defense of the plateau scrambled back to the ranch and its outbuildings for a final stand. General Wool rode up to Zachary Taylor and announced "General, we are whipped." However, the American commander laconically surveyed the battlefield and replied, "that is for me to determine." Taylor noted the arrival of his reserves from Saltillo and determined to employ them to save the day. Several companies of sharpshooters were assigned to man every roof and window on the ranch and give covering fire to the men pulling back from the plateau. When the advance units of Santa Anna's army began to charge down on the hacienda, the newly deployed riflemen peppered the attackers with well aimed shots and forced a temporary Mexican fallback.

Taylor could see a large enemy force deploying for a much larger assault, so he immediately assigned Davis' Mississippi Rifles and Colonel James Lane's reorganized 3rd Indiana regiment to smash the Mexican advance before it fully developed. Several hundred American riflemen formed into an inverted V with the open end toward the enemy. A huge force of Mexican cavalry supported by General Pocheco's infantry division swept forward toward the still forming American position. Just as the lancers closed on the formation, General Torrejon sensed the Americans were setting up a trap and he ordered a sudden halt to the charge. The mounted brigade was ripped to pieces by volleys of rifle fire as Torrejon rode frantically to restore his men's cohesiveness. Suddenly the Americans swept forward and drew out six shooters, Bowie knives and hatchets and began hacking and shooting the panic stricken horsemen. Just as the Mexican infantry began to advance to support their comrades, Captain Braxton Bragg's artillery battery clambered up the plateau from Buena Vista and opened a devastating fire on Pacheco's men.

Santa Anna realized that three of his divisions had been stopped by the enemy defenders, but he still controlled a fourth division that had not been fully committed. The Generalissimo hurriedly shifted this force toward the series of ridges four miles away that would provide another approach to Buena Vista. Luckily for the American defenders, Taylor had just appreciated the possible danger of an attack from this direction and Davis, Lane and much of the available artillery were re-deployed to hold the ridge line while a scratch force of dragoons, sharpshooters and recently arrived gunners was positioned to guard against a renewed attack across the plateau.

When the Mexican advance along the ridges ground to a halt in the face of the re-deployed American riflemen and artillery, Santa Anna shifted the focus of the battle back to the plateau which was now only thinly held by Taylor's army. A small force of dismounted dragoons, sharpshooters and several companies from the 1st Illinois regiment were on the verge of being overwhelmed when Lieutenant George Thomas' gunners arrived to plug a widening hole in the line. The future "Rock of Chickamauga" gained just enough time for Taylor to initiate a massive concentration of every artillery unit he could deploy. Washington's guns were dragged over from the pass, Bragg's cannon were moved from the ridge line and additional units were brought up from the ranch. Just as the Mexican host was breaking through the line of American infantrymen, a massive volley of grapeshot tore gaping holes in the advancing line. The American gunners had set up a monumental crossfire which broke the back of the Mexican advance and ended Santa Anna's last major gamble of the day.

Santa Anna's bold attempt to annihilate the American northern army before Scott could land in Vera Cruz had resulted in a colossal disaster to the Mexican army. Taylor had lost 673 men in a day of extremely desperate fighting, but the Mexican total of over 4000 casualties was an appalling price to pay for so little military gain. While the controversial once and future president of the republic would have several more opportunities to regain his reputation on the road to Mexico City, Zachary Taylor had fought his last battle. The next campaign that Old Rough and Ready would direct would be an ultimately successful advance on the White House.

CHAPTER 20

# Winfield Scott's War

## The Southern Campaign in the Mexican-American Conflict

$T$he battle of Buena Vista proved to be the last major engagement in the northern theatre as the focus of the war shifted to a struggle for the Mexican capital city between Antonio Lopez de Santa Anna and Winfield Scott. The first significant step in the American expedition to Mexico City developed in October of 1846, when Scott began a campaign to convince President Polk that victory for the United States was contingent on the capture of the enemy capital. Polk and Secretary of War Marcy were beginning to realize that victories in northern Mexico alone would not bring their adversary to the bargaining table and the administration gave its reluctant approval to Scott's plan to land 20,000 men at the port of Vera Cruz and then march inland to seize Mexico City.

On February 21st, 1847, as Santa Anna's lancers began the first stage of the battle of Buena Vista, Winfield Scott arrived at his invasion staging area at Lobos Island, about 50 miles south of the Mexican port of Tampico. The American commander had planned his expedition on the basis of 20,000 men utilizing 150 specially constructed landing vessels to secure a beach-head for the move inland. However, the War Department never seemed to fulfill its promises and by early March, Scott was faced with the prospect of attempting the assault with only 12,000 men and 65 landing craft. Scott decided to make the best use of the assets that he had and on March 2nd the commanding general stood on the deck of the steamer *Massachusetts* and reviewed a fleet of 80 paddle wheelers and sailing vessels, which carried his expeditionary force 200 miles to the south. Three days later the Americans saw the spires of Vera Cruz and the officers took special note of the imposing fortifications of Fort San Juan which guarded the sea approaches to the city. The air was so clear that Scott and his staff could make out the outline of 15,000 foot Mount Orizeba, almost 50 miles inland. The American commander knew that his men must either have pushed inland that far by April or they would be exposed to the terror of the annual outbreak of yellow fever that would afflict the coastal lowlands and probably decimate his army. All of his military calculations revolved around this looming threat.

While most of the army marked time until the start of the landing, Commodore David Conner, commander of the American naval squadron supporting the assault, invited Scott and his staff to survey possible landing sites from a small patrol boat. This tiny vessel ventured too close to the guns of Fort San Juan and soon salvos of shells were dropping around the American craft. Several shells came within a few feet of sinking the vessel and this event would have not only changed the course of the Mexican-American war, but also influenced the outcome of the future war between North and South. Not only was Scott and every American division commander aboard this vulnerable boat, the group also included George Meade, Robert E. Lee, Joseph Johnston and Pierre Beauregard. Conner wisely ordered an immediate withdrawal to safer waters, and the general and commodore agreed on a landing site called Collada, which was a small beach near the city that offered an excellent staging area for the construction of siege batteries.

At one o'clock on the afternoon of March 9th, Conner's bombardment squadron stood in place offshore and began to shell the Vera Cruz defenses, while seven smaller gunboats armed with grapeshot moved in to cover the landing craft. A few hundred Mexican lancers rode nervously along the beach but the first American salvo sent them riding inland, and moments later General William Worth stepped ashore at the head of 4500 regulars, who were serenaded by naval bands playing "The Star Spangled Banner" as they jumped into the surf, waded in and sprinted up to the sand dunes, where they raised the American flag. The landing craft went back to the fleet for additional men and by midnight Scott had a 10,000 man expeditionary force on shore without the loss of a single soldier.

A beachfront council of war the next morning placed Scott in vehement opposition to a number of his senior division commanders, who insisted that he should launch an immediate infantry assault against Fort San Juan and the city defenses. However, the American commander was determined to keep casualties to a minimum and he ordered the initiation of a formal siege. American soldiers, toiling in ankle deep sand, dragged the siege artillery into position along a series of sand hills behind the city. Scott occupied an investing line that stretched for 8 miles and featured four batteries of cannons interspersed with infantry fortifications. However, the War Department's promise to deliver much heavier siege guns for the operation was never fulfilled, and the available guns were not large enough to blast down the walls of Fort San Juan. Scott eventually accepted Conner's offer to employ land based naval guns in the bombardment, but just as the operation was about to begin, the commodore went home on sick leave and was replaced by Commodore Matthew Perry. Perry was just as cooperative as his predecessor and his only proviso for supplying naval artillery was that sailors had to man the guns. Three 6300 pound monsters were designed to fire 32 pound solid shot, while three more guns began lobbing 62 pound explosive shells into the city. Vera Cruz was now encircled in a sheet of fire from naval vessels and land based artillery, and by March 25th, 180 shells an hour were pounding the Mexican defenses. The day and night bombardment panicked city residents, destroyed both private and public buildings and encouraged the English, French and Prussian consuls to convince the city's commander, General Morales, to open negotiations for an honorable capitulation or evacuation. Scott ultimately provided a number of face saving gestures which allowed the defenders to march out with full military honors and receive immediate parole, while the civil and religious rights of all civilians were guaranteed. On March 29, 1847, at a cost of 67 casualties, the American flag was raised over the first city on the route to the fabled capital city of the Mexican republic.

Scott's initial inland objective was the town of Jalapa, which was 75 miles from Vera Cruz and formed an important crossroads on the National Road that led to the capital. However, the War Department continued its increasingly long string of foul-ups and supplied only one quarter of the number of horses required to move the entire army from the coast. The American army became split into isolated divisions as the soldiers trudged through the swampy, sandy lowlands on their way to higher ground.

On the same day that the American expeditionary force landed at Vera Cruz, the surviving elements of Santa Anna's army staggered back into San Luis Potosi after retreating from Buena Vista. Desertions and deaths from exposure had whittled several thousand more soldiers from the already decimated army, so that only half of the 20,000 man force that had marched out from Mexico City in January returned. The canny Generalissimo however displayed a variety of captured American cannons and regimental flags on his return to the capital and simply declared a great victory, while issuing vague casualty figures for the battle that he had "won." The Mexican commander left most of his army at San Luis Potosi under the direction of General Galencia, hurried to Mexico City to shore up his political base, and then moved east toward Jalapa with 12,000 men culled from the capital's garrison. Santa Anna was never tempted to share the privations of his enlisted men and he was delighted to be able to establish his command center at his own ranch near the town. The Generalisssimo leisurely developed plans to meet the oncoming American expedition and finally decided that a town and hill both named Cerro Gordo was the most strategically important location in the region. Cerro Gordo Hill dominated a pass through the National Road that Scott would be utilizing in his march to Mexico City. This defile was situated with the Rio de Plan on the right flank and Cerro Gordo screening the left flank so that the Americans and Mexicans found themselves in a mirror image of Buena Vista. This time the

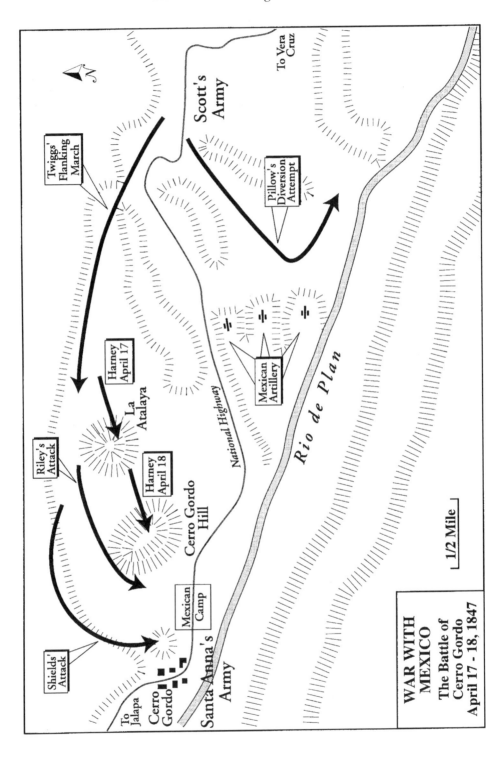

N

To Vera Cruz

Scott's Army

Twiggs' Flanking March

Pillow's Diversion Attempt

Harney April 17

La Atalaya

Mexican Artillery

Riley's Attack

Harney April 18

Cerro Gordo Hill

National Highway

Rio de Plan

Mexican Camp

Shields' Attack

To Jalapa

Cerro Gordo

Santa Anna's Army

1/2 Mile

WAR WITH MEXICO
The Battle of Cerro Gordo
April 17 - 18, 1847

Americans would have to force their way through a heavily defended pass with Santa Anna's men enjoying the advantage of terrain and position.

The first two American divisions to arrive within striking range of Cerro Gordo were commanded by David Twiggs and Robert Patterson, who detested one another. Although Patterson was the senior general present, he had himself placed on the sick list and in his absence Twiggs began toying with the idea of a massive bayonet charge right through the pass. When Patterson was informed of Twigg's less than sophisticated plan, he promptly dispatched young engineering officer, Lieutenant Pierre Beauregard, to try to discover a way around the mountain and into the rear of the Mexican camp near the town of Cerro Gordo. The Louisiana Creole undertook a dangerous scouting mission which uncovered a second fortified hill named La Atalaya, which in turn fronted a dense wooded area that contained a narrow footpath that might be used to move a column to the rear of the Mexican defenses. While Beauregard tried to convince Twiggs to postpone his frontal assault, Scott arrived in camp and dispatched Captain Robert E. Lee to gather further information about the terrain. Lee worked his way through the woods and along the path until he came to a spring where he almost crashed into a Mexican patrol coming from the opposite direction. The future Confederate general quickly hid behind a log which was soon used as a seat for several enemy soldiers, who came within a few feet of at least temporarily ending the Virginian's military career. When darkness fell, Lee crept away and informed an elated Scott that the path led right into the rear of the Mexican camp.

On the morning of April 17th, 1847 Scott deployed his 8000 available men in an operation designed to flank a Mexican army that now most likely outnumbered his force by at least two to one. While most of the army demonstrated in front of Cerro Gordo hill, Twiggs' division worked its way along the wooded path until Mexican troops stationed on La Atalaya observed the march and called in artillery fire, while preparing to charge down the hill into the enemy columns. Twiggs ordered Colonel William Harney's brigade to attack the Mexican position before the enemy could bring up more reinforcements. Harney's men charged up the ridge and smashed through the Mexican lines, forcing the defenders to pull back toward their camp to reorganize for a counterattack the next day. Scott knew that he was heavily outnumbered, but he was convinced that he could flank the Mexican defenses and smash Santa Anna from his unprotected rear. The American commander ordered General Worth's division to support Twiggs' flanking movement toward the town of Cerro Gordo, while Gideon Pillow was ordered to deploy his brigade in a march along the river bank that would hopefully allow the Americans to get behind the forward Mexican batteries that were defending the pass.

The battle of April 18th began when Pillow's force of two Tennessee and two Pennsylvania regiments marched along the bank of the Plan river under cover of some groves of trees. Unfortunately, the inexperienced volunteers let out constant war whoops and cheers and even fired their guns in the air as they conducted their "secret" march on the enemy artillery emplacements. Suddenly batteries of Mexican guns slashed through the trees and while Pillow engaged in a shouting match with his officers as to who was responsible for the lack of silence. Meanwhile, the volunteers were milling around under a hail of grapeshot. Suddenly Pillow went down with a minor wound and as the brigade commander left the field, the cohesion of the regiments simply collapsed and the remaining colonels ordered their men back to safer ground. The diversionary attack designed to distract the Mexican defenders from the threat of a flank attack had failed miserably, and a more energetic Mexican commander might have concentrated his more numerous forces and smashed Twiggs and Worth while they were most vulnerable. However, fortunately for the Americans, Santa Anna failed to make any decisive decisions and Pillow's failure had no permanent impact on the battle.

While Pillow's diversionary attack was collapsing, General Twiggs ordered the brigades of Colonel James Shields and Colonel Bennett Riley to swing right as they marched down the slopes of La Atalaya, in order to attempt to get at the Mexican camp near the town of Cerro Gordo. The two brigades became separated in the woods and while Shields managed to work his way toward Santa Anna's headquarters, Riley veered too far to the left and his men were quickly caught by fire from Cerro Gordo hill. The Mexican defenders started sweeping down the ridge and began surrounding Riley's outnumbered men, when Colonel Harney shouted for his regulars to initiate a bayonet charge to save their comrades. The bluecoats went down Atalaya hill screaming at the top of their lungs, swept across the gully separating the two hills, and charged up the slopes of Cerro Gordo. This sudden wave of steel started to turn the tide in the Americans' favor, and when several front line cannons were abandoned by the Mexicans, Captain John Magruder's gunners turned the pieces around and swept the enemy fortifications.

While the defenders of Cerro Gordo were withdrawing gradually toward the opposite slope of the hill, Shields' men burst into the rear of Santa Anna's headquarters tents and peppered his personal coach with rifle and pistol fire. Shields' advance force was only 300 strong, but they were concentrated around the Mexican commander's tent and the Generalissimo promptly fled the battlefield on foot with most of his staff. Thousands of Mexican soldiers now followed their general's lead and began a panicky stampede that one eyewitness described as "safety alone being the object, all became involved in a frightful whirl." The defenders of Cerro Gordo enjoyed a two to one superiority over the relatively small American assault force, but in an authentic reproduction of the Yankee retreat at Bladensburg three decades earlier, thousands of disgruntled Mexican soldiers streamed back toward their capital city as the victorious invaders continued a leisurely pursuit of their defeated opponents. Euphoric American soldiers broke into the Mexican supply depot, helped themselves to mountains of rations and counted a prisoner contingent that soon passed 3000. At a cost of 63 killed and 367 wounded, Winfield Scott had inflicted over 4000 casualties on his adversary and secured a new, healthier base of operations for a renewed advance toward Mexico City. However, the American general was soon undergoing a decimation of his small army that was far greater than any loss his opponent could inflict.

Winfield Scott had won substantial victories at Vera Cruz and Cerro Gordo with relatively light losses to his army, but by early May of 1847 his expedition was threatened by the imminent expiration of the enlistment terms of most of his volunteer regiments. Most of these men decided that it was time for someone else to fight for the United States, and beginning on May 6th, seven regiments marched out of Jalapa on their way back to Vera Cruz and transport home. The American invasion force was now reduced to fewer than 7000 men and while Scott pushed his remaining divisions to the town of Puebla, another sixty miles closer to Mexico City, Santa Anna began to concentrate the Mexican army to intercept the Americans before they reached the capital. The Mexican commander called in 4000 men from General Valencia's northern army, 3000 men from the army of the south, and 10,000 men from the National Guard, to augment the 14,000 man garrison of the capital and provide the Generalissimo with a 4 to 1 manpower advantage over his adversary.

The American army spent most of the summer of 1847 in Puebla, waiting for new contingents of reinforcements to arrive and lessen the Mexican numerical superiority. The aging Duke of Wellington had been following the progress of Scott's campaign, and while he applauded his initial victories, he was now convinced that the American general was in serious jeopardy, as he noted "Scott is lost, he cannot capture the city and he cannot fall back upon his base." The American army was adrift in a hostile nation of 7 million people, facing the daunting prospect of attempting to capture an enemy city of over 200,000 people defended by a garrison which far outnumbered the attacking army. However, at no point did Scott seem to lose his confidence in ultimate victory, and by early August he had scraped together an army of over 10,000 men and was prepared for his next advance.

Santa Anna decided to attempt to stop the American invaders before they could deploy against the immediate defenses around the city, and an August 10th thousands of National Guardsmen were cheered by large throngs of citizens as they marched though the streets of the capital toward a prominent mountain ten miles outside of the city known as El Penon. The Mexican general placed 7000 men and 30 guns along this ridge which dominated the National Road as it approached the capital city. However, when Scott's army marched toward the imposing mountain, the general ordered Captain Robert E. Lee to locate an alternate road that could get the invaders around El Penon without a frontal assault. Lee probed toward Mexico City and reported back with information that he had discovered a small path that wound around Lake Chalco and led to the town of San Agustin which was directly south of the enemy capital. While Twiggs' division demonstrated against El Penon's garrison, the remaining three divisions marched along the narrow road and captured San Agustin before Santa Anna could respond to the move.

When the Mexican commander received the news from his excited scouts that the enemy had slipped around his carefully prepared roadblock, Santa Anna rushed back to the capital and began erecting a new defensive line in the south based on the Churubusco River. An army of almost 16,000 men was deployed along a series of fortified haciendas and hastily constructed redoubts that stretched from a left flank anchored on Lake Xochimilco to a right flank screened by a strange looking molten sea of solidified lava called the Pedregal.

Scott's scouts informed him that the only direct north-south road that led from San Agustin to the Churubusco River was located between the Lake and Pedregal and he assumed correctly that his adversary would deploy most of his forces to meet that threat. Therefore the American general quickly called for the ever present Lee to take a small reconnaissance force and try to discover a way through the lava bed that would allow the Americans to strike from a less defended direction. Lee probed around the molten sea and finally located a tiny track that wound through the lava bed and came out at the right end of the Mexican defense line at a small town called San Angel, which appeared to have been initially occupied by the Mexican army and then, incredibly, had been abandoned. Lee could not know that the American army had just gained an enormous dividend from the almost ritualistic rivalry of the Mexican high command. Santa Anna had entrusted the defense of the right flank of his line to his most senior subordinate, General Gabriel Valencia, commander of the army of the north. Santa Anna and Valencia, who had each served terms as president of Mexico, despised one another and when Valencia was assigned to fortify San Angel, he took one look at the position and promptly marched his 6000 men about 3 miles further south to Papierna Hill, near the town of Contreras at the very edge of the lava bed.

The Americans had now been presented with a fantastic opportunity to roll up Santa Anna's undefended right flank but at the cost of a new danger as the path through the molten sea wound dangerously close to Valencia's new position. Scott's engineers quietly spent the morning of August 19th improving the small path through the Pedregal, and at noon Twiggs' division started to push through the lava toward San Angel. Valencia's men on the nearby ridge quickly observed the enemy march and a battery of Mexican guns began lobbing shells toward the American column. At this point General Gideon Pillow arrived on the scene with his division, and even though he was thirty years younger than Twiggs, he was senior general present and began to take command of the operation, emphasizing his determination to keep Scott out of the action. Thus the engagement termed the Battle of Contreras began as a contest between two subordinate adversaries who each despised their commander and each desperately wanted to have a victory with no interference or aid from a superior. Valencia and Pillow also matched each other for the high level of incompetence that they amply demonstrated. Pillow immediately reacted to the Mexican threat by resorting to the now traditional ritual of calling in the mobile artillery units. Captain John Magruder's battery was promptly wheeled into action to the blast the enemy from Padierna ridge, but this time the tables were turned as Valencia moved his mobile artillery into position and he soon had the Americans outgunned by 22 cannons to 6 pieces. Magruder was eventually forced to withdraw his guns, but Valencia was so focused on his emerging victory in the artillery duel, that he ignored two American infantry brigades as they used this action as a diversion to march through the lava bed and seize control of the San Angel road. Pillow now matched his opponents' incompetence by failing to move the rest of his command north through the lava bed to support his now isolated advance units.

The end of the first day of the battle left both sides with few clear cut advantages. Two American brigades were able to occupy the town of San Angel but they were too weak to move any further and they were out of supporting distance from the rest of Pillow's command. Valencia's men held Padierna Ridge, but they had no idea whether Santa Anna would march from Churubusco to trap the Americans between them. The most energetic commander on the scene for either army was Brigadier General Persifor Smith, who dispatched Captain Lee back to San Agustin with dispatches of the action for Winfield Scott, and then, on his own initiative, marched his brigade to San Angel and took command of the American defenses. Lee and a few men picked their way across the rocks and gullies of the lava bed in the middle of an enormous thunderstorm and when the Virginian stumbled into Scott's headquarters, the American commander sprang into action to retrieve the situation. The commanding general ordered Worth's division to move up the main road from San Agustin to the town of Churubusco to convince Santa Anna that he was attacking toward the Mexican left flank, which the rest of the army was deployed to support Smith on the San Angel Road.

At dawn on August 20th, the defenders of Padierna ridge waited for the expected reinforcements from Santa Anna's main force. However, the Generalissimo apparently decided to let his arch rival handle the American threat himself and the only soldiers seen marching toward the Mexican position turned out to be Americans attacking from San Angel. In only seventeen minutes, Valencia's position simply collapsed as the disheartened defenders panicked and were overrun by an American bayonet attack. Seven hundred dead and wounded and eight hundred prisoners littered the hill while the assault had cost less than sixty American casualties. Valencia's force was now removed from the military chessboard and the second phase of the battle was initiated. Scott now ordered the Padierna assault force to sweep up to San Angel road to hit Santa Anna's right flank while Worth's column moved up from San Agustin to strike the Mexican left. The sight of the Mexican army being rolled up from both flanks encouraged Santa Anna to begin pulling his forces over to the north side of the Churubusco River while a few key fortifications on the south side were expected to delay the American advance. The main bridge across the river was located in the town of Churubusco which featured a well constructed redoubt and formidable stone walled San Mateo Convent guarding the span. While most of the Mexican army was streaming across the river, several elite units held these two fortifications against a massive American attack. A combination of effective artillery support, superior close-in weapons and an unusual superiority in numbers allowed five American regiments to overwhelm the 700 Mexicans holding the bridge redoubt. The Convent was now isolated from Santa Anna's main force, but the defenders, including the largely Irish contingent of the San Patricio Battalion, fought with pistols, clubbed muskets and knives until only 80 men from the garrison were still alive. By 3 P.M. on August 20th Santa Anna's Churubusco River line was crumbling and 4000 Mexican soldiers had been either killed, wounded or captured. The vicious fighting had cost Scott over 1000 casualties, but the southern approach to Mexico City was now, at least temporarily, vulnerable to a massive American final assault.

The American forces could probably have smashed their way into Mexico City on the afternoon of August 20th, but apparently Winfield Scott was haunted by the specter of a house to house battle which would further mangle his already decimated army. Therefore, he consented to President Polk's personal representative, Nicholas P. Trist, opening negotiations with the Mexican government. However, as the peace talks dragged on with little hope for a breakthrough, Santa Anna utilized the truce to strengthen the capital's defenses. Scott finally ended the truce and began to develop a plan to capture Mexico City. The American general's first priority was to capture a foundry near Chapultepec Castle that was allegedly turning church bells into large numbers of additional cannons that would be deployed in the city's defenses. Scott ordered General Worth to take over 3000 men and capture the foundry, called Molino del Rey and its supporting fortification, the Casa de Mata.

Worth moved out the morning of September 8th, deploying one brigade to cut off possible reinforcements from the castle and placing a squadron of dragoons to hold off any cavalry attack from the West. However, Santa Anna fully expected an attack on the foundry, and he had quietly hidden brigades of infantry in the buildings, while 4000 lancers were deployed in a ravine just out of sight of Worth's column. Thus when a storming party of picked men under Major George Wright closed on the foundry, a hail of Mexican rifle bullets and artillery shells cut down half of the attackers and 11 of the 14 senior officers. Colonel Alvarez's lancers then emerged from their ravine and threatened to slash Worth's flanks to pieces. However, at this moment the 270 available American horsemen launched a mounted charge at the startled Mexicans and delayed the attack long enough for reserve batteries of American artillery to repel the enemy advance. Finally, as the massed American guns began to pound the Molino and its outbuildings to rubble, the Mexican defenders began to withdraw back to Chapultepec Castle after inflicting almost 800 casualties on Worth's division. Total Mexican losses were nearly 2000 killed and wounded and 700 captured but Santa Anna had far more reserves than Scott, and one American officer noted "we were like Pyrrhus after the fight with Fabricus—a few more such victories and the army would be destroyed."

Five days after the battle of Molino del Rey, Winfield Scott called a council of war in a small church near his headquarters tent outside of the capital. The assault on the foundry had cost him 25% of the attack force and the Americans had discovered that the building wasn't even being used to construct cannons. The invading army simply could not afford another useless bloodletting and Scott was desperate to locate the most vulnerable part of the city defenses. The commanding general admitted his personal preference for using the newly captured foundry as jump off point for an assault on Chapultepec Castle, but he opened up the discussion for other opinions. Gideon Pillow gave a long, rambling argument for an assault on the southern defenses of the capital which would concentrate on San Antonio Gate. Robert E. Lee and almost all of the generals agreed with Pillow's reasoning, with only Pierre Beauregard offering major dissent. Beauregard, who was not particularly fond of Scott, was convinced that Santa Anna had deployed most of his elite troops exactly where Pillow suggested the attack, and he believed that Chapultepec Castle was much more vulnerable than it initially appeared. General Franklin Pierce added his support to Beauregard, and Scott supported their argument and exclaimed, "gentlemen, we will attack by the western gate."

The morning of September 13, 1847 dawned with the promise of a perfect late summer day as the small American expeditionary force prepared to storm the capital city of the Mexican republic. General John Quitman led his division in a massive demonstration attack against the San Antonio causeway, while the rest of the army moved out from the cover of the Molino del Rey and slipped across the marshes and parkland that adjoined Chapultepec Castle. The castle stood on a 200 foot hill and was surrounded by enormously thick walls, but the main building could only hold about 250 defenders while the surrounding ramparts were manned by an additional 600 men. The garrison commander, Colonel Nicholas Bravo, implored Santa Anna to deploy a much larger force on the causeways approaching the fortress, but the Generalissimo focused most of his attention on San Antonio Gate.

The American assault began under cover of a massive artillery bombardment which allowed an attack force under Gideon Pillow to charge through the park grounds and concentrate along the base of the castle wall. While

Pillow's men traded shots with Mexican sharpshooters, Franklin Pierce's troops waded through a cypress swamp and began to scale the castle walls. When most of the garrison was fully engaged with these units, a regiment of gray coated voltigeurs under Joseph Johnston struggled over the opposite walls of the castle defenses and waited for the arrival of scaling ladders to help them get into the main building. The first ladders in place were toppled but soon enough ladders arrived to allow fifty men to climb simultaneously and a battle for the fortress ramparts that was reminiscent of the Alamo began to take shape.

Bravo and his men were gradually pushed from the walls into the buildings of the Military College that occupied part of the fortress. The 80 cadets, aged 13 to 19, that had insisted on remaining during the assault fought ferociously for their flag and their school and at least six of the "Los Ninos Heroicos" were killed in the melee. One cadet dueled bayonet-wielding attackers up the steps of a college building to the roof where a Mexican tricolor still fluttered. The cadet went down in a last defense of the colors and Lieutenant George Pickett gained a moment of fame when he stepped over the fallen teenager and hauled down the enemy flag and raised the Stars and Stripes, in one of the most emotional moments of the war. When Bravo finally surrendered his surviving defenders, American troops began to pour into the capital proper as they shouted themselves hoarse in their conquest of the Halls of Montezuma.

At noon on September 14, 1847, General Winfield Scott rode triumphantly through the City Square of Mexico City and supervised the raising of the American flag over the Grand Plaza. The United States had now indeed "conquered a peace" that would add 1.2 million quare miles of territory to the dynamic American republic, and yet, ironically, light a fuse that would soon propel thousands of men from North and South to engage in a far bloodier conflict that was soon looming on the horizon.

# CHAPTER 21

# Alternative Strategies and Outcomes

## *Mexico and the United States 1836-1848*

$T$he chronicle of the conflict between the United States and Mexico presents one of the relatively rare instances in modern history in which one nation defeated its adversary in every major battle of a moderately extended struggle. However, the outcome of the war was certainly not a pre-ordained American triumph, as the republic of Mexico enjoyed the advantages of a much larger and much more experienced army at the outset of the conflict. Thus a summary analysis of the Mexican-American War might reasonably focus on three inter-related problems. First, why did a consistently outnumbered American army fighting largely on enemy soil win virtually every engagement? Second, what are some of the alternative outcomes that might have emerged in Mexico's conflict with the Texan rebels and the United States Army? Finally, to what extent was the American experience in the war with Mexico a precursor of the far more colossal struggle between Union and Confederacy just over a decade after the end of the conflict with the other major republic in North America?

The record of American military engagement in the contest against Mexico presents some startling contrasts. On the one hand, only 930 regulars and 600 volunteers were killed in action during the course of the war. However, 6000 volunteers and 5000 regulars died of disease or accidents while an additional 9000 volunteers and 4000 regulars were so badly wounded that they had to be discharged from the army and sent home. Thus almost one American in four who volunteered for service in the Mexican war either went home seriously injured or didn't go home at all. While these losses did not approach the carnage of the Civil War or even World War II, they are, proportional to the overall population, remarkably similar to the American involvement in World War I, which also presents a very similar time span of combat for United States forces. Thus the United States gained a complete military victory and the acquisition of substantial new territories at a moderately high cost in total casualties. However, even though the tangible benefits of war with Mexico far surpassed the essentially drawn conflict with Britain in 1812, the margin of superiority in the performance of the United States compared to three decades earlier was not all that substantial.

While the sense of triumph in Washington in 1848 largely compared with the euphoria in the Northern states in the spring of 1865, several aspects of the war with Mexico are more analogous to the second war with Britain than to the Civil War. For example, while 116,000 men were recruited for service in the Mexican War, the government and War Department were little more successful in concentrating troops at the field of battle than their predecessors of three decades earlier. Zachary Taylor and Winfield Scott were placed in command of armies that never exceeded 12,000 men and frequently numbered fewer than 6000. The total population of the United States in 1846 was almost identical to the population of the Union in 1861, yet the size of most field armies was a throwback to the War of 1812. The Union in the Civil War was consistently able to field armies that numbered over 100,000 men, and at the beginning of the 1864 campaign deployed two forces that broke the 100,000 barrier. Yet Taylor and Scott were forced to engage relatively large Mexican armies with contingents only one tenth the size commanded by Grant or Sherman.

A second throwback to the War of 1812 was the penny pinching attitude of the American government in its support of the armies in the field. The United States in 1846 was certainly a nation that was wealthy enough to supply its soldiers with the very latest weaponry and equipment that could be purchased. For example, the excellent Model 1841 percussion rifle was already being manufactured, as was the equally advanced Colt revolver. One of these weapons provided reliable long range accuracy while the other offered an incredibly rapid rate of fire for close-in combat. However, the War Department decided to depend largely on the obsolescent muskets filling its warehouses, leaving most of the regulars to fight the Mexicans with less than superb weapons, while volunteer regiments smart enough to purchase the new rifles and six-shooters went to war at the cutting edge of mid-19th century technology. This parsimonious attitude plagued the American commanders time and again. Scott's siege of Vera Cruz was complicated by the failure of promised siege guns to arrive from New Orleans, while only the cooperation of the navy allowed the American army commander to destroy the enemy defenses. Both Taylor and Scott were plagued with shortages of horses, pack mules, wagons and any other form of transport. Compared to the cornucopia of supplies and equipment provided in the Civil War and World War II, the Mexican War was definitely the outlet store model of warfare.

The authors believe that the American forces were able to overcome the shortcomings imposed by Polk and Marcy's theory of discount warfare because of two invaluable assets enjoyed by the United States Army at this time. First, the leadership skills exhibited by Zachary Taylor and Winfield Scott were absolutely first rate. These two titans of the war with Mexico were certainly blemished heroes. Both men consistently underestimated the fighting potential of the Mexican army and when that army actually rose to its potential a number of near disasters ensued. Taylor and Scott also displayed a voracious appetite for turning every military victory into another way station on the road to the White House, and their correspondence is filled with references to the conversion of battlefield triumphs into political capital. However, both of these commanders also exhibited an exhilarating combination of personal bravery, clear judgement, decisiveness and energy that allowed them to overcome lack of numbers, poor supply lines and indifferent subordinates to win a series of stunning victories over a nominally superior adversary. Unlike many Civil War generals who burned the telegraph wires with demands for more men, more supplies or more horses before they moved another mile, Taylor and Scott improvised and made do with what they had on hand.

Zachary Taylor's attitude before Buena Vista represents a posture that Abraham Lincoln could only dream about in the early campaigns of the Civil War. Taylor shrugged off Scott's requisition of virtually his whole force of regulars and then proceeded to command an army of raw volunteers to a smashing victory against an army that outnumbered him more than three to one. Scott consistently out-maneuvered and outfought a number of far larger Mexican armies around the capital city, and was able to capture Mexico City even though half of his army had gone home and he faced a formidable fortified city garrisoned by an army far larger that his own.

The positive traits of the two highest ranking generals was enhanced enormously by the second major asset available to the American army—the corps of excellent junior officers that had graduated from the relatively new United States Miliary Academy. These young West Pointers played a prominent role in most of the victorious engagements and were particularly valuable in their roles as artillery and engineering officers. The success of the horse artillery during the war demonstrated the value of mobility and justified the extensive training that had been imposed on the American artillery arm. Future generals such as Braxton Bragg and George Thomas as well as a number of less historically prominent West Point trained gunners utilized the American guns so effectively that they essentially neutralized the enormous Mexican advantage in infantry units. In a similar context, junior officers serving in engineering units such as George Meade, Robert E. Lee and Pierre Beauregard, provided vital reconnaissance, scouting and map making services, which proved to be an invaluable aid in locating routes around enemy fortifications, determining vulnerable points in the Mexican defenses and providing technical expertise regarding the construction of vital roads and bridges.

These invaluable assets to the American cause were enhanced by at least two significant weaknesses in the Mexican war-making capability. First, the unstable nature of the Mexican government during the course of the war encouraged the antics of Antonio Lopez de Santa Anna during the key battles of the conflict. The authors feel that even the modest praise given to the Generalissimo by a number of historians is far too generous. Quite simply Santa Anna was an egotistical opportunist who enjoyed only one major success over American opponents, and that was in the assault on the Alamo where he enjoyed a 20 to 1 numerical superiority and still managed to lose almost half of his assault force. The Mexican commander's barbaric treatment of the small number of prisoners captured at the Alamo and the far larger contingent from Goliad was one of the main factors in creating American hatred for Mexico that encouraged the outbreak of war a decade later.

While Santa Anna was able to raise large armies during the conflict with the United States and was certainly adept at making disastrous defeats appear to be victories, his performance in the key campaigns of the war was incredibly incompetent. He lost more men on the march from San Luis Potosi to Buena Vista than Zachary Taylor had in his whole army; at Cerro Gordo he panicked and fled the battlefield when a small advance force of Americans shot up his personal carriage, at Contreras he held back a relief force for General Valencia that would have trapped a large portion of the American army; and at Mexico City he deployed most of his army to defend San Antonio Gate while the enemy was attacking Chapultepec Castle. Santa Anna may have been a colorful leader and a good showman but he was a terrible military commander, who managed to continually squander advantages of numbers and terrain.

The impact of Santa Anna's incompetence was magnified by the parsimony of the Mexican government in prosecuting the war against the United States. The war department in Mexico City made even Polk and Marcy look profligate in their spending as they conducted a classic bargain basement war. Mexican soldiers suffered through a never ending series of problems with obsolete muskets, malfunctioning cannons, defective gunpowder and mediocre cavalry mounts, which largely negated their advantage in numbers. The government seemed to be able to furnish warm bodies for the Mexican army but then marched them into battle with such poor equipment that it was common for the soldiers to either shoot from the hip or close their eyes while firing, which hardly aided the prospects for victory. In essence, the Mexican republic was attempting to fight an 18th century war against an adversary that was clearly comfortable with the technology and weaponry of the mid-19th century.

While the conflict between America and Mexico offers fewer possibilities of alternative outcomes than either the earlier conflicts with Britain or the later contest between North and South, there were at least a few situations where key events might have emerged quite differently. Perhaps the most fascinating possibility of an alternative outcome revolves around the most heavily chronicled event of the whole period—the siege of the Alamo. The exploits of Travis, Bowie, Crockett and their 180 compatriots in the crumbling mission at Bexar fired the imaginations of Americans at the time and for a century and a half afterward, and stimulated discussion of alternative outcomes that might have resulted in a Texan victory.

One of the ironies of the siege of the Alamo was that the Texan rebels were attempting to hold the mission in a period that immediately preceded technological breakthroughs that began to provide enormous advantages to men deployed in a defensive position. If the siege of the Alamo had occurred even a decade later, it is probable that the garrison would have been armed with fast firing six-shooters and even some breech-loading rifles in lieu of the awkward and slow firing muzzle-loading pistols and rifles they possessed in 1836. Thus a theoretical assault on the Alamo in 1846 would have matched a Mexican army that had employed virtually no technological advances in the intervening decade against a garrison that might have been armed with impressive short range firepower. Two hundred men equipped with revolvers and breech-loading rifles could inflict terrible casualties on a more primitively armed attack force which in turn may have led Santa Anna to simply declare victory and either go around the mission or retreat back to Mexico.

Since the Texan rebels were faced with defending the mission before the availability of the new weapons, the only other hope for deliverance seems to have been the arrival of reinforcements from Goliad. Colonel James Fannin actually attempted to march his 400 men the 90 miles to San Antonio, but quickly gave up the expedition when his wagons began to break down. A more energetic and flexible commander might have altered history by pushing on toward Bexar with whatever men and equipment he could move without the aid of wagons. Since Santa Anna's army maintained a rather loose siege of the mission, a relief column, with proper support from a sortie by the garrison, might very well have been able to triple the size of the rebel defense force and present the Mexican army with a far more complicated challenge.

A Texan garrison of 600 men would have created two enormous problems for a prospective Mexican assault. First, the Alamo contained an artillery complement of nearly 30 guns which represented the largest concentration of cannons between New Orleans and Mexico City. The main problem that Travis faced was that his garrison was simply too small to man all of the cannons and also provide riflemen to hold the mission walls. Thus only a fraction of the Alamo's guns were actually used against Santa Anna. A substantially larger Texan garrison would have allowed the rebels to throw enormous artillery firepower at any assault and also negate the arrival of additional Mexican cannons which Santa Anna expected on March 8th or 9th. Second, since the actual Texan garrison was able to inflict perhaps 500 casualties on the Mexican army before they ever got over the mission walls, it is reasonable to expect that a much larger contingent of riflemen could have inflicted virtually unacceptable losses on Santa Anna's assault. A garrison of 600 men could have swept every approach to the mission with incredibly intense fire that might have doubled or even tripled Mexican casualties as they attempted to reach the Alamo walls. Since the attack was at the point of disintegrating against the much smaller actual garrison, Santa Anna would have been forced to re-evaluate his whole strategy. While the Generalissimo could have taken the time to concentrate all of his available units for a continued siege of the Alamo, it is equally probable that the defenders could have expected additional reinforcements from units that eventually fell under the command of Sam Houston. Thus rather than the climax of the Texan War of Independence occurring on the fields of San Jacinto it is not unlikely that the critical engagement for Texan freedom may have occurred around the mission walls at Bexar.

While the timely arrival of reinforcements may have tilted the assault on the Alamo against the Mexican attackers, there are at least two battles during the Mexican-American war in which the course of the war might have been altered in favor of the Mexican republic. The first opportunity to dramatically enhance Mexican prospects for a more advantageous termination of the conflict occurred in February of 1847 when Winfield Scott stripped Zachary Taylor's northern army of virtually all of its regulars. Taylor initially failed to consolidate his remaining units and Santa Anna was able to concentrate an impressive force of 20,000 men to overwhelm the American army. However, Santa Anna's nonchalant attitude toward the welfare of his soldiers resulted in a poorly organized march through desert terrain that ultimately reduced the assault force by 25%. Once the Generalissimo's army arrived at Buena Vista, the army was able to almost achieve a critical breakthrough of Taylor's increasingly extended lines. At the moment of crisis, when the American general had committed virtually all of his reserves, Santa Anna simply wasn't able to achieve an overwhelming concentration that would have smashed the enemy defenders. If the Mexican commander had been able to utilize an additional 5000 men that he had frittered away in his march north, it is not unreasonable to expect that he might have destroyed or captured a large segment of Taylor's army and subsequently placed enormous pressure on the Polk administration to reconsider the validity of American war aims.

A second window of opportunity for the Mexican republic most likely emerged during August of 1847 as Winfield Scott directed the American campaign against the capital city's defenses. Gideon Pillow, Polk's close friend who emerged as an incompetent leader in two successive wars, provided Santa Anna with a golden opportunity for victory when he mismanaged the opening phase of the battle of Contreras. Pillow's attempt to move through the imposing barrier of the molten sea resulted in the first day of the battle ending with one contingent of 3000 Americans deployed out of supporting distance of Pillow's remaining 3000 soldiers. These two isolated columns were essentially bracketed by General Valencia's 6000 men on Padernia ridge to the west and Santa Anna's main army of 14,000 men deployed near the Churubusco River to the east. A well coordinated assault by Valencia and Santa Anna would have rolled up the heavily outnumbered American force at San Angel and then could have turned on Pillow's remaining units with devastating results. Elimination of these two columns would have left Winfield Scott in the almost ludicrous position of "besieging" an enemy capital with only 4000 men facing a defending army more than seven times his size. Under these conditions, it is not unreasonable to imagine that a negotiated peace far more favorable to the Mexican republic would have been the major result of a Mexican victory at Contreras. However, Valencia ignored Santa Anna's orders to attack. The Generalissimo held his own force back from any offensive operations, and the far more energetic Scott was able to put in motion a counterattack that would eventually place the American flag in the Halls of Montezuma.

Since the Mexican-American conflict was followed slightly more than a decade later by the far more sweeping War Between the States, most chronicles depict the war in terms of its impact on the strategy and tactics of the upcoming trial by fire between Union and Confederacy. The authors agree with this concept in its general emphasis on the fact that many of the senior generals in the Civil War received their first taste of combat and their first responsibility of command fighting Mexico. However, a detailed examination of the relationship between the two wars reveals a distinctly Southern tinge to both the war with Mexico and its impact of decision making during the war of secession. While support for a conflict with Mexico was more broad based and less regionalized than the War of 1812, it is equally evident that the war was primarily a Southern adventure. While each state in the Union made some attempt to provide volunteer regiments for the national army, relatively few Northern units were actively involved in the major campaign. In fact, Brigadier General Franklin Pierce was able to establish a thriving political career that led to the presidency based on his unique status of being a combat general from New England.

The conflict with Mexico was largely initiated by a Southern president, armies were commanded by Southerners Zachary Taylor and Winfield Scott, and Southern born junior officers such as Robert E. Lee, Joseph Johnston and Pierre Beauregard emerged as rising stars during the battles. A wide spectrum of Northerners including Abraham Lincoln, Ulysses Grant, and John Quincy Adams expressed serious reservations about the morality of fighting with their neighboring republic, yet most Southerners were extremely enthusiastic about the onset of hostilities with Mexico. Within this context, the Mexican War experience became an important part of the Southern mind set as the region lurched toward secession and confrontation with the north.

The American victories against the Mexican armies inspired Southerners of the early 1860's to convince themselves that the North's superior numbers could be defeated by a better organized, better led Confederate army; thus much of the mythology that "one Southerner can whip ten Yankees" was actually a restatement of beliefs concerning Mexican fighting ability in the 1840's. The Mexican War experience also seems to have convinced many potential Confederates that Northern opposition to war in the 1890's automatically translated into a reluctance to fight the South a decade and a half later. The dangerous idea that unmanly, soft, effete Yankees opposed any fighting in preference to making money convinced far too many potential secessionists that the North would never deploy an army large enough and persistent enough to force their "erring sisters" back into the Union. Finally, the Mexican War imprinted an indelible set of emotions on the most important Confederate of them all—Jefferson Davis. The hero of Monterrey and Buena Vista returned home with an inflated sense of his leadership abilities and command of military tactics. He subsequently spent much of the Civil War convinced that he was more than just the president of the Confederacy, he was also a true commander in chief who could replicate the victory over Mexico with a victory over the north. While Jefferson Davis saw the Mexican War as the defining moment of his military career and used that experience as a point of reference for his tenure as leader of the Confederacy, his adversary, Abraham Lincoln, was quick to realize that his earlier military experience as a militia captain in the Black Hawk War provided little insight into managing the prosecution of an operation as vast as the Union effort in the Civil War. Thus in at least some respects, the very war with Mexico that so enormously expanded the potential territory of the slave states also encouraged a series of Southern misconceptions that substantially influenced the ultimate collapse of the Confederate States of America.

# CHAPTER 22

# The War of Amateurs

## Fort Sumter to Manassas

*D*uring the pre-dawn hours of April 12, 1861, Major Robert Anderson of the First United States Artillery Regiment walked with three members of General Pierre Beauregard's staff to the small wharf adjoining Fort Sumter. In an emotional farewell, Anderson shook hands with Colonel James Chestnut, Lieutenant Colonel James Chisholm and Captain Stephen Lee and whispered in a choked voice, "if we never meet in this world again, God grant that we may meet in the next." The three officers of the new army of the Confederate States of America were rowed through the darkness of Charleston harbor toward the dozens of bonfires that lighted a ring of rebel artillery batteries. The Southerners manning these guns were waiting for a signal to open a bombardment against a fortress that now flew a flag that was no longer the emblem of seven former states of the American Union.

Beauregard's aides ordered their small boat to steer toward the gun emplacements at Fort Johnson and when the men alighted they advised Captain George Jones to prepare a seacoast mortar to be fired as a signal to commence the general bombardment. Soldiers fell in for roll call, guns were trundled into position and all along Charleston's rooftops, wharves and beaches hundreds of residents tried to locate the best vantage point from which to watch the unfolding drama. At 4:30 A.M., seventy minutes after the Southern officers had delivered their final ultimatum to Anderson, the signal mortar was ready to fire. One of the witnesses to this preparation was Virginia Congressman Roger Pryor, who was ready to savor a moment that he had been urging for almost a decade. However, when Jones asked the congressman if he would accept the honor of firing the first shot in the war for Southern independence, Pryor shook his head and whispered that he couldn't start the conflict himself. Thus Lieutenant Henry Farley, the gun commander, stepped forward and fired the piece and a moment later there was a flash of light and a dull explosion as the glowing red shell arched high in the humid darkness and exploded squarely over Fort Sumter. The citizens of Charleston responded to the explosion with a wide spectrum of emotions ranging from loud cheers to whispered prayers—few people could possibly imagine they were witnessing the opening moment of the most bloody conflict in the entire American experience.

Unlike the "shot heard round the world" on a similar April morning in Lexington, Massachusetts 86 years earlier, this equally momentous explosion was identifiable, planned and certainly not accidental. The American experiment in self-government born on that earlier spring dawn was now about to face the greatest and most dramatic challenge imaginable, as four years of bloody conflict would alter forever the hopes, fears and future of virtually every citizen of the now separated halves of the United States. This arching mortar shell was the culmination of a series of events that had begun in the wake of Abraham Lincoln's election to the presidency just over five months earlier. When South Carolina and then six other cotton states seceded from the "perpetual union" that had been formed in 1787 and started their own rival American republic, there were immediate demands from the new Confederate government that all United States posts in those states should be evacuated as quickly as possible. By the spring of 1861, the Stars and Stripes continued to wave over four military fortifications—three small forts in Florida and the much larger, thought unfinished, Fort Sumter. Two companies of Federal troops had occupied that fort since the day after Christmas when Major Anderson, conducting a daring night time expedition, transferred his 85 men from the almost indefensible Fort Moultrie to the much more imposing fort in the middle of Charleston harbor. While Anderson ignored demands from the South Carolina government to return to Moultrie, he knew that even Sumter could not hold out indefinitely as supplies would be exhausted by the middle of April. Outgoing President James Buchanan's attempt to re-supply the garrison by dispatching the steamer *Star of the West* to Charleston failed when Confederate shore batteries drove off the vessel, and Abraham Lincoln was handed a looming crisis when he took the oath of office on March 4, 1861.

While Lincoln's new administration debated the impact of abandoning or re-enforcing the fort, Major Anderson used his small garrison to maximum effectiveness, as he deployed over 60 pieces of artillery in the lower level casemate and on the upper level barbette, while bricking up the whole middle tier of gun ports due to a lack of gunners. Anderson faced some of the same challenges confronted by William Barrett Travis 35 years earlier at the Alamo; the garrison had far more artillery than they could effectively utilize, while the besieging force had an overwhelming number of potential attackers. However, while the defenders of the Alamo were facing an enemy army that was only a few hundred yards away, Anderson knew that Beauregard's 7000 men would have to be ferried across the harbor to physically assault the fort, and Sumter's guns could decimate the Southern attackers even if they wouldn't actually prevent their eventual victory. As

Lincoln drafted plans for a rescue operation and Jefferson Davis moved toward delivering an ultimatum for surrender, the people of North and South awaited the climax of the crisis. The Charleston *Mercury* noted with satisfaction that "the gage is thrown down and we accept the challenge. We will meet the invader and God and Battle must decide the issue between the hirelings of abolition hate and Northern tyranny and the people of South Carolina defending their freedom and their honor!"

The recourse to "God and Battle" soon became a reality as President Davis dispatched an order to General Beauregard to demand from Anderson either the evacuation of the fort or acceptance of the consequence of a massive Confederate bombardment. Lieutenant Farley's signal gun was the culmination of that threat and within minutes every gun emplacement around Charleston harbor was prepared to reduce Fort Sumter to rubble. It is reasonably probable that the first shot of the actual bombardment was fired by a secessionist fire-eater whose state still hadn't seceded. Crusty old Edmund Ruffin, a seventy-year-old Virginia planter and anti-Union agitator had traveled down to Charleston and enlisted in a local artillery battery so that he could be one of the first people to shoot at the hated Yankees. Ruffin, an eccentric looking person who was tall, gangly and displayed shoulder length white hair, was invited by Captain George Cuthbert to fire the first gun manned by the Palmetto Guards and contemporary eyewitnesses generally, though not unanimously, agreed that this was the first shot that actually hit the Federal fort.

Major Anderson could see no particular reason to waste his limited supply of ammunition firing at targets that were still shrouded in darkness, so his gunners ate a leisurely, if meager, breakfast of pork and water and then one of the battery commanders began to sight the guns at about 7:30 A.M. Captain Abner Doubleday personally directed the aiming of a Federal battery and gave the order to fire the first Federal shot in the defense of the shattered Union. While Federal and Confederate shells sailed through the hazy April sky, Charleston spectators dragged out well supplied picnic hampers and cheered their local units to an expected Southern victory. According to some Federal defenders, the crowd's cheering became so obnoxious to the garrison that, when no officers were looking, two veteran sergeants swung a pair of forty-two pounders around and fired at the civilians congregating along one of the beaches. The cannon shells sailed over the picnickers but slammed into the Moultrie Hotel, which was flying a hospital flag but didn't contain any patients. Southern newspapermen had their first good atrocity charge of the war, the sergeants had released their pent-up frustration, and the spectators gradually returned to their rudely interrupted lunches.

The battle of Fort Sumter soon settled into an unequal artillery duel between the heavily manned Confederate gun positions and the tiny Federal garrison, which was content with demonstrating that they wouldn't surrender without a fight. The Union defenders were briefly encouraged when they spotted a Federal relief force streaming on the horizon, but the steamship *Baltic,* which carried supplies and reinforcements, wouldn't attempt a run into the harbor without heavy naval support and the main support ship hadn't yet arrived. Thus Anderson's men spent the afternoon and night of April 12th watching Confederate mortars drop dozens of shells into the middle of their gradually crumbling defenses while debating whether the first boats they spotted would be the Union relief force or Beauregard's attackers.

The morning of April 13th dawned with the American flag still flying over Fort Sumter, but the garrison's hours were clearly numbered. Huge holes were appearing in the outer walls, the officers' barracks was on fire, the lower casemates were filling up with smoke and a major fire was raging out of control and heading for the fort's main powder magazine. At noon a Confederate shell smashed Sumter's flagpole and the repairs to the staff progressed so slowly that Confederate observers began to wonder if the fort had surrendered. Beauregard dispatched Captain Lee and Congressman Pryor to investigate the lowered flag and ask Anderson if he needed any assistance in fighting the obviously spreading fires. However, while these two men were being rowed out to the fort, another of Beauregard's numerous aides, former Texas senator Louis Wigfall, had already arrived at the fort without specific orders and was negotiating with Anderson for the evacuation of the fort. While the two newly arrived Southerners were surprised to meet Wigfall in the fort, they all readily agreed that the terms offered were still in force, and Anderson agreed to surrender the post on condition that his men could fire a final salute to the United States flag and have a free passage to a Northern port.

The next morning, April 14th, while Charleston civilians were ferried past the smoking ruins of the fort at 50 cents a person, the American flag was raised one last time and an artillery salute was initiated. Up to this point, the thousands of shells fired by each side had failed to even seriously injure one member of either army, but now a burning fragment of a powder bag was caught by the wind and dropped on a pile of ammunition stacked behind a cannon; a sudden explosion ripped through the Federal formation and Private David Hough became the first fatality of the war. Hough was buried in a service presided over by a Confederate chaplain, while a company of South Carolina volunteers presented arms. The garrison band then struck up the airs of "Yankee Doodle," and Major Anderson's command embarked on a waiting transport as the Confederate and Palmetto flags were raised over the newly acquired fortress. As all the guns in Charleston harbor fired a jubilant salute to an almost bloodless victory, the telegraph wires to the North were crackling with the awesome details of the first major armed confrontation of the secessionist crisis.

On that same Sunday afternoon, as news of Sumter's surrender reached the White House, Abraham Lincoln called an emergency cabinet meeting to discuss other options available to the Federal government. The next morning the President issued a call for 75,000 state militia to serve a 90-day enlistment, in order to deal with "combinations too powerful to be suppressed by ordinary law courts." On this bright Monday morning in April, 26 states still belonged to the Union, but the response of those states to Lincoln's call quickly demonstrated the diversity of sympathies of these remaining entities. While Oregon and California could offer little more than moral support because of their distance from the scene of the crisis, the other 16 states that no longer permitted slavery entered into a festival of patriotic fervor that quickly over-subscribed individual state quotes for militia and demonstrated that the potential military strength of the North was enormous. The specter of Fort Sumter was seen as a humiliation that could only be erased by a sudden and total military subjugation of the secessionist rebels and the destruction of their infant government.

On the other hand, the states that had not yet seceded but still permitted slavery reacted in a dramatically different fashion to Lincoln's call for volunteers. Delaware, which had fewer than 2000 slaves and relatively little in common with the other slave states, merely informed Washington that since the state had no organized militia units, it could not respond immediately to the president's call. Maryland, which was divided between a pro-slavery Chesapeake region and an anti-slavery western area, agreed to provide a quota of troops provided that the regiments only served in Maryland or the District of Columbia. However, the other six still-loyal slave states responded with unanimous virulence to the presidential proclamation. Governor Berick Magoffin of Kentucky informed the president that "Kentucky will furnish no troops for the wicked purpose of subduing her sister Southern states." Tennessee governor Isham Harris insisted "Tennessee will not furnish a single man for the purpose of coercion but 50,000 if necessary, for the defense of our rights and those of our Southern brethren." Governor John Letcher told Lincoln that "the militia of Virginia will not be furnished to the powers at Washington for any such purpose as they have in mind. You have chosen to inaugurate a Civil War, and having done so, we will meet it in a spirit as determined as the administration has exhibited toward the South." The governors of North Carolina, Arkansas and Missouri responded with very similar messages on the illegal and unconstitutional nature of Lincoln's call, and it soon became apparent that if Fort Sumter was pushing Northerners to a rediscovered military fervor in defense of the Union, the Federal response to the fort's surrender was also instrumental in encouraging some or even most of the border states to cast their lot with the new Confederate republic.

Of all the responses of the individual border states, the action of the governor and legislature of Virginia had the most significant impact on the nature of the upcoming conflict. On April 17th, an already sitting state convention voted to take the Old Dominion out of the Union and subsequently offered the new Confederate government the use of Richmond as the capital of the Southern republic. The next day, several companies of militia closed in on the Federal arsenal at Harpers Ferry and as the tiny garrison of 47 soldiers fled, they botched a demolition attempt that left huge supplies of muskets and machinery behind for the arriving Confederates. On April 19th, a larger militia force marched toward the even more important prize of Gosport Navy Yard near Norfolk. This base contained over 1200 cannons, extensive repair facilities and 10 warships, including the powerful forty gun steam frigate *Merrimack,* which was probably the most powerful vessel in the United States Navy. Commodore McCauley refused to evacuate the ships until it was too late to save them and then bungled a half hearted attempt to destroy the base. Most of the guns and ships would be used against the Northern forces and the *Merrimack* would be converted into the legendary CSS *Virginia.*

The secession of Virginia not only provided the rebels with a splendid arsenal and naval base, it also turned a badly overmatched league of cotton states into a much more powerful adversary for the Unionists. The Old Dominion was the most populous state in the South, had an industrial capacity nearly as great as all seven states of the deep South, and contained the Tredegar Iron Works, the only plant in the secessionist states capable of providing heavy ordnance. The enormous influence of Virginians in founding the American republic now essentially made Washington, Jefferson and Madison honorary Confederates and strengthened Southern contentions that they were the real American republicans, engaged in rescuing the heritage of the founding fathers from the distorted form of radical democracy and rampant capitalism promoted by Yankee abolitionists and businessmen. While a succession of deceased Virginians would provide much of the legitimacy for the so-called second American Revolution, a number of living residents of the Old Dominion would increase the possibility that this war for independence would be as successful as the original contest. Joseph Johnston, A.P. Hill, Jeb Stuart and Thomas Jackson would soon demonstrate a variety of military talents on a number of battlefields. Most notable of the Virginians who left Federal service to defend the interests of their state was, of course, Robert E. Lee. Lee would not only provide the tactical genius that almost single-handedly rescued the Confederacy from almost certain destruction on a number of occasions, he also provided an aura of dignity, chivalry and honor that gained adulation from fellow Southerners and even grudging admiration from his Northern adversaries.

The addition of Virginia to the Confederate coalition not only provided the new republic with talented generals, hard fighting regiments and invaluable industrial assets, but it also enormously complicated the defense strategy of the infant nation against Federal attempts to restore the Union by force. Montgomery, Alabama, the first capital of the Confederacy, had terrible hotel accommodations, poor railroad facilities and the atmosphere of a frontier town, but at least it was hundreds of miles from any Union territory and relatively difficult to capture. On the other hand, Richmond was barely 100 miles from the rival capital of the United States and any sort of determined military expedition marching out from Washington could threaten the new capital within a very short time. Jefferson Davis and his advisors became more and more committed to the defense of Richmond and its adjoining counties, often to the point of ignoring the enormous Union forces that were confronting the rebels elsewhere. Davis assigned the best generals and the best equipment to the Virginia front and allowed the Unionists to gradually strangle the Confederacy almost everywhere else, until the Confederate "nation" was eventually reduced to a glorified city-state of Richmond and its suburbs. While the secession of Virginia certainly placed Washington within much closer striking range of a Confederate army, in the primarily defensive strategy that the outnumbered rebels would generally adopt, Richmond would be much more susceptible to attack than the District of Columbia.

If the secession of Virginia provided a variety of long term assets to the Confederate cause, the secessionist impulse among a large number of Marylanders provided the South with the more immediate possibility of isolating Lincoln and his government in an untenable capital city before they could even begin to organize a military response to the rebels. While Maryland was still officially in the Union, large numbers of its citizens were determined to ensure that the state would eventually ally itself with the new Confederacy. On April 19th, the first fully equipped northern regiment to respond to Lincoln's proclamation entered Baltimore on its way to Washington. Unfortunately, Baltimore didn't have a cross town railroad link between President Street station and Camden Street station, so the men from the 6th Massachusetts regiment were forced to disembark from one train and then begin a shuttle operation of individual cars over the city horse-drawn trolley system. Most of the regiment was ferried across the city as a secessionist mob began to yell curses and throw stones at the transported train coaches, but when the Southern sympathizers were finally able to barricade the trolley tracks, four companies of Massachusetts men were forced to form ranks and begin to march across the city. As the men marched to the accompaniment of catcalls and cheers for Jefferson Davis, someone unfurled a Confederate flag, which seemed to encourage at least some of the secessionist to push and jostle the Yankee soldiers and grab their rifles. At this point the Unionists began double timing, which simply incited the crowd to more blatant violence as rocks and then bullets began to fly. The New Englanders quickly formed a firing line and blasted the crowd and within two or three minutes four soldiers and twelve citizens were dead, while scores of injured men were staggering away from the scene of the riot.

The clash between Union militia and secessionist sympathizers produced enormous repercussions for the Lincoln administration in Washington. The mayor and chief of police of Baltimore decided to prevent any more troops from entering the city by ordering the destruction of the railroad bridges from Philadelphia and Harrisburg while Marylanders who supported the rebel cause were busy cutting down telegraph lines from Washington and

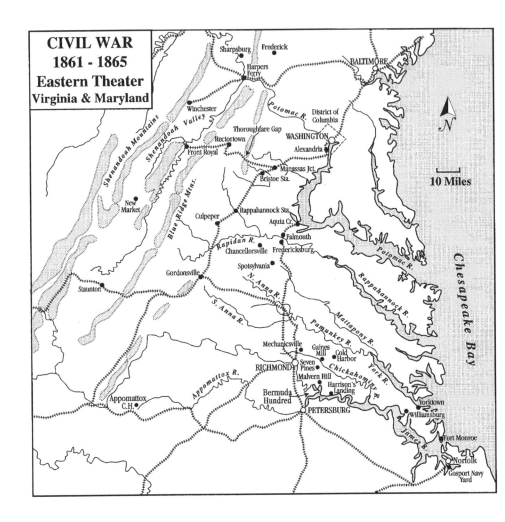

CIVIL WAR
1861 - 1865
Eastern Theater
Virginia & Maryland

barricading railroad routes leading North. Since the national capital was bordered on one side by an already belligerent Virginia and on the other three sides by a potentially hostile Maryland, the President and his advisors were caught in a virtual state of siege with nearly all contact with the loyal states now cut off. The Washington garrison consisted of the recently arrived 6th Massachusetts, a few companies of partially armed Pennsylvania militia, and a handful of regular soldiers. Until and unless communications with the North could be restored, the national capital remained extremely vulnerable to a determined Rebel attack pushed across the Potomac from Virginia.

While the new President stared anxiously out of the White House windows wondering whether Union or Confederate troops would be the first units to march down Pennsylvania Avenue, an extraordinarily controversial politician-general from Massachusetts was making a series of key decisions that would retain the capital for the Federal side. General Benjamin Butler, a fast-talking, eccentric politician who had managed the incredible feat of counting both Jefferson Davis and some of the most radical abolitionists among his friends, arrived on a steamboat at Annapolis, accompanied by a regiment of Massachusetts volunteers and a burning desire to make political capital from the upcoming war. Butler ignored Governor Hicks' pleas to postpone a direct march toward Washington and organized the many former railroad employees among his men to repair a number of sabotaged locomotives and replace ripped up sections of track. While his Massachusetts volunteers reopened the Baltimore and Ohio route to Washington, Butler took charge of a newly arriving New York regiment and hustled them by train to the national capital. On the morning of April 25th, six days after the "siege" of Washington had begun, the New Yorkers arrived in the capital city, formed ranks, and marched along Pennsylvania Avenue toward the White House. The week of panic for Washington Unionists had now ended and the rebels had just missed a golden opportunity to appropriate the national capital as the new seat of Confederate government.

Once it became apparent to the Lincoln administration that the District of Columbia would not be re-designated the District of Dixie in the near future, attention began to shift toward the capture of the enemy capital before the Confederate Congress could hold its opening session, scheduled for July 20th, 1861. Northern newspapers, spearheaded by Horace Greeley's *New York Tribune* published dozens of "on to Richmond" editorials and Lincoln felt increasingly compelled to order his new field commander, General Irvin McDowell, to organize an expeditionary force to march toward the Rebel capital as quickly as possible. When McDowell and his superior, commanding general Winfield Scott, protested to Lincoln about the lack of time to train the raw recruits, the President simply responded, "you are green, it is true, but they are green also. You are all green alike." Thus on July 16th, 1861, under considerable pressure from the Federal government, Irvin McDowell ordered fifty regiments of infantry, ten batteries of field artillery and one battalion of cavalry to march out from their camps along the Potomac River and proceed in the direction of Manassas Junction about 30 miles away.

While the upcoming disaster at Bull Run tainted McDowell's reputation for decades, in reality the young general was an intelligent and sophisticated officer who had designed an excellent plan for maximizing the effectiveness of his extremely raw troops. What Lincoln could not yet realize, but McDowell fully understood, was the fact that even though the Rebel forces were as inexperienced as the Federal army, it was much easier to order green troops to simply deploy along already selected defensive positions than to march 30 miles in blazing heat and then launch a large scale attack against an entrenched enemy. McDowell immediately developed a plan to reduce this imbalance. First, because almost all of the militia regiments were commanded by men totally without experience in war, he organized the army into small brigades, each of which would be commanded by a regular army colonel who in turn would be assisted by as many junior regular officers as might be available. Second, the commander largely ignored the government's priority of capturing Richmond and focused on capturing Manassas Junction and interposing his army between to the main Confederate forces and the Southern capital.

If all went well, McDowell's plan had a real chance to succeed. The Union attack force of about 32,000 men would initially confront General Beauregard's army of only 18,000 men deployed along the Bull Run river near Manassas. However, the Northern army would only enjoy this substantial numerical advantage if a second Union force under General Robert Patterson could hold General Joseph Johnston's Shenandoah army in place and prevent any reinforcements from reaching Manassas. Unfortunately, the sixty-nine-year-old Patterson, a veteran of the War of 1812 and the Mexican War, was already befuddled about how to use his 14,000 men to deflect Johnston's 8000 rebels from any eastward movement. Johnston had the great good luck to have the services of two future heroes of the Confederacy, who were able to use their originality and daring to more than compensate for lack of numbers. Colonel Thomas Jackson, an eccentric professor at Virginia Military Institute, was utilizing his new command to disrupt Northern transportation lines from Harpers Ferry, by sending raiding parties out to capture over 40 locomotives and 500 freight cars, which left increasingly large segments of Patterson's army as semi-permanent railroad guards. While Jackson drew off one part of the Yankee army, a young Rebel cavalry colonel named James Ewell Brown Stuart launched a series of mounted attacks on Federal supply routes which convinced Patterson that he was about to be attacked by a massive Confederate army. While the Union forces flailed at both real and spectral attackers, Johnston quietly began to load his men on every available eastbound train and began a massive shuttle of reinforcements to Beauregard.

Irvin McDowell had expected the Union advance from the Potomac to Manassas to take two days, which would have allowed him to confront

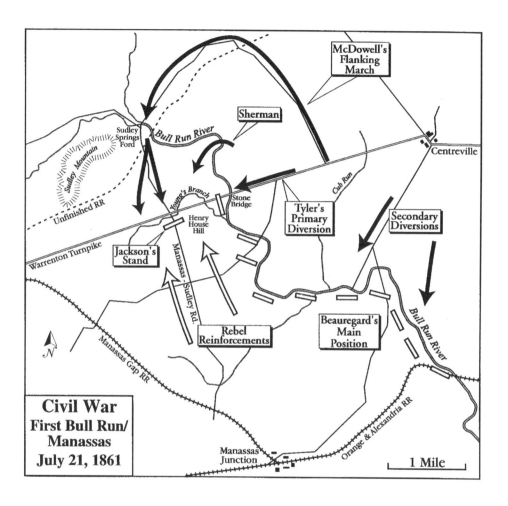

McDowell's
Flanking
March

Sherman

Sudley
Springs
Ford

*Bull Run River*

Centreville

*Sudley Mountain*

Young's Branch

Stone
Bridge

*Cub Run*

Tyler's
Primary
Diversion

Secondary
Diversions

*Unfinished RR*

Henry
House
Hill

*Warrenton Turnpike*

Jackson's
Stand

*Manassas - Sudley Rd.*

Rebel
Reinforcements

Beauregard's
Main
Position

*Bull Run River*

N

*Manassas Gap RR*

**Civil War**
**First Bull Run/**
**Manassas**
**July 21, 1861**

Manassas
Junction

*Orange & Alexandria RR*

1 Mile

Beauregard's outnumbered army well before any of Johnston's men arrived. However, the raw regiments set a pace that startled McDowell and his staff. The first day's march only covered an incredible three miles, as the shuffling blue coated columns came to a halt practically in sight of the camps they had left that morning. During the next three days the army ambled toward the town of Centreville with frequent stops to loot nearby towns and farms, interspersed with naps and swimming excursions. While Federal volunteers dragged commandeered mattresses, mirrors and clocks along the route of march, Beauregard began to integrate the first of Johnston's regiments into his own defenses. The arrival of the Shenandoah troops was supplemented by the transfer of Theophilus Holmes' detachment from Aquia Creek, and Wade Hampton's mixed legion of infantry, artillery and cavalry on its way up from Richmond. This steady stream of reinforcements was gradually swelling Beauregard's army to approximately the same 32,000 as McDowell commanded, and the first major engagement of the war would be perhaps the most evenly matched contest of the conflict.

Beauregard enjoyed the advantage of placing his men in pre-selected defensive positions where the men knew the ground and the approaches to the battlefield. On the other hand, the Confederate advantage was at least partially nullified by the fact that McDowell was accompanied by 7 companies of regular cavalry, 8 companies of regular infantry and of 9 batteries of regular artillery which, if deployed to maximum advantage, could possibly tip the balance of the battle in favor of the Federals. Also, while McDowell was not aware of this, Beauregard was seriously considering abandoning the advantage of holding defensive positions in order to attack the Yankees, in an attempt to swing behind the Union army and place Confederate troops between the Federals and the Potomac River. Thus, in this possible scenario, the Rebel troops might well have smashed into the far better trained Union regulars, who would probably have inflicted enormous casualties on the poorly organized Southern attackers.

McDowell's army finally deployed around the village of Centreville late on Saturday, July 20th, and by 2 A.M. the next morning a complicated Union assault plan had been set in motion. The Union commander had no intention of launching a head-on attack with untrained men who might evaporate in the face of heavy casualties; he wanted to get a large detachment beyond the Confederate left flank and then hit the Rebels from behind as he rolled up the Southerners regiment by regiment. McDowell's complex plan envisioned a force of 14,000 men marching off on a wide circle to the right, fording the Bull Run river at Sudley Springs Ford several miles west of Beauregard's main army, and then hitting the Rebels from behind when they least expected an attack. While this main force was attacking Beauregard and simultaneously keeping Johnston from intervening, a diversionary force would feign an attack against Beauregard's extreme left flank, which was deployed along a stone bridge across the river, while two smaller forces would advance in such a way as to convince the Rebel general that his center and right were also threatened.

The complex four-part Union advance began in the early morning hours of Sunday July 21st, 1861. While several regiments deployed to form a reserve position around Centreville, the forces designated to distract Beauregard's center and right flank units slowly moved into their assigned positions. While none of these forces were setting any speed records for the deployment of troops, they were apparently moving much more quickly than McDowell's two other detachments, that were virtually crawling toward the Bull Run. The Union commander had based much of his plan on the assumption that his forces would be across the river before it was light enough to spot them, but the Federal troops took almost nine hours to march from their campsites to the relatively nearby stream. While the main force fumbled across the stream at Sudley Ford, the primary diversionary unit commanded by General Daniel Tyler arrived at the approach to the stone bridge. Tyler's force was opposed by an under-strength brigade of two small regiments commanded by General Nathan Evans, who initially deployed his force to confront what seemed to be the main Union effort of the battle. However, Tyler's men managed one of the worst diversions of the war and were so lackadaisical and half hearted in their feigned "attacks" that Evans started to suspect a Yankee ruse. These suspicions were heightened when a Confederate signal officer, Captain E. Porter Alexander, sent a message from a nearby signal tower that a Federal column was already across the river and was threatening the Confederate left flank.

Evans left four companies to cover the stone bridge and then rushed the remainder of his South Carolina and Louisiana troops, along with two artillery pieces, through a series of fields and streams to intercept the Union flanking column. The Confederates came panting and winded to a farm house a half mile from the Warrenton turnpike and hastily deployed a battle line only minutes before the lead elements of McDowell's force arrived. The first Federal brigade to cross the Bull Run and move along the Warrenton road was Ambrose Burnside's mixed brigade of New York, New Hampshire and Rhode Island regiments. Burnside, accompanied by wealthy young Rhode Island governor William Sprague, observed the Confederates form-ing for battle and quickly ordered his four regiments to advance. The result was the first of a series of mismanaged attacks that would plague Burnside for most of the war. The Yankee 4 to 1 advantage was frittered away in piecemeal assaults that made no real progress until McDowell ordered up two batteries of artillery to support the advance. The regular army gunners started tearing huge holes in Evans' line and the whole position was on the verge of crumbling when General Barnard Bee arrived on the scene with one of Johnston's brigades that had been brought in by railroad to Manassas Junction. Bee's initial inclination was to re-assemble a Confederate battle line on a nearby ridge, but he reluctantly acceded to Evans' determination to hold his present position and, for a time, the Union advance was checked.

While the reinforced rebels dueled with the ever-increasing Union flanking force, one of the future heroes of the North was in the process of turning the battle against the Confederacy. Colonel William Tecumseh Sherman, who commanded one of the regiments assigned to Tyler's diversionary force, discovered that he could get his men across the river upstream from the stone bridge. Sherman's men waded across the river and suddenly smashed into the right flank of Evans' line when the Rebels least expected an attack from that direction. The Southern defenses simply collapsed as hundreds of men began running through fields, splashing through a muddy stream called Young's Branch, and climbing the slopes of an elevation called Henry House Hill. This hill, dominated by the farmhouse owned by a former officer of the famous U.S.S. *Constitution*, now became the focal point of the first major battle of the war. McDowell's plan seemed to be on the verge of success as the whole left flank of the Confederate army had evaporated into a disorganized mass milling around Henry House Hill, while Beauregard was still deploying his main force to counter a non-existent Union threat to his right flank. One more solid Federal push would probably have crushed the rebellion and turned the war of Southern secession into a single summer of crisis that would eventually be compared to Shay's Rebellion and the Whisky Rebellion of the early days of the Republic. However, just as Sherman was demonstrating the initiative and energy that would prove so destructive to the Confederacy three years later, an equally bold and energetic Southerner was about to turn McDowell's plan into a disaster for the Union.

Brigadier General Thomas Jackson, who had already given General Patterson fits in the Shenandoah Valley, was now in the process of forming his five regiments of Virginia infantry near the crest of Henry House Hill. While the rest of the Confederate forces seemed to be disorganized and panic stricken, Jackson calmly formed his men behind the crest of the hill and prepared to meet the oncoming Yankee advance. While General Bee was attempting to reorganize his own brigade, he observed the perfect order of the Virginians and shouted to his own men, "Look! there is Jackson standing like a stone wall! Rally behind the Virginians!" A moment later Bee went down with a mortal wound, but the legend of "Stonewall" Jackson was born and the Union attack up the hill began to waver.

While Bee, Evans and Jackson were attempting to organize a defense of the threatened hill, Johnston and Beauregard were observing the struggle from a hill several miles distant. Beauregard had continued to toy with the idea of his own flank attack against the Federals all morning, but it was becoming increasingly apparent that the crisis of the battle would occur far away from his proposed point of assault. Finally, Johnston pointed to the distant smoke and exclaimed "the battle is over there. I am going," and the senior general on the field rode toward Henry House Hill. Beauregard remained behind just long enough to organize a redeployment of his right flank units toward the left and then followed Johnston toward the scene of

the fiercest fighting. While Johnston expedited the unloading and disposition of his brigades that were just arriving on the trains pulling into
Manassas Junction, Beauregard went directly to Henry House Hill and
began to cobble together a more formidable defensive line.

The Creole general remarked later that the intensity of the fighting was
far beyond what he had expected, as "the political hostilities of a generation
were now face to face with weapons instead of words." Just as additional
Union regiments climbed up the ridge to attempt a sweep of the crest, Wade
Hampton's legion arrived and blocked the Yankee advance. What had
begun as a battle of motion, of outflanking, advance and retreat now became
a bloody shootout on a hilltop that was bare of trees, devoid of ditches or
vales and was merely an open field where hundreds of men loaded and
fired, cursed and fell. Two lines of riflemen were essentially stalled less than
a hundred yards from each other and men from New York, New Jersey and
Massachusetts simply stood and blasted away at soldiers from Virginia,
South Carolina and Louisiana as the wounded crawled back to collapse in
the grass and new units arrived to take the place of their fallen comrades.
The Yankees were convinced that if they could sweep past this one army
they would march into Richmond and initiate the almost immediate collapse of the rebellion, while the Confederates were just as certain that if the
Federal army was decimated on this field, the Unionists might never again
attempt an invasion of the sacred soil of the South.

McDowell's attack probably hit its high water mark when several batteries of regular artillery obliterated part of the Henry farmhouse and the
defenders who were attempting to hold it. Among the Southern casualties
killed in the barrage was Judith Henry, an eighty-four-year-old widow who
had been evacuated from the house before the battle but insisted in
returning to her own bedroom before the crisis swirled around her home.
Once the prominent farmhouse was captured, two of the Federal batteries
were redeployed too far from their supporting infantry and became a prime
target for a Confederate counterattack. McDowell ordered two reinforcing
units, the New York Fire Zouaves and a battalion of newly recruited
Marines, to move up toward the artillerymen, but as they advanced along
the plateau they were suddenly attacked by Jeb Stuart's cavalry who quickly
routed the untrained men. A few minutes later the exposed gunners cheered
as they watched another regiment of blue coats approach their position, but
their cheering was quickly cut short when the new "reinforcements" proved
to be a Virginia regiment that hadn't been able purchase gray coats as yet.
While the Federal gunners waved and yelled, the rebel colonel ordered his
men to take aim and fire, and within seconds 49 of the 50 battery horses and
most of the gunners were shot down. The Rebels then charged with bayonets
and Bowie knives and in a brutal melee the Federal artillery units simply
disintegrated. A Confederate officer who observed the incident noted that
"it seemed as though every man and every horse of that battery just laid
right down and died right off."

McDowell was startled to see two of his best artillery units wiped out by "friendly" troops, and the commanding general quickly climbed the stairs to the top floor of the Henry House to get a better feel for the situation of his other units. The Union general probably realized that his plan was in serious jeopardy when he observed hundreds of fresh Rebel soldiers approaching Henry House Hill from at least two directions. Joseph Johnston had hustled one of his best units, a brigade commanded by Edmund Kirby Smith, from the Manassas railroad station to the scene of the battle in a remarkably short time, while Brigadier General Jubal Early had pushed his regiments 8 miles from the original Confederate right flank to the crisis point in an equally rapid march. Now these two units smashed into the tiring Federal forces from two separate directions and the Northerners began to give ground. Beauregard simply kept feeding new units into the battle line and extending his ranks further and further around the Union flank until huge Rebel forces were threatening the Federal rear. The Confederates had now probably concentrated more men at the scene of the fighting than their Union counterparts and the raw Yankee militia were used up beyond their capacity to fight. Burnside's brigade had already pulled back to a grove of trees, most of Tyler's detachment had collapsed panting in the grass, and the fresh reserve regiments were still in Centreville too far away to be of any help. Thus somewhere between 4 P.M. and 5 P.M. on this hot, humid, July afternoon, larger and larger units of the Federal army simply decided that they had fought enough for one day and began to disengage from the battle. Platoons, companies and then whole regiments began a steady retrograde march toward Centreville and equally exhausted Confederates began to realize that they would hold the field and, at the very least, win a narrow victory.

At about five o'clock on this Sunday afternoon Irvin McDowell probably realized that he wouldn't destroy Beauregard's army, but he would console himself with the facts that he had inflicted more casualties than he had taken and he could reorganize his still intact army at Centreville for another attack in the near future. However, a few minutes later the check at Bull Run transformed into a disaster. The prospect of a spectacular Sunday confrontation between Federals and Rebels had encouraged hundreds of Washington legislators and civilians to pack picnic lunches and take a carriage ride toward the expected battle site. These spectators emulated the enthusiasm of the Charleston citizens three months earlier, while at least ten Congressmen and six Senators drove down to place their personal stamp of approval on the crushing of the rebellion. The spectators made themselves comfortable on a series of slopes between the Bull Run river and a small creek called Cub Run about a mile east of the battlefield and settled down to watch the largest battle ever fought on American soil. The smoke and haze obscured most of the action but most of the series of military couriers seemed optimistic enough to encourage most people that a Union victory would be confirmed by supper time.

This atmosphere of optimism began to erode when the first retreating units marched suddenly past the civilians as they pulled back toward Centreville. Then, just as a long line of Union supply wagons and artillery caissons began crossing Cub Run bridge, a Confederate battery maneuvered close enough to start dropping shells near the stream. A Federal wagon went careening across the bridge at high speed, lost control, and overturned, creating a traffic jam worthy of 20th century holiday weekends. Exploding shells, screaming women and children, cursing men and panic stricken horses created a scene of chaos which quickly infected the retreating army units and initiated a stampede that sent men running all the way back to the Potomac River. McDowell still had 5000 men and 20 artillery pieces deployed around Centreville and he expected this force to serve as a rallying point for the retreating bluecoats. However, the Union general finally realized that most of his army was a confused, demoralized mob, and he started conjuring up images of a Confederate counterattack cutting his army off from the Potomac, and Rebel generals riding into Washington to dictate peace terms in the White House.

While the battle reached it dramatic climax, the presidents of the rival American republics experienced the roller coaster of emotions that was a feature of the rapidly shifting nature of this battle. Abraham Lincoln spent much of this hot Sunday reading a series of optimistic telegrams from McDowell's headquarters and even Winfield Scott admitted that a Union victory seemed probable. The President decided to go for a late afternoon carriage ride while he awaited more complete reports, but when he returned to the White House he was informed by an agitated aide that Secretary of State Seward had stopped in with terrible news. Lincoln rushed over to the War Department just in time to read a new communique which stated "General McDowell is in full retreat through Centreville. The day is lost. Save Washington and the remnants of the army." The now thoroughly shocked President returned to the White House and spent the rest of the night on a sofa in the Cabinet room, while a steady stream of politicians who had returned from the battlefield brought him their eye-witness accounts of the opening disaster of the war to restore the Union.

While Lincoln's mood swing downward from modest euphoria to bone-numbing depression over the course of the day, Jefferson Davis experienced an opposite range of emotions. When the Confederate president confirmed that a battle was underway, he took a special train from Richmond to Manassas Junction and then mounted a horse for the ride to the battle site. The president was initially shocked at the sight of dozens of retreating soldiers warning him to go back, as the Federals had defeated the army. However, when Davis got closer to Henry House Hill he began glimpsing the Union retreat and soon encountered an enthusiastic Stonewall Jackson, who insisted that he could capture Washington with 10,000 fresh men. However, when the president arrived at Beauregard's headquarters, the two senior Confederate generals insisted that their troops were as disorganized and exhausted as the blue coats, and that a confused, hungry, tired army would be unable to threaten a still numerous Federal force. Confederate cavalry units were in the process of snapping up hundreds of Yankee stragglers and Davis was unwilling to reconcile himself to allowing the Union army to retreat to the safety of the Potomac, where it could refit and launch another threat to the Confederate capital. However, a combination of unenthusiastic commanding generals and the beginning of an increasingly intense rainstorm soon after dark eliminated any initiation of a controversial and long debated follow-up attack to destroy the Union army and plant the Confederate flag in Washington.

The largest and best equipped army in the history of the American republic staggered back toward Washington after losing just under 10% of its total strength. McDowell's army had suffered a casualty rate that was relatively low by the standards of later Civil War battles, but was huge by the benchmark of earlier American wars. Four hundred and eighty-one Federal troops had been killed in action, eleven hundred and twenty-four were wounded and something over fifteen hundred blue coats had been captured. The Southern loss in killed and wounded was actually somewhat higher than the Federal casualty rate—as three hundred and eighty seven rebels were killed and fifteen hundred and eighty-two were wounded, but only eight Confederate soldiers were listed as missing or captured. Beauregard and Johnston also garnered twenty-eight captured Federal artillery pieces, five hundred late model rifles, half a million rounds of ammunition and nine regimental battle flags which could be prominently displayed in Richmond.

As the last of the beaten Yankees retreated to the fortifications around Washington, the citizens of the new Southern republic celebrated their victory and offered prayers of thanksgiving for their deliverance from the abolitionists. The citizens of the secessionist republic generally believed that their independence was now assured, as their "grand and holy cause" was at last fulfilled. However, less than a hundred miles to the north, a so far badly underestimated president of the United States had quite different ideas about admitting that the divorce between the two sections of the country that he called the "last, best hope on earth" was permanent and final.

CHAPTER 23

# The Response to a Clash of Arms

## Union and Confederate Strategies and Resources

$S$oon after the details of the battle of Manassas were transmitted to towns and cities across America, newspaper editors began to discuss the probable impact of the Southern victory on the Confederate bid for independence. Horace Greeley, the mercurial editor whose *New York Tribune* had taken the lead in the "On to Richmond" frenzy, almost immediately wrote a letter to Abraham Lincoln which virtually implied that the Union cause had been defeated in that single battle. Greeley told the president that "on every brow sits sullen, scorching, black despair... if it is best for the country and for mankind that we make peace with the Rebels at once and on their own terms, do not shrink even from that." On the other hand, most newspapers in the South were decidedly more upbeat as they discussed the now inevitable prospect of Confederate independence. The Mobile *Register* predicted that the Union army "would never again advance beyond cannon shot of Washington" while the Richmond *Whig* noted that "the breakdown of the Yankee race, their unfitness for empire, forces dominion on the South. We are compelled to take the scepter of power. We must adapt ourselves to our new destiny."

While many newspaper accounts grossly exaggerated the long term impact of a single battle, cooler minded men in the meeting rooms of Washington and Richmond realized that the confrontation at Bull Run was merely a beginning, not an end, to the secessionist conflict. By the morning after Manassas, Abraham Lincoln had recovered from his initial shock at the Union disaster and had begun to draw up a list of priorities for winning the war. In some respects Lincoln and his cabinet were in a position that was similar to the one faced by George III and his ministers after they had received the news of the initial fighting in the American colonies. Both the 18th century British monarch and the 19th century American president recovered from their initial shock at an early rebel success to prepare a memorandum on how the breakaway provinces could be restored to the central government. The United Kingdom of 1775 had a population of about 9 million compared to about 2½ million colonists of which about 2 million were free whites. The states that remained in the Union in the summer of 1861 counted a population of about 22 million citizens opposing a southern population of about 5½ million whites and 3½ million slaves. Each rebel force was opposed by a central government that had something around a four to one advantage in a pool of eligible males who could be recruited for military service. Thus, in theory, Lincoln and his military commanders could place an army in the field that had the same type of numerical superiority that George III's forces enjoyed during most of the War of Independence.

However, while the Unionists shared this numerical superiority with the 18th century redcoats, they also faced one of the major challenges faced by Lord North and his king as they embarked on their quest to restore royal authority to America. The American Unionists, much like the British imperial forces in 1775, would be faced with the daunting task of attempting to restore central authority to a number of breakaway provinces that were spread over a vast territory and would be almost impossible to physically occupy on a permanent basis, and, even if these provinces were restored, that conquest would probably be useless if the territories were littered with the bodies of former countrymen and the burned out houses and farms of the inhabitants. A ravaged and desolate rebel territory was of equally little use to the growth-oriented British society of 1775 or the American republic of 1861.

While the British government of 1775 and the Federal government of 1861 shared certain common advantages and challenges, the secessionist crisis also presented Lincoln and his administration with a situation that contained substantial differences from the earlier confrontation between crown and colonies. On the positive side, while the British ministry of 1775 was faced with the daunting prospect of transporting men and supplies across a 3000 mile wide storm ravaged ocean, the Union government was facing an adversary that could literally be seen from the windows of the White House. However, while Lord North never had the fear that rebel troops might seize London as a bargaining chip for recognizing independence, Lincoln was faced with an ongoing threat of a Confederate strike against Washington. The Unionists were also faced with the prospect of initiating hostilities with only 16,000 regular soldiers and 42 ships, while the British government of 1775 could deploy over three times as many soldiers and the largest, most powerful fleet in the world.

There is little doubt that many Americans, and probably most Europeans, saw the task of restoring Federal authority to the secessionist states as being so daunting as to present a virtual impossibility. However, the Union of 1861 was far from a helpless entity. The Northern states in 1861 contained an intelligent, energetic, highly adaptable population that had developed a fantastically efficient agricultural system and was experiencing enormous industrial and technological progress. The Federal government could not only raise more troops than the Confederacy; they could keep them better armed, better fed and better clothed than their adversaries and they could support them with a powerful industrial and agricultural base. The Northern states had twice as many miles of railroad, six times as many factories, ten times as many industrial workers and twelve times the financial wealth as their Southern antagonists. If the impending conflict was truly going to be the first modern war rather than just a slightly updated version of Napoleonic campaigns, all of these assets would play a critical role in encouraging a Unionist victory.

While the North had more men, more money and more factories than the South, the Confederacy enjoyed its own particular set of wartime advantages. One of the few things that such diverse rebel leaders as Jefferson Davis, Pierre Beauregard and Joseph Johnston could agree upon was the fact that few people ever attempted to secure their independence with more advantages than enjoyed by the Southern states in 1861. As Johnston insisted almost twenty years later, "that (southern) people was not guilty of the high crime of undertaking a war without the means of waging it successfully." The most visible advantage held by the secessionists at the outbreak of hostilities was the enormous cotton production that by 1860 had reached a value of $190 million a year and constituted almost 60% of the entire worth of exports from the United States. If cotton wasn't quite an absolute king in 1861, it was certainly a viable member of royalty, as the factories and mills of Dickensian England had developed a seemingly insatiable appetite for the Southern product and the sales of that commodity, could, if properly managed, buy enough guns, cannons, ships and bullets to counteract much of the Northern advantage in industrial capacity. Cabinet officials and ordinary citizens generally agreed that the virtual monopoly of a crucial commodity of the Industrial Revolution would allow the new republic to simply purchase the technologically advanced weapons systems of Great Britain that were thought to be more powerful than anything the Northern factories could produce.

The substantial asset of possessing a valuable commodity that could be used to purchase weapons was enhanced enormously by the solid military credentials of many of the men who would be called upon to lead the Confederate forces. Almost 700 officers from the United States army and navy had resigned their commissions to join the South and many of these men were viewed as the top flight members of their former organizations. Robert E. Lee, Albert Sydney Johnston, Pierre Beauregard and Joseph Johnston composed much of the upper tier of influential officers in the pre-war Federal army and their commander in chief had been regarded as an excellent Secretary of War in the 1850's. This substantial corps of West

Point and Annapolis graduates was dramatically enhanced by the fact that seven of the eight military colleges in the United States were located in the slave states and schools such as Virginia Military Institute and The Citadel could provide large numbers of alumni who could instantly step into key command positions. For example VMI alone provided almost 1800 officers to the Confederate army and at one point in 1861, one third of the field officers in the state of Virginia had graduated from the school in Lexington. Thus when Lincoln insisted to General McDowell that Northern and Southern forces were "green alike" in their lack of military experience, this was certainly not the case in the officer corps of the contending armies.

The initial recognized Southern advantages of the dominance of cotton and the better experience of the Confederate officer corps were expected to be supplemented by two major assets that were envisioned as emerging once the war began in earnest. First, careful examination of available private and public correspondence among Confederate officials indicates that few of these men seriously expected the "Second American Revolution" to stop at the secession of eleven states. Just as the infant republic had expanded from seven to eleven states after the Fort Sumter crisis, most Southern leaders expected the ineptness of the Lincoln administration to push virtually all of the remaining states into the arms of the Confederacy before the end of the first year of the war. Thus most Confederate political and military leaders were not really expecting to be outnumbered 4 to 1 indefinitely; they expected that the addition of the remaining border states was just a matter of time.

The addition of Virginia, Tennessee, North Carolina and Arkansas had almost doubled the potential military strength of the infant republic between April and June of 1861, and the expected secession of Missouri, Kentucky, Maryland and possibly Delaware would shift the manpower balance even further away from the Union. A third tier of seceding states would add over 3 million new citizens to the Southern Confederacy and, because of the relatively limited number of slaves in those states, almost all of the young males would be eligible to serve in the Rebel army. This additional reservoir of manpower would reduce the Federal military advantage to about 2 to 1 and would quite possibly convince even Lincoln and his advisors that the North simply didn't have the resources, energy or soldiers to reconquer a land area that was actually larger than the remaining Union states. Since Oregon and California were too distant to provide much more than moral support anyway, any mass secession of the remaining border states would leave the balance of contiguous states at only 16 Union to 15 Confederate and push the northern borders of the new republic all the way to the Susquehanna and Ohio rivers.

The expected expansion of the Confederacy in the short term was generally viewed as the prelude to a slightly longer term addition of one or more European allies to ensure the confirmation of Southern independence. Southerners were keenly aware that what they considered to be a basically greedy, self interested French nation had helped their forefathers in the War of Independence mainly to get even with England for its victory in the Seven Years War. Thus Southerners reasoned, if a French nation that had little in common with the American colonies was willing to aid the 18th century rebels against their oppressors, was it not infinitely more likely that a far more culturally and politically similar Great Britain would spring to the aid of its Anglophile cousins in the American south? Large numbers of secessionists were convinced that, sooner or later, the United Kingdom would support the Confederacy against the Unionists. Not only did Southern planters assume that the people who really counted in the British government were aristocratic landholders just like themselves; they believed that Great Britain would be so desperate to obtain Southern cotton that they would go to almost any lengths to protect their supply of this invaluable commodity. As an additional bonus to stir British interest in support for the Confederacy, it was assumed that the British empire could benefit substantially from dividing its most important economic rival into two smaller entities, one of which would be enormously grateful for British aid in its time of birth and development.

Just as the secession of the remaining border states and the positive intervention of Great Britain were counted by Southern leaders as two of the most important keys to ultimate independence, the prevention of those two outcomes headed the list of priorities for the Lincoln administration, if it held any reasonable hopes of restoring the Union. The emergence of the additional threats of an even larger Confederacy to the south combined with a belligerent British presence in Canada and on the Atlantic was a nightmare that struck horror into the hearts of the President and his advisors. Furthermore, if the border states could be held in the Union and Britain and the rest of Europe enticed to maintain a neutral posture, Lincoln could than begin to look for opportunities to enhance the favorable balance of numbers even further to the Union's favor. The first possible new asset that could be utilized under the proper conditions was the pool of Union loyalists who made up a portion of virtually every state in the new Confederate republic. The proportion of white Southerners who maintained an active desire to see their states restored to the Federal Union was far less than Lincoln's wildly optimistic conviction that South Carolina was the only state that truly contained a majority of secessionists. However, especially in the mountain regions far removed from the tidewater plantations, there was extensive opposition to Confederate authority and an opportunity to not only deny invaluable manpower to the Rebel alliance but also add significant units to the Union armed forces. People who owned few, if any, slaves, and despised the power of tidewater families, could see little advantage in becoming citizens of a secessionist republic and would be particularly open to Union recruitment if they had a Federal army present in their region. Ultimately, every state but South Carolina was represented by loyalist regiments in the

Union army, and these units were particularly valuable in their first-hand knowledge of local terrain, geography and other vital information.

An even more radical possible enhancement of the Federal manpower advantage was the recruitment and enlistment of former slaves into the Northern army. While this concept started very slowly and provided few manpower advantages before the summer of 1863, the enlistment of black soldiers, especially men who were living in the South, not only increased the size of the Federal army but also deprived the Rebels of workers who could build fortifications, drive supply wagons, and repair railroads and bridges in an increasingly labor deficient Confederacy. The combination of pro-Union whites and former slaves entering Federal service provided something over 300,000 men to the Northern army, and went a long way in at least partially negating the impact of the 450,000 men from Virginia, Tennessee, North Carolina and Arkansas who served in the Confederate army after the post-Fort Sumter wave of secessions.

Once the two contending societies had made an inventory of their present assets and possible future reinforcements, the next logical step was to devise a strategy to win the war as quickly and cheaply as possible. Unlike many of the more recent wars of the preceding century or so, the initial war aims of North and South didn't seem very amenable to the idea of partial victory. The Union could only consider the war a success when the Rebel states had nullified their acts of secession and rejoined the republic; while the Confederates could only claim a victory if their new nation was recognized as a fully sovereign state. However, if these initial goals seemed almost impossible to become negotiable, they were actually relatively straightforward when compared to the additional objectives that were added by each side in the upcoming two years. Confederate definition of victory was gradually ratcheted upward from simply "being left alone" in 1861 to a demand for the "liberation" of most of the border states by 1863. Confederate leaders increasingly equated a truly successful military effort as one in which the Union acknowledged the secession of Maryland, Kentucky and Missouri. This acknowledgment in turn would force a Federal government that was willing to admit Southern victory to allow hundreds of thousands of Unionist residents of the border states to be either dispossessed from their homes and farms or forced to live under a regime they despised, while the addition of those states to the Confederacy would almost certainly entail evacuation of the District of Columbia as the Federal capital, with the added humiliation of Northern citizens being forced to watch the Confederate flag raised over a capital named after the founder of a whole republic which would now be permanently dismembered.

On the other hand, after the implementation of Lincoln's Emancipation Proclamation, Northern victory could only be defined in terms of a restored Union and abolition of slavery, and Southern admission of defeat would automatically entail surrendering the accumulated wealth of the most important families in the region, since the slaves were the most valuable tangible property that they owned. Thus, while a belligerent United States and equally adamant Great Britain had gradually abandoned their initial war aims in the conflict of 1812, the Union and Confederacy went in exactly the opposite direction and kept raising the stakes until only a total military victory on the part of one army or the other would terminate the conflict. There would be little chance for an equivalent to the Peace of Christmas Eve ending the War Between the States.

The gradual realization on both sides of the Mason-Dixon Line that this war would not be a single summer campaign but a long and arduous contest forced citizens of both republics to consider the assets and liabilities of their respective presidents as military commanders-in-chief. Jefferson Davis entered the conflict with the sort of "can't miss" label given to high first-round professional football and basketball draft picks in modern society. In 1861 few Americans seemed to be better prepared for the role of leader of a wartime nation than the Mississippi planter. He had a West Point education, regular army experience, had commanded both regulars and volunteers, held both administrative and elective offices and was widely read on military affairs. The new president was supported by some of the most talented officers from the pre-war United States army while being opposed by Union generals who were largely more noted for their business and industrial successes in the decade before the war.

However, while Davis could count many positive points both in his own character and in the qualifications of the men who would assist him, he was almost immediately thrust into the difficult situation of espousing a largely defensive war among a people who were far too aggressive, hot blooded and impatient to tolerate a defensive role in any aspect of their lives. After the enormous success at Manassas, Davis and his generals toyed with the idea of taking the war onto Northern soil and smashing the Union armies before they could get another chance to march south. As the Richmond Examiner noted, "the idea of waiting for blows instead of inflicting them is altogether unsuited to the genius of our people." Pierre Beauregard developed a detailed plan for an offensive in which the Confederate army at Manassas would be doubled from 30,000 to 60,000 men and then be utilized in a wide sweep around Washington which would either force the Union army to leave its defenses or allow the Rebels to march perhaps all the way to Lake Erie.

This bold plan to carry the war to the North before the Unionists could fully utilize their wealth and manpower essentially disintegrated because of two emerging problems in the new republic. First, the Confederacy of 1861 was essentially a league of autonomous republics banded together in a fairly loose union. The concentration of forces that Beauregard proposed would stack most of the army in Virginia, leaving large parts of the other ten states exposed to Yankee invasion. This situation was a virtual political impossibility for the Davis administration. Second, Southern manufacturing capabilities at this time were wholly inadequate to provide the modern weapons needed for a Confederate army that was on the offensive, while a combination of the Union blockade, a poorly managed overseas procurement program, and delays in finalizing contracts to purchase weapons in Europe meant that most of the best arms were still on the wrong side of the Atlantic. Thus even if troops could be recruited for a major northward thrust, there wouldn't be enough weapons or equipment to provide the Confederates with any reasonable chance of beating the Yankees on their home ground.

Once the opportunity for offensive warfare had faded, the next, and vitally important, strategic controversy focused on which areas of the Confederacy the government should most stoutly defend. Davis, Robert E. Lee and a number of Virginia officers gradually emerged as allies on the supreme importance of keeping the Confederate capital out of Yankee hands and holding as much of the Old Dominion as possible. These leaders believed that every successive northern thrust toward Richmond had to be met by deploying the largest field army possible, even if it meant stripping dozens of secondary targets of their garrisons. Since the North had a 4 to 1 manpower advantage, they could only match the strength of a Union invasion force by concentrating almost every available man in one army, and then hope to beat at least one Yankee army somewhere, preferably in Virginia. This strategy would frequently collide at different points in the war with a coalition of politicians and generals who were ultimately labeled the "western concentration bloc." These Southerners, including Joseph Johnston, Pierre Beauregard and Senator Louis Wigfall, viewed Richmond's defense as only desirable, not vital, to the continuation of Confederate sovereignty, and insisted that a preoccupation with protecting the capital would drain off resources and manpower from the really crucial challenges, such as holding Missouri and Kentucky for the Confederacy and ensuring a Southern presence on the Mississippi River.

While Confederate strategists debated the merits of an offensive or defensive deployment and the concentration of forces in east or west, the Union government was simultaneously reviewing its strategic options. Abraham Lincoln's resumé for the job of commander in chief of the largest army in the western world at this time was, on the surface, almost laughable. Lincoln had served for a few weeks as captain of an Illinois militia company in the Black Hawk War of the 1830's, but had admitted that he had never seen any fighting and even had been forced to carry a wooden sword as a punishment for incompetence in his duties. However, outside observers such as London *Times* correspondent William Russell sensed that behind the ungainly, awkward exterior was a leader who could learn the military craft quite quickly. The Republican president possessed a happy blend of a personality which allowed him to get along with people, combined with the ability to cut to the heart of a problem very quickly, and he gradually developed a level of self-confidence that encouraged him to believe that his basic grasp of strategy was at least as good as the initial corps of military commanders who answered to him.

On the afternoon after the disaster at Manassas, Lincoln sat at his desk and wrote down a set of plans on how the Union army could reverse the negative impact of its initial defeat. The memorandum included plans for expanding the naval blockade, maintaining the Federal toehold on the Virginia peninsula, ensuring the loyalty of the population of Baltimore, securing Union control of Missouri, and preparing offensives from Cairo, Illinois toward Memphis and from Cincinnati toward East Tennessee. This operational plan actually meshed fairly well with commanding general Winfield Scott's controversial "Anaconda Plan," which had been initially ridiculed in the emotions surrounding the "On to Richmond" frenzy. Scott doubted that the war could be won in a single campaign directed against the enemy capital, and proposed a plan that was based on recruiting and training an army of at least 300,000 three-year volunteers. The Federal government would impose an increasingly rigorous blockade on the South-ern coast while a powerful army, accompanied by a flotilla of naval vessels, would move down the Mississippi, seize New Orleans and establish a firm grip on the river all the way to the Gulf of Mexico. This operation would "clear out and keep open the great line of communication... so as to envelop the insurgent states and bring them to terms with less bloodshed than by any other plan." Lincoln's memorandum and Scott's plan provided a fairly workable blueprint for a Union victory assuming that three absolutely critical challenges could be dealt with successfully. The North would have to design a strategy that would fully utilize the region's enormous supe-riority in manpower; the Federal strategists would have to minimize the distracting influence of becoming obsessed with capturing the enemy capital city; and the President would have to eventually discover a field commander who could maximize the use of Federal power before the Northern public grew discouraged at the human and financial cost of the war. If any one of these challenges was not fully solved, the war would be extended, and if all three of these challenges remained unsolved, it was very probable that the Confederacy would achieve its independence.

The first of these challenges revolved around the simple truth that if the North recruited and enlisted the same proportion of its available males as the South, the Federal army would always outnumber the Confederates by a ratio of 4 to 1. However, if the Rebels were allowed to use their interior lines, access to railroads and generally superior cavalry to concentrate their unit at individually threatened points, they could deploy an army that nearly equaled the size of the Union force on each battlefield. To a large extent, Lincoln grasped the impact of this situation more rapidly than his generals. "I state my general idea of this war to be that we have the greater numbers and the enemy has the greater facility of concentrating forces upon the point of collision, that we must fail, unless we can find some way of making our advantage an overmatch for his; and that this can only be done by menacing him with superior forces at different points, at the same time; so that we can safely attack, one, or both, if he makes no change; and if he weakens one to strengthen the other, forbear to attack the strengthened one, but seize and hold the weakened one, gaining so much." Unfortunately, although Lincoln's strategic theories were absolutely correct, it was far more difficult to coordinate a series of offensives led by generals with different temperaments and conducted over vastly different terrain. However, if this coordination was ever successfully accomplished, the Confederate defense system would simply have to crumble somewhere along the line and Federal armies could plunge deep into the heart of the Rebel nation.

The second key challenge revolved around the proximity of the two rival capitals to one another. A significant element of Civil War strategy seems to have been focused on the "capture of the flag" objective of marching into the opposing capital city and thus encouraging the adversary to sue for peace. The leaders of both sections often seemed to forget their common heritage of the War of Independence, when the British capture of Philadelphia had a minimal impact on the continuation of colonial resistance. Although General Howe's message to George III that he had captured the rebel capital had encouraged the king to convince himself that the war was finally over, George Washington had merely shrugged off the loss of the city and camped his army 20 miles outside of Philadelphia until the enemy evacuated the town. If the Americans of the Revolutionary era could simply cart the Liberty Bell to another town, remove the official government papers and transfer the legislative debates to another venue, it seems quite probable that the Confederate government could have accomplished the same thing and continued to resist the Yankees from other locations. The key to Union victory was the destruction of the Rebel armies, not the capture of Richmond, and whether Irvin McDowell, George McClellan or Joseph Hooker had captured the capital in 1861, 1862 or 1863, any reasonably competent Confederate general, and Beauregard, Johnston and Lee were certainly all competent, could merely have marched the army somewhere else and continued the war from another site. It seems that, early in the war, Lincoln was as guilty of "On to Richmond" fever as any of his advisors but, to his credit, the President gradually shifted away from this preoccupation toward a more realistic concern with the destruction of enemy armies and the securing of the Mississippi River. In this respect he grew more sophisticated than his Confederate counterpart, who seems to have maintained his pre-occupation with defending Richmond until the last few weeks of the war.

Finally, and perhaps most important, the Union strategy for victory was based on the eventual success of discovering a Northern general who could orchestrate the increasingly massive, but often poorly coordinated, Federal war effort. The 22 loyal states were rich enough, populous enough and productive enough to provide Union generals with what was undoubtedly an awesome military machine by the standards of the mid-19th century. However, this well equipped, numerically superior and generally sophisticated army was simply not going to crush their formidable, though outnumbered, adversaries until a general emerged with the ability to use this awesome power properly. McClellan was too cautious, Halleck too pedantic, Buell too inflexible and Hooker too unstable, to fully utilize this power even if each of these men should be given credit for at least some degree of success during the war. The Union cause was fortunate that its President had the self-confidence, decisiveness and intuition that allowed him to quickly remove incompetent generals and permit him to gradually discover a whole new team of winning generals. This process would not be short or easy, as for every Grant, Sherman, Thomas or Sheridan who emerged from a sea of Federal officers, there always seemed to be a Fremont, Burnside, Banks or Pope who would invariably find a way to lose a winnable battle and thus extend the life of the Confederacy for another season. However, all things being equal, once the right resources, the right objectives and the right commanders were all meshed in a proper sequence, the Union cause would have an excellent, though by no means inevitable, opportunity to win the war.

# CHAPTER 24

# The Stride of a Giant

*The Great Union Offensive of 1862*

$O$n New Year's Day, 1862, two rival presidential mansions a hundred miles apart were the sites of festive public receptions. In both Richmond and Washington, cabinet members, army and navy officers in full regalia and a host of influential private citizens celebrated the onset of a new year and compared notes on the appearance, personality and demeanor of their respective chief executives. Guest at Jefferson Davis' soiree found the Mississippian looking relatively healthy and appearing quite friendly, although more careful observers found him distracted and felt that his cordiality was largely for show. Visitors at the White House in Washington seemed to think that Abraham Lincoln's friendliness and warmth were more genuine, but he seemed as pre-occupied by the war as his Confederate rival. William Russell, correspondent for the *London Times*, acknowledged the warmth and sincerity of the President but added, "this poor president is to be pitied. He is trying, with all his might, to understand strategy, big guns, the movement of troops and exterior and interior lines," hardly the usual purview of a professional politician.

While each of these men shared a common challenge of leading a nation in a time of military crisis, Davis and Lincoln probably viewed the events of 1861 with quite different feelings. Jefferson Davis continued to worry about the continued shortage of weapons and supplies for the Confederate armies, and instinctively realized that a long war would allow the North to mobilize far more men and resources than his Southern republic commanded, but the first phase of the war had clearly favored the secessionists. The new republic had won a spectacular victory at Manassas and had gained a potentially decisive diplomatic coup when rebel envoys James Mason and John Slidell had been plucked from the British steamer *Trent* by an over eager Federal naval captain. The most talented military leaders from the old army had generally sided with the South. Thus a combination of proven Southern battlefield superiority in 1861 and the distinct possibility of British retaliation against the United States seemed to offer bright prospects for the Confederacy in 1862.

On the other hand there were few bright spots on the horizon for the President of the United States. The newly appointed commander in chief of the Federal Army, George B. McClellan, was stricken with typhoid fever and was totally incapacitated for the foreseeable future; the two commanders of the western armies, Don Carlos Buell and Henry Wager Halleck, had each telegraphed repeated messages to Washington that it would be impossible for either one to cooperate in a concerted offensive against the Rebels; Joseph Johnston's army in Virginia was so close to Washington that his advance pickets could see Lincoln's bedroom window in the White House. Late in the afternoon of December 31st the troubled President went to the office of Quartermaster General Montgomery Meigs and discussed the condition of the Union. "General, what shall I do? The people are impatient; Chase has no money and tells me he can raise no more. The General of the Army has typhoid fever. The bottom is out of the tub. What shall I do?"

Ironically, within five months of this first wartime New Year the President who believed that "the bottom is out of the tub" would be reading a continuous stream of dispatches detailing sensational Union victories, while the executive who had expressed confidence in his new republic would be evacuating his family from the capital and preparing special trains to remove the government archives from Richmond. The events of the winter and spring of 1862 turned the course of the war almost entirely in favor of the Union cause, as a massive, although not particularly coordinated, series of Federal offensives that one observer called "the stride of a giant" almost, but not quite, ended the Civil War before it could turn into the all encompassing conflict that it would evolve into by 1865.

Abraham Lincoln may have been afflicted with sick generals, slow generals and pompous generals in this early stage of the war, but the subordinate officers and enlisted men who were going to do the really serious fighting in the upcoming campaigns were already developing into first rate soldiers who would at least be a match for their Rebel adversaries. The defense perimeter of the Confederacy in early 1862 was exposed to four possible Union thrusts, each of which could permanently cripple the power of the secessionist republic. First, a Yankee move against the long Confederate defense line from eastern Kentucky to the Mississippi River would allow the Northern armies to push far into the interior of the deep South; second, an amphibious strike at the Atlantic coastline and its ports would seal off Rebel interchange with Europe and wreck the Southern economy; third, a Federal offensive on the Mississippi River would threaten the key cities of Memphis and New Orleans and split the Confederacy in two; and finally, a thrust at Virginia would threaten the largest Rebel army and provide the opportunity for the Unionists to capture the nerve center of the rebellion. Each of these operations would present the Union forces with enormous challenges but equally impressive opportunities for ending the war in one series of campaigns.

The first significant step in the great Federal offensive of 1862 occurred in the rain-swept, barren countryside of eastern Kentucky around Cumberland Gap. This sparsely populated region was the eastern anchor of a defensive line set up by western theater commander Albert Sidney Johnston, a long-time friend of Jefferson Davis, who called him "the greatest soldier, the ablest man, civil or military, Confederate of Federal then living." Johnston had been supplied by the War Department with a colorful and diverse group of subordinates, but he was essentially expected to hold an area the size of France or Germany with fewer than 70,000 men and a pitiful supply of modern weapons. General Earl Van Dorn assumed responsibility for the trans-Mississippi defenses with 20,000 Confederate regulars, Missouri militiamen and Indian braves confronting a Federal army of 30,000 men. The left flank of the main defense line was established at Columbus, Kentucky, where Episcopal bishop turned Confederate general Leonidas Polk commanded 17,000 men screening Ulysses S. Grant's 20,000 troops based in nearby Cairo, Illinois. General William Hardee assumed command of the central force of 25,000 men at Bowling Green, Kentucky who were menaced by 60,000 Yankees under Don Carlos Buell at Louisville. Finally, the extreme right flank of the western theater featured a 4000 man force under General Felix Zollicoffer which protected Cumberland Gap against Union General George Thomas' 8000 troops camped in Barbourville, Kentucky. Thus Johnston was attempting to hold an enormous swath of territory with only 66,000 men, who were facing 118,000 Federals. The Confederate army was stretched far too thin, and it was only a matter of time until it was pierced at one or more places by any Federal commander who had the audacity to take the offensive.

The first significant Union advance occurred on the eastern end of this tenuous line when the Union loyal Virginian George Thomas began to lurch toward the rebel defenders of Cumberland Gap in January, 1862. Zollicoffer was a well respected Tennessee newspaper publisher who ardently supported the Confederate cause, but had minimal aptitude for military affairs. When Zollicoffer received intelligence that Thomas was preparing to move, he shifted his small army to the north bank of the Cumberland River, which placed him in the potentially disastrous position of facing an army twice his size with a major river at his back and no ready avenue for retreat. When Richmond dispatched General George Crittenden to the region to supervise Zollicoffer's activities, the Kentuckian was shocked to discover that his field commander had placed his army in an almost certain trap. Before Crittenden could rectify this error, Thomas, ignoring terrible roads and horrendous rainstorms, began marching straight toward the vulnerable Rebel camp. However, Crittenden received two pieces of good news which crystallized his plans. Thomas was only advancing with half of his army and he had temporarily halted his march along Fishing Creek, and apparently had deployed his army in two wings on opposite sides of the flooding stream. Since Thomas' camp near Logan's Crossroads was only nine miles from Zollicoffer's vulnerable force, Crittenden decided that the smart move was to stage an all night march and slam into the divided Federals before they could re-unite for a continued southward advance.

During the night of January 18-19, 1862 4000 wet and miserable Rebels slogged through shin deep mud during a torrential rainstorm, in order to launch a pre-dawn surprise attack on the Yankees. However, as was typical for this stage of the war, the pace of the march was far slower than planned, and at daybreak Federal cavalry patrols discovered the enemy columns early enough to give an alarm. The Confederates were still able to launch a powerful assault on one wing of the Federal army and the Yankees were forced to backpedal against a strong tide of gray coats. However, after an extremely promising start, the whole Confederate assault began to unravel. First, the nearsighted Zollicoffer was unable to wear his spectacles in the pouring rain and managed to ride right into the middle of a Federal unit that he assumed was part of his command. Seconds later the white coated Confederate general was shot by a Union rifleman and large numbers of Rebels were disconsolate at the loss of their popular commander. Confederate morale sank even lower when the Southerners began to realize that the "impassable" creek wasn't all that flooded, as Union troops waded from the far bank to help their threatened comrades. When the reunited Yankees began to form up for a well organized counterstroke, the Rebels were quickly handicapped by their far inferior weapons, which included hundreds of flintlock muskets that were useless in wet weather. As the Confederates realized that they were becoming hopelessly outgunned, the cry "betrayed!" started to rise through the Rebel ranks and suddenly the whole Southern line simply began to disintegrate.

The Rebel army had virtually ceased to exist as a functioning military force and only the atrocious roads and even worse weather prevented Thomas from bagging the whole lot. Even so, it was a first class Confederate disaster as over 500 Southerners were captured along with 12 cannons, and dozens of other Rebels were killed or wounded compared to a total Union loss of fewer than 200 men. The rain, fog and mud prevented Thomas from making an immediate thrust at Knoxville for the redemption of the East Tennessee loyalists, but the Union had won its first significant victory of the war and a new Union star was just beginning to emerge.

Soon after George Thomas displayed his military talents at Fishing Creek, another, even more impressive, future hero of the Federal cause, was showing a similar aggressiveness on the western anchor of Johnston's tenuous line. Ulysses S. Grant had gone from almost complete failure in a succession of civilian jobs to a commission as a brigadier general under Henry Halleck's command in the early weeks of 1862. Halleck and his counterpart, Don Carlos Buell, had been feuding about responsibility for initiating some form of Union offensive in the vicinity of Nashville, and when Grant requested permission to take 15,000 men and capture the key Confederate ports of Fort Henry and Fort Donelson, Halleck was more than willing to let his subordinate try his luck if it would discredit his rival.

On February 3rd, 1862, Grant sent a brief message to Halleck in St. Louis simply noting, "will be off up the Tennessee at six o'clock. Command, twenty-three regiments in all." Grant may have been energetic, calm under fire and confident of his abilities, but he also had the great good luck to be facing an enemy that had quite literally managed to put one of its key forts in exactly the wrong place for a battle. The Confederate engineering officers who chose the location for Fort Henry must have missed the most important academy classes on fortifications, for they determined to build a post that could only be garrisoned by amphibians. General Lloyd Tilghman, a Kentuckian who was given initial responsibility for both Fort Henry on the Tennessee River and nearby Fort Donelson which shielded the Cumberland River, must have stood in disbelief when he inspected a fort that was already partially under water and seemed to be becoming more water-logged with each passing day. Tilghman's 3400 defenders stacked sandbags, shifted gun positions and pumped out barracks buildings, but by early February the flooding of the river had left only nine cannons still above water. Thus when Ulysses Grant and his naval counterpart, Andrew Foote, approached the fort with 15,000 men and seven gunboats, Tilghman decided to merely use his guns to buy enough time to evacuate most of his men to Fort Donelson.

While Tilghman organized the fort's evacuation, 2 officers and 54 men of a Tennessee artillery regiment cited their batteries and waited for the Federal onslaught, as they responded to their commander's request to delay the Yankees for at least an hour. Foote's four ironclads and three wooden gunboats crept up to within 1700 yards of Fort Henry, and let loose with 54 guns that started blasting huge gaps in the Rebel fort. The Union naval commander was convinced that his ships were still not as effective as they could be, and he ordered the range closed to 600 yards. At this point the Rebel guns could finally be fully utilized, and within minutes the *Essex* staggered out of control as a Confederate shell ruptured a steam line and scalded dozens of Federal sailors. However, while the Confederates were able to inflict some damage on the Federal ships, the Yankee guns gradually eliminated the Rebel batteries and after a two-hour duel Tilghman decided that honor had been saved and it was time to capitulate. The water level had risen to a point where the fort's main magazine was about to be submerged, and when Federal naval officers came to accept the surrender, they merely rowed into the fort's main entrance in a naval launch. Foote had lost 39 sailors killed and wounded, compared to 5 Confederates killed, 11 wounded and about 40 other prisoners; but despite the relatively small casualties, the Union had scored an impressive victory by eliminating one of the major barriers to Federal capture of the vital supply depot at Nashville. An ecstatic Halleck wired McClellan in Washington that "Fort Henry is ours, the flag of the Union is re-established on the soil of Tennessee. It will never be removed."

Albert Sidney Johnston was shocked by the loss of Fort Henry and he considered a number of options to restore the situation. His new second in command, Pierre Beauregard, suggested a concentration of every available Confederate soldier in the vicinity of Fort Donelson in order to attack Grant's army while the Yankees marched the 12 miles that separated the two forts. General William Hardee urged just the opposite tack, a complete evacuation of Donelson with a general fall back into southern Tennessee to await an opportunity to strike the Federals where they would be most vulnerable. In essence, Johnston decided to split the difference, and in a highly controversial move, he ordered about half of his 34,000 available troops to reinforce the threatened bastion while the other half were ordered to withdraw toward Nashville. Three Confederate generals, John Floyd, Gideon Pillow and Simon Bolivar Buckner were sent to Donelson, and within a few days the Rebels had close to 20,000 men in the immediate vicinity of the fortress. While this was an impressive garrison, Johnston's reasoning is still extremely questionable, since Confederate intelligence reports insisted that Grant could concentrate something like 30,000 men for an assault, and thus the Confederate army would be too small to stop the Federals but too large a force to lose in a disaster.

Grant was far too optimistic about his ability to march on Donelson and capture it in a very short campaign. After the surrender of Fort Henry, he wired Halleck "I shall take and destroy Fort Donelson on the 8th and return to Fort Henry with the forces employed." However, the advance took much longer than Grant could ever have imagined. First, the roads which Generals McClernand and Smith were ordered to use for their march were in terrible condition with almost non-stop torrential rains having turned them into seas of mud. Also, Foote's ships had been damaged badly enough in the assault on Fort Henry that they were forced to move back up to the Ohio River for repairs and then back over to the Cumberland to provide naval support. Thus when Grant's two divisions finally approached Donelson on the evening of February 12th, 1862, the Union's 15,000 besiegers were actually outnumbered by the Confederate defenders. The Union commander deployed his forces in a semi-circle around the land side of the fort while he sent a dispatch back to Fort Henry for General Lew Wallace to bring up his division and he asked Foote to speed up the arrival of naval support units.

On the morning of February 14th, while Wallace's men were deploying in their new positions, Foote's gunboats moved along the Cumberland River and prepared to attack Donelson's water defenses. The Union commodore opened fire almost a mile from the fort and traded long range shells with the defenders, but while the Navy was inflicting fairly heavy damage on the fort, Foote was too far away to fully realize his success. Thus, just as at Fort Henry, Foote moved into closer range in this case, to less than 400 yards. Donelson's 15 river defense guns were far better sited than their Fort Henry counterparts, and they were able to direct a plunging fire that could penetrate the decks of armored vessels, while many of their guns were at such an elevation that the gunboats could only hit them with their mortars. At about 3:30 P.M. the Union vessels closed in for the kill, and suddenly much of the fleet was a shambles. The flagship *St. Louis* was hit 59 times while Foote received a wound that would eventually kill him; *Louisville* was disabled and drifting out of the battle and *Pittsburgh* was on the verge of sinking. The Union fleet was forced to withdraw, and the Confederates, who had suffered no casualties, went wild in celebration. Grant had been watching the disappointing engagement on a nearby ridge and he now realized that he would have to settle down to traditional siege operations. However, his trio of adversaries had other plans.

While Grant responded to an urgent call for a consultation with Foote; the Confederates Floyd, Pillow and Buckner agreed to use their impressive victory as a springboard to a surprise assault that would open an escape route, and allow the garrison to evacuate before Grant called in even more reinforcements. The basic plan revolved around Pillow launching an assault on the right wing of the Yankee line, while Buckner's men held the fortification; then once the Federal flank had been pushed back, Buckner's command would swing out of their fortifications to man the captured Union position, while the rest of the army withdrew down the Dover-Charlotte Road with Buckner's men than forming a rear guard. The night of February 14-15, 1862 was one of the coldest in memory in the region, with a temperature hovering around 12 degrees and a blinding snowstorm reducing visibility to near zero. As a result, the Federals had almost no advance warning of the Rebel assault and suddenly, just as the snow began to taper off at dawn, thousands of graycoats charged out of their fortifications and crumpled McClernand's right flank. Soldiers from both armies slipped on the ice and groped toward one another in the snow, but at first momentum was clearly on the Confederate side. Grant, who had been consulting with Foote, arrived just in time to see his flank on the point of collapse, but Lew Wallace had already extended his center division far enough to cover McClernand's withdrawal and fuse a new line. The future author of *Ben Hur* conferred with his commander and both agreed that the Rebel position on the right had to be retaken. While Wallace organized a counterattack on his flank, Grant rushed over to General Charles Smith's left flank position and ordered him to break into Donelson's fortifications from that direction. Smith immediately called together his regimental commanders and personally led a wild charge into a hail of Confederate bullets, as his men smashed their way through entrenchments and abatis and occupied a substantial portion of the Rebel line by nightfall. Ironically, Smith survived several near misses in this melee only to die a few weeks later, when he cut his leg on a jagged piece of metal while entering a small boat and subsequently died of blood poisoning.

Despite the quick thinking of Wallace, Smith and Grant, the Confederate offensive had accomplished its primary mission; the Dover road was now open and the Confederate garrison still had time to escape while the Federals were trying to reorganize their forces. Incredibly, after losing scores of men trying to open an escape route, Pillow called the whole thing off and ordered his flabbergasted men back into their fortifications. Buckner, who was just on the verge of moving his men out of the fort, was startled with Pillow's order and stormed in to confront Floyd, who supported Pillow. Neither Pillow nor Floyd ever offered a consistent reason for their actions; they insisted that either their men were too exhausted for a night march, or the Federals would cut them off before they could get very far, or the weather was too miserable for an evacuation. Whatever their reasoning really was, it was obvious that Smith's lodgement in their entrenchments made the fort untenable and the three generals agreed that surrender was the only option. Floyd was already under indictment in the North for his questionable activities as James Buchanan's Secretary of War and he had no desire to become a Federal prisoner. Once he passed the command on to Pillow, that largely incompetent officer decided he didn't want to be the first Confederate general to be captured, so he passed the honor to Buckner who, as a personal friend of Grant's, probably expected to negotiate a relatively palatable surrender.

During the frigid night of February 15-16 Floyd evacuated several of his Virginia regiments by steamboat, Pillow escaped toward the river with his personal staff, and the colorful cavalry commander Nathan Bedford Forrest swore oaths at his commanding generals and led his horsemen through a series of frigid streams and creeks to safety. Meanwhile, Buckner sent a messenger to his Union adversary to request terms of surrender. Grant thought for a few minutes and penned a reply that would startle Buckner but make him a hero in the North; "no terms except an unconditional and immediate surrender can be accepted; I propose to move immediately upon your works. Buckner, protesting at such "ungenerous and unchivalrous terms," knew that he must comply, however reluctantly, with Grant's demand, and on February 16th just under 15,000 Confederate soldiers and 40 cannons passed into captivity while the battle itself had cost an additional 2000 Southern and 3000 Federal casualties. All over the North church bells began ringing in celebration of the first major Union victory of the war and Abraham Lincoln requested Congress to confirm Grant's promotion to major general.

While Northerners toasted their new hero, a large number of people throughout the South were demanding the resignation of Albert Johnston although Jefferson Davis refused to even consider such a move. Johnston ordered Nashville abandoned and gradually withdrew to the important rail center of Corinth, Mississippi, which was a depot for both the Mobile and Ohio and Memphis and Charleston railroads. Cities such as Mobile, Pensacola and New Orleans were stripped of troops to provide the western theater commander with 45,000 men who would be used for a counteroffensive against the slowly advancing Yankees. By late March Grant, after a series of disputes and a near firing by Halleck, had assumed command of six Union divisions deployed in the vicinity of Pittsburg Landing, Tennessee, about 20 miles north of Corinth. Halleck had just assumed command of the entire western theater and he had ordered his subordinate to remain where he was until Don Carlos Buell's large army could link up with him for a concerted drive on the new Rebel bastion.

Johnston knew that several departments had been stripped of troops mainly to provide him with the means of striking the Federals as quickly as possible and with maximum impact. The Confederate commander's response was a plan to strike Grant at Pittsburg Landing before Buell's reinforcements could arrive. Confederate scouts reported that Buell's army was making slow progress as it marched south through Tennessee and at least one of Grant's divisions had been deployed at least five miles away from the rest of the army. Thus Johnston would have over 44,000 men in an assault force that would confront perhaps 35,000 Federals in the immediate vicinity of the Landing.

At dawn on April 3rd, 1862 the advance elements of the Confederate army moved through the streets of Corinth at the beginning of a twenty-mile march. Johnston expected to arrive near the Federal camps before dawn on April 5th. Almost immediately the march degenerated into a Southern version of Irvin McDowell's fiasco approach to Manassas. Men from William Hardee's lead corps were delayed by supply wagons that jammed the main exit from the town, and then elements of Braxton Bragg's corps became so intermingled with Leonidas Polk's regiments that the whole advance almost ground to a halt. A combination of traffic jams, bad roads and extensive straggling insured that the army wouldn't even approach Pittsburg Landing until late Saturday afternoon, April 5th; close to a full day behind schedule.

The Confederates may have muffed an opportunity to accomplish a rapid strike against their opponents, but the Federals easily matched their adversaries in questionable tactics. Grant, who would emerge as one of the most talented commanders in American history, was still capable of making significant mistakes, as he clearly displayed at this crucial moment of the war. Rather than remaining with his army, he established his headquarters at Savannah, Tennessee, eight miles north and on the opposite side of the river, primarily to expedite the link up with Buell. He failed to appoint any of his division commanders as his field general in his absence, so each unit pretty much operated and deployed as an independent entity. Finally, he failed to use his 3000 cavalrymen in any serious scouting capacity while compounding the error by neglecting to order his men to intrench.

Thus when Johnston and his senior commanders conferred in the early evening of Saturday, April 5th, the Confederate theater commander was faced with a perplexing challenge. His army seemed to have lost the element of surprise by arriving behind schedule and then by approaching the Federal camp with cheers and firing weapons. Beauregard was so convinced that the Yankees were completely ready for them that he encouraged his superior to simply give up the whole plan as a bad gamble, march back to Corinth, and wait for a better opportunity for victory. On the other hand, Braxton Bragg and Leonidas Polk were convinced that they would surely be defeated if they allowed Grant and Buell to unite and a slashing attack next morning might very well prevent that from happening. Johnston quickly sided with their reasoning by exclaiming, "Gentlemen, we shall attack at daylight tomorrow. I would fight them if they were a million. They can present no greater front between these two creeks than we can, and the more men they crowd in there, the worse we can make it for them."

Confederate scouts had reported that the Union army was deployed on a three mile front between the Snake Creek and its tributary the Owl Creek on the north and the Lick Creek to the south. Raw, untrained divisions commanded by William T. Sherman and Benjamin Prentiss formed an irregular front line in front of Shiloh Church, which was about three miles inland from the river, while three more divisions commanded by William Wallace, John McClernand and Stephen Hurlbut occupied campsites closer to the 200 foot high bluff which was adjacent to Pittsburg Landing. Johnston's basic plan was to take advantage of the lack of a continuous Federal front and the haphazard deployment of the divisions to hurl Hardee, Bragg and Polk, each with about 10,000 men, in a column attack that would provide enough mass to smash the Federal front lines and push the Yankees back toward the river. Then John Breckenridge would use his 6500 man division to locate the most vulnerable spot on the Union left flank and push through to the river, maneuvering the Federals back toward Snake Creek and away from their vital supply base at Pittsburg Landing. Theoretically, the enemy army would be trapped with its back against the Creek and be forced to surrender, which would then allow the victorious Confederates to turn on Buell's army just as it was arriving.

A few minutes before 5 A.M. on Sunday morning, April 6th, Major James Powell was leading a reconnoitering party of three companies that had been ordered out by his brigade commander Colonel Everett Peabody. While most of the Federal commanders deployed around Pittsburg Landing were convinced that no serious Confederate threat existed, Peabody was suspicious of reports of enemy movements and he wanted more information. Powell's scouting force quickly found more than it bargained for when these Missourians encountered the lead elements of Hardee's assault force, which threatened to overwhelm the Yankees. As the scouting force pulled back they received support from two of Prentiss' regiments, but this force was no match for thousands of screaming Rebels who smashed through the blue-coats' advanced lines and charged into the Federal encampments. Braxton Bragg noted that the surprise was so great that "the enemy was found utterly unprepared, many being captured in their tents, and others, though on the outside, were in costumes better fitted to the bedroom than to the battlefield." Another Confederate officer observed that "the breakfasts were on the mess tables, the baggage unpacked, the knapsacks, stores, colors and ammunition abandoned."

Ulysses Grant was having breakfast at his headquarters at Cherry Mansion in Savannah when he heard the distant rumble of gunfire and assumed correctly that a major battle had started. The Union commander requisitioned a steamboat and started toward Pittsburg Landing, with a brief detour to Crump's Landing to warn Lew Wallace to be ready to march to the support of the rest of the army. When Grant reached Pittsburg Landing he was shocked to see a large number of his men huddled panic stricken below the bluffs at the river's edge, with hundreds of other bluecoats staggering back from the front lines. The Union commander then began to visit each of his division commanders to evaluate the situation. Prentiss' left flank had been nearly annihilated by the initial assault and the remnants of his division had fallen back almost two miles to link up with Stephen Hurlbut's and William Wallace's commands. On the other hand, while large numbers of Sherman's new recruits had simply disappeared, the Ohio general still held a ridge line that focused on Shiloh Church. Grant and Sherman quickly agreed that this would be the key spot on the battlefield as this ridge dominated the main road from Corinth to Pittsburg Landing and also provided access to the bridge over Snake Creek which Lew Wallace's division would need to use when it arrived. Sherman had blended his units with John McClernand's more veteran forces and had cobbled together a defense line around the meeting house that could be held at least temporarily.

Probably one of the reasons that Sherman was able to hold his position was that Johnston was far more anxious to smash through the Federal left flank and drive straight for the Tennessee River. Prentiss, Hurlbut and William Wallace were all throwing up temporary blocking positions, but all morning long the Confederate attackers were pushing closer to the river. Finally, when part of the Federal army tried to hold a position between a large peach orchard and the nearby Lick Creek, Johnston himself organized and led a wild attack on the enemy position. However, while the western commander was riding around to organize another, larger, push he gasped at a sudden pain and almost fell from his horse. Tennessee governor Isham Harris was accompanying the general and he quickly laid him on the ground and frantically began to search for a wound. Finally, Harris discovered that Johnston had been hit in an artery near the knee but before a doctor could be located, the Confederate general bled to death, and thus removed much of the psychological edge enjoyed by the Rebel attackers. Johnston died at about 2:30 P.M. and from that time on, the battle at first almost imperceptibly began to shift in the Union's favor.

Beauregard now became commander of the Confederate army, but he had been near the rear of the army organizing each of the successive Rebel attacks. While the Creole began to organize himself for his new leadership role, the Southern army was losing thousands of men in a series of desperate, but not totally successful, assaults. Parts of Prentiss' and William Wallace's divisions had set up a formidable defensive position behind a sunken road and a dense concentration of trees that provided extensive cover for the Federal riflemen. Confederate troops had launched an incredible 11 separate assaults on the position that they had nicknamed the "Hornets Nest," yet in late afternoon the Yankees were still definitely holding their ground. Finally, Confederate General Daniel Ruggles took charge of clearing out the Union salient and managed to concentrate 62 cannons to fire on the single enemy position. The Yankee defenders watched in silence as battery after battery of Rebel guns were wheeled into position for the great barrage. Suddenly, a firestorm of metal smashed into the sunken road and woods and hundreds of Federals either ran for their lives or died where they stood. Wallace was able to lead part of the force out of the trap, although at the cost of his own life, but Prentiss and about 1500 Unionists were trapped and forced to surrender when the Confederate infantry launched its final assault.

Prentiss' surrender opened a potentially fatal gap in the Union defense line, and some Confederate cavalry units were able to thrust all the way to the river, thus fulfilling their dead general's predictions that "tonight, we will water our horses in the Tennessee." However, the Rebels had lost enormous numbers of men in taking each Federal strong point and Beauregard was having problems locating units that were fresh enough to push even further. Meanwhile, Grant was organizing a fall back position almost literally at the edge of the cliffs. Grant's artillery chief, Colonel Joseph Webster, had been deploying every available siege gun in a final defense line about 500 yards from the river. As retreating units fell back in this direction, Webster commandeered every available cannon and formed them into a lethal ten battery firing line. Then the Union gunboats *Tyler* and *Lexington* steamed close to shore to add their impressive firepower to the Union defense. Thus, just as the Confederates were finally able to launch a major assault toward the river, a succession of field artillery, siege guns and naval cannon ripped through the graycoats and provided time for the Federals to deploy their infantry. While Grant reorganized his own units, General William Nelson's lead division of Buell's army crossed the Tennessee and formed on the vulnerable left flank of the Federals. Then, just as darkness was closing in, Lew Wallace's division, which had taken a roundabout series of roads and had only just arrived, marched on the field to support Sherman and the right flank. The Union line, which had been ready to evaporate a little while earlier, was now becoming stronger by the minute, and Beauregard was faced with a crucial decision.

The Louisiana general was strongly tempted to risk everything on the single roll of an all out night assault across the whole battle line. However, his men had now fought for 13 hours with almost no relief and already large numbers of his men were drifting back to the food and booty of the captured Federal campsites. While Rebel soldiers read their adversaries letters to sweethearts and wives, sampled the generally superior enemy food and hunted the grounds for souvenirs, Beauregard's possibility of penetrating the Union lines was gradually evaporating. Therefore, the Creole reluctantly ordered his units back to the captured tents and began contemplating a new offensive for Monday morning.

Beauregard may have been convinced that he could resume the assault on the Federal lines after his men had a good night's sleep, but Grant was receiving a steady stream of reinforcements and the Confederate army had been decimated by their spirited attacks all day Sunday. The next morning, Buell's fresh divisions took the left flank, Lew Wallace's division took the right flank and the survivors of the previous day's fighting at Pittsburg Landing took the center, and an almost irresistible mass of bluecoats began an inexorable march toward the Rebel positions. Beauregard, who had been assured that General Earl Van Dorn was about to arrive with 20,000 reinforcements, maneuvered desperately to hold Shiloh Church and the nearby road to Corinth so that Van Dorn could intervene in the nick of time. The Southerners contested every foot of the peach orchard, pulled back through the swamps near Lick Creek and withdrew through enormous lines of captured tents in a mirror image of Sunday's battle. The Rebel commander sent some of his best units wading through waist deep water in Water Oaks Pond that almost, but not quite, demolished Grant's flank. However, by 2 P.M., just about 24 hours after Johnston's death, Beauregard realized that no help was coming and his main objective became the salvation of the army. A two hour running battle ensued as graycoats backpedaled from Shiloh ridge toward the Corinth road, and when they finally cleared away from the battlefield the exhausted Federals simply let out a huge cheer and let them go without much further disturbance.

The battle of Shiloh was the first major battle in the west and the engagement emerged as one of the most controversial battles of the war. The Union army had paid for being surprised by losing a staggering 13,047 men, while the ferocious Confederate assaults had cost their army an almost as severe 10,669 casualties. The battle could probably be considered a tactical draw to the extent that the Confederates failed to annihilate the Federal army but were in turn able to withdraw with almost no pursuit from the enemy. However, in a strategic sense, the authors believe that Shiloh was an enormously important Union victory. Johnston's basic battle plan was excellent, and the attack almost worked. However, the simple truth is that the Confederate assault failed to destroy Grant's army before Buell arrived, and for this failure, the Rebels paid a heavy price. Not only was it easier for the Union to replace its losses than the Confederacy, but the concentration of forces for this offensive had so stripped other threatened points that the lack of victory at Shiloh prompted other significant disasters for the South. The combination of losses from Fort Donelson and Shiloh eliminated about one third of the effective fighting force in the Confederate west and allowed the Federals to score significant victories at Island Number 10, Fort Pillow and more importantly, New Orleans. The loss of the Crescent City was a numbing defeat for the new Confederate nation, as it represented the richest, most populous, most cosmopolitan city of the South, which made Richmond look like an overgrown village in comparison. The enormous losses inflicted on the Confederates at Shiloh, when combined with the surrender of Fort Donelson and the loss in rapid succession of Nashville, Memphis and New Orleans, forced the Rebels in the western theater to fight at an enormous disadvantage for the rest of the war.

The Federal offensives toward Nashville, Memphis and New Orleans in the west were matched by George McClellan's even more imposing drive toward Richmond. During the last week of March, 1862, the commanding general of the army of the Potomac directed the embarkation of more than 400 passenger ships, naval transports, ferry boats and barges to carry his 100,000 man army from the wharves at Alexandria to the landing beaches at Fort Monroe, at the tip of the Virginia Peninsula. By early April the soldiers and a cornucopia of supporting materials including siege guns, observation balloons, portable telegraph systems and thousands of tons of food, were safely landed and the Union army lurched forward toward Richmond. Officials in Washington were so convinced that McClellan would capture the enemy capital and thus end the war, that Secretary of War Stanton ordered the termination of all recruiting activities for the Federal army and Washington civilians eagerly waited for dispatches that would signal the Union victory in Virginia.

The first significant barrier on the road to Richmond was the old Revolutionary War fortification of Yorktown which was defended by General John Magruder. The Confederate general, nicknamed "Prince John" because of his fondness for amateur theatricals, had only 13,000 men but compensated for his lack of numbers by having an impressive imagination and a flair for hoodwinking his adversaries. Magruder planted dummy cannons, marched men back and forth across the same defense lines a dozen times and generally convinced McClellan that he was facing an enormous number of defenders. "Prince John" didn't fully realize it yet, but he was striking at his adversary's major vulnerability; McClellan's ability to multiply the number of opponents who faced him soon became legendary. One massive thrust might have smashed right through the Rebel defenses but the Union commander wasted almost a month hauling up his huge siege train and then watched his opponents vanish just as he was ready to open the first major bombardment. McClellan sent back euphoric messages proclaiming his first "victory," but more than a few Northerners, including Abraham Lincoln, began to wonder about the general's definition of a triumph.

The Army of the Potomac was able to close in on the outer suburbs of Richmond after a brief, furious battle at Williamsburg, but just when McClellan had a clear shot at a poorly defended enemy capital the caution that would contaminate the otherwise talented leader's career began to dominate his thinking and planning. The initial attack plan that McClellan had presented to a somewhat dubious President was based on the assumption that all four corps of the Army of the Potomac, about 155,000 men, would be transported to the Peninsula while something like 60,000 troops would be left behind to defend Washington against a possible Confederate counterstrike. However, McClellan had done some extremely creative accounting exercises which essentially double counted some of his assault troops as defenders of the capital as well. When Lincoln and Stanton conducted their own count of defenders, they were startled to that find over half of the garrison was actually not present. Lincoln was convinced that even a temporary Confederate capture of Washington would drag Britain and France into the war on the Rebel side, so a furious President quickly recalled Irvin McDowell's corps, which had not yet embarked for Fort Monroe. An equally furious McClellan suddenly realized that 25% of his army was being taken from his command which would create a possible disaster since his intelligence chief, railroad detective Allan Pinkerton, had already "identified" 180,000 Confederates around Richmond with more units streaming in every day. A running feud between McClellan and Lincoln regarding McDowell's deployment kept the telegraph wires burning and eventually determined the whole nature of the emerging campaign.

The President finally agreed to a compromise plan in which McClellan could have McDowell's men, but only if they marched overland from Fredericksburg and constantly remained interposed between Richmond and Washington to fend off a Rebel offensive. McClellan was happy to get the reinforcements, but there was a stiff price to pay for this concession. The Army of the Potomac commander was becoming increasingly more attracted to shifting his base of operations from the York River to the James River, which would provide more immediate naval support and allow the Federals to assault the capital from its seemingly vulnerable south side. However, in order to make contact with McDowell's expected reinforcements, he would have to deploy his army on both sides of the Chickahominy River which was currently flooding its banks on an alarming basis. The river that McClellan would call the "confounded Chickahominy" would be the key to the struggle between Yankees and Rebels for several critical weeks during the late spring and early summer of 1862, and ultimately change the course of the war for the immediate future.

The commander of the Richmond defenses during the spring of 1862 was Joseph Johnston, one of the heroes of Manassas, and an extremely popular commander among his men. Much of Johnston's reputation during the Civil War, for better or worse, revolved around his defensive operations. However, in this case even Johnston quickly realized that once McClellan was able to invest the city and bring up his far superior heavy artillery, "the rest will merely be a matter of guns" in which the Southerners could not hope to win. Thus when Confederate scouts reported the Federal army was now stretched across two sides of the Chickahominy, his prayers were answered, and the energetic Rebel general carefully devised a plan to annihilate part of McClellan's army while the rest of the Yankees looked on in helpless futility.

Johnston had been quietly concentrating Rebel forces from all over the east coast and by late May he had 28 assault brigades in position for a surprise attack on the southern wing of McClellan's army. The Rebel commander's first inclination had been to attack the Federal northern wing detachments before they could link up with McDowell's force, but when cavalry commander Jeb Stuart returned from a spectacular raid behind McClellan's lines, Johnston quickly shifted gears. Stuart confirmed reports that McDowell's corps had gotten to within 30 miles of McClellan's army and then had turned back toward Fredericksburg, thus eliminating, for a time, a threat from that direction. The new Confederate plan focused on the two Federal corps deployed south of the swollen Chickahominy. That waterway was now at its highest flood stage in 20 years, so that the Union corps commanded by E.D. Keyes and Samuel Heintzelman were isolated from reinforcement and deployed in a line that left a gap of two miles between the Federal flank and the raging river. Keyes' front lines ran from the left flank anchor of White Oak Swamp to a right hand position that ended at Seven Pines Crossroads, near the Fair Oaks railroad station. Heintzelman's divisions had been posted toward the rear of Keyes' men and would require a two or three mile march to support their comrades. Johnston planned to hurl most of his army, four divisions of about 60,000 men, against the 37,000 Federals on the south bank, while two divisions of 15,000 men guarded Richmond against an attack by McClellan's northern contingent.

On paper, the plan seemed almost foolproof, as the Federal line was flawed by the inviting gap between Fair Oaks station and the Chickahominy which would allow the Confederate attackers to get around the Yankees' right flank and then smash them in the rear, while the flooded river prevented McClellan from dispatching reinforcements. However, as was the case in about 90% of Civil War battles, the "perfect" plan began to disintegrate about the time the first soldier moved toward the enemy. The battle of Seven Pines is probably in competition for the award of worst coordinated battle of the war, even though the Confederates still almost won the battle. The foul-ups began almost as soon as the four assault divisions moved out along their assigned attack routes. Johnston ordered his divisions to approach Seven Pines by marching along three parallel roads that would enable the Rebels to form a huge pincers, that would close in on Keyes' two divisions from front, flank and rear. James Longstreet's division would march down from Fairfield racecourse, along Nine Mile Road to the Union rear at Fair Oaks train station, while Gustavus Smith's division deployed along that same road to guard against any attempt by the Federals to send reinforcements across the Chickahominy. D.H. Hill's division would march out on the Williamsburg road and deliver a frontal assault to keep the Yankees deployed at Seven Pines, focusing on their front while Benjamin Huger's division took the more southerly route along Charles City Road and came up behind Keyes on the edge of White Oak Swamp. Thus three Confederate divisions would smash into two Union divisions at Seven Pines and then, when Smith's division moved up in support, a total of 23 brigades could crash into the remaining two divisions that were further back under Heintzelman.

Apparently the plan began to unravel when Longstreet, who was subordinate to Smith, asked Johnston's permission to "assume command of the forces on the right as the next senior general." For some reason the Confederate commander agreed to this rather vague request and Longstreet promptly decided to shift his brigades to the Williamsburg Road just as Huger's men were using the same route to march down to their assigned avenue. While Huger and Longstreet argued about seniority and disputed which division had the right of way, Hill's division had marched far ahead of the pack and was already slamming into the Federals at Seven Pines, assuming that Longstreet and Huger would be launching supporting assaults from Fair Oaks station and White Oak Swamp. Harvey Hill, a forty-year-old general who was as dyspeptic and humorless as his brother-in-law Stonewall Jackson, led his men over an imposing series of natural and man-made barriers as they struck Keyes' advance guard and then stormed through Seven Pines Crossroads, capturing eight cannons and scores of Federal soldiers. Keyes' units almost disintegrated in the developing rout, but the Federals were finally able to pull back to a second line of fortifications about two miles east, with Hill's men in hot pursuit.

Johnston's plan was working perfectly in respect to the timing and accomplishments of the frontal assault, but the rest of the plan began to disintegrate in a rapid succession of events. First, Huger's division, which had already been severely delayed by its entanglement with Longstreet on Williamsburg Road, now discovered to its horror that the supposedly narrow but passable path along the edge of White Oak Swamp had been turned by the recent heavy rains into a morass that was almost as bad as the swamp itself. Huger's men would never arrive in the Union rear in time to coordinate with any other unit's assault. Second, Longstreet's move on the Union right flank in the vicinity of Fair Oaks station was so far off schedule that it allowed time for part of Heintzelman's corps to rush forward in support of Keyes and turn that Confederate thrust into a bloody stalemate. Finally, just as Smith's division prepared to move up in support, the Rebels were startled to discover Edwin's Sumner's corps making its way across the Chickanominy on a pair of repaired bridges. The spans were rickety and threatened to collapse at any moment, but they enabled the Federals to check Smith's advance and deprive Johnston of the force he needed to smash the Union line.

While each of these events was depriving Johnston of his expected triumph, the Confederate commander himself was knocked out of the fight when he was hit in the shoulder by a sniper and then struck in the chest by a shell fragment while he was falling from his horse. Jefferson Davis and his military aide, Robert E. Lee rode up just in time to see Johnston being carried from the field, with the command temporarily going to Gustavus Smith as the senior division commander.

Smith prepared to engage the Federals in a second day of battle on June 1st, but he quickly realized that Harvey Hill's division was decimated, three other divisions were deployed in vulnerable positions, and the best that he could do was to organize a fighting withdrawal that left the Federals in possession of almost all of the ground they had lost the day before but at least allowed the Confederate army to retreat without even more ruinous losses. The South had lost 6000 men compared to only 5000 casualties for McClellan, but they had at least encouraged the Union commander to reconsider the wisdom of an immediate attack on Richmond. As the second day of the battle of Seven Pines drew to a close, Davis and Lee were riding near the battlefield discussing the changed command situation. After a brief silence, Davis turned to Lee and offered him the command of the vulnerable, but still confident, Confederate army defending Richmond. Perhaps no other decision by the Southern president would have the long-term impact of what transpired on that otherwise gloomy early June afternoon.

# CHAPTER 25

# Oh, But That He Was Ours!

## *Robert E. Lee and the Redemption of Richmond*

*F*ew Americans, whether unionist or secessionist in their sympathies, realized at the time that the two months of May and June, 1862 would change the course of the Civil War from an imminent Federal victory to the beginning of a Northern crisis that would come close to providing the Confederate States of America with its independence before Halloween. During those two crucial months, just as two enormous Union armies were on the verge of securing their primary objectives, the tide of the war would alter to push one army ever further from its target while the other force would quickly discover that the capture of its objective was at best, a hollow prize.

While George McClellan's Army of the Potomac had been inching its way up the Virginia Peninsula to threaten Richmond, his western counterpart, Henry Wager Halleck, had been moving at an equally glacial pace toward the important Mississippi rail center at Corinth. After the battle of Shiloh, Halleck had taken field command of Grant's Army of the Tennessee, Buell's Army of the Cumberland, and John Pope's Army of the Mississippi and ordered this concentrated mass of 15 divisions and 120,000 men toward Corinth. Pierre Beauregard had withdrawn the survivors of the attack on Pittsburg Landing back to that rail hub and then tried to formulate a response to the Union advance. The Creole had plenty of time to think as Halleck was approaching at a rate of less than one mile a day, with a daily extravaganza of entrenchment building to avoid another surprise like Shiloh. Halleck must have employed intelligence agents with the same counting abilities as McClellan's men, because he was convinced that the Rebel garrison of Corinth was slightly over 200,000 men which, when combined with the 200,000 Rebels that McClellan insisted were around Richmond meant that these two generals thought they were encountering more men than the entire Confederacy ever deployed even at its peak strength.

Beauregard actually had only about 52,000 effectives available to confront Halleck, but he had an imagination and flair for the dramatic worthy of Prince John Magruder, and he eagerly launched a campaign of disinformation that almost halted his adversary in his tracks. First, the Louisianan dispatched volunteer "deserters" into the Union camp who cheerfully confirmed Halleck's estimate of vast hordes of Rebels just waiting to pounce when he approached Corinth. Then, as the Federals crept closer to Corinth, Beauregard ordered his men to fortify a series of ridges along a creek three miles from town where he intermingled real and dummy cannons along the line. On May 25th the Creole held a conference with Bragg, Van Dorn, Hardee, Polk and Breckenridge in attendance and these Confederate luminaries debated their options. While none of the Rebel generals were enthusiastic about a withdrawal, they reluctantly agreed that they simply didn't have enough defenders to provide a reasonable chance of victory and an evacuation toward Tupelo was their only legitimate course.

On the evening of May 28th, while Joseph Johnston was organizing his desperate assault on McClellan, his western counterpart began one of the most successful charades of the war. While front line troops crept out of their entrenchments under cover of darkness, additional dummy guns and dummy soldiers were deployed along the line. A large and noisy band spent the night marching up and down the deserted trenches playing taps at nightfall and reveille at daybreak at different points along the line. Camp-fires were left burning with drummer boys stocking the flames, while all night long a single train of empty freight cars rattled back and forth along the tracks, stopping at intervals to blow its whistle, which was a signal for a special detail of soldiers to cheer at the top of their lungs as they welcomed "reinforcements." A thoroughly shaken General Pope wired Halleck "the enemy is reinforcing heavily by trains in my front and on my left. The cars are running constantly and the cheering is immense every time they unload in front of me and I have no doubt, from all appearances, that I shall be attacked in heavy force at daylight."

The sun rose on May 29th, and needless to say, the Confederate response wasn't quite as ferocious as Pope and Halleck expected. While a series of explosions announced the demolition of the main railroad yards, Federal soldiers picked their way through dummy cannons manned by dummy graycoats. The Yankees marched into a rail center that was almost devoid of military or civilian inhabitants and Union officers began to realize that after seven weeks of organizing, planning, marching and digging, Henry Halleck was the proud owner of several batteries of fake artillery pieces and one badly smashed up railroad depot. While Halleck congratulated his men for "a victory as brilliant and important as any recorded in history," a Chicago newspaper retorted "General Halleck has achieved one of the most barren triumphs of the war."

Halleck may have scored a hollow victory, but at least he had captured his objective, while his eastern counterpart was spending the weeks after Seven Pines trying to discover a foolproof plan to get inside Richmond's defenses while not being annihilated in the process. While McClellan ruminated and conferred, Robert E. Lee was taking definite steps to make sure that his adversary never got close enough to direct a pitched battle in the streets of the capital. Although much of the literature about the most famous general of the Confederacy emphasizes the suddenness of Lee's appointment after the injuries to Johnston, in reality, the Virginian had been quietly exercising power for several weeks since Jefferson Davis had appointed him his military advisor. While Johnston directed the defense activities around Richmond proper, Lee was already responding to longer term threats that would be sure to develop when the 75,000 Federals in northern Virginia and the Shenandoah Valley were able to concentrate against the capital in support of the Army of the Potomac.

The armies commanded by John Fremont, Nathaniel Banks and Irvin McDowell were relatively widely scattered, but the Confederates had fewer than 20,000 men to block any determined Union advance. While McClellan was advancing toward Richmond, Lee secured Davis' permission to combine the diverse Confederate detachments in a more concentrated striking force under Stonewall Jackson and Richard Ewell.

Jackson and Ewell were a pair of generals who were unusually eccentric even in a war that produced eccentric leaders by the score. Ewell was a forty-five-year-old bachelor who had a series of real or imagined stomach ailments that limited him to a grim diet of buttermilk and cracked wheat, while his bald head, sharp nose and habit of leaning his head to one side encouraged his officers and men to identify him with a variety of species of birds, none of them complimentary. Ewell's superior, Stonewall Jackson, was, if possible, even more eccentric, as he battled even worse dyspepsia with an odd menu of plain bread, raspberries and a seemingly inexhaustible supply of lemons. Contemporary artists must have been either enormously imaginative or enormously nearsighted when they painted portraits of Stonewall with glittering swords, scarlet capes and expensive gauntlets, as Jackson's real wardrobe consisted of a VMI cadet cap that was both ill fitting and had a broken visor, and his left-over Mexican War uniform that hadn't been cleaned or repaired in over fifteen years.

These two generals had a collection of weird personality traits that exasperated more than one Confederate officer, but in the crucial spring of 1862 they directed one of the most heavily discussed campaigns of modern warfare. While Ewell's detachment of about 8000 men discouraged a rapid advance on the part of Nathaniel Banks, Jackson, with 9000 men swung wide around Union cavalry patrols and came crashing down on Fremont's advance units about 25 miles from the Shenandoah Valley town of Staunton. On May 8th 1862, at the crossroads town of McDowell, Stonewall sent several Union regiments scattering in panic toward their main army with the Rebels snapping at their heels. Then, just when Fremont thought that he was certain about the direction from which the Confederates were approaching, Jackson marched south toward Richmond and then suddenly loaded his troops on several trains and shuttled them back toward Staunton from the opposite direction. While Fremont's army withdrew away from this new threat, Jackson switched direction again and came down hard on one of Banks' divisions which was also thrown into a panic stricken retreat.

Jackson was now determined to annihilate Banks' entire force and he began to put into practice the credo that would win him a special niche in the pantheon of military commanders. Stonewall insisted that the keys to victory were relatively simple, "always mystify, mislead and surprise the enemy and when you strike and overcome him, never let up in the pursuit so long as your men have strength to follow; for an army routed, if hotly pursued, becomes panic stricken and can then be destroyed by half their members." Banks became a primary victim of this tactic as he desperately attempted to concentrate his 9000 available Federals to contest the advance of Jackson's now united army.

On the evening of May 22nd, Jackson prepared his first strike on Banks when his army deployed on the outskirts of Fort Royal, Virginia, which was held by 1000 men from Banks' advance guard. Rebel cavalrymen circled around the town and cut the telegraph lines to prevent requests for Federal reinforcements, and then tore up the railroad tracks and covered the roads leading into the town. Shortly after lunch the main Confederate assault began, and after a brief resistance the Federal garrison commander ordered his men to retreat across the Shenandoah River to withdraw back toward the main army 10 miles away. Suddenly wave after wave of Rebel cavalry jumped his retreating troops and in 15 minutes almost the entire Union detachment was eliminated at a cost of 904 killed, wounded or captured, compared to 50 Confederate casualties.

Jackson's now famous "foot cavalry" remained in Front Royal only long enough to gather fresh supplies and then started another march designed to cut Banks off from the Potomac River and destroy him in detail. Union squads, platoons and companies were dribbled away in rear guard actions and Confederate ambushes as Banks attempted to discover a point at which he could make a stand and delay Jackson long enough to make a final sprint to the safety of Maryland. The Federals won the race to the key town of Winchester and Banks ordered his men to make a stand in front of the town while he sent urgent dispatches for help to Fremont and McDowell. However, while a brigade of Louisianians launched a direct assault on the imposing Federal artillery concentration, a mixed unit of cavalry and infantry swept around both sides of the Union-held ridge and hit the Yankees simultaneously from two flanks just as the Louisiana shock troops hit the front line. The whole Northern line disintegrated and the 7000 surviving Federals lost almost half their number in a wild 36 mile running battle back to the Potomac, while Jackson's pursuit force lost only 400 men.

The Confederate army now seemed to be poised for a direct attack on Washington, and the Northern telegraph wires hummed with government directives to counter this new threat. Jackson's fast moving army would spend much of June continuing to bedevil three Union armies that were desperately needed for the Richmond campaign. Before he was ordered to bring his own army to the vicinity of the Confederate capital, Stonewall's army had captured over 4000 men, 10,000 muskets and hundreds of wagon loads of supplies, and had marched over 700 miles, to effectively neutralize 70,000 Union soldiers at extremely modest loss to his own 17,000 men.

While Stonewall Jackson was clearing the Shenandoah Valley of Union forces, Robert E. Lee was quietly planning a master stroke to not only push McClellan from the gates of Richmond, but quite possibly destroy the Union army in the process. The new commander of the Army of Northern Virginia had come to his new position with an inaccurate reputation as an overly cautious commander who had been nicknamed "Granny Lee" and "The King of Spades" by his earlier subordinates. However, future artillery commander E. Porter Alexander became one of the first Confederate officers to sense that Lee's true personality was far more aggressive than advertised. While riding with staff officer Colonel Joseph James, Alexander received a preview of the new commander's boldness. James responded to his colleagues misgivings by insisting "if there is one man in either army, Confederate or Federal, head and shoulders above every other in audacity, it is General Lee. His name might be audacity. He will take more chances, and take them quickly, then any other general in the country, North or South and you will live to see it."

The new Confederate commander who impressed subordinates officers and enlisted men alike with his "dignity of character, intellectual power and his calm self reliance," was stripping virtually every rebel garrison in the east to concentrate the largest single Southern army of the war, 85,000 men, to smash into the Union army, before it could enter a capital that was so close that Federal pickets could hear Richmond clocks strike the hour. On the afternoon of June 23rd, 1862 a dusty, exhausted Stonewall Jackson entered Lee's headquarters on the outskirts of Richmond. Jackson had ridden all night on a relay of five horses to answer Lee's summons to a summit meeting of his talented young assault commanders. While the commanding general attended to some last minute paperwork, James Longstreet, Harvey Hill, Ambrose Hill and Stonewall Jackson discussed Lee's proposal fro a surprise attack on McClellan. All four generals had been cadets at West Point at about the same time and though each man wore a long beard that hinted at maturity, in reality they were all only in their late thirties or very early forties. These young commanders quickly hammered out the details of a plan in which almost 60,000 Rebel soldiers would be concentrated against the only Union corps that was still camped north of the Chickahominy, General Fitz-John Porter's V Corps, which was deployed behind an imposing series of fortifications on Beaver Dam Creek.

The key to Confederate opportunities for success revolved around the sudden appearance of Jackson's foot cavalry behind Porter's defenses which had apparently been constructed primarily to deflect a Rebel frontal assault. While Ambrose Hill and Longstreet kept Porter's attention with a forward thrust, Jackson would sweep down from the north and strike from the rear while Harvey Hill's force swung wide around Beaver Dam Creek and confused the Yankees still more. This concentrated assault would eliminate almost 25% of the Union army in one day, provided that two developments went as expected. First, the attack would have to be perfectly coordinated; Porter's defenses were almost impervious to an unsupported frontal attack and only a threat to his rear could force him into an open battle. Second, this attack left only 25,000 men to hold Richmond against almost 75,000 Yankees deployed on the south side of the Chickahominy. If McClellan happened to make his threatened big push against the capital at this particular moment, the Rebel victory north of the river would be more than counterbalanced by the loss of Richmond.

Lee was not the only commanding general planning an intricate assault for the last week in June. George McClellan had used the Confederate surprise attack at Seven Pines as a catalyst for re-thinking his whole strategy for capturing Richmond, and by the time that Lee and his generals were planning their new offensive, McClellan had begun to finalize plans to shift his base of operations from the York River to the James River, with an ultimate objective of attacking Richmond from its back door entrance of Petersburg. Since the Union general was still convinced that the enemy had almost 200,000 men guarding the capital, he determined to shift his base to Harrison's Landing where he could obtain much more direct support from the navy, and then strike at the vital rail depot at Petersburg which, if captured, would sever Richmond from its main sources of food. Thus on June 25th, the day before the Confederate offensive was due to begin, McClellan ordered Samuel Heintzelman's corps to advance down the Williamsburg Road to test enemy strength around Old Tavern as a prelude to a more general move. A confused and savage fight erupted when Benjamin Huger's Confederates disputed the Yankee advance, and each army lost about 500 men in an engagement that would mark the first day of a solid week of battle between blue and gray.

The Seven Days campaign represented one of the most complex, contro-versial military confrontations of the Civil War. Ever since that confusing series of engagements, historians have debated whether Robert E. Lee forced an almost triumphant Union army back from the gates of Richmond very much against its will, or whether George McClellan merely carried out a change of base that he was planning anyway and proceeded to bleed the Confederate army white in the process. No matter which of these conten-tions is more accurate, the fact remains that Lee's reputation for audacity was initiated by this campaign and, until U.S. Grant arrived from the west, a succession of commanders of the Army of the Potomac would lie awake in their beds wondering what the crafty Virginian had in store for them the next time the rival armies fought.

Thursday, June 26th, 1862 dawned clear, sunny and hot and president Jefferson Davis, wearing his usual suit of Confederate Gray and a Panama hat, rode out with his staff to confer with Lee and watch the upcoming battle. While Yankees sprawled on front porches and under trees that dotted the landscape around the village of Mechanicsville, Lee and Davis sat on their horses waiting anxiously for the sound of distant firing that would signal the arrival of Stonewall Jackson in Porter's rear. At 8 o'clock the pair of Confederate leaders were simply mildly surprised at the delay, at noon they were genuinely concerned and at 3 o'clock in the afternoon they were exasperated as the wide fields behind Beaver Dam Creek remained ominously quiet. Several miles away George McClellan, who was expecting a Rebel attack, inspected Porter's lines and admitted to his subordinate that he had mixed feelings about whether he wanted a fight on that particular day. After a leisurely lunch he went back to his headquarters and wired Edwin Stanton "all things very quiet on this bank of the Chickahominy. I would prefer more noise."

McClellan's wish would soon be granted; Ambrose Powell Hill finally tired of waiting for Stonewall to begin the engagement and at a little past 3 o'clock his screaming graycoats smashed into Porter's lines without the supporting rear assault. The initial shock of the attack pushed the Federals through the streets of Mechanicsville as they gradually withdrew toward Beaver Dam Creek beyond the town. Once Hill's men had captured the village, Lee sent orders to avoid attacking the main Union position unless an approach that offered some semblance of cover could be found. Hill largely ignored that directive and send his men slamming into a defense line that McClellan and his engineers had carefully constructed and, the result was easily predictable. Scores of Rebels were shot down with little observable effect on the Union defenses and even when Longstreet and Harvey Hill joined the assault the Federals didn't budge. Porter was one of the most talented defensive-minded generals in the National army and he had his men deployed exactly where he wanted them to be.

While Longstreet and the Hills were being decimated by Porter's front lines, Stonewall Jackson was nowhere near the Yankee rear. His detachment was crawling along at the rate of one mile an hour and didn't arrive at their jump-off point of Hundley's Corner until after 5 o'clock. They were now within three miles of Beaver Dam Creek with three hours of daylight remaining, but, almost incredibly, Jackson called a halt to the march and ordered his men to set up camp for the night. The engagement at Mechanicsville, Lee's first crucial battle, was now effectively over, and it was little short of a disaster. Hill had attacked without using any cover, and Jackson had not attacked at all, and the result was almost 1400 Confederate casualties, almost quadruple the Union loss. Lee's worst nightmare, a Union thrust on Richmond while most of the army was occupied with Porter, had not occurred, but the capital was still threatened and Lee would try again the next day.

At dawn on Friday, June 27th, the Confederate assault forces charged toward the Union lines and found only empty entrenchments. During the night Porter had pulled back to a new position on Powhite Creed which fronted a large brick and timber structure known as Gaines Mill. Powhite Creek provided plenty of high ground and ample sheltering woods on its east bank, and Lee expected that his opponent would strongly contest a Confederate crossing. However, just as A.P. Hill's troops repeated their thrust of the day before, the Union soldiers faded back into the woods after token resistance. Why would the Federals abandon a formidable position after only a short defense? Lee and his generals found out soon enough, as the Confederate attackers charged past the far side of the creek and ran into a hail of artillery fire as dozens of cannons tore the Rebels to pieces. McClellan and Porter had combined their defensive genius to construct a triple tiered defensive network along a boggy creek called Boatswain's Swamp, which was about a mile east of Powhite Creek and located near a scene of future horror—Cold Harbor. This marshy land was dominated by an elevation called Turkey Hill, which was now studded with cannons but wasn't even located on most Confederate generals' maps.

Lee's assault troops were confronting a challenge that would plague the Confederates during the whole week of fighting; they had very little idea where they were and even less knowledge of the topography of the enemy strong points. Even Southern general Evander Law expressed his admiration for the Federal superiority in map making and reconnaissance. "The real trouble was that the Confederate officers, even those in command, knew little or nothing of the topography of the country in which they were operating. The Federals, on the other hand, knew the country thoroughly; they had occupied it for several weeks, and during that time their engineer officers had inspected it thoroughly. There was no earthly reason why the Confederate authorities should not have possessed the same information." Here was a paradox of the Confederates fighting grimly on their own territory and knowing less about the region than the Yankee invaders!

Lee rode into the hail of shells and bullets and, observing the panic and confusion around him, informed his staff officers, "gentlemen we must rally these men." A new thrust against Turkey Hill was organized while the commanding general set out to find Stonewall Jackson, who had again failed to threaten the enemy rear. The two men conferred briefly and at about 5 o'clock Jackson led a bayonet charge against the far end of the ridge while Harvey Hill hit the center, and Longstreet and Ambrose Hill swept in from the right. Lee finally had all of his men where he wanted them and they heavily outnumbered the Union defenders. However, at least at first, the general assault was less than a spectacular success. Harvey Hill's men slammed into George Sykes' division of 6000 Federal regulars, who turned that part of the attack into a giant target practice in which their section of the line wasn't even dented. Porter rode up and down his line directing reserves to threatened points, secure in the knowledge that McClellan had insisted that this was a mere holding action and he only had to hang on until nightfall before being evacuated.

As the early summer sun reached the horizon, it was becoming increasingly clear that the Federals had won the battle and that the Confederates would have a disaster matching Mechanicsville. However, John Bell Hood's Texas brigade and Evander Law's brigade of men from Mississippi, Alabama and North Carolina had just arrived on the battlefield after a series of delays and Lee was determined to try one last roll of the dice. Lee rode over to the tall, blond Texan commander and asked him if he could break the Union line in one final charge, and Hood agreed to try. Just as the twilight was covering the field, these two brigades of graycoats charged through the growing darkness and broke through the first line of Federal defenders. Over a thousand Rebels went down in less than 10 minutes, but the survivors got in among the startled Yankee gunners and the rest of the Confederate line now swept forward.

The Federal withdrawal was anything but a panic-stricken retreat, as the Union troops withdrew toward the Chickahominy with every confidence that they had accomplished their general's mission of delaying the Rebels. As the Confederates pressed closer to the retreating Yankees, two of Sumner's brigades crossed the river and set up a final defense line near the Chickahominy. While Sykes' regulars hammered at the Rebel flanks to discourage another Confederate charge, the entire V Corps of the Union army was safely evacuated to the south bank. The Southern attackers had been able to cut off several Union units and by nightfall Lee could inform Jefferson Davis that he had over 2000 prisoners and several pieces of captured artillery. However, claims of a Confederate victory were wildly exaggerated, since Lee's army had lost a staggering 9000 men in their assault while Porter's outnumbered Federals had lost only 2500 killed and wounded. While Lee exulted that "we sleep on the field and shall renew the contest in the morning," in reality, the Confederate general had sacrificed over 10,000 men in two days merely to push McClellan from a position that he was going to abandon anyway. However, at least in a psychological sense, the initiative was clearly passing over to the Confederates.

The next three days presented a dramatic and violent panorama of Confederate thrusts against an enormously encumbered Federal army, set against the backdrop of exploding railroad locomotives, burning warehouses and demolished wagons that would do credit to the Hollywood set of *Gone With The Wind*. While McClellan attempted to change his base from White House on the York River to Harrison's Landing on the James River, Lee sent his divisions snapping at the Yankees' heels, constantly attempting to close a trap that just wouldn't quite stay shut. McClellan still had no idea that Richmond was almost stripped of defenders and that a lunge toward the capital would have totally untracked Lee's careful plans, but his eyes were focused on the James River, not the spires of the city. Even the Army of the Potomac's more aggressive generals were deceived by Prince John Magruder's continuing theatrics as, for example, "Fighting Joe" Hooker excitedly telegraphed his chief, "they have it in mind to advance on us I can be whipped before the reserves will get up." As long as McClellan and his generals believed that 200,000 battle hardened Rebels were waiting to annihilate them if they attacked Richmond, a successful retreat to the James River was probably about the best that could be hoped for.

The great Federal change of base began soon after Porter's fallback from Gaines Mill as Franklin, Sumner and Heintzelman were directed to hold the Chickahominy river line while Keyes and then Porter marched through White Oak Swamp to cover the passage of over 5000 wagons. All day Saturday June 28th, Lee tried to discern whether McClellan was planning an assault on Richmond, a retreat back down the Peninsula, or a move to the James, and he was forced to keep his army scattered to meet any of these contingencies. Finally, on Sunday morning, Confederate scouts reported that the enemy was neither advancing on Richmond nor marching toward Williamsburg, so the Confederate commander could now begin to deploy his men to annihilate the Federals as they moved through the quicksand, bogs and marshes of White Oak Swamp. Lee's basic plan was to send Magruder's division out from the Richmond entrenchments to move along the railroad line, to attack the Union rear guard from one direction while Stonewall Jackson would sweep in from the opposite side after his men had repaired the Grapevine Bridge and crossed the swollen Chickahominy. While these units were smashing into McClellan's rear troops, Benjamin Huger's division would move along the Charles City road to slash at the Federals that were just emerging from the other side of White Oak Swamp, while Longstreet and A.P. Hill would execute a wide sweep and hit the Yankees from the other side once they had turned to meet Huger. McClellan would discover his army getting hit from four different directions while he was forced to defend his wagons and fight without the cover of the breastworks that had decimated the rebels at Mechanicsville and Gaines Mill.

Lee would have preferred a coordinated attack from all directions simultaneously, but he realized that Longstreet and Hill could not possibly attack until sometime Monday because of the distance they would have to march to get into position. Therefore, the Confederate commander decided that Magruder and Jackson should smash into McClellan's rear on Sunday afternoon, since this would force McClellan to turn in mid-march and fight a rear guard action north of White Oak Swamp, possibly allowing more time for the other assault units to get into position. Magruder spent most of Sunday afternoon marching his 13,000 men along the railroad line while trying to locate the Federal rear guard. Finally, just short of Savage Station railroad depot, the Rebels came under intense Federal artillery fire and Prince John ordered an attack on the Yankees, who were deployed all around the station and its auxiliary buildings. For four hours, until a violent thunderstorm and the onset of darkness put a halt to the action, Magruder's men attacked a Union force that had more artillery and better cover. Meanwhile, Jackson, who was supposed to sweep in from the north, spent virtually the whole day repairing Grapevine Bridge and never arrived for the battle. Each side had lost about 500 men, but Magruder's force hadn't even dented the Federal lines and McClellan had been given an extra day to withdraw and prepare his new base on the James.

The commander of the Army of Northern Virginia was disappointed at the failure to injure the Federals on Sunday, but he was convinced that Monday would provide a far better opportunity for the climactic victory that he expected. When McClellan's lead units emerged from White Oak Swamp, and began to march through the crossroads village of Glendale, four Confederate divisions would smash into his flank while Jackson would hurl three more divisions at his rear. If everything went according to plan, over 70,000 Confederates would hit the Federals in the open, strung out along miles of roads and forced to defend their precious wagon trains with no advantage of cover.

Monday, June 30th, was expected to be the crucial day of the entire campaign to annihilate the army threatening the Confederate capital. As one Confederate general noted years later, "it was the opportunity of a lifetime for Lee; the Confederacy was in its prime with more men available than ever before or after; at no other period would the moral or the physical effect of a victory have been so great as upon this occasion." Lee had ordered all of the coordinated assaults to begin at dawn, and he had personally conferred with Stonewall Jackson, who confirmed that he was ready to move at first light. Jefferson Davis and his staff rode out to watch the battle with Lee, and as was so frequently the case in the confusing week, absolutely nothing happened. The first assault of the day might have come when Huger's men smashed into the Federals just as they were emerging from White Oak Swamp, but when the Yankees observed the Rebels marching to intercept them, they simply began felling trees to delay the enemy march. Huger was forced to enter a construction contest that he couldn't win. As one Confederate leader noted, "it seems incredible that this division could have been allowed to spend the whole day in a contest of axmen, wherein the Federals, with the most axes, had only to cut down and the Confederates, with the fewest, had to cut up and remove." Thus in this sector, the Union army clearly won the race to redeploy before the enemy hit them in the open.

While Huger's men were hacking through the woods, Stonewall Jackson's men seemed to be moving so slowly that they spent the day snapping at Federal units just as they marched out of range. Jackson finally pushed his forces into the marshy swamp land and managed to deploy over 30 guns on a ridge that allowed him to target part of the Union wagon train. However, while the initial Confederate salvos were very effective and about 50 Yankee wagons were destroyed, a Federal screening force of artillery quickly wheeled its guns into position on a nearby elevation and utilized their longer range weapons to decimate the Rebel batteries. Jackson quickly decided that Tuesday would be a better day for the major confrontation with the Federals and he suspended operations as hundreds of Union wagons creaked on their way out of the swamp.

The main action of June 30th occurred as the Federals were marching through the town of Glendale. Four divisions of Union soldiers were in front of the village, on the fields of Frayser's Farm, with orders to screen the wagons as they emerged from White Oak Swamp and headed for the James River. Longstreet and A.P. Hill took most of the day to approach Glendale, but by 6 P.M. they were driving in the Union pickets and had begun a savage battle that continued after nightfall. The Confederates captured 18 Federal guns, made a prisoner of Yankee division commander George McCall, one of Longstreet's close friends, and engaged in a furious hand to hand fight with bayonets, knives and even fists, marking a battle that surged back and forth across the farmyards. As full darkness descended on the field, the Federals withdrew to the south, but they had delayed the Rebels long enough to save McClellan's supply train and had inflicted over 3300 casualties at far less cost to their own force.

The last hours of June had also been the last hours in which Lee had possessed a real chance to annihilate the Federal army. The Yankees had been pushed back ever farther from Richmond, but the army was still quite intact and was even now fortifying the almost impregnable lines along Malvern Hill. As Porter Alexander insisted much later, "I have often thought that no one day of the whole four years should seem more unfortunate than June 30, 1862." The chance for a battle of annihilation had been frittered away and McClellan had been able to deploy his army back in the entrenchments that the general always used to so much advantage. Now the rebels would be forced to fight another battle on Little Mac's terms.

One of the reasons why Robert E. Lee is not only a celebrated general but a fascinating individual is that behind the marble exterior of a Virginia aristocrat, there lurked the personality of a riverboat gambler. Lee knew throughout his tenure as a general that the Federal army always had more manpower and resources than he would ever enjoy, so he often used audacious gambles to attempt to even the odds or even stack the deck in his favor. However, these stupendous risks brought uneven rewards for the Confederate cause. During the battles of Second Manassas and Chancellorsville the large gamble brought equally large success, while the order for Pickett to advance on Cemetery Ridge at Gettysburg resulted in a critical defeat. The final act in the drama of the Seven Days campaign was not as disastrous as Pickett's charge but it was hardly the shining moment of Lee's career.

On Tuesday morning, July 1st, George McClellan was directing the organization of his new base at Harrison's Landing, while much of his army was occupying a temporary position along Malvern Hill. When Lee surveyed the Union position he developed a state of mind that was remarkably similar to his mood on an equally critical morning one year and two days later as he studied a very similar ridge containing a very similar adversary. In both of these instances, Lee was convinced that his opponent had been badly injured and was on the verge of total annihilation if only one more well, timed blow could be delivered. Ironically, while it would be James Longstreet who expressed extreme reservations about the risk of attacking George Meade on Cemetery Ridge, on this occasion the commander's old war horse was fully supportive of the assault. While a small group of Confederate generals studied the features of Malvern Hill with their telescopes, Harvey Hill carefully noted the rows of Federal artillery and insisted to Lee "if General McClellan is there in strength, we had better let him alone," while Longstreet quipped "don't get scared men that we have get him whipped!"

Lee would have his massive assault, but as was the norm for this complex campaign, the attackers began to advance several hours after they had received their orders. While the Confederate divisions spent most of the morning attempting to deploy for assault, Union artillery officers carefully sited hundreds of field guns and siege cannons in several tiers of almost impregnable positions while Federal gunboats on the James River prepared to slaughter any Rebels who broke through the Federal lines. Finally, at a few minutes past 1 P.M., six Confederate divisions began to move through a broad wheat field toward the 150-foot ridge while Southern gunners frantically wheeled their cannons into supporting range. General William Pendleton, Lee's chief of artillery, insisted that every reserve cannon in the Army of Northern Virginia should be utilized to support the infantry charge, but the orders to advance never reached most of the rear artillery batteries, and the Confederates were forced to commit their guns on a piecemeal basis rather than in a massive barrage.

For over two hours individual batteries of Rebel guns would be deployed to duel the Yankee guns, and the eager Federals would simply aim as many of 50 of their own cannons at the Southern battery and blow it to pieces, after which it would eventually be replaced by another single battery. The outcome of this one-sided artillery duel was a disaster for the Confederates. At one point twenty Southern guns were destroyed in twenty minutes and one artillery unit lost 60 of its 80 men and all but one gun in five minutes. However, the erratic Confederate barrage did have one noticeable effect on the battle; the Rebel shells encouraged General Sumner to pull part of his infantry back to a less exposed position and as Federal skirmishers began to withdraw, Lee was convinced that the enemy was on the verge of breaking. As one observer noted, "as if moved by a reckless disregard of life equal to that displayed at Gaines Mill, with a determination to capture the army or destroy it by driving them into the river, brigade after brigade rushed at the ridge." The charge was magnificent, but the Union cannons were parked hub to hub and they simply shifted from one target to another as the wheat field filled up with writhing graycoats. When the Confederates moved closer to the imposing hill, the Yankee infantry raised their rifles and annihilated squads and platoons before the Rebels could even begin to respond. Huger's division scored a small breakthrough at one part of the line, but just as Lee shifted Magruder's division the Union guns also shifted position and tore huge gaps in both units. Harvey Hill watched the bloody panorama with a mixture of awe and terror and later recalled "it was not war, it was murder." Dusk finally brought a halt to the valiant but useless charge and another 6000 Confederates were added to the butcher's bill for the week, while only 2000 Union soldiers joined them on this bloody list.

While Lee was visibly shaken by the extent of casualties that he had suffered to no apparent purpose, a number of Federal generals surveyed the battlefield and sensed an opportunity for much greater dividends. Several corps commanders, including even the commander's closest friend, Fitz-John Porter, begged McClellan to suspend his move to Harrison's Landing and launch a massive thrust toward Richmond before the Confederates could recover from the shock of their losses. A less cautious commander would have seen the opportunity of a lifetime, but McClellan could still only picture those 200,000 phantom Rebels crushing his army as they were lured into the trap of attacking the capital; and in at least one sense, Lee had won again, since two more years would pass before a Federal army ever got this close to Richmond.

Lee's bold strike at the Union army during the last week of June, 1862 resulted in a series of battles that were at the same time exciting, confusing and controversial, and provide a glimpse of the reason that the Civil War has such a fascinating hold on Americans almost a century and a half after the conflict. Did Lee win a spectacular victory or bleed his army white for little gain? Was McClellan forced into an ignominious retreat by a smaller army or conducting a brilliant change of base under very adverse circumstances? Was Fitz-John Porter the savior of the Federal army or was Stonewall Jackson the culprit for the lack of total Confederate victory? Of course, there is no answer that everyone can agree upon, but a dispassionate view of a passionately fought campaign reveals some possible implications. First, the authors believe that the fact that after this battle Lee's star was in the ascendancy and McClellan's career soon to be in eclipse has somewhat colored evaluations of this campaign. In a sense it is much more fun to describe the exploits of an audacious gambler who exalts the attack than an overly cautious defensive genius who mainly pulls an army back from one series of fortifications to another. However, in a fair evaluation of this crucial series of engagements each commander was partially successful and a partial failure. Lee's willingness to take the offensive with a smaller army definitely saved Richmond from imminent capture and eliminated the last really serious Union opportunity to enter the capital until the summer of 1864. Northerners who read newspaper reports of millions of dollars of Federal weapons and equipment being demolished or abandoned, Jeb

Stuart's almost effortless ride around the whole Army of the Potomac, and long lines of Union soldiers marching into captivity were hardly going to welcome the campaign as a "successful change of base." The outcome of the re-deployment might have been successful but the images that movement produced reeked of defeat and embarrassment. When loyal unionist civilians read the accounts of Lee's exploits and saw pictures of the incredibly photogenic and heroic appearing Virginian in their pictorial weeklies, it was no wonder that in a moment of ambiguous emotions, people could exclaim "oh but that he was ours." Here was a chivalrous yet audacious cavalier who was the personification of many of the most positive characteristics of all Americans before the nation was divided, and it didn't seem fair that the region that supported an abomination such as slavery deserved to get a Lee (or a Stonewall Jackson) while the men who fought for a nobler cause were saddled with Fremonts, McDowells and Butlers.

On the other hand, while Lee had more flair, more audacity and more drive than his adversary, George McClellan had done much more than backpedal from Richmond during a series of violent engagements with the new commander of the Army of Northern Virginia. At Beaver Dam Creek, Boatswain Swamp and Malvern Hill, the Rebel army had been decimated in attempting to break through incredibly formidable Union defenses. The assaults had cost Lee over 20,000 men who were simply irreplaceable given the limited manpower reserves of the South and, as a stark reminder of that fact, the Army of Northern Virginia would never again field as many men as were deployed for the Seven Days campaign. McClellan's loss of 16,000 men was not only a much smaller percentage of his army, but it was also top heavy with men who were captured and would soon be exchanged, while the number killed in action was little more than half the Rebel total. Thus, far more of the men "lost" from the Northern army would return to duty than the Confederates, who could ill afford these losses in the first place. Lee had at least temporarily saved Richmond, but McClellan had made him pay dearly for the privilege, and it was ultimately much more the failures of men in Washington than the "Young Napoleon" that allowed the Confederates to turn this temporary check into a gambit that very nearly won the whole game.

CHAPTER 26

# A Long and Strong Flood

## *The Confederate Counter-Offensive of 1862*

*I*ndependence Day of 1862 was a particularly unsatisfying celebration for most citizens of the Northern states. The Union cause had raised two magnificent armies that were so large and so well equipped that Marlborough and Wellington would have envied their commanders. And yet, on this patriotic festival, these two armies of almost a quarter million men were doing precisely nothing to end the rebellion. A few weeks before this 4th of July, it had seemed that the Confederacy was a doomed experiment that would simply shatter into pieces if the Rebel armies were defeated once or twice more. However, ironically, just a few weeks after this holiday, the tide of battle would change so dramatically that most Southerners, many Northerners, and not a few influential Europeans, were convinced that the war was indeed virtually over, but with independence for the South virtually assured. From Mississippi to Virginia the Northern engine of war was losing momentum and several energetic Southerners were perfectly prepared to fill this void of power.

The western army of the Union had accomplished its initial objective of capturing Corinth, but its cautious commander, Henry W. Halleck, had promptly thrown away even the hollow victory he had secured by dismantling an army that could have marched anywhere it cared to in the heart of the secessionist republic. Don Carlos Buell was ordered to march toward Chattanooga with four divisions, but the need to almost literally rebuild the whole railroad line for several hundred miles promised to make this advance an excruciatingly slow campaign. William T. Sherman was sent west with three divisions to garrison Memphis and repair that region's railroads with an eye to restoring the cotton trade from that city. John McClernand was given two divisions and sent to Jackson, Tennessee to repair the railroad lines back to the North, while Halleck would remain with the rest of the army and supervise railroad repairs in Mississippi. Thus an army of 120,000 men was almost literally turned overnight into a mega-sized road crew that would be pounding railroad spikes rather than shooting at Confederates. However, one of the most prominent members of this western army wasn't even given the opportunity to lead men in railroad repairs. Ulysses S. Grant seemed to be a permanent resident of Halleck's dog house, and he was becoming so frustrated at his figurehead second in command status that only the last minute emotional appeal of Sherman prevented the hero of Fort Donelson from resigning his commission and heading back to dubious civilian employment.

While the western army was being fragmented into glorified construction gangs, Abraham Lincoln and Edwin Stanton were attempting to go in the opposite direction and consolidate the scattered armies operating in northern Virginia. Lincoln was convinced that McClellan would be in no hurry to attack Richmond from his new base on the James River, but the President was convinced that the Army of the Potomac could still play the role of an anvil if he could only construct a hammer to strike the enemy capital from above. The President's hammer was going to be a newly designated Army of Virginia which would be formed from the consolidation of the armies of Fremont, Banks and McDowell. This army would move south towards Richmond and gradually catch Lee in a pincers between these advancing Federals and the imposing forces under McClellan based at Harrison's Landing. All that Lincoln really needed was an energetic, fearless director for this hammer and he finally concluded that a general from the victorious army of the west would be the best candidate. Lincoln could and should have selected Ulysses Grant for the position and the appointment might very well have shortened the life of the Confederacy. Grant was strongly considered, but Halleck's insinuations that his subordinate was back on his drinking binges encouraged Lincoln to back off and select the seemingly just as successful John Pope instead.

John Pope shared much of the energy and fearlessness that would eventually make Grant so invincible, but while Grant was quiet and self-effacing, Pope was an egotistical blowhard who managed to gain the disrespect and hatred of both his Confederate adversaries and his Yankee colleagues within the space of an incredibly short time. Pope came east in late June and enthralled Congress with his plans, told his army that they would never retreat and threatened to treat Southern civilians in territory he occupied as little more than guerillas and bandits. Down in the Richmond area, two prominent generals were determined to see this man fail; Robert E. Lee began plans to "suppress" this pompous adversary who seemed to be going beyond the acceptable limits of mid-19th century warfare, and George McClellan probably secretly wished the Southern general well in his suppression.

Lincoln may have picked the wrong commander, but his plan was an excellent one and, at first, everything went well for the new Army of Virginia. Pope's major objective was to seize the key railroad depot at

Gordonsville, cut the Virginia Central Railroad which brought supplies from the Shenandoah Valley to Richmond, and then force Lee to come out and fight with at least part of his army while McClellan struck the now less heavily defended capital. However, unfortunately for the Unionists, the two Federal armies were being commanded by men who were each saddled with enormous flaws. Pope couldn't wait to slash his way through a Rebel army he was convinced was led by an overrated general while McClellan was so awed by the power of the Confederates that he wouldn't move. Then, just to make sure that the probability of success dropped to near zero, as the new campaign began, Lincoln promoted Henry Halleck to the command of all Union armies and let him run the operation from his desk in Washington, thus producing probably the worst leadership mix of any Northern campaign of the Civil War. McClellan counted phantom Rebels, Pope dismissed real Rebels, Halleck sent contradictory telegrams to both of his field commanders, and the Southern Confederacy very nearly won the war in the process.

The summer campaign that would eventually produce the Union fiasco known as Second Manassas, actually had its genesis when Henry Halleck, in his new capacity as commander of Federal armies, made perhaps the single most stupid decision of the war on the Union side. Halleck visited McClellan at Harrison's Landing to discuss the upcoming move against Richmond, and when the Army of the Potomac commander would only guarantee success if he was provided with an additional 30,000 men, Halleck went back to Washington and changed the course of the war. The Federal commander simply gave up trying to cajole McClellan into advancing and instead ordered him to abandon his base on the James and withdraw his army back to northern Virginia to ultimately link up with Pope for a single, concentrated advance. McClellan fumed and stammered and responded, "here directly in front of this army is the heart of the rebellion. It is here that all our resources should be collected to strike the blow which will determine the fate of the nation. It matters not what partial reverses we may meet with elsewhere. Here is the true defense of Washington. It is here, on the banks of the James, that the fate of the Union should be decided."

McClellan may have been far too cautious to be a really great general, but in this instance he was absolutely right and Halleck had unknowingly guaranteed that Richmond would not be seriously threatened again for two years. A Confederate general later noted the error of this Union maneuver. "On August 14, 1862 began the evacuation of the only position from which it could have forced the to evacuation of Richmond. They were only to find it again after two years of fighting and the loss of over 100,000 men; and they would find it then, only by being defeated upon every other possible line of advance." However, not only did Halleck's order insure that the Federals would simply have to repeat the whole grisly process of investing Richmond again two years later, he also provided Robert E. Lee with a brilliant opportunity to smite Pope. As long as McClellan's army was sitting on the

James River, Lee couldn't really go anywhere with the bulk of his army; there was always the chance, however slim, that the Yankees would march into Richmond if Lee denuded the capital of troops. However, McClellan's enforced evacuation was exactly the mistake that the Confederates could capitalize upon, as the Rebels could use their interior lines to strike Pope before the slower Union naval vessels could transport the Army of the Potomac in its intended linkup with the Army of Virginia. For at least a few days, Pope would be extremely vulnerable and Lee would have a real opportunity for a battle of annihilation.

While Pope waited for McClellan's corps to move north and reinforce him, the commander of the Army of Virginia deployed his army between the Rapidan and Rappahannock rivers near their point of confluence. The Union general's infantry and cavalry scouting units were so inept that he didn't know that his opponent had quietly marched most of his army up to the cover of Clark's Mountain and was even now preparing to spring a gigantic trap on the Yankees. Lee's initial plan was to send most of his cavalry to the west to destroy the huge railroad bridge at Rappahannock Station, which would cut off the Union army from its main supply depot at Manassas Junction. Then, when Pope moved to re-establish his lines of communication, the Confederate infantry would spring from their hiding place and gradually push the Federals back into the cul-de-sac formed by the two rivers, which would force Pope to either surrender or be annihilated. However, just as during the Seven Days Campaign, communications broke down at the key moment and equally important, the Union cavalry made one of its few major contributions this early in the war when a force of mounted Yankees surprised Jeb Stuart, captured his famous plumed hat and cape and, more importantly, acquired a general plan of Lee's orders. Pope was now warned of the trap and was able to pull his men back behind the Rappahannock before Lee could strike.

Pope had escaped one near disaster, but Lee was almost immediately at work devising a new scheme to "suppress" this despised opponent. The Confederate commander now sent Stonewall Jackson and 24,000 men on a wide flanking movement to come down on Pope's rear at Manassas Junction and force the Union army to fight on ground of the south's own choosing. While Lee remained with Longstreet's 30,000 men along the upper Rappahannock to occupy Pope's army Jackson led his men on a 56 mile march past Carter Mountain and down through Thoroughfare Gap toward Bristol rail depot. On the evening of August 26th, after two days of intense marching, the Confederates pounced on the rail yards and captured two long supply trains before the Federals discovered the trap. A third train saw the rebels closing in just in time to reverse power and back up furiously along the tracks in time to alert the garrison at Manassas Junction. The small Federal garrison put up a brief but spirited resistance, but by early morning of August 27th Jackson's corps was at least temporarily in possession of almost a full square mile of Union supplies and rations. The famished, ragged

Rebels probably had the attitude of a modern child who wins the grand prize of a contest that provides 30 minutes in a toy store to cart out all you can carry. One startled Confederate private recounted his feelings as he saw the Federal supply depot. "What a prize it was! Here were long warehouses full of stores; cars loaded with boxes of new clothing; camps, sutler's shops etc. In view of the abundance, it was not an easy matter to determine what we should eat or drink and wherewithal we should be clothed; one was limited in his choice to only so much as he could personally transport." After almost a full day of searching, looting, bartering and packing, the glare of bonfires lit the countryside for miles around as anything that couldn't be carried was put to the torch.

Pope promptly set his army to the chase but Jackson was far too experienced and far too elusive to be found until he wanted to be discovered, and Federal brigades scattered around Manassas and Centreville trying to find a phantom army. Stonewall finally deployed his corps in a heavily wooded area near the village of Groveton and prepared to snare any unwary Federals, while he waited for Longstreet and Lee to join him. While 34 brigades of Union soldiers groped through the Virginia countryside all day on August 28th, Longstreet's men started their approach to Thoroughfare Gap, and Jackson became increasingly confident that he could smash any Federal unit that approached him. While Rebel troops dozed, played cards and continued to gorge themselves on their cornucopia of captured rations, their commander stood on a nearby ridge to keep watch for a bluecoat column. Just as the sun was dropping to the horizon, John Gibbon's brigade of newly recruited regiments from Indiana and Wisconsin, followed by two of Abner Doubleday's regiments, marched into sight of Stonewall and his staff. Suddenly, as the 2800 Federals began to tramp through the edge of the woods, three batteries of Confederate artillery let loose and hundreds of Rebels led by the elite Stonewall Brigade swarmed down the slopes toward the startled bluecoats.

The surprised Midwesterners were facing a far larger force of Rebels, but rather than retreating in panic they formed tight ranks and blasted the oncoming Confederates. Neither side would budge in this bloody confrontation as the 2nd Wisconsin lost 300 of its 500 men, while only 425 members of the Stonewall Brigade emerged unhurt from the two hour battle. Finally, after each side had lost about 1000 men and total darkness had descended, the Federals pulled back across the Warrenton turnpike and Gibbon sent out messengers to Pope to converge on this spot. While Pope was rushing every available division to the fields around Groveton, Stonewall Jackson was quietly pulling his men back toward the almost impregnable position dominated by an unfinished railroad cut beyond the turnpike.

The morning of August 29th dawned clear and hot and John Pope prepared to throw every man he could find against what he believed was Jackson's "trapped" corps on the opposite side of the road. Pope assumed that the concentration of his own Army of Virginia and the arrival of part of the Army of the Potomac would allow him to smash into Stonewall with about 70,000 men, who should easily overrun a third as many Rebels. However, the arithmetic of this battle was going to develop far less congenially, for the Federal commander Porter's corps was marching far too slowly to arrive in time to start the battle, and McDowell's corps was still chasing phantom Confederates around Manassas Junction. On the other side of the ledger, Longstreet's corps had arrived in the vicinity of Thoroughfare Gap the night before and were now poised to deploy next to Jackson's divisions.

The battle began with Pope throwing the corps of Franz Sigel, Jesse Reno and Samuel Heintzelman toward Jackson's lines in a series of disjointed, poorly coordinated attacks. The Union commander was convinced that his opponent was only trying to escape him and he couldn't understand why his men couldn't penetrate the Rebel front. However, Jackson's troops were in a strong defensive position and would be as difficult to overrun as the Federals on Malvern Hill a few weeks earlier. For at least a while the Yankees had a large enough manpower advantage that they could make the battle touch and go, and at one point General Maxcy Gregg's South Carolina brigade was holding the whole Confederate left flank against an entire Union division, but Jackson rushed in reinforcements just before the Rebel line totally disintegrated.

Sometime after 1 P.M. Longstreet's regiments started to arrive at the battle scene and file in on Stonewall's right, but Pope ignored this deployment as he was still unaware that the rest of the Confederate army was even through Thoroughfare Gap. Lee suggested that "Old Pete" should use the men he had already brought up to charge the enemy flank when they least expected it, but Longstreet was unenthusiastic about this strategy since part of his corps was still strung along the roads and he hadn't had time to study the ground in front of him. On the other hand, at least one senior Union corps commander was just as reticent to attack the Confederates. Fitz-John Porter, a close friend of McClellan and a person who despised Pope, was ordered by the Army of Virginia commander to "press forward into action at once on the enemy's flank and, if possible, on his rear." Pope was sure that Jackson was preparing to retreat and that Longstreet hadn't arrived, but Porter insisted that his 9000 men would be annihilated by what seemed to be a huge Confederate reinforcement that had been arriving all afternoon. Pope fumed that his subordinate's reticence might cost him the battle. Actually, Porter was totally correct in his assessment. Longstreet already had 25,000 men in position and would have annihilated the heavily outnumbered bluecoat assault force. Porter, who was perhaps the most talented Federal general on the defensive, was ultimately relieved of command and thrown out of the army, a response that a number of Confederate generals, who admired their adversary's abilities, considered one of the major bonuses of Second Manassas.

Pope's army hadn't gained the expected breakthrough on the first day, but the commanding general was positive that he had Jackson on the ropes and would finish the job on August 30th. The next day, Pope ordered all of his divisions to concentrate for the "pursuit" of the "beaten" Rebels and the result was nearly the annihilation of the Union army. It had taken most of the morning and early afternoon to deploy the last arriving brigades, but at 2 P.M. on this sultry August afternoon a wall of blue started toward the Confederate positions. Longstreet stood on a ridge with his gaze alternating between the advancing Yankees and the 18 artillery pieces he had carefully hidden during the morning. Suddenly, Longstreet's hand went down and the whole front erupted in fire. The Federal lines were being shattered by guns they couldn't see and the momentum of the attack simply evaporated while Pope bellowed for his men to keep advancing. Suddenly, thousands of concealed infantrymen sprang out of the woods and obliterated the Federal left flank, which was now caught in the jaws of a pincer delivered by both Jackson and Longstreet. The most exposed Yankee regiments simply disintegrated as a gray tide swept over them and a seemingly inexhaustible column of Rebels kept sweeping out of the woods.

Pope's "pursuit" had only lasted for a few minutes, but to his credit, once he realized that he had been tricked, he quickly moved to save his army even if he couldn't save the day. The general used his freshest units to form a defensive line back at Henry House Hill of First Manassas fame, and this desperate stand allowed most of the army to retreat across Bull Run creek at the equally famous Stone Bridge. However, over 6000 Federals were captured during the retreat, and the field was littered with 20,000 rifles and 30 cannons that the Confederate army would immediately put to use. Lee's army had lost about 9000 men but had inflicted over 16,000 casualties, and John Pope's blustering promises of imminent destruction of the rebels were permanently silenced as he was transferred to Minnesota to fight Indians.

Second Manassas was not only a major Confederate victory; it also dramatically shifted the direction of the war in Virginia. In a sense, Pope's furious assaults on Jackson's railroad embankments at Groveton were the last gasps of a huge Federal offensive that began in April when McClellan marched north from Fortress Monroe. While the Confederates had certainly launched localized attacks on the Yankees between April and August, most of the engagements revolved around Federal attempts to either directly or indirectly eliminate the Southern defenders of Richmond. As late as 2 P.M. on August 30th, John Pope was still thinking in terms of "On to Richmond" as the next logical move. However, as the Union soldiers marched in the rain from Manassas to the Washington fortifications, much as they had done just over a year earlier, the balance of power had clearly shifted. A panic stricken Halleck, and a somewhat calmer but still shaken President, were now thinking merely of the safety of their own capital, not the capture of the Confederate seat of power. If Robert E. Lee could simply conjure up one more spectacular victory, European intervention might guarantee the permanent separation of the Union.

Lee and Jefferson Davis fully appreciated the opportunities created by the victory at Second Manassas, but each opportunity also incurred a decided risk. The Confederate army could remain on the defensive around Manassas and Centreville, but this allowed the Federals time to regroup and try another lunge at Richmond. The Southern forces could make their first serious attempt to capture Washington, but if they gave the Federals time to reorganize their units, the Union capital would be very difficult to capture. Finally, Lee could invade the North and draw the enemy army from Virginia during the crucial harvest season. Ultimately, the Confederate high command agreed on the latter course, and Lee refined the plan to include a thrust toward Harrisburg in order to destroy the enormous Pennsylvania Railroad bridge across the Susquehanna River. Destruction of that span would cut off the main route by which western reinforcements could be sent east, and possibly allow the Confederates to threaten Philadelphia or Baltimore while forcing the Yankees to fight the Southerners at a place of Lee's choosing. A decisive victory over the Army of the Potomac combined with even a temporary occupation of one of the North's major cities would quite possibly induce Britain and France to recognize the Confederacy.

Lee's plan had merit, and was probably the best alternative open to the Confederacy in September of 1862. However, three significant events would turn this promising campaign into a climactic battle that at best produced an unsatisfying draw for the Rebels and at worst very well might have annihilated the Army of Northern Virginia. These three events were: first, the ability of the Union army to recover from the debacle of Second Manassas far more rapidly than Lee imagined; second, the unwillingness or inability of large numbers of the Army of Northern Virginia to accompany Lee on his invasion of the North; and third, the Union possession of a document that gave the Yankee commander virtually the same information about Lee's intentions as the Virginian's own subordinates.

The first complicating factor in the Confederate invasion of Union territory was the re-emergence of George Brinton McClellan as commander of the primary army of the American republic. During the aftermath of Second Manassas, contrary to the advice of most of his Cabinet members, Lincoln restored the Young Napoleon to command in order to prevent a feared Confederate capture of Washington. Lincoln was hardly enthusiastic about the move, but his response to criticism was quite blunt; "we must use what tools we have. There is no man in the army who can man these fortifications and lick these troops of ours into shape half as well as McClellan. If he can't fight himself, he excels in making others fight." The Union troops marching back from Bull Run creek did not share their President's reservations. When a small party of clean uniformed, confident looking officers rode toward the retreating army, men passed the word down the ranks from regiment to regiment and soon cheers were exploding across the fields as George McClellan gratefully acknowledged the ovation from "his" army. A soldier in these ranks still remembered the day vividly twenty years later, "the scene that followed can be more easily imagined then described. From extreme sadness we passed in a twinkling to a delirium of delight. A Deliverer had come. A real 'rainbow of promise' had appeared suddenly in the dark political sky. Men danced and frolicked like school-boys and threw their caps high into the air, so glad were they to get their old commander again. General McClellan may have had opponents elsewhere; he had few, if any, among the soldiers he commanded."

While "Little Mac" secured Washington from attack and reorganized and revitalized shattered regiments to produce an army that was growing in power, the fighting strength of Lee's army was rapidly diminishing. The Confederate forces had been fighting an almost non-stop campaign against superior numbers for most of the spring and summer and large numbers of men were physically exhausted. The Southern quartermaster and commissary systems had almost totally collapsed when the army marched northward, so that thousands of men were barefoot and thousands more were subsisting on ears of green corn. Thus when Lee and his generals splashed across the Potomac River, possibly one fourth of the soldiers remained behind too tired, too hungry or too barefoot to really desire a fight with the Yankees on Northern soil. Most of these men didn't exactly desert; they simply waited around until their army came back south, but in the meantime, Lee was marching into enemy territory with only about 40,000 men, his lowest strength until the final march to Appomattox.

The third impediment to Confederate success was the famous "Lost Order." While the Rebel army was occupying Frederick, Maryland, Lee issued Special Orders 191 which narrated an ambitious series of simultaneous convergences which would support the Southern drive toward the Susquehanna River. The orders provided a detailed description of the disposition of the Confederate army for the next several days, and was sent to the division commanders who were scattered around different parts of Maryland. Apparently an unidentified member of Harvey Hill's staff decided to keep an extra copy of the orders as a souvenir, but then unaccountably used the paper as a wrapper for his cigars. Several days later, on Saturday morning September 13th, Federal troops marched into the town and used the same grounds for their campsite. Two Indiana soldiers spotted the welcome gift of several fine cigars and then noticed that the wrapper was marked with official Confederate stationary. This fantastic discovery was quickly moved up the chain of command to McClellan's headquarters, and one of the general's staff officers authenticated the handwriting of the Confederate officer who had made the copy. Little Mac exulted, "here is a paper with which if I cannot whip Bobby Lee I will be willing to go home."

Lee had provided his adversary with an opportunity that most commanders could only dream about. The Confederate advance toward the Susquehanna River while maintaining a line of communication back through Harpers Ferry down into Virginia had forced Lee to not just split his army into two detachments, but even more obligingly for an opponent, divide the Army of Northern Virginia into five highly vulnerable units. McClellan had a copy of his adversary's battle plans, could deploy over 80,000 men for an engagement and had the advantage of fighting on his home ground. All he had to do was move quickly and destroy the scattered elements of the rebel army one by one. However, the same caution, passion for detail and meticulous attention to organization that made McClellan an excellent defensive commander ensured that Lee would have more time to salvage this situation than most other Union generals would have given him. McClellan leisurely put his army corps in motion toward the passes through South Mountain that shielded the Confederate detachments, while heavily outnumbered units of Southerners tried to delay the Federal juggernaut.

The main body of the Union army began plunging through Turner's Gap and Fox's Gap, while a smaller force under William Franklin was dispatched several miles south to smash through Crampton's Gap and relieve the threatened Federal garrison at Harpers Ferry. Lee quickly dispatched Longstreet and Harvey Hill to temporarily delay the enemy coming through the northern passes, while Evander Law's column was rushed up from the Harpers Ferry assault force to confront Franklin. The contest for the passes occupied most of the day on September 14th, with the Confederates giving ground grudgingly as they bought time for Stonewall Jackson's men to invest Harpers Ferry and prepare to assault 12,000 Federals who had been ordered by Halleck into an almost untenable position. Franklin's corps was unable to smash through Law's defenders and the next morning, after the Union garrison commander was killed in the opening bombardment, a white flag was raised over the town and Lee had scored his most tangible gain of the invasion. At this point the Confederate commander probably should have realized the danger he was in, declared a victory with the capture of Harpers Ferry, and marched back into Virginia with his prisoners and booty. The loss of 12,000 men was almost as severe as the Union losses at Shiloh and Second Manassas, while up to this point, Southern casualties were extremely light. However, Lee seemed to revel in the idea of a confrontation with McClellan, and he ordered his scattered detachments to concentrate on Antietam Creek near Sharpsburg, Maryland, which was only a short distance from the Potomac River.

Lee's decision to fight was complicated and controversial. His entire army, even if it could be concentrated, was outnumbered 2 to 1 and was deployed with a major river to the rear which had only one ford in the vicinity. Probably the best that the Confederates could hope for was a drawn battle, yet Lee didn't even seriously consider a fallback to Virginia. Sharpsburg Ridge was a good defensive position to the extent that the high ground commanded the approach that McClellan would have to use to assault the Rebel army. However, if the Yankees ever managed to penetrate the Southern defense line, the Rebel army would be trapped and face almost certain annihilation. The climax of the first Confederate invasion of the North was an exciting and dramatic contest between two contending armies attempting to bring every possible man onto the battlefield before the critical period of the engagement.

At one point on the early afternoon of September 15th, McClellan had over 60,000 men facing only 18,000 Confederates across Antietam Creek, but the Northern commander wanted more men deployed, and as the newly arriving Federal troops filed into their assigned positions, the sun sank toward the horizon and Lee was spared for at least another day.

September 16th dawned clear and warm, a perfect day for a battle, but McClellan spent the day doing what the Young Napoleon did best. He organized, he supervised, he drew up complex plans of attack and he peered regularly at the Rebels through a powerful telescope. In fact, he did everything but fight. Much of Lee's army had still not reached the field and, whether he knew it or not, Little Mac had the manpower to overwhelm the Rebels and perhaps virtually end the war before nightfall. McClellan developed a solid plan, but waited just a little too long to implement his strategy. Hour by hour, the odds were narrowed as exhausted graycoats marched into Sharpsburg. The Northern battle plan revolved around seizing control of the three bridges that spanned the Antietam in the vicinity of Sharpsburg. McClellan ordered Hooker to march his corps across the upper bridge late on the 16th and deploy along a ridge about two miles above the town. This force would be in position to move down to Hagerstown Pike at dawn the next day and roll up Lee's left flank. While Stonewall Jackson's men on the left were being overwhelmed by Hooker, Ambrose Burnside would push across the lower bridge, about a mile and a half below Sharpsburg, and begin to roll up the enemy right flank, which seemed to be the most thinly occupied part of the Rebel defense line. Then, depending on whether Hooker or Burnside was making the most progress, the third portion of the Federal army would rush across the middle bridge, penetrate the Confederate center position and then sweep either left or right, depending on which flanking force arrived first to link up with them. McClellan was convinced that Lee simply didn't have enough men to hold all of his line in any depth, and when he tried to rush reinforcements to meet one threat, the Federals would merely break through somewhere else. If all the attacks were properly coordinated, the Union army could sweep toward the Potomac and demolish the Rebels before they could escape to Virginia.

While Lee spent most of the night of September 16th-17th peering toward Harpers Ferry as he waited for additional troops to arrive, his cavalry scouts reported Hooker's thrust across the upper bridge and forced the Confederate commander to respond to his first crisis of the battle. Jackson was reinforced with some newly arrived units and Stonewall concealed much of his force in the dense East Woods near the small Dunker Church, and then deployed the rest of his men adjacent to a cornfield on the grounds of the Miller Farm. Just as dawn broke on September 17th, Federal guns on a bluff on the far side of Antietam Creek began to pour shells into the relatively few Confederate units that were actually visible, and Hooker's men moved out from their cover of the West Woods to charge down Hagerstown Pike and gain control of the ground around the meeting house. The Federals were in the process of smashing through the forward defenders of the Confederate line when the commander of the center position, Harvey Hill, took an enormous gamble and rushed three of his brigades to help his brother-in-law. The Yankees swept down the turnpike, overran another Confederate position, and charged into the cornfield. As the Federals pushed their way through the shoulder high cornstalks, John Bell Hood's Texas Brigade rushed forward, leaving their unfinished breakfasts behind, and slammed into the startled bluecoats. Entire ranks of Yankees dropped from the Texans' first volleys, but then a brigade of Pennsylvanians under General George Meade hit the Lone Star men from another angle, and the 1st Texas regiment lost almost 190 of its 220 men to earn the dubious distinction of suffering the heaviest casualties of any unit during the war.

The bluecoats pushed their way through rows of corn that contained equally neat rows of dead and wounded soldiers, but when they came out the other side and headed for the Dunker Church, Jackson's carefully concealed units jumped up and chased the Unionists right back into the cornfield. However, this see-saw engagement quickly changed direction again when the Rebels came within range of a large number of Federal batteries deployed hub to hub and capable of annihilating any further southern advance. The morning was still young, and already men from both armies began to sense that this would be a particularly brutal struggle. As Hooker noted in a dispatch, "in the time that I am writing, every stalk of corn in the greater part of the field was cut as closely as could have been done with a knife, and the slain lay in rows precisely as they had stood in the ranks a few moments before. It was never my fortune to witness a more bloody, dismal battlefield." A few minutes later Hooker became one of those casualties, and as he was carried off the field, hope for a Union breakthrough in this area passed to General Joseph Mansfield's corps, which was now attempting to jump start the stalled Federal offensive. At about 7 A.M. Mansfield rode along his front line and shouted to the men of his XII Corps to finish the work started by Hooker's now exhausted 10 brigades. The Union corps commander went down in one of the first volleys and as the dying general was carried to safety, his men launched a furious charge at Jackson's main defense line.

Jackson sent Lee a desperate request for reinforcements, and the commander now robbed his right flank of its already thin screen of defenders to plug the growing gap in Stonewall's line. Mansfield's men burst through the Rebel lines at several places, but there were simply too many concealed Southerners bringing down bluecoats who couldn't locate their enemies, and finally Mansfield's men pulled back from the field with a loss of one quarter of the corps. Two Federal corps had been decimated with little gain except for an almost as appalling tally of Confederate casualties inflicted, and now McClellan deployed the largest corps in his army for a third attempt to smash Jackson. Edwin Sumner was brave, loud and not particularly subtle, but he was convinced that his men could break the stalemate, if they could only strike before the Rebels could recover from the first two rounds of the battle. Sumner hustled his men through a series of dense woodlands and he was able to achieve the rapid movement that he felt he needed. However, huge portions of his corps couldn't keep up and got lost in the woods, so that by the time that Sumner emerged to do battle he was down to a single division. John Sedgwick's bluecoats sprinted for the white church but Jubal Early's men slashed from one flank and Lafayette McLaws' troops jumped up from their cover and a third Federal attack simply evaporated. Before 9 o'clock on that bloody day, the Union army had lost 7000 men in three futile attacks and the Confederate flank was probably stronger than before the opening of the battle. If McClellan was going to make good on his prediction to whip Bobby Lee, he would have to win the battle from another location.

When the bloody confrontation north of Sharpsburg sputtered to a close, the next immediate threat to Lee's position developed along the Confederate center. Harvey Hill had ended up sending so many men to assist Jackson, that even when some new regiments arrived on the field, he could only deploy 7000 men to hold the line directly in front of the town. Most of these men were deployed in a sunken road which had been made into a stronger position when the Rebels dismantled every fence they could find to construct breastworks in front of the depressed line. Just as Hill's men were attempting to deflect Union attackers coming across the middle bridge, Sumner's two "lost" divisions came charging out of the woods and threatened to overwhelm the Rebel line. General Richard Anderson's division arrived from its long march from Harpers Ferry just in time to blunt a near breakthrough, but a few minutes later Anderson became one of the 18 Confederate and Union generals to be killed or wounded in this deadly contest. Hill gave orders to his units to refuse their lines by redeploying reserve regiments, but in the confusion of this maneuver part of Robert Rodes' brigade mistook the command for an order to retreat and pulled back long enough to leave an inviting gap in the Confederate defenses. Union Colonel Francis Barlow quickly spotted the hole and charged with two regiments, occupied a position of the sunken road, and smashed Confederates to left and right with a devastating enfilade fire. Lee's front line had essentially been sliced in two and any major thrust of McClellan's reserves across the middle bridge would have annihilated the remaining defenders. However, no fresh troops crossed the Antietam and the center of the battlefield entered the same stalemate as the left flank. Now the main Union hope was Burnside's four divisions who were expected momentarily to roll through the weak Confederate right and cut off the rebels from their sole Potomac crossing point.

Of the three major Union thrusts at Lee, this attack from the lower bridge was the most likely to succeed. The Confederate general had spent most of the morning stripping this already thin flank of most of its best units, until Burnside probably held a 20 to 1 advantage if he cared to use it. At around

9 A.M. the first of the 10,000 Union assault troops started running across the bridge, and promptly retreated when General Robert Toombs' 600 defenders opened fire. For almost six hours Burnside's exasperated engineers insisted that the Federals could simply wade across at a less defended point, but the Rhode Islander became more stubborn and insisted that he was going to take the bridge at all costs. Finally, at about 3 P.M. a fuming Pennsylvania colonel simply marched his regiment a short distance downstream, pushed his men across the relatively shallow stream and then encouraged a New York unit to come across and join him in a thrust at Toombs' rear. The Georgia brigadier realized that he had already more than accomplished Lee's expectations, and as he fell back Burnside finally got his priceless bridge.

A luckier general than Burnside still would have emerged as a hero, because the Rebel right flank had now almost vanished and his men could simply march over the river leading to the town and attack Lee in his unprotected rear. However, Burnside had the dangerous combination of little talent and even less luck, and just as his army was sweeping toward Sharpsburg, A.P. Hill's panting, exhausted soldiers completed a 17 mile march from Harpers Ferry in less than 8 hours and smashed into the unsuspecting Federals. Burnside had no idea that Hill was nearby and suddenly found his men retreating from thousands of rebels who came so hard and so fast they just wouldn't give the Yankees time to organize for a real fight. The bluecoats were soon back on the banks of Antietam Creek, happy to have escaped destruction and the third great Federal penetration had fizzled out into another stalemate.

Lee's line had been able to hold, but the Confederate general had committed every soldier he had to the battle and was now a general without reserves. On the other hand, McClellan had over 25,000 totally fresh troops but he was a general without audacity. A number of Union generals pleaded with the commander to thrust his rested brigades across the Antietam where they were sure to smash through Lee's defenses somewhere and, with any luck, reach the Potomac less than two miles away before the enemy could even attempt a withdrawal to Virginia. However, Little Mac was convinced that the always crafty Lee was hiding a large party of reserves in one of the dense woodlands and that when his men crossed they would be ambushed and annihilated. As McClellan noted, "at that moment—Virginia lost, Washington menaced, Maryland invaded—the national cause could suffer no risks of defeat." Several corps commanders almost convinced the Young Napoleon to change his mind but when he turned to his closest friend on the field, Fitz-John Porter, the defensive-minded corps commander shook his head and said "remember general, I command the last reserve of the last army of the republic" a wildly exaggerated statement that was able to convince McClellan to call it a day.

Lee's army was decimated, outnumbered, and barely able to man its lines, but almost in defiance, the Confederate general kept his army on the field all through the next day and almost dared his adversary to come out and get him. McClellan, in a decision that epitomizes this general's complex personality, finally concluded that he would attack Lee as soon as an additional 10,000 troops marching toward Sharpsburg arrived, which was expected to be two days later. However, before the Federals could make a move, Lee, as if he had proved his point, withdrew his army across the Potomac and prepared for the inevitable next campaign in Virginia. Lee had captured 12,000 Yankees, thrown a major scare into the Union government, and fought a much larger Federal army to a draw. However, the 11,000 men that the Confederacy lost on that single bloodiest day of the war would be much more difficult to replace than the 12,000 Northerners who had fallen on what one observer called "a landscape turned red!" McClellan had muffed the opportunity of a lifetime as he should have annihilated his opponent and essentially left Richmond open to Union capture. McClellan had certainly not won as much as he should have, but he did blunt one of the two prongs of Confederate invasions that could have led to Rebel independence. Now Lee would have to pull back toward Richmond, Abraham Lincoln would have the technical victory that he had needed to preface his Emancipation Proclamation, and the onus of invading the North would fall squarely on the Confederacy's western armies.

While Robert E. Lee was conjuring his vision of Confederate troops hanging the Stars and Bars from the city hall of Philadelphia or Baltimore, General Braxton Bragg was developing his own plan for having Southern bandsmen play "Dixie" in the public squares of Louisville or Cincinnati. Bragg had succeeded to the command of the largest Confederate army in the west when Pierre Beauregard, in the wake of his skillful withdrawal from Corinth, had taken a self-authorized sick leave which destroyed the last tenuous bonds of civility between the Creole general and his president. Braxton Bragg was appointed as the new commander of the Army of Tennessee and the prickly but energetic former artillerist attempted to confront a much larger, but increasingly scattered Union menace.

When Henry Halleck had been summoned to Washington to become the new commanding general of the army, his western command was essentially divided between Ulysses Grant and Don Carlos Buell. Grant had been named commander of a department embracing North Mississippi, West Tennessee and part of Kentucky, with 80,000 men under Generals McClernand, Sherman and Rosecrans available to him. However, during the summer of 1862, while Grant was already attempting to develop a strategy to capture Vicksburg, the key Confederate position on the Mississippi River, a combination of massive Rebel cavalry raids destroying railroad lines and a severe drought which made the Tennessee River useless as a supply line virtually immobilized this impressive force.

At the opposite end of the western theater, Buell was crawling eastward along a series of vulnerable railroad lines toward his ultimate objective, the capture of Chattanooga and the liberation of largely pro-Union East Tennessee from Confederate rule. Since Grant seemed immobilized while Buell was moving, albeit at a glacial pace, Bragg ultimately concluded that he could hold the hero of Fort Donelson in place with small forces under Generals Earl Van Dorn and Sterling Price, while the bulk of the Confederate army confronted the Army of the Ohio. Bragg's response to the Union advance was, on the whole, a masterful operation. First, during July Bragg rushed a small reinforcement to the garrison commander at Knoxville, Edmund Kirby Smith to hold that city in case Buell suddenly gained speed. Then he unleashed John Hunt Morgan and Nathan Bedford Forrest deep into the Union rear to cut supply lines, tear down telegraph systems and destroy railroad bridges vital to the operation of Buell's army. While the Yankees were occupied deflecting cavalry raids and repairing railroads, Bragg initiated the first large scale transfer of Confederate troops by railroad of the war. While artillery and cavalry units used their horses to travel from the Confederate base at Tupelo, Mississippi to Chattanooga, almost 30,000 infantrymen were handed seven days' cooked rations, ordered aboard a pre-assigned train and sent on a roundabout journey to Eastern Tennessee.

The combination of Federal occupation of large areas of the South and a rickety, poorly coordinated system of rail lines forced a journey of almost 800 miles all the way down to Mobile, Alabama and then back up through Georgia into Tennessee. The trip was roundabout but still far faster than marching, and the first units that had left Tupelo on July 23rd were in Chattanooga four days later. For several days a procession of jam-packed trains carrying cattle cars, freight cars, flat cars and passenger cars chugged around Missionary Ridge and rolled into the Confederate assembly point. Bragg arrived in Chattanooga on July 30th and Kirby Smith quickly rode down from Knoxville to plan a strategy for dealing with Buell. Bragg now began to finalize a plan that would not only take care of the Army of the Ohio, but recover Kentucky for the Confederacy and plant Rebel soldiers on the far side of the Ohio River. The western commander proposed a thrust up through Kentucky which would recruit thousands of Southern sympathizers in that state, capture the state capital of Frankfort so that a Confederate government could be installed, and then drive for Louisville before Buell could stop him. At that point the Confederates could pick the best possible ground to turn and smash the advancing Yankees and then leisurely proceed across the Ohio to capture Cincinnati and create panic throughout the Midwest. Bragg had perhaps the least cheery disposition of any leader in the Confederate army, but he realized that his gamble of staging a huge railroad born re-deployment had stolen a march on Buell and he gushed "everything is ripe for success; the country is aroused and expecting us. Buell's forces are much scattered and from all accounts much demoralized."

During much of August and September of 1862, Bragg's unusual cheerfulness was amply justified by a wave of Confederate successes. First, on August 30th while the Union army in Virginia was initiating the disastrous attacks against Stonewall Jackson, Edmund Kirby Smith's 12,000 veteran Confederates were thrusting toward the state capital of Kentucky. Union

General William Nelson, a lively, 300 pound former naval officer was roused from his bedroom in Lexington to rush south to Richmond, Kentucky and take charge of a 7000 man division of raw recruits who were the only significant troops in Smith's path. Nelson arrived just in time to see his command disintegrating as it withdrew toward the Richmond town limits with the Rebels slashing at their flanks. Nelson managed to set up a brief resistance around the town cemetery as the green Yankees used graveyard fences and headstones for cover. However, Nelson was wounded twice, the defense line collapsed, and almost 5200 Federal soldiers were lost at a cost of less than a tenth as many Rebel casualties.

Nelson escaped capture, but a short time later Buell lost this talented division commander when the ex-sailor got into a shouting match with a fellow general with the improbable name of Jefferson Davis. Nelson and Davis shared thin-skinned personalities and hair-trigger tempers and when the ex-mariner threw a crumpled up calling card in Davis' face, the Indiana political general retaliated by borrowing another officer's pistol and shooting his tormentor in his Louisville hotel. This loss was followed on September 16th with another battlefield disaster. Colonel J. T. Wilder had been assigned 4000 men to guard the key railroad depot of Munford, Kentucky from Rebel cavalry raids. Wilder had managed to beat back a Southern mounted attack, but just when he was congratulating his men on their success, the graycoat horsemen returned with most of Bragg's army and snapped up another large Federal detachment at virtually no loss. Thus by nightfall on September 16th, the eve of McClellan's thrust at Antietam Creek, Buell had lost one of his most talented generals and almost 10,000 men while inflicting almost no injury on the Confederate invaders.

The highwater mark of the Confederate thrust toward the Ohio River probably occurred at exactly noon on October 4th, 1862. At that moment the honorable Richard Haines was being sworn in as the Confederate governor of Kentucky in a demonstration of the bluegrass state's alliance with its Southern sisters. However, while Braxton Bragg looked on approvingly at the most tangible symbol of the success of his invasion, the whole illusion of an imminent drive beyond the Ohio came crashing down around the saturnine general. At about 1 P.M., as Haines delivered his inaugural speech lauding the now "permanent" bond between Kentucky and her sister states to the south, artillery fire drowned out the address and startled spectators turned to watch Union cannon shells drop into the suburbs of the town. Bragg had captured the Kentucky capital, but Buell had beaten him to Louisville and was concentrating every available bluecoat to throw the Rebels out of the state.

Buell had thrown a single division of green recruits to demonstrate against the Confederates in Frankfort, and Bragg mistakenly believed that the whole Union army was marching to recapture the state capital. Meanwhile, while over half of the Confederate army deployed to protect their new provisional government, most of Buell's army marched out of Louisville and headed directly for the remaining Rebels, who were scattered to the south of the city. The Union feint had worked to perfection and now 55,000 Federals in three corps were closing in on Leonidas Polk's badly outnumbered Southerners, with much of the rest of the Rebel army too far away to help him. While much of the driving force behind the future collision at Gettysburg was a Confederate search for shoes, the confrontation at Perryville was largely motivated by a Federal search for drinking water. The ongoing drought had eliminated most available water supplies and Union troops quickened their march when scouts brought back word of significant water available at Doctor's Creek outside the town of Perryville. However, while the Federals were hustling toward the stream, Polk's Southerners were determined to get the creek for their own use. Thus, during the late afternoon of October 7th, the Confederate invasion of Kentucky came to its climactic point in a furious battle for a minor body of water.

Leonidas Polk and William Hardee were able to concentrate about 16,000 Confederate soldiers on the outskirts of Perryville and by midnight on October 7th their desperate fighting had forced the Yankees to withdraw from the stream. However, all night long fresh units of Federals were converging on the far side of the creek, and in the pre-dawn hours of October 8th a massive Union charge threw the Southerners back into the woods. The stream itself had been captured by Brigadier General Philip Sheridan, who only a few months earlier had been a bored supply captain with little expectation for the future except becoming a bored supply major by the end of the war. However, a series of political maneuvers in this most political of wars propelled the thirty-one-year-old West Pointer to a general's stars only nine days before the battle, and the son of Irish immigrants was determined to prove that his promotion was no fluke. Sheridan's division gained extensive ground as it rolled up the Confederate defenders and soon the Yankees were astride Springfield Road which led directly into town.

While the massive Federal army began to deploy for a general advance, Bragg arrived on the field and began to quietly organize a stunning counteroffensive even though his men were outnumbered almost 4 to 1. At about 1 o'clock, with no advance warning, the Rebels burst from the cover of a dense woodland and smashed into General McCook's corps on the Federal left flank. Suddenly the whole Union advance came to a halt as the mostly inexperienced recruits of this Yankee unit raced toward safety in the rear. Two of the Federal commanders, James Jackson and William Terrill, were killed within minutes as Confederate generals Benjamin Chatham and Simon Bolivar Buchner drove their men through the panic-stricken recruits. Hundreds of Yankees surrendered, 15 cannons were captured, and only the timely intervention of Sheridan's well placed guns slowed the Rebel charge.

Bragg was pulling off a sleight of hand trick worthy of Robert E. Lee, as he was able to keep the Union center corps occupied with only 2500 of his own men, while the 23,000 men of the Federal right flank were discouraged from intervening by only Joseph Wheeler's 1200 cavalrymen and two fast moving Confederate cannons. The result of this deception was that the main part of the battle of Perryville was actually contested between about 13,000 Federals and a similar number of Confederates in a confused and fluid battle that inflicted enormous numbers of casualties. While the blue and gray lines ebbed and flowed, at least one Union brigade commander reported to Leonidas Polk for orders, and was promptly captured, and Polk himself tried to rally an Indiana regiment and barely escaped becoming a prisoner himself. Bragg simply didn't have enough men to annihilate the Federals and Buell didn't have enough talent to annihilate the badly outnumbered Rebels. Many of Buell's subordinates urged their commander to launch a night assault before the Confederates could bring in more units, but the general refused with a promise to consider an attack at daybreak. The next morning the Federals were ready to advance but Bragg was gone, as the Confederates withdrew toward an expected link-up with Kirby Smith and the rest of the army. In a strict sense, the Confederates had won the battle by inflicting 4300 casualties on their adversaries compared to only 3400 of their own, while preventing a much larger enemy from destroying them. On the other hand, the Confederate invasion of Kentucky and the corresponding hope of thrusting across the Ohio River into the heart of the North had now essentially died.

Bragg had been highly successful in turning the Federal army away from its objective of recapturing East Tennessee for the Union. Buell had to content himself and the government with merely throwing the Rebels out of Kentucky and preventing Confederate soldiers from marching into a panic stricken city of Cincinnati. On the other hand, the thousands of muskets that Bragg had carted into the commonwealth to distribute to Kentuckians eager to fight for the secessionist cause largely remained unused, as only a trickle of residents accepted the invitation to join the Rebel army. Once Bragg realized that no groundswell of recruits would be forthcoming while Buell was pulling in thousands of reinforcements from the threatened Midwest, all hope of breaking through to the Ohio River vanished and the Confederate commander started considering the advantages of spending the winter in more friendly territory.

During a two-week period around Halloween of 1862, two of the most organized, intelligent but overly cautious generals of the Union army were dismissed by an exasperated Abraham Lincoln. Don Carlos Buell and George Brinton McClellan had refused to accelerate their leisurely pursuit of two retreating Confederate armies and the more aggressive, but possibly less talented, William Rosecrans and Ambrose Burnside were given their chance to crush the Rebels and achieve hero status in the north. Buell and McClellan are fascinating figures to consider in the overall context of the war because neither man could be blamed for a fiasco on the level of Fredericksburg, Chancellorsville or Cold Harbor. Each of these men played a major role in blunting the most serious Confederate invasion of Union territory during the war, which was nothing less than an attempt to bring

Kentucky and Maryland into the Southern alliance, capture significant commercial centers in the North, and above all, secure British and French recognition of the Confederate States of America as a legitimate nation. Lee and Bragg had each escaped near annihilation when their opponents bungled golden opportunities to destroy a much smaller army. However, these Rebel armies were forced to withdraw back into the Southern heartland with numerous casualties who would be difficult to replace. Citizens of Maryland and Kentucky had waved a few Rebel flags, handed out cookies and buttermilk and even cheered a Southern army as it marched by, but few of these border states residents were willing to take the much larger risk of putting their lives on the line for the Confederate cause. This lack of enthusiasm in the border states merely exacerbated the disappointment among the Southern generals at not being able to reach the Susquehanna River or the Ohio River. How, as autumn chill really set in, the still famished, still ill-clad graycoats marched back into their own territory. A very calculating British government took a careful look at the just ended campaigns and decided to wait for another time to consider recognizing the Confederate nation. Meanwhile, a combination of a brilliantly timed Emancipation Proclamation and two crucial battles to be fought the next summer in Pennsylvania and Mississippi would guarantee that the potential day of recognition would never be so close at hand again. Buell and McClellan were gone, and their successors would throw the North into a crisis of confidence in the upcoming winter and spring, but the pendulum of war was gradually swinging in the Union direction. The most audacious Confederate gamble of the war had failed, and the Federal juggernaut would only be delayed, not stopped.

CHAPTER 27

# Alternative Strategies and Outcomes

## *Union and Confederate 1861-1862*

$T$he inability of either Union or Confederate offensives to end the conflict in 1862 ensured that the Civil War would be far bloodier and all-compassing than most people had imagined when the first shell arched high over Charleston harbor the previous April. The first year and a half of the war, from Fort Sumter to Perryville, caused more American casualties than the Revolution, War of 1812 and Mexican War combined, and yet was merely the opening act of an even more brutal bloodletting that would terminate at Appomattox Court House. However, while this period was only one stage of a larger conflict, it is fascinating to speculate about the implications for the future of American society if either Union or Confederacy had been able to win a clear cut victory, before the nature and scope of the war began to change in the wake of the Emancipation Proclamation and the even greater mobilization of men and resources that began in 1863.

A consideration of possible alternative scenarios of events that occurred in 1861 and 1862 virtually encourages that ever tantalizing question—could either North or South have actually won the Civil War during its early stage, and if that is the case, which factors might have produced this quite different outcome? While the Civil War fits into a four-year epoch that coincidentally also almost perfectly spans the Presidential term of Abraham Lincoln, there is nothing in historical precedent that defines civil wars as four-year struggles. The Spanish Civil War of the 1930's lasted only little more than half as long as the American version while the English Civil War, measured from the rising of the King's standard in 1642 to the execution of Charles II in 1649 was nearly twice as long as the War Between the States. Thus, theoretically, the Civil War could have ended in one campaign in a sort of bloodier version of Shay's Rebellion or the Whiskey Rebellion, or could have degenerated into a decade-long guerilla war that would have devastated even more of the American republics. The authors believe that there are several points during 1861 and 1862 in which either Union or Confederacy could definitely have won the war with even a modest improvement of leadership skills, fighting skills or even luck at a key moment of crisis.

There appears to be at least two battlefield situations in which the South might have turned a single military victory into a much more comprehensive triumph against the Union government and both of these opportunities revolve around the engagements near Manassas. The first significant opportunity for Confederate independence seems to emerge in the hours immediately following the Union retreat from Henry House Hill and the ensuing withdrawal toward Washington. Most accounts of the aftermath of this battle stress the disorganized status of the victorious Confederates, the onset of a rainstorm on the night of the battle and the reluctance of Joseph Johnston and Pierre Beauregard to strike immediately at the enemy capital. However, the arguments against the feasibility of an immediate Southern counter-offensive seem to ignore a number of key points. First, the victorious Confederates didn't really need to re-organize their whole army for a strike at Washington. When Stonewall Jackson insisted to Jefferson Davis that he could capture the capital with 10,000 fresh troops he was probably not being unrealistic. Forty-seven years earlier a British expeditionary force had captured Washington with only 4000 men, even though they had been opposed by far more Americans who were also far more disorganized. Substantial numbers of Confederate troops had not been committed during the battle of Bull Run and if presented with a clear cut objective—an assault on Washington—they might have found the road to the capital and the White House relatively open in the immediate aftermath of the battle. Second, while it was raining immediately after the battle, there is no reason to expect that the roads were impassable, both Confederate and Union armies frequently marched long distances under far worse conditions at other points during the war.

Quite simply, the victorious Confederate army didn't have to permanently capture Washington; all they had to do was destroy much of the credibility of the new Lincoln administration by either capturing the President or, at the very least, forcing the Republican administration into an embarrassing flight from the city similar to the event that haunted the Madison presidency a half century earlier. Irvin McDowell was not the incompetent bumbler that some contemporary accounts described, but it is unlikely that he had the talent to rapidly re-organize a panicky, disgruntled army to meet an immediate, slashing attack of victorious Rebels against the Union capital. The sight of a Confederate flag waving over the Capitol or White House, for even a brief time, would hardly have gone unnoticed in European seats of power, and it is just possible that even temporary loss of Washington in the aftermath of the chaos and panic at Manassas might have encouraged influential Northerners to pressure the administration to negotiate the least embarrassing separation possible. However, the window of opportunity for the Confederates was relatively brief, because once George McClellan arrived and took command of the defenses of Washington, the capital city became virtually invulnerable to Rebel assault. Over a year would pass before a Confederate battlefield victory would provide the opportunities for exploitation that First Manassas offered.

This window re-opened for a time during the summer of 1862, when John Pope took over command of the newly established Army of Virginia and Henry Halleck became the new commanding general of the American army. Pope shared much of Lee's energy and audaciousness and, despite his numerous character flaws, seemed aggressive enough to use the large Union numerical superiority to the best advantage. However, once Halleck ordered the Army of the Potomac to evacuate its base on the James River, Lee almost literally began to run circles around Pope and his army. The Army of Virginia commander spent most of August, 1862 moving one step ahead of annihilation. His deployment of his forces in the dead end position of the confluence of the Rappahannock and Rapidan Rivers almost allowed Lee to trap the whole force; his poorly coordinated charges against Jackson's corps at Groveton, with virtually no knowledge of the whereabouts of Long-street's men, invited disaster and the poorly organized retreat toward Washington could have been turned into a rout if the Rebels had been able to get around his flanks in more strength.

While many accounts of the Civil War emphasize the Confederate opportunities in their two-pronged invasion of the North in the autumn of 1862, the authors believe that the key to possible Southern success was actually in the period immediately before this offensive. When Lee and Bragg advanced into Maryland and Kentucky, their opportunity for major military success was probably considerably less than commonly assumed. Each Rebel commander was essentially invading enemy territory with an army of 40,000 men while Buell and McClellan could draw from manpower pools that were at least three times as large. Lee was hindered by the fact that a large portion of his army was straggling through Virginia when he crossed the Potomac, while Bragg was handicapped by the need to leave almost half of his army behind in Mississippi to counter any threat from Grant. Thus the Confederate offensive of 1862 committed far less than the full strength of the Southern armies, and ran the risk of subjecting either Lee or Bragg to virtual annihilation if the Federals were able to concentrate their forces and cut off a Rebel retreat back to their own territory. A much more achievable scenario would have been an all out attempt to destroy Pope's army on its way back to Washington after Second Manassas with a strike at the capital before McClellan arrived to restore the city's defenses. During the very end of August and the very beginning of September, 1862, the capital was at one of its most vulnerable points and a major propaganda victory that would have been achieved by even a temporary capture of Washington was probably more achievable than the riskier, and ultimately unsatisfying, longer range invasion of the North.

While the Confederates seem to have had two major opportunities to turn battlefield victories into war winning campaigns, it appears that the Unionists had at least three noticeable possibilities of winning the war before the end of 1862. First, while the aftermath of First Manassas presented a spectacular opportunity for the Confederacy, the initial stage of the Bull Run campaign held enormous possibilities for an early Federal victory in the war. Irvin McDowell's basic strategy to get between the armies of Joseph Johnston and Pierre Beauregard before they could concentrate was actually an excellent plan that provided a real opportunity for defeating the two fractions of the Confederate army in detail and then marching on Richmond and capturing the city before the Rebel Congress ever had a chance to hold an official session. If Patterson's army had accomplished even part of its mission of occupying Johnston in the Shenandoah Valley, and if McDowell's army had marched at a leisurely instead of a glacial pace and arrived at Centreville even a day earlier, the Union army would have almost definitely had the upper hand in a battle that the Federals almost won anyway.

A second tangible opportunity for total Union victory emerged in the late spring of 1862, culminating in McClellan's advance on Richmond. Despite the brave speeches of Jefferson Davis that the South would fight to its last soldier, it is abundantly clear that the Confederacy was on the ropes by May of 1862 and the capture of Richmond at that time might very well have ended the war with the restoration of the Union. The first four months of 1862 had produced a succession of losses or near defeats for the Rebels and it appears that a significant number of Southerners were questioning the whole concept of a secessionist republic, while at the same time the Federal government was offering peace terms that essentially restored Southern citizens to all of the rights they had enjoyed in 1860. Thus the specter of a disorganized Confederate government in flight from the captured Rebel capital combined with extremely generous peace terms might have encouraged the reversal of the process of secession and the end of the war, before emerging Southern heroes such as Robert E. Lee and Stonewall Jackson began to convince Southerners that maybe they actually could defeat the Yankees in open battle. McClellan's retreat from the gates of Richmond was not so much a military disaster as a propaganda victory for the Davis government, which proved it could defend its capital and produce an emerging genius such as Lee in the process.

The final opportunity for the Union to win the war before the onset of the Emancipation Proclamation and its attendant complications occurred during the Antietam campaign. The authors believe that Lee made one of his greatest blunders of the war in his underestimation of McClellan's ability to concentrate an army quickly enough to severely threaten the Confederate invasion of Maryland, and in his subsequent insistence that he could defeat the Yankees at Sharpsburg with only a fraction of their strength. An earlier

Federal assault, a better coordinated actual Union attack or a willingness on the part of McClellan to commit his massive corps of reserves at the climax of the battle should have annihilated a large portion of the Rebel army and quite probably trapped the whole Confederate force on the wrong side of the river. The authors are convinced that the elimination of Lee and his Army of Northern Virginia from the chessboard of the war could only have resulted in a far earlier Confederate defeat. This army was simply irreplaceable and would have left the defense of Virginia to a scattering of regiments that even the cautious McClellan could not resist attacking. The war again came tantalizingly close to ending on that bloody September afternoon, but McClellan's partial failure ensured that another such opportunity would not emerge for many months to come.

While the prospect of turning a battlefield victory into a maneuver to end the war is the most visible example of alternative scenarios, the authors believe that each side also possessed a "secret weapon" that, if properly utilized, might have produced a victory before the end of 1862. For the South, this weapon was "King Cotton" and its potential impact on dramatically strengthening the Confederate arsenal at a key period of the war. During the early months of the War Between the States, the Confederacy essentially held two crucial advantages over the Union adversary. First, the South had a large number of males who were far more experienced in riding, shooting and marching than their Yankee counterparts. Second, the South possessed the most valuable source of obtaining hard currency in North America, a virtual monopoly on one of the most vital ingredients of the ongoing Industrial Revolution—cotton.

Modern oil producing nations frequently utilize their enormous petroleum assets to purchase weapons systems that they may not be able to manufacture within their own society. The result, in at least some cases, is a country with relatively few factories but possessing extremely advanced armaments. The authors believe that the Confederacy of 1861 had a similar opportunity to utilize the nation's enormous cotton assets in order to purchase the most advanced naval and military weapons from European manufacturers. While the Davis administration, generally supported by popular opinion, decided to withhold their cotton supplies from France and England in order to provoke those nations to force their way through a largely paper Union blockade, the much more effective use of their primary asset would have been to purchase ironclad rams, fast firing rifles and modern artillery pieces from Europe. At that point, the Confederates could have entered the early battles with the Yankees with superior weapons and a much better chance to win the many relatively evenly contested engagements of 1861 and 1862.

The Confederacy that was challenging the power of the United States in 1861 was faced with a predicament similar to the Japanese Empire in 1941. Each nation essentially had to win a rapid, early series of victories over an unprepared adversary, before the enormous economic and industrial might of that nation was fully mobilized. If the Confederacy had been able to arm and equip the many volunteers it had to turn away early in the war; and even better, arm and equip them with weapons and material that was superior to the Federals, they would have had a much better opportunity to win the conflict at that time than when, two or three years later, the United States was fully geared up for a truly modern war effort. The authors feel that one of the most devastating mistakes on the part of the Davis administration was the failure of that government to convince the South's planters to trade their cotton crop for Confederate bonds and then use that product to gain a military advantage when it most counted. An army that turned away thousands of volunteers for lack of weapons, and then armed many of the men it did accept with flintlock rifles, shotguns and fowling pieces had almost voluntarily thrown away one of its few tangible advantages.

The authors believe that the Federal government also had access to a "secret weapon" which, at least during the first stage of the war, was frittered away just as idiotically as the Confederates jettisoned the cotton weapon. At the outset of the war, at least seven armaments companies approached the Federal government with offers to mass produce either single shot breech loaders or repeating rifles. The prospect of arming the Union army with these new weapons offered the possibility of an enormous advantage over the rebel adversaries, since the Confederates had no capability of manufacturing breech loading weapons. The muzzle loading rifled muskets that dominated the arsenals of both armies at the outbreak of war presented two significant disadvantages. First, they simply did not fire very rapidly. Under battle conditions, a typical infantryman could get off about two rounds a minute which was no better than soldiers of a century earlier. Second, it was very difficult to reload a muzzle loading weapon without somehow exposing yourself to enemy fire and even more difficult to load while you were running across a battlefield. On the other hand, the newly developed breech loaders largely overcame both of those handicaps. A single shot Sharps breech loader could fire 10 to 12 rounds a minute, a Spencer repeating rifle could get off 7 shots in 10 seconds, and a 16 shot Henry magazine rifle was designed for a rate of fire of 120 rounds in 3-5 minutes, which provided one soldier with the firepower of ten opponents armed with muskets. Equally important, it was possible to fire breech loaders from a prone position to provide additional cover from enemy marksmen while an attacking unit could fire on the run rather than stopping every few feet to reload or merely depend on a bayonet.

The ability of Northern manufacturers to mass produce this latest generation weapon was one of the most substantial potential advantages the Union held over the Confederacy, and yet the Federal government virtually ignored the potential implications of these rifles. While Lincoln expressed some genuine interest in this weapon, his Secretary of War and commanding general bent over backwards to make sure these weapons weren't introduced. Simon Cameron spent most of his term in Lincoln's Cabinet with the

vague odor of corruption hanging around him and apparently the manufacturers of the standard muzzle loaders had the ear of the Secretary and were
able to ensure that their contracts would be given priority over the "new
fangled" producers of breech loaders. Also, the seventy-five-year-old Winfield Scott, who admittedly still had a clear grasp of the intricacies of
strategy, simply couldn't conceive of commanding an army that didn't have
its trusty muskets. As Scott insisted, "the muzzle loader is, has been, and
always will be the American soldier's primary weapon. Breech loaders are
not practical for military usage. They would spoil our troops by allowing
them to be too fast, thus wasting ammunition."

The result of this short sighted and parsimonious perspective was that
hundreds of thousands of Union volunteers went off to war well clothed,
well fed and well shod, but carrying weapons that were essentially totally
obsolete. Quite simply, the Federal armies went into battle without the
benefit of the latest generation of weapons that was then available to a
modern, industrialized nation and thus squandered an enormous military
advantage that was clearly available. A number of historians have lauded
the dependability and firepower of the last generation of muzzle loaders—the percussion rifled-musket. These were excellent weapons, for muzzle loaders, but commending their suitability is very similar to commending
an American government in 1941-42 that would have gone to war with
Germany and Japan still using the last generation of biplanes as its first line
fighters and bombers. The last generation of biplanes were excellent war-
planes when compared to World War I model Nieuports and Sopwith
Camels, but the policy makers of 1941 realized that even the latest model
biplane was no substitute for the monoplanes that were already in general
use by Britain, Germany and Japan.

As leaders such as Cameron and Scott resigned or retired, the Federal
government began to change its policy by initially providing cavalry units
with breech loaders and then supplying the new weapons to a growing
number of infantry regiments in the last stage of the war. The impact of this
transition was clearly evident in the battles of Cedar Creek, Franklin and
Nashville in which units armed with the new weapons were able to inflict
casualties at a rate of over 4 to 1 over the numbers they lost. It is fascinating
to imagine the implications of a similar advantage of firepower in the earlier
battles of the war. General E. Porter Alexander perhaps best summarizes the
awesome potential of this weapons system from a Confederate point of
view. "There is reason to believe that had the Federal infantry been around
from the first even with the breech loaders available in 1861, the war would
have terminated within a year."

If we assume that the Union of Confederacy actually could have won the
war before the end of 1862, the next logical question must be; what would
have been the consequences of a victory by either South or North at this
particular point in time? Each scenario provides the possibility of a quite
different path for the development of North America. First, the authors

believe that a Confederate victory relatively early in the war may have produced different implications than even a Rebel victory in 1863 or 1864. For example, we believe that a Confederate nation that received its independence in the wake of a Democratic victory in the North in 1864 would have had far more modest ideas concerning the extent of Confederate territory than a Davis administration that was dictating terms from a captured White House in 1861 or 1862. A Rebel victory during the first stage of the war that had been gained from battlefield successes would most likely have emboldened the Confederate government to demand the annexation of Maryland, Kentucky and Missouri as legitimate slave state members of the Southern republic, even though a probable majority of the population of those states was pro-Union. In addition, since the District of Columbia would then be fully surrounded by Confederate states, it is equally likely that the Federal government would have been forced to cede the capital to a Southern government that firmly believed that it was the real descendant of the original American republic. The authors feel that this scenario would have produced a better than even chance of some form of renewed warfare in North America within a decade of Confederate independence.

The annexation of the border states and the national capital would have created a festering feeling of ill will between the newly separated republics, not unlike the hostility between France and Germany between 1870 and 1939. The border states would like have become the American equivalent of Alsace and Lorraine, with Northern newspapers publicizing the misery of loyal border state Unionists who were forced to either live under an alien yoke or leave their homes and farms forever, while Southern journals insisted on the historic solidarity of all slave states. This emotional tinderbox would have been fanned regularly by the sight of the Confederate flag waving over the White House and Capitol, a constant reminder to Northerners that their noble experiment had been amputated and the city named after their greatest hero occupied by a foreign power.

Even in the unlikely situation that this daily provocation couldn't start a renewed conflict, there might have been ample opportunity for Northerners to lash out in a totally different direction. There is a fairly high probability that any triumph of the secessionist cause in the first two years of the war would have been tied to some level of European, especially British, recognition or intervention in the conflict. If the British government had used a theoretical series of Confederate victories to place diplomatic, naval or military pressure on the Union to concede Southern independence, it is not unlikely that the citizens of the United States would have been clamoring for revenge against Perfidious Albion. The most likely target for American vengeance would have been the Canadian provinces, whose forcible annexation to the Union would not only have allowed revenge against Britain but would have provided some compensation for the loss of the seceded states. Thus the prospect of a replay of the War of 1812, with larger armies, upgraded weapons and naval duels between steamships and ironclads might have been the closing drama of the duel at Fort Sumter.

The Union cause had an equal chance to triumph in 1861 or 1862 and that event might have produced an equally fascinating series of alternative developments. A Confederate surrender before the end of 1862 would have produced a reunion of North and South under very different circumstances than the conditions imposed after Appomattox. Southerners who were reconciled with the Federal government during 1861 or 1862 would have come back into the Union with the legal ability to own slaves and with a significant voice in the next Congressional and Presidential elections. Thus it is possible that the person who would have gained the most mileage out of a Union victory early in the contest would not have been Abraham Lincoln but his Democratic opponent in the 1864 election. While Lincoln would certainly have gained the valuable aura of the President who restored the Union, it is also a statement of fact that a reunited American republic had more Democrats than Republicans on its voting lists and if the Democrats could have been able to avoid the factionalism of 1860 in the next election, they might very well have won. The authors believe that if the Union had won the war at any point in 1862, it is almost certain that the Democratic nominee would have been the same person who actually did carry the standard in 1864—George Brinton McClellan. The Young Napoleon's luke-warm attitude about abolition, belief in avoiding making war on noncom-batants and generally conciliatory policy toward Southerners most likely would have gained him far more votes below the Mason-Dixon Line than Lincoln and very well may have propelled him to the term in the White House that he barely missed in the actual election of 1864.

A second irony of a theoretical Union triumph during the first stage of the war is that a Confederate surrender would have left untouched the very cause of the conflict in the first place—the institution of slavery. The authors believe that any termination of the secessionist movement before the end of 1812 would have encouraged Lincoln to pursue his stated beliefs of 1860, which were the prohibition of slavery in the territories and the support for some form of gradual, compensated emancipation. Thus many Northern abolitionists would have been thrown into the uncomfortable position of realizing that the very success of the Union cause would have slowed down the impulse toward the immediate emancipation of the slaves. If large numbers of Americans during the 1990's expressed dissatisfaction with the outcome of a Persian Gulf war that produced victory for the United States but failed to unseat the tyrant who was acknowledged as the primary cause of the conflict; it is not difficult to imagine the frustration of significant numbers of anti-slavery Northerners who watched the victory parades in their town squares and then observed slave owners restored to their positions of power in Washington.

A final irony of this first stage of the war is that what was perhaps the most critical event of this period, the succession of Robert E. Lee to command of the Army of Northern Virginia after the wounding of Joseph Johnston, not only insured that McClellan wouldn't capture Richmond, it also guaranteed a far more devastated South than if the Young Napoleon hadn't been prevented from virtually ending the war at that decisive moment in time. Lee's audacious and brilliant leadership during the Seven Days campaign saved the Confederacy from almost certain defeat and purchased an additional 33 months of existence for the Southern republic. However, the cost of that 33 months of life was exorbitant, for the Southern people suffered almost 1500 deaths for each extra week of nationhood and in the end suffered a shattering destruction of their whole society and way of life. Lee bought time for his imperiled republic, but this talented general was not quite able to prevent the Confederacy from succumbing to the power of the Union. A less superb commander might have failed to prevent a Rebel defeat in 1862, which in turn would have forced the Southern states to return to the Union in a far healthier state than they exhibited three terrible years later.

CHAPTER 28

# The Winter (and Spring)
# of Union Discontent

## 1862-1863

$T$he first snowstorm of the oncoming Virginia winter provided a backdrop
for the first in a series of events that would make the winter and spring of
1862-63 one of the bleakest periods of the war for Union sympathizers. Late
on the night of November 7th, 1862, General C.P. Buckingham arrived in a
blinding snowstorm at Rectortown, Virginia after a harrowing train ride
from Washington. Buckingham went to the tent of General Ambrose Burnside and the two men then walked over the icy paths to the headquarters of
George Brinton McClellan, with the purpose of notifying him that Lincoln
had relieved him of the command of the Army of the Potomac. Three days
later McClellan waved farewell to his army in one of the most emotional
episodes of the war. One Union officer insisted "every heart was filled with
love and grief; every voice was raised in shouts expressive of devotion and
indignation; and when the chief had passed out of sight, the romance of war
was over for the Army of the Potomac."

McClellan's removal was the final part of a two-stage purge of Federal
army commanders put in motion by Abraham Lincoln two weeks earlier
when he had fired Don Carlos Buell from command of the Army of the
Cumberland for his lack of vigor in pursuing Braxton Bragg after the battle
of Perryville. Now it was McClellan's turn to meet the fate of generals who
Lincoln determined were afflicted with "the slows." The President summed
up his feelings about his most exasperating general when he insisted, "he is
a pleasant and scholarly gentleman. He is an admirable engineer, but he
seems to have a special talent for a stationary engine." Now bolder but
somewhat unproven men such as William Rosecrans and Ambrose Burnside
would get their opportunity to become the heroes of the hour.

Burnside was honest, popular and modest, but his appointment was a surprise to both Union and Confederate generals. His handling of a brigade at Bull Run had been less than superb, his failure to capture Lower Bridge at Antietam had probably cost the North a victory, and his highly publicized victories in North Carolina were often won against feeble opposition. Burnside didn't really want the command and felt that he was not qualified for such an enormous responsibility, but when rumors began to seep out that Joseph Hooker was also in contention, a number of Union generals begged the Rhode Islander to take the post if offered. Contrary to the popular conception that McClellan had given up any thought of forcing the enemy to battle before spring, the Young Napoleon had been in the process of finalizing a strike at one wing of the Rebel army based at Culpeper before Jackson's detachment camped in the Shenandoah Valley could respond to the threat. As General Longstreet noted "this was the move about which we felt serious apprehension and we were occupying our minds with plans to meet it...... by interposing between the corps of Lee's army he would have secured strong ground and advantage of position." However, once McClellan was dropped, the plan dropped with him and Burnside secured a reluctant approval from Lincoln and Halleck for an entirely different venture.

The new Union commander proposed to ignore Lee entirely and instead move down the Rappahannock to Falmouth, which was opposite the colonial town of Fredericksburg. Burnside assured Lincoln that if he could use pontoon bridges to get across the river at top speed, he would be nearer to Richmond than Lee was and by advancing along the railroad he could compel his adversary to fight in the open or else capture Richmond before the enemy could get into the entrenchments. While Lincoln seemed pleased to have an aggressive general who couldn't wait to march his army southward, the President was already coming to the conclusion that capturing Richmond was far less important than destroying Lee's army, and Burnside's plan seemed to reverse that order of priorities. Nevertheless, the new general was given the go-ahead and the newly reorganized three grand divisions of the Army of the Potomac lurched toward Falmouth with the assumption that the crucial pontoons would be waiting for them on arrival. Unfortunately, orders from Washington were delayed seven days, the necessary mule trains arrived late, and it was November 27th before there was any equipment available to span the Rappahannock. By this late date the Confederate regiments were already filing into almost impregnable positions on the far side of the river, and Lee was handed a golden opportunity for an easy victory which was so obvious that Joseph Johnston complained of his eastern counterpart, "what luck some people have! Nobody will ever come to attack me in such a place!"

A more talented and imaginative Union general would have written off the non-arrival of the pontoons as bad luck and immediately initiated a process of developing an alternative plan to get around the rebels. However, Burnside was neither talented nor imaginative and he soon became fixated on the drama of marching his whole 119,000 man army across on the delayed pontoon bridges and confronting the Confederates in front of their six miles of fortified ridges. The result was a disaster waiting to happen as the Rhode Islander simply wasn't sophisticated enough to understand that Lee had packed 78,000 men and 250 guns on a stretch of high ground that offered such a clear field of fire that Confederate artillerist E. Porter Alexander noted, "a chicken could not live on that field when we open on it."

During the pre-dawn hours of the frigid morning of December 11th, the 1600 Confederate defenders who had remained behind in the town of Fredericksburg began to hear the distinctive sounds of engineers constructing a pontoon bridge on the far side of the Rappahannock. As each successive pontoon was launched over the creaking layer of ice that coated the river, William Barksdale's Mississippians fired a few blind shots into the darkness and waited for sunrise for the real action to begin. By 10 o'clock engineers were dropping at regular intervals into the river and the increasingly impatient Burnside ordered Henry Hunt's 150 guns on Stafford Heights to bombard the town. In less than an hour 5000 shells smashed into the town as walls crashed down, houses crumpled and roofs collapsed, but the Rebel sharpshooters were well protected in cellars and piles of rubble and only a risky cross river assault by four regiments using the pontoons as landing craft even began to threaten the defenders. All that Thursday afternoon a vicious house to house fight swayed back and forth through the town until Barksdale was ordered to pull back to the main defenses after dark.

Burnside spent most of December 12th marching his enormous army across the river into the newly occupied town while Lee carefully surveyed his imposing defense line. The Union commander finalized an attack plan in which Sumner's Grand Division assisted by most of Hooker's command would launch a thrust against the Confederate left anchored by a ridge called Marye's Heights, while Franklin's Grand Division and the remainder of Hooker's men would assault Stonewall Jackson's forces on the Southern right. Burnside seems to have had some vague assumption that Franklin's men would be able to smash through their objectives and then wheel and hit Longstreet's part of the line from the flank, while the main Union assault force kept the rebels occupied from the front. As General Alexander noted, "the Confederates were facing the strongest and best equipped army that had ever stood upon a battle-field in America. But our army was better organized and stronger than ever before, concentrated at exactly the right moment and was as confident and elated as if the victory had already been won."

Saturday, December 13th, 1862 dawned foggy and cold with a fresh dusting of snow enhancing the surrealistic atmosphere created by the sound of marching bands and thousands of boots moving on the ground that could not be seen from the heights above. Suddenly, around 10 A.M., the fog lifted to reveal one of the most dramatic spectacles of the war—over a hundred thousand blue coated warriors advancing in perfect unison as if on a parade. These thousands of assault troops were focusing their attention on the imposing Confederate positions along the barely visible ridges that were separated by about 1000 yards of open field from the Yankee soldiers marching out of Fredericksburg. However, the Federals didn't yet realize that Longstreet had placed much of his firepower behind a quarter-mile-long stone wall at the base of the ridge. This shoulder-high barrier, which fronted one of the ubiquitous sunken roads that every other Civil War battle seemed to feature, was packed with four ranks of riflemen who were under orders to fire in relays to maximize their impact. The result of this deployment was that Charles Sumner's perfectly aligned bluecoats were about to get a preview of the carnage that would decimate a future generation of Europeans on the battlefields of the Great War.

The Federal assault was dramatic, energetic, and the outcome was never in doubt. The attack was a fearful succession of attempted advances by increasingly fragmented units which were fed into a killing machine in a piecemeal fashion that kept running up a larger body count by the minute. Howard's corps lost 900 in 30 minutes of futile charges, while French's single division lost 1200 men in ten minutes less. Winfield Scott Hancock's division soon topped that count in a futile forward thrust which left 2000 bluecoats dead or wounded in a quarter of an hour. During the last few assaults wounded Federals tried to grasp the legs or ankles of the next wave of attackers to keep them from advancing, while Lee, who seemed genuinely stunned by the extent of the slaughter, made his famous remark that "it is well that war is so terrible or we would grow too fond of it."

Only on Jackson's front was there the slightest possibility of a Union success, since this part of the line offered less natural protection and a lesser density of men on the firing line. General George Meade's division actually burst through a vulnerable point in the Rebel defenses, but his 4500 men received no backup support and they were only saved from an annihilating counterattack when they ran back to the cover of the Union artillery. Burnside alternated between extreme grief at the fate of so many of his men and an obstinate desire to attack again the next morning, but a group of his subordinates calmed their commander down enough for him to digest the enormity of the disaster. The casualty count was one of the most one-sided of the war, as almost 13,000 Federal troops were lost in this useless assault, while the Confederate defenders had suffered slightly more than 4000 killed and wounded. The victory was so complete that when Lee went to Richmond to suggest new military operations, a number of legislators and cabinet members insisted that the war was virtually over and that "in thirty or forty days we will be recognized and peace proclaimed." While Lee did not share this level of optimism, it would be hard to fault those Southerners who felt that the Union cause was tottering on the brink of disaster.

While Burnside engaged in his disastrous attempt to maneuver his way into Richmond, his western counterpart, Ulysses S. Grant, was facing an equally frustrating challenge in his approach to the Mississippi bastion of Vicksburg. If Richmond was the nerve center of the Confederate government, Vicksburg was the bridge between the tenuously linked wings of the Confederate republic. A successful Federal advance on this high bluffed city meant that the eastern half of the secessionist republic would lose forever the livestock, food and military recruits that the vast trans-Mississippi region could provide, while the Yankees could then squeeze the remaining states from both east and west. However, during the final month of 1862, Grant's plan to capture this vital objective was unraveling at an alarming rate.

During the fall of 1862 Grant had begun following the line of the Mississippi Central Railroad southward in an attempt to come in on Vicksburg from the east, while his most trusted subordinate, William Tecumseh Sherman, was organizing an amphibious expedition that was designed to strike the "back door" of the city via the Yazoo River. Grant's basic plan was to keep Confederate General John Pemberton's main army occupied with his 30,000 men threatening the rebel base at Grenada while Sherman's 30,000 troops slammed into a minimally defended Chickasaw Bayou that was on the outskirts of Vicksburg. However, each element of the plan fell apart in rapid order.

First, Grant's initial manpower advantage over Pemberton was greatly diminished when Jefferson Davis ordered one of Braxton Bragg's strongest divisions to march west and shore up the defenses of Vicksburg. Bragg's loss of 25% of his infantry would produce repercussions very shortly in Tennessee, but 9000 additional graycoats provided an enormous complicating factor for Union aims in Mississippi. While Grant adjusted his plans to take into account the Rebel reinforcements, his rear was being threatened by another part of Bragg's command. The Union supply line stretched all the way from Grant's advance base at Oxford, Mississippi back to Columbus, Kentucky, over 175 miles away. This over-extended line practically invited a Confederate attack and the emerging Rebel cavalry leader Nathan Bedford Forrest was preparing for one of his most dramatic exploits.

Forrest, a self-made millionaire who carried the unsavory aroma of his slave trading activities, was a natural born military leader who consistently bested opponents with far more formal military training, and would ultimately attain virtual legend status in the Confederate pantheon. On December 11, 1862, as Burnside's men were pushing their pontoons across the Rappahannock, Forrest left Columbia, Tennessee with 2100 newly recruited horsemen, who were mainly armed with shotguns and flintlock muskets. Four days later the Rebel cavalrymen crossed the Tennessee River on two flatboats that Forrest later sank in a nearby creek, in case he needed them on his way back. Seven days before Christmas, the Confederate riders ripped through Colonel Robert Ingersoll's combined force of artillery, cavalry and infantry and then began to demolish 60 miles of the vital Mobile and Ohio railroad line between Jackson and Union City, Tennessee. Paroled prisoners constantly exaggerated the size of the Confederate raiding force and soon the bleak winter countryside was covered with Union pursuit forces that finally converged at Parker's Crossroads and tried to block the Rebel escape. When the Union forces surrounded Forrest's command, he ordered his officers to "charge both ways" and launched two massive attacks in two entirely opposite directions. While 300 Rebels were captured before they could get back to the Tennessee River, the rest of the force refloated the flatboats, crossed the river and carried with them 10,000 new rifles, a million rounds of ammunition and a parole list of 2000 captured Federals. More important, Grant's vital supply line was shattered and his army seemed totally dependent on the forward supply dump at Holly Springs, Mississippi.

However, while Forrest was devastating the northern axis of the Union supply line, General Earl Van Dorn was leading 3500 Confederate horsemen on a mission to destroy Grant's advance depot. Van Dorn headed east from Grenada, skirted the Federal flank and then headed north in a feint towards Corinth. Suddenly, the graycoats rode down on the 1500 man garrison holding the huge supply base and captured the defenders with minimal losses. The result of the attack was a virtual replay of the Manassas Station revels as the Southern horsemen helped themselves to a cornucopia of foods, uniforms and boots and then torched anything they couldn't carry off. Back in Oxford, Grant was shocked at the ease with which Van Dorn had destroyed his depot while noting "the news of the capture of Holly Springs and the destruction of our supplies caused much rejoicing among the people remaining in Oxford. They came with broad smiles on their faces indicating intense joy, to ask what I was going to do now without anything for my soldiers to eat." The Union general quickly turned the citizens' smiles into scowls of astonishment when he countered that he was already sending troops out with wagons to collect all the food and forage they could find within 15 miles of the town. However, Grant was still forced to backtrack to Memphis, which allowed Pemberton to shift desperately needed troops back to the Vicksburg garrison just in time to challenge Sherman's Yazoo River expedition.

A Federal fleet of 50 transports moved over 30,000 Union soldiers to within 12 miles of Vicksburg, and on Saturday, December 27th, Sherman's four assault divisions began sloshing ashore in the swampy Yazoo bottoms, while Rebel snipers kept up a hot fire from behind the almost impenetrable foliage. While the city of Vicksburg itself was held only by a skeleton force of one Louisiana regiment, General Stephen Lee was busy organizing rapidly arriving reinforcements along a series of imposing ridges called Chickasaw Bluff. Sherman intended to use all four divisions in a frontal attack all along the Confederate lines, while actually concentrating his assault forces on two supposedly vulnerable points about a half mile apart.

On Monday morning, December 29th, the bluecoats slogged through the swamps of Chickasaw Bayou under cover of a massive artillery barrage. Suddenly Rebel gunners unmasked their hidden cannons while concealed riflemen jumped up from cover and caught the Yankees in a devastating crossfire, as the Northerners groped for a way to climb the steep bluffs. Sherman blamed one of his division commanders, General George Morgan, for failure to properly support the other assault units, but in reality the attack probably never had a chance to succeed. Federal troops began scooping out with their hands caves in the steep bank which sheltered them against the Rebels until the graycoats held their muskets vertically and fired down on their adversaries. The men who survived this fire were forced to wait until darkness before they could scurry back to the main lines and dozens of men were either killed or captured before they could fall back. Even Sherman admitted "our loss had been pretty heavy, and we had accomplished nothing, and had inflicted little loss on our enemy." While the 1776 Union casualties were far fewer than the Fredericksburg fiasco, the Confederate losses were only one ninth as high at 207, and it was clear that Chickasaw Bluff wasn't the open back door to Vicksburg that the Federals had hoped. Soon after the battle Pemberton could wire Jefferson Davis a telegram brimming with confidence, in which the Pennsylvania born Confederate general exulted "Vicksburg is daily growing stronger, we intend to hold it."

The last hope for Union progress before the end of winter lay with the Army of the Cumberland, but in certain respects William Rosecrans was facing an even more daunting challenge than Grant or Burnside. This army of the center was so tied up with the defense of railroad lines around its base at Nashville that its commander could only spare 44,000 men for an advance on Bragg's defenses near the town of Murfreesboro. However, when Federal intelligence confirmed the transfer of Bragg's largest division to Mississippi, Rosecrans set in motion a post-Christmas advance on the enemy. While Rosecrans and Bragg were both moderately competent army commanders, the Northern general was a mercurial figure who had earned the warm affection of most of his men, while Bragg was a humorless disciplinarian who had few friends among his fellow generals and few admirers among his enlisted men.

On December 30th, 1862, the Union army was approaching Stones River on the outskirts of Murfreesboro, and the corps of McCook, Thomas and Crittenden were deployed along a series of small ridges and hills almost exactly opposite the Confederate army that was still largely hidden in the woods. Rosecrans and Bragg spent the evening mapping out their plans for an assault, and by a strange irony they came up with the same idea. Each general planned to hold fast on his right flank while concentrating the bulk of his force in a massively reinforced left flank that would land a crushing blow at the opponent. A perfectly coordinated attack by each army would have produced a fascinating situation in which the two forces essentially would have pivoted on each other and occupied the enemy's lines to start the business all over again. However, while Rosecrans' concept of a "dawn assault" meant an advance after breakfast, Bragg's idea of a "dawn assault" was an attack at first light. Therefore, when New Year's Eve dawned cold and windy after the obligatory torrential rain that seemed to plague so many Civil War armies in the "sunny South," the Rebels got in the first major blow of the day and very nearly won the battle because of it.

The dawn assault on McCook's corps allowed William Hardee's Confederates to smash the extreme flank of the Union line while Leonidas Polk's graycoats slashed toward the hinge connecting McCook to George Thomas' men. The two extreme right flank divisions commanded by Generals Johnson and Davis were virtually annihilated as waves of Rebels poured through weak spots in the Union lines, but rising star Phil Sheridan not only held his own with his division but for a time threw the Southerners back with a spirited counterattack. As this single division became the target for much of the Rebel assault, Rosecrans sent Sheridan an urgent message telling him to hold on where he was in order to buy time for a new defensive line to be constructed. Sheridan later noted "from this I judged that the existing conditions of the battle would probably require a sacrifice of my command," and the successive Confederate assaults did result in the loss of all of his brigade commanders and a number of his regimental leaders.

Sheridan's division was gradually whittled down to a fraction of its original strength, but a new Union line that very much resembled a half closed pen-knife began to take shape. The new crisis point of the battle now became the angle where the two bent back wings of the Federal army joined. If the Confederates could break through this salient, they would split the army in two and be able to smash each fragment in turn. However, while Sheridan's stand bought valuable time for the defenders, George Thomas had been fortifying the vital hinge with every cannon he could find. This part of the battleground was a four acre clump of tightly packed cedar trees that was called the Round Forest and by the time that Bragg realized that this was the main objective of the battle, more than 50 Union guns were deployed among the trees. Just before noon, a Mississippi brigade became the first unit assigned to clear out the woodland and over 2000 graycoats let out the shrill Rebel yell and charged into the forest. Battery after battery of Federal guns created a storm of wooden splinters flying through the frigid air as the survivors plugged their ears with cotton from nearby bushes to drown out the horrifying noise of this barrage. A Tennessee brigade was promptly double-timed to support the attack and the Federal gunners simply shifted their angle of fire and pulverized the Volunteer State infantry. When Confederate casualties started to approach 75% in some of the assault units, Bragg reluctantly conceded that any hope of a breakthrough now lay in a charge toward the opposite end of the enemy line—the Union left flank.

General John C. Breckenridge had been given responsibility for holding the right flank against any Union assault across Stones River, and Breckenridge continued to be convinced that Federal demonstrations in his direction were merely the prelude to a massive enemy attack across the river and into his position. Thus the Kentucky division commander only released his units in driblets while holding as many men as possible in readiness for the expected Union attack. The two brigades that Breckenridge released were linked up with part of Polk's original assault force and as the sun began to dip below the horizon, 6000 graycoats made the final attempt of the day to pierce the Federal defenses. A Union staff officer who observed the attack noted the spectacle of the approach as "on they came in splendid style, full six thousand strong. Case-shot tore through their ranks, but the gaps closed up. Volley after volley of grape shot was sent against them and the 6th and 26th Ohio, taking up the refrain, added the sharp rattle of rifles to the unearthly din. They staggered but quickly re-formed and.... advanced again to the charge. The battle had hushed on the extreme right, and the gallantry of this advance is indescribable!" However, the Rebels continued to be staggered by a sheet of fire and finally wavered and fell back, in the last significant clash of the bloody year of 1862.

Braxton Bragg spent most of the last night of the year calculating a list of Rebel casualties that soon reached the 9000 mark while he listened with great interest to the sound of hundreds of Federal wagons rolling back up the turnpike to Nashville. The Confederate army had been seriously damaged, but Bragg was convinced that the Yankees had suffered even heavier losses and he assumed that the wagons signified Rosencrans' decision to retreat northward. The saturnine Southerner sent Davis an unusually sanguine telegram that concluded "a complete victory" has been achieved in order to ensure a happy New Year in the South. However, early the next morning Bragg was startled to see the Union army defiantly in their defenses seeming to dare the Rebels to try another expensive assault. Rosecrans had sent his wounded men back to Nashville for treatment, but the uninjured survivors were still very much in position. Bragg spent most of January 1st hoping that the Federals would be the first side to blink in this confrontation, but when dawn of the 2nd revealed the Yankees still in place the Confederate general realized he either had to break the enemy line or withdraw himself.

John Breckenridge, who had already seen part of his division mauled in the first day of the battle, was now summoned to Bragg's headquarters and told that his remaining fresh brigade would now be expected to be the shock force that would penetrate the Yankee defenses. The Confederate com-mander decided to throw three brigades of Rebels against Union General Van Cleve's part of the Federal line only 30 minutes before sunset, and then use Breckenridge's newly captured positions as the springboard for a more general Rebel attack the next morning. The Kentuckian insisted that the hill he was to attack was almost impregnable, but despite his protests 5000 graycoats started down from their own ridge and marched steadily across a field that separated them from the Federals. However, Union artillery commander John Mendenhall had crammed almost 60 cannons on the flanks of the targeted ridge and filled every gun with double charges of grapeshot. The resulting Confederate charge was dramatic, brave, and doomed to failure. Five dozen Union guns sent over a hundred rounds a minute smashing through the thinning ranks of rebels and only the oncoming darkness allowed slightly more than half of the assault force to stagger back to their original positions.

Rosecrans was able to hang on to his frozen rifle pits and artillery emplacements, but his losses in an essentially defensive battle for the Federals was an astronomical 13,000 men, or almost one third of his army. Bragg had lost slightly more than 10,000 men from his smaller army, although his total of killed and wounded exceeded the Union army which counted 4000 men captured in its casualty list. The Confederate commander's initial determination to hold his position at any cost gradually eroded, as his subordinates began to lobby for a retreat southward before reported Union reinforcements augmented Rosecrans' army. While Bragg withdrew to a new base at Tullahoma, Rosecrans breathed a sigh of relief, sent an upbeat victory message to Washington, and virtually put the Army of the Cumberland in suspended animation for six months.

After a long string of Federal disasters in this gloomy winter season, Lincoln and his advisors accepted Rosecrans' message of victory with a euphoria that went far beyond the limited gains of the engagement. Stanton wired the general "the country is filled with admiration of the gallantry and heroic achievement of yourself and the officers and troops under your command." Henry Halleck gushed "you and your brave army have now the gratitude of your country and the admiration of the world... all honor to the Army of the Cumberland." Some months after the battle, Lincoln wrote Rosecrans in another period of crisis, "I can never forget, while I remember anything, that about the end of last year and beginning of this, you gave us a hard earned victory which, had there been a defeat instead, the nation could scarcely have lived over." While the narrow victory at Stones River provided a temporary boost to Union morale, the remainder of winter and early spring provided a different form of depression among Northerners than the recent series of military fiascoes. Rosecrans' army was decimated, short of wagons and horses, and attempting to operate in a region that seemed to produce only one commodity in abundance in winter—mud. In fact, a Confederate staff officer inspecting Bragg's fortifications around Tullahoma noted that even the name of this town was linked to that brown substance as he sarcastically noted that *Tulla* was a Greek word for mud while *Homa* was a term for more mud.

This substance was very much a feature of Ulysses Grant's operations around Vicksburg that winter and early spring, as a series of projects to bypass the defenses of the city by digging alternate canals or channels sent thousands of bluecoats into the ooze and mud of the bayou country. Seven different attempts that Grant blandly called "experiments" gradually sank into the morass of muddy swamps and rivers that always seemed to be too high or too low for effective use. When spring returned to Mississippi, the Federals were essentially no closer to capturing Vicksburg than they had been a full year earlier and even Lincoln, who already admired Grant's energy, was beginning to wonder if the river bastion led the same charmed life as Richmond.

If Grant and Rosecrans were making little headway in their attempt to attack their adversaries, at least conditions in these two armies were enormously more positive than the showcase army of the Union—the Army of the Potomac. Ambrose Burnside followed up the fiasco of Fredericksburg with another offensive that, while far less costly in lives, was, if possible, even more embarrassing than the December operation. On January 19th, 1863, the Union army commander became convinced that the onset of winter would largely tie Lee to his Fredericksburg defenses so the Federal army might have an opportunity to move up the Rappahannock and slash the Rebels from the flanks. The next day the army started to march, and for perhaps four hours everything ran smoothly. Then a torrential rainstorm turned the approach roads into quagmires and the whole Yankee operation almost literally ground to a halt as wagons, cannons and horses disappeared into waist-deep mud. Confederate troops on the far side of the river had a ringside view of the disaster and let out derisive cheers for the Federal soldiers as they fished wagons out of the mire. The rebels held up signs that mockingly pointed arrows with "Richmond this way" on them. When the Union troops staggered back into their camps after this Mud March, the fighting effectiveness of the Army of the Potomac probably had dropped to its all time low point. The army was losing almost the equivalent of a regiment a week in desertions, scurvy was rampant due to poor quality rations, and Burnside was becoming increasingly distrustful of his subordinates. Finally, when the Rhode Islander confronted Lincoln with a choice of firing nine senior officers or accepting his resignation, the President terminated Burnside's command and placed arch-rival Joseph Hooker in charge.

Hooker came to his position with a well deserved reputation as a hard drinking, womanizing, manipulative officer who shocked the sensibilities of more puritanical soldiers. However, once he took command of the army, the general surprised and delighted his men with an almost immediate make-over of the whole organization. Fresh vegetables, soft bread and similar luxuries started pouring into the camps along with the additional bonus of six months' back pay for every soldier. The unit and army drills and reviews that McClellan had popularized were re-instituted. Each corps and division in the army was given its own distinctive color coded badge to promote identification with a particular unit. By the end of April, a seemingly "played out" army was at a peak strength of over 133,000 men and its commander was convinced that he had developed the strategy that would finish the Rebels once and for all.

Hooker's plan was based on his ability to keep Lee's eyes fixed on a potential attack across the Rappahannock at Fredericksburg, while half of the Union army slipped out of it Falmouth camps and crossed the river well upstream, where the Confederate defenses were far weaker. To a large extent, Hooker's idea was quite similar to William Howe's battle plan when he confronted George Washington at Brandywine Creek—keep the defending army occupied with a demonstration attack on the front while part of the attacking army crossed the river at a ford beyond the enemy's perimeter of defense and then come slashing down on the defender's exposed flank. However, Hooker, unlike his British counterpart, had the additional advantage of outnumbering his adversary almost two to one, so that each of the wings of the Federal army would be as large as Lee's entire force. If the Virginian threw most of his army against the threat to this flank, the force opposite Fredericksburg could easily penetrate the Rebel defenses and hit Lee from the rear, while if the Southerners heavily engaged in their front, the contingent advancing from upstream could maul the enemy from the flank. In either case, it seemed highly likely that the Confederates would be either badly cut up or forced to withdraw toward Richmond over open country, with a much larger Federal army snapping at its flanks all the way to the Confederate capital.

While Hooker was in fact a far less heroic figure than either Lee or Grant, the fact remains that, up to a point, his plan was brilliant and did work extremely well in its initial stages. On April 27th, Hooker crossed the Rappahannock at Kelly's Ford, 27 miles from Fredericksburg, with 42,000 men, and then marched rapidly toward Lee's flank while 10,000 Yankee cavalrymen were tearing up the Confederate railroads and supply lines leading to Richmond. Hooker was exultant as he insisted, "the rebel army is now the legitimate property of the Army of the Potomac,"

The Union army, still receiving heavy reinforcements as it marched, arrived at the crossroads hamlet of Chancellorsville on the morning of May 1st. Chancellorsville was essentially nothing more than the family farmhouse of the Chancellor family augmented by a few outbuildings, and located about eight miles from Fredericksburg. However, this new headquarters for the Army of the Potomac was also in the middle of a gloomy, heavily forested region called the Wilderness, which stretched for about 15 miles in an otherwise abundant region of the Old Dominion. The Federal army had actually stolen a march on the wily Lee, and even dour General George Meade, who was certainly no fan of Hooker's, exclaimed, "this is splendid! Hurrah for Old Joe! We are on Lee's flank and he doesn't know it!" Meade and fellow corps commander Henry Slocum were ordered to advance the remaining four miles to the edge of the Wilderness and then locate the flank defenses of the Confederate army.

George Sykes' division of regulars spent much of this beautiful Friday morning and early afternoon pushing through Confederate scouting parties and picket lines, but suddenly they crashed into a large force from Anderson's division, who were quickly lapping at both Federal flanks and forcing Sykes to send a call for assistance. Winfield Hancock's division promptly rushed up in support, and the power of two advancing Union formations allowed the Yankees to gain control of a series of ridges near Tabernacle Church. When senior corps commander Darius Couch arrived at the scene of the battle, he agreed with Meade and Slocum that a significant Northern victory seemed to be developing, and Lee's army was now at its most vulnerable point of the past year.

The Union advanced units were now colliding with a Confederate army which was in the middle of an emerging re-deployment that represented the first of a series of gambles that Lee attempted during the next few days. When the Southern commander finally confirmed that Hooker really was threatening his western flank, he quickly went into his riverboat gambler mode and entrusted his entire position on Marye's Heights to Jubal Early's single division modestly augmented by Barksdale's brigade and the Washington Artillery—a total of 10,000 men who would be facing between 50,000 and 60,000 Federals at this particular moment. Lee then wheeled his remaining 42,000 to face Hooker's advance, just as the Federals were advancing along the Orange Turnpike and Orange Plank Road in their attempt to secure Banks' Ford and grab all the high ground they could locate in the vicinity. Two brigades commanded by Paul Semmes and William Manone had double timed into position just in time to contest Sykes' advance, but there just weren't enough Confederate units available to beat off a really serious advance by Hooker's whole striking force. However, the desperate Rebel attack was the first in a series of crises which the Union commander disastrously mishandled or misjudged.

Hooker's plan was based on the presumption that Lee would remain more or less stationary in his entrenchments while the Federals pitched into the vulnerable Rebel flank. However, the enemy had pulled their first surprise by smashing into the Union advance, and quite simply, the Yankee commander lost his nerve. Once Hooker received word of the Confederate attacks, he sent urgent orders to his corps commanders to halt their advance toward Banks' Ford and withdraw back to Chancellorsville. When Darius Couch went storming back to his commander questioning this move, Hooker rather lamely insisted that he wanted Lee to take the offensive and smash his army on the Union breastworks. However, Meade asked his fellow corps commander "if he thinks he can't hold the top of a hill, how does he expect to hold the bottom of it" while Couch agreed that "I retired from his presence with the belief that my commanding general was a whipped man."

The commander of the Army of the Potomac may have continued to bluster that "the enemy is in my power and God Almighty cannot deprive me of them," but in reality the initiative had passed to the Confederates and would never again be relinquished in this battle. Lee was fighting this battle at a terrible disadvantage, as he had dispatched James Longstreet and two of his best divisions to gather supplies in North Carolina and southern Virginia, but he still had Stonewall Jackson and the eccentric former professor was determined that Hooker could still be defeated. While Lee and Jackson sat on a pair of Federal hardtack cases, they received the results of Jeb Stuart's reconnaissance of the Union lines. Hooker had already made a serious tactical error in withdrawing his army into the tangled forest around Chancellorsville. Now the superb Union artillery, which was probably the most powerful combat weapon the North possessed, was forced to deploy in a region that prevented its optimum use. In essence, the Federals deploying in the Wilderness were confronting the same challenge faced by American forces in the jungle battles in the Pacific theater of World War II, in which the powerful American superiority in armor was often negated by the terrain. Hooker had imposed another limitation on himself when he dispatched virtually his whole cavalry force on to raid enemy communications, which left the Union infantry groping blindly against an adversary that very much still had use of their excellent horse soldiers. Finally, Hooker compounded these errors by bragging about the impregnable nature of his defenses and then promptly providing Lee with a golden opportunity to penetrate them.

The Federal army occupied an imposing series of breastworks that were six miles long and anchored on one flank by the Rappahannock river. However, for reasons that are still lost in the fog of history, the Union line ended well short of its other natural anchor, the Rapidan River. Hooker was apparently convinced that Lee's army would never be able to swing so far west that it could possibly strike his right flank. This attitude bears a remarkable similarity to the attitude of the designers of the R.M.S. Titanic who failed to extend their watertight bulkheads to the top deck of the ship, because they assumed that no conceivable crash could possibly destroy enough watertight compartments to send seawater slopping from one bulkhead over to the next to the point of sinking the vessel. The assumption of these engineers would threaten the lives of 2000 passengers while the similar approach by Hooker would ultimately risk the lives of his 70,000 defenders.

When Stuart brought back the startling news that the enemy right flank was "in the air" Lee and Jackson promptly agreed on the next gamble of the battle—the Confederate army that was already divided once would be divided into two more fragments. While Lee took command of 14,000 men and 100 guns that would occupy Hooker's main army for most of Saturday, Stonewall Jackson would march 28,000 men in a wide sweep around the Federal line in order to smash into the exposed flank sometime during the afternoon. At sunrise on May 2nd Jackson and Lee made what would become their final exchange of good wishes, and 70 regiments of graycoats, marched to the crossroads of Brock Road and the Orange Plank Road and then swung northeast to make their wide circuit around the Union army. Their target was Oliver O. Howard's XI Corps of primarily German volunteers who were camped in the Wilderness around Dowdall's Tavern.

Howard's corps had no support on its right flank, which petered out in the surrounding forest, but the left flank was secured by Daniel Sickles' III Corps whose line extended toward Hooker's headquarters at the Chancellor House. Sickles was a highly influential New York politician who had a mercurial temper and had already shot and killed a man caught dallying with his wife, and would soon become the centerpiece of one of the most emotional controversies of the upcoming Gettysburg campaign. On this sunny Saturday Sickles was his usual high-strung self and when his scouts reported evidence that part of the Confederate army was marching near his lines, he pulled two of his divisions from their positions supporting Howard and sent them charging against the reported Rebels. Sickles men were actually colliding with Jackson's rear guard, and they quickly gobbled up an entire Georgia regiment. However, the rest of the Rebel column was able to withdraw to safety, and when Sickles sent word of his engagement to Hooker, the Union commander accepted the report as proof that Lee was retreating and that he had won the battle. This assumption, in the John Pope school of victory over phantoms, was simply one more bonus for Stonewall and his men.

At 5 P.M. on Saturday afternoon a two mile long line of graycoats stood three deep in the woods near Dowdall's Tavern. Stonewall Jackson peered through a group of thickets at the Federal soldiers cooking their suppers and playing cards as he prepared to give the orders for the final spectacular action of his life. Fifteen minutes later 28,000 Rebels screeched and charged against 9000 bluecoats who simply didn't know what had hit them. The Rebel surprise was complete, but these Federals were not untrained militia, and they fought much harder than Civil War mythology gives them credit for. However, these largely German-speaking Yankees were badly outnumbered and the best that they could accomplish was a bloody rearguard action that cost them 25% of their unit, but slowed down the Rebel advance to about one mile an hour. Jackson had assumed that the advantages of surprise and numbers would enable him to annihilate Howard's corps and then cut off Hooker from the fords across the Rappahannock, but by 7 P.M. it was becoming increasingly obvious that this was not going to happen. Just as the first Rebels started to come within range of the Chancellor house itself, Union cavalry general Alfred Pleasanton formed an impenetrable stop line at a small ridge called Hazel Grove, where a combination of dismounted horsemen firing Spencer repeating rifles, saber wielding mounted cavalry and tenacious gunners manning double-shotted cannons pulverized the lead Rebel units and held open an escape route for Howard's survivors.

Jackson was initially toying with ordering a rare night assault to regain his momentum, but it was clear that his men were exhausted, so he settled for a personal reconnaissance in order to locate a vulnerable spot in the defenses that could be exploited Sunday morning. While Stonewall and his staff were riding along the fringes of the battle line, pickets from a North Carolina regiment mistook the horsemen for a Federal cavalry unit. They fired a volley that wounded Jackson badly enough to cause the loss of his arm and his subsequent death from pneumonia on the following Sabbath. Now, with Jackson and his chief subordinate A.P. Hill down with wounds, the Confederate advance on the Federal right flank would be entrusted to cavalry leader Jeb Stuart who would have to confront a Union army that had used a crucial reprieve to strengthen its defenses and extend its line to the Rapidan. As the sun rose on Sunday, May 3rd, Hooker still had over 60,000 fresh troops dug into an imposing series of defenses, that would be attacked by fewer than 40,000 Confederates in two separated wings. However, Lee continued to profit from a combination of bad luck and poor decisions that continued to plague his opponents.

First, as long as the Yankees held Fairview plateau and nearby Hazel Grove, Federal artillery could sweep the enemy approaches and slaughter any attacking units, as they had already demonstrated on Saturday. However, in a moment of indecision and then panic, Sickles became convinced that a series of Rebel attacks was about to overrun these artillery concentrations and he ordered the position abandoned for a fallback to a "safer" line. Stuart knew a gift when he saw it, and he promptly occupied the spot with almost 50 Confederate guns, which promptly enfiladed the Union defenses and started blasting into the Chancellor house itself. One of these shells stuck a column on the porch where Hooker was standing and knocked him senseless, an injury which seemed to affect his judgement for the rest of the battle. No one seemed ready to take immediate command of the Army of the Potomac, and by 10 A.M. Lee had linked his two wings back together and now had to determine whether to keep pushing the Federals that were in front of him or turn around and smash the other Union column that was approaching from Fredericksburg.

Once it became apparent early on that Sunday morning that the Rebels were going to continue their offensive, Hooker had ordered John Sedgwick to use his wing of the army to storm Marye's Heights and then catch Lee from the rear . Sedgwick was finally able to carry the Confederate position after several attempts had failed, but by the time he had chased Early's division a few miles south, Lee had turned to confront him with 22,000 men, while leaving the remainder of his army to keep Hooker occupied behind his latest set of trenches. About six miles east of Chancellorsville, in a set of fields surrounding Salem Church, Lee's graycoats smashed into the unsuspecting Sedgwick's flanks, and sent him reeling back to Bank's Ford in order to hold open his most accessible escape route. As the sun set on the third day of the battle of Chancellorsville, Lee had taken the initiative and was in a position where he could choose to strike either of the separate wings of the Union army.

Lee decided during the night to "attend to Mr. Sedgwick" and on Monday morning he rode out to Salem Church to finalize his attack plan with his assault commanders. Jubal Early had reoccupied Marye's Heights during the night, and his division would now become one flank of a complex advance that would feature Lafayette McLaws' division striking Sedgwick from the opposite side while Richard Anderson's division lunged at the Union center holding the road to Bank's Ford. However, while the past two days had featured well coordinated, hard hitting Confederate assaults, the fourth day of the battle of Chancellorsville was a series of missed opportunities for the South. Sedgwick held a rectangular line of defenses about three miles in length and generally placed on high ground that dominated the approaches. Early's men floundered through a series of deep ravines and suffered heavy casualties while Anderson's men didn't arrive in time to add support to McCaws' division which got lost in a maze of thickets, and by the time his men were ready to attack, a heavy fog began to shroud the fields and a coordinated attack became impossible. Lee began to think of ordering a night assault, but as the Rebels groped through the fog toward their jump-off points the Confederate commander decided to suspend operations and see what morning brought.

When Confederate pickets moved toward the Union lines the next morning, they discovered that Sedgwick had abandoned his lines and retired across the river, a move which now gave Lee's undivided attention to Hooker. However, at midnight Tuesday, as Sedgwick was ferrying his men across the Rappanhannock, Hooker called a council of war to determine whether or not the rest of the army should retreat in the same direction. Interestingly, not one corps commander voted to do what Lee most expected, remain in their defenses and allow the graycoats to attack. Howard, Meade and John Reynolds all voted to attack Lee before he could launch his own assault, Sickles voted to fall back across the river, Couch gave a reluctant assent to a withdrawal and Slocum didn't arrive in time to vote. Hooker thought over his options, and promptly ignored his generals' advice while ordering a retreat to "save the capital and save the army."

Historians have debated for almost a century and a half over the probable outcome of a Confederate attack on Hooker's lines on May 5th, 1863. If Pickett's charge was the most controversial assault of the war, this spring Tuesday provided the most controversial non-assault of the conflict. The Union army had the advantage of holding a solid defensive line with about twice as many defenders as Lee had attackers—a truly unusual situation for an offensive. On the other hand, Hooker was at least somewhat affected by his earlier injury and couldn't seem to focus on the problem at hand, while refusing to delegate full authority to anyone else. Thus some analysts are certain that Lee could have slashed through a Union army that was fighting only to stave off defeat, while other scholars are equally sure that the Confederates would have confronted another Malvern Hill or Cemetery Ridge, in which thousands of Rebels would have been annihilated by Federal musket volleys and artillery shells. However, since the Union generals seemed eager only to either attack Lee or retreat, it is probable that this fascinating scenario was not terribly likely unless the Confederates struck before Hooker could either lunge forward or pull back.

Hooker pulled his army back across the Rappahannock, congratulated his men for an alleged triumph and sent the government in Washington into one of their most emotional hand, wringing episodes of the war. Charles Sumner of Massachusetts simply groaned "all is lost" at the news of the withdrawal while an "anxious and harassed" Lincoln walked around his office exclaiming "My God, My God, what will the country say?" The largest concentration of Federal power at any point in the war had been beaten by an army that was only half as large and another 17,000 Federal casualties had been added to the seemingly endless list. Lee had probably fought his greatest battle, although the 13,000 Confederates lost were far higher than the toll at Fredericksburg, and even the commanding general admitted that he couldn't keep fighting this kind of battle of attrition for much longer. If Hooker and his subordinates hadn't muffed a long list of opportunities, the Rebel army might very well have been annihilated and Joseph Hooker, not Ulysses S. Grant, might have emerged as the national hero. Now the Confederacy had another splendid victory and Northern morale was pushed to one of its lowest points of the war. However, this gloom would soon be pierced by two enormous benefits to the Union occurring from an otherwise horrendous series of events.

First, among the 13,000 Confederate casualties was General Thomas Jackson, who was undoubtedly the most brilliant tactical genius the South would ever put into the field. Another man could be promoted to lieutenant general and given command of Jackson's corps, but there was simply no one who had Stonewall's peculiar talent for smashing Northern armies. Lee and Jackson were a team for which there were no substitutes and now the Southern commander would head for a rendezvous with destiny in Pennsylvania without the subordinate who helped him to get that far in the first place. The Army of the Potomac commander George Meade would still face an imposing foe in the Army of Northern Virginia on the fields of Gettysburg, but that army was made substantially more beatable when Jackson took his last breath in Guiney Station.

Second, Earl Van Dorn's destruction of Grant's vital forward supply base at Holly Springs was a devastating short term blow to the Union advance on Vicksburg, but as the Yankee army was forced to forage through the countryside to feed itself as it withdrew northeast, the highly adaptable commander was making mental notes on the supply situation. As Grant acknowledged later, "this taught me a lesson which was taken advantage of later in the campaign when our army lived twenty days with the issue of only five days rations by the commissary. It showed that we could have subsisted off the country for two months instead two weeks and our loss at Holly Springs was more than compensated...by the lesson taught." Thus while the South lost the general who was most able to move swiftly and strike where he was least expected, the North gained an emerging hero who was about ready to undertake a campaign that the fallen Stonewall could fully appreciate, and perhaps, grudgingly admire.

CHAPTER 29

# The Summer of the Titans

## *Climax at Vicksburg and Gettysburg*

On the warm, moonless night of April 16th, 1863, Ulysses S. Grant and his wife Julia sat down on deck chairs on the upper deck of the steamer *Magnolia* and watched a fantastic display of lights flashing in the sky while their two young sons let out gasps of awe and excitement. During peacetime the Grant family might hag been watching a shoreline fireworks show but this was the middle of the Civil War and the explosion and flashes indicated far more serious business. About three miles away Commodore David Porter was aboard his flagship *Benton* directing the actions of 11 Federal vessels as they attempted to run past the Confederate batteries protecting Vicksburg on the bluffs 200 feet above the Mississippi River. Confederate gunners scored hit after hit on the specially prepared armored gunboats and steam transports, and a few minutes into the dash the *Patrick Henry* was totally wreathed in flames and beginning to explode as its crew abandoned ship. However, the other 10 ships came through the gauntlet more or less intact and the first giant step in the final campaign against the "Gibraltar of the West" had now been accomplished.

Porter's daring gamble was the result of an agreement between the commodore and his army counterpart that the only way to break the stalemate around Vicksburg was to have the army cross from Louisiana into Mississippi, well to the south of the main enemy defenses, which in turn would require the services of the fleet. Once the naval vessels made their successful run, Grant ordered McClernand's and McPherson's corps to march the 50 miles from Milliken's Bend to a plantation named Hard Times which was opposite an east side landing at Grand Gulf, Mississippi. However, when Porter's gunboats attempted to eliminate the enemy shore positions they were repulsed with heavy casualties. The situation looked bleak until an escaped slave came into Grant's headquarters with the vital information that there was an alternate landing beach 10 miles south at

Bruinsburg, which was virtually undefended by the Rebels. By the evening of April 29th a motley fleet of ironclads, tinclads, gunboats, river steamers and barges began a ferry service which placed over 30,000 Federal soldiers on the eastern bank of the river and within striking distance of the more vulnerable landward approaches to Vicksburg.

General John Pemberton, the Pennsylvania officer who had sided with the Confederacy at the outbreak of hostilities, had over 50,000 men assigned to the defense of Vicksburg, but Union diversions were rapidly scattering this force. First, Colonel Benjamin Grierson, a music teacher turned cavalry leader, led a detachment of 1700 bluecoat horse soldiers on a wild raid that slashed its way through the railroad lines and supply depots of eastern Mississippi and prompted Pemberton to deploy almost a full division of Rebel defenders in an ineffective attempt to ambush the Yankee raiders. At a cost of only 24 casualties, Grierson's raid had not only severed vital Confederate rail links, but diverted a substantial portion of the Vicksburg garrison away from Grant.

While Grierson was creating havoc in the eastern part of the state, Vicksburg's northern flank was being threatened by William Sherman. The energetic redhead had been ordered by Grant to make a demonstration attack against Rebel defenses on the Yazoo, and then quickly pull back when the Southern general had committed a sizeable force of defenders to meet this phantom threat. Sherman seemed to enjoy this charade immensely, and 10 Union regiments were duly landed near the mouth of the river, Yankee guns opened up a showy artillery bombardment and Confederate troops from a 60 mile radius were force, marched to the scene of the "battle." By the time the show had finished, only 8000 Rebels remained in Grant's front as he began his new offensive.

On May 1st the Union army smashed into General John Bowen's thin line of defenders around Port Gibson and the aggressive Confederate general used every steep ridge and every deep ravine to fight a skillful defensive battle that delayed the Yankee advance all day. However, there were simply too many Federals and too few Confederates, and Bowen had to retreat toward the Big Black river as he expected Grant to begin a march directly toward Vicksburg. However, the Union commander now initiated a series of maneuvers that would be studied with admiration over the next century. While the Confederate commander prepared to lunge at Grant's apparently vulnerable supply line, the Union general told his men to stock up on all the coffee, sugar and hardtack they could carry and then abandoned his line of communications. While Pemberton groped around trying to demolish a supply line that no longer existed, Grant ignored Vicksburg, shifted the direction of advance, and lunged for the state capital of Jackson, which was the main rail center used to funnel reinforcements from the east toward the Vicksburg garrison.

While Sherman was ordered to hurry south to link up with the main army, the other two corps of the army smashed through a Confederate roadblock

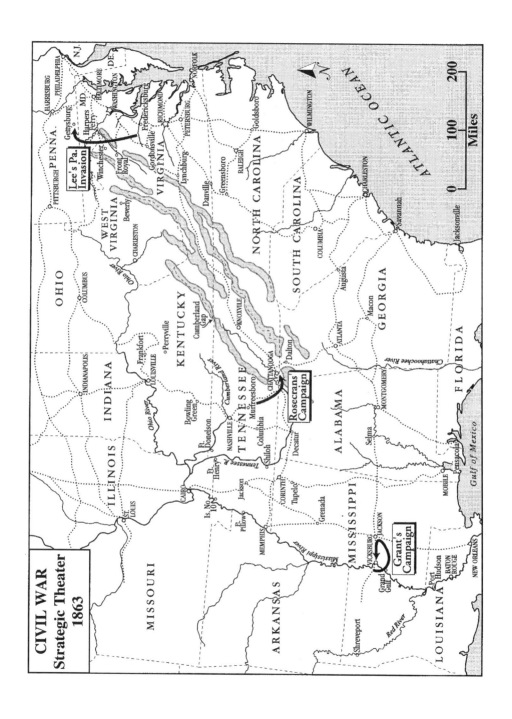

CIVIL WAR
Strategic Theater
1863

Lee's Pa.
Invasion

Rosecrans
Campaign

Grant's
Campaign

at Raymond and marched toward the Mississippi capital, which had just become the headquarters of Rebel theatre commander Joseph Johnston. Johnston had been promised substantial reinforcements by the War Department but in mid-May he had only 6000 men on hand, and after a token resistance he abandoned Jackson and retreated northward. Grant led the Yankee army into the town, spent the night in the same hotel room that had been used by Johnston the evening before, and promptly ordered the destruction of the railroad and any factories capable of manufacturing military equipment.

Back in Vicksburg, Pemberton was facing an insoluble quandary. Joseph Johnston had virtually ordered the Pennsylvanian to pull together a large mobile attack force, ignore the Federal threat to Vicksburg, and march east along the railroad line to link up with Johnston's force in order to crush Grant. On the other hand, Jefferson Davis had sent Pemberton a series of telegraph messages emphasizing the need to hold the city at any hazard and promising major reinforcements if the Rebel general simply sat tight behind his breastworks. At this point, Pemberton made a fatal compromise. He assembled about half of his garrison, 18,000 men, and marched out from the defenses while leaving two divisions behind to man the city defenses. Not only was the Rebel army much smaller than Grant's current total of 40,000 men, the Union commander had the additional advantage of knowing his adversary's intentions. A Unionist resident of Memphis had been loudly branded an arch secessionist by the local Union commander and with great fanfare thrown out of the town. Actually the whole drama was a ruse to place the man in the Confederate camp and he was promptly rewarded for his "sufferings" by becoming one of Johnston's couriers. The agent quickly provided Grant with copies of key correspondence between the two Rebel commanders, and the Union general quickly responded to this invaluable intelligence by leaving Sherman to finish the destruction of much of Jackson while the rest of the army lunged toward the cautiously advancing Pemberton.

When the Confederate general realized that Grant was ignoring Johnston and throwing most of his army against him, he quickly established a defensive position on a ridge called Champion's Hill which was almost exactly at the mid-point of the 45 mile route from Jackson to Vicksburg. On the morning of May 16th Grant and the pursuing Federals arrived at this ridge that backed up to the swollen Baker's Creek, and the Union general began launching a series of probing assaults in order to locate some vulnerable point in the Rebel line. After about three hours of skirmishing, a Yankee division under Indiana lawyer Alvin Hovey attempted a seemingly suicidal drive straight up one of the steep embankments, and to everyone's surprise, the Confederates panicked and abandoned almost a dozen cannons. Pemberton quickly concentrated every spare unit he could find to throw the Federals back off the ridge, but while the graycoats were able to push the Union force right back down to the foot of the hill, another division under John Logan got around the northern end of the ridge and discovered that the main path leading toward the creek had been left undefended. However, just as Logan was preparing to take advantage of this startling discovery, a messenger galloped up with news that Hovey's force was in danger of annihilation, and these troops were needed to march to the rescue. Grant later admitted that pulling Logan's men back from the process of closing off the escape route of Pemberton's army was one of his most significant mistakes of the campaign. He insisted "had I known the ground as I did afterwards, I cannot see how Pemberton could have escaped with any organized force."

There were simply too many Federal attacks in too many directions to permit the Confederates to pull out a victory, and Pemberton gradually began to think in terms of saving his army. As the sun went down behind the ridge, the Confederate divisions were disengaged one by one, as rear guard units covered the retreat over the creek. The Rebels had inflicted 2400 casualties on their tormentors, but the Southern loss was far more devastating. Not only did the graycoat casualty list creep toward 3600, but an entire Confederate division was cut off from the rest of the army during the retreat and soon found Grant's troops between themselves and Pemberton. While this large unit was able to join Johnston's force, an additional 5000 men were now knocked out permanently from the garrison of Vicksburg, which would swing the odds even more dramatically in Grant's favor.

Pemberton's army marched eight miles closer to Vicksburg in their all-night retreat and on the morning of May 17th reached the Big Black river. The key to this new Confederate position was a huge railroad bridge that spanned the river. The Rebel defenders threw up a series of rifle pits and barricades made of cotton bales, designed to command the approaches to the bridge on the east side of the river, while a second series of fortifications provided additional artillery and infantry fire support from the west bank. Grant had no intention of throwing his whole force into a frontal attack on this maze of defenses, and instead he ordered Sherman to march north along the river, cross the water several miles north at Bridgeport, and then march south on the opposite shore in order to smash Pemberton's left flank. While much of the Confederate energy was directed toward this new threat from the north, Brigadier General Michael Lawlor took off his coat and vest and led his men through a seemingly impenetrable swamp that covered the Confederate positions on the east bank. When the graycoats saw this assault from an unexpected direction, they initially rallied enough to hit 200 Yankees in less than five minutes while they were wading, but when Lawler's force began to lunge toward the railroad bridge, the whole Rebel line collapsed as men retreated westward leaving a burning span behind them. A large segment of Pemberton's army was trapped on the wrong side of the river and almost 2000 prisoners and 18 captured guns hit the defense of Vicksburg another body blow.

As a result of the battles of Champion's Hill and Big Black river, over half of Pemberton's mobile force was now out of commission and the victors and the vanquished now raced to arrive in Vicksburg first. Colonel S. H. Lockett, Pemberton's chief officer of engineers, rushed back to the endangered city and mobilized the defenders for an imminent assault. Lockett shifted dozens of shore defense guns to the landward defenses, deployed the two fresh divisions that had remained behind, and positioned each gun that had accompanied the mobile force as the retreating army made its way back into the city barely ahead of the pursuing Federals. On the morning of May 19th, as the Yankees overran the newly abandoned outer defenses of the city, Grant gave the go-ahead for a continued advance and the Union troops pushed on to the main Rebel emplacements. Pemberton and Lockett had filled these works with the freshest troops they had while the more disorganized men who had been caught in the retreat were held in reserve. Suddenly the bluecoats were encountering well-rested, confident adversaries and the result was a small scale Union disaster.

Three days later Grant's troops had closed to within 800 yards of the Rebel lines and a coordinated army-navy attack smashed against the defenders from both river and land approaches. In several instances Union soldiers gained footholds on the Confederate earthworks, but a combination of crude hand grenades made out of cannon shells, exploding powder barrels that served as mines, and the massive fire of over 100 cleverly positioned guns eliminated each precarious Federal foothold. However, while Pemberton was sending enthusiastic messages to Richmond chronicling this dramatic repulse, William T. Sherman's corps was steadily sweeping into the key positions around Haynes Bluff and Chickasaw Bayou, and routing the undermanned defenders in the northern tier of defenses. While the Confederates still held the city proper, Sherman's maneuver allowed the Union navy to stream down the Yazoo River and deliver inexhaustible streams of supplies and reinforcements to Grant's army. Johnston now in effect ordered his subordinate to evacuate the city in order to save the garrison, but in one of the most controversial decisions of the war, the Pennsylvania Confederate stuck to Davis' demand that the city be held at all costs, and accepted gratefully his president's assurances that help would soon be on the way. Thus as May neared an end, Pemberton and his besieged soldiers and civilians peered anxiously eastward, waiting for a tangible sign of deliverance.

The 5000 civilians and 32,000 soldiers who shared the danger of an ever-tightening siege were not being ignored in the meeting rooms of the Confederate capital. A group of senior Confederate military and government officials were busy finalizing a draft proposal to organize a relief of the Gibraltar of the West. Secretary of War James Seddon and General James Longstreet had developed a plan in which Longstreet's corps would either be transported by rail to Mississippi to link up with Johnston and attack Grant from the rear, or else travel to Tennessee to augment Bragg's army for a strike against Rosecrans, which would be expected to drain Federal troops from the Vicksburg trenches. Davis' significant concern for the need to prevent the Confederacy from being sliced in two initially encouraged him to support this plan, but his most successful general had other ideas. Robert E. Lee insisted that the torrid summer climate of Mississippi would so enervate the Yankee troops that offensive operations around Vicksburg should soon sputter out. This hiatus meant that the best employment of the victorious Army of Northern Virginia would be an invasion of Pennsylvania with every soldier that could be concentrated for the offensive. Such a move, he reasoned, would keep the Federals out of Virginia for the crucial growing season, while there was also a distinct possibility that Hooker could be lured into a battle under conditions favoring the Southern army. A massive Confederate victory on Union soil offered the twin possibilities of European recognition and the capture of a major city such as Baltimore or Philadelphia, which would probably force the Lincoln administration to rush large segments of the western armies back to protect the northeast.

Lee had certainly become the Confederacy's best general and his army was on a significant winning streak, but the Virginian was basing his plan on a number of highly questionable assumptions. First, the heat of the Mississippi summer was having little effect on Grant's army, which was now well supplied, large enough to rotate soldiers in and out of the siege lines, and psychologically in far better shape than the Rebel defenders. Second, Lee was significantly overestimating the impact of Chancellorsville on the Army of the Potomac. Most Union soldiers were convinced that they had been robbed of a possible war-ending victory by upper level bungling and were eager to get another crack at the Rebels under better circumstances. A fight on their own ground supported by the cheers of sympathetic Northern citizens would hardly be a terrible experience for the Yankee army. Finally, once Lee crossed the Potomac, his army would have only a relatively limited time to conduct offensive operations in hostile territory. If some form of spectacular victory or capture of a major city didn't happen fairly quickly, the Rebel army would be forced to retreat back into Virginia, after which it was quite probable that the Federal government would use its seemingly inexhaustible manpower reserves to initiate another campaign to besiege Richmond.

The most famous military campaign ever fought on the American continent began with little fanfare in early June, as the first of Lee's 37 brigades quietly slipped away from their camps on the Rappahannock and began using a series of well screened routes to march toward the Potomac. The Army of Northern Virginia that invaded Pennsylvania was, in many respects, very differently constituted than the force that had defeated Hooker at Chancellorsville. The death of Stonewall Jackson had forced Lee to re-evaluate the command structure of his army and the first result was an expansion from two to three corps. James Longstreet maintained his position as commander of the First Corps, but his force was reduced to three divisions. Jackson's Second Corps command went to Stonewall's most senior division leader, Richard Ewell, while a newly formed Third Corps was entrusted to Ambrose Powell Hill, who Lee believed was his best division commander.

By stripping coastal garrisons, re-deploying part of the Richmond defense force, and bringing some of the wounded from Chancellorsville back to active duty status, Lee had brought the effective strength of the Army of Northern Virginia up to 75,000 men, which was almost twice the strength of the army that had invaded Maryland the previous fall. However, while this army was confident of its abilities and far larger in total strength than in most previous or subsequent battles, it was still marching north without the irreplaceable Jackson. Ewell and Hill were reasonably competent officers, but they were both suffering from significant physical challenges. Ewell had lost a leg the previous year and was still far from recovered from the trauma of amputation. He tired easily, generally couldn't ride a horse, and was constantly battling excruciating pain. A. P. Hill's ailments were far less publicized, but it is almost certain that he was suffering from a sexually transmitted disease that left him weak and helpless for days at a time. While two of the corps commanders were significantly affected by physical ailments, James Longstreet was psychologically devastated by the staggering blow of the recent death of three of his children in a single week. Rarely in history has an army entered into its most critical campaign of the war with so many of its key leaders suffering such a range of physical and mental handicaps.

The army that Lee was about to confront was experiencing its own set of crises during the hot, sultry days that marked most of that memorable June and July of 1863. First, the strength of the Army of the Potomac had dropped to one of its lowest points of the war. While Lee's army was peaking in strength, a combination of casualties at Chancellorsville and the expiration of enlistments of dozens of two-year and ninety-day volunteers dropped the field strength of the army from 115,000 to 85,000 men. Thus the 2 to 1 advantage that the Federals had enjoyed in a number of battles was reduced to virtual parity at one of the most decisive moments of the war. Second, the command of the army seemed to be in flux as Lincoln and Halleck had lost confidence in Joe Hooker, and by the time that Lee was known to be on the offensive it was obvious that the President was looking for a new field commander. While Hooker made noises about advancing on Richmond while Lee invaded Pennsylvania, the administration began creating so many impediments to the general's operations that he requested a resignation that was instantly accepted. On June 28th, only a matter of hours before the huge collision of forces would begin, George Gordon Meade was awakened from a deep sleep and told that he was the latest in a lengthening line of men who could call themselves commander of the Army of the Potomac.

Lee's invasion of Pennsylvania was an initial psychological triumph for the embattled Confederacy, but almost as soon as the graycoats scattered across the southern counties of the Keystone State, the Confederate plan of campaign began to come apart. First, Jeb Stuart had convinced his commander to let him take most of the Southern cavalry corps on a massive expedition intended to pass behind the Union rear and disrupt enemy communication and supply lines, while also feinting toward the Washington defenses. This was almost exactly the task Hooker had assigned to the Union cavalry during the Chancellorsville campaign and the results were disastrous in both instances. Stuart's men charged through towns on the outskirts of Washington, captured Federal wagon trains, tore up Yankee railroads and gained fantastic publicity opportunities. They also left Lee virtually blind in enemy country, much the same as a 20th century army advancing into hostile territory without either aerial or armored reconnaissance forces. It is small wonder that Lee seemed to spend most of the Gettysburg campaign asking virtually everyone who arrived at his headquarters if he knew the whereabouts of his cavalry commander.

While Lee waited for the "eyes and ears" of his army to show, he dispatched Ewell's corps on a mission to capture the state capital of Harrisburg. However, when Early's division started advancing from York to the Susquehanna River, Pennsylvania militia units demolished the main railroad bridge and left the Rebels just short of their objective. Then, while the Confederate advance force studied other ways to cross the river, one of Longstreet's scouts informed the Rebel commander that the enemy was north of the Potomac and organizing to intercept the Southern invaders. The Virginian reacted quickly to this startling news and immediately ordered a concentration of all three corps at Cashtown.

George Meade did have his cavalry available and he had a good idea of his opponent's activities. The Pennsylvania general's first inclination was to have his engineers construct a formidable defense line along Pipe Creek just south of the Maryland-Pennsylvania border and make Lee attack him in what would become a mirror image of Fredericksburg. However, a Union general who wanted information and a Confederate general who wanted shoes would soon present the brand new commander of the Army of the Potomac with one of the most difficult decisions of the Civil War.

General John Buford was leading two brigades of Federal cavalry on a mission to locate Lee's army, and on Tuesday June 30th, the 2500 bluecoat horse soldiers rode into the sleepy college town of Gettysburg. While Buford noted the strategic importance of a town that was the terminus for a half dozen major roads, his scouts reported the approach of a large body of Confederate infantry. The Rebel foot soldiers were General Johnston Pettigrew's brigade of Henry Heth's division, and they were approaching Gettysburg in order to appropriate a large number of shoes that were reported to be located in the town. Pettigrew saw the bluecoats deployed in the town, but he mistook his adversaries for Pennsylvania militia and informed Heth that he would launch an attack Wednesday morning. Heth, who was a distant cousin of Lee, determined to sweep the town of militia, grab all the shoes he could find and then determine what he should do next.

While Pettigrew was waiting for reinforcements from Cashtown, Buford deployed his 2500 men along McPherson's Ridge on the western fringe of the town and sent couriers to the nearest infantry unit, John Reynold's I Corps, that he expected the Confederates to attack in force the next morning. Buford told Reynold's that he would hold the high ground as long as possible in order to give the infantry a chance to fight a battle where, for once, the Federals would have the geographical advantage.

Lee and Meade had each given their corps commanders orders to avoid inciting a major battle until their respective armies could be concentrated, but A. P. Hill and John Reynolds were unknowingly collaborating to bring on a major confrontation in a place where neither commanding general really expected it. A dawn collision of two small fractions of the contending armies would rapidly expand to encompass virtually the entire effective strength of the two premier armies in the Civil War. Buford know that dismounted cavalry wasn't expected to be able to defeat infantry in open battle and he would be further handicapped by the fact that he had to detach 25% of his men to hold the horses of the men who were fighting. However the Kentucky-born former Indian fighter also knew that his men were equipped with new Spencer seven shot carbines that could fire at least ten times as rapidly as Confederate muskets, while he would have the additional advantage of choosing his own ground for the fight.

As the sun rose on what was to be a stifling hot Wednesday morning, the advance units of the two armies began to open fire on one another and soon Rebel infantry and Yankee cavalry were engaged in a bitter contest for control of the high ground around Gettysburg. Confederate troops smashed their way past the Union pickets on the first of a series of hills, Herr's Ridge, but were initially stopped cold by the Yankee fast-firing rifles when they attempted to storm McPherson's Ridge. However, by 11 A.M. Confederate reinforcements were threatening to swamp Buford's position. The Kentucky Unionist climbed the stairs to the cupola of the Lutheran seminary on the next ridge over, and watched nervously as his flanks showed signs of crumbling. As he started down the stairs he was met by Reynolds, who asked him the situation. Buford quickly replied that "there is the devil to pay here" but was relieved when he learned that significant Union infantry units were beginning to arrive.

Reynolds arranged some of his hardest fighting units, including the already famous Iron Brigade of black hatted Midwesterners, in an attack formation that ambushed Archer's brigade of graycoats and captured the first of Lee's generals to surrender, alone with most of his unit. The Pennsylvanian was in the process of flanking the rebel assault force when a southern sharpshooter killed the I Corps' commander. While the battle would continue to ebb and flow for the rest of that torrid Wednesday afternoon, the death of the Lancaster native was a calamity from which the Federals could not fully recover during the first days of fighting. Abner Doubleday took an energetic lead in reforming the I Corps while Oliver O.

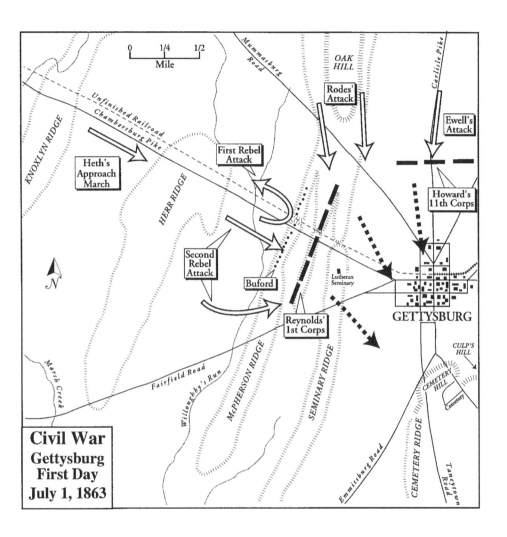

0   1/4   1/2
Mile

Mummasburg Road

OAK HILL

Carlisle Pike

Rodes' Attack

Ewell's Attack

Unfinished Railroad

Chambersburg Pike

KNOXLYN RIDGE

Heth's Approach March

HERR RIDGE

First Rebel Attack

Howard's 11th Corps

Second Rebel Attack

Buford

Lutheran Seminary

N

McPHERSON RIDGE

Willoughby's Run

SEMINARY RIDGE

Reynolds' 1st Corps

GETTYSBURG

CULP'S HILL

CEMETERY HILL

Cemetery

Marsh Creek

Fairfield Road

Emmitsburg Road

CEMETERY RIDGE

Taneytown Road

**Civil War**
**Gettysburg**
**First Day**
**July 1, 1863**

Howard's XI Corps soon arrived on the battlefield to provide a temporary manpower advantage for the Northern army. The one-armed Howard took command of the entire field army and began to organize a new defensive position around the seminary and its adjoining ridge, while part of the Federal army continued to battle around McPherson's farm and its high ground. By 3 P.M. Pettigrew's and Iverson's Confederate brigades had been badly mauled by well coordinated Union counterattacks and over 5000 Rebel soldiers had been captured. However, just as the battle was clearly swinging in the North's favor, Richard Ewell's corps completed its march back from the aborted assault on Harrisburg, and smashed into an unsuspecting Union army. Suddenly Confederate troops were pouring out of the woods onto the bluecoat flank positions and McPherson's Ridge was quickly made untenable.

Lee arrived at the scene of the battle just in time to watch the beginnings of a Federal rout. Henry Heth's men splashed across Willoughby Run and tore the Iron Brigade to pieces, as one Michigan regiment was reduced from 500 men to 96 soldiers in ten minutes and the 600 survivors of the brigade fled down the back side of the ridge only steps ahead of their ecstatic pursuers. Meanwhile, Robert Rodes' division led Ewell's corps in a sweep down the length of Seminary Ridge whose defenders now collapsed and started a panicky retreat down the side of that ridge and into the town itself. While bluecoats and graybacks fought a desperate battle in the streets of Gettysburg, Winfield Scott Hancock arrived at the gates of the town cemetery which dominated the last in the series of ridges in the area. Herr's Ridge, McPherson's Ridge and Seminary Ridge were now all in Confederate hands; if Cemetery Ridge went as well, the battle would be a total Southern victory. Hancock, who was the same type of energetic, decisive leader as his fellow Pennsylvanian Reynolds spent the remaining daylight hours deploying every riflemen and artillery piece he could find on a wide, hookshaped arc running from Culp's Hill on the right to Cemetery Ridge on the left.

While the Federals who had survived the street battles and newly arriving units from Maryland were all filling in the last ditch defense line, there were still major gaps in the position and the hill on which the town cemetery was located was still weakly defended. Lee saw this hill as a possible key to the battle and ordered Ewell to launch another all out assault and take Cemetery Hill "if practicable" while also cautioning his new corps commander to "avoid a general engagement until the arrival of the other divisions of the army." These two qualifiers to Lee's order have encouraged an emotional debate for almost the entire period since that late Wednesday afternoon in July of 1863.

Richard Ewell couldn't pretend to have the relationship with his chief that Stonewall Jackson had enjoyed and he was new to this level of responsibility. On the one hand Lee's orders were too conditional and the commander didn't really supervise its execution all that closely. On the other hand, Ewell didn't really expend too much energy in determining whether he could take the hill and he didn't really appreciate the enormity of the opportunity that was slipping away. Whether Lee or Ewell should be labeled as the main culprit, the fact remains that at nightfall on July 1st, the Union army, battered as it was, still held the high ground that would dominate the conduct of the battle. Nine thousand Federals were killed, wounded or captured and one of the most talented leaders in the entire Union army was dead, but Lee could not claim victory as long as the United States flag flew over any part of Gettysburg cemetery.

Between the final shot fired on Wednesday evening and the opening of action on Thursday morning, the commanders of both armies were faced with truly significant decisions. George Meade wasn't even on the scene at the first day's engagement, and for much of that Wednesday he saw the Gettysburg action merely as a device to buy time until his Pipe Creek defenses were completed. However, he had dispatched Hancock to take charge of the battle and evaluate the situation, and when his fellow Pennsylvanian sent back a message that the college town was the better place to have the showdown, Meade left his Maryland headquarters and rode most of the night to arrive at Cemetery Ridge about an hour before daylight on July 2nd. As directions went out to the remaining corps commanders to concentrate at Gettysburg, Meade effectively dropped his Pipe Creek strategy.

Robert E. Lee had the advantage of being on the scene for the climax of the first day's battle, and he quickly grasped the opportunity the initial victory provided for the South. However, while the Virginian kept thinking in terms of simply renewing the offensive the next morning and capturing the last of the series of ridges, James Longstreet insisted that this was exactly what Meade wanted him to do. The burly Georgian strongly urged his commander to consider a move in which the Confederate army would sidle around the Union flank near the Round Tops and re-deploy to the south between the Army of the Potomac and Washington, forcing the Yankees to hit the Southerners on ground of Lee's own choosing and, hopefully, producing another Fredericksburg which might very well crush the already shaky Northern morale. However, at the end of the conversation, Lee simply pointed to Cemetery Ridge and said, "the enemy is there and there I will strike him, I will either whip him there or he will whip me."

The Union position that Lee was pointing toward has frequently been described as a huge three mile fish hook that began with Culp's Hill and then continued through Cemetery Hill, over Cemetery Ridge and down to Little Round Top and Round Top at the stem. The enormous advantage that the Federals had by holding this line was that around 80,000 men and 350 guns were holding a three-mile line, while the Confederates would essentially be fighting the second day of the battle with only 50,000 men and 270 cannons on hand to deploy along a line that was about five miles in extent. This meant that the Union line was about three times as densely manned as their opponents while any break in the line could be quickly filled in by reinforcements who had only to come a relatively short distance from their old position. Beyond this advantage, Yankee- held Cemetery Ridge was higher than Rebel-held Seminary Ridge, which allowed the Federals to keep a close watch on at least some aspects of the Southern maneuvers.

Meade essentially accepted his opponent's fairly obvious desire to continue on the offensive, knowing that he could use his interior lines to keep ferrying reinforcements back and forth between threatened points. However, the new Yankee commander was also convinced that Lee would primarily threaten his right flank when the Virginian was actually planning exactly the opposite approach. Lee's basic plan for July 2nd was to initiate a serial attack in echelon starting on the extreme left flank of the Federal army and working its way eventually to a grand finale on the extreme right at Culp's Hill. First Longstreet's corps would smash into the Federals, then Hill's men would pick up the action, and finally Ewell's troops would deliver a blow at the other end. If all went well, Meade simply couldn't rush reinforcements to each threatened position in time, and the Union line would crumble and be rolled up along the flanks.

Lee's plan wasn't bad, but it was far less imaginative than his tactics of the past year and failed to properly consider two major problems. First, Lee seems to have ignored the lessons that Malvern Hill and Fredericksburg should have taught him about frontal assaults against an army that held the high ground and was supported by plenty of artillery. Almost exactly a year ago a Rebel army had been decimated by slamming into a Yankee position that looked uncomfortably similar to this one. Even more damning, a Southern army at Fredericksburg had easily held off a Federal assault force that was twice as large as their own force and yet now the defenders were the ones with the huge numerical advantage. Lee's troops were good, but not good enough to negate that kind of handicap. Second, the Confederate attack's possible success was dependent on pinpoint timing based on an early initial assault and excellent coordination of each further action in the series. In this instance, the whole timetable simply fell apart. The initial assaults were to be carried out by Hood's and McLaws' divisions, but they had spent most of the night marching to Gettysburg and there was no way they could launch a sunrise attack. Once the graycoats actually got marching, the Confederate commanders were so concerned about the operation being spotted by Federal observers on Round Top that the exhausted Rebels marched, counter-marched and then marched again in an exhausting 12 mile marathon in 95 degree heat in order to set up for a thrust against enemy positions that were only about a mile from their start point.

Almost 12 hours after the sun rose on this torrid Thursday, the men of the Confederate assault force were still trying to get in position for their attack while, unknown to them, two decidedly amateur Union officers were about to wreck their timetable in even more dramatic fashion. The first of these two Yankees to frustrate Lee's plans was a New York businessman and engineer named Hiram Berdan. Berdan had married a wealthy New York

City socialite and was traveling in the inner circles of Gotham society when the outbreak of war thrust him into a very different role. Berdan's engineering mind drew him toward a conviction that the Federal government was virtually insane to try to beat the rebels with obsolete muzzle loaders when breaching loading rifles were now available, and with significant help from generous donations by his business associates, he held nationwide auditions to join his experimental regiment of sharpshooters. Only the best marksmen were offered a place in this elite regiment of men dressed in green uniforms and equipped with brand new Sharps breech loaders. On the afternoon of July 2nd, Berdan and 100 of his 1st United States Sharpshooters were deployed in a heavily wooded area along Pitzer's Creek with their eyes peeled to spot the beginning of an expected Confederate advance.

Several regiments of Alabamians in the vanguard of Longstreet's corps were marching rapidly in an attempt to restore some semblance of the Confederate timetable when, as they approached the creek, Berdan raised and lowered his right hand and a solid sheet of flame erupted from the fast-firing rifles. The Rebels were blasted backwards as if swept by an invisible scythe and Pitzer's Creek turned crimson before the startled graybacks even knew what had hit them. In an engagement that even Longstreet called "a clever fight," the well camouflaged, green coated Federals dropped dozens of their adversaries and threw back a succession of attacks that even further disrupted the Confederate schedule. Finally, when Berdan sensed that his men were being outflanked, he gave the signal to withdraw and the sharpshooters faded into the woods. At a cost of 19 men, Berdan had bought a precious 40 minutes for Union reinforcements to deploy.

The Alabamians' objective was occupation of the two Round Tops, and if their timing had been better, they might have captured two virtually unoccupied hills. After regrouping from their vicious firefight with the greencoats, William Oates' men scrambled hand to hand up over the huge boulders and dense underbrush on the side of Round Top and finally made it to the crest, panting and exhausted. Oates peered across to the crest of the smaller hill and was pleasantly surprised to see it occupied by nothing more than a detachment of Federal signalmen who were wigwagging messages to other points on the field. The Rebels now began a charge down Round Top with the intention of rushing across the small clearing between the hills and climbing up Little Round Top before the Yankees recognized their peril.

However, while the rebels were racing down Round Top, Federal soldiers were rushing up the slopes of the other hill in an dramatic race that might very well give the battle to the victor. General Gouverneur Warren, Meade's chief engineering officer, had just made his way to the top of Little Round Top and had realized that no one had bothered to deploy any combat units on this obviously critical position. Thus while Rebel soldiers ran down Round Top, Warren dragooned Colonel Strong Vincent's brigade into marching part way up the smaller hill, while deploying Stephen Weed's brigade on the crest to confront a possible Rebel attack from another direction. The Federals had won the dramatic race, but just barely, and at this moment the second talented Yankee amateur would even more fatally disrupt the Rebel plans.

Colonel Joshua L. Chamberlain's major military experience before the Civil War had been confined to the study of Greek and Roman heroes, in his capacity as a classics and religion professor at Bowdoin College in Maine. Chamberlain had taken a leave of absence from the college to "study abroad," but quickly enlisted as second in command of the 20th Maine regiment, and during the late spring of 1863 assumed command of the unit. When Colonel Vincent began to deploy his brigade after they had won their race to Little Round Top, he assigned Chamberlain's men the most challenging task—to hold the left flank, which was in reality the left end of the entire Union line. The regiment of just over 300 men hastily constructed breastworks as two large enemy regiments numbering over 1000 men climbed up the hill to attack these loggers and fishermen. Their former college professor commander probably thought at least momentarily of the analogy to King Leonidas' stand with 300 Spartans at Thermopylae, as the far larger number of Rebels began to advance toward his line. Over 120 defenders were killed or wounded and the survivors were rapidly running out of ammunition, when the graycoats formed for their supreme effort. In a moment of brilliant decisiveness the Maine professor ordered a totally unexpected downhill bayonet charge which sent the Rebels hurtling back down the slopes and ended the immediate opportunity to flank the Union defenders.

Berdan and Chamberlain had each provided an invaluable boost to the Federal defenders, but the fight for the Round Tops was in reality only the first act in a drama that would seesaw back and forth right into the humid summer night. A third Northern amateur, certainly far more controversial than these two men, would provide the Confederates with a golden opportunity to more than compensate for their initial frustration on this decisive day. General Daniel Sickles, the colorful commander of III Corps, was a New York politician whose career had survived everything from accusations of corruption to a sensational murder trial after he had shot his wife's lover in a fit of passion. Sickles never failed to voice an opinion and he was certain that his commander had put him in the wrong place for Thursday's battle.

Sickle's corps had been assigned to defend the southern portion of Cemetery Ridge and was adjacent to Hancock's corps, which was responsible for the northern part of the line. The lower portion of the line had far less elevation than the upper part, contained large stretches of marshy ground and didn't seem to provide an effective position for his artillery. Sickles was basically looking uphill at the ground in front of him, and he decided to abandon his line and deploy further forward before the Rebels attacked. Ten thousand bluecoats marched several hundred yards west and took up a position hedged in between Emmitsburg Road and Plum Run Creek and notable for the presence of three distinguishing features; a wheat field, a peach orchard and a jumble of enormous boulders that the locals fittingly called Devil's Den. Now Sickles had the position he wanted, but a huge gap had now opened on Cemetery Ridge and the Federal III Corps was about to be hit with a monumental assault.

If Sickles' men had stayed where Meade deployed them, the Rebels marching in alignment with the Emmitsburg Road would have been decimated by a wall of fire from Cemetery Ridge. However, at this moment luck had sided with the Rebels and instead it was the new Yankee salient that was smashed from three sides. Brigade after brigade of Southerners struck the Peach Orchard salient from south and west, left the Wheatfield strewn with Federal corpses, and overran Devil's Den in a bloody assault that ended Sickles' active military career when a Rebel shell cost the New Yorker his leg.

Meade had seen the potential for disaster in Sickles' unauthorized move, and as the III Corps refugees started streaming back from their doomed salient, the Pennsylvanian displayed an excellent ability to rush reinforcements to the right place at the right time. As the Federal line around the Peach Orchard crumbled, William Barksdale's Mississippi brigade made a furious dash for an obvious gap on Cemetery Ridge. However, just as the colorful white-haired general was leading his men over the last stretch of field, hundreds of fresh Federal riflemen and several batteries of cannons were rushed onto the ridge in time to mortally wound the general and leave half of his assault force writhing in pain on the bloody ground. Each division in this serial attack had much the same experience, as they poised to strike an opening in the Yankee line and then seemed to strike just hordes of bluecoat reinforcements deployed along the vulnerable spot. One Confederate attacker asked in amazement, "have we got all Creation to whip? Attention, Universe! Nations into line! By Kingdoms! Right Wheel!"

Meade's numerical advantage wasn't quite as large as that one Southerner imagined, but it was becoming increasingly clear as the sun dropped on the horizon that the Confederate attackers were too uncoordinated to secure the level of penetration that could win the day for the South. When Ewell's twilight assaults on Culp's Hill and Cemetery Hill sputtered to an end with no permanent breakthrough accomplished, Lee's hope to win the battle by Thursday night faded with the daylight. The Confederate army had almost broken through the Union line on several occasions, but each time just enough Yankees had arrived to blunt the thrust and save the Union position until the next threat emerged. The Rebel army now held the Wheatfield, the Peach Orchard, Devil's Den and a few tenuous footholds along the line, but their assault forces had suffered fifty percent casualties, significant generals such as John Hood, William Barksdale and Paul Semmes were either dead or badly wounded, and the Federals still held the high ground. At least one Confederate leader noted that the outcome was really no longer in doubt. As E. Porter Alexander insisted, "one is tempted to say that thus ended the battle of Gettysburg. For the third day it must be said, as was said of the charge of the Six Hundred at Balaclava, "'Magnificent, but not War!'" Robert E. Lee still had a chance to turn the course of the battle back in the Confederacy's favor, but he had little margin for error as Friday dawned.

The final outcome of the most decisive battle in the East now depended on the decisions made by Meade and Lee in their mile-apart headquarters during the short period of darkness that separated Thursday and Friday. George Meade convened a council of his corps commanders in his small farmhouse and his subordinates presented him with a relatively unanimous series of recommendations. Virtually every general agreed that the Army of the Potomac should remain on the defensive and allow Lee to attack them in their excellent defensive positions. The only disagreement focused on the length of time that the army should wait before assuming that the enemy was not going to attack and initiating an alternative strategy. On the other hand, Lee seems to have pretty much made up his own mind on the next day's strategy and that decision was entirely offensive. The Virginian was convinced that Meade had stripped his center to meet Thursday's attacks on the left and right and he assumed that the middle of Cemetery Ridge was held by no more than 5000 men. Thus Lee determined to throw 15,000 men from Longstreet's corps on a do-or-die assault which would follow the most concentrated artillery bombardment of the war. The general's assumption was that the Federal line would be split in two and the Rebel penetration force could then sweep over the ridge and essentially have a clear road to Washington.

Lee's audacity and commitment to the offensive had carried him to a position as the Confederacy's most successful general, and he had no intention of totally changing his personality for the most eventful day of the war. However, the Virginian was clearly making some major miscalculations as he approached the climax of the battle. First, although his estimate of 5000 Federals manning the center of the line was only a few hundred short of the actual number, Lee didn't fully appreciate the firepower of the Union artillery, which could launch a vicious crossfire as the Rebel troops marched over nearly a mile of open fields where they would be an inviting target for far too many minutes. Second, Lee badly underestimated the number of men that would be needed for this sort of monumental enterprise. The Virginian was essentially risking a number of men that was too large to replace in case of disaster but too few to do the job intended. Fifteen thousand men simply weren't enough to both penetrate the Union defenses and exploit the breach they made. A more realistic figure would probably have been something like 30,000 men, or most of two of the three army corps. This was certainly a far greater risk, but offered far more opportunity of being rewarded. Finally, a series of last minute changes in the organization of the assault force actually reduced the number of first line attackers to something like 11,500 men, which reduced the Confederate superiority at the point of contact from Lee's assumed 3 to one to an actual 2 to 1—a crucial weakening of the potential impact of the offensive. Each of these miscalculations would add substantially to the possibility of failure in the upcoming charge.

While the third day of the battle of Gettysburg has always been linked with the drama of Pickett's Charge, Friday's action started on the ground around Culp's Hill and Cemetery Hill. Ewell's units had achieved toeholds on those positions during Thursday's fighting, and almost the moment the sun rose the opposing armies began contesting the Federal right flank position. However, five hours of intensive fighting found the graycoats being gradually pushed back to their own lines and it soon became obvious that Lee's hope that Ewell could divert attention away from the main Confederate objective was fading. The prospect of support from an additional infantry assault was now gone, the next hope for weakening the Cemetery Ridge defenses rested with the Rebel artillery.

Colonel E. Porter Alexander, the twenty-eight-year-old commander of Longstreet's reserve artillery, was given essential responsibility for the twin objectives of forcing the enemy guns to pull back from their best positions while either scattering the Federal infantry or at least making the bluecoats keep their heads down while the Southerners made their mile-long advance. The West Point trained Georgian was expected to deploy 80 guns, which in tandem with an additional 60 cannons of Hill's corps, would concentrate enormous firepower on the stone wall and nearby grove of trees that were the focal point of the center of the Union position. At precisely 1:07 P.M. 140 rebel guns lobbed shells into the startled bluecoats and signaled the climactic point of the battle. The bombardment, which could be heard over 200 miles away in Pittsburgh, smashed Meade's headquarters, blew apart Federal wagons, ripped through Yankee supply dumps, and slaughtered dozens of Union horses. However, while one effect of the barrage was a spectacular visual demonstration of Confederate firepower, very few front line infantrymen or cannons were hit.

Essentially, this massive bombardment was hitting the wrong targets, as the intended purpose was to clear the front lines, not strike panic among Union quartermasters and bandsmen. However, when Federal artillery chief Henry Hunt began to pull back most of the batteries deployed on the cemetery grounds in order to conserve ammunition, Alexander assumed he had accomplished his mission and sent a message to Pickett, "for God's sake, come quick or my ammunition will not let me support you properly." The colorful, perfumed Pickett now took center stage in the planned assault. In one sense, the term "Pickett's Charge" is not totally accurate, since the former last-place graduate of West Point commanded only 4700 of the 11,500 front line assault troops. However, he has certainly emerged as the energetic driving force behind the charge, while Isaac Trimble and Johnston Pettigrew were essentially substitute commanders who were much less identifiable with their units. Each of the four leading figures in the division of Virginians that would make the charge had some form of emotional imperative in this desperate enterprise. Pickett himself had arrived too late for Manassas, commanded reserve troops at Fredericksburg and had been deployed in southern Virginia during Chancellorsville. Thus this assault would be his first real opportunity to lift himself out of relative obscurity. Brigade commander Richard Garnett was still under a cloud caused by Stonewall Jackson's violent reaction to his withdrawal of his unit at the battle of Kernstown, which had resulted in a court martial that had been constantly postponed with no clear cut decision. James Kemper had served as speaker of the Virginia House and probably saw the charge as a giant step toward the Governor's mansion which he would ultimately attain. Lewis Armistead knew that his closest friend from the Old Army, Winfield Hancock, was defending the position that he was ordered to assault. As these four generals and thousands of enlisted men collected their thoughts before the great advance began, the bluecoat defenders crouched behind their stone wall and probably hoped desperately that their supporting artillery could smash the huge mass of Rebels before they slammed into Cemetery Ridge and broke a Federal line that seemed a bit too thin to withstand the assault that seemed to be brewing.

At about 3 o'clock on Friday afternoon, July 3rd, a mile wide formation of Southern soldiers marched out from their position in the woods, received the eager salutes of their cannon-firing comrades and advanced toward the looming enemy ridge at about 100 yards a minute. Within three or four minutes the first Federal shells began to plunge into the gray ranks and in some cases an entire squad would go down with one explosion. Eight hundred yards from the stone fence the Rebels began to reform their increasingly gap-filled line, and while this process was underway the Yankee gunners stepped up their rate of fire to an even higher level. While Kemper's men were being riddled by the guns on Little Round Top, Johnston Pettigrew's left flank regiments were being decimated by almost 30 Federal cannons that had been deployed on Cemetery Hill. At this point, in an unprecedented action at this point in the war for the Army of Northern Virginia, four of these regiments simply turned around in a mass and rushed back to the cover of Seminary Ridge.

The left flank of the assault was now crumbling from mass retreat, and the right flank was being annihilated as men tried to move forward, and the net result was a rapidly developing disaster for the Confederacy. In Pickett's division generals Kemper and Garnett were shot and ultimately 34 of the 35 ranking officers in the assault force would be killed or wounded. Casualties among field officers in Trimble and Pettigrew's units were rising toward 90% while captains tried to rally survivors of regiments for the final push forward. Armistead, the last of Pickett's brigade commanders who was still unwounded, urged his men forward with the insistence that "home is over beyond those hills!" while his old friend Hancock set in motion a flanking movement that began tearing the Rebels to pieces. Armistead made it over the stone wall with about 300 of his men, but volley after volley of Federal musket fire mortally wounded the brigadier and virtually annihilated the small band of Rebels who constituted the "high tide of the Confederacy" when they reached Cemetery Ridge.

Robert E. Lee, James Longstreet and George Pickett were each watching the climax of the charge from a different vantage point but they all saw the same disaster. Something like 7500 of the 11,500 front line assault troops were now dead, wounded or captured, and when Pickett made his famous response to Lee concerning the disposition of his division, "Sir, I have no division," he wasn't all that far off the mark. Pickett had lost all of his brigadiers, all of his colonels and nearly two-thirds of his men. On the other hand, the Federals had captured 38 regimental flags and 4000 prisoners at a cost of only 1500 casualties. The three-day engagement had resulted in about 23,000 Union casualties, but their opponents had lost closer to 28,000 men and the Confederacy was clearly unable to replace this level of casualties. What made this loss doubly grievous was that just as Pickett's men were being slaughtered, the climactic campaign in the West was about to end even more disastrously for the Confederate republic.

Lee had not only lost the battle of Gettysburg, but his operations in Pennsylvania had also failed to have any impact on drawing Federal troops away from the tightening noose that Ulysses Grant was drawing around Vicksburg. Grant's army had spent the preceding six weeks preventing Pemberton's garrison from securing supplies or reinforcements from the outside, while digging trenches that had now virtually reached the gates of Vicksburg. Confederate soldiers were reduced to one biscuit a day supplemented by a variety of mule, dog and rat carcasses which were themselves rapidly becoming luxury items. By June 28th the Rebel supply system had almost totally collapsed and Pemberton received a strongly worded circular from "many soldiers" which bluntly stated, "if you can't feed us you had better surrender us...! rather than suffer the whole army to disgrace themselves by desertion. I tell you plainly, the men are not going to lie here and perish."

The Pennsylvania Confederate subsequently received a dispatch from Joseph Johnston saying that he would make a diversionary attack on Grant's lines on July 7th to enable the garrison to break out, but Pemberton and his lieutenants now realized that their men were too weak to do any more than stand in their rifle pits and the best that could be hoped for was a generous capitulation agreement. The Confederate commander still held one ace and he used it brilliantly. The Rebels had broken the flag code between the Federal navy and army, which they discovered was based on Edgar Allen Poe's "The Gold Bug." They knew that Commodore Porter was becoming adamant about his desire to avoid using his ships to transport a surrendered garrison to Northern prisoner of war camps. Thus, Pemberton reasoned, "Unconditional Surrender" Grant might settle for considerably less than those terms, especially if the capitulation could be signed on Independence Day. The Philadelphian told his Southern subordinates, "I know my people. I know we can get better terms from them on the Fourth of July than any other day of the year."

White flags began to appear along the Confederate trenches on the afternoon of July 3rd and although Grant quickly rejected Pemberton's initial offer to abandon the city if the Rebel army could march out with its arms, he finally relented enough to allow the Southerners to receive an on-the-spot parole while officers could keep their horses, swords and pistols. As at least one Federal division gave a hearty cheer "for the gallant defenders of Vicksburg," 32,000 graycoats stacked their arms and marched out of the city. At a cost of just under 5000 casualties, Ulysses Simpson Grant had eliminated one of the three main armies of the Confederacy and captured the single most important point in the secessionist republic, while attracting increasing attention to himself as the person who was most likely to oversee the coordinated operations that would be vital to the hopes of an eventual Union victory.

The dramatic first few days of July, 1863 permanently changed the course of the War Between the States. In a little more than a week the Confederate invasion of Pennsylvania had been smashed and the Mississippi River bastion of Vicksburg along with its southern supporting defenses around Port Hudson had been captured, effectively slicing the southern republic in two. Nearly 70,000 Rebel soldiers were killed, wounded or captured between July 1st and July 9th and this loss represented nearly one-third of the front line troops available to the Confederate government. The Confederate war department could and would rob Peter to pay Paul in a gigantic shell game of redeploying Rebel regiments, divisions and even corps to meet the latest potential breakthrough along the enormous perimeter of the republic. However, replacements for the losses of July, 1863 would increasingly be found among teenage boys, middle-aged men and wheezing, reluctant militia clerks, none of whom could really match the fighting ability of the thousands of men in their prime who were now in their graves or limping around their homes with newly amputated limbs. The South was still capable of brutally convincing overly optimistic Yankees that the war was far from finished, but the conqueror of Fort Donelson and Vicksburg was about to move to center stage and no single person in the Confederacy was exactly sure how to prevent Ulysses Simpson Grant from turning Mr. Lincoln's armies into the agents of ultimate Confederate disaster.

# CHAPTER 30

# The Duel for Chattanooga

## *The Emergence of U.S. Grant*

While Ulysses Grant was recovering from a near-fatal riding accident and George Meade was groping through Northern Virginia in a vain attempt to trap Lee's army, a small group of Confederate officials were debating a variety of plans designed to provide the South with a decisive victory to at least partially nullify the negative impact of Gettysburg and Vicksburg. During the weeks after those two disasters had occurred, William Rose-crans' Army of the Cumberland had shaken off six months of almost total inactivity, and through a series of brilliant maneuvers, had forced Braxton Bragg's Army of Tennessee to abandon its base at Tullahoma and withdraw rapidly toward the vital rail center of Chattanooga. Unless this latest Federal drive was halted, the Yankees would soon enter Georgia and capture Atlanta, which would divide the northern and southern sections of the Confederacy in the same way that the fall of Vicksburg had split the republic into separate eastern and western sections a few weeks earlier.

Secretary of War Seddon and General James Longstreet once again proposed the plan that they had submitted after the victory at Chancellors-ville; namely, that at least one corps of the Army of Northern Virginia be transported west by rail to reinforce Bragg's army and overwhelm the Federals threatening Chattanooga and Atlanta. While Robert E. Lee had been able to veto this plan in May, this time Jefferson Davis approved the idea and Major Frederick Sims was ordered to work out the logistics of moving three Confederate divisions 550 miles from the Rapidan River to Chattanooga. However, while Sims was working out the calculations for this massive transfer, an army under General Ambrose Burnside captured Cumberland Gap and Knoxville. This forced the Confederates to reroute their expedition through the Carolinas, then to Augusta, Georgia, north to Atlanta and then finally toward the rapidly shifting lines of Bragg's army—a total of almost 1000 miles along the creaky, poorly maintained Southern railway system. As Longstreet prepared his men for their long journey, he was informed of two additional changes of plan. First, the Confederate authorities had decided that George Pickett's division had been too badly mangled at Gettysburg to make the trip, and second, that Rosecrans had just captured Chattanooga and the link-up of eastern and western forces would have to occur somewhere in northern Georgia.

On September 8th, as Federal troops advanced toward Chattanooga, the first units of Hood's and McLaws' divisions boarded a series of trains sitting on sidings at Orange Court House and began the bone jarring journey through a shrinking Confederate republic. Horses were shoved and pulled up ramps and into boxcars, cannons and caissons came creaking and groaning aboard flatcars, and graycoat infantry squeezed onto an odd assortment of passenger coaches, baggage cars, mail cars and flatcars as the engines started chugging at the beginning of an originally expected four-day journey that soon stretched well beyond a week. While the expeditionary force was in no danger of setting any speed records, the Confederates were helped by poor Federal intelligence, which the Northern War Department had convinced that Bragg was actually going to be moved east to reinforce Lee, while the absence of two Rebel divisions went unnoticed by Meade's army for almost a week. Braxton Bragg would enjoy the luxury of both surprise and superior numbers when he confronted an overconfident Rosecrans, and if all went well, the summer defeats would be avenged.

Bragg had already almost annihilated Rosecrans without Longstreet's help when the Northern commander unwisely divided his army into three separate detachments as the Federals plunged headlong into Georgia chasing the "defeated" Rebels. However, the Confederates were far from defeated and only a last minute realization that the Southerners had baited a trap caused the Union commander to hurriedly withdraw while he began the difficult task of concentrating his forces. Rosecrans pulled back to the valley of Chickamauga Creek on the western slope of Missionary Ridge, about 12 miles south of Union-occupied Chattanooga. The Confederate commander responded to this move by ordering his army to smash into the Federal left flank and thus cut the Yankees off from their only escape route back to the city—the road through Rossville Gap. On the afternoon of Friday September 18th, the Army of Tennessee, now reinforced by the first of five eastern brigades that would arrive in time to influence the battle, started attacking the northern end of Rosecrans' defense line in a massive push to get control of an many Chickamauga bridges as possible. However, a combination of well positioned Yankee artillery and the rapid fire of several Union regiments armed with new Spencer repeating rifles slaughtered dozens of the attackers and allowed the bluecoats to gradually pull back away from the creek to a new position along the Lafayette-Chattanooga road.

At dawn on Saturday, as the Rebels tried to move more units across the creek, Union corps commander George Thomas started sending his bluecoats in brigade sized assault teams designed to smash the Rebels before they could consolidate on the west side of the Chickamauga. Two of these brigades caught legendary Confederate cavalry commander Nathan Bedford Forrest's men in a pincers that threatened to annihilate the dismounted graycoat horsemen, until an infantry division led by a commander with the appropriate name of, States Rights Gist, crashed into the Federals' flanks and turned the battle into a seesaw affair that spilled back and forth through the woods adjoining the creek. The Union troops always seemed to have enough firepower to stop Rebel assaults just short of their final defenses, but the Confederates had enough of a manpower advantage to discourage the Yankees from charging back across the Creek. Finally, as the sun went down on a bloody but indecisive Saturday, the bluecoats began to pull out their spades and axes and throw up an ever larger line of breastworks along the Lafayette road, while Bragg sulked in his headquarters and tried to figure out a way to penetrate an ever stronger enemy line. At about 11 P.M. Saturday night James Longstreet himself arrived at the battlefield after nearly walking into the headquarters of a Union brigade. Bragg proposed an attack on Sunday at dawn utilizing whatever eastern reinforcements had arrived by that time, in an echelon type attack starting from the north and moving progressively toward the southern end of the Union line. Since almost half of Longstreet's infantry and all of his artillery were still in transit, Bragg probably would have been wiser to delay the attack 24 hours until he could fully employ the force that the Confederate government had spent so much time and energy standing to his support. However, the Army of Tennessee commander insisted that he couldn't delay any longer and Longstreet was assigned six divisions to form the right wing of the Southern army, while Leonidas Polk was assigned five divisions to initiate the assault with the left wing.

At dawn on Sunday September 20th Bragg stood outside his headquarters waiting for the sound of firing that would signal the Rebel attack against the Union left flank. Nine months earlier the Army of Tennessee had almost annihilated Rosecrans when the Rebels attacked at first light while the Yankees were still earing their breakfast. However, unlike the engagement at Stones River, this time Bragg stood impatiently as the minutes ticked by and absolutely nothing happened. An eager staff officer dispatched to find Polk found the Episcopal bishop-general on the porch of a farmhouse with his feet propped up, reading the paper and waiting for a hot breakfast. Another messenger found General Harvey Hill unaware that any assault had been ordered, and not even sure what the bishop's plans for the day actually were. These incredible foul-ups gave the Union defenders plenty of time to perfect their breastworks, and when Polk's wing finally got around to attacking, Thomas' divisions blasted them to pieces and no graycoat got to within 30 yards of the Yankee lines.

By late morning Polk's disjointed attacks had fizzled out, and if the battle had ended at that point, the North could have claimed a substantial victory.

However, Longstreet's wing hadn't launched its assault and the burly Georgian now decided to ignore Bragg's order for an echelon attack and risk everything on one throw of the dice—a gigantic hammer blow launched with every man hitting the Federal line at once. While Longstreet aligned his shock troops in the safety of the nearby woods, Rosecrans and his aides were riding along the Federal center and right flank congratulating themselves on a superbly fought defensive victory on Thomas' left flank. In an ironic twist of fate, Captain Sanford Kellogg was riding down a portion of the Federal line just after General John Brannan had become dissatisfied with the deployment of his division, which prompted him to pull his men back to a more defensible position in a wooded area to the west. Kellogg didn't see Brannan's new position and instead, rode back to headquarters and reported a huge gap in the Union lines. Rosecrans didn't bother to personally investigate the problem and instead ordered General Thomas Wood to pull out of his place in the line and plug the "gap" further north. Just as Wood's men had disengaged from their position and had begun marching north, a tidal wave of Rebels smashed into a now all too real hole in the bluecoat lines and promptly split the Union army in two.

Sixteen thousand rebels who were well rested and enjoyed excellent cover on their approach drove into the most vulnerable point in the enemy line and began shredding Union regiments into pieces. General Bushrod Johnson, an Ohioan who had joined the Confederate cause, noted "the scene now presented was remarkably grand. The resolute and impetuous charge, the rush of our heavy columns sweeping out from the shadow of the gloom of the forest into the open fields flooded with sunlight, the glitter of arms, the dash of artillery and mounted men, the retreat of the foe made up a battle scene of unsurpassed grandeur." Union general Philip Sheridan had a slightly less romantic view of the onslaught. "A horde of Confederates overwhelmed us and sliced two of my brigades to pieces my troops were driven back with heavy losses."

The next hour was 60 minutes of chaos for the Union army as screeching Rebels rolled up the right flank and center of the Federal line, thousands of panic stricken bluecoats retreated northward and Rosecrans and his staff became caught up in the blue tide of stragglers. However, as the Yankee regiments began to disintegrate as organized units, General John Wilder's brigade of Spencer equipped mounted infantry interposed themselves between the fleeing Federals and the advancing Rebels and poured a sheet of flame into the cheering graycoats. Wilder's men were outnumbered 10 to 1 and the check they could inflict on the on the Southerners would only be a temporary one, but just as their line began to become engulfed a supporting force under twenty-five-year-old Colonel Charles Harker came rushing up and slammed into John Bell Hood's elite Texas brigade. Hood himself went down with a shattered thigh that would add an amputated leg to his already useless arm, and the sudden Union attack at least temporarily slowed the gray onslaught.

At this point in the battle, one of the most ironic events of the Civil War occurred as both commanding generals in effect relinquished control of the battle while still unhurt from the fighting. Rosecrans assumed that battle was lost and essentially entrusted a rear guard action to Thomas, while he rode back to Chattanooga to supervise the preparations for what he felt would an imminent Rebel follow-up assault. Amazingly, Bragg was equally convinced that the Confederates had lost the battle after Polk's assaults had failed, and the Army of Tennessee commander retired toward the rear, leaving Longstreet in effective field command. Both Thomas and Longstreet were more than willing to take responsibility for the rest of the engagement and each general prepared for a climactic afternoon. Longstreet tallied his gains so far: two square miles of battlefield captured, 40 enemy cannons overrun, thousands of bluecoat prisoners and even more thousands of captured rifles. However, about a mile further back in this heavily wooded field George Thomas was furiously constructing a new Federal line. This position, centered around a spur of Missionary Ridge called Snodgrass Hill, blocked the way to Confederate control of vital Rossville Gap, and the Virginia Unionist would be incredibly difficult to dislodge.

Confederate units under Joseph Kershaw, Bushrod Johnson and Thomas Hindman converged on the Union last ditch line, and while the Yankees were able to smash the first series of assaults, most of the bluecoats were now almost out of ammunition. However, a prickly, bad tempered Union general was about to radically alter this situation. General Gordon Granger had been assigned by Rosecrans to hold the road to Rossville Gap while the rest of the army deployed along the Chickamauga. While the battle raged four miles to his south, Granger fretted and paced, cursing his bad luck that caused him to be out of the action. After climbing a tall haystack to get a glimpse of the action through his binoculars, the general decided to essentially ignore Rosecrans' orders and march most of his force to the sound of the guns. After a harrowing encounter with large numbers of Forrest's cavalrymen, Granger fought his way through to Snodgrass Hill with two fresh infantry brigades and thousands of rounds of spare ammunition. Suddenly, empty Yankee rifles were reloaded and as the usually taciturn Thomas warmly shook hands with his unexpected savior, the advancing Rebels were engaged from a totally unexpected direction.

However, just as the battle surged back in the Federals' favor and Thomas became optimistic that he could hold his position through the night, two Confederate generals, both with close ties to the North, provided the margin for Rebel victory. William Preston, a former United States Congressman from Kentucky and a prominent Harvard alumnus; and Archibald Gracie, a member of a prominent New York family that would eventually give their name to the home of New York City mayors, organized 3000 relatively fresh graycoats for a last, desperate charge against the Federal position. About half of these Rebels went down in another ferocious hail of Yankee rifle fire, but the defenders of this part of the line had again run out of ammunition and it became obvious to Thomas that he could no longer keep the Confederates at bay. Exhausted and outflanked, Northern soldiers ditched knapsacks, haversacks and rifles and trudged back to Rossville Gap while a few rearguard units held the Rebels at a respectful distance. The bluecoats had left behind 51 guns, 23,000 rifles and several thousand of their comrades, but while Forrest closed in on Chattanooga and started bobbing shells into the city, no infantry support arrived for a final engagement. Longstreet hurried back to Bragg's headquarters pleading for permission to continue the offensive but Bragg simply shook his head and said that only a traditional siege could take the city.

The Confederates had finally gained their first substantial victory in the West, but it was one of the most hollow triumphs of the war. Bragg had finally sent the bluecoats running in panic from a battlefield but he had suffered a mind-numbing 21,000 casualties to accomplish his objective. Almost half of Longstreet's assault force had been killed or wounded, while the total number of Union killed and wounded was only a little over 11,000. Only the surrender of 5000 Yankees during the retreat evened the casualty total somewhat, but the simple fact was that a Confederacy that had just lost 60,000 men at Vicksburg and Gettysburg was far too undermanned to lose another 20,000 even in a victory. Chickamauga could only have been defined as a really decisive victory if Bragg had been able to force the surrender of Rosecrans' army after besieging Chattanooga. However, very shortly the Army of the Cumberland wouldn't be Rosecrans' to command and the Army of Tennessee would soon be facing a far more dangerous Northern leader.

The debacle at Chickamauga not only provided Ulysses Grant with an opportunity to display his military talents to Lincoln and his military advisors in Washington, it also demonstrated dramatically the logistical and technological superiority of the Union military machine. When the War Department received word that the Army the of Cumberland was besieged at Chattanooga, Lincoln was roused from his bed and called a late night conference to consider plans to relieve the crisis. The authors believe that the ensuing few weeks demonstrated the enormous war-making capacity that the Union would increasingly employ during the final two years of the War Between the States. Orders were immediately dispatched to George Meade to prepare the XI and XII Corps of the Army of the Potomac to be detached under the command of Joseph Hooker in order to be transported for the relief of the Army of the Cumberland. Early in September the Confederacy had been able to turn the tide at Chickamauga by sending 7500 Rebel troops 900 miles in nine days. Now the North would send 20,000 men 1200 miles in about half the time in order to turn the campaign back in favor of the Union.

While this large contingent from the main eastern army was riding westward, Grant and his conquerors of Vicksburg were organizing for an eastward trek for the same purpose of saving the Army of the Cumberland from a humiliating surrender. Grant had been badly injured during an inspection tour of New Orleans. His horse had become alarmed at an approaching train and had thrown the general in a fall that caused a probable fractured skull and massive leg injuries. As Grant slowly recovered from this near fatal accident, he received orders to proceed to Louisville to confer with a designated "officer of the War Department." The officer proved to be none other than Secretary of War Edwin Stanton, who after mistaking Grant's physician for the general, settled down to confer command of virtually all forces east of the Alleghenies on the hero of Vicksburg. Grant promptly removed Rosecrans from command, substituted Thomas as leader of the Army of the Cumberland, and made his way painfully over the miserable roads that gave access to the besieged army in Chattanooga. Once Grant arrived in that vital city, the days of Confederate siege-making were already numbered.

At the same time that the Union army was gaining new leadership and more confidence, the besieging Confederate army was slowly self-destructing at the top. Bragg had never been a popular commander at the best of times, and now most of the significant generals of the Army of Tennessee were convinced that their commander had botched the greatest opportunity of the war. Bragg-bashing became so pronounced that Jefferson Davis was forced to put his mountains of paperwork aside and travel westward to sort out the mess in his currently largest field army. Nathan Bedford Forrest had already stormed into Bragg's headquarters virtually threatening to kill the general if they ever served together again. Then newly suspended corps commander Leonidas Polk cornered his close friend Davis and swore that he would never serve in the same army with the bad tempered commander. When the Confederate president finally reached Army of Tennessee headquarters in the outskirts of Chattanooga the atmosphere was tense as charges and counter-charges volleyed between Bragg and most of his subordinates. The result was a surrealistic conference where Bragg sat silently and listened to his subordinates categorize his failings to Davis. Bragg offered to resign, the president loudly refused and the next morning quietly began interviewing successors to the commanding general.

Longstreet was offered the command after a day-long conference with the president, but "Old Pete" responded that "in my judgement, our last opportunity was lost when we failed to follow the success at Chickamauga and capture or disperse the Union army, and it could not be just to the service or myself to call me to a position of such responsibility." In other words, command of this army was a disaster waiting to happen and when Longstreet countered with a suggestion of Joe Johnston for the position, Davis went into a tirade concerning one of his least favorite generals as "the suggestion of that name only seemed to increase his displeasure and his severe rebuke." After this less than satisfying exchange with Bragg's senior lieutenant, the president sounded out Hardee, Hill, Buckner and Cheatham about accepting the position and each general politely declined the honor, although none of them wanted Bragg to remain in command either. Davis finally took the path of least resistance and kept Bragg in command while the commanding general retaliated against his subordinates by sending Harvey Hill back to Virginia, packing off Buckner on a "voluntary" leave of absence and relieving Cheatham from his temporary corps command. Bragg was also particularly anxious to dispose of Longstreet, but his key role in the recent victory combined with his friendship with the powerful Lee encouraged the general to bide his time and wait for a better opportunity, which ironically would greatly add to his own eventual undoing.

Soon after his arrival in Chattanooga, Ulysses Grant and his subordinates went out on an inspection tour of the Union defense lines and the Confederate emplacements nearby. Rebel artillery had effectively closed off the main water route, the main railroad and the major turnpikes into the city, but one of Grant's West Point classmates, General William "Baldy" Smith, proposed a plan to reopen the supply line by seizing enemy occupied Brown's Ferry on the opposite side of the Tennessee River. Smith proposed that a Union brigade would utilize 60 newly constructed pontoon boats to float down the river and seize the ferry landing, while a second force of Joseph Hooker's Army of the Potomac reinforcements would march from their base at Bridgeport, move along the railroad tracks during the night, and knock out the Confederate defense on Raccoon Mountain in order to deter a counterattack on Brown's Ferry. Grant quickly gave Smith operational control of the assault and on the night of October 26th, 1863, General William Hazen's 1500 troops boarded the pontoon boats and began a circuitous six-mile run down the Tennessee, river knowing that if they were spotted by Rebel pickets on the other shore they could well be annihilated with almost no effective defense.

At 5 o'clock in the morning the first of Hazen's men waded ashore, surprised the Confederate guards, and set up a defensive perimeter around the ferry landing. While Union engineers started to construct a pontoon bridge back to the Federal side of the river, several poorly coordinated enemy assaults were launched with each one being thrown back in confusion. Meanwhile, Hooker's men had been marching all night and were making good time until daylight revealed their activities to Rebel observers on 700-foot-high Lookout Mountain. Bragg and Longstreet were hurriedly called to the observation post and while Bragg favored an energetic follow-up attack on Brown's Ferry, Longstreet was convinced that Hooker's rear guard was the most inviting target. Therefore, while Hooker's main force was allowed to link up with Hazen, a rear guard division under General John Geary was attacked by Hood's old division, now led by General Micah Jenkins. However, Jenkins' men became lost in the woods during their approach march, several hundred Federal mules broke loose and stampeded into the graycoats just as they began to charge the Union force, and Geary's men set up a withering fire that decimated an attack force that was actually slightly smaller than the defenders. By the time the attack had sputtered out, Brown's Ferry was solidly in Union hands and a "Cracker Line" was established to ensure that the besiegers of Chattanooga would shortly be transformed into the besieged.

Braxton Bragg still commanded a formidable force of about 60,000 men on Lookout Mountain and Missionary Ridge to confront Grant's reinforced Federal army of 75,000 troops, but in one of the most controversial decisions of the war, the Army of Tennessee commander began to strip his defenses just as his enemy was preparing to attack him. Bragg was still fuming over Longstreet's failure to support him in the earlier meeting with Jefferson Davis, and when dispatches arrived informing the general that Northern forces were moving on Knoxville, the dour general quickly assigned his chief subordinate 15,000 badly needed men to recapture East Tennessee from the Federals. While Longstreet's men were marching away from the Confederate lines, William Tecumseh Sherman's troops were marching into Chattanooga and the balance of power was rapidly tilting toward the Union.

Grant and Sherman spent several days climbing through the hilly terrain trying to find a vulnerable spot in the enemy defense line. The two generals assumed that Bragg would concentrate most of his artillery and best infantry units along the center of Missionary Ridge, which stood 300 feet above the Tennessee River. In order to avoid a probably fruitless frontal assault at that point, Grant drew up plans in which Sherman would march four divisions around to the extreme northern end of the ridge to hit the right flank of the enemy line, while Hooker would demonstrate against Lookout Mountain, and George Thomas' Army of the Cumberland would menace, but not assault, the Confederate center. Grant and Sherman were convinced that Hooker and Thomas would keep most of the Confederate army occupied while Sherman would have a clear path to seize the northern edge of the ridge and then roll down the crest, sweeping startled Rebel troops before him.

The Union would gain a spectacular victory in this campaign but almost nothing in this battle went according to the original game plan. At 2 P.M. on November 23rd, Philip Sheridan's division moved out from its positions east of town and linked up with Thomas Wood's troops at the edge of an open field that separated the Union lines from the Rebels on Missionary Ridge. The bluecoats formed so openly and in such perfect formation that the Southern guards along the crest were convinced that the Yankees were staging a parade. However, the Federals suddenly cheered and broke into a run as they charged toward the enemy lines. These troops were not yet interested in attacking Missionary Ridge, their objective was a smaller hill called Orchard Knob which was about a mile from the main Confederate lines. The Rebels had a few regiments stationed on the Knob and they fought a short, determined delaying action in which each side lost about 1000 men. However, when no graycoat reinforcements were sent in support, these defenders retreated toward Missionary Ridge and the Yankees celebrated their opening triumph with a mass of cheers from the rest of the Federal army.

Grant quickly moved his headquarters forward to Orchard Knob and ordered Hooker to prepare his diversionary attack and Sherman to initiate his main attack at dawn the next day. At 2 A.M. on November 24th, 116 pontoon boats carried the first wave of Sherman's assault force across the Tennessee River well upstream from the main Confederate lines. The Yankees scrambled up the river bank, waded through thickets and bushes with a rifle in one hand and a shovel in the other and began throwing up entrenchments to counter an expected Rebel assault. When no assault materialized, Sherman ordered his men forward through a depressing combination of fog, mist and drizzle and directed his troops to begin climbing what was assumed to be the northern edge of Missionary Ridge. Unfortunately for the redheaded Ohioan, Federal maps were woefully inaccurate, and his bluecoats were actually overrunning a totally separate hill that was cut off from the vital railroad tunnel at the north end of Missionary Ridge by a deep ravine and almost impenetrable undergrowth on the far side of the gorge. An annoyed and perplexed Sherman ordered his men to fortify the positions they held while he came up with a new attack plan that wouldn't be carried out until the next morning.

If November 24th was a less than spectacular day in Sherman's rising career, this rainy Tuesday was a major comeback opportunity for Joseph Hooker. Hooker's initial orders were nothing more than to occupy as many Confederate troops as possible on Lookout Mountain while Sherman's men rolled up the enemy right flank and won the battle. However, while the redheaded general's troops were wandering around trying to find the right hill to assault, Hooker's men accomplished far more than they originally planned. Twelve thousand assault troops crossed swollen Lookout Creek early on Tuesday morning and advance units began a gingerly move toward Confederate rifle pits at the base of the mountain. However, when the defenders provided only weak opposition and fled, larger groups of Federals started climbing a series of paths that led part way up the heavily timbered mountain and converged part way up at Craven's Farm. Brigadier General Edward Walthall managed to deploy most of his regiments around the farm but visibility was poor and his men couldn't see Federal attackers until they were almost on top of them. At this point, while Walthall sent for reinforcements, the overall Confederate commander on Lookout, General John Jackson, seems to have largely disappeared from the scene. General Jackson, derisively called "Mudwall" because of his ineptness compared to the other Jackson, kept wavering between supporting his subordinate and abandoning the whole mountain, and for most of the battle seemed to maintain an incredibly low profile.

As the clouds lowered on this murky day, Hooker's troops pushed past the farm buildings and moved toward the peak, out of sight to spectators below. By now thousands of otherwise unengaged Yankee soldiers were watching this high altitude drama unfold and when the action moved up out of sight only the rattle of rifles gave a clue to what was happening. Finally, in one of the most dramatic moments of the war, "the Battle above the Clouds" came to an ear splitting climax just as the clouds lifted and a weak late fall sun peeked through. Union soldiers gasped with delight as they saw regimental flags moving toward the now visible peak. At a cost of about 600 casualties, Joseph Hooker and his sometimes derided "paper collar" soldiers from the east had won a spectacular victory, and that evening Union campfires lit the sides of the mountain "looking like lightning bugs on a dark night." At first light Wednesday morning, six men from the 8th Kentucky regiment raised an oversized Stars and Stripes on the top of the peak in the Civil War version of the similar event at Iwo Jima 82 years later. Thousands of bluecoats waved their caps in the air as they prepared to embark on the final phase of the Battle of Chattanooga.

Despite Hooker's spectacular operation, Grant's main objective was still the northern end of Missionary Ridge, and Sherman was expected to supply the punch that would roll up Bragg's army once and for all. However, the dour Southerner had actually improved his chances of holding Missionary Ridge when he had initiated another incomprehensible move. While Grant was launching his first moves toward the Confederate defenses, Bragg had been busily dispatching two additional divisions to East Tennessee to support Longstreet's growing siege of the Union garrison holding Knoxville. When the Federal threat began to crystallize, one of the divisions was already too far down the railroad line to be recalled, but Patrick Cleburne's crack division was rerouted and marched back toward Tunnel Hill at the northern end of Missionary Ridge. This was exactly the spot that Sherman needed to capture to roll up the Confederate lines, and Cleburne quickly deployed his men on the heights above the ravine to counter the Yankee advance.

Sherman's men started down the side of the ravine leading to Tunnel Hill early on Wednesday morning, expecting only token initial resistance. However, Cleburne commanded what was probably the best division in the Army of Tennessee and his men were deployed in a perfect position to counter the Yankee thrust down the ridge. Wave after wave of bluecoats tried to climb up the far side of the ravine, but a hail of cannon balls, rifle bullets and even rolling boulders and rocks dropped over 1500 Federals and brought the operation to a halt. Grant initially hoped that Hooker's recently victorious easterners might be able to take some of the pressure from Sherman, but when these bluecoats wound their way down the winding, narrow roads of Lookout Mountain they were abruptly halted by the swollen waters of the Chattanooga River, which now contained no crossing points as the Rebels had demolished every bridge. While Hooker's men scoured the countryside to find building materials, Grant chewed on one unlit cigar after another and tried to devise an operation that could free Sherman's stalled troops from their stalemate. Finally, the Union commander turned to George Thomas and said "don't you think its about time to advance against the rifle pits.?" The Union commander was essentially ordering the Army of the Cumberland to launch a limited advance to capture the lowest line of Confederate defenses along Missionary Ridge, which would hopefully siphon some of the defenders of Tunnel Hill away from Sherman. Before the afternoon was out, far more than this would be accomplished.

At about 3:30 on that Wednesday afternoon, four divisions of bluecoats totaling about 25,000 men lined up in front of Orchard Knob in a two mile wide battle formation. As one awestruck observer noted "it was a scene never to be forgotten—a panorama to stir the blood into wild tumult." An officer in the line of march insisted "it was one of the grandest spectacles ever seen, an experience never to be encountered twice in a lifetime." As thousands of bayonets caught the late afternoon sunlight, Federal soldiers jumped over gullies, climbed over felled trees, moved around rocks and stumps and let out one huge resounding cheer as they closed in on the Rebel rifle pits at the foot of Missionary Ridge. Dozens of Bragg's 170 available cannons blasted at the advancing Yankees but Federal batteries emplaced on Orchard Knob not only silenced many Rebel guns but blew Bragg's headquarters to rubble just after the general had stepped out to direct the defenders. When the Union troops got to within pistol range of the rifle pits, Confederate fire from the crest became useless as friend and foe intermingled in a melee of bayonets, clubbed rifles and fists which the far more numerous bluecoats were clearly winning.

As the surviving Rebels rushed part way up the ridge to their next level of defenses, the victorious Yankees were suddenly thrown back into mortal danger as the defenders were once again free to blast the attack force from the heights. While Grant had ordered the Cumberland men to take the first line of rifle pits he hadn't really directed them to advance any further, and soon the troops were milling around in confusion. Confederate fire became so intense that it was obvious they couldn't stay where they were, the nearest Federal lines were several hundred yards back over open ground, yet rows of Southern rifles and cannons loomed menacingly from the crest. At this point reality and myth become hopelessly intertwined. One fact is clear, a significant number of Federals began to realize that they couldn't stay for long in the rifle pits without getting shot by the Rebels on Missionary Ridge crest, so at some point an increasingly large number of these bluecoats decided that it would be safer to take their chances with a second stage assault rather than be hit staying where they were or in a retreat. It seems fairly likely that no high ranking commander ever gave the initial order to charge; for example Grant stood on Orchard Knob watching the assault unfold while he muttered that heads would roll if this unauthorized charge was annihilated. What seems most probable is that groups of soldiers recognized the danger they were in while occupying the rifle pits and decided either singly or in small groups to continue the attack while picking up either the enthusiastic or tacit support of company level officers on their way up the mountain. Once this advance started to gain momentum, higher ranking officers probably stepped in to more fully organize the direction of the attack, giving orders to the men as they clambered up toward the second line of Rebel entrenchments half way up the hill.

Luckily for the Yankees, the Confederate density of fire was nothing like Cemetery Ridge at Gettysburg. Twenty-five thousand bluecoats, more than twice Pickett's strength on July 3rd, were charging up a hill that was dangerously short of defenders due to detachments sent to Longstreet and the deployment of men to meet threats from Hooker and Sherman. The Southerners held good ground, but most officers reported that their men were spread so thinly that at some points the Rebels were six feet apart—far too wide a deployment to provide really concentrated rifle fire. Yankee attackers were getting shot by the hundreds but color bearers, adjutants and junior officers kept urging the men forward. Seven color bearers who scaled Missionary Ridge and planted their flags on the crest won Congressional Medals of Honor while the young adjutant of the 24th Wisconsin put his name in the history books when he yelled "On Wisconsin!" and carried what might have been the first regimental flag to reach the crest. John MacArthur would go beyond Missionary Ridge to a highly successful military career while fathering a son in Douglas MacArthur who would produce enough fame, success and controversy to be worthy of any Civil War general.

Once the uphill charge got underway, normally mercurial generals such as Gordon Granger and Phil Sheridan really got into their element as they organized massive thrusts against the final rebel line. The Confederates rolled boulders and fused artillery shells down the cliffs, emptied pistols, swung clubbed muskets and gradually retreated in the face of overwhelming numbers of bluecoats. Bragg ran up and down the line imploring his men to stand firm while groups of soldiers either insulted him or ignored an obviously defeated leader. Soon the Rebels began to tumble down the opposite side of the ridge as they dropped knapsacks, rifles and even precious food supplies to avoid being engulfed by the blue tide. Only the last minute intervention of Cleburne's versatile troops protected the gray flanks long enough to allow Bragg and most of his men to escape down the roads into Georgia, but they could not prevent the Army of Tennessee from suffering its most decisive defeat up to this point in the war.

The disparity in casualties between the victors and vanquished was relatively minor, Grant lost 6000 men, Bragg lost 7000, but the psychological impact to both sides was far greater. The panic stricken retreat from Missionary Ridge completely nullified the positive aspects of the Confederate victory at Chickamauga. Bragg had been heavily reinforced from other manpower-short Southern armies in other to defeat Rosecrans and retake the vital city of Chattanooga. Two months later the Army of Tennessee commander had not only lost the last opportunity to recapture the city, he had also suffered 28,000 casualties who couldn't be replaced and was now on a seemingly permanent retrograde movement. Not only was Chattanooga irrevocably lost to the Confederacy, the even more vital city of Atlanta was now within striking range of the advancing Federals.

Beyond the geographical implications of Bragg's failure, the retreat from Missionary Ridge was a brutal lesson to the many Southerners who always assumed that only Yankees engaged in panic stricken routs. As one correspondent for the *Richmond Dispatch* noted, "for the first time since our struggle for national independence our defeat is chargeable to the troops themselves and not to the blunder or incompetency of our leaders!" One of the retreating soldiers admitted that "the troops ignominiously left a field which could have been theirs had they but nerved their hearts to take it, instead of this they fled panic stricken from the enemy." Four days later the disaster at Missionary Ridge was compounded when James Longstreet's siege of Knoxville ended in the worst imaginable result. "Old Pete" had thrown over 3000 Confederate assault troops against a Federal redoubt at Fort Sanders which was defended by only 400 Yankees. The attackers became entangled in loops of telegraph wire strung out along the approaches, men slipped on sleet and ice as they attempted to cross a ditch in front of the fort, and regiments never received the assault ladders they had been promised for the final push over the top of the redoubt. When the debacle was over, Longstreet had suffered 813 casualties compared to an incredibly low Federal total of 5 men killed and 8 wounded. Now both Chattanooga and Knoxville were gone and the Federal juggernaut increasingly seemed unstoppable.

The news of Lookout Mountain and Missionary Ridge encouraged wild celebrations all through the North as Unionists celebrated their third major triumph since the beginning of July. A war that seemed unwinnable in May seemed to be entering its final stages by November. This victory inspired two very different ceremonies during the next few months. First, President Lincoln had already called for the fourth Thursday in November to be celebrated as Thanksgiving Day throughout the nation, and the news of Chattanooga became a tangible point of thanks in this first national celebration. Second, several months later, as the oncoming winter finally in turn gave way to the earliest days of spring, Ulysses S. Grant was summoned to the capital and given a rank that no one since George Washington had enjoyed. Newly promoted Lieutenant General Grant was now the commander of all armies of the republic and most people in Washington and throughout both halves of the divided nation began to realize that sooner or later this Yankee champion would contend directly with Robert E. Lee and the fate of much of North America would hang in the balance.

# CHAPTER 31

# The Confrontation Between Grant and Lee

## *The Spring of 1864*

*I*n late March of 1864 two bearded, cigar smoking men in blue uniforms checked into the Burnet House in downtown Cincinnati and placed a very visible "do not disturb" sign in front of their room—an armed sentry was posted at the door. These two men, Ulysses S. Grant and William T. Sherman, had now become second only to Abraham Lincoln in the exercise of power in the United States, and they had checked into this hotel to discuss how they could use their enormous power to crush the secessionist movement in one final spectacular campaign. They removed their coats, pulled an ample supply of cigars from their pockets, and spread maps all over the floor as they tried to find the key to restoring the divided Union. As Sherman recounted 25 years later, the most important decision made in this room was that "Grant was to go for Lee and I was to go for Joe Johnston. That was the plan."

Sherman's terse statement was an accurate statement of the heart of the Union strategic plan for the campaign of 1864, but it doesn't do justice to the complex series of operations that the new commander of the Federal armies devised during the early spring of that critical election year. Lincoln and his two leading generals had all agreed that the main reason that the North hadn't been fully able to utilize its enormous manpower advantage was that the Yankee armies never served to operate in concert. When one army went on the offensive, it always seemed as if the rest of the Union forces were largely milling around waiting for that particular campaign to finish until the next operation began with a different army. The Confederates always seemed to be able to utilize their interior lines to shuttle reinforcements from a quiet sector of their perimeter to a more threatened point, which substantially closed the manpower gap in actual battles. Now Grant was determined to end this ongoing shell game by launching five coordinated offensives against the Confederacy on the same day and then dare the Rebels to meet every thrust at once.

Sherman was expected to use an army group of 110,000 men from the Army of the Ohio, Army of the Tennessee and Army of the Cumberland to strike southward toward Atlanta, which would put him in direct confrontation with the Confederate Army of Tennessee now under the command of Joseph Johnston. Johnston would have only 55,000 men but would be fighting in a hilly, wooded country that heavily favored a defensive army. Also, Johnston had a ready reservoir of reinforcements in Leonidas Polk's 20,000-man Army of Mississippi which could be shuttled north in case of an emergency. Grant hoped to prevent those troops from reaching Georgia by ordering a 40,000-man army under Nathaniel Banks to launch an assault on Mobile, Alabama, operating in Johnston's rear and presumably keeping most of Polk's men facing this new threat.

While Johnston's army and the city of Atlanta were the prizes in the Western theatre, the Army of Northern Virginia and Richmond were the main targets in the East. In this theatre three separate columns would converge against the Confederate capital from three separate directions. The main Federal army, the Army of the Potomac, would move south from the Rapidan River to engage Lee's 65,000 men with 120,000 bluecoats. Meanwhile, Franz Sigel's 20,000-man army would move up the Shenandoah Valley and threaten Richmond from the west while destroying vital Southern food supplies. Benjamin Butler's 30,000-man Army of the James would move up the Virginia Peninsula and attempt to smash its way into Petersburg, which provided Confederate access to the railroads entering Virginia from the deeper South. Thus Lee might very well lose Richmond even before his army could deploy southward to defend the capital.

Once either Lee or Johnston had been disposed of, the Union army that had won this victory would be shuttled either eastward or westward to overwhelm the surviving Confederate army with the power of two enormous Yankee hosts. Grant didn't really care whether Lee or Johnston was defeated first, or whether Richmond or Atlanta was the initial city to surrender; all the resources of the Union would simply converge on the remaining objective and finish the war. The shock of multiple, coordinated Federal offenses would allow the Rebels little opportunity to attack or shuttle forces from one area to another. This would deny or at least delay Lee from receiving substantial reinforcements from even nearby detachments such as Breckinridge or Beauregard. At the same time, manpower, supplies and treasure would be gradually destroyed by Union forces or exhausted by Confederate armies until the South was compelled to accept total surrender and ultimate defeat. As Sherman noted enthusiastically, "that we are now to act on a common plan, converging on a common center, looks like enlightened war."

While Grant and Sherman were studying their maps and attempting to

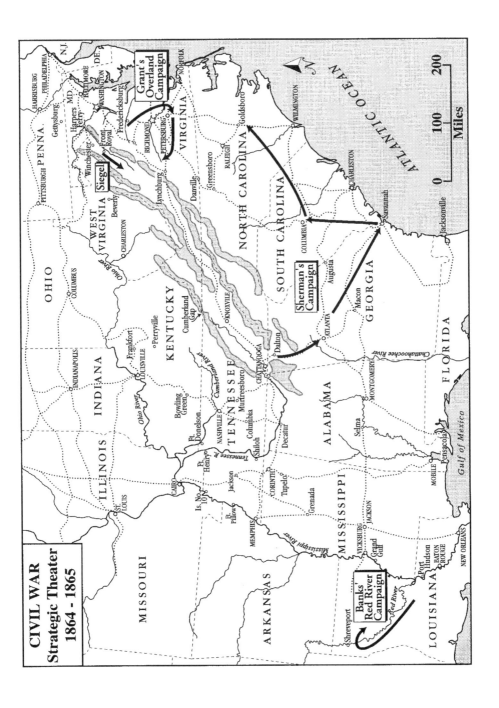

coordinate a complex series of offensive thrusts, Jefferson Davis and his generals were viewing the upcoming campaign from a very different perspective. The previous year had provided a roller coaster of emotions for Southerners, as early triumphs had given way to the disastrous summer of Vicksburg and Gettysburg and the temporary comeback at Chickamauga had been shattered by the rout at Missionary Ridge. Confederate casualties had been so heavy during 1863 that the government was forced to dip in its reservoir of boys under 18 and older men over 50 to support a military establishment that was threatened along a huge front. The 200,000 front line soldiers that the South could field in the spring of 1864 was opposed by well over a half million bluecoats who could in turn be reinforced by thousands of other men who hadn't yet volunteered or been conscripted.

However, while the Southern manpower situation was hardly bright, the situation was not totally bleak. The year 1864 would see a Presidential election in the North, and if the Confederacy could simply hold its own on the battlefield, there seemed to be a good chance that a Democrat more amenable to a negotiated peace would replace the warlike Lincoln. The South didn't have to achieve any spectacular victories; all the Rebels had to do was prevent the Yankees from gaining a significant triumph that would convince the Northern voters to stick with the current administration during a war that would then seem to have a discernible end.

The showcase campaign of 1864 would center around the Army of the Potomac in its now traditional attempt to destroy Lee's army and/or capture Richmond and, hopefully avoid its equally traditional drubbing on the soil of the Old Dominion. McDowell, McClellan, Pope, Burnside and Hooker had all marched through the Virginia countryside, fought a major battle or series of battles and ended up back north of the Rappahannock with another defeat and a new general appointed to try his luck at this tiresome contest. The spring of 1864 brought both continuity and change to this process. On the one hand, Grant would still have to march an army through a landscape that always seemed to favor the defenders, he would face the most formidable general that the Confederacy could field, and he would be hounded by newspaper reporters who wanted to know the exact date for the capture of Richmond. However, Grant was the first general in this theater who enjoyed the full confidence of a President who, unlike the reporters, fully expected the capture of the enemy capital to take almost a year. If Grant lost a battle or two, it was highly unlikely that he would be dispatched west to fight Indians or reduced to a corps commander in the Trans-Mississippi. Also the new Federal commander was not obsessed with capturing Richmond and agreed with Lincoln that Lee and his army were the real objective of the campaign.

As the date of the opening of the spring campaign approached, Grant was forced to choose between two possible avenues in which to attack the Army of Northern Virginia. One option was to try to get the Union army around Lee's left flank by crossing the Rapidan upstream from the Confederate main defenses. This move would probably be less expected by his adversary because it would entail abandoning the Union line of communications and the attendant naval support that went along with an advance near the coast. However, an operation around the enemy left flank compensated for these disadvantages by allowing the Federals to march over terrain that would maximize the employment of superior Union numbers and artillery, and offer an excellent opportunity to surprise Lee and get in his rear before he could fully react to this threat. In essence, this operation offered the possibility of a replay of the Vicksburg campaign, since it would entail the abandonment of supply lines but allow the Federals to move rapidly and force Lee into attacking Grant in a position chosen by the Union commander.

Grant initially favored this maneuver, but after he considered the implications of two complicating factors he jettisoned the operation. First, a flank march to the Union right could theoretically provide an opening through which Lee could launch an all out attack on Washington, a city that was now increasingly vulnerable since the Yankee general had largely stripped the capital of supporting defense units. Second, while Grant knew from experience that the Mississippi countryside contained ample provisions for his army to live off the land, he had been warned that Virginia had already been largely picked over for both Confederate and Federal supplies and the local farms might not be able to feed an enormous army. Although Grant eventually rejected this plan, he remained intrigued by its possibilities and later admitted that he would have risked implementing this operation. He noted "I thought of massing the Army of the Potomac in moveable columns, giving the men twelve days rations and throwing myself between Lee and his communications. If I had made this movement successfully, if I had been as fortunate as I was when I threw my army between Pemberton and Joe Johnston, the war would have been over a year sooner. I am not sure that it was not the best thing to have done, it certainly was the plan I should have preferred."

From the comfortable distance of well over a century, it seems clear that even though Lee would have proven himself a much tougher adversary than Pemberton or Johnston, this sweep around the Rebel left flank would have very likely succeeded. While Lee had slammed into every previous invasion force with some unexpected offensive, Grant was far less likely to have been panicked by his adversary's audacity than his predecessors, and had a much better prospect of meeting his enemy's gambit with one of his own. However, the supposedly apolitical general was keenly aware of the tenuous nature of Lincoln's possible re-election, and he reluctantly conceded that any move toward the Confederate right would better protect the capital that the North could not afford to lose even on a temporary basis at this particular critical point in the war. As Grant insisted, "if I had failed, it would have been very serious for the country and I did not dare take the risk." The new general was not yet aware of the capabilities of his leaders and his men and if he badly miscalculated, the Stars and Bars might well be waving over the White

House while the Army of the Potomac tried to emerge from an enemy trap. Grant admitted "if it had been six months later when I had the army in hand and knew what a splendid army it was, I would not have hesitated for a moment."

On the south side of the Rapidan, Robert E. Lee sifted through every piece of intelligence that he could acquire and tried to divine his new opponent's intentions. On a beautiful Monday morning, May 2nd, 1864, Lee and his lieutenants climbed to the top of Clark's Mountain and viewed a spectacular panorama of Union encampments on the far side of the river. Lee raised a gauntleted hand and pointed to a six-mile stretch of the river between Ely's Ford and Germanna's Ford and said to his generals, "Grant will cross by one of these fords." The Virginian knew that if his adversary crossed the river at either of these points he would have to enter the 100 square mile Wilderness that had so disrupted Hooker's offensive almost exactly a year earlier. Once Grant entered that dark and forbidding region, his superior numbers and his artillery would become useless and, with luck, the Confederates could send still another defeated, panic stricken Yankee army running back toward Washington, with a strong possibility that they wouldn't come south again before election days.

As midnight on Wednesday, May 4th, just as Lee had predicted, Union engineers waded through the waist deep water to throw pontoon bridges across Germanna Ford and Eby's Ford while Philip Sheridan's cavalry splashed across the shallow points and established beachheads on the Confederate side of the river. By mid-morning five bridges had been thrown across the Rapidan and bluecoat infantry was advancing further and further into the tangle of trees and bushes that ran for about 10 miles and then ended abruptly near Spotsylvania, about 50 miles north of Richmond. General Winfield Hancock's II Corps crossed at Ely's Ford and marched to a camp at Chancellorsville about five miles from the river. General Gouverneur Warren's V Corps crossed at Germanna and marched six miles south to Wilderness Tavern. General John Sedgwick's VI Corps covered the river crossings and then prepared to move south between Hancock and Warren. General Ambrose Burnside's IX Corps remained on the north side of the river ready to provide support wherever needed. Grant was in excellent spirits as his men crossed the river with almost no opposition from the Rebels and he later exclaimed "this I regarded as a great success; it removed from my mind the most serious apprehension I had entertained of crossing the river in the face of an active, large, well appointed and ably commanded army."

However, Grant was facing much the same challenge that American generals would face in the island campaigns of the Pacific in World War II. Lee had deferred an initial confrontation along the landing zone in order to gain the advantage of being able to use superb defensive terrain once his adversary moved further from the river. Grant had some expectation that his opponent might not seriously contest his advance until both armies were much closer to Richmond, but this hope was soon to be convincingly shattered. The Army of the Potomac was encumbered with over 50,000 horses and mules and over 8,000 wagons, and while these slow, vulnerable vehicles crawled through the narrow roads of the Wilderness, Lee would have ample opportunity to smash into a Yankee army that had no idea of the location of its nemesis. The Virginia general knew that in this jumbled region with its poor visibility his army would have all the advantages and he was determined to add still another triumph to his impressive string of victories in the Old Dominion.

The whole key to Confederate success in the Wilderness was the control of the road network which wound its way through the dense growth of shrubs and trees. In order to get the enormous Yankee supply train safely through the region, the Federals would have to maintain their position along the Germanna Road, which wound southward until it reached Wilderness Tavern, where it transformed into Brock Road. This north-south avenue was intersected by the two east-west roads that connected Fredericksburg with Orange Courthouse, the Orange Turnpike and the Orange Plank Road. Lee's basic plan was to push Ewell's corps along the Turnpike and A.P. Hill's corps along the Plank Road in order to attack the Union forces holding the Germanna Road near the Wilderness Tavern. The dense undergrowth would severely restrict the Yankees' ability to maneuver and prevent the bluecoats from forming an accurate picture of the location and strength of the attackers. Thus relatively unseen Rebels could blaze away at their opponents and the enemy would become more and more panicky during a battle with no front lines as they wondered where the Southerners would strike next.

Lee's plan was a good one, but it was partially negated by two complicating factors. First, Longstreet's corps had been camped too far away to reach the battlefield until Thursday morning, so that the planned Wednesday assault would have to be carried out with only two thirds of the already outnumbered rebel army. Second, Lee didn't know that the aggressive Grant had already planned his own offensive toward the east-west roads and thus the Rebels wouldn't be able to slam into a stationary target. The result was one of the most disorganized, confusing, terrifying engagements of the war in which, one participant noted, "no men saw or could be seen; a battle of invisible with invisible."

The first day of the battle of the Wilderness, May 5th, 1864, was simply bushwhacking on a grand scale in which platoons and companies groped through the woods and blasted at equally small units on the other side. A consistent line of battle was simply impossible to form and the bluecoats and graycoats lurched into one another in a seesaw contest that surged back and forth across the crucial roads. Musket shots firing into the tinder-dry underbrush ignited fires in many spots which created a supreme horror for men too badly wounded to crawl out of the path of advancing flames. The Federals actually came the closest to achieving a significant breakthrough when Hancock's entire 28,000 man corps rumbled toward a Confederate position held by Harry Heth's 7000 man division. However, Hancock had no idea how many graycoats were actually in front of him, so he ordered his troops to build a series of backup fortifications just in case they walked into an ambush. This delay of over an hour allowed Lee to rush enough reinforcements to the threatened position to hold the Rebel breastworks until nightfall and the two armies settled down to a fitful rest while their leaders planned the next day's operations.

During the evening of May 5th-6th both commanding generals assumed that they were close to winning a decisive victory. Grant assumed that his offensive operations had badly damaged the Confederate army and he ordered Burnside's men to cross the river to add support to an all out offensive on the 6th. On the other hand, Lee knew that Longstreet's men were on their way and he intended to use his "Old Warhorse" for a surprise flank attack on Grant's right wing the next morning. The Union assault was the first to get underway, and Hancock's corps rolled right through two Rebel divisions and were kept at bay only by the massed fire of four batteries of Rebel guns that raked the Yankee line as it closed in on Lee himself. While Hancock's men tried to organize another assault the Virginian placed himself at the head of a brigade of Texans and prepared to launch his own counterattack, until some cooler headed men escorted Lee and his horse back to comparative safety. At this point Longstreet's hard marching troops began to arrive on the field and they were able to re-form a Confederate battle line.

Lee wanted far more than a stalemate, and Longstreet, who was ecstatic about escaping the dreary western theatre and the even more dreary Braxton Bragg, was eager to show his commander that his men hadn't lost their fighting skills in Georgia and Tennessee. When Lee's chief engineer, General M.L. Smith, returned from a scouting mission with the exciting news that an abandoned railroad cut provided an unobserved route into the exposed left flank of Hancock's corps, Longstreet assigned his young aide, Georgia colonel Moxley Sorrell, to the task of leading four brigades through the cut into the middle of the unsuspecting Yankees. The twenty-six-year-old former bank clerk couldn't believe his good luck at drawing such a critical assignment and by 11 A.M. he had positioned 5000 eager Rebels in a perfect position to sweep the field.

A huge line of screaming graycoats simply pulverized the poorly positioned Yankee flank units and several bluecoat regiments disintegrated in the first 10 minutes of the attack. Hancock admitted to Longstreet later on that "you rolled us up like a wet blanket." However, two developments saved the Federals from a defeat on the same level as Chancellorsville. First, Hancock quickly remembered the fortifications that he had ordered constructed the day before, and he deftly withdrew his surviving units behind these breastworks where they could at least delay the Rebel surge. Once the Union soldiers were able to stem the gray tide, Longstreet and his staff rode onto the field to attempt to locate a way around the enemy defenses. In one of the major ironies of the war, Longstreet was shot by mistake by his own soldiers only a short distance from the spot where Stonewall Jackson had been mortally wounded by friendly fire a year earlier. The Georgia general was much more fortunate than his Virginia counterpart; he would survive a ghastly but treatable series of injuries, but his services were lost to the Confederacy for several months, and the removal of their leader took much of the steam out of the Rebel's offensive.

The Union left flank had been able to hold together by the narrowest of margins, so Lee quickly shifted his attention to a Yankee right that was equally exposed. Another young Georgian, brigade commander John B. Gordon, had discovered the fact that there was a sizeable gap between John Sedgwick's Federals and the Rapidan River that they were guarding. Gordon had spent most of Thursday imploring his superiors, Jubal Early and Richard Ewell to hit the Union army in this exposed position, but both generals kept shaking their heads and ordering the young brigadier to hold his position. However, at about 6 o'clock, Lee and his staff arrived at this portion of the battlefield and by now the commanding general was desperate for a major breakthrough. When Lee heard about Gordon's proposal, he quickly assigned him a second brigade, and the two Rebel units smashed into Union general Truman Seymour's men, capturing the general and many of his soldiers. By nightfall, Gordon had pushed his way right through two crumbling Yankee divisions and killed, wounded or captured over 1000 men at a paltry loss of 50 graycoats. A few more hours of daylight might have produced a major Confederate triumph, but darkness ended the battle, and with it, Lee's hopes for a decisive thrust. Neither side yet knew it, but the battle of the Wilderness was over, yet the campaign for Richmond had just begun.

At first glance, it appeared that the Union army had suffered one of its bloodiest setbacks of the war. The Army of the Potomac had lost over 18,000 men and Grant assumed that because of the ferocity of the battle that Lee had lost almost as many Rebel soldiers. However, the Confederates had lost only 8,000 men, which made the Wilderness the most one-sided battle in the East since Fredericksburg. While the Union commander had retained his composure for almost the entire two-day engagement, by late Thursday Grant was so overcome with the emotion of his enormous losses that according to his aide "he threw himself face downward on his cot and gave way to the greatest emotion" in a tear filled breakdown of his usually stoic demeanor. As Charles Francis Adams, Jr., son of the ambassador to Britain noted to his father "I never saw a man so agitated in my life." However, while Joseph Hooker had taken one look at similar casualties and pulled back across the river, Grant startled the army by ordering the men to march southward towards Richmond. The whole pattern of Union advance, Union defeat and Union retreat had now been broken, and with this break from tradition, the war suddenly took on a dramatic new guise. A sergeant in a Virginia artillery unit summarized the shock of seeing the Yankees attempt an entirely new strategy. "I remember surprise and disappointment were the prevailing emotions in the Army of Northern Virginia when we discovered, after the contest in the Wilderness, that General Grant was not going to retire behind the river and permit General Lee to carry on a campaign against Washington in the usual way but was moving to the Spotsylvania position instead. We had been accustomed to a program which began with a Federal advance, culminated in one great battle, and ended in the retirement of the Union army, the substitution of a new Federal commander for the one beaten and the institution of a more or less offensive campaign on our part. This was the usual order of events, and this was what we confidently expected when General Grant crossed into the Wilderness. But here was a new Federal general, fresh from the West, and so ill informed as to the military customs in our part of the country that when the battle of the Wilderness was over, instead of retiring to the north bank of the river and awaiting the development of Lee's plans, he had the temerity to move by his left flank to a new position, there to try conclusions with us again. We were greatly disappointed with general Grant, and full of curiosity to know how long it was going to take him to perceive the impropriety of his course."

The soldiers of the Yankee army may have been almost as shocked as their graycoat adversaries at Grant's break with the tradition of retreat after a bloody engagement. However, as the Federal soldiers started to realize that the direction of their next march was south, not north, rounds of cheering broke out among the bluecoats and they were infused with a new sense of purpose. They sensed that they had been badly mangled during the Wilderness battle but they were still marching toward Richmond and their commander seemed to be fully in charge of the situation. They were also engaged in a race with their adversaries to reach the town of Spotsylvania Court House. A Union army astride this sleepy town's roads would cut off Lee from his capital and force the Confederates into a frontal assault against a much larger army. As the Northern regiments were hustled through the final few miles of the smoky woods of the Wilderness they started to realize that another mammoth confrontation might be only hours away. Robert E. Lee most have hoped that the punishment that he had inflicted on the Federals in the Wilderness would encourage his adversary to pull back across the Rapidan to regroup, but he probably sensed that Grant hadn't become the premier general of the Union by retreating, so he wasn't shocked when his scouts brought word that the battered Yankees were continuing to march south. Lee had already planned for that eventuality when he had ordered his engineers to build a new shortcut access route to Spotsylvania while the battle in the Wilderness was still raging. Although Grant had the advantage of gaining a head start on his adversary when he quietly pulled his men out of their Wilderness fortifications, Lee's men now had a shorter road to the south and the result was a race that would be decided by a few minutes. Poor coordination between Union infantry and cavalry units began causing delays along the Yankee march route while Confederate foot soldiers had no such impediments, and when the Federals finally broke out of the woods into the open country approaching Spotsylvania, they were greeted by the site of entrenched Rebels waiting for them.

During most of Monday, May 9th and Tuesday, May 10th, Grant conducted an operation that included flanking movements that never quite located a vulnerable spot in the Confederate breastworks, and frontal assaults that simply piled up bluecoat bodies in front of the Rebel trenches. Finally, on Tuesday afternoon, a young brigade commander, Colonel Emory Upton, managed to convince his superiors to try an entirely new approach. Upton had been watching the futile Union attacks all day and he was convinced that they had failed because the men were expected to load and fire their rifles while they were in the process of running, a delay that gave to Rebel riflemen far too much time to shoot the attackers. Upton proposed to substitute speed for firepower, and he was finally given 12 regiments to attempt his theory. This assault force would be divided into four assault lines: the first group would secure a limited penetration and then fan out left and right to widen the breach; a second force would plunge straight ahead to deepen the penetration; a third and fourth line would move in whichever direction enemy resistance seemed to be crumbling. Upton's objective was a salient in the Confederate lines which Ewell's men had occupied in order to deny the Federals possession of some high ground which could be used for enfilading artillery fire. This salient was studded with ample Confederate artillery units but the Union colonel was determined to get among the guns before the crews could fire more than one round.

At 6 o'clock on the evening of May 10th, Upton's 12 regiments sprinted across the open ground and overran the Rebel riflemen and gunners. Dozens of startled Confederates threw up their hands in surrender while the support groups fanned out left and right to widen the breach. Upton had assumed that the Rebels would attempt a massive reinforcement of the gap in their lines, and for this purpose a full division under General Grisham Mott had been assigned to launch a supporting assault designed to occupy the most likely Southern reinforcements. However, Mott's troops became bogged down in their diversionary attack and this failure allowed Ewell to rush every available unit to confront Upton's men. When the young colonel saw thousands of graycoats organizing a huge counterattack, he gathered together his men and their 1200 prisoners and hastily pulled back to the Union lines. Grant took this partial setback in stride and simply muttered "a brigade today, we'll try a corps tomorrow."

The scheduled assault actually took slightly more than a day to organize, but during the rainy night of May 11-12, the troops of Hancock's II Corps were deployed 20 deep in a large scale version of Upton's attack force. The torrential rain not only screened the formation from Rebel observers, it dampened the powder of many of the defenders' rifles, and when the Yankees charged forward at dawn, Edward Johnson's division of Rebels was virtually annihilated. The Confederates had just been in the process of redeploying over 20 guns that had been temporarily removed from this sector, and the cannons were overwhelmed before most of the startled gunners could get off a shot. Lee realized that had a first class disaster on his hands, and he personally rode up to take charge of a counterattack, being pulled back to safety only seconds before he was within range of the advancing Federals.

The initial Union attack had worked almost flawlessly, but the Yankees actually suffered from a surplus of assault troops. At one point there were more than 20,000 attackers attempting to push their way through a relatively small gap in the Confederate lines and as bluecoats waited their turn to push through the enemy trenches, Lee was able to rush in significant reinforcements. As the Northern troops fanned out from a newly captured series of angled Confederate breastworks a massive Rebel counter thrust smashed into the blue lines. One Yankee participant noted "under cover of the smoke laden rain the enemy was pushing large bodies of troops forward, determined at all hazard to recover the lost ground. They were crawling forward under cover of the smoke, until, reaching a certain point, and raising their usual yell, they charged gallantly up to the very muzzles of our pieces and reoccupied the angle."

The Federals pulled back to the other side of the breastworks, and what followed was one of the most intense periods of fighting of the whole war. Thousands of contending troops were separated only by a thin strip of breastworks that allowed men from both sides to push their rifles through the wall and fire blindly into the packed mass of soldiers on the other side. Other men became so caught up with the orgy of violence that they would climb up on the parapets and fire into the enemies below, while being handed freshly loaded rifles until they were invariably shot down by a volley of enemy guns. Lee's engineers worked desperately through the rain-swept morning and afternoon to construct a new set of fortifications at the base of the punctured salient that soon became famous as the "Mule Shoe." Meanwhile, up at the vital breastworks some of the survivors in the front ranks of the armies fired over 400 rounds each as a line of soldiers stacked up over 40 deep passed an unending supply of loaded rifles to the relatively few men who could get off a shot. This position quickly became nicknamed the "Bloody Angle" as, for 20 hours, thousands of bluecoats and graycoats fired at one another through a torrential rainstorm. Wounded men slumped into a mire of oozing mud and in many cases either drowned or were crushed by their own comrades. One participant described the inferno he witnessed, "the mud was half way to our knees, and by our constant movement the fallen were almost buried at our feet. The dead and wounded were torn to pieces by the canister as it swept the ground where they had fallen. Our men went down by the score; all the artillery horses were down; the gallant Upton was the only mounted officer in sight. So continuous and heavy was our fire that the head logs of the breastworks were cut and torn until they resembled hickory brooms. Several large oak trees were completely gnawed off by our converging fire, and at about 3 o'clock in the day fell among the enemy with a loud crash." Finally, just past midnight, after almost 20 hours of non-stop firing, the dazed Confederates pulled back to their newly constructed positions and the equally stunned Yankees sank into exhaustion toward their own lines. Five thousand bluecoats and four thousand graycoats has been killed or wounded in the furious struggle, although the initial surrender of over 4000 Confederates in the first moments of the battle gave the Union a technical "victory" in this otherwise useless engagement.

The duel over Spotsylvania would continue for several more days with fighting at various levels of intensity, and when it was over another 18,000 Yankee names were added to the casualty lists. However, as Grant was conferring with an Illinois congressman about his future plans, he spoke words that would reverberate through both North and South. Rather than even consider any sort of fallback, he exclaimed "I intend to fight it out on this line if it takes all summer!" This bold statement made for great newspaper headlines but virtually at the same time that the newspapers were being sold, Grant abandoned this line and sidled around Lee's right flank in another race toward a key objective. This time the prize was the North Anna River, and once again, the Confederates barely won the race. Lee set up a trap to spring on the unwary Federals when they prepared to cross the river as he practically conceded the Yankees a landing point, and then hid much of his army both upriver and downriver to catch the bluecoats in between when they crossed. However, Lee went down with an intestinal ailment and his subordinates weren't quite able to spring the trap, which cost the Union forces "only" 600 men.

The two armies now began another race, to the barren, dusty crossroads of Cold Harbor, which was located near the old Mechanicsville battlefield from the Seven Days campaign. This time the Yankees won the race and Sheridan's cavalry captured the local tavern, dug in along the road and pleaded with Grant to rush every infantry unit forward. However, near 100 degree heat and a near total burnout of men who had been fighting non-stop for almost a month slowed the infantry advance to a crawl, while Lee's engineers fortified a nearby ridge line and constructed a fearsome array of breastworks and artillery emplacements.

Sheridan's horsemen had occupied Cold Harbor on the afternoon of June 1st, and if any substantial infantry forces had arrived to support them they would have discovered an open road to Richmond less than 10 miles away. Some Federal units marched into position during the next morning, and even all-night construction activities by the Rebels had not created a solid defensive front. However, Meade and Grant seemed to take turns issuing short-term postponements of the assault as they kept waiting for additional units to show up in the camps. A noon attack became a 1 P.M. assault which became a 4 P.M. advance which became a twilight charge, while all that time more and more Confederates were filing into the Rebel defenses. When Grant finally assented to a postponement until dawn of June 3rd, he still believed that he had enough men and enough firepower to shatter the Southern lines and drive for downtown Richmond. His men knew better, and began attaching pieces of paper with names, addresses and units on their uniforms so they could be identified after the charge.

At daybreak on the oppressively hot morning of June 3rd, 1864, a somber preview of the mindless carnage of World War I was about toe be played out. Confederate artillerymen stood by their pieces as Rebel riflemen cocked their weapons and watched an awesome attack force of 80,000 bluecoats advance across an open plain to attack the ridge. Suddenly every Southern cannon and rifle exploded in a fury that roused people out of their houses in nearby Richmond. A sheet of flame engulfed five corps of Union assault troops and only eight minutes later 7000 of those men were dead or wounded. Confederate general Evander Law held a portion of the Rebel line that day and was shocked by the enormity of the slaughter. He noted that "line followed line until the space of the old salient became a mass of writing humanity upon which our artillery and musketry played with cruel effect. The men in our trenches were in fine spirits, laughing and talking as they fired. I had seen the dreadful carnage in front of Marye's Hill at Fredericksburg, and on the old railroad cut which Jackson's men held at Second Manassas; but I had seen nothing to exceed this. It was not war; it was murder." Five acres of bleeding and dead bluecoats sprawled in the June heat while cowering Federals prayed that they could survive the barrage long enough to surrender. The few Confederate casualties of the battle occurred when Union troops overran some fringe areas of the enemy lines, but only tiny numbers of the defenders in the trenches suffered even minor wounds. Lee had abandoned all thought of holding back any reserves and had lined his breastworks with every man who could fire a rifle. Now the great Union offensive seemed to have ground to a permanent halt near a decaying ramshackle tavern.

Up to this point in the war, much of Grant's reputation had been based on his ability to surprise enemy defenders, flank them out of their entrenchments, or cut off their supply lines and force them to surrender. On this awful day, however, Grant had resorted to a brute force that very nearly ruined his army and which he admitted was the greatest mistake he had made in the war. In a month of phenomenally bloody fighting Grant had lost 55,000 men, nearly half the strength of the Army of the Potomac, and he now faced a victorious Confederate army that was sitting confidently behind a series of breastworks that might take another 55,000 casualties to overrun. Unless momentum began to shift dramatically in favor of the Union cause, it was quite likely that both Lincoln and his commanding general would be repudiated in just over 20 weeks.

# CHAPTER 32

# The Final Turn of the Tide

## *The Crisis Summer of 1864*

*T*he campaign of 1864 produced a number of emotional low points for the North, in which the attempt to restore the Union seemed to be doomed to ultimate failure. However, the authors believe that June 3rd, 1864 would be an excellent candidate for the dubious distinction of the single day during that year when a Federal victory seemed most unattainable. When 7000 Yankee soldiers fell in only 8 minutes at Cold Harbor, even Ulysses Grant began to realize that the Union cause simply couldn't afford to endure many more utterly futile assaults that offered not even a hint of comparable injury to the enemy. By the afternoon of June 3rd all three thrusts at the Confederate capital had come to a screeching halt. Franz Sigel's advance up the Shenandoah Valley had been emphatically stopped at the battle of New Market, when a collection of Confederate regulars, local militia and young VMI cadets had thrown the bluecoats into a panic stricken retreat back toward the Potomac. Ben Butler's march up the Virginia Peninsula had petered out in a series of indecisive battles near Bermuda Hundred where 8000 rebel soldiers had stalemated the Army of the James' 30,000 men and according to Grant, "left Butler's army as completely shut off from further operations directly against Richmond as if it had been in a bottle strongly corked."

The bloody repulse at Cold Harbor had now halted the advance of the third and largest Federal army in Virginia, and had convinced Jefferson Davis and Robert E. Lee that their strategy of simply holding the Yankees at bay until the November elections seemed to be working. Grant had already lost more men in a month than the Federal casualties at First Manassas, Second Manassas, Fredericksburg and Chancellorsville combined, and yet was no closer to downtown Richmond than McClellan had been two years earlier. The authors believe that Davis and Lee's optimism at this moment was certainly justified; the Confederacy probably had a better chance of securing its independence in June of 1864 than the American patriots had in

June of 1781, which was only weeks before the initiation of the decisive Yorktown campaign. The rebels of the summer of 1781 were facing the bleak prospect of the imminent termination of French assistance combined with the fact that Lord North's government in London faced no prospect of an immediate election challenge to its leadership. Before the chain of events that led to Yorktown, time was probably more on the side of the British than the patriots. On the other hand, in June of 1864 the Southern rebels knew that if their adversaries didn't attain some form of major victory in the next five months, it was probable that a more peace oriented Democratic president would assume office and quite possibly recognize Confederate independence. Up to this point in 1864 the South had avoided any really serious defeats since the beginning of the year, and Grant and Sherman both still seemed a long way from defeating their respective opponents. If the South could avoid a decisive setback for about 150 more days, long term prospects would appear bright.

At this critical point in the war, both Ulysses Grant and William Sherman were able to orchestrate a series of maneuvers that would decisively turn the tide of the war back in favor of the Union and ultimately guarantee Lincoln's re-election, with a subsequent prosecution of the war to total victory. While Sherman's exploits would gain far more favorable attention, Grant's next gambit would be equally important to the long term success of the overall Federal plan.

After the disaster at Cold Harbor, Ulysses Grant became increasingly concerned that Lee would keep the Army of the Potomac pinned opposite the formidable Confederate breastworks while the Virginian shuttled substantial reinforcements to strike Sherman's western army in the rear. The whole premise of the Union offensive in both theatres was based on the expectation that each Federal commander would prevent his adversary from shunting troops to the other Confederate army. Thus even if Grant couldn't immediately capture Richmond, it was imperative that he at least pin Lee to the defense of the capital rather than setting up the conditions for another, and even more disastrous, Chickamauga. Grant's response to this challenge was a rapid and unexpected shift of his army to the south bank of the James before Lee fully realized the implications of his opponents' maneuvers.

Between nightfall of June 12th and dawn of June 13th, army engineers assembled pontoon bridges to span the half mile wide James River, transports and gunboats raced up and down the river, and thousands of bluecoats marched quietly from the killing fields at Cold Harbor to embarkation points on the north side of the James. On the morning of June 13th Confederate pickets found that the enemy army had vanished, and Lee was still unsure where Grant was headed. According to Confederate general E. Porter Alexander, Grant's surprise change of base was one of the decisive moments of the war. As Alexander emphasized, Lee expected that his adversary would merely cross the Chickahominy and take position on the north bank of the James at Malvern Hill, adjoining Butler on the south bank at Bermuda Hundred. This would unite the two armies at the nearest point to Richmond. However, Grant elected to cross the James at Wilcox's Landing, 10 miles below City Point and entirely out of Lee's observation, and then more directly upon Petersburg with his whole army. This move was totally unexpected in the Confederate camp. "This involved the performance of a feat in transportation which had never been equaled, and might well be considered impossible, without days of delay. It was all accomplished without mishap and in such an incredibly short time that Lee for three days refused to believe it."

Thus for three days Lee remained with most of his army in the woods on the north side of the James River, while the Army of the Potomac passed in the rear of Butler's army and came swooping down on the extreme right flank of the Confederate defense system, the trenches around Petersburg. This vital rail center was initially defended by only 2500 men under Pierre Beauregard, who was attempting to hold perhaps the best system of fortifications in the Confederacy with almost no men. As Alexander insisted, "had Longstreet's troops manned the entrenchments of Petersburg when Grant's troops first appeared before them, his defeat would have been not less bloody and disastrous than was the one at Cold Harbor. Grant here escaped a second defeat more bloody and more overwhelming than any preceding."

The Union army smashed into the skeleton force holding the Petersburg trenches and nearly captured the city before Lee knew what had hit him. The most advanced Federal corps, 16,000 men under W.L. "Baldy" Smith, arrived in front of the Confederate breastworks on the morning of June 15th. Smith was opposed by barely over 2000 Rebels stretched out thinly along a line of 55 forts connected by six foot breastworks and an outer ditch six feet deep and fifteen feet wide. The capture of Petersburg was the key to imminent Federal victory since the town, 20 miles south of Richmond, contained virtually every railroad line that passed into the Confederate capital. A Yankee occupation of the town would cut off food supplies for the city and Lee's army, at which point the Confederacy's days would be numbered. However, Smith and his men had endured the holocaust of Cold Harbor less than two weeks earlier, and the Union general was convinced that thousands of well-armed Rebels were concealed in the breastworks just out of view. Smith spent most of the day studying the defenses and didn't order an attack until nearly dusk. As the sun began to drop on the horizon, three assault divisions, spearheaded by General Edward Hincks' division of African-American bluecoats, swarmed over the ditches, pushed through the numerous obstacles and overran several of the redoubts while capturing 300 men and 12 guns. Hincks' men had captured almost a mile of entrenchments and now had a clear path all the way to downtown Petersburg and its vital rail stations. However, when Hincks sought permission to follow up his initial assault, Smith backed off and ordered the men to hold their positions until Hancock's corps arrived.

Once Hancock had marched his men across the James at Windmill Point, he expected orders to march immediately for Petersburg in time for a late morning assault. However, Benjamin Butler sent orders for the corps commander to wait in position until 60,000 rations arrived. Not only was the supply train delayed for hours, Hancock's men didn't need the food anyway, and a furious corps commander finally ordered his men to move out at around 10:30 A.M. The march was complicated by inaccurate maps which consistently put the Federals on the wrong roads so that they didn't arrive until late that day. By the time that Hancock's men arrived there were perhaps 8000 rebels around Petersburg, but now there were close to 40,000 Union attack troops and Hancock wanted to launch a night assault. However, the II Corps commander couldn't get definitive orders to attack and the frustrated general and his men were forced to postpone an operation that had an excellent chance of success. As one observer noted, "the rage of the enlisted men was devilish."

During the morning of June 16th the Union assault forces were able to carry several more redoubts, but no general attack could be launched until either Meade or Grant arrived. By the time that Meade arrived on the scene, Lee had realized the enemy intentions and was pouring every graycoat rifleman he could find into the Petersburg trenches. The Federals could never quite coordinate their assault and bluecoats always seemed to crash into a part of the line that had been empty 10 minutes earlier but was now full of panting, but deadly, Rebels. At one point early in the day Beauregard had noted that "it seemed that the last hour of the Confederacy had arrived," but a steady stream of boxcars filled with Southern reinforcements gradually tilted the battle in the Rebels' favor. The next two days would see a continuation of poorly organized Yankee assaults fended off by the timely arrival of graycoat reinforcements and by nightfall of June 18th Petersburg was no longer in danger of imminent capture. Beauregard had orchestrated a masterful defense of a position in which he was sometimes outnumbered almost 10 to 1 and his talents had bought the Confederacy another nine months of existence. However, despite the loss of several thousand additional men in the poorly coordinated assaults, Grant had achieved a significant gain for the Union cause. A follow-up series of Federal assaults would end in bloody repulses which would reach a crescendo on July 30th with the fiasco at the Crater. Jefferson Davis would conduct business in the Confederate White House into the Spring of 1865. But Federal engineers were also rapidly building a chain of permanent siege works that would hem in the Army of Northern Virginia and never again permit Lee to campaign in the region of the Old Dominion for which his army was named. For the time being, Lee could hold Petersburg and Richmond, but a Confederate army in Georgia that could sorely use Virginia reinforcements would now never receive them, and if Grant was stalemated in front of Richmond, William T. Sherman was most certainly not stalemated in his drive toward that other great Union prize—Atlanta.

While Union engineers were laying pontoon bridges across the Rapidan River in Virginia, William T. Sherman's bluecoats were beginning the first stage of their Georgia campaign. Sherman's adversary, Joseph Johnston, had spent the winter of 1863-64 perfecting his defenses around Rocky Face Ridge, which protected his main base at Dalton, Georgia. Johnston assumed that Sherman would make his major effort against the gaps in the ridge nearest the Confederate headquarters, but the Ohioan had no intention of hitting his adversary where he was the strongest. Instead, the red-headed general planned to use John Schofield's Army of the Ohio to threaten the railroad lines east of Dalton, while George Thomas' Army of the Cumberland launched a diversionary attack at Buzzard Roost Gap and Dug Gap where Johnston was expecting an assault. This would leave General James McPherson's 25,000 men Army of the Tennessee free to slip further south and pass through thinly defended Snake Creek Gap and then capture the enemy rear supply depot at nearby Resaca. This would leave McPherson astride the railroad between Dalton and Resaca, and force Johnston to attack him in place while the rest of the 110,000 man Federal army swarmed in behind him. As long as McPherson held the railroad line, Johnston had no escape route.

If Grant's overall strategy had been fully implemented, Sherman's plan would probably have worked. Since Nathaniel Banks' army was expected to keep Leonidas Polk's Army of the Mississippi occupied by a thrust at Mobile, the Episcopal bishop-general wouldn't be able to reinforce Johnston's badly outnumbered army. However, in one of the truly crackpot schemes of the war, Lincoln and Stanton decided to divert Banks' army to a Red River expedition designed to re-capture part of Texas and the Mobile assault was postponed indefinitely. Thus as soon as Sherman's bluecoats marched toward Johnston, the Virginian sent a hasty call to Polk for reinforcements. Polk's soldiers were beginning to arrive at the Resaca railroad depot when McPherson's men pushed through Snake Creek Gap, and even though only 4000 additional Rebels had arrived, McPherson was expecting no opposition and was startled to blunder into well-fortified Rebel positions. The Army of the Tennessee commander made a half-hearted attempt to destroy part of the railroad line, and then pulled his men back into the Gap to await requested reinforcements. This delay gave Johnston just enough time to pull his whole army back to Resaca, and soon the rebels were throwing breastworks all along the nearby Oostanoula River, the first water barrier on the way to Atlanta.

Sherman was convinced that his adversary would set up his next defensive position on the south side of the river, and when the bluecoats attempted to enter Resaca they were shocked to meet stiff resistance. Soon after lunch on May 14th, 1864, Union soldiers started advancing over a broken terrain of ravines and creek beds which allowed the Rebel riflemen plenty of time to pick off dozens of attackers. John Bell Hood used the ensuing stalemate to launch a two-division counterattack on the Federal left flank which Sherman had left dangerously exposed. Hood's initial attack routed several brigades of Yankees, but a single six gun battery of Indiana artillery utilized hundred of rounds of double charged canister to bring the 5000 screaming Rebels to an absolute halt. At this point some of Joe Hooker's former Army of the Potomac troops were rushed in to fill the gap and hold the Rebels in position while Thomas Sweeney's division crossed the river several miles downstream at Lay's Ferry and threatened Johnston's rear. The Virginian's plans for another counterattack were quickly shelved as the Army of Tennessee was withdrawn southward while engineers demolished most of the Oostanoula bridges. The Union commander had now forced his opponent to abandon two formidable positions at a relatively modest cost of 4000 Federal and 3000 Confederate casualties, but as Johnston withdrew toward the next major barrier, the Etowah River, he was rapidly developing a plan to ambush his somewhat overconfident adversary.

The Union commander's advance was becoming increasingly predictable. He kept dividing his army in order to use parallel roads, and in this case part of his force was marching down the road that let to Kingston while the rest of the units were assigned a route that led to Cassville. Johnston set up his retreat so that the largest Union force, the armies of McPherson and Thomas, would be pursuing a small force of Confederates, while Polk's and Hood's corps, pursued by Schofield's relatively small detachment, would suddenly halt their retrograde and turn on their opponents just before they reached Cassville.

On the morning of May 19th the trap began to close. While Polk's men wheeled around to strike back at the front of the bluecoat column, Hood's force swung around the Yankee flank and prepared to hit Schofield from the rear. Suddenly, Hood's scouts reported a large enemy force closing in on the rebel right flank and the Texan started to fear that it was the Confederates that were marching into a clever ambush. Actually, the graycoat scouts had mistaken a small force of bluecoats who had become lost in the woods for a more substantial threat. Hood gave the order to cancel the attack and the frustrated rebels pulled back to a line south of Cassville while Johnston and his corps commander argued whether the enemy threat had been real or a mirage. Even more controversy erupted in the Southern camp when Polk and Hood ganged up on their commander and insisted that his newly chosen defense line north of the Etowah River was too easy to outflank, and Johnston petulantly pulled the whole army southward, leaving the Chattahoochie River as the only major water barrier between Sherman and Atlanta.

For the next several weeks the campaign became a predictable ritual of Union flank maneuvers, subsequent Confederate withdrawals from a succession of defense positions, followed by another series of Yankee flank moves. Sherman could never quite get between his opponent's army and Atlanta, but Johnston could never quite find a position that could halt the enemy advance. Constant skirmishing produced a moderate number of casualties on both sides, including the death of Leonidas Polk in one Union artillery barrage, but the Union army kept advancing through an endless series of torrential rainstorms and flooded roads and creeks, creeping ever closer to the last major position in front of the Chattahoochie, the formidable 700 foot peaks of Kennesaw Mountain.

Sherman was rapidly losing patience with the time-consuming flanking maneuvers that never seemed to bring on a decisive battle, and when the Ohioan concluded that his opponent might actually fight to hold Kennesaw, an all out Union assault was ordered. At 8 A.M. on June 27th, 1864, all three Federal armies advanced on a seven-mile-long assault line, designed to hold the Confederates in position along the center of the ridge while the bluecoats moved around the enemy flanks. The result was a miniature version of Cold Harbor. As one Union general noted "officers and men fell thick and fast" as Yankee attackers tried to pick their way through trees and boulders lining the approaches to the Kennesaw breastworks. A Confederate witness noted that "as they came up through an open field their ranks closed up into a solid phalanx and appeared as so many living walls of blue. Their arms glistened in the sunlight and the columns advanced as steadily as though they were on dress parade." On the receiving end of the marching column, a Union soldier exclaimed that "the air seemed filled with bullets, giving one the sensation experienced when moving swiftly against a heavy wind and sleet storm."

This particular form of deadly sleet killed or seriously wounded the usual quota of regimental and brigade commanders, who waved their men forward with their swords and then became listed as "gallant leaders" after being shot down by enemy riflemen. A situation very similar to the terror of the Wilderness developed, as the dry grass caught fire during the fighting and spread flames that threatened to engulf wounded Yankees who couldn't crawl to safety. However, the scenario had a happier ending than in Virginia, as Confederate Colonel William Martin tied a white handkerchief to a ramrod and shouted to the Union attackers, "we won't fire a gun till you get your wounded men away. Be quick." Martin and some of his men than went out to personally rescue some of the trapped bluecoats, an act of gallantry that encouraged a Union major to present his Confederate adversary with a set of expensive pistols, insisting that the colonel accept them "with my appreciation of the nobility of this deed."

Sherman at least had the good sense to realize when a frontal attack was not going to be successful and he admitted later, "by 11:30 the assault was in fact over and had failed, and we had not broken the rebel line at either point.... while McPherson lost about 500 men and several valuable officers and Thomas lost nearly 2000 men." The total Union loss was actually closer to 3000 men including Schofield's casualties, while only one-fourth as many Confederates were hit, most of them being lost among the outer pickets. The mercurial Ohioan had learned the same hard lesson as Grant at Cold Harbor, although at somewhat fewer casualties. Once the enemy had a chance to perfect a series of breastworks, a frontal assault was doomed to failure. Just as Grant saw the crossing of the James River as his alternative to this unrewarding slaughter, Sherman viewed a sudden crossing to the south bank of the Chattahoochie as the key to his continued advance.

On July 8th, 1864, while most of the Union army sparred with the retreating Rebels, Colonel Daniel Cameron's brigade discovered a submerged fish dam that extended all the way across the Chattahoochie, and offered a crossing point that was just about fordable without a bridge. Cameron quickly realized that he had one of the keys to the campaign in his hands, and the bluecoats sloshed through water up to their chests and then scattered a small Rebel guard force on the other side of the river. Jefferson Davis was in the middle of a meeting with a Confederate senator who had just returned from Atlanta with Johnston's assurances that he could keep the Yankees on the north side of the river for another eight weeks, when a messenger quietly handed the president a telegram that Federal troops were on the south bank of the Chattahoochie. Davis almost immediately concluded that he had chosen the wrong man to defend Atlanta and quickly sounded out Robert E. Lee on his opinion of John Bell Hood as Johnston's replacement. Lee's response was so full of qualifications and subtle warnings that Davis should have thought twice about his plan, but he largely ignored his most famous general and placed the young former commander of the Texas Brigade in command of the second largest army in the Confederacy.

Feelings about the startling change in leadership were electric on both sides of the battle line. Johnston was an extremely popular commander among his men, while Hood was at best an unknown quantity who didn't seem to be a very sophisticated military strategist. On the other hand, two Federal army commanders, Schofield and McPherson, had graduated with Hood at West Point, and both men had been close friends of the Kentucky-born Texan. Schofield had been the new Confederate commander's roommate and had coached him in mathematics when Hood was on the point of being thrown out for too many failures. When Sherman asked his subordinate's opinion of the new adversary, he responded, "he'll hit you like hell, now, before you know it" and warned him that he was "bold, even to rashness and courageous in the extreme." Sherman quickly realized that the whole nature of the campaign would soon change dramatically and he wrote home that "I confess I was pleased at the change."

John Bell Hood was ecstatic at his appointment as the second most powerful general in the Confederacy, and he was confident that his aggressive brand of fighting would soon force the Yankees to run for their lives back into Tennessee. Within hours after he assumed command, he had devised a bold plan to strike back at the advancing Federals. On July 19th Confederate scouts had informed the new general that George Thomas' Army of the Cumberland was in the process of crossing Peachtree Creek almost within sight of Atlanta. The scouts reported that the Union crossing was proceeding very slowly and it appeared that Thomas' men would be divided by the Peachtree most of the following day. Hood quickly devised a plan where Benjamin Cheatham's corps of infantry, Joseph Wheeler's cavalry and 5000 short-term Georgia militia would divert the Army of the Tennessee and the Army of the Ohio, while William Hardee and A.P. Stewart's corps would lunge into the Cumberland men before they could reunite on the south bank of the Creek.

For some reason the usually aggressive Hood decided to maintain his headquarters in Atlanta while he appointed Hardee to oversee the actual assault. This is particularly strange because Hood already believed that Hardee was far too cautious and was too timid to carry through on costly assaults. Thus the general whom Davis had selected for his aggressiveness was nowhere in sight when the Rebel columns quietly marched out of the city and advanced toward their attack positions. Bit by bit the whole Confederate plan began to unravel. First, McPherson's army had marched much closer to Atlanta than originally thought, and Cheatham was forced to incline southward to cover this threat, which in turn left a huge gap in the Confederate battle line. Hardee decided that the gap was too dangerous to be ignored and called a halt to the planned assault while the Rebel line was re-deployed, thus giving Thomas a golden present of an additional two hours to get all of his men across the Peachtree and into hastily constructed breastworks.

The graycoat assault finally lumbered forward during mid-afternoon of July 20th and William Loring's division advanced toward wooded ground that scouts had reported was undefended by the Federals. Suddenly the Rebels collided with the 33rd New Jersey regiment that had just taken position in the woods, and the whole Southern assault stalled as the Confederates gradually worked their way around the enemy regiment's flanks. The New Jersey men lost half their strength in opposing the overwhelming number of Rebels, but their delaying tactics bought time for Thomas' army to complete their entrenchments and the result was a bloody check to the gray tide, in which 2500 Rebels were killed or wounded in a frustrating attack that dropped only1600 bluecoats and gained no penetration of the Union line.

Hood was disappointed at the outcome of Peachtree Creek but he was convinced that it was the execution, not the plan itself that was defective. The Texan quickly shifted his attention to McPherson's army and developed a plan to annihilate his old classmate's force before the rest of Sherman's men could rush to their assistance. McPherson's men had assaulted and occupied Bald Hill on July 21st, and this important prominence near the Georgia Railroad provided the Yankees with a vital ridge overlooking the Atlanta defenses. However, Wheeler's scouts had reported that McPherson's reserve ammunition, reserve artillery and most of his supply wagons were still about three miles away in the town of Decatur, while his new position hadn't been linked up with the rest of Sherman's army. Hood's response was to order Wheeler to capture Decatur and cut off McPherson's vital ammunition supplies, while Hardee smashed into the Federals' exposed left flank in a repetition of Jackson's surprise attack at Chancellorsville. Stewart would occupy the rest of Sherman's army while Cheatham struck McPherson from the front and annihilated an enemy force now cut off from reinforcements and ammunition.

On the sultry night of July 21st, thousands of already exhausted Confederate troops left their defensive positions in Atlanta and began a 15-mile march toward Bald Hill to the east of the city. However, while the sweating Rebel troops lurched toward a supposedly unguarded Yankee left flank, General Grenville Dodge was at that very moment marching his bluecoat divisions and much of the reserve ammunition train back to Bald Hill after destroying the enemy railroad terminus and track at Decatur. Thus when the sleepless graycoats began their sweep against a supposedly vulnerable Union line on the morning of July 22nd, they smashed into a well-fortified enemy position that wasn't supposed to be there. While two Confederate divisions were startled by their collision with a surprisingly powerful Union flank force, two more Rebel divisions found themselves prevented from advancing by a huge array of briar patches that fronted a mill stream on their approach route. When division commander W. H. Walker requested permission to shift his route of attack, an already irritated William Hardee refused to alter the plans and left Walker's men sweating and cursing their way through the briars.

The result of this assortment of fiascoes was entirely predictable. Federal riflemen quickly spotted Walker's men struggling through the bushes and dropped scores of them, including the division commander, who was planning to challenge Hardee to a duel until he was killed. Dodge deftly shifted his reserves to meet an assault by William Bate's division with a hail of grapeshot from massed batteries, which began to rival the fire that decimated Pickett at Cemetery Ridge. The only tangible success of the day occurred when Patrick Cleburne's division poured through a newly discovered gap between Dodge's men and the rest of McPherson's army. The assault resulted in the death of McPherson as he was trying to organize a new defense line, but the dead general's successor, fiery John Logan, personally led a counterattack that closed the gap.

The climax of the battle occurred around 3 o'clock when Cheatham's corps finally got their orders to launch their frontal assault on Bald Hill. Cheatham's men began to penetrate the Yankee defenses along the ridge, but in a perfect example of poor coordination, just as these Rebels were breaking through in one place, Hardee's men were retiring from their unprofitable flank attack. Logan quickly shifted the men holding the flank to the new threat in front, and the whole gray tide began to recede. This appallingly hot July 22nd was probably the key day of the entire Atlanta campaign, as Hood lost 8000 men in an attack which cost Sherman only 3500 men and failed utterly in its objective. The Federal commander was now convinced that if he simply continued to destroy Atlanta's railroad links that

Hood would come to him and batter himself to annihilation in a series of unsophisticated assaults against a much larger Union army. Sherman now decided to move west to destroy two more of Atlanta's vital rail links and he both hoped and expected that his opponent would come out of his trenches after him.

Hood quickly realized what his adversary was attempting to accomplish, and he ordered the newly appointed 30-year-old corps commander Stephen Lee to seize the crossroads of Lick Skillet Road and Marietta Turnpike to block the enemy advance, while Stewart's corps would be deployed to hit the advancing Yankees in the flank. However, the Federals outmarched the Rebels and occupied the vital crossroads town of Ezra Church, throwing up a series of breastworks that included the pews from the church. At 10 A.M. Lee arrived on the outskirts of Ezra Church convinced that the Yankees had only beaten him by a few minutes and eager to sweep through the "unfortified" enemy. The Rebels lunged forward, shot hundreds of holes in the overturned pews but hit almost no Federal defenders. When Lee started running out of unwounded assault troops he borrowed one of Stewart's divisions and threw every man he could deploy against the church building. Union commander General Oliver O. Howard had ringed the church with nearly two dozen cannons, and 50% of the Confederates went down in a hail of artillery fire. One of the Yankees crouching behind the overturned pews noted "we whipped them awfully. Their dead were left almost in line of battle along our entire front. I am tired of seeing such butchery, but if they charge us this way once a day for a month, this corps will end the war in this section."

Lee blamed the disaster on the timid nature of his troops, but an army that could lose 5000 men assaulting a single church was hardly timid. The Union loss was an incredibly smaller 600 men, and even loyal Confederates began to call Hood's operational plan "disgusting" and a "travesty." Hood had managed to lose 16,000 men in just over a week of fighting, while inflicting only 6000 casualties on a far larger enemy force. On July 29th he ordered the army's survivors back into the Atlanta fortification and at this point the fabled "siege of Atlanta" of *Gone With the Wind* fame really began. The "siege" wasn't a truly classic operation because the city was never fully surrounded by Federal troops. Sherman was able to initiate a fairly spectacular bombardment of the city, but the shelling had relatively little impact on the city's fortifications and the Union general seems to have become bored with the whole operation about 24 hours after it began. Sherman kept the siege guns firing, but his real objective was to cut off the last railroad links from Atlanta to Macon. While the Union commander initiated a huge cavalry raid to destroy the Confederate railroads, Hood coincidentally launched an equally large Rebel cavalry raid to demolish the Union rail links to the North. Each raid had spectacular charges, flashing sabers and eager horsemen tearing up tracks and blowing up railroad bridges, but neither side's trains were permanently put out of action, and Sherman finally concluded that only infantry could put the Rebel railroads out of business for good.

On August 25th, 1864, the Union infantry wheeled into motion under orders to capture the vital rail depot at Jonesboro, which would cut the Macon-Atlanta connections. Hood needed little encouragement to initiate a massive response to this threat and long columns of graycoats marched to the nearby town of Rough and Ready with orders to slam into the Yankee troops approaching Jonesboro. On the afternoon of August 31st Rebel scouts reported that the Federals were deploying around Jonesboro, and two corps under Hardee and Lee lurched forward to attack. Once again Hood remained behind in Atlanta while a subordinate that he now despised orchestrated the attack. Hardee managed to deploy his men for the now traditional unsophisticated, frenzied assault, and, as usual, the two corps attacked at different times allowing the Yankees to simply shuttle troops back and forth between threatened positions. Most Rebels never got within 50 yards of the Union lines and an ominous number of graycoats simply surrendered rather than attempt to storm a position that seemed impregnable. Two thousand more members of the Army of Tennessee were added to the growing casualty list while only, 180 Federals were killed or wounded.

While one portion of the Northern army was relatively effortlessly smashing Hood's latest sortie, the rest of the bluecoats were furiously tearing the Confederate rail lines to pieces. By 3 o'clock on August 31st the last links between Atlanta and the outside world were cut off, and when Hood lost telegraphic contact with his field army he started to realize that the end of the Atlanta campaign was near. Hardee was able to throw up a temporary defensive line outside of Jonesboro and delay an immediate Union advance on Atlanta for a few hours, but by the early morning hours of September 2nd Hood decided to evacuate the city, and the ground shook with terrific explosions until the pre-dawn sky flowed with a bloody fire and black smoke caused by the massive inferno of a dying city.

Six miles away in Jonesboro, Federal soldiers began to realize that the climactic moment of the campaign had arrived. One Union artilleryman noted that "late on the night of September 1st while I was on picket duty, I heard in the direction of Atlanta what at first I thought was artillery. The rumbling kept increasing in intensity until it seemed like the heaviest firing I had ever heard. Finally, a number of terrific explosions lit up the air. At six miles distance they seemed like bright flashes of lightning." The scene was now the chaotic panorama of Margaret Mitchell's celebrated chronicle of Scarlett and Rhett. Locomotives exploded, boxcars caught fire, buildings turned into infernos, wounded soldiers begged for rescue and civilians tried to find any possible escape from a doomed city. The next morning a delegation of city officials led by the mayor rode out and surrendered the city to the advancing Yankees, and a jubilant Sherman rushed to his telegraph operator and ordered a dispatch to Washington that "Atlanta is ours and fairly won." In cities throughout the North crowds celebrated the news with church bells, band concerts and fireworks while Ulysses Grant ordered a 100 gun salute fired into the Confederate lines at Petersburg.

Jefferson Davis, who had repeatedly called Atlanta one of the two most important points in the Confederacy, quickly retracted his earlier statements and insisted that the fall of the city really wasn't all that critical. Few Southerners agreed with him. The Confederacy had stripped other vital points in order to hold this vital rail terminus and manufacturing center. Now Atlanta was gone and with it went almost half of the irreplaceable Army of Tennessee. Now Grant's ability to hold Lee in place at Petersburg and prevent him from reinforcing the western army seemed to look like a much more positive accomplishment. The fall of Atlanta, enormously enhanced by David Farragut's spectacular victory at Mobile Bay and Philip Sheridan's string of triumphs in the Shenandoah Valley, began to shift the electorate toward an affirmation of Lincoln's plan for total victory. If the first Tuesday in November produced a re-election of the Republican chief, the days of the Southern experiment in secessionism would be clearly numbered.

Tuesday, November 8th, 1864, brought an unwelcome preview of winter to Washington. Cold rain dampened the spirit of many residents but Abraham Lincoln and his principal advisers grew more elated as the day continued. Telegraph dispatches of the voting in the Northern states brought the welcome news that Democratic candidate George McClellan would carry only New Jersey, Delaware and Kentucky, while every other loyal state opted to continue Lincoln's presidency. In one of the many ironies of the war, the Union soldiers gave a solid majority of votes to a president who had vowed to continue the war to the bitter end, thus keeping those bluecoats in danger. Now, at least substantially due to those soldiers' ballots, Lincoln had received a firm mandate to continue the war until every trace of Confederate government in the South had been eliminated. A Confederacy that still had a strong chance for permanent existence in June of 1864 now had nothing but hope for some miracle to save it from an increasingly inevitable demise, as Grant, Sherman, Thomas and Sheridan gathered their armies for one last massive drive deep into the heart of Dixie.

# CHAPTER 33

# Alternative Strategies and Outcomes

## *Union and Confederate 1863-1864*

$A$ period of just over 22 months separated the arrival of two vital telegrams at the Confederate White House. The first message, sent in the early hours of New Year's Day, 1863, informed Jefferson Davis that the Southern army had won the first round of fighting at Stones River and that Braxton Bragg was confident that he would rout Rosecrans' army in the next assault. The second message, received on the morning of November 9th, 1864, related the first news of President Lincoln's re-election on a platform of continuing the war until the Confederate republic had been totally dismantled.

This period of just under two years represents less than one percent of the existence of the United States as a nation, yet the events that occurred during that span of time largely decided the future of the American republic. During the first hours of January 1st, 1863, it appeared that the Confederacy was clearly winning its bid for national independence, and yet by November of the following year the course of secession was all but lost with only the final date of termination yet to be determined. The intervening period provided both adversaries with clear opportunities to change the nature and outcome of the War Between the States; any one of a series of events might well have given the North a decisive victory many months before Appomattox, while other actions might have ensured a continued existence for the Confederate republic.

A large number of narratives of the Civil War emphasize the importance of the titanic struggle at Gettysburg as the most promising opportunity for the South to have won its independence during the final two years of the war. However, the authors contend that while Gettysburg marked the high tide of the Confederacy in a psychological sense, the most promising

446

opportunities to permanently change the direction of the war in favor of the South actually occurred before Buford's cavalry and Heth's infantry clashed over the fields of McPherson's Ridge. Even as Lee observed the beaten Federals withdraw through Gettysburg toward their last stand at Cemetery Ridge, John Pemberton had essentially accepted the fact of imminent surrender of Vicksburg and its 30,000 defenders. Thus no matter what the Rebels accomplished during the next 48 hours in Pennsylvania, the best they could hope for was to counter the devastating blow in the West with a spectacular triumph in the East. A major victory at Gettysburg would still not have won a war against a Union that had just succeeded in splitting the Confederacy in two.

It seems fairly apparent that a far better opportunity for a Confederate military victory actually occurred six months earlier in the frozen fields around Murfreesboro, Tennessee when Braxton Bragg's Army of Tennessee decimated Rosecrans' army at Stones River and threatened to annihilate the Yankees in the final hours of 1862. Burnside's debacle at Fredericksburg, Sherman's bloody repulse in front of Chickasaw Bluffs and Grant's forced withdrawal from his Mississippi base produced a series of disasters that sent Northern support of the war plummeting in the last few days of the old year. A Confederate annihilation of the Yankees at Stones River, a definite possibility in the early stages of the battle, might have produced a ground-swell of opinion in the North that the war was unwinnable and that it was time to negotiate the best deal possible with an independent Confederacy.

The apparent failure of the Union war effort coincided with an initial negative response to Lincoln's Emancipation Proclamation that threatened to isolate the Northeast, especially New England, from the Midwest and the border states. While the Proclamation served as a long-term asset to the Northern cause, the short term impact was far more negative. On January 3rd, 1863, Governor Oliver Morton of Indiana warned Edwin Stanton that his legislature was considering a resolution acknowledging the Southern Confederacy and urging the Midwestern states to dissolve all relations with New England in anticipation of a possible alliance with the South. Many Midwesterners openly expressed their admiration for Stonewall Jackson and John Hunt Morgan; rallies for Jefferson Davis were widespread; and Iowa Governor Samuel Kirkwood was forced to ask for additional arms for 5000 troops to attempt to suppress pro-Confederate activities in his state. Even Lincoln admitted at this bleak New Year that "the Almighty is against us and I can barely see a ray of hope." The authors believe that this was the closest that the Union cause came to surrender, and one more spectacular Confederate victory might have sealed the fate of Northern attempts to restore the Union by force. Thus it was Braxton Bragg, not Robert E. Lee, who had the opportunity to produce the decisive victory at exactly the right moment to convince the people of the North that their cause was hopeless. Fortunately for the Union side, Bragg was no Lee and he essentially squandered a golden opportunity to produce the victory that might have ended the war. William Rosecrans was no Grant or Sherman, but he had just enough talent to turn a seemingly disastrous defeat into a precarious victory by holding a battlefield that his adversary chose to abandon. Thus in a sense it was not Pickett's Charge that was the "high water mark" of the Confederacy, but John Breckinridge's equally gallant but futile assault on January 2nd that marked the closest the South could get to winning the war outright.

The other major opportunity for the South to win the war during 1863 revolved around the complex deployment of forces that was debated during the Vicksburg campaign. After the battle of Chancellorsville, Lee was able to convince Jefferson Davis to reinforce the Army of Northern Virginia for his proposed invasion of Pennsylvania which he promoted as the best way to safeguard the defenses of distant Vicksburg. Lee may or may not have really believed that his march into Pennsylvania would offer significant relief to Pemberton, but there is little doubt that Davis accepted the wrong advice. A coalition of such diverse leaders as Pierre Beauregard, Joseph Johnston, James Longstreet and Secretary of War Seddon all insisted that the only legitimate way to help save Vicksburg was to use the interior lines and railroads of the Confederacy to move troops into the Western theater. Hooker had little desire to engage Lee in the near future after the fiasco at Chancellorsville, and Rosecrans' army had been so decimated at Stones River that it was out of action for months. Thus the only Union army that presented any immediate threat to the Confederacy in the spring of 1863 was the force commanded by Ulysses Grant. If Grant captured the vital fortress of Vicksburg, the temporary occupation of Harrisburg, or even Philadelphia would be small compensation for the permanent division of the Confederacy.

The authors believe that the most advantageous strategy for the Confederacy in the spring of 1863 would have been to enhance Longstreet's original idea of moving two of his divisions into the western theatre. The move that would have been most threatening to the Union cause would have been the concentration of Longstreet's corps (13,000 soldiers), two divisions from Bragg's army (11,000 men), two divisions from Kirby Smith's Trans-Mississippi army (11,000 men) and the garrison of Port Hudson (8000 men) with Joe Johnston's mobile force near Jackson, Mississippi. This entire force would then have numbered 66,000 men and when combined with Pemberton's 34,000 man garrison, would have provided 100,000 Confederates to oppose Grant's army that at this time was less than 40,000 strong. Grant was a talented general, but odds of this extent would have been difficult to counteract and there would have been a real project for a significant Rebel victory in Mississippi.

A Confederate victory in Mississippi in the spring of 1863 would have opened up fascinating possibilities for the South. First, if Grant had been defeated or forced to retreat northward, a large part of the Mississippi army under either Johnston or Longstreet would have been free to combine with Bragg for an offensive against Rosecrans or could have been shuttled back to the East to link up with Lee. In either case the prospects for another Confederate victory would have risen dramatically. Quite simply, the Confederacy in the spring of 1863 had enough manpower to defeat the North by concentrating much of its army to win in the West and then shifting back to face the Army of the Potomac. However, the South did not have enough men to defeat Grant, Rosecrans and Hooker or Meade simultaneously, and yet, ultimately, this was the prospect that Davis faced. The Confederate president vacillated between two or three plans during the critical window of opportunity for the South when he should have concentrated on checking Grant while allowing his superior eastern commander to hold the line until the threat to Vicksburg could be eliminated. Davis ultimately chose the strategy with the least probable return for the risk taken, and when this gambit failed the Confederacy was thrown into a permanent strategic disadvantage.

Once the Confederates permitted Grant and Sherman to initiate their southern offensives in the spring of 1864, the opportunities for outright Rebel military victory plummeted. However, the South still had a legitimate opportunity to secure its independence until the last week of August. The Confederacy could simply inflict unacceptable casualties on the Yankee invaders and encourage Northern voters to nominate a peace-Democrat for the presidency and then elect that nominee to the highest office. Jefferson Davis knew that the fall of either Richmond or Atlanta might very well produce a wave of enthusiasm in the North that would carry Lincoln to re-election, and yet he faced a daunting challenge; he had only one absolutely reliable, brilliant general and yet needed two men to direct the defense of the two threatened cities.

Davis' appointment of Joseph Johnston was criticized both then and later because of the Virginian's inherent caution and tendency to favor retreat over battle. However, it should be noted that the Army of Tennessee was at the point of disintegration after the fiasco at Missionary Ridge, and Johnston performed virtual miracles in restoring the army to fighting trim by the spring of 1864. The more disastrous presidential decision occurred several months later, in July of 1864, when Davis replaced Johnston with John Bell Hood. Davis was quite rightly concerned that Johnston seemed to have no definitive plan to keep Sherman from capturing Atlanta, and the authors believe that the Virginian indeed was planning to evacuate the city at the point of his dismissal. However, we feel that Davis actually had another far more intriguing option that might have changed the course of the war; the replacement of Johnston with Robert E. Lee. While the thought of Lee commanding the Army of Tennessee may shock Civil War purists who can't conceive of this legendary general fighting outside the Old Dominion, the utilization of this general's talents in defending Georgia may have made an enormous difference in what became the decisive campaign of 1864.

By early July 1864, when Davis first seriously considered relieving Johnston, the war in the East has settled into a stalemate around Petersburg. Grant was unable to penetrate the formidable Confederate defenses, but

Lee's army was too weak to get at a Yankee army that was deployed behind defenses that were almost as strong as the Rebels'. Lee was a great symbolic presence during the defense of Richmond, but he couldn't perform the kind of audacious maneuvers that had made him a legend. Either Pierre Beauregard or A.P. Hill was perfectly competent enough to hold the lines around Petersburg while Lee slipped west to assume command in Georgia. The Virginia commander could even have brought much of Jubal Early's corps with him, since these men were already operating outside of the Richmond trenches and could have gone into a more defensive posture with a far smaller contingent. Thus it is not unreasonable that Lee and 10,000 men could have arrived in Atlanta before Sherman was able to consolidate his position on the south side of the Chattahoochie River. While the authors do not feel that Lee and 10,000 additional men would have been enough to actually defeat the Union army in Georgia, the Confederates, at the very least, would have had a higher possibility of holding Atlanta until the November elections, after which the loss of the city would have been far less catastrophic. Hood simply threw his army away in a series of poorly planned and poorly executed sorties. It is far more likely that the brilliant Lee would have come up with an alternative strategy that might have frustrated Sherman's intentions during the crucial late summer and early fall. Once Grant fully implemented the siege of Petersburg, Lee could no longer influence the outcome of the war from the East, a timely transfer to Georgia might have been a far better use of the Virginian's many talents.

The opportunity for the Confederacy to win a military victory dropped enormously after the twin disasters at Vicksburg and Gettysburg, but the South could have escaped absolute defeat by securing a negotiated peace that was still possible through most of 1864. If Jefferson Davis and the more hawkish members of his government had been both more realistic and more flexible, the South could have traded reunion with the North for a congenial series of Yankee concessions including probable compensation for slaves that would be emancipated, some role for major Confederate government and military leaders in United States policy-making, and protection of Southern property and investments. The most favorable period for the opening of negotiations would probably have been during June or July of 1864 when expectation of outright Confederate military triumph was low, yet Lincoln's hopes for re-election weren't much better. It seems likely that the Northern president would have been eager to orchestrate a reconstruction of the Union before the elections, even if he had to make significant concessions to the South to achieve this end.

Another alternative scenario might have developed if George McClellan had won the election. The election of 1864 was much closer than most modern Americans realize, and even relatively small shifts in voting patterns in a few key states could have provided the Democrats with a narrow victory. The authors are convinced that a McClellan victory would not necessarily have given the Confederacy its independence. The "Young

Napoleon" had not spent a long period as commander of the Army of the Potomac just to practically give the South an independence that it hadn't achieved in battle. However, McClellan was definitely a "soft war" man who would have offered the Confederacy virtually everything short of permanent separation to end the conflict. McClellan's view on the status of slavery in the autumn of 1864 is fairly vague, and the situation was complicated by the fact of 180,000 African-Americans serving in the Union army and thousands of slaves leaving their plantations as the Yankees edged closer to many Southern communities. However, it seems likely that even a substantial number of concessions that a McClellan government might have offered a Confederacy that was willing to re-enter the Union would have been rejected by a Jefferson Davis who didn't even think that the loss of Richmond and the surrender of his two main armies were mortal wounds to the Southern republic. The leaders of the South had a number of opportunities to make the "Lost Cause" much less "lost," but for a number of leaders and a sizeable fraction of the people, the fight for the last ditch seemed the only appropriate ending to a struggle that was much of the time more spiritual than material in nature. Perhaps different leaders with different agendas would have seen a successfully negotiated peace as an acceptable consolation for being unable to win the military conflict.

The Confederacy may have muffed several opportunities to either win the war or at least secure a more congenial peace, but the Union was no slouch in squandering opportunities to secure victory before Appomattox. Since 3000 Americans were dying each week that the war continued, even a modest advancement of the end date of the war would have been a major accomplishment. The authors believe that the North had four recognizable opportunities to significantly accelerate the onset of victory: the Chancellorsville campaign of May 1863, the pursuit of Lee after Gettysburg in July, 1863, the initial stage of the Atlanta campaign in May 1864 and the first phase of the battle of Petersburg in June of 1864. Each of these episodes presented the North with a clear opportunity to so cripple the Confederate war effort that the days of the secessionist republic would be clearly numbered, yet at the critical moment, each opportunity failed to produce expected results.

The first clear cut opportunity for Union victory in this time period occurred when Joseph Hooker orchestrated a flawless movement around Lee's flank at Fredericksburg and threatened to place the much larger Federal army between the Virginian and the Confederate capital. "Fighting Joe"'s opportunity for a war-winning victory was spectacular. Lee's army was more outnumbered than usual, caught off guard and threatened at its most vulnerable point. The authors believe that this was the closest that the Army of Northern Virginia came to outright destruction between the beginning of 1863 and Appomattox, as every single initial factor in the campaign was in Hooker's favor. If the Rebel army really had become "the legitimate property of the Army of the Potomac," as Hooker boasted, it is difficult to see how the Confederacy could have long survived the elimination of its primary field force.

The other primary confrontation in the East during 1863, the Gettysburg campaign, presents a more complex series of possible alternate outcomes. Emotional debates have raged since the summer of the battle regarding George Meade's decision to pass up the opportunity of a counterattack in the wake of the annihilation of Pickett's Charge. The authors contend that while an immediate Federal counterstroke did have some chance to succeed and possibly annihilate the Army of Northern Virginia, such an assault would have been an enormous risk. The authors agree with Meade's contention that a Federal army charging up Seminary Ridge may have experienced the same devastating casualties as the Rebels who had just assaulted Cemetery Ridge. Lee had used only a relatively small fraction of his infantry in his desperate afternoon attack, and thus much of the Confederate army was still well deployed to meet a Yankee thrust. The key element in this equation is the Southern artillery. Most accounts of the battle stress the dwindling supply of ammunition on the Rebel side after the dramatic early afternoon artillery duel. If the graycoat gunners were actually almost literally out of ammunition, the Union troops would have enjoyed a far better chance to overrun the Confederate positions. On the other hand, even a few available rounds for each gun could have wreaked havoc on a Yankee advance across those open fields. Meade's principal charge was to screen the major eastern cities from Confederate capture and keep his army between Lee and Washington. He had fully accomplished that charge by the late afternoon of July 3rd, although at the cost of nearly 25,000 casualties. After witnessing the carnage imposed on Federal armies in earlier ill-advised attacks on defended ridges and having just observed the decimation of a Confederate army attempting to do exactly the same thing, there is little wonder that a general who had only been in command of the most important army in his nation for a few days would think long and hard about throwing away his considerable gains with one more throw of the dice.

The authors contend that Meade's real opportunity to further wreck the enemy army actually occurred ten days later, on July 13, 1863. By this time the dispatch of Federal reinforcements had made good most of Meade's losses while the badly battered Rebel army was backed up against a flooded Potomac River near Williamsport, Maryland. Lee's army held a decent, though not formidable, defensive position that was far more modest than either army's deployments at Gettysburg. The authors feel that the Williamsport line was far more vulnerable than the Seminary Ridge line and Lee was further handicapped by having a unfordable river immediately in his rear. Meade now had a higher manpower advantage than he enjoyed at Gettysburg, his casualties had been replaced, Lee's had not, and if he secured a major breakthrough, there was nowhere for the Confederates to retreat.

This point seems to be the climactic moment of the whole 1863 campaign. Grant had just captured one entire Confederate army nine days earlier; if

Lee's army was destroyed, the Confederacy could not survive until the end of the year. Meade favored an attack which very well may have succeeded, but when a majority of his corps commanders advised a more cautious approach, the commanding general postponed the attack until the next day. The next morning, Federal troops advanced to find Lee's army had crossed over hastily constructed bridges back into Virginia, and the moment for spectacular victory was delayed almost two years. Meade's total haul in this postponed offensive was exactly two Rebel cannons that had been stuck in the mud when the Rebels withdrew.

The bloody campaigns of 1864 also provided at least two significant opportunities for the Union army to dramatically shorten the war by scoring a spectacular triumph. Sherman and Grant each experienced a golden moment in which the enemy seemed ripe for destruction and yet, somehow, escaped to fight again. Sherman's opportunity occurred very early in the Georgia campaign when his attempt to distract Johnston with two armies while a third army passed through Snake Creek Gap and trapped the Rebels from behind, worked to perfection in its first stage. Johnston really was fooled and James McPherson was able to deploy over 25,000 men astride the Rebels' only route of retreat. Thus, in one of the most agonizing muffed opportunities of the war, McPherson allowed a tiny force of 4000 newly arrived graycoats to panic him into abandoning his perfect position and allowing Johnston to escape with his army intact. There is a strong possibility that a completely trapped Rebel army that was surrounded by an overwhelming number of Yankees would have capitulated, allowing Sherman to walk into Atlanta and then shuttle much of his army eastward to smash into Lee.

Grant's major opportunity occurred a few weeks later near the dusty roads approaching Petersburg, Virginia. When Grant was able to move his army south of the James without Lee's knowledge, the Confederate defenders of the vital rail center of Petersburg were placed in one of the most difficult positions of an army in the war. During the early days of the siege of Petersburg, the Federals enjoyed numerical superiority that ranged between 4 to 1 and 10 to 1 and should have resulted in the almost immediate capture of the city and its vital rail lines. The authors are convinced that this outcome would have placed Lee in an untenable position which would have forced him to attack an overwhelmingly superior Union army deployed behind formidable breastworks, just in order to have a chance to escape the doomed capital while the immediate fall of Richmond itself would have become a virtual certainty. In this case it was Beauregard and a small number of Confederate defenders that bought the Confederacy an additional nine months of existence.

Each side could have produced alternative outcomes that might have substantially changed the direction of the war. However, in a curious sort of balancing act, each army seems to have squandered a relatively equal number of opportunities which guaranteed that the war would continue into a fourth bloody year. However, after the re-election of Abraham Lincoln the opportunities for alternative scenarios became substantially limited. The margin and superiority of North over South had become so great that it seemed that almost no amount of last minute Confederate triumphs or last minute Union fiascos could alter the final outcome.

# CHAPTER 34

# The Death of Confederate Independence

## *The Birth of the Lost Cause*

On Monday, November 7th, 1864, the day before the presidential election in the North, the Confederate Congress was welcomed back in session by a message from Jefferson Davis. The Confederate president tried to minimize the catastrophic loss of Atlanta by emphasizing that even the loss of every major city in the republic would leave the Southern people eager to continue their struggle for independence from the rapacious Yankees. "There are no vital points on the preservation which the continued existence of the Confederacy depends. Not the fall of Richmond, nor Wilmington, nor Charleston nor Savannah nor Mobile nor all combined can save the enemy from the constant and exhaustive drain of blood and treasure which must continue until he shall discover that no peace is attainable unless based on the recognition of our indefeasible rights."

Less than five months after Davis wrote those words of perpetual continuation of the struggle, not only would the "hard war" President of the United States be inaugurated for a second term in office, but the Confederacy itself would be reduced to an enclave of territory in southern Virginia and upper North Carolina defended by armies that were losing hundreds of men to desertion every week. This period of time, from the re-election of Lincoln to the surrender at Appomattox, was the death struggle of a Confederacy that had been doomed by a devastating series of defeats between late summer and mid-autumn and was now fighting on with virtually no hope of final victory. A nation reeling from the defeats at Mobile Bay, Atlanta and the Shenandoah Valley, would soon discover even more humiliating setbacks during Sherman's march to the sea, Hood's debacle-strewn invasion of Tennessee and the final collapse of the Richmond defense at Five Forks. The South would certainly go down fighting, but in that fight it was mainly Southerners whose lives were either ruined or ended.

The first element in this triple series of disasters began to develop when William T. Sherman finally realized that the psychological impact of his recent capture of Atlanta had been at least partially negated by the escape of a large part of the garrison. The Army of Tennessee may have been badly mauled during the summer, but they simply would not go away, as Hood launched a series of strikes on the Union supply and communication lines while thousands of bluecoats scattered over the Georgia countryside in a vain attempt to bring the Rebels to decisive battle. When Hood's infantry was attacking Union railroad depots, cavalry forces under Joe Wheeler and Nathan Forrest were shooting up trains and ripping up rails and even threatening to carry their operations north of the Ohio River. Sherman was increasingly frustrated at this inability to engage the enemy in one open battle that he was confident he could win and soon his fertile mind turned to less conventional solutions to his dilemma. The red-headed general finally charged his adversary with wildly eccentric behavior as "I cannot guess his movements as I could those of Johnston who was a sensible man and did sensible things."

Sherman's solution to the problem was in itself rather eccentric. He proposed to Grant that the Union army would simply ignore Hood and his exasperating activities and instead concentrate on devastating the war-making capacity of Georgia. As far as his attitude toward Hood and the Army of Tennessee, the victor of Atlanta exclaimed, "if he will go to the Ohio River I will give him rations.... let him go North. My business is down South." In reality, Sherman's proposal wasn't quite as extreme as it seemed. The western commander actually intended to send part of his army north to Nashville in order to link up with General George Thomas' garrison and provide the Union-loyal Virginian with over 70,000 men to keep Hood's 40,000 from capturing any vital points.

Meanwhile, Sherman would organize a force of just over 60,000 of his best men into a vast expeditionary force that would march eastward from Atlanta toward the Atlantic Ocean. His army would "sweep the whole state of Georgia" on its way to Savannah. The general impressed upon Grant that "such a march would be more than fatal to the possibility of Southern independence. They may stand the fall of Richmond, but not all Georgia." While Grant was still squeamish about allowing his favorite subordinate to leave a still dangerous opponent in his rear while he marched toward unknown ambushes and traps in hostile territory, the commanding general finally relented, and by late October Sherman was putting the final touches on this grandiose scheme. On November 16th, on the same day that Hood issued orders for his army to march north into Tennessee, Sherman sat on his horse on Bald Hill outside Atlantic and watched the smoke rise from the doomed city. The Union general had ordered most civilians to leave the city and then began to demolish anything that might be of use to the Confederate war effort once the Federals marched east. While Sherman's original intention was not to destroy the whole city, a combination of Union troops who liberally interpreted their orders and a stiff breeze that quickly spread flames from public buildings to private residences turned much of the town into a raging inferno. One of Sherman's staff officers noted, "all the pictures and verbal descriptions of hell I have ever seen never gave me half so vivid an idea of it as did this flame wrapped city." Sherman himself noted simply, "behind us lay Atlanta, smouldering and in ruins," while ahead lay a 300 mile march that would obliterate every vestige of Georgia's capacity to continue to support the dying Confederate cause.

The March to the Sea would blacken Sherman's reputation in much of the South for generations, but despite his fiery rhetoric about "making Georgia howl," the expedition was a relatively bloodless operation. On the one hand, the army was expected to supplement its wagon loads of supplies by "foraging liberally on the country during the march," but soldiers were officially ordered to refrain from entering the dwellings of local inhabitants, especially when no overt opposition to the march was encountered. The march was conducted by two columns of about 30,000 men each pushing eastward along a 60-mile front that avoided the larger cities of Augusta and Macon. While the Confederates were busily moving their limited number of troops to defend those two population centers, Sherman's men slipped between the Rebels and occupied the state capital of Milledgeville which became the fifth such capital to fall to the Union Army. While the Union forces regrouped for their next eastward push, the Confederate government in Richmond and the governor of Georgia predicted the total annihilation of the Yankee hordes within the next few days.

The great Confederate counterstrike featured a 3000 man force of second line militiamen which closed in on General Osterhaus' rear guard near Griswoldville on November 22nd. Late that afternoon the 1500 Yankees of the rear units detected a heavy column of infantry moving through the nearby town and the bluecoats quickly threw together some hastily built breastworks to confront the Rebel army. The graycoats managed three violent attacks on the outnumbered Federals, but the poorly trained, poorly equipped Southerners were smashing into a confident, superbly equipped detachment of defenders who mowed down almost 600 attackers at a loss of only 60 men. When the Rebels finally gave up and retreated back toward Macon, the Federals ran out onto the field to count the enemy casualties and were startled and somewhat sickened to see that most of their opponents had been either boys or old men. As one Illinois soldier insisted "I was never so affected by the sight of dead and wounded before. I hope we will never have to shoot at such people again."

The engagement at Griswoldville was the only significant infantry clash before the Union army pushed to the outskirts of Savannah. However, Judson Kilpatrick's bluecoat horsemen constantly skirmished with Joe Wheeler's Rebel cavalry in a contest which allowed the Confederates to do little more than pick off Yankee stragglers and perhaps convince the citizens of Georgia that at least some resistance was being made to what increasingly appeared to be an irresistible wave of Yankee intruders. Four weeks into the march, 218 well-fed, confident Union regiments approached the Atlantic coast in a virtual holiday atmosphere. On December 13th Sherman climbed to a Federal signal station constructed atop a rice mill and saw "a faint cloud of smoke gliding as it were along the horizon above the tops of the ridge toward the sea, which little by little grew till it was pronounced to be the smokestacks of a steamer." For almost a month the only reports that Lincoln, Grant and most people of the North had received concerning Sherman's army had come from captured Confederate newspapers that emphasized the furious assaults on the Yankee column by Rebel troops and the imminent annihilation of the whole bluecoat horde. Now, while the jubilant Union soldiers read weeks-old mail brought in by the Federal navy, anxious friends and relatives were startled and gratified by the almost bloodless triumphal march through the heart of Dixie.

A Confederate garrison at Fort McAllister still blocked Sherman's entry into Savannah proper, but when a naval vessel asked the general if the fort had been taken, the redhead quickly sent back a brief reply; "not yet but it will be in a minute." Actually the capture of Fort McAllister took more like 15 minutes, as William Hazen's division swarmed out of the woods, charged across ground that had been strewn with "torpedoes," pushed through the abatis and engaged in a wild melee with the 250-man garrison. Hazen lost 134 men, captured the entire garrison, and signaled the fleet that Savannah was now open.

William Hardee, former senior corps commander in the Army of Tennessee, had been given the unenviable task of attempting to scrape together enough men to prevent Sherman's army from capturing Savannah. Old Reliable commanded a scratch force of 15,000 convalescents, militiamen, new recruits and cavalrymen, and he immediately rejected Sherman's demand for surrender. However, when Richmond refused Hardee's request for more regulars to engage the far larger Union army, the Confederate general began a Johnston-like evacuation of anything that was mobile enough to be salvaged. The Yankees entered the city on December 22nd after a series of minor skirmishes and the politically aware Sherman quickly wired Lincoln "I beg to present you, as a Christmas present, the city of Savannah with 150 heavy guns and plenty of ammunition, also about 25,000 bales of cotton." At a cost of 103 killed and 428 wounded, the Ohio general had essentially knocked one of the most important states in the Confederacy out of the war while threatening the Carolinas with even worse devastation. The only army that could have seriously challenged this Federal juggernaut had been conducting a totally separate war 500 miles to the west and the climax of this campaign would present yet another Christmas gift to the newly re-elected President.

John Bell Hood had received Jefferson Davis' enthusiastic support for his proposal to march the Army of Tennessee northward, destroy the huge Union supply depot at Nashville, and then push forward across the Ohio River into the heartland of the Yankees. Hood and Davis reasoned that a successful offensive might very well impel Sherman to abandon his march to the Atlantic or, even if that general wasn't halted, the Army of Tennessee could swing eastward and threaten Grant in his Petersburg siege lines. Neither the Confederate general or president could fully understand that Union manpower superiority had become so substantial that Sherman could easily make his famous march while at the same time dispatching significant units to confront Hood in Tennessee.

On Sunday, November 20th, Hood crossed the Tennessee River at the head of 32,000 infantry, 6000 horsemen and 108 cannons, and attempted to get between General John Schofield's 34,000 men camped at Pulaski and General George Thomas' similar force garrisoning Nashville. Hood realized that he enjoyed a slight numerical advantage over each of his potential opponents, and if he could get control of the bridges across the Duck River between Pulaski and Nashville he could strike either enemy force and then turn to destroy the remaining army. The initial part of the march was carried out in complete security as Forrest's horsemen were able to prevent any Yankee cavalry units from penetrating his screen and discovering the Rebel general's intentions. However, just when it appeared that the Confederates would win the race for the river, a small Union cavalry patrol observed the direction of Hood's march and warned a startled Schofield that his army was about to be outflanked. The Rebels had a head start toward the Duck, but Schofield had access to a more direct route over a much better road, and advance units of his army were able to seize the vital crossroads town of Columbia just before Forrest's horsemen came charging into the village.

Hood's initial inclination was to simply throw each of his infantry units into his old West Point roommate's lines and hope that superior aggressiveness would carry the day. However, the Texan suddenly changed his mind and decided to implement a more sophisticated plan. A. P. Stewart's corps was ordered to use almost all of the army's artillery batteries to make a demonstration against the Union army on the north side of the Duck, holding them in place while the other two corps made a forced march, crossed the river several miles upstream, and occupied the town of Spring Hill 12 miles north of Columbia. Schofield's retreat route to Nashville would be cut off, and he would be caught between two segments of the Army of Tennessee. As an early season snowstorm blanketed the countryside, the men of Chatham and Lee's corps marched north to spring the ambush while Hood exulted, "the enemy must give me a fight or I'll be in Nashville tomorrow night."

General James Wilson was out on this snowy night with his Federal cavalrymen and the young general soon realized that much of Hood's army was no longer south of the Duck River. When Schofield was warned of the developing trap, he left part of his army to deal with Stewart while his 800 wagons and most of his 62 guns were escorted up the turnpike by General David Stanley's detachment. Brigadier General George Wagner's division double-timed into the town of Spring Hill just in time to help the town's small garrison defend against the first Confederate cavalry charge. Then Stanley, leaving part of his force to guard the wagons, rushed into town with 5000 men and 34 guns. These reinforcements were enough to hold off three vicious Rebel assaults and Hood decided to halt his offensive until he could better organize his forces the next morning.

The Confederates quickly started fires to ward off the 12 degree temperature and passing snow flurries, but while they huddled for warmth, Schofield's army quietly marched up the turnpike only 200 yards away. The Rebels were so close to the road that dozens of Federals were captured when they came up to enemy campfires to either warm themselves or light their pipes, but no one in authority guessed that these men were more than a minor group of stragglers. The next morning, a shocked Hood discovered that the enemy that he believed was hopelessly trapped was actually well on its way north to Franklin. The Confederate commander ranted to his subordinates that their incompetence "ruined the best move in my career as a soldier" while Forrest snarled back that only Hood's crippled condition prevented him from killing him on the spot.

After this not-so-congenial group of gray-clad generals threatened a few duels and hurled a few insults at one another, the army was marched northward toward Union-occupied Franklin. Schofield did not really expect Hood to attack before he reached the far more strategically important Nashville, but he had deployed his 34,000 men in an imposing series of defenses backed up by formidable artillery positions on the north side of the Harpath River above the town. Hood halted his own army two miles south of Franklin on an elevation known as Winstead Hill and surveyed his adversary's position. The former commander of the Texas Brigade was now obsessed with the concept that his men were too timid to assault breastworks and were therefore useless to the Confederacy unless they could show more raw courage. Therefore the general, who was hardly known for his sophisticated tactics in the best of times, ordered most of his army to line up in formation and advance over two miles of open fields to smash into the Yankee defenses.

Schofield's men could hardly believe their eyes as at 4 P.M. in the fading sunlight of a beautiful Indian Summer November 30th, 18,000 Rebels and a number of their bands lined up below Winstead Hill for a frontal assault. Several Yankee brigades that were newly equipped with repeating rifles estimated how many Rebels they could drop before the enemy got to within 100 yards of their positions and the gunners manning 15 batteries of Federal artillery prepared to drop a hail of canister on the advancing men in butternut and gray. The Confederate army may well have been annihilated before it ever got close to Franklin, except that one major Union blunder gave the rebels a brief opportunity to turn the tables. General Wagner had ordered one of his brigades, commanded by Emerson Opdycke, to fall back into the town to guard the huge Yankee wagon train but his orders for his other two brigades were either garbled or never communicated. The result was that several regiments of bluecoats now formed a dangerous salient between the main Union position and Winstead Hill. The charging Rebels were startled to discover this knot of Union defenders deployed far too forward to be supported by their comrades and with a chorus of high pitched yells, the graycoats smashed into the hastily erected breastworks and either captured or dispersed the whole Yankee detachment. When most of the Federals bolted to the rear to get back to their main position, the Confederates began shouting, "lets' go into the works with them!"

A crisis point in the battle had now arrived as the intermingling of Rebels and Yankees prevented the imposing Union artillery from blasting the advancing men, and soon thousands of graycoats were trying to claw their way into the main Federal position. At this point, Opdycke realized that the remainder of his brigade's parent division was in danger of annihilation and he quickly abandoned the wagons for a double quick march up to the point of greatest Rebel penetration. Two Confederate divisions led by generals Cleburne and Brown were just in the process of exploiting a breakthrough in the line when Opdycke's men smashed into them from a totally unexpected direction, and the battle began to surge back and forth over the grounds of the Carter family mansion.

While the left flank of the Confederate assault force was engaged in a wild battle that kept shifting momentum, the Rebel right flank divisions of Walthall and Loring were being torn to pieces by the Yankee artillery smashing into them from Fort Granger on the north side of the river. Once the surviving graycoats ran through a torrent of cannon fire they were halted by a series of Osage hedges that held them in position just long enough for the Spencer equipped Yankee brigades to begin an operation that was only one step short of target practice. One Union participant marveled at the ability of the repeating rifles to "blaze out a continuous sheet of destruction," and within minutes captains were left in charge of brigades and sergeants were leading regiments as a dozen generals and 54 colonels went down in the hail of fire.

The talented Patrick Cleburne and the aptly named States Rights Gist joined four other generals in receiving mortal wounds while several other division or brigade commanders were captured or severely wounded. The forward-most Confederate regiments had simply been annihilated, and when the right wing assault simply stopped dead in its tracks, the left flank troops who were still fighting were also forced to pull back or be overwhelmed by Yankee firepower.

Hood's idiotic idea of forcing allegedly "timid" soldiers to conquer their fears by a totally unsophisticated frontal assault produced one of the most one-sided Confederate defeats of the war. Not only did the 6000 total Rebel casualties far outnumber the 2000 Yankees lost, the nearly 2000 graycoat dead exceeded the 180 fatally wounded Federals by an astonishing margin of over 10 to 1. The authors believe that the battle of Franklin was the definitive warning to Southerners that the War Between the States had now clearly become the Lost Cause. A Union army that already far outnumbered its adversaries and was now rapidly being issued the latest generation of available weapons was now starting a process of inflicting casualties that were so much higher than Yankee losses that the conflict couldn't even be defined as a war of attrition anymore. A few more debacles like Franklin would simply annihilate the entire Confederate army at relatively small cost to Union forces.

John Schofield had no further interest in holding Franklin; he was only interested in linking up with Thomas' army at Nashville; and when the Yankees slipped away during the night, Hood congratulated his army on their hard won "victory" even though there were now only about 22,000 unwounded infantrymen left to celebrate the "triumph." The Confederate general started his men up the turnpike toward Nashville, but not until he had matched Braxton Bragg's blunder of the previous autumn and detached a combined force of 6000 infantry and cavalry to threaten the 9000-man Union garrison at Murfreesboro. This left Hood with about 19,000 infantry and a small force of cavalry to confront Schofield and Thomas' combined army of almost 65,000 men deployed in almost invulnerable fortifications around Nashville. The aggressive Texan set up an almost laughable "siege line" around the Tennessee capital but he only had enough men to cover a small part of the city's circumference. Hood's main ally was a stretch of horrendous weather in which snow, sleet and freezing rain made offensive maneuvers almost impossible and forced Thomas to postpone a planned attack until the ground was passable.

In one of Ulysses Grant's least brilliant moves of the war, the Union commander repeatedly threatened to relieve Thomas if he didn't immediately attack Hood. The former hero of Chickamauga actually had every intention of launching an assault, but not until the ground was decent enough for him to fully utilize his cavalry and artillery. Finally, on the evening of December 14th, the Union general left a wake-up call for 5 A.M. At his St. Cloud Hotel room the next morning the general calmly packed his own bags, checked out, and mounted his horse to orchestrate the largest battle of his career. All over Nashville thousands of citizens, most of them still Confederate sympathizers, lined every high point in the city to watch the expected spectacle that was unfolding. The onset of warmer weather had clashed with the icy ground to produce a dense ground fog, but by a little past 8 o'clock the first Union regiments slammed into A. P. Stewart's left wing. A combined force of Wilson's cavalry units and several infantry brigades climbed up a small incline and smashed into Chalmer's and French's Rebel divisions. These two units had been almost annihilated at Franklin and now deployed fewer than 1000 men between them, while the Union assault force was twenty times as large. When these divisions began to crumble, the whole graycoat left began to disintegrate and of the four roads that the Confederates controlled at dawn, only two were still in Rebel hands at noon. By mid-afternoon 48,000 Yankees were smashing into a diminishing left flank that was held by only 4800 graycoats, and the only thing that prevented a total rout was the early onset of darkness.

Hood's army was now outnumbered nearly 4 to 1 and only two escape routes, Granny White Pike and Franklin Pike, were still in Rebel hands. However, the Confederate commander continued to insist that Thomas would make some grievous error the next day which would turn the tide of the battle, and the campaign. The Confederates spent the entire long winter night throwing up a formidable series of breastworks and early the next morning the battle re-opened with the first major assault by black troops in the western theater. General John Steedman's two brigades of U. S. Colored Infantry smashed into the Confederate right flank in a desperate attempt to capture Franklin Pike and cut off a possible avenue of retreat, but Hood had placed most of his artillery and his most intact units in this part of the breastworks and large numbers of black soldiers were shot during a series of attempts to penetrate the strongest point of the Confederate line. One unit, the 13th U.S. Colored Infantry regiment, suffered 221 killed and wounded during the attack, the highest regimental loss on either side during the battle, but their loss ultimately served a purpose.

Hood had become so alarmed at the ferocity of the attacks on his Franklin Pike positions that he started shuttling more and more units from his seemingly less threatened left flank over the more precariously held right. A new series of sleet and rain showers began during this re-deployment and the Confederate commander began to assume that the worst of the crisis was past, when suddenly his diminished left wing was overwhelmed by Thomas' carefully organized final assault of the day. One Confederate division lost all of its brigade commanders in the first five minutes of the new assault, and thousands of Rebels simply threw down their rifles and streamed down Granny White Pike while Union forces snapped at their heels. The exultant bluecoats quickly captured 53 Confederate guns and over 3300 prisoners and were in the process of swooping down on the dazed survivors when ice and darkness ended the fight. In his final major battle, Hood had lost another 6000 men compared to 3000 Union casualties and Thomas emerged anew as a genuine Union hero, as he shouted to cavalry commander Wilson "dang it to hell Wilson, didn't I tell you we could lick em?" The return of new rounds of ice, sleet and snow prevented Thomas from annihilating the remnants of Hood's force, but the Army of Tennessee was finished as a significant piece on the military chessboard. An army that had counted 65,000 men under Johnston in May of 1864 had fewer than 10,000 soldiers still present for duty by Christmas. Hood's poorly conceived Atlanta and Tennessee campaigns had simply eliminated one of the two major Confederate armies from the strategic picture, which left Robert E. Lee's Army of Northern Virginia as the only significant military force remaining in the South. On the other hand, Thomas, Sherman and Grant each commanded a huge Federal army, with the first two forces now free to march virtually anywhere in the Confederacy. As Sherman's army moved its mobile base of operations from Georgia to the Carolinas and Thomas prepared to launch slashing cavalry assaults into the Deep South, the operational control of Jefferson Davis and the Confederate Congress was essentially reduced to a glorified city-state of Richmond and its suburbs. During the long, cold winter of 1864-1865, Lee's lines were being stretched more thinly by each successive Federal thrust and by late March it was only a matter of when and where the defenses of Richmond would finally crumble.

On Saturday morning March 25, 1865, exactly three weeks after Lincoln's second inauguration, Robert E. Lee set in motion the last offensive of the Army of Northern Virginia. The Confederate commander had abandoned any hope of holding the Rebel capital for more than a few weeks, and was now interested merely in providing an open route for his army to link up with Joseph Johnston's scratch force that was attempting to counter Sherman's advance in North Carolina. Lee hoped to combine the two remaining Southern armies, smash Sherman's force, and then turn on Grant in a desperate gamble to turn the tide at the last moment. The first step in this long-shot attempt would be an attack by 12,000 Confederates led by General John Gordon against an apparent vulnerable spot in the Yankee siege line at Fort Stedman, halfway between the Crater and the Appomattox River, and only 150 yards from a bulge in the Rebel works. Lee's plan was to use 50 axmen to chop a path through the Union outer defenses, pounce on the four-gun Federal fort, and then utilize three special attack groups of 100 men each to seize three smaller forts in the rear whose guns would then be turned on the Yankee flanks to widen the breach. The main assault force would then smash its way toward City Point, which contained the main Union railroad depot, supply base, and Grant's headquarters. Thus a successful attack would at the very least force the Federals to weaken their flanks to meet this threat, which in turn would allow the Rebels to hold open the main route to North Carolina. At best, if the attackers were really lucky, they might capture Grant in his headquarters, which could influence the entire course of the war.

At 4 A.M., as Lee watched from a hill just in the rear of the Rebel trenches, the initial assault force, all wearing strips of white cloth to identify them in the darkness, charged through the outer defenses of Fort Stedman and overwhelmed the position's 300 defenders. Gordon quickly advanced with his main body and, just as dawn was breaking, the Confederates captured Battery Number 10 and Battery Number 11 on the Union line. However, within a few minutes the offensive began to fall apart. The advance units came panting back with the startling news that the three targeted "forts" were actually nothing more than abandoned ruins of old Confederate works and contained no cannons that could be turned on the enemy. Then the bluecoats in the adjoining Batteries 9 and 12 repulsed determined Rebel assaults and began sweeping the newly captured trenches with canister charges. Every available mobile Union artillery battery was soon being wheeled into a massive firing line which met every subsequent Rebel attack toward City Point with a sheet of flame. At 8 o'clock Gordon realized that he couldn't penetrate the Union line, and he ordered a retreat. However, Grant was now convinced that his adversary must have stripped his flank defenses in order to concentrate men for the assault, and he ordered a major assault on the Southern right flank at Hatcher's Run, which pushed Federal soldiers dangerously close to the vital Southside Railroad, which was Richmond's last link with the rest of the country. Lee's attack and Grant's counteroffensive had cost the Virginian another 5000 irreplaceable soldiers compared to only 2000 Union casualties, and the Yankees now had the beginning of a penetration that would ultimately mean the doom of Richmond.

Three days later, on Tuesday, March 28th, four of the most powerful men in the United States shook hands and took seats in the lounge of a passenger steamer that was moored only a short distance from Saturday's bloody assault. Abraham Lincoln, Ulysses Grant, William Sherman and Union naval chief David Dixon Porter combined a lively series of personal stories with the more serious business of planning the final offensive of the war. While Lincoln counseled his generals to let the nearly defeated Confederate armies "down easy" and strongly hinted that he wouldn't mind Jefferson Davis' escape to another country, Grant and Sherman outlined their plans for the final defeat of the two principal Rebel armies.

Lincoln was still somewhat concerned that Lee would slip out of the Richmond trenches and combine with Joe Johnston to hit Sherman, but the red-headed general seemed confident that his 100,000 men, now camped about 150 miles to the south, could handle two Rebel armies that even together numbered little more than half his force. Sherman also assured the President and the commanding general that his men would initiate their spring offensive no later than April 10th with a thrust against Johnston's army near Raleigh and a subsequent advance into Virginia, which would permit a linkup with Grant and provide the two generals with nearly a quarter-million men to capture Richmond. However, Grant was reasonably confident that he could exploit his newly won position near Hatcher's Run to begin the final offensive much earlier and thus force the crumbling Army of Northern Virginia southward almost into the arms of the waiting Sherman, even if the Rebels weren't annihilated before they got out of Virginia. A few hours later, when the conference adjourned, Sherman hopped aboard a fast steam packet to rejoin his army while Grant set in motion his own final offensive.

The next day, Wednesday, March 29th, while Jefferson Davis began the first phase of the evacuation of Richmond by placing his wife and children on a train bound for Charlotte, Philip Sheridan's cavalry began to slash their way toward Dinwiddie Court House in the first step toward the severing of

Richmond's remaining rail links. Sheridan's major objective was the vital crossroads of Five Forks, which covered the approach to the Southside Railroad just under three miles to the west. Lee had deployed George Pickett and three brigades of Rebel infantry along with most of his remaining cavalry to hold the crucial position, and during the last three days of March Sheridan and Pickett dueled with one another for possession of the crossroads with both armies hampered by torrential rains.

Finally, on April 1st, a combination of dry weather and the arrival of infantry reinforcements allowed Sheridan to organize a late afternoon assault that caught the Rebels by surprise. George Pickett and cavalry commander Fitzhugh Lee had accepted fellow Virginian Thomas Rosser's invitation to a shad bake several miles from the Confederate lines and neither general had bothered to give his subordinates any idea of where he was going. While the Rebel generals enjoyed their picnic, Sheridan personally led an assault that sent the graycoats tumbling backwards and very nearly cut off all five of Pickett's brigades. At a cost of 600 Union casualties, another 5000 Confederates were wiped from Lee's active duty roles, and by the time that the picnickers got back to their units, Five Forks and with it the Southside Railroad, were no longer Confederate possessions.

News of this latest debacle convinced Robert E. Lee that the time had come to evacuate Richmond and he immediately began drawing up plans for the evacuation of his army. The next morning, while Jefferson Davis was attending communion services at St. Paul's Episcopal church, a messenger quietly walked up to the presidential pew and handed the chief executive a brief note from Lee advising him to evacuate the government. Davis left a group of increasingly agitated worshipers and hurried to the Confederate White House to direct the loading of two special trains, one to carry the nation's gold reserve and the other to evacuate the president and his cabinet. While Rebel midshipmen loaded money and papers aboard the trains, Lee attempted to direct a holding action to keep the Yankees at bay for a few more hours. Confederate corps commander A. P. Hill went down with a mortal wound while organizing a defense line and 200 Rebel defenders of Fort Gregg fought an Alamo-like battle as they tried to prevent 4000 Yankee assault troops from smashing through and capturing Lee. As Sunday evening gradually turned to total darkness, the surviving units of the Army of Northern Virginia crossed the Appomattox River and began their final retreat.

The last hours of Confederate control of Richmond presented scenes very similar to Atlanta eight months earlier. Confederate troops trying to demolish essential war supplies and munitions paid little attention to the spreading fires they created and huge sections of the capital went up in flames. One Confederate arsenal containing almost a million rounds of rifle and cannon ammunition exploded in a ferocious blast that took much of downtown Richmond with it. While Lee led his army west toward Amelia Court House and Davis led his cabinet to Danville, the first Federal soldiers appeared at dawn and the horse soldiers of an African-American cavalry unit rode cautiously into a now abandoned capital of secessionism.

While Jefferson Davis made frequent speeches along the train route, telling his audiences that the Rebels now had gained the strategic initiative because they no longer had to worry about defending their capital, Lee's shattered but still defiant army trudged toward the expected supply trains at Amelia Court House. The trains were in the depot as Lee had ordered, but through some bureaucratic foul-up the only supplies available were artillery shells and rifle bullets, at this point the last thing the starving graycoats needed. Lee was forced to halt his retreat for a day while foragers scavenged the countryside for whatever meager rations they could discover, and this delay was all that Grant and his generals needed. Federal infantry and cavalry units were deployed as if engaged in a gigantic chess match as the Union commander tried to seal off every potential escape route. Meanwhile, in the Confederate camp, hundreds of soldiers went out on foraging expeditions and simply never returned as they headed for home instead. As one Confederate officer noted, "our army is ruined I fear" and when his letter was subsequently captured by a Yankee cavalryman, Phil Sheridan redoubled his efforts to get his horsemen in front of the crumbling Rebel army.

On April 6th, as the hungry Confederates staggered toward an expected re-supply at Appomattox Station, a huge Federal pursuit force caught the Southern rear guard at a small stream called Sailor's Creek. The Rebels were able to beat back a vicious Yankee assault but then launched an ill advised counter-attack just as even more Federals arrived on the field. A huge flanking movement caught an entire Confederate corps in a giant pincers and resulted in the capture of 8 generals and 8000 men. Lee watched the debacle from a distant vantage point and exclaimed "My God, has the army dissolved?"

The surviving elements of the Southern army renewed their westward march that afternoon but while the graycoats were making their way across the spectacular High Bridge that spanned the Appomattox River, General Edward Ord's Army of the James marched up to support an already deployed Federal cavalry screen that was closing Lee's escape route. During most of Friday and Saturday Rebel units tried to penetrate ever stronger Union battle lines in an attempt to discover a vulnerable point that might allow the army to break through to Lynchburg. However, one by one the original weak points were filled in by thousands of newly arrived Yankees who now sensed that the climax of the war was at hand.

After nightfall on April 8th Lee called a final conference of his generals to discuss the shortening list of options that were open to the Army of Northern Virginia. As General John Gordon remembered, "there was no tent, no tables, no chairs and no camp stools. On blankets spread upon the ground or on saddles at the roots of trees we sat around the great commander." One of Lee's youngest generals, artillerist E. Porter Alexander, voiced an opinion that guerilla war was the most viable remaining option. "We could take the woods and bushes with orders to rally on the Governors of the respective states. If we surrender this army it is the end of the Confederacy. We have the right to ask of you to spare us the mortification of having you ask Grant for terms and have him answer that he had no terms to offer." Lee discouraged talk of guerilla warfare as he insisted "the men would become mere bands of marauders..... they would be compelled to rob and steal in order to live." However, the commanding general agreed that unconditional surrender was equally intolerable, although he hoped for far better terms. A series of dispatches between Lee and Grant addressed this concern when the Union commander offered far more favorable terms that included immediate parole of the whole army in exchange for a prompt surrender. Even the younger members of Lee's staff admitted that this proposal allowed the army to keep its honor intact and Lee finally agreed to meet with his adversary "though I would rather die 1000 deaths."

On Sunday morning, April 9th, Robert E. Lee rode to the McLean house in Appomattox Court House which was already crowded with Grant and a dozen of his officers. After some small talk about mutual experiences in the Mexican War, the two generals got down to the business of formalizing Grant's proposed terms. The Union general informally agreed to his adversary's request that Confederate cavalrymen and artillerymen could keep their horses and also offered to supply 25,000 rations for Lee's almost starving army. Formal terms allowed officers to retain their swords, pistols and horses and permitted the entire army to return to their homes as soon as they signed parole forms. These terms were quite generous and Lee admitted "this will have the best possible effect upon the men. It will be very gratifying and will do much toward conciliating our people." The two greatest military leaders of a now reconciled country shook hands and Lee mounted his horse with the genuine admiration of his enemies accompanying him. As Philip Sheridan observed "he mounted his chunky gray horse and lifting his hat as he passed out of the yard, rode off toward his army, his arrival there being announced to us by cheering, which as it progressed, varying in loudness, told us he was riding through the bivouac of the Army of Northern Virginia." When Union guns started to fire in celebration of the surrender, Grant ordered his officers to stop the shooting as he insisted, "the war is over, the rebels are our countrymen again, and the best sign of rejoicing after the victory will be to abstain from all demonstrations on the field."

On the gray, cheerless morning of April 12th, 1865, the 28,000 surviving members of the Army of Northern Virginia marched along the old stage road with Federal soldiers lining both sides of their route. The Confederates were marching between the lines to lay down their arms for the last time. General Joshua Chamberlain, one of the heroes of Gettysburg, who had survived near-fatal wounds to achieve both division command and assignment to accept the Confederate surrender, marveled at the demeanor of his former adversaries. "Before us in proud humiliation stood the embodiment of manhood, men whom neither toils and sufferings, nor the fact of death nor disaster nor hopelessness could bend from their resolve." Out of respect for these courageous opponents, Chamberlain ordered the assembled Federal troops to "carry arms" which was a sign of salute and honor. General John Gordon, who was in front of the Confederate formation quickly realized the intent of his former foe and "caught the sound of shifting arms, looked up and facing his own command gave word for his successive brigades to pass us with the same position of the manual—honor answering honor." No trumpet, drum or cheers pierced the stillness of a climactic moment in American history, but as Chamberlain noted "the erect men with eyes looking level into ours, making memories that bound us together as no other bond; was not such manhood to be welcomed back into a Union so tested and assured?"

# CHAPTER 35

# Why Was the "Union Forever"?

## *The Strategy and Tactics of Northern Victory and Southern Defeat*

$O$nce it became apparent that the formation of a Southern Confederacy would be challenged militarily by the United States, the majority of European military analysts, most Southerners, and not a few citizens of the states remaining in the Union became convinced that the Rebels would win any war between the two sections. Yet, four years later the capital of the Confederacy was occupied by Yankee troops, much of the South lay in ruins and the superb soldiers of the Confederate States Army were either dead, deserted or paroled prisoners of war. The question of how the North won and why the South lost has been one of the most prominent and fascinating topics in American studies since the *Richmond Examiner*'s editor Edward Pollard's *The Lost Cause* was published in 1866, and accused Jefferson Davis of being the single most important factor in Confederate defeat. Subsequent books over the next thirteen decades have offered stimulating, often controversial reasons for the outcome of the War Between the States and few historians have fully agreed on the most important factor that decisively influenced the final outcome. The authors feel that this question of why one side won and the other side lost might be discussed more profitably within the context of three inter-related questions. How did the Union achieve military dominance over the Confederacy? To what extant did the match-up of military commanders influence this outcome? Did the Confederacy really have a realistic chance to maintain its independence?

The first question, "why did the North win?" is a paradox of simplicity and complexness. First, it must be emphasized that the North won a complete, definitive military victory over the adversary that was as all-encompassing as the Allied victory over the Axis in World War II. The Lincoln administration essentially dictated the terms of peace, captured the entire enemy army and totally occupied the defeated side's territory. However, in one major respect, the pattern of Union victory over the Confederacy is very different from the American experience in the Second World War. After an initial stage of shock inflicted by Pearl Harbor and a succession of subsequent defeats in the Pacific, the American army and navy won virtually all of the remaining battles of the war.

For example, after the capitulation of Corregidor in May, 1942, the American land forces in the Pacific never surrendered another major unit for the rest of the war and essentially never retreated from an inexorable forward drive against the Japanese mainland. American naval forces in the Pacific never experienced another tactical defeat after the battles around Savo Island in the fall of 1942 and, in fact, spent the rest of the war scoring almost unbelievably one-sided victories over the Imperial Navy. The only significant defeat that the German army secured against their American opponents was at Kasserine Pass in February 1942; from that point on the best that Hitler's forces could attain was temporary advantage, such as in the Ardennes offensive which still ultimately resulted in an overwhelming German defeat.

The Civil War seems to present a very different rhythm. On several occasions the Union forces seemed just about on the verge of winning the war and then suddenly, the whole momentum of the conflict would swing toward the Confederacy. American civilians studying newspaper maps during Wold War II could observe a monthly, and sometimes daily, advance of their armies toward Berlin or Tokyo, and calculate how far the forces had advanced and how many miles remained until what seemed to be an assured victory. On the other hand, the Union army was further away from Richmond in May of 1864 than it had been in May of 1862 and Confederate cavalry units were still raiding into Northern territory very late in the war.

The sense that the war was moving perceptibility toward victory, which brightened the mood of Americans during much of World War II, was simply not evident in the North until very late in the war, probably sometime after the fall of Atlanta. A few days before the fall of Richmond, Lincoln urged Sherman to hurry back to his army in North Carolina, still fearful that the Confederates would pull some spectacular feat that would turn the war around once again even at what seemed to be the last minute. Therefore, while the pattern of World War II was one of continuous, determined American advance toward final victory, the Civil War was much more of a roller coaster of emotions. There are points at which Jefferson Davis and Abraham Lincoln share almost identical feelings of imminent victory or imminent defeat literally on the same day when it is obvious that both sides can't be winning (or losing) at the same time!

The Union may have won the war, but it won only a small majority of the battles and actually lost more men than the defeated Confederates. Thus while the end result of victory was overwhelming, the margin of victory seems much slimmer than it was in the 1940's. The authors feel that there is a very tangible reason for this narrow margin of victory. Quite simply, the Civil War was a conflict in which Americans were fighting themselves.

We feel that the emphasis placed on the differences between the cultures of North and South as the war approached have been grossly exaggerated, at least in a military sense. The cliches of "pasty faced Yankee clerks vs. manly Southern outdoorsmen" or "ingenious Yankees vs. stupid, indolent rebels" was great propaganda for both sides but was also mostly myth. The Civil War was long, bloody and emotionally draining simply because each side fielded an army of incredibly talented, courageous, patriotic men, who were willing to undergo horrendous privations, appallingly severe wounds and ultimately death by the thousands in order to support a cause they believed was right. This is dramatically different from many other major wars. For example, in the spring of 1940 a smaller army of highly motivated, superbly commanded Germans annihilated a larger army of Frenchmen that was plagued by enormous internal political divisions and led by virtually senile commanders. This was simply not the case in the War Between the States. While the Rebels did possess an initial advantage in horsemanship and the Yankees did enjoy an initial superiority in engineering activities, by later in the war there were dozens of superb bluecoat cavalry regiments and scores of talented Confederate engineering units. Even the most successful leaders on each side shared the same prototypically American shunning of pomp and show. Grant, Sherman, Lee and Stonewall Jackson may have had completely different personalities, but they all shared a kind of businesslike pragmatism that differed substantially from 19th century European military leaders. Grant invited common soldiers to ride in his personal railroad coaches on the assumption that not utilizing the ample extra seats was wasteful. Lee virtually never posted sentries in front of his very spartan headquarters tent and was widely seen as extremely approachable by enlisted men. Sherman and Jackson shared an aversion to fancy uniforms and went into battle with mud-splattered shoes, worn-out hats and second-hand frock coats.

Thus the Civil War was essentially fought by men who shared most of the same habits, hopes, fears and eccentricities as their opponents and generally saw their adversaries as equally competent, equally courageous and equally dangerous. Therefore, in order for the North to win the incredibly evenly matched battlefield contests, the Union army would have to find some other advantages that the enemy either could not or would not employ. The authors believe that the North ultimately utilized at least four advantages in their advance toward ultimate victory. First, while both sides opened the war with relatively evenly matched talents in infantry combat, the respective Confederate and Yankee advantages in cavalry and artillery provided a net gain for the North. The common wisdom that the Rebel horsemen were generally superior to their bluecoat counterparts is generally valid, at least for the first two or three years of the war. Cavalry geniuses such as Jeb

Stuart, Nathan Forrest and Joe Wheeler smashed Union supply lines, captured outposts, destroyed railroads and wreaked havoc with communications. The problem with this advantage was that by the 1860's the horsemen could seldom directly influence the course of a conventional battle. During the 18th and early part of the 19th century riders carrying sabers and lances could often break up lines of infantry before the short range muskets could drop very many men from their horses. However, by the Civil War, any decent infantryman could use his rifle to shoot a cavalryman well before he could close in to do any real damage. In fact, while the Union horsemen were no better at this type of attack than the Confederates, the issue of repeating rifles to bluecoat cavalry actually allowed them to dismount and become a fast firing shock force on a battlefield, which the shotgun-armed Rebels usually could not accomplish as well.

On the other hand, mid-19th century artillery could still very much influence certain aspects of a battle, and the Union superiority in this arm made a major difference during a number of decisive engagements. The role of field guns in Civil War assaults was limited by the fact that unprotected gunners were too often easy targets for the long range rifles of the defenders. However, on those occasions when the Northern army was on the defensive and had time to properly protect the gunners, cannon fire could be a devastating blow to the Rebel attackers. During the battles of Shiloh, Malvern Hill, Atlanta and Franklin, Confederate attacks were stopped cold by Union massed artillery and the pendulum of the battle shifted toward the Yankees. Of course, in the most famous of these scenarios, it was Henry Hunt's massed artillery that allowed a relatively small number of Union infantry in the center of Cemetery Ridge to smash Pickett's desperate charge at Gettysburg. On the other hand, Confederate artillery barrages on that decisive afternoon damaged Meade's headquarters, killed dozens of horses and terrorized rear echelon troops, but did almost nothing to weaken the Federal defense lines. Confederate artillery could be effective in certain instances, but it seldom turned the course of the battle in the same way that it did for the Union.

Second, the North won because the Federals developed and utilized a far better naval arm than their Southern adversaries. The British forces in the Revolution used naval superiority to some advantage against the American rebels, but not nearly to the extent that the Union vessels impacted the engagements of the Civil War. The introduction of steam power enabled the Federals to not only prevent the Confederates from obtaining badly needed supplies from abroad as the blockade became more effective during the course of the war, it also allowed the Yankees to penetrate deep into the Confederacy by using the vast river networks to Northern advantage. Union gunboats provided vital fire support in victories such as Fort Donelson and Shiloh; a naval flotilla captured the largest city in the South, New Orleans; naval transports placed Grant's army on the "right" side of the Mississippi River during the Vicksburg campaign. The Confederates achieved spectacular but strategically unimportant successes with their steam rams, torpedoes and submarine while the somewhat less glamorous Union naval forces provided the Yankees with a firepower and mobility that in some respects more than negated the mobility of the Rebel cavalry.

Third, the North utilized a combination of superior manufacturing capacity and superior technology to excellent advantage as the war progressed. There has always been a kind of romantic aura surrounding the ill-clothed, barefoot, half starved Rebel soldier continuing to fight simply on raw courage. However, the romantic aspects of this image simply don't win wars. Quite simply, the Confederate government failed miserably in its feeble attempts to properly arm, clothe and feed the men who were expected to defend the secessionist movement. When a circular letter from the Rebel defenders of Vicksburg was given to General Pemberton, their demand that "if you can't feed us then you had better surrender us" is a damning indictment of Southern war effort. Rebel soldiers living on one biscuit and four ounces of corn meal a day were simply not going to fight as well as properly supplied soldiers. The chronicle of the war includes numerous instances of Confederate generals canceling offensives because their artillery horses were starving, or their men hadn't eaten in three days, or supply wagons had never arrived. In many cases these delays allowed the Yankees to take the initiative and win crucial battles.

On the other hand, not only were Union soldiers generally well clothed and well fed, as the war continued they were issued weapons that began to give them a huge advantage over their adversaries on the battlefield. For example during the last two years of the war almost 300,000 single shot breach loaders and more than 100,000 repeating rifles were issued to Union troops. By the autumn of 1864 Federal brigades armed with repeaters were devastating Rebel armies at Cedar Creek, Franklin and Nashville, and inflicting casualties of almost 10 to 1 in key parts of these engagements. The North's better fed, better clothed, better transported and better armed soldiers were increasingly likely to beat equally brave opponents who had none of those advantages.

Finally, the North won the Civil War because it possessed anything from slightly more competent to significantly more talented leaders in the crucial leadership positions that determined the outcome of battles, campaigns and the war itself. The South produced a number of first rate military commanders, most notably including Jackson, Stuart, Forrest and Lee, but by the summer of 1864 Jackson and Stuart were dead, Forrest was being poorly utilized in marginally important cavalry raids, and Lee was caught in a siege that prevented him from using most of his talents. On the other hand, during this critical period of the war, the four most significant Union generals, Ulysses Grant, William Sherman, George Thomas and Philip Sheridan were all not only very much alive but engaged in significant operations that would have a major bearing on the outcome of the war.

# Grading the Generals

The South could field talented generals, but through a combination of battle deaths and injuries and poor military decisions at the presidential level, the best men were generally not available in the most critical period of the war. For example Nathan Forrest was often less than superbly utilized by Braxton Bragg and John Bell Hood, Patrick Cleburne, the most talented division commander in the West, was never given an opportunity for corps command, Stonewall Jackson was killed and James Longstreet was wounded by their own men at the climactic moment of decisive battles, and even Lee was not placed in command of all armies until the last weeks of the war. On the other hand, while the North certainly had its share of incompetent generals, a large number of talented men had moved up the ladder of command during the war to orchestrate the final defeat of the Confederacy in the final year of the conflict. Grant, Sherman, Thomas and Sheridan were all extremely minor figures in the earliest stage of the war, and yet by the autumn of 1864 these four men were operating a juggernaut that was tearing the Confederacy apart. Just as the American patriot cause in the War of Independence produced just enough talented generals to defeat the British, the Union side in the Civil War identified enough superb men who could fully utilize the manpower advantage that the North had already enjoyed but didn't fully understand how to implement it. A comparative rating of the dozen most prominent generals on each side demonstrates this modest, but decisive, Union advantage.

The Confederate general who had ultimate responsibility for the two opening confrontations of the Civil War, Fort Sumter and First Manassas, was also one of the most colorful yet underestimated leaders on either side. Pierre Beauregard was vain, prickly and convinced of the brilliance of every one of his battle plans but he was also a major asset to the Confederacy in a number of crisis situations. The Creole played a substantial role in the Rebel victory at Bull Run, conducted a masterful withdrawal when Henry Halleck's enormous army advanced on Corinth, orchestrated a first rate defense of Charleston in 1863 and provided Lee with vital time to move the main army into the trenches at Petersburg.

The Louisianan's strategic plans have been criticized by some historians as being unrealistic, given the resources of the Confederacy, but a closer examination of his ideas reveals a number of ideas that might very well have dramatically aided the Southern cause if they had been implemented.

A number of flaws prevent Beauregard from being rated as a truly great general. His command of the Confederate army at Shiloh after the death of Albert Sidney Johnston was lackluster, his self-appointed sick leave during the summer of 1862 was poorly timed, and his abysmal relations with the equally prickly Jefferson Davis encouraged the president to ignore what were otherwise good strategies. Beauregard must be considered a generally able commander who deserves a solid "B" grade.

A general who not only shared command with Beauregard at Manassas but also shared his poor relations with the president was Joseph Johnston. Johnston was an enigma in the Confederate military camp; he was a cautious general in an army of aggressive, offensive minded leaders. One of the problems in rating the complex Virginian is that the number of either clear cut victories or absolute defeats under his leadership is minuscule. His success at Manassas is complicated by his co-commander status; his initial gains at Fair Oaks were negated after he was severely wounded; his attempt to link up with Pemberton outside of Vicksburg was canceled by the Pennsylvanian's surrender and he was relieved of command in Georgia just as the Atlanta campaign entered its decisive phase.

Johnston never lost a significant part of his army, but never destroyed a significant contingent of Yankees. He was extremely popular with his men and possessed excellent organizational skills, but his obsession with seniority of rank caused enormous difficulties with the president and other senior generals. This close balance of assets and liabilities points to a final "C" grade.

If Joseph Johnston was the bane of Jefferson Davis' existence, the other Johnston, Albert Sidney, was the epitome of the president's assertion of the superiority of Southern leaders. Johnston was expected to become the focal figure for the defense of the entire western theatre of the Confederacy, and he did become the central person but not quite in the way that Davis intended. Johnston's command in the West started with the embarrassing Rebel defeat at Fishing Creek, which lost most of eastern Kentucky to the Confederate cause. This setback was followed by the stunning debacle of Forts Henry and Donelson which inflicted almost irreplaceable losses on the western theatre. The former Republic of Texas general developed a decent operational plan for the assault on Grant at Pittsburg Landing, but the timing of the attack allowed the Union army to be massively reinforced by Buell's fast marching troops just as the Confederates threatened to win the battle. Johnston's death during the battle of Shiloh ended his career before he had an opportunity to rescue his reputation, but there is no reasonable prospect that the South would have won the battle even if their field commander had lived. The defeats at Fort Donelson and Shiloh effectively eliminated a third of the western field army and led directly to the loss of New Orleans, the largest city in the Confederacy. Since there were no tangible victories to compensate for these decisive defeats, Albert Sidney Johnston must be assigned an "F" grade.

While Albert Sidney Johnston emerges as a sympathetic but failing commander, Braxton Bragg was neither particularly successful nor sympathetic. The number of Bragg admirers has always been minimal, for the simple reason that there is very little likeable about this ill tempered, dyspeptic general. While Bragg was in command at the only significant Confederate victory in the West, Chickamauga, in reality it was James Longstreet who directed the decisive part of the engagement while the commanding general sulked in his tent. On the minus side of the ledger, Bragg frittered away apparent Confederate victories at Perryville and Stones River and totally wasted the positive impact of Chickamauga through the embarrassing fiasco at Missionary Ridge. Bragg was a generally good organizer but his men loathed him, his subordinate generals seemed to spend most of their time plotting to get rid of him, and when he resigned his command he left an army that was in shambles. This is another general who so badly hurt the Confederate war effort that he deserves an "F" grade.

Bragg's ability to destroy the fighting ability of the second largest army in the Confederacy was given an ample run for its money by his eventual successor, John Bell Hood. This Kentucky-born Texan was a classic example of a fairly good brigade and division commander who was promoted far beyond his capabilities and proved to be one of Jefferson Davis' most disastrous appointments. Hood's Atlanta and Nashville campaigns resulted in the loss of one of the most vital points in the Confederacy of 1864 in the first campaign, and the virtual annihilation of the Army of Tennessee in the second round of battles. When Lee not so subtly warned Davis to avoid appointing Hood, the president should have listened. Hood's rating as a commanding general can only be an "F."

The damage inflicted on the Confederate cause in Tennessee and Georgia by Bragg and Hood was matched in the vital Mississippi region by John Pemberton. The appointment of the Confederate-sympathizing Pennsylvanian was another of Davis' less than brilliant decisions in which a marginally competent brigade or division commander was simply incapable of leading an army to victory over a master such as Ulysses Grant. There is something almost pathetic about Pemberton's desperate thrusts against a Union supply line that no longer existed, while Grant tore through Mississippi and beat his opponent at every turn. Pemberton never should have allowed himself to be trapped in a city that couldn't be supplied, and he bears the onus of commanding the single largest army surrendered during the war while losing the most strategically important site in the South. Here is another clear cut "F" rating.

The only significant Confederate general who served primarily in the West and emerged from the war as a legendary leader was Nathan Bedford Forrest. Forrest was the embodiment of the ability of the western Rebel horsemen to disrupt Union strategy with relatively limited numbers and relatively primitive weaponry. When Yankees called the western cavalry leader "that devil Forrest," they were paying the ultimate compliment to one of the most genuinely original and brilliant military strategists of the time. However, through no fault of his own, the mediocre western commanders probably never took full advantage of Forrest's talents and his fantastic string of successes still weren't enough to turn the tide of the war in the West. Forrest undoubtedly deserves an "A" grade, but he was clearly a Confederate star that wasn't fully utilized.

The personification of the ongoing Confederate sense of superiority over their opponents in the East, especially when compared to the exact opposite view in the West, was Stonewall Jackson. This eccentric former college professor was probably the most feared man in the Union army between the spring of 1862 and the spring of 1863, and his activities have justifiably become textbook examples of surprise, daring and mobility. Even if Jackson had lived, it is unlikely that he ever would have made an ideal commander of a full size army. His difficulty in dealing with subordinates and lack of interest in mundane details of running an army were exasperating and potentially counter-productive. However, when in tandem with "senior partner" Robert E. Lee, Jackson was simply devastating in most of his engagements, with the curious lethargy of the Seven Days campaign the only notable exception. The conduct of the Valley campaign, Second Manassas and Chancellorsville were simply brilliant and the authors feel that Jackson's death during the last named battle was so devastating to the Confederate cause that it actually provided the North with a technical victory despite Hooker's retreat. This military genius easily scores an "A" rating.

The magnitude of the loss of Jackson to the Southern cause is particularly evident in an evaluation of Stonewall's direct successor in corps command, Richard Ewell. While Jackson and Ewell shared eccentricities, the newly appointed commander never came close to matching his predecessor's talent. A combination of significant physical disabilities and a not particularly imaginative approach to battle relegated Ewell to a mediocrity that the outnumbered and outgunned South simply couldn't afford. His conduct at Gettysburg was lackluster at best and disastrous at worst, as his failure in a variety of attacks did much to set up the conditions for Pickett's annihilation. During the crucial campaign of 1864 Ewell had good days and bad days but never came close to a Stonewall-like spectacular. This general represents one of Lee's weakest appointments and probably deserves no more than a "D" rating.

While Ewell seems to bear significant responsibility for the Confederate defeat at Gettysburg, James Longstreet was assigned most of the blame in the post-Civil War South. The authors believe that this Georgian was far too harshly judged and was actually a definite asset to the Confederate cause. Longstreet's *de facto* command of the Rebel army during the crucial phase of Chickamauga produced the only significant Confederate victory in the West, although his subsequent activities in the siege of Knoxville produced an embarrassing, if relatively minor, defeat. This general's main reputation was won in the East and his contributions were generally solid, if not as spectacular as Jackson's. Longstreet probably had a better idea of the opportunities and limitations of the Pennsylvania campaign than Lee, but was unable to convince his chief to fight a more defensive engagement. His subsequent actions in the Wilderness almost produced a decisive Rebel victory until the Georgian's untimely injuries robbed the assault of much of its momentum. Longstreet can not be realistically evaluated as a brilliant commander, but a solid "B" seems a reasonable grade for Lee's "Old Warhorse."

The eastern counterpart to Nathan Bedford Forrest was Jeb Stuart, who epitomized the flair and audacity of Rebel cavalrymen in the Virginia engagements. In most campaigns between 1862 and 1864 Stuart provided excellent support for Lee's infantry operations, with the only significant blemish being the Pennsylvania campaign. Stuart's harassment and capture of Yankee supply trains didn't compensate for the absence of screening and scouting activities just as Lee made his deepest thrust into enemy territory. However, there is still considerable disagreement as to exactly how much of a role Stuart's late arrival played in the ultimate outcome of Gettysburg and the Virginia cavalier provided superb service during most other battles. He also proved himself to be an excellent infantry leader when he temporarily took command of the fallen Jackson's corps at Chancellorsville. This was a superior general who deserves an "A-" rating.

One of the many ironies of the Civil War is that the most legendary, admired general of the conflict commanded the army that lost the war. Robert E. Lee has been placed on a pedestal that he may share only with fellow Virginian George Washington, and yet Yorktown and Appomattox present two very different dramas in which one general became legendary in victory while the other commander became legendary in defeat. Lee certainly had the personality for Olympian status; he was gallant to non-combatants, chivalrous to enemies, courteous to his subordinates and genuinely worshiped by his men. His relations with Jefferson Davis were excellent, while even Abraham Lincoln and many other Northerners openly admired a man they would have welcomed as their own commander.

There is little doubt that it was Lee who extended the life of the Confederacy, although that extension was certainly a mixed blessing. He was a field commander who won most of his battles even though he was almost always outnumbered, and was forced to waste much of his energy simply attempting to feed, clothe and arm his men. However, while Lee was almost definitely one of the most successful battlefield generals on either side, his impact on the outcome of the war was limited by his almost exclusive focus on his native Virginia. There is little doubt that Lee placed the probable impact on the defense of Virginia as the first priority of any strategic planning. It would be fascinating to speculate on how these plans may or may not have been altered if the capital of the Confederacy had remained in Montgomery, Alabama.

This parochial attitude of "Virginia first" represents a significant difference from Ulysses Grant who was much more able to view the war in an almost continental frame of reference, which allowed him to reluctantly accept a stalemate in Virginia as long as other bluecoat armies were making progress in their campaigns. Lee was the most brilliant *theatre* commander of the Civil War, but by the time he had responsibility for all of the Southern armies there was virtually no Confederacy left to defend. Lee certainly deserves an "A" grade as a general, but that rating must be qualified by a localism of strategy that Grant was able to transcend.

The Union general who had the dubious distinction of being responsible for the first debacle of the war is Irvin McDowell. McDowell shares certain common characteristics with Albert Sidney Johnston, a bright, energetic, extremely professional officer who was simply expected to do too much. McDowell actually developed an excellent plan of operations for the Manassas campaign, and then had to stand by and watch his incredibly slow moving army provide ample time for the Rebels to checkmate his moves. The resulting fiasco on Henry House Hill brought the Union cause to the brink of disaster and almost secured Confederate independence in one battle. McDowell's attempt to recoup his reputation occurred against Stonewall Jackson in the Valley campaign and his failures in that arena guaranteed an "F" grade for a general who passed out of the limelight almost as quickly as he entered.

McDowell's disaster at Manassas paved the way for the emergence of a general who the authors insist was the most exasperating commander of the Civil War, George Brinton McClellan. It seems that no one is neutral about this wealthy Pennsylvanian who did so much to create the unique personality of the Army of the Potomac. On two separate occasions this general rebuilt a shattered army that might have crumbled under the blows of one more Confederate offensive and led these men to two of the most controversial campaigns of the war. McClellan was probably the only Federal general who enjoyed the level of affection from his men that Rebel soldiers demonstrated for Lee, yet his relations with Lincoln and Stanton were appallingly immature and short sighted.

McClellan's Peninsula campaign has been criticized frequently; but in reality, he was able to place his army in about the same spot that it took Grant 60,000 casualties to achieve two years later. The resulting Fair Oaks and Seven Days engagements were essentially tactical draws that still left the Union army on Richmond's doorstep, until Henry Halleck panicked and ordered the James River positions abandoned. In turn, the Antietam campaign was also a tactical draw that pushed Lee out of Union territory but failed to recover much of Virginia. Thus, in a technical sense, McClellan never either won or lost a campaign. However, in the strategic sense, especially from a long term perspective, the Pennsylvanian would have to be considered moderately successful. The Seven Days and Antietam cost Lee almost 40,000 casualties, which were difficult for the manpower-short Confederacy to replace. Lee could only make good these losses by stripping other points in the South of their defenders, which in turn made them more vulnerable to Federal attack. While McClellan was certainly not on the verge of capturing Richmond when he was relieved of command, he had inflicted more casualties than he had lost, an accomplishment that few Eastern commanders could emulate. McClellan's huge ego, over-cautious nature and consistent overestimation of the enemy facing him are substantial blemishes on his record, but he was still a moderately successful general who deserves a solid "B" rating.

The general who initially succeeded McClellan and then in turn was replaced by him was a leader who had a personality that made the Pennsylvanian look positively saintly. John Pope parlayed a modest, but ultimately important, victory over Confederate Island No. 10 on the Mississippi into an Eastern command of the newly formed Army of Virginia. The result of this appointment was almost unmitigated disaster for the Union. Pope turned the Virginia countryside against him with draconian edicts, barely escaped Lee's ambush near the Rapidan, and then blundered into a battle near Manassas where he kept assuming that he had virtually annihilated an enemy that was actually close to annihilating him. Pope was boastful, cranky, overconfident and loathed by officers and men, and only escapes total failure due to his western victories that did add substantially to Union power in the Mississippi theater. Thus this unpleasant commander escapes with barely a "D."

Pope was the first in a trio of Union generals who would suffer embarrassing defeats at the hands of Robert E. Lee. The second member of the triumvirate was Ambrose Burnside. This pleasant Rhode Islander exhibited none of Pope's false bravado, but he wasn't any better at beating Lee. Like Pope, Burnside came to command with a modest, but relatively important, victory under his belt. Burnside's expedition against Roanoke Island had captured a strategically important spot and netted several thousand Rebel prisoners who would be difficult to replace. However, his plan of operations against Confederate defenses around Fredericksburg was totally unimaginative and resulted in one of the most one-sided Rebel victories of the war, and added significantly to an end-the-war groundswell of opinion in late 1862. Burnside had a few modest successes in lesser commands during the next 18 months but was at least partially responsible for the fiasco at the Crater in 1864. Burnside had just enough success to squeeze through with a final "D-" grade.

The third member of this gallery of Lee's victims is Joseph Hooker. While Pope and Burnside conducted battles that they had virtually no chance to win, Hooker actually devised a plan that almost worked, and could have possibly ended the war. Hooker's performance at Chancellorsville was far from superb, but Lee's victory cost him extremely heavy casualties and the loss of Stonewall Jackson, which really gave the South little to show for merely pushing the Yankees back across the Rappahannock River. Hooker's failure at Chancellorsville is also at least partially mitigated by his excellent ability to improve the organization and morale of the Army of the Potomac, the provision of that army with its first effective cavalry arm, and a significant contribution to the victory at Chattanooga through his actions at Brown's Ferry and Lookout Mountain. Hooker might have emerged as an outstanding general if he had been more even-tempered, but he still should be graded as a modest "C-" general.

The spotty record developed by Hooker's actions is somewhat matched by another mercurial leader, William Rosecrans. During the early winter of 1862-63 this emotional, talkative general performed a decisive service for the Union cause by turning a seemingly certain Confederate victory at Stone's River into a slight, but highly publicized, Northern triumph. On the other hand, Rosecrans was also responsible for the most significant Federal defeat in the West at Chickamauga where he not only provided Longstreet with an opportunity to retrieve a lost battle, but then unwisely left the defense of the field to subordinate George Thomas. Rosecrans was a decent general who had only average talent and would leave the really decisive battles of the West to future commanders. This general is a classic example of a "C" rated leader.

Rosecrans' withdrawal from the Chickamauga battlefield provided a golden opportunity for George Thomas. The authors believe that the Union-loyal Virginian is one of the most underrated generals of the Civil War. He scored the first significant Union victory of the war at Fishing Creek, saved the Army of the Cumberland from possible annihilation at Chickamauga, performed superbly during the Atlanta campaign, and then won one of the most lop-sided battles of the war at Nashville. Thomas' only blemish is that Grant didn't particularly like him, and in this case it appears the fault was with the supreme commander. While Lee would have been the most important Virginian to side with the Union if he had accepted Lincoln's offer of command, George Thomas was an excellent second prize for the Northern cause. This general deserves an outstanding "A" rating.

While George Thomas was cautious, phlegmatic and successful, fellow western general William Sherman was mercurial, fast talking and equally successful. Sherman was not universally successful in battle; his operations at Chickasaw Bayou, Missionary Ridge and Kennesaw Mountain were embarrassing setbacks, but his grasp of what it would take to defeat the South was brilliant, and he provided enormous talent to the Union cause. The Ohioan's fantastically successful Atlanta campaign and the subsequent March to the Sea turned a still defiant Confederacy into a severed republic that was on its last legs by Christmas of 1864 and provided Grant with the luxury of conducting a long term siege of Richmond. Sherman won decisive campaigns with modest losses and became one of the most indispensable men in the Union cause with an "A" emerging as the only possible grade.

The first general who significantly turned the war in the East in favor of the Union was the often underrated George Meade. In an ironic twist of fate that is amply demonstrated in the film *Gettysburg*, this Pennsylvanian was doomed to be far less famous in winning the decisive battle of the Civil War than his adversary would become in losing the engagement. While the film features Lee in a large number of sequences from the Confederate perspective, Meade is on camera for little more than a minute. Meade's subsequent reduction to a secondary role with the coming of Grant sometimes obscures the simple fact that this general decisively defeated the best Confederate army, led by the best Confederate general, in a battle where the North enjoyed only minimal numerical superiority. Meade's only blemish was that he failed to ignore his corps commanders and attack Lee before he could get back across the Potomac. However, a very solid "A-" should still be awarded to the first Federal general who proved that Lee could be beaten.

The other Union general who was most responsible for the decisive victory at Gettysburg was another Pennsylvanian, Winfield Scott Hancock. Hancock became the *de facto* field commander of the Union army in the first crucial stage of the battle, and then assumed responsibility for the most volatile spot on the field during the ensuing action. While it was Meade's excellent judgement that deployed the Federal army in the right place at the right time, it was Hancock's on field brilliance that gave the Yankees the decisive positional advantage. After Gettysburg, Hancock continued to serve as an excellent corps commander despite his severe injury during the battle, and at one point commanded as many men as an army commander would have led earlier in the war. Like Meade, Hancock tended to be somewhat overshadowed after the arrival of Grant, and he didn't fully exploit the opportunity to overwhelm Beauregard's lines at Petersburg, but a general nicknamed "Hancock the superb" deserves a nearly superb "A-" grade.

While Jeb Stuart and Nathan Forrest epitomized the flair and audacity of the Confederate cavalry, Philip Sheridan came closest to providing a Yankee equivalent for boldness. Sheridan is somewhat of a hybrid general as he commanded infantry units, led cavalry forces and at times orchestrated combined arms operations. Whatever kind of units this diminutive Irishman led, he was invariably successful, ranging from vital supporting role performances at Perryville and Stones River to decisive command situations at Cedar Creek and Five Forks. Sheridan's aggressive cavalry tactics during the spring of 1864 resulted in the death of Jeb Stuart and the gradual elimination of spectacular Rebel mounted exploits, at least in the eastern theater. Sheridan was both talented and lucky and definitely rates an "A" grade.

The final place in the Union pantheon must, of course, go to Ulysses Grant. While Lee was seen as a budding superstar from the day he resigned his commission to go South, Grant emerged from unbelievable obscurity to command the largest army in the history of the republic, mainly through constant growth and a brilliant perception of the nature of an opponent. Grant shared his principle adversary's audacity, flexibility and perception that the enemy could be panicked into stupid moves. Grant also matched Lee in coolness, persistency of purpose and confidence in his own abilities. However, the Union commanders' single most important asset that was not exhibited by Lee was his ability to envision the conflict in progressively wider geographical and political horizons. Grant could see that an army stalemated on one front could still be valuable if it tied down possible enemy reinforcements for another front. He also realized that the war was as much a political as a military struggle, and that perception of victory by the civilian population was as important as accomplishment of victory on the battlefield. Thus, for example, he was willing to parole Pemberton's army in order to immediately occupy Vicksburg, since the combination of a still= surrendered enemy army and the capture of the main citadel on the Mississippi was just as impressive in a psychological sense as marching an already disintegrating Rebel army into prison camps.

Grant, like Lee, was not successful in every battle and on occasion suffered bloody repulses when he grew impatient. However, he relied on attrition much less than some of his critics suggest. Up until the campaign of 1864, Grant had clearly inflicted far more casualties than he suffered, and during the final struggle with Lee the only absolutely unsophisticated, brute force assault was the debacle at Cold Harbor which was quickly followed by a brilliant maneuver south of the James. Grant was not a perfect general, but he was exactly the right commanding general at the time of ultimate decision in the War Between the States and deserves his clear cut "A" rating.

The authors selected what we considered to be the 12 most influential battlefield commanders on each side during the Civil War for this comparison. Obviously, once a finite number is selected, the question of "other significant leaders" begins to emerge. We felt that marginal Union political generals such as Ben Butler and Franz Sigel were more or less canceled out by not particularly talented Southern amateurs such as Felix Zollicoffer and Leonidas Polk. Henry Halleck was a timid commanding general but an excellent chief of staff under Grant, yet is difficult to grade because he was seldom in command during a battle. Similarly, A. P. Hill is difficult to rate because he was ill so often that he didn't participate in the decisive moments of several key battles. Confederate John Gordon and Yankee James Wilson were potentially brilliant leaders who were only beginning to emerge at the end of the war. Don Carlos Buell and William Hardee were meticulous, intelligent generals who always seemed to be overshadowed by more prominent army commanders who demonstrated more audacity than they could manage. Thus the 24 generals selected seemed to be the men, for better or worse, who determined the outcome of the decisive battles of the war and a comparison of the collective ratings on each side provides some evidence of Union superiority.

First, during the final ten months of the war, the Federals had five "A" rated generals active in the field as Grant, Sherman, Sheridan, Thomas and Meade all exercised significant authority, with Meade's influence probably the most marginal of this group. On the other hand, during that same period, the only outstanding Confederate generals still active in the field were Lee and Forrest while Forrest was marginalized by his exclusively cavalry status. Thus as least four superior Union generals were directing operations against a Confederacy that could field only one absolutely outstanding battlefield commander. Lee could not be everywhere at once; a collective team of Federal generals could be.

Second, the authors rated four Confederate generals as failures because they suffered catastrophic defeats with no even modest victories to partially compensate for their losses. Sidney Johnston and John Pemberton were responsible for the loss of an entire army at Fort Donelson and Vicksburg, and Braxton Bragg and John Bell Hood between them virtually eliminated the Army of Tennessee as an effective fighting force. On the other hand, no significant Union commander managed to lose an entire army and only Irvin McDowell failed to compensate for a major defeat with some sort of victory in another engagement. Pope, Burnside and Hooker were not good generals, but they at least contributed in some tangible way to Union victory even if that contribution was somewhat modest. An overall comparison of these two sets of ratings reveals a collective "B-" for the Northern commanders and a "C" for the Confederate generals. In a war where an outnumbered Confederacy needed to compensate for Union numerical superiority by fielding superior generals, the overall rating of "average" simply wouldn't be enough.

The North's advantage in field commanders was echoed by an equally decisive superiority in the military decision making of the respective presidents. Jefferson Davis was selected as the first president of the Confederate States of America based on his relatively moderate views on secession and relations with the North, and his reputation as the most talented military mind in the South. Davis had actually hoped to become commander of the Southern armies, and he continued to be attracted by the possibility of some form of field command throughout the war. The Mississippian was sophisticated enough to realize that the North would probably fight to maintain the Union, and that the ensuing war would be long and costly. However, Davis began to make significant mistakes as soon as he was directly confronted by the newly inaugurated Lincoln. The Confederate president promptly allowed his Yankee adversary to maneuver him into firing the first shots in the war, which in turn allowed Lincoln to utilize the attack to mobilize public opinion on the side of armed intervention. Davis then began to appoint cronies such as Albert Sidney Johnston and Leonidas Polk to key positions, while allowing the prickly natures of more talented men such as Joe Johnston and Pierre Beauregard to color his thoughts on deploying armies and generals.

Davis compounded his poor personnel decisions with an obsessive attention to detail that forced him to spend far too much energy on rather unimportant issues that clerks could have handled just as well. The president should have been spending his time thinking about how to raise more men and how to develop a winning strategy, rather than concerning himself with the number of uniforms requested for the Georgia militia. This sort of stubborn attention to detail also produced mixed results in his famous loyalty to perceived friends and undying hatred of alleged enemies. The president appointed and supported the brilliant Robert E. Lee when newspapers were decrying the abilities of "The King of Spades," but on the other hand, Leonidas Polk, Braxton Bragg and John Pemberton were maintained in command well after it appeared that their abilities were not commensurate with their positions. Davis clearly allowed John Bell Hood's cloying flattery to influence his choice of a replacement for Joe Johnston, even after Lee strongly recommended against the move.

Davis was an honorable, incorruptible chief executive who was handicapped by two significant weaknesses that would both harm the Confederate nation. First, he spent far too much of his presidency "indisposed" with a variety of illnesses and afflictions. There were far too many periods when Davis simply wasn't making decisions, and yet a besieged Southern republic couldn't afford the luxury of an incapacitated executive. Just as far too many Confederate generals seemed to be physically incapable of exercising command during crucial battles, their commander in chief was often just as unable to provide timely leadership for the Confederacy.

The second major flaw was the frequent separation of Davis' perceptions from the reality of the situation, especially in the later stages of the war. A more realistic, pragmatic executive would have realized by the summer of 1864 that chances of military victory were dwindling rapidly and a negotiated peace would be in the best interests of Americans both North and South. However, Davis simply ignored the reality of crumbling armies, captured cities and devastated farmlands, and increasingly conjured up military responses that were simply illusions. Lincoln was a flexible enough adversary who would have been willing to offer generous peace terms to end a war that the Union seemed destined to win at some unforeseen point. Yet even after the surrender of both Lee and Johnston, Davis was dreaming of scenarios that would create a last minute victory long after the overwhelming majority of his countrymen realized that the cause was lost. Jefferson Davis was not necessarily a failure as president, but he was only a marginal chief executive who deserves a "D" rating.

The presidency of Abraham Lincoln presents a very different image of the chief executive as a military leader. The Illinois lawyer spent much of the first year of the war ordering a semi-trained army to march on Richmond far before it was prepared to fight; overestimating the loyalty of a Southern population that contained far fewer Union sympathizers than he imagined; and ordering a coordinated advance of all Federal armies in a Washington's birthday offensive that produced absolutely no forward movement anywhere in the country. However, one of the major differences between Lincoln and Davis was that the Yankee amateur kept learning from his mistakes while the Southern expert didn't think that he had made any mistakes from which to learn.

Lincoln appointed incompetent generals, poor administrators and mediocre staff officers to important commands, but he was equally willing to dispose of these men if they served no long-term purpose. Lincoln began to realize the importance of defeating Lee's army over the capture of Richmond well before most of his generals caught on to this fact, and he gradually nurtured and promoted men such as Sherman and Grant who could allow him to remove himself from the day-to-day conduct of the war. By the summer of 1864 the team of Edwin Stanton as Secretary of War, Henry Halleck as chief of staff and Grant and Sherman as principal field commanders produced a group of men whose diverse personalities and attributes combined to form a juggernaut that was becoming irresistible in nature. Once Lincoln had this collection of men in place, supported by equally competent subordinates, the whole power of a rich, populous, modern society could be properly mobilized by a president who knew when to take command and when to merely sit back and make suggestions. Lincoln, as a war president, was able to steer through a political minefield of radical Republicans, Copperhead Democrats, prickly political generals and jealous, conniving Cabinet members to lead the Union to ultimate victory. This accomplishment can only produce an "A" grade for the 16th President.

\* \* \*

No analysis of the Civil War would be complete without that century old question, "Could the South really have won the war?" Our answer to this query is a resounding "Yes!" The authors feel that the Confederate States of America had a greater chance of gaining their independence in 1861 than the patriots had in their break with Britain in 1776. The patriots of 1776 were facing the most powerful army in the world supported by the equally imposing Royal Navy, while their own force was a motley collection of farmers and artisans led by largely amateur officers. On the other hand, the South opened hostilities with a slightly superior officer corps compared to the Yankees, a majority of the most talented generals and an army that was no worse in training or experience than the Federals. The Union navy was still small and filled with obsolete ships, the North didn't have any particular advantage in military technology, and Jefferson Davis was considered to have a better military mind than Abraham Lincoln. Thus it seems apparent that the most opportune moment for the South to force Northern recognition occurred during the first year of the war. Some combination of scenarios featuring the capture of Washington after First Manassas, the annihilation of Grant's army at Shiloh, a successful ambush of Pope's army near the Rapidan or a major penetration of Union territory on a semi-permanent basis might have created enough shockwaves in the North to encourage the Federal government to drop the whole idea of forcibly reconstituting the Union.

However, sometime between the autumn of 1862 and the spring of 1863 the odds against a Confederate military victory gradually lengthened. The war started to become an endurance contest that the North could better hope to survive in the long term, and Unionists were less ready to forfeit the idea of reunion after only one significant defeat. The authors believe that after the first year of the war, the South needed to win a minimum of three major victories in at least two different theaters within a short period of time to have a real chance to destroy Northern will to continue the war. For example, if Lee's impressive victory at Fredericksburg had been followed up by a successful offensive against the Army of the Potomac which in turn had been supplemented by a massive victory by Bragg over Rosecrans at Stones River, this series of shocks may have forced Lincoln to reconsider his policies. Or, alternatively, if Lee's victory at Chancellorsville had been followed by a successful invasion of Pennsylvania and supplemented by Grant's defeat in Mississippi, the pressure for Northern accommodation of Confederate independence might have grown irresistible. As the war continued, and the Union was able to mobilize more and more of its manpower and industrial strength, the odds of this triple play kept dropping. If, on the other hand, the Civil War had gone into the history books as a relatively brief conflict, there is an even chance that the Confederate States of America would have become a permanent sovereign republic.

The Civil War was the defining moment of the American experience during the 19th century, but the impact of the conflict has reached unabated into our own generation. The War Between the States not only forcibly terminated a particularly odious relationship of master and slave, it created a far more unified nation than the coalition of states that had called themselves America before 1861. A permanent split between North and South would have resulted in a much smaller banner of freedom to encourage oppressed people in other societies and a much smaller "arsenal of democracy" to challenge the tyrants that sprouted worldwide in the 20th century. Edward Porter Alexander, the brilliant young artillery commander in Lee's army, was one of the last generals to accept the concept of Confederate capitulation. However, almost a half century later this Georgian had the opportunity to see what restoration of the Union had produced. Alexander lauded the courage of his fellow Rebels, but had second thoughts about the merits of Confederate victory. "We now enjoy the rare privilege of seeing what we fought for in retrospect. It no longer seems as desirable. It would now prove only a curse." The mature citizen of a reunited 20th century nation viewed the outcome from a new perspective as he insisted that independence "would now prove only a curse. We have good cause to thank God for our escape from it; not alone for our sake but for the whole country and even the world. Had our cause succeeded, divergent interests must soon have further separated the States into groups and this continent would have been given over to divided nationalities, each weak and unable to command foreign credit. It is surely not necessary to contrast what would have been our prospect as citizens of such States with our condition now as citizens of the strongest, richest, and, strange of us to say who once called ourselves "conquered" and our cause "lost," the freest nation on earth. These are but the first fruits of what the future will develop, for our Union is not built to perish. Its bonds were not formed by peaceable agreements in conventions, but were forged in the white heat of battle in a war fought out to the bitter end and are for eternity."

The Civil War not only liberated a people who deserved to be free, it reunited a society that deserved to be whole and it ultimately guaranteed that at least one nation would have the combination of population, resources, ingenuity and courage to prove to the chieftains of totalitarianism that their warped and bloodthirsty mockery of normal relations among people would not become the final legacy of the 20th century.

# Index